Preface

Tourism continues to reach out in to space and time. Implicit within the trite phrase of 'tourism is the world's largest industry', it *appears* that everyone is either a tourist or a potential tourist, everywhere is someone's destination and no human activity is immune from the fleeting glimpses of transient eyes. Appearances, of course, can be deceptive.

Ironically, change, movement, development and growth are the norms that characterise a phenomenon that many still see as an opportunity to slow down, relax and do little. The new millennium will undoubtedly see more tourists, more tourism, more travel, more impacts, more to market, more to manage. Core human traits of creativity and curiosity, desires to consume and commune, along with the need to survive, remain as the fundamental, and often conflicting, drivers for this thing we label tourism. Tourism is an important subject of academic inquiry *precisely* because it is an extension of our humanity and the cultures we inhabit, and because of the rapidity of change and growth that now typifies it.

This series of six volumes arose out of a major international conference held at Sheffield Hallam University, UK, in September 2000. Organised by the Centre for Travel and Tourism, University of Northumbria and the Centre for Tourism Sheffield Hallam University, **Tourism 2000: Time for Celebration?** was designed to reflect on, evaluate and anticipate the growth and development of tourism from its roots in pilgrimage and exploration, to its present and future role as a vast and complex social and cultural activity, a diverse international industry, and a focus for academic discourse. The conference attracted tremendous interest from academics, policy makers and practitioners from across the world and in itself was a touristic experience. These books contain 173 of nearly 200 papers presented at the conference.

The importance of this series lies in its diversity as well as its dimensions. We believe it to be important that authors from differing disciplines, perspectives, nationalities and cultures are able to reflect on the many facets of tourism. With diversity, however, comes problems of categorisation and hard editorial decisions. We trust that in the main we have managed to produce a reasoned and manageable breakdown of papers.

The production of one book can generate a plethora of problems. Not surprisingly the production of six volumes involving so many contributors and from such a diversity of locations has not been without anguish. Differing interpretations of the word 'deadline' is a common source of editorial angst! Technology too, though we are indebted to it, has frequently been the object of derision – the email delivery failure, the server that is down, the lost file, the scrambled text, and the ever popular 'pressing the wrong button.'

Fortunately there are those amongst us that appear to take problems in their stride and who sail on through the waves of worry. Thanks must go to Richard Shipway for his help in chasing the most elusive of authors. Thanks also to Jill Pomfret for her help in the editing process and to Amanda Miller for her assistance. Central to this bout of thanks are the staff at Business Education Publishers Ltd (BEP), who have been down this road with us many times now and continue to deliver a service second to none. Without the professionalism, commitment and good humour of Andrea Murphy, Moira Page and everyone who has worked on this series at BEP, you would not be reading this.

Finally our thanks go, as ever, to all the contributors to the series. Reflections on International Tourism provides a home for over 200 researchers, thinkers, critics and practitioners from nearly forty countries who have been through the processes of contemplation and reflection – those precious intellectual spaces between doing and being.

The important thing that all our authors now offer us through the work contained in these pages, is an invitation for you, the reader, to engage in your own process of reflection.

Mike Robinson
Sheffield, 2000

Introduction

The tourism industry commonly seeks to identify, measure, understand and reach large numbers of people, many of whom share at least some identifiable motivational and behavioural characteristics. Also, academic researchers need to define, classify and categorise phenomena so they can be analysed in a meaningful way. Cultural, social, and (inter-) personal factors that may influence tourist motivations and behaviour and assist in the definition of tourist types are therefore a central concern for many researchers in tourism.

These motivational and behavioural factors are also of major importance for the tourism industry from planning, marketing and visitor management perspectives. Attempting to define, categorise and identify the wants and needs of various tourism market segments is therefore of interest both to the industry and to academic analysts. Industry applications of such research include, for example, the packaging of inclusive tour products that aim to anticipate and meet perceived new forms of demand that are associated with cultural changes in tastes and fashion. The development of 'arts-', 'urban-', 'clubbing-', and 'eco-tourism' products, destinations and experiences are examples of such an application. For others in the tourism industry, the interest may be concerned with understanding and managing the patterns, wants and needs of visitors from particular national markets. An example is the design, presentation and content of interpretative materials in the Japanese language at heritage attractions in Europe. A further, more general consideration that is of interest both to academic researchers and the tourism industry is the extent to which changing values and lifestyles in the 'consumer society' have consequences and implications for types of tourist demand and behaviour.

The development of new consumer goods and services, including travel and tourism products, and people's desire and motivation to possess them is today a central dynamic of socio-economic life. Many people, particularly in North American and north European countries, live in societies where individual identities, motivations and behaviour are related to their consumption patterns. Inter-personal judgements are often based on lifestyles that are created by our patterns of consumption. These consumption patterns include our travel purchases, destination choices and tourist behaviour. Consumption is widely seen as being a means towards personal development, self-realisation and self-fulfilment.

The tourism marketing literature has made significant contributions to an understanding of consumption patterns in the areas of market segmentation, consumer behaviour, and marketing to nationals of other countries. However, marketing theory commonly assumes that the tourism industry aims to satisfy people's inherent wants and needs for tourism products, as opposed to creating them. Perspectives from other academic disciplines such as, psychology, anthropology, sociology and cultural studies thus offer different insights into what motivates people to travel (and *not* travel), past and present patterns and explanations of tourist behaviour, and new tourist typologies. These perspectives include; explorations of the tourist desire to recover a sense of meaning that is absent from everyday home life, the condemnation of tourism as a frivolous activity, with increasingly knowing tourists seeking out and participating in 'pseudo-events', the creation and reinforcement of 'myths' about destinations and people brought about by the experience of travel, and different categorisations of tourists based, in part, on anthropological study.

A number of other social explanations have been advanced that go some way towards an understanding of past and present influences on tourist motivation, behaviour and types, at least in 'developed' societies. Some researchers have focussed on people's educational experiences and the nature of the school and college curriculum, with particular attention focussed on the perceptions that are communicated and learned about other countries and peoples and about tourism specifically. Changes in family and household structures, for example in terms of poverty, relative divorce rates, and the growth in the number of one-parent households, have also been examined for the effects of these social trends on tourism motivation, behaviour and demand.

Social and cultural influences on tourist demand and behaviour are, of course, not fixed. Changes in the shared and accepted values of a society, if such values exist, can be linked with changes in tourist motivation and behaviour and demand for tourism products and destinations. As far as western (North American, Australasian and north European) societies are concerned, these changes in values include the relative demise of traditional gender and family relationships. The distinction between work and leisure activity, including tourism, is also increasingly problematic in contemporary society. The old certainties about full-time jobs for life with fixed and separable holiday periods have been hard to sustain, with many changes in the nature and location of employment. Changes to the motivational and behavioural patterns and demand for tourism that are associated with this de-differentiation between work and leisure require further research.

A number of key research questions therefore exist in the field of tourist motivations, behaviour and types. This volume contains work that examines many of these key research issues. The adaptation and application of theories and methods that have been developed to explain and explore other dimensions of social structures and changes, for example, offers fresh insights into tourist motivation and behaviour. The vast range of established and emerging, 'niche' forms of tourism product and tourist experience highlights the breadth of conceivable tourist motivations and behaviours and emphasises the complexity and richness of this area of research. Tourist expectations and motivations categorised by age, gender, sexual orientation, and the social status of the traveller offer further new directions for researchers in the identification of emerging categories of 'sub-cultural' tourists. The combination of altruism, education and pleasure may also provide some fresh appreciation of people's multiple motivations as travellers. New insights may also be developed in terms of the social carrying capacities of destinations and the effects of the physical proximity of other tourists on travellers' behaviour. The role of the media, including television, film and the arts, and information and communication technologies, as agents in the promotion of national and global tastes and fashion, and in the representation of places and people, is another important contemporary influence on tourist motivation and behaviour.

Scope therefore exists for new and fascinating reflections on the motivational and behavioural life of the tourist and the identification of new and adapted types. This is an area that will continue to attract researchers in the tourism field.

Table of Contents

In search of the grape: Towards building a motivational framework for International wine tourists to Australia

Jane Ali-Knight

Curtin University, Australia

Abstract

In 1994 about 10% of total international visitors made a visit to an Australian winery, an increase of 20% on the 1993 figures. The majority of these were long-haul European and North American tourists. This growing market is further emphasised in the International Visitor Survey (IVS). In 1996 the IVS identified 5% of total responses of factors influencing a decision to come to Australia as 'to visit Australian wine regions.' This data highlights the potential of wine tourism to be a significant export market for Australia and the importance of international wine tourism to Australian Wineries.

Some researchers expand this to define a key determinant of wine tourism is as a form of consumer behaviour in which wine lovers and those interested in wine regions travel to preferred destinations. Key researchers in this emerging field of wine tourism have commented on the lack of published research material available into the behaviour and characteristics of the winery visitor or tourist. There is even confusion over the definition of the wine tourist. Little research has been published based on surveys of wine tourists, all derived information on wine tourists has originated from interviews with winemakers. Very little is known therefore about the wine tourist with regards to key issues such as motivations, expectations and satisfactions.

This paper will present the justification of the research process and a review of current literature focusing on consumer motivation theories. Needs-based motivational theories such as those used by Maslow and Freud will then be applied to the wine tourism consumer and will then be applied to the different attributes which constitute the consumer experience at the winery. This motivation model will help determine the methodology to be used in future research and to design the exploratory survey instrument. Within Australia several wine regions will be chosen to act as case studies. Regions will be chosen which have a high percentage of international winery visitors. This research will attempt to address these important areas of inquiry and add to the limited body of work available.

Introduction

Wine Tourism has been defined as 'visitation to vineyards, wineries, wine festivals and wine shows for which grape wine tasting and/or experiencing the attributes of a grape wine region are the prime motivating factors for visitors.' (Hall 1996, cited in Johnson 1997: 61). Both the wine and tourism industries have achieved high levels of growth within Australia in the 1990s, and as invisible exports are significant contributors to the GDP. Australia had a record 72 707 hectares of vines in 1995 and exported 113.6 millions litres valued at a record $385.3 million (Australian Bureau of Statistics (ABS), 1996.) According to the Bureau of Tourism Research (BTR) IVS 390 400 International visitors visited wineries during their stay in Australia in 1996. The majority of which were long-haul European and North American tourists. The Wine makers Federation of Australia estimates total wine tourism figures to be in the order of 5.3 million visits per annum worth $428 million in 1995 which is expected to grow substantially to around $1100 million by 2025. This data highlights the potential of wine tourism to become a significant export market for Australia.

Tourism represents a significant dimension of the business of many wineries as many smaller wineries rely on cellar door as their sole method of distribution. By definition, their target market comprises regional and international visitors that have an interest in wine. (WAWTS 1999) The value-added element of the industry fosters regional development through job creation and enhances both wine exports and increases tourism dollars. These economic benefits however are often lost to both the wine and tourism industries through a lack of understanding about its potential and the needs of this emerging new client base.

This importance is also reflected in the fact that within Australia, support from a governmental level has led to a National Wine Tourism Strategy having just being released, with one to follow shortly from the West Australian government. National Wine Tourism Conferences are also planned over the next three years with the inaugural International Wine Tourism Conference being held in Margaret River, WA in 2001.

Wine tourism, as explained previously, is a growing research area that is attracting attention and support both from the wine and tourism industries as well as academics. However compared to other special interest tourism areas, such as eco-tourism there is a lack of industry-focused research, especially when considering the growing importance of wine tourism to a country's economy (Hall and Johnson 1997).

The relationship between tourism and wine is merely one of many socio-cultural influences which affect buying and consumption patterns worldwide. A quick survey of those countries with the highest per capita consumption of wine shows a close association with those countries that are major tourism destinations countries and are also significant wine producers i.e. France, Spain and Italy (Ritchie et al. 1999). However, this does not mean that wine and tourism are intrinsically linked in the consumers' mind and it is this area that requires extensive research.

On the demand side, successful wine tourism is dependent on attracting the wine tourist (Dowling 1998). Information on tourist behaviour derived from segmentation studies is an essential component of marketing and development (McCool 1987). Wineries attract a whole host of different visitors the majority of whom visit wine regions for their rural ambience, rather than the possibility of drinking wine. Getz (1998) expands this to define a key determinant of wine tourism is as a form of consumer behaviour in which wine lovers and those interested in wine regions travel to preferred destinations. However key researchers in this emerging field of wine tourism (Getz 1998, Hall and Johnson 1997, Macionis 1996) have commented that despite the unprecedented interest in the *development and marketing of wine tourism,* there is a lack of published research material available into the behaviour and characteristics of the winery visitor. None of the literature consulted examines in any depth the role and importance of tourist motivation in the wine tourist market.

There is confusion over the definition of the wine tourist; for example McKinna (1987) identifies wine tourists as 'the passing tourist trade who thinks a winery crawl is just a good holiday'. McKenzie, however, (1987:7) describes wine tourists as wine aficionados who seek out 'trendy, exclusive or almost unattainable wines direct from the producer.'

Any research also needs to try to define the wine tourist in the context of international wine tourism. Research conducted so far by Hall (1996) into the New Zealand Wine Tourist focused on who visits wineries, what motivated them, and the implications of winery visitation and future purchasing behaviour. Research by Morris and King (1998) into the Margaret River wine region in Western Australia has focused on purchasing behaviour at cellar door sales and neglected wider issues of motivation and expectations. However no behavioural research has been published based on surveys of wine tourists, all derived information on wine tourists has been from interviews with winemakers.

Wine tourism is a developing field of study and publicly available research into this sizeable niche market is limited. Very little is known to date about the wine tourist with regards to key issues such as motivations and expectations. This paper therefore attempts to provide a current picture, albeit sketchy, of who the wine tourist is in Australia, in the context of motivation and attempts to close some gaps that exist in the overall framework of understanding.

Methodology

In order to produce this paper secondary material has been analysed from sources such as the BTR, ABS, various State tourism and wine industry publications and the work of an emerging group of authors who have published in this and related fields. Reference is also made to previous research done by the author in the field of wine education examining the role and importance of the educational winery experience (Ali-Knight and Charters 1999).

This paper is exploratory in nature and aims to provide a snapshot of the progression of current wine tourism research into defining the VALS (values, attitudes and lifestyle attributes) of international wine tourists. Existing work on domestic wine tourists in Australia and overseas will be used, as a starting point and this will be examined against the context of tourist motivation.

This exploratory paper will form the basis for focus group research to be conducted with a group of West Australian domestic wine tourists identified in previous research activity in subsequent months. Focus group research will aim to research visitor motivation, expectations and purchasing behaviour. A brief presentation on the aims and objectives of the project will be used alongside structured informal interview/group discussion. Questions will be open ended in order to elicit as much information as possible in the time required. A number of key research questions will be addressed:

1. Who are the best wine tourist consumers and how are they motivated?

2. What elements and combinations in the wine tourism system work best to attract and satisfy different target markets?

3. Are wine consumers just interested in purchasing wine or in the totality of the experience?

4. What impact does being a wine tourist have on their role as a wine consumer?

The focus group research will help to develop the motivational model that will then be applied and tested in wine regions in Australia with a significant number of international visitors.

Motivational theory

The classic definition of motivation is derived from the word 'motivate', which is to cause a person to act in a certain way or stimulate interest inducing a person to act. Maslow's (1970) needs hierarchy is probably the best known theory of motivation. This proposed a form of a ranking, or hierarchy of individual needs (see Figure 1).

Figure 1   Maslow's Hierarchy of Needs

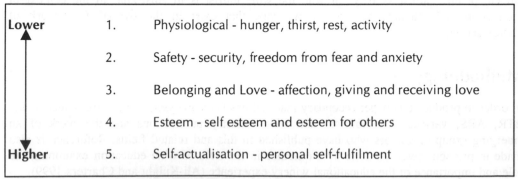

Lower	1.	Physiological - hunger, thirst, rest, activity
	2.	Safety - security, freedom from fear and anxiety
	3.	Belonging and Love - affection, giving and receiving love
	4.	Esteem - self esteem and esteem for others
Higher	5.	Self-actualisation - personal self-fulfilment

Maslow identified two motivational types of sequence mechanism in motivation which can be greatly simplified as deficiency or tension reducing motives and inductive or arousal seeking motives. A person tries to satisfy the most important need first, it then ceases to be a motivator and the next most important need will come into play. He treated his needs levels as universal and innate, yet only those behaviours which satisfy physiological needs are unlearned

McGregor (1960) proposed two distinct views of the nature of human beings: a basically negative view, labeled *Theory X*, and a basically positive view, labeled *Theory Y*. Theory X assumes that lower order needs dominate individuals. Theory Y assumes that higher-order needs dominate individuals. Unfortunately there is no evidence to confirm that either set of assumptions is valid or that accepting theory Y assumptions and altering ones action accordingly will make someone more motivated.

Freud's theory of motivation assumes that people are largely unconscious about the real psychological forces shaping their behaviour. Thus, he suggests that a person does not fully understand his or her motivation. These urges are never eliminated or under perfect control; they emerge in dreams, in slips of the tongue, in neurotic an obsessive behaviour, or ultimately in psychoses. For example, if a person wants to purchase a holiday to the Maldives they might describe their motive as to get away from work and relax, at a deeper level they may be trying to impress people with their choice of an unusual destination and at a still deeper level they might be purchasing the holiday as a means of feeling exotic and independent.

What motivates tourists?

Critical of understanding all marketing activity which aims to develop, promote and sell products is an understanding of consumer behaviour. Swarbrooke and Horner (1999) identify consumer behaviour research as the study of why people buy the product they do and how they make their decisions examining a range of internal and external influences on decision making. Current wine tourism research has focused on external variables such as demographics, reference groups and cultures; this paper however will focus on the internal variable of motivation. This type of research activity is important to the wine tourism industry as it helps to provide valuable insights into who the wine tourist is, what motivates them to visit a winery, take a guided tour, purchase wine and why (Mitchell, Hall and Macintosh 1999).

Motivation research remains a useful tool for marketeers seeking a deeper understanding of consumer behaviour (Kotler 1998). The theories of Freud and Maslow, as described above, have been applied to tourist behaviour. While a great deal of tourism demand theory has been based upon Malsows approach, it is not clear from this why he selected five basic needs, why they are ranked as they are and how he can justify this model. It is not that he has been extended or distorted by tourism theorists but simply he has provided a convenient set of containers, which can be relatively easily, labelled (Cooper et al 1995). The notion that a comprehensive coverage of human needs can be organised into an understandable hierarchical frameworks has obvious benefits for tourism theorists as tourism activity addresses each of the levels of needs from basic needs in the hospitality sector and self actualisation though the advent of tourism products such as adventure tourism. It would be interesting to discover which needs wine tourism activity addresses.

The study of motivation in tourism has led to a diversity of approach, some of which are outlined below. Dann (1981) identifies seven areas of tourist motivation:

- Travel as a response to what is lacking yet desired.

- Destinational pull in response to motivational push.

- Motivation as fantasy.

- Motivation as classified purpose.

- Motivational typology's (ie: sun lust, wanderlust).

- Motivational and tourist experiences.

- Motivation as auto definition and meaning.

It is obvious that most tourists would be motivated by a combination of the above approaches.

McIntosh and Goeldner (1986) condense the above and utilise four categories of motivation:

- Physical motivators including refreshment of body, mind and health.

- Cultural Motivators including desire to see and know more about other cultures.

- Interpersonal motivators including desire to meet new people, visit friends and relatives and seek new and different experiences.

- Status and Prestige motivators including a desire for personal development with the desire for recognition and attention from others.

Plog (1974) developed a theory whereby the US population could be classified by a number of psychographic types:

- Allocentric - Adventuresome and individual exploration.

- Mid-centric - Individual travel to areas with facilities and growing reputation.

- Psychocentric - Organised package holiday to 'popular' destinations.

While Plogs' model is a central pillar within tourism theory and is useful to apply, it is too simplistic in its approach as tourists will travel with different motivations on different occasions, they may typically engage in *mid centric* tourist behaviour but due to prestige motivators may decide to embark on an *allocentric* holiday. Smith (1990) also tested Plogs model in seven different countries to verify whether there are cultural differences associated with the model. Smith questioned the model but due to the reliability of his data further studies are required to test the hypothesis fully and to apply it to distinct tourism consumers such as wine tourists.

Although the literature on tourism motivation is still being developed it has been shown that there is a strong link between motivation and demand and Cooper et al (1995) identify the following dimensions:

- Travel is essentially need related and this manifests itself in terms of motivational or push as the energiser of action.

- Motivation is grounded in sociological and psychological norms, attitudes, cultures, perceptions leading to person specific forms of motivation.

- The image of a destination created through induced or organic communication channels will influence motivations and subsequently affect the type of travel undertaken.

Comparisons can be made with research conducted by Turner and Reisinger (1999) into shopping behaviour of Japanese tourists to the Gold Coast. Shopping has been recognised as an important motivator to travel, although shopping is seldom mentioned as a primary reason for travel. It is perhaps the most universal of tourist activities, and of great economic importance to the local community. The same can be said of wine as a key component of shopping purchase behaviour - the wine regions create an attractive and inviting environment and incentive to travel, develops an attractive tourism product and is a source of pleasure and excitement. Jansen Verbeke (1990) discussed the difficulties in defining leisure shopping behaviour and consumer attitudes have been related to personal characteristics and Lesser and Hughes (1986) segmented shoppers into seven types: active, inactive, traditional, service, dedicated, price and transitional. It is unclear at present whether wine tourists would fall into similar categories but what is apparent is that the purchasing of wine products at the cellar door is a primary motivating factor for a winery visit (Ali-Knight and Charters 1999)

An understanding of consumer needs and motivation is critical for successful marketing and travel can be seen to satisfy many physical, social and psychological needs. Travel motivation can therefore be both general and specific. Tourists experience the general drive to get away from their normal routine while at the same time displaying individual motivations to see specific destinations and undertake specific activities whilst on holiday. They seek to satisfy not one single need but a number of quite distinct needs simultaneously. The most successful tourism products as Holloway and Robinson (1995) state are therefore those which respond best to this bundle of needs within a given market segment

In search of the grape?

After discussing the importance of an understanding of motivational theory to organisations such as wineries delivering tourism products it is important to try and examine what motivates wine tourists. Is it their love of wine or a bundle of other attractions such as climate, the environment and culture that lures them to a wine tourism destination?

There is no doubt that there is no single 'wine tourist'. Wineries are perfectly realistic about the segmentation of their market at the cellar door - although their analysis of the segments is generally based on general awareness rather than any accurate method of data collection.

Earlier research by the author (Ali-Knight and Charters 1999) showed that WA wineries offer segments such as the 'casual' tourist who looks to taste and little else. Estimates of the size of this group vary from 5-30% of all visitors. Another proffered category is the 'sophisticated drinker' who is hungry for as much information as s/he can obtain. Winery estimates of the numbers in this group vary from 5% upwards.

Most wine tourists however clearly fall into some middle category - those who claim no special knowledge, interested in experience as much as learning, but who also drink wine regularly enough to make planned visits to a winery.

This intuitive approach to segmentation adopted by wineries is mirrored in the academic literature on the topic. Hall (1996, in Hall and Macionis 1998), on the basis of discussions with representatives of the supply side, posited three categories: the *'wine lovers'*, the *'wine interested'* and *'curious tourists'*, and provides some indicators pointing towards the profile of each. This is a useful starting point, but focuses on the perceptions of the winery owner/managers rather than the tourists themselves. European researchers have followed a similar line - in one instance proposing 'the formal wine tourist', the 'tourist with an acknowledged interest in wine' and the 'general tourist'. However the structure of each form of tourism differs; for instance in Europe the 'formal wine tourist' is perceived to travel in an organised tour, whereas in Australia and New Zealand the highly wine-educated tourist is much less likely to do this than the 'wine interested' or 'curious tourist'.

Dodd and Bigotte (1997) used cluster analysis, following a consumer perception survey at Texas wineries. Using the data obtained they could only satisfactorily suggest two consumer segments - based only on age/income. One group was older, with a higher mean income than the other. Various differences between the two groups emerged, and it was suggested that these tended to result from the different stages in the family life-cycle that each group represented.

Other researchers have asked consumers to 'self-categorise'. Maddern and Golledge (1996 in Johnson 1997) asked visitors to determine whether their wine knowledge was 'advanced', 'intermediate' or 'basic'. The problem with knowledge is that it is only an indicator of their motivation as a wine tourist. A visitor may be knowledgeable without being enthusiastic, and knowledge is probably less useful as an indicator of their activity levels as wine tourists, and their relationship with the local tourism market.

Dodd and Bigotte give broad differences between two groups of wine tourists. Others have tried to give an overall general profile of them. Getz (1998 using data from the South Australian Tourism Commission) describes them as being

> *Couples with no children and those with higher education and incomes in professional occupations.*

He also quotes Dodd and Bigotte (1997) who suggest that income is one of the best predictors of wine consumption - and therefore wine tourists will not be "on cheap package deals."

There have been a number of studies developing a profile of the wine tourist and a variety of references have been used to suggest a more holistic picture of who the wine tourist is. Williams and Young (1999) in their research on Australian wine tourists pulled together the following snapshot of the average wine tourist:

- Drink wine frequently.

- Not considered wine experts.

- Likely to spend around $50 at cellar door, but do not buy from all wineries.

- Predominantly mature age bracket: aged 30 to 60.

- Even split between men and women but women are younger.

- Usually couples without dependent children.

- Have a tendency to originate from urban areas.

- Often university educated although a large number with only secondary education.

- Tend to visit wineries 2 or 3 times a year.

- Large number plan to visit a specific winery before leaving home and thus purpose driven.

- Base their choice of winery visited in the wine/style and reputation/name.

- Seeking a winery experience in a social, possible educational environment, likely to enjoy a combination of food and wine. Authenticity of meeting wine maker enhances the experience.

- More likely to stay in Bed and Breakfast or luxury accommodation.

From this snapshot they developed two types of wine tourist based on a continuum (see figure 2). Halls (1996) and Ali-Knight and Charters (1999) definitions can also be placed on this. Although simplistic in approach, as this does not take into account different wine regions and new emerging markets, it provides a framework within which winery operators and wine regions can develop individual consumer profiles and target future marketing activity.

Figure 2   Wine Tourist Continuum

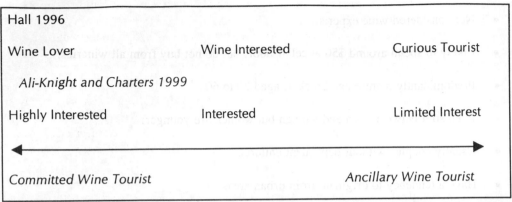

Williams and Young (1999) develop their hypothesis against the profile of the national Australian wine drinker to link the committed and ancillary wine tourist to primary (taste/preference, consumption and price) and secondary (age and gender, packaging and wine experience) indicators. There appeared to be considerable support from various secondary sources (ABS) to imply that primary indicators are relevant however further investigation is needed in the area of the secondary indicators in terms of demographics and pyschographics.

Several wine tourism researchers (Hall 1996, Hall et al 1999; Johnson 1997) have identified motivations in terms of internal (behavioural) and external (pull) factors. Several of the internal motives identified such as socialising, relaxing, learning about the wine and meeting the winemaker show that motivations are deeply rooted in the VALS (value, attitudes and lifestyles) of the visitor.

The typologies of the wine tourist discussed could therefore be analysed in terms of internal and external motives and the relative size of each of the markets needs to be examined.

Conclusion

Data relating to the development of psychographic profiles of wine tourists is relatively scarce. Although existing information, as discussed above, provides considerable insight into a *suggested* wine tourist it is still generalistic, originates from the wineries perspective (ie: supply side) rather than from the tourists (demand side) and does not focus on any specific nationality or wine region. Thus winery owners and tourism operators have difficulties in distinguishing the level of interest and commitment of the winery tourist to their region.

Existing literature is also limited to a focus on new world wine regions with very little research being conducted into the 'old world' (ie: Europe) which constitutes the majority of international visitors to Australian wine regions. There is obviously a nexus of research that can be conducted to compare these two distinct groups in terms of their motives to visit a wine tourism destination.

Any study of the wine tourist also has to be considered in the light of existing literature on tourist motivation. Where do wine tourists lie on Maslows needs continuum? are the 'committed' wine tourists allocentric?; are they driven by cultural, physical, interpersonal or prestige motivators?; can they be categorised by Danns seven areas of motivation?; are there cultural differences between tourism generating countries for wine tourism? Any future research centering on the motivation of the wine tourist obviously has to address these types of questions in order to build up a profile of both a countries domestic wine tourist and more importantly its international wine tourist.

Research into wine tourist motivation would not only help winery operators and wine regions identify potential customers but also help ensure that their product offerings are meeting the needs of their particular wine tourist. As stated earlier, research into wine tourist consumer behaviour has an obvious link to more effective marketing activity and ultimately increased sales at the cellar door, brand loyalty and repeat visitation.

In summary the wine tourist is an important though neglected part of the wine and tourism market of any wine producing country. It can be seen that the profiles discussed are not motivated purely by a love of wine but by a complex interrelationship of internal and external factors. Future research, beyond the scope of this paper, will therefore aim to identify who the international wine tourist to Australia is, liken them to the developing domestic profile and identify a motivational framework to compare them against.

References

Ali-Knight and Charters, (1999), Wine Education in a West Australian Wineries Context, *International Journal of Wine Marketing*, Vol. 11, No. 1 pp7 - 18.

Ali-Knight and Charters, (1999), Wine Tourism - A Thirst for Knowledge, *First European Wine Tourism Conference*, University of Surrey, UK, 1st – 4th Sept.

Australian Bureau of Statistics (ABS), (1997), Wine Consumption, Wine and Grape Industry, 1329.0.

Australian Bureau of Statistics (ABS), (1996), 1995 Australian Wine and Grape Industry Compendium, Cat. 1329.0, Canberra.

Cambourne, B. (1998), Wine Tourism in the Australian Capital Territory. Wine Tourism: Perfect Partners, *Proceedings of The First Wine Tourism Conference*, Margaret River, Western Australia, 7 – 9 May.

Cooper, C. Fletcher, J. Gilbert, D. and Wanhill, S. (1995), Tourism Principles and Practices, Longman, Malaysia.

Dann, G. M. S (1981), Tourist Motivation: an appraisal *Annals of Tourism Research* Vol. 8 No. 2 pp. 187 – 219.

Dodd, T. and Bigotte, V. (1997), Perceptual Differences Among Visitor Groups to Wineries *Journal of Travel Research* Winter 1997, pp.46 – 51.

Dowling, R. (1998), Wine Tourism – an emerging industry. Wine Tourism: Perfect Partners, Proceedings of The First Wine Tourism Conference, Margaret River, Western Australia, 7 – 9 May.

Dibb et al. (1994), 'Marketing concepts and strategies.' Houghton Mifflin, 2nd European Edition.

Getz, D. (1998), A Global Overview of Wine Tourism. Wine Tourism: Perfect Partners, Proceedings of The First Wine Tourism Conference, Margaret River, Western Australia, 7 – 9 May.

Hall, C. M. (1996), Wine Tourism in New Zealand in G. Kearsley (ed.) Tourism Down Under II Conference – Towards a more Sustainable Tourism Conference Proceedings (pp 109-119) Centre for Tourism, University of Otago.

Hall, C. M. (1997), Wine Tourism in New Zealand: Large Bottles or Better Relationships? in J. Higham (ed.) *Trails, Tourism and Regional Development Conference Proceedings.* Centre for Tourism, University of Otago, Dunedin.

Hall, C. and Macionis, N. (1998), "Wine Tourism in Australia and New Zealand." in Butler, R., Hall, M. and Jenkins, J. (eds.) (1998). *Tourism and Recreation in Rural Areas.* England: John Wiley and Sons.

Holloway, J. C. and Robinson, C. (1995), Marketing for Tourism 3rd Edition Longman Singapore.

Jansen-Verbeke, M. (1990), Leisure and shopping-tourism product mix, in Marketing Tourism Places (G.Ashworth and B. Goodall eds.) Routledge, London, pp. 128-137.

Johnson, G. (1997), Surveying Wine Tourism in New Zealand in Johnson G (editor) *Quality Tourism: Beyond the Masses, Proceedings of the First National Tourism Students Conference.'* Conference, Tourism Club, Dunedin.

King, C. and Morris, R. (1997), The Cellar Door Report: Margaret River Region Winery/Tourism Research. For the Margaret River Wine Industry Association and the Margaret River Tourism Association, Bunbury.

Kotler, P. (1988), 'Marketing Management and Strategy: A reader.' Prentice Hall, 4th Edition.

Kotler, A. P. A., Bowne, J., Makens, J. (1998), Marketing for Hospitality and Tourism 2nd Edition, Prentice Hall.

Lesser, J. A. and Hughes, M. A. (1986), Towards a Typology of Shoppers *Business Horizons* Vol. 29, No. 6, pp. 56 – 62.

Macionis, N. (1996), Wine Tourism in Australia in G. Kearsley (ed.) *Tourism Down Under II Conference – Towards a more Sustainable Tourism Conference Proceedings* (pp 264-286) Centre for Tourism, University of Otago.

Maslow, A. H. (1970), Motivation and Personality 2nd Ed New York Harpers and Row.

McCool, (1987), 'Tourists and tourism in Montana: The Basics of a viable Industry.' *Western Midlands 13, p.7-11,* in Harris, C et al. (1990) 'A Comprehensive Method for Studying Leisure Travel.' *Journal of Travel Research, p.39-44.*

McGregor, D. (1960), The Human Side of Enterprise New York Mc Graw Hill.

McIntosh R. W. and Goeldner C. R. (1986), Tourism: Principles, Practices and Philosophies New York, Wiley.

McKenzie, M. (1986), The premier wine state set to fight back. *Grapevine,* South Australian Tourism News. December pp.6-7.

McKinna (1987), Developing Marketing Strategies for Wines. Mc Kinna Pty Ltd. pp.119-113.

Mitchell, R., Hall, M., and McIntosh, A. (1999), Wine Tourism and Consumer Behaviour in forthcoming text *Wine Tourism around the World.*

Plog, S. C. (1974), Why destination areas rise and fall in popularity *Cornell Hospitality Review Quarterly* Vol. 14. No 4 pp 55 –8.

Ruberto, A. (1996), Visitors to Wine Regions in *Tourism Update,* summer 1996, BTR, Canberra.

Ries, A., and Trout, J. (1981), 'Positioning: The Battle or your Mind.' Mc Graw Hill.

Ritchie, C., Jones, E., and Pritchard, A. Tourism and other Socio/Cultural Influences on Wine Consumption within the UK, *First European Wine Tourism Conference,* University of Surrey, UK, 1st – 4th Sept.

Smith, S. L. J. (1990), A Test of Plogs Allocentric/Psychocentric Model: Evidence from Seven Nations *Journal of Travel Research* Vol. 28 No. 4 pp. 40-3.

South Australia Tourism Commission, (1997), Wine and Tourism: A Background Research Report, Adelaide.

Turner, L. W., and Reisinger, Y. (1999), The Determination of Shopping Satisfaction for Japanese Tourists Visiting the Gold Coast, Australia *CAUTHE Conference,* Adelaide 10th – 13th February.

West Australian Wine Tourism Strategy, (1999), West Australian tourism Commission.

Williams, A., and Young, I. (1999), Wine Tourists: white wine casks or bottled reds? 2nd *Australian Wine Tourism Conference, Rutherglen, Victoria, 15 – 17th August.*

Charity challenges and adventure tourism in developing countries - who dares wins?

Sue Bleasdale

Middlesex University, UK

Sponsoring someone to undertake a task in order to raise money for charity is a widely used means of fundraising in the UK. We are all familiar with the London Marathon and similar events and many of us will have supported sponsored silences as School fundraising events. Charity challenges are a recent development of this form of fundraising. These usually involve travel to a distant location to undertake, as part of an organized group, some physical activity ranging from the relatively undemanding to the arduous.

Over the last few years the number and variety of these Charity Challenges has increased quite noticeably. The number of trips and participants, the range of locations, the charities and the physical activities involved have all been extended to the point where this is now a recognizable and distinct form of tourism operating in a clearly defined market niche within adventure tourism. Questions inevitably arise concerning the efficacy, ethics, impact and sustainability of this new form of tourism and yet there is little published material on the topic(Warburton-Lee, 1999). This paper will seek to identify and explore some of the key issues relating to charity challenges overseas from a UK perspective. It should be seen as an exploratory paper which will provide the basis for further research.

Why has this form of tourism emerged in the late twentieth century?

There are a number of reasons behind this burgeoning popularity. Charity challenges have emerged within the wider tourism sectors of adventure tourism and sport-related tourism which have been growing in recent decades particularly in the USA, Australia and more recently in Europe and the UK (Tallantire, 1993, Gibson, 1996, Zurick, 1992). There are no specific statistics on adventure tourism but the growth of the sector is evidenced by the existence of extensive advertising of activity holidays in the UK press (e.g. the Guardian travel pages have a defined section for activity holidays) and by the existence of magazines that cater specifically for those seeking to combine physical activity and adventure with global travel (e.g. Global Adventure), as well as regular coverage in more general magazines such as Wanderlust and Geographical. The explosive growth of new sports such as snowboarding and mountain (or all terrain) cycling has also characterized the 1990s both reflecting and fueling the demand for travel and excitement in combination especially among the young adult age group (17-30). The activities of organisations such as the Dangerous Sports Club also reflect the growing demand among certain sectors of the public for adventure and travel. In the USA physical activities known as 'extreme sports' are incorporated into 'thrill seeking' vacations. Television and radio advertisements also attest to the growth in popularity of these activities (as for example in the Pepsi Max campaign on TV and the Sanatogen radio advertisements) . The tourism and travel industry have been quick to respond to this specialized demand and the popularity of the annual Independent Travellers World show in the UK further reflects the growth of this sector.

This growth can be explained by a range of factors. One is the growth of tourism in general and in particular the emergence of an expanding range of niche sectors. New forms of tourism emerge frequently in response to the increasing sophistication of tourist demand and behaviour. Lifestyle concerns and improved health of the population in the main originating countries have led to an increased demand for activity based holidays. Hall (1992) argues that the emergence of adventure and sport-related tourism is a response to urbanism and twentieth century living and reflects also the search for a healthy lifestyle. Such holidays are often located in the more remote countryside and according to Gibson (1996) this can add to the element of perceived risk by incorporating a sense of the struggle against nature. The developing countries and other remote unpopulated areas are perceived to have a comparative advantage in this context as they can provide numerous locations which are ideally suited to adventure tourism activities. The very fact of these being at a considerable distance from the countries originating the adventurers merely adds to the sense of adventure. Adventure tourism has been divided into 'hard' and 'soft' categories based upon the degree of danger, risk and physical discomfort involved.

Charity challenges have emerged in this context. Charities are constantly seeking new and more effective ways of raising funds. This has particularly been the case in the 1990s which has seen the emergence of 'donor fatigue'. In addition in the UK charities have now to compete with the National Lottery for disposable income. The charity challenge is a response to the need to revitalize fundraising from the general public. They exploit the growth in demand for personal and physical challenges. Many businesses and corporations support the participation of members of their workforce in such activities as they are seen to have good team building potential. Charity fund-raisers can therefore seek to promote the charity challenge both to individuals and to corporations. As a highly organized and structured group activity the charity challenge is arguably a good example of 'soft' adventure tourism.

The nature of the charity challenge sector

There are discernible trends in the charity challenge sector even though it is relatively youthful. One charity claims to have initiated the first international charity cycle ride some eight years ago. These trends, which are dominantly expansion and growth, reflect the capacity of charities and tour organisers to respond to increases in, and the changing nature of, consumer demand. The fact that the sector is changing so rapidly indicates a very dynamic market within which both the consumer and the industry are constantly in pursuit of something new and different. This is likely to have implications for the future vitality of the sector. It may be that the charity challenge has a limited shelf life and will quickly become economically unsustainable. This would have serious implications for any community that has become dependent on the passage of such groups unless alternative economic activities are available. It would also have serious implications for the charities involved.

The range of activities and locations for charity challenges is wide. Many activities are UK based, single day events such as the Three peaks, parachute jumps, bungee jumping, bike rides. These occur in numerous locations throughout the British Isles. Many others are linked to big city marathons around the world. For this paper however the focus is upon charity challenges overseas, especially in the developing countries and other remote, less visited parts of the world. Details have been gathered since 1997 from magazines, newspapers, the web, charities, tour operators and personal contacts and this information gives a clear picture of the sector.

On average, participants pay £200 as a non-refundable deposit and then raise some £2000 in sponsorship for the charity. Recently some 'special offers' have appeared reducing the deposit to £99 for 'early booking' or offering a 10% reduction. This probably reflects increased competition and may be the first sign of market saturation. Some advertisements emphasize the possibility of a 'free' trip (for a higher level of sponsorship).

Initially, challenges focused on bike rides and trekking but the range of activities now includes scuba diving, white-water rafting, four-wheel driving, swimming, kayaking, canoeing, horse riding, whale and dolphin watching. Multi-activity trips are becoming more common and some challenges are putting more emphasis on the arduousness of the physical challenge.

All the challenges are organized as a group activity. This explains to a considerable extent why they are supported as a corporate activity. Group size varies and seems to be adjusted according to the location and activity involved. For Alaska the group size is limited to 10 whilst for a cycle challenge in Jordan or Russia the group may involve 80-100. However most seem to have 30-40 members in a group. A group based challenge may seem safer and offer greater possibilities for social benefits. Whilst it may seem that groups will have a greater impact on communities and the environment than individuals a concentrated impact may be easier to manage than a dispersed one, and groups can be easier to control and manage in remote or dangerous environments. Clearly, the group format is essential to the success of the challenges for fundraising, being more cost effective.

The charity challenge is multi-faceted having a physical component and a social component (fundraising). Both are substantial tests requiring a high level of commitment and motivation over several months. Stamina and determination are needed to fulfill both aspects of the challenge. For the participants therefore successful completion will bring a substantial reward in terms of personal achievement.

Apart from the charities and the challenge participants who are the other stakeholders who stand to benefit from these events? Certainly there are several tour operators who have become specialists in setting up and organizing these events. Most charities use a tour company to make practical arrangements, undertake liaison in the event region and provide logistic support. Tour companies may also research and promote new destinations and itineraries. It does seem to be a competitive field and there are issues concerning the amount charged to cover costs and profit for the tour company. Since these events are promoted as charity fund-raisers this is a valid area of concern. An alternative approach would be to follow the example of LEPRA which had lower levels of sponsorship for its events in India, Brazil and Nepal (£1050-1470) but asked participants to cover the full costs of their involvement. The total costs were much the same as other events £2-2500 but all of the sponsorship money raised went to the charity. However it is probably the case that initially this approach would not look as attractive to participants.

The country and region where the event takes place will also expect to benefit from the activity. These benefits will mainly be in the form of increased tourist revenue, helping to boost the foreign exchange earnings of the host country but there will also be expected benefits in employment and through the provision of local services such as porterage and accommodation. In addition, Governments may see such activities as having a role in their tourism development strategy - adding diversity, exploiting comparative advantage, assisting in regional development strategy and helping to build an international image in the tourism industry. An important question is the extent to which these expected benefits are realised.

Advertisements tend to be high profile - often appearing in prominent positions in the broadsheets, such as the Guardian, as well as in the magazines mentioned above. However the case study survey showed that advertising in the Big Issue and in local papers are also effective in recruitment. Recruiting among existing charity supporters is also a significant source of participants. The advertisements emphasize location, using the physical characteristics of the location as a key element in promoting the event and in attracting participants. The advertisements also focus on activity and low cost. The emphasis is on doing something exciting in an exotic location whilst also doing something worthwhile by raising money for charity. Some even seem to throw down the gauntlet of a challenge ('Have you got the bottle?', 'Be warned - this ain't no picnic' - Macmillan Cancer Relief). The challenges clearly target those with a social conscience but advertisements mainly target those who are physically and touristically adventurous and who may have a competitive streak or a strong desire to be different and avoid the ordinary (e.g. references in the publicity material to following in the footsteps of Ghenghis Khan, or being one of few people to visit the hidden regions of Alaska). On the other hand the fact that the challenges are organized group activities makes them appear 'safe'. Hall (1992) sees adventure tourism through organized packages run by tour operators as the entry point into adventure tourism for many and he hypothesizes that many will later become independent adventure tourists. This may not hold true for charity challengers for whom the motivation may be different.

Challenges predominantly, but not exclusively, take place in developing countries, involving remote and relatively little visited regions that are not associated with mass tourism and package holidays. Brochures emphasize the exotic nature of these environments drawing attention to the unique physical characteristics of the area alongside the attractions of experiencing different cultures and visiting unique historical features (for example the Amazon and Borneo are presented as 'jungle' adventures, Peru is characterized under the banner of the Machu Pichu or the Inca trail.) Several organisations refer to 'the experience of a lifetime' further emphasizing the uniqueness of the challenge experience. Original locations in Egypt, Nepal and Jordan have been extended to include Kenya, Kazakhstan, Ladakh, Brazil, Cuba, Zimbabwe, Russia, Romania, Patagonia, Borneo, China, Peru,

Ecuador, Namibia, Morocco, Alaska, the Grand Canyon, Iceland, India, Sri Lanka, Malawi, Mexico, Costa Rica, Mongolia, Thailand, Vietnam and most recently Madagascar. A number of these locations have fragile or vulnerable physical environments and most involve travel through areas where the population is predominantly rural and living what can be described as a traditional way of life. The impact of groups of adventure tourists passing through these areas may be considerable and should be investigated. There is a strong expectation that charitable organisations and those who support them will and should exercise responsibility to areas that are contributing significantly, if rather indirectly, to their fundraising. Several of those surveyed were making definite efforts to employ local people, use local transport, buy local food and to minimize environmental impacts but there must still be a concern about the impact of the rapid rise in numbers visiting some areas.

Just as the range of activities and locations have expanded rapidly so the number of charities running challenges has increased. Most are well known national charities with a pre-existing high profile. Many support work with children and/or the disabled. Many others have a focus on a health issue. Most are UK-based charities raising money for UK projects. Very few brochures or information leaflets have any reference to work overseas and quite a number explicitly state that the monies raised will be spent on projects in the UK. There are a small number of charity challenges raising money for work overseas e.g. Sightsavers, Save the Rhino, Friends of Russian Children, the Whale and Dolphin Conservation society, Tasca Trust, Lepra, Land Aid, Womankind and AFS International Youth Development. Ironically although most of the challenges take place in 'developing' countries none of the big agencies working in development issues have, as yet, become involved in charity challenges but this may just be matter of time. The challenges are obviously a very effective way of raising, quite quickly, quite substantial sums of money which is and not ring fenced for specific projects (this gives useful flexibility to the charity). Although the precise proportion varies in all cases surveyed at least half the sponsorship money goes to the charity. In some cases the figure is over 70%. The totals raised can be considerable. Friends of Russian Children expected to raise ,600,000 from their challenges in 1999. Sense raised 500,000 from their Nepal treks in 1997 and expected to raise ,200,000 from the Borneo challenge in 1999 while the Sightsaver Mount Kilimanjaro climb in 2000 was expected to raise ,40,000.

Several charities use challenges as a major component in their fundraising and now organize several challenges a year. Warburton-Lee (1999) sees SCOPE as the market leader and notes that Mencap plan to run 14 events in 2000. Charity based sources provide the information that in 2000 Whizz Kidz is planning 11 overseas challenge events, Norwood Ravenswood will run 8 events and at least one event will run on three occasions, One to One plan 6 events, NDCS 7, AFS plan 3 and Sense hope to run 6. Most of the organisations spoken to are planning more for 2000 than they ran in 1999, reflecting the success of these events as fund-raisers.

There may be a good reason for the bias towards UK charities. It is possible that UK residents prefer to raise money, and find it easier to raise money, for UK projects (charity begins at home). The recent history of UK charity donations would give some support to this hypothesis and feedback from some of the organisations named above also supports the view that it can be more difficult to raise sponsorship for an overseas project. This may explain why some of the brochures are quite explicit about money raised being spent in the UK.

Given the profile of the charity challenges outlined above, what are the key questions to emerge? Do challenge participants fit the profile of the adventure tourist or do they have a different set of characteristics? What motivates individuals to participate in these events and what are the implications of this motivation for the challenge and its impacts? Do those raising money for a challenge have an awareness of the impacts of the event? Do the challenge organisers monitor the impacts? Do they try to ensure benefits for the host communities? A further issue that has already been raised in a number of arenas concerns the proportion of the sponsorship money reaching the charity, going to the tour operator. Related to this is the matter of money raised for sponsorship being used to subsidize participants' expenses. Clearly these are complex issues and the information collected suggests a diversity of practice. There is some evidence of a growing awareness among charities and tour operators of the need to address these issues and seek transparent solutions. Quite a number of information packs make explicit pledges concerning the maximum amount of sponsorship money that can be allocated to costs or guarantee to give a specific amount of sponsorship to charity projects. Some treks are using locally based tour operators , thus ensuring that more of the challenge costs stay in the host country. Others are using a non-profit tour operator where the tour profits, as distinct from the sponsorship, is dedicated to local community projects such as schools, clinics and clean water provision. Most are aware of the need to create local employment.

Case study

A case study was undertaken among those participating in a sponsored trek in Nepal in 1999 for the Imperial Cancer Research Fund. 31 trekkers (out of a group of 40) completed a questionnaire during or immediately after the trek. The questionnaire sought to gather information on the characteristics of the participants but also investigated issues of motivation and awareness of impacts. The fact that participants are willing to accept the challenge of raising significant sums of money for charity indicates individuals who are highly motivated and who have a well developed sense of social responsibility. One question that arises is whether this sense of social responsibility is also active in the context of the trek or cycle. Do participants have a realistic awareness of the impact of their presence on the areas visited? Do participants see a need for the challenge to deliver benefits to the 'host' communities as well as to the charity being sponsored? Does the fact that the challenge involves trekking mean that the participants will be environmentally aware?

Trekker characteristics

58% of the trekkers were male and 38% female (one no response was returned). This skew towards men is perhaps not surprising for a physical challenge. However one respondent did comment that she felt that charity challenges of this type were a safe way for a single woman to participate in this kind of travel. There may be scope for more targeting of single women.

The age distribution of the trekkers showed a pattern rather different from other adventure tourist groups. Gibson (1996) identifies young adulthood as the main period for 'thrill-seeking' but among the trekkers surveyed the dominant group was the 30-40 age group (38%). It could be that more mature adults have a greater sense of social responsibility, or a wider network in which to fund raise or are motivated by the desire to do something adventurous 'before it's too late'. The responses on motivation support these hypotheses. The 50 plus age group was also well represented (29%). Gibson (1996) also reports a rise in participation among the fifty plus age group. Again the responses from the survey support the view that for some the desire to do something adventurous before it's too late was part of the motivation. However the survey more forcefully reflects the fact that many in the fifty plus age group were very strongly motivated by personal experiences relating to cancer. Lowest participation level was among the 40-50 age group. This may reflect life cycle factors as this is a period when many people are highly committed in terms of career and family. The low numbers in the 20-30 age group may reflect the fact that this is a key period for career building , but it may be that the 20-30 age group would see the charity challenge as too 'soft', preferring independent travel and a more extreme physical challenge. As a group travel experience for the under 30's the charity challenge is clearly unable to compete with Club 18-30 and other mainstream travel alternatives.

All of those interviewed classified themselves as 'white', 41% identified themselves as Christian. No other religions were represented with 58% claiming to be inactive or of no religion. The group was dominated by people with high level educational qualifications - 70.9% had A levels or higher (19.3% had a post-graduate qualification) and the occupational mix showed a high proportion in professional or managerial positions (64.5%). There were six respondents from law and finance, four service industry managers, two civil servants and six high level technicians. Education was not well represented with two respondents, but the trek did take place in term time. The picture presented by these characteristics reinforces the stereotypical image of the British charity supporter as being dominantly white and middle-class but it could be simply a reflection of the way in which participants were recruited. There were three retired persons, two unwaged (both housewives) and three manual workers.

In terms of geographical spread there was a degree of clustering. While participants from the south-east dominated (13 out of 31 - 41.9%) there was also a strong contingent from Scotland (10 out of 31 - 32.2%) and the north-west (5 out of 31 - 16.1%). There were no participants from the Midlands. Looking at the responses to questions on age, occupation and motivation there is no obvious explanation for the clustering but it could be related to the effectiveness of the Imperial Cancer Research Fund support groups in the two dominant areas. Only further research would clarify this.

When asked about their concern for environmental issues 64.5% said they were concerned 'quite a lot' about the environment and the remaining 35.5% stated that they were sometimes concerned about environmental issues. 54.8 % said they were interested (quite a lot) in non-western cultures and societies and 45.2% said they were 'a little' interested. This represents quite a high level of interest which should be reflected in a high level of awareness of the impacts of the trek on the area visited.

Trekker motivation

18 of the 31 (58%) had strong personal motives for choosing a challenge in support of Cancer research and 7 (22.5%) were strongly supportive of the charity though for more impersonal reasons. Of the rest only four seemed relatively indifferent to the charity - three stating they would have been happy to support any good cause and one that his wife had

chosen it. This would seem to indicate that challengers are very focused and likely to be very selective about participating in such an event. The challenge does not seem to be perceived as just another opportunity to travel - the link with the specific charity is very important. Only one trekker did not specify this as a powerful motivator as they had 'won' the trek in a draw. Four trekkers specifically said that they did not regard the event as a holiday and therefore would not see the event as tourism.

Despite the strong link with the charity most of the trekkers had multiple motives for undertaking the trek. These can be divided into several categories. Firstly the fundraising motive (the desire to do something worthwhile, to help a good cause, to benefit others, to raise awareness), secondly the physical challenge motive (enjoyment of walking, hill walking, preference to cycling, long held ambition to trek in the Himalayas - some 24 (77.4%) trekkers had this kind of motivation) and thirdly the personal challenge motivation (sense of achievement, experience of a lifetime, rewarding experience, adventure, achieving a lifelong ambition, self- discovery - 58% of trekkers). Only three trekkers did not express any personal motivation. There were other motivations which could perhaps be categorized as travel motivations. These included experiencing other cultures - this was mentioned by nine trekkers (29%). For a large number the opportunity to visit Nepal and the Himalayan region was a strong motivation. Several mentioned a lifelong ambition or dream to visit the area, others mentioned the scenery, the culture, natural beauty and remoteness. In total only 8 out of 31 (25%) had not specifically chosen Nepal. They had chosen the challenge and it happened to be in Nepal. Finally social motivation was also mentioned by a few (group bonding, meeting new friends, meeting like minded people - 19.34%).

Most of those surveyed had multiple motivations combining a desire to challenge themselves physically, to support a worthwhile cause and to achieve some kind of personal goal. This makes the challengers seem rather more complex in terms of motivation than the 'ordinary' adventure tourist.

Trekker views of the challenge impact

Trekkers were asked to comment on the impact of the event on Nepal, on the people in the communities on the trek route and on the environment. The responses showed an appreciation among many of the trekkers of the positive and negative aspects of such events for Nepal and its people. Most trekkers recognized the financial benefits of tourism in the form of money, increased income, business opportunities and investment. Many also mentioned the creation of jobs and tourism related employment (e.g. porters, cooks and cleaners). In all 26 trekkers (83.8%) specified the economic benefits. Only two felt there would be no impact on Nepal. Three had only vague ideas about possible impacts. Two mentioned the benefit from the wider exposure of Nepal from the publicity relating to the trek and two expressed the view that contact with other cultures (namely western culture) would be beneficial.

Despite this widespread recognition of the economic benefits many also expressed doubts and reservations. The main points raised included the danger of exploitation, the need to distribute benefits and to alleviate poverty, the need to channel the revenue into health, water and children's projects, the fear of government corruption absorbing all the revenue and the need to ensure money is spent in the rural villages. Several also mentioned the need for the government to control and manage the trekking industry in order to get more benefit from it and to ensure its sustainability (by preventing overuse of pathways and protecting both the culture and the environment).

In response to the question on the impact on the people living in the communities visited there was a diversity of views. Three trekkers felt there was little or no impact and two felt unable to comment. Most other comments related to the impact of money and the jobs arising from trekking and to the impact of contact with other cultures, specified as westernisation in some responses. Whilst some felt this would be interesting or beneficial some commented on the danger of the local culture being destroyed or changed and two raised the possibility of trekking leading to resentment of outsiders. There was a very strong recognition among most of the responses that trekking would lead to cultural change and one or two commented that there was little evidence at the level of the village of benefits from tourism. In one case the negative impact of contact with the west was perceived not only in rather emotional terms but was seen to be having a direct effect on the dental health of the children through the practice of giving the children sweets brought in from the UK.

With reference to the environmental impact seven trekkers felt there was no impact. Of the 24 who did see an impact five felt the impact was negligible, six felt that the environmental impact could be controlled with good management and some already saw signs of good management and responsible trekker behaviour. Clearly there is a positive role for the charity and tour organisers in this area - both through prior education of the participants and through management on the trek. Some trekkers did feel that the trek organisers did make an effort to be environmentally responsible by limiting the number of campfire singsongs and encouraging 'take your litter home' behaviour. The environmental dangers most widely recognized were litter and waste pollution, path erosion. Two or three trekkers felt that the litter problem stemmed from Nepalese culture as well as irresponsible trekker behaviour. If this is the case then the solution must include attempts to educate the local people as well as the trekkers. Some explicitly recognized the fragility of the environment and several recognized the importance of increased numbers for footpath wear and tear.

Overall there seemed to be more concern for the impacts on the local communities and a slightly more positive view regarding the environmental impacts. Some did comment that they thought the trek organisers had tried hard to minimize the environmental impacts (e.g. by limiting the number of campfires to one evening).

A final question asked the trekkers to assess the impact of the trek on Imperial Cancer Research. Whilst most focused on the financial benefits (estimated by the trek organiser at between £170-180,000) ten trekkers said that they thought the event also resulted in increased awareness of the organisation and there was reference to an improved image. However one trekker felt that the charity would need to be careful to avoid any possible claims that the treks exploit 'Third World' countries and also felt that there is a need to address the issue of sponsorship money subsidizing participants costs. One or two also raised the question of market saturation. The feeling is that if the number of such events rises too steeply their fundraising capacity will be undermined. This seems to imply that this type of activity does have a limited market appeal and there is some feeling that they are most effective whilst they can still be seen as something new and different.

Conclusion and recommendations

Whilst the research so far has raised more questions than it has answered it is nevertheless still possible to draw some general conclusions and to make some recommendations both for further research and for charity challenges.

One aspect of the charity challenge development that has become clear is that the challenger is rather different from the mainstream adventure tourist, being older and more likely to have an established professional occupation. Changes to the advertising policy of challenge organisers could broaden the participant base. It is also clear from the case study that participants have quite a well articulated concern for the impact of the challenge on the areas visited. Whilst challenge organisers also seem to exhibit some concern to manage and minimize the negative impacts of the challenge events it is also clear that more could be done, particularly to ensure a higher level of benefits to the host communities. There is little evidence of any active attempt to deal with the question of using sponsorship money to subsidise participation.

It has not been possible in the research to date to explore the response of the host communities to the passage of the challenge groups. This will be pursued in a future research project. It is possible that there could be a discrepancy between the attitude of government bodies and local people. Government bodies may favour the operation of challenge events in their territory for reasons of publicity and foreign exchange. Local people may not see any long lasting benefit. It is important that challenge organisers work with both levels so that the potential for causing resentment at the local level can be avoided.

Organisers could also do more to educate the challengers before the event. Most of the literature in the packs given to challengers focuses on giving information about living conditions, required fitness levels and training programmes and making suggestions about fundraising activities. There is little in these packs about the need for cultural sensitivity or appropriate environmental behaviour. One pack suggests taking sweets and pens to give to children, a practice that many who are experienced travellers to developing countries would question on the grounds that it encourages begging. However it is also recognised that some consideration of appropriate behaviour may be given in the group meetings rather than in the packs. Of the organisations interviewed some are clearly more aware of the ethical issues raised by charity challenges than others.

In conclusion the main recommendation is that a code of practice should be developed for challenge organisers. This could be accompanied by a set of guidelines. The production of these guidelines and code will necessitate collaboration between tour companies, charities, National Tourist Boards and local community representatives and might be facilitated by a third party organisation such as Tourism Concern or the Institute of Fundraising Managers. The aim should be to provide a framework within which charity challenges can be organised to ensure a fair distribution of benefits and the positive management and minimization of negative impacts.

Acknowledgments

The author gratefully acknowledges the help given in the preparation of this paper by a number of charities and tour operators. Middlesex University provided the funding which supported the questionnaire survey but special thanks are due to the two trekkers who added to their trekking and fundraising challenges by agreeing to undertake the questionnaire survey. Thanks go to Pauline Wilkinson and Jane Fuller for their enthusiastic help.

References

Gain, J. (1999), *Charity Begins Abroad*, paper presented at the Royal Geographical Society Conference on Changing Tastes, Changing Places , 28.10.1999.

Gibson, H. J. (1996), Thrill seeking vacations: a lifespan perspective, *Loisirs et Societe*, 19 (2): 439-458.

Hall, C. M. (1992), Adventure, Sport and Health tourism, in Weiler B and Hall C M (editors) *Special interest tourism,* Belhaven Press, London.

Tallantire, J. (1993), Happy holidays or conservation nightmares? *Geographical*, November, pp.53-56.

Warburton-Lee, J. (1999), All in a good cause, *Geographical,* June, pp. 35-39.

Zurick, D. (1992), Adventure travel and sustainable tourism in the peripheral economy of Nepal, *Annals of the Association of American Geographers,* 82 (4): 608-628.

An assessment of tourist motivations within a multiple holiday taking context

Short Breaks

David Bloy

Sheffield Hallam University, UK

Abstract

Much research within the tourist motivation field is based upon the assumption that tourists have one set of holiday motivations and seek one type of holiday to satisfy them.

Using the interim results taken from a series of qualitative interviews held with cycle tourists who also undertake other types of holidays as its example, this paper argues that current theoretical models ignore the possibility that a person may have holidaying behaviour that looks to satisfy a range of needs over a number of holidays.

Introduction

In the area of tourism, the desire to understand and predict the behaviour of holiday makers has led a range of authors to purport motivation to be amongst the most fundamental areas to be studied (Crompton, 1979; Card and Kestel, 1988; Mansfield, 1992; Parrinello, 1993; Pearce, 1993; Fodness, 1994).

In many cases, research within the tourist motivation field has made the assumption that a person has one set of holiday motivations and seeks one type of holiday to satisfy them (Card and Kestel, 1988; Dunn Ross and Iso Ahola, 1991). At its extreme, the view of motives as static and fixed has been expressed in tourist typologies that classify individuals into groups based upon the clustering of psychological attributes (Plog, 1994). In addition to the basic premise that people within one group can be considered homogenous, the assumption is that individuals belong to and remain within one classification. Pearce (1982, 1991, 1993) does offer a dynamic model of motivation in his Travel Career Ladder but postulates that changes occur over time in an individual as a result of touristic experience (i.e. the total number of holidays undertaken) (Ryan, 1998).

In their critique of static typologies, Swarbrooke and Horner (1999) state that individuals can move between groups but attribute this to changes in circumstance such as health, income, leisure time and family and work commitments. This assessment, although potentially valid, fails to take account of the growth of multiple holiday taking and thus ignores the hypothesis that a person may take a number of holidays over a period of time and may look to satisfy a range of different needs with those holidays. This is a possibility that Swarbrooke and Horner (1999) themselves identify:

> *"the main holiday ...may well be used for relaxation, stress release and the recharging of the tourist's batteries. The extra holidays may normally be shorter, more active and more specialist in nature."*

Likewise, Urry (1990), quoting Feifer's (1985) earlier work on the concept of the 'post-tourist' adopts a similar position:

> *"Now he wants to behold something sacred: now something informative, to broaden him, now something beautiful, to lift him and make him finer; and now something different, because he's bored."* (1985, pp269)

Despite highlighting the concept of different holidays satisfying different needs within one individual, both sets of authors offer no theoretical context for their assessments. In so doing they demonstrate the paucity of current tourist motivational research in being able to accommodate a dynamic model of intra-personal motivation. They also illustrate the need for applied research to be undertaken within the tourism field in order to test the hypothesis that an individual's motives can vary over a number of holidays.

Aims of the paper

The aim of this research is to develop a methodology to enable levels of intra-personal motivational heterogeneity/ homogeneity across multiple holidays to be identified and compared.

The objectives are to:

- Identify scale item pools and motive dimensions to be used to measure holiday motivations in general and the motivations present in the sampling frame selected.

- Identify weaknesses in current motivation theories with regard to accommodating multiple holiday taking behaviour.

- Develop a methodology for measuring and comparing intra-personal motivations for undertaking different types of holidays.

- Assess levels of reliability and validity of the instrument(s).

- Apply the methodology to a sample of tourists who exhibit multiple holiday taking behaviour.

- Develop and test a theoretical model of motivation based on the results of the study which accommodates the levels of motivational homogeneity / heterogeneity identified in the study.

This paper presents the progress made on Stages 1 to 3 of the research programme. The conference presentation will include an update on the research.

Conceptual framework

As has been highlighted, research within the tourist motivation field has tended to make the assumption that a person has one set of holiday motivations and seeks one type of holiday to satisfy them.

Given the focus of this study, this research takes as its conceptual basis the few studies that make reference to the presence of multiple and distinct motives being satisfied over a range of holidays (Urry, 1990; Swarbrooke and Horner, 1999).

As these authors offer cursory observations rather than fully developed and rigorously tested motivational models, the first stage in the research has been to extrapolate testable hypotheses from these exploratory studies. A diagrammatic representation of one such hypothesis appears below.

Figure 1 Hypothesised Intra-personal Motivational Profile for Multiple Holiday-Taking Behaviour

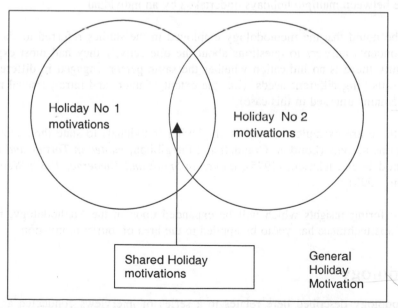

It should be noted that for the sake of graphical simplicity, multiple holiday-taking is represented by only two holidays. The research study itself will look at the extent of motivational homogeneity between a greater range of holidays taken by the sample selected. Figure 1 illustrates the hypothesis that there exists two categories of motivations. These are;

(i)   motives present to a significantly greater degree in the desire to undertake some holidays rather than through others (Holiday No. 1 and No. 2 Motivations)

(ii)   motives which are present to approximately the same degree in all types of holidays (shared holiday motivations), indicated by the intersection between the two.

This hypothesis amalgamates the work of authors stated previously with work in the leisure sector that identifies the presence of the same two distinct categories of motives (Tinsley and Barrett, 1977;Tinsley and Kass, 1978,1979; Baldwin and Tinsley, 1988).

The latter studies identified only a low level of general motives with, in one case, 42 out of 45 motives significantly differing across different activities. Differing findings have been derived in studies resulting from the application of the General Activity Model, which hypotheses that there exists a co-variance or substitutability between recreation activities (Smith and Macaulay, 1980). Underlying this hypothesis is the assumption that there is "an interchangeability of recreational activities in satisfying participants' motives, needs and preferences." (Hendee and Burdge, 1974, *quoted in Smith and Theberge, 1987*). These studies would support an assertion that the level of intersection illustrated in Figure 1 is greater than that shown.

Whilst Figure 1 illustrates a case in which there exists an intersection between holiday motivations, the research's aims do not assume such a relationship. Indeed, given the seemingly contradictory findings of studies referred to above, a key element of this research is to ascertain the extent, if any, of general holiday taking motivational intersection or covariance between multiple holidays undertaken by an individual.

It should be noted that the methodology employed in the studies referred to above is based upon respondents answers to questions about the one activity they had most experience in. Consequently there is no indication whether the same person engaged in different activities would be satisfying different needs. (i.e. the extent of inter- and intra-personal motivational variance remains untested in this case).

However there are examples of studies employing individuals to state their motivations for more than one activity (London, Crandall and Fitzgibbon, *quoted in Tinsley and Kass, 1978*; Ditton, Goodale and Johnsen, (1975), *quoted in Smith and Theberge, 1987;* Wann, Schrader and Wilson, 1999)

Although offering insights which will be expanded upon in the Methodology, it should be noted that this technique has yet to be applied to the area of tourist motivation.

Methodology

The methodology described here relates to a series of interviews conducted as part of the pilot stage of a larger study into tourist motivation within a multiple holiday taking context. Details of further research to be undertaken is given at the end of the section.

Context

A literature review of applied research on motivational research reveals two main elements to motivation research instruments – (i) item pools and (ii) motivational dimensions (Stewart and Carpenter, 1989; Fodness, 1994; Markland and Hardy, 1997; Ryan and Glendon, 1998).

Item pools are defined as the specific questions that are asked of a particular sampling frame whilst motivational dimensions are made up of groupings of item pools that are identified by the researcher to be in some way similar and hence indicative of the existence of a more fundamental motivation.

Reference to applied motivational studies offers insight into the methodologies employed by authors to develop item pools and motive dimensions. (see Table 1).

Table 1   Methodologies employed to generate item pools and motive dimensions

Studies	Methodology Employed			
	Adapted from other studies	Theoretical literature Review	Qualitative Research	Generated own items (e.g. Brain-storming)
Csikszentmihalyi (1975)	✓		✓	
Hollender (1977)			✓	
Knopp, Ballman and Merriam (1979)	✓	✓		✓
Pearce & Caltabiano (1983)		✓	✓	
Ruskin & Shamir (1984)	✓	✓	✓	
Ewart (1985)	✓			
Baldwin & Tinsley (1988)		✓		
Sato (1988)	✓	✓		
Winiarski (1988)	✓	✓		
Stewart & Carpenter (1989)	✓	✓		
Clough, Shepherd & Maughan (1989)	✓	✓	✓	
Dunn Ross & Iso-Ahola (1991)	✓			
Polovitz- Nickerson & Ellis (1991)	✓	✓		
Ragheb & Tate (1993)	✓			
Masters, Ogles & Jolton (1993)	✓			
Weissinger & Bandalos (1995)		✓		
Manfredo, Driver & Tarrant (1996)	✓	✓	✓	
Corey, R.J (1996)	✓	✓	✓	

As Table 1 illustrates, the majority of studies have developed items and motive dimensions based, at least in part, on previous research and theoretical literature. This methodology can be seen as a response to criticisms made by Knopp, Ballman and Merriam, (1979) and Pearce (1993), that earlier research in the area contains inconsistencies in the language used to define motive clusters or dimensions resulting from the grouping of items. He and other authors purport that this is the result of a failure to build upon the research of others (Masters, Ogles and Jolton, 1993; Ryan and Glendon, 1998)

In an attempt to circumvent such a failing in this research, motivational dimensions to be used in the primary research phase have been gleaned from a wide range of applied research. This includes motivational research in the activity holiday, general holiday and recreation fields (Crompton, 1979; Tinsley and Kass, 1979; Crandall, 1980; Leisure Consultants, 1992; Countryside Commission, 1995; Simonsen & Jorgensen, 1996; Ritchie, 1997; Ryan & Glendon,1998).

Population

This study explores the issue of multiple holiday taking using as a starting point a tourism product typically consumed as one of a number of holidays taken by an individual in a year. Whilst more narrowly focussed than a study attempting to explore the entire multiple holiday phenomena, such a methodology is more likely to provide reliable and valid results.

Whilst there is scant research on the patterns of multiple holiday taking, there are a number of reports that indicate that takers of independent cycling holidays in the UK often do so as part of a short break holiday of four days or less. (Beioley, 1995; EETB, 1996; Lumsdon, 1996b; Cope and Doxford, 1998; Downward and Lumsdon, 1998). For the purposes of this study, cycle tourists are defined as people who undertake a holiday that includes at least one overnight stay and for which cycling is the main purpose of the holiday (Countryside Commission, 1989).

Further justification for the selection of cycle tourists as the population for study is derived from the fact the cycle tourism market in the UK is in a significant and sustained period of growth (Countryside Commission, 1995; Beioley, 1995; Lumsdon, 1996a, 1998; Sustrans, 1997)

Sampling frame

In this case, no comprehensive sampling frame existed in published form. Consequently a sampling frame was developed from people ordering cycle route maps by mail from the cycling charity Sustrans. In selecting this sampling frame, the research utilises a non-probability method of sampling.

The sample was gained by devising a mail questionnaire which was slipped inside a clear plastic wallet that protects Sustrans route maps. Given that it was likely that some of the sampling frame did not fall into the category of cycle tourists, a number of filter questions were developed to identify relevant members of the sampling frame.

It should be noted that there are some people who go on cycle holidays but who (i) do not purchase Sustrans maps to help guide them (ii) buy Sustrans maps but not via mail order. The aim will be to overcome this potential bias by sampling cycle tourists whilst on cycle routes (Hurst, 1994), whether or not they have purchased a map from Sustrans or not.

Introducing this element of data triangulation into the research is one method of improving the reliability of the method (Maykut and Morehouse, 1994; Ward, 1997; Decrop,1999)

Sample selection

From those members of the sampling frame that indicated a willingness to take part in future research (approx. 70%), a convenience sample of 12 interviewees were contacted by telephone to ascertain whether they would agree to participate in an interview about their holiday taking behaviour over the last 2 years. Of those contacted, 11 agreed to be interviewed and a questionnaire was sent out prior to the interview to gain basic demographic information and details of holidays taken.

Research instrument design

The research was carried out using a semi-structured approach, with a list of questions constructed prior to the interview. Such pre-structuring is favoured over a loose, undefined methodology by Mason (1996); Miles and Huberman (1994). The reasons they give are multifarious but include the ability to focus data collection, the ability for different field workers to apply the same set of questions to a series of respondents and the fact that we as researchers bring some background knowledge to the area of study.

The questions drawn up sought respondents' motives for undertaking a cycling holiday and their motives for going on other types of holiday.

Motivations were investigated by constructing two main types of questions, those that asked for unprompted recall of motivations and the presence or otherwise of a number of prompted motivations. Unprompted motivations were ascertained by asking interviewees the reasons for taking each holiday and by using a methodology advocated by Pearce (1983), which asks for the worst and best experience whilst on holiday. Pearce states that it is possible to analyse the resulting answers to ascertain the dominant motivation, although it is proposed to use the method in this case to identify multiple motivations and not solely one dominant motivation.

In addition to eliciting unprompted statements concerning the interviewees motivations, the interview schedule also sought to use prompted recall of motivations to test the presence of a specific number of motivational dimensions. This was to allow for consistent comparison of motivations across a number of holidays. The dimensions to be used were derived from the previous studies highlighted earlier. These include:

- Achievement

- Physical

- Exploration

- Stimulus Avoidance

- Solitude

- Nature

- Psychological

- Hedonism

- Prestige

- Environmental

- Kinship

The nature of the motivation dimensions above is expanded upon in the results section.

Data collection

11 qualitative interviews were conducted in the respondents' homes during January and February 2000. Interviews lasted for an average of 45 minutes and were recorded and later transcribed.

Preliminary data analysis

Following the conducting and transcribing of a qualitative interviews, the data from the interviews has been subjected to preliminary analysis based on a three stage process developed by Miles and Huberman (1994). This consists of data reduction, data display and conclusion drawing/verification.

Data reduction refers to the process of simplifying, abstracting and selecting information from the transcript. Much of this process was carried out by the drawing out of themes using marks in the margins of the transcript and by highlighting relevant text.

The display of data is presented in the following section. For ease of interpretation, holidays have been split into two groups, cycling holidays and non-cycling holidays. A more detailed analysis, based upon a segmentation that reflects more accurately the range of holidays taken by the sample, will be undertaken in due course.

Given the main hypothesis to be tested is whether motivations are general to all holidays taken by an individual or whether differences exist between holidays, the results are presented in two sections, motivations where differences appear and motivations where no discernible difference was present.

Motivational dimensions displaying differences between cycling holidays and non-cycling holidays

Achievement

The concept of challenge was the most often cited reason given to undertake a cycling holiday. There was a high degree of physical challenge, with references to hills, climbs and terrain being given as the source of the challenge. However, in tandem with this, there was a more personal expression of the idea of challenge, with cycling holidays offering a challenge on other levels including the overcoming of illness and disability or the effects of ageing. Rather than avoid such challenges, the respondents sought out these aspects, and in many cases drew great personal pride from overcoming such challenges.

Challenge was rarely cited as a motivating force in undertaken non-cycling holidays. Even where other activity holidays were undertaken, these tended to be of a less challenging nature (e.g. walking).

Exploration

The chance to explore an area was important although a distinction was made between exploring an area and exploring specific attractions. Few used cycling holidays to explore specific attractions or places, it was more the serendipity of coming across places along the route. When probed as to why this was so, the pressure to reach daily destinations and/or mileage was given. There was also evidence that cycling holidays were taken in new destinations or destinations where cycling had not been undertaken by them before.

Cycling holidays contrasted with other types of holiday, where itineraries included more sight-seeing of specific attractions. These typically included historic ruins, museums and scenic towns and villages. There was also likely to more risk-averse behaviour on non-cycling holidays with return visits to destinations.

Physical

Cycling holidays were not generally seen as a way of getting fit, although there was an acknowledgement that the holiday was physically active. Fitness was often quoted as a reason for cycling per se rather than going on a cycling holiday.

The desire to exercise featured less strongly in non-cycling holidays, though many respondents reported that holidays included activities such as canoeing, walking and swimming.

Kinship

Enjoying the company of others whilst riding was an important aspect of cycling holidays. Cycling holidays were generally taken with friends rather than family. Reasons for the non-inclusion of family members included absence of an interest in cycling, differing standards of cycling and that it *"not their idea of a holiday"*. Groupings of friends tended to be either two people or a larger group. In the case of the larger groupings, there was a shared interest in cycling established prior to the holiday. Only in one case was a cycling holiday undertaken alone.

Non-cycling holidays were far more likely to have been taken with family members, however spending time with family members did not feature so heavily in reasons why these holidays were undertaken. Non-cycling holidays were typified by more social encounters outside of those actually taking the holiday together. This was most prevalent in holidays centred around visiting friends and relatives.

Stimulus avoidance

Despite their physical nature, cycling holidays were considered relaxing. Some interviewees drew a distinction between physically relaxing and mentally relaxing, considering cycling to be the latter. Other respondents preferred to describe them as exhilarating and engendering a sense of wellbeing. There was only moderate agreement that cycling holidays were a *"get away from it all"* holiday.

"A chance to wind down"," *somewhere to relax"* - these were comments that typified the non-cycling holidays. There was also a stronger sense of the *"get away from it all"* aspect. There was little evidence that the sample undertook beach-based holidays, favouring instead holidays with some activities and a considerable amount of independently organised sight-seeing.

Nature

Scenery featured prominently in descriptions of the best experiences whilst on holiday. Further questioning identified that the lack of people and the relative wildness of the scenery were the important factors that underlay their enjoyment.

Respondents also made reference to the fact they experienced nature in a different way whilst on a bike. They felt that they saw things that they wouldn't be able to see if exploring by car and went to places they couldn't get to by other modes of transport.

The importance of scenery was not stated as strongly in non-cycling holidays. Foreign destinations were selected for the weather and their ability to provide specific leisure opportunities (e.g. skiing).

Psychological

The sample reported cycling holidays as being a chance to do something for themselves. It was seen as an escape from their familial role as mother or father. However, more research is needed to ascertain whether this attribute can be aligned to a concept such as self-actualisation (Maslow, 1943), which tends to typify this motivational dimension.

Interviewees tended to take non-cycling holidays with family members and indicated that there was a high degree of the vacation representing a compromise between the needs of the various family members. There was also a degree of vicarious enjoyment, with the interviewees' enjoyment derived from the enjoyment of their children.

It is again open to interpretation whether these factors intimate that a low level of self-actualisation was possible.

Prestige

Cycling holidays were a great source of discussion with family and friends. Anecdotes of challenging experiences often featured in post-holiday conversations. Where cycling holidays were taken with friends, the holiday remained a topic of discussion throughout the year.

Non-cycling holidays were occasionally talked about upon the return from holiday.

Motivational dimensions showing no difference between cycling holidays and non-cycling holidays

Environmental

Even when prompted, there was little evidence that cycling holidays were undertaken because of their perceived environmental benefits. This was a pattern repeated in other holiday taking behaviour undertaken by the sample.

Hedonism

The desire to have fun was a major factor in the selection of both cycling holidays and non-cycling holidays.

Ration Being

The desire to have an inexpensive holiday was not conveyed strongly for any holidays that were undertaken. This is despite the fact cycling holidays tended to be centred around youth hostel or bed and breakfast accommodation, rather than hotels.

Solitude

Relative Solitude was important for both types of holidays, but there was no significant difference in the desire for this across the two holiday types being studied.

Table 2 displays motivation dimensions using a checklist matrix, a methodology suggested by Miles and Huberman (1994). The authors state that it is a useful format for analysing field data on a major variable or general domain of interest. The matrix also includes a crude rating of the strength of presence within the text of each motivation domain.

Table 2   Strength of Presence of Motivational Dimensions: Comparison of Cycling and Non-Cycling Holidays

Motivational Dimension	Cycling Holidays	Non-Cycling Holidays
Achievement	High	Low
Physical	Moderate	Low
Kinship	High	Moderate
Stimulus Avoidance	Moderate	High
Nature	High	Low
Psychological*	High	Low
Environmental	Low	Low
Hedonism	High	High
Rational Being	Low	Low
Solitude	High	High
Prestige	High	Moderate

As has been stated, further research needs to be undertaken with regard to this dimension in order to ascertain whether the aspects identified during the interviews can be said to constitute self-actualisation.

Conclusion drawing/verification

It would appear from the interviews that there is some evidence to support the main hypothesis, that individuals in this sample do possess different patterns of motivations for taking cycling holidays when compared with other, non-cycling holidays.

At this stage in the research, this would lead one to question work within the tourist motivation field that assumes that a person has one set of holiday motivations and seeks one type of holiday to satisfy them (Card and Kestel, 1988; Dunn Ross and Iso Ahola, 1991). It also brings into question tourist typologies (Plog, 1974) and the time and experience-related model of dynamic motivations put forward by Pearce (1982, 1991,1993).

The preliminary results presented here concur with the previous cited work of a number of authors working in the recreation field that identifies a level of motivational heterogeneity across activities (Tinsley and Barrett, 1977;Tinsley and Kass, 1978,1979; Baldwin and Tinsley, 1988).

The results also point to a multiple motive explanation of tourist behaviour and hence concur with the elements of the motivational theories of Pearce (1993) and Murray (1938).

Validity and reliability

It should be stressed that these results are based only on a preliminary analysis of a small number of qualitative interviews, selected via a convenience sampling method.

Whilst these are not untypical of qualitative research methods, these characteristics have led a number of authors to identify this as an unavoidable limitation (De Groot, 1986), Miles and Huberman (1994).

Considerable further research is planned in order to develop and validate these initial findings. As such it is unwise that any unequivocal conclusion be drawn from this stage of the study. A schedule of proposed further research is presented below.

Future research

Development and analysis of a quantitative research instrument

The results of analysis from the qualitative interviews, together with results of the literature review, will be used to produce a research instrument designed to measure motives as they relate to cycling holidays and other forms of holiday taken. The instrument will be constructed using the Total Design Method that aims to maximise response rates of postal questionnaires (Dillman,1978).

A non-probability sample of approximately 800 respondents from the sampling frame of UK cycle tourists selected for the preliminary stage of research will be selected and the research instrument administered by post.

Data from the research instrument will be analysed using two main methods of multivariate analysis.

(i)   A selection of appropriate factor analysis methods will be undertaken in order to identify the existence of any co-variance amongst holidays undertaken.

(ii) Cluster analysis will also be performed, a technique which, unlike factor analysis, does not make the assumption that there are underlying motivational dimensions that all holidays have in common. (Beaman 1975, *quoted in Smith and Theberge, 1987*).

Reliability and validity

Reliability and validity will be increased by pilot testing the items included in the research instrument that are generated from the qualitative interviews, as well as the ones derived from previous studies.

The pilot study will also pre-test the items generated and reject those that are not rated as important by the sample, a method seen by Manfredo, Driver and Tarrant (1996) as a reasonable alternative to including all items in the final research instrument. Also in line with their methodology, all motivational domains will be assessed with more than one item. This will avoid the increase in sampling error that would result from the use of limited item pools (Clough, Shepherd and Maughan, 1989). The exact number to be included will be based on the results of a multivariate analysis to ascertain levels of variance covered by a particular item. A minimum acceptable level of variance that will act as a cut off point for the inclusion of items will be set with reference to studies dealing with the subject (Clough, Shepherd and Maughan, 1989; Fodness, 1994; Manfredo, Driver and Tarrant, 1994)

In order to test the validity of the instrument itself, item-to-scale correlations will be assessed for all motivation dimensions previously identified. Reliability of the dimensions themselves will be tested by identifying item-to-item correlation levels (Thomas and Butts, 1998; Wann, Schrader and Wilson,1999).

Critique and model formulation

Conclusions drawn from the data analysis will be used as the basis of a critique of motivation theories and their application to a multiple holiday taking. It is anticipated that a model of motivation able to accommodate multiple holiday taking will be presented and tested.

Opportunities for further study

This exploratory study investigates the concept of multiple holiday-taking motivations from a starting point of people who undertake UK cycling holidays in addition to other holidays. Further research opportunities exist in developing a more wide ranging study looking at multiple holiday-taking motivations of a wider sample. There is also the scope to develop research instruments that could be applied to other tourism products that are typically consumed within a multiple holiday-taking context.

A programme of theory testing could also be explored, scrutinising specific motivation theories using the methodology developed in the original study.

References

Baldwin, K. S. and H. E. A. Tinsley (1988), An Investigation of the Validity of Tinsley and Tinsley's (1986) Theory of Leisure Experience, *Journal of Counselling Psychology*, 35, 263-267.

Beioley, S. (1995), On Yer Bike - Cycling and Tourism, Insights, B17-B31.(Abstract).

Card, J. A. and C. Kestal (1988), Motivational Factors and Demographic Characteristics of Travellers To and from Germany, *Loisir et Societe*, 11, 49-58.

Clough, P., J. Shepherd and R. Maughan (1989), Motives for Participation in Recreational Running, *Journal of Leisure Research*, 21, 297-309.

Cope, A. M., D. Doxford and T. Hill (1998), Monitoring Tourism on the UK's First Long-Distance Cycle Route, *Journal of Sustainable Tourism*, 6, 210-223.

Corey, R. J. (1996), A Drama-Based Model of Traveler Destination Choice, *Journal of Travel and Tourism Marketing*, 5, 1-22.

Countryside Commission (1995), The Market for Recreational Cycling in the Countryside (Abstract).

Countryside Commission (1989), Recreational Cycling in the Countryside (Abstract).

Crandall, R. (1980), Motivations for Leisure, *Journal of Leisure Research*, 11, 3, 165-181.

Crompton, J.L. (1979), Motivations for Pleasure Travel, *European Journal of Marketing*, 6, 408-424.

Csikszentmihalyi, M. (1975), *Beyond Boredom and Anxiety*, Jossey-Bass Inc. San Francisco.

Decrop, A. (1999), Triangulation in qualitative tourism research, *Tourism Management*, 20, 157-161.

De Groot, G. (1986), Deep, Dangerous or Just Plain Dotty?, in Qualitative Methods of Research: A Matter of Interpretation, proceedings of a seminar held in Amsterdam 5-7 Feb 1986, ESOMAR.

Dillman, D. A. (1978), *Mail and Telephone Surveys: The Total Design Method*, John Wiley and Sons Inc, New York.

Downward, P. and L. Lumsdon (1998), Cycle and See: Developing a Cycling Package for Visitors, *Insights*, July 1998,

Dunn Ross, E. L. and S. E. Iso-Ahola (1991), Sightseeing Tourists' Motivation and Satisfaction, *Annals of Tourism Research*, 18, 226-237.

East of England Tourist Board (1996), England's Cycling Country: A Cycling Tourism Strategy for the East of England 1996-1999, (Abstract)

Ewert, A. (1985), Why People Climb: The Relationship of Participant Motives and Experience Level to Mountaineering, *Journal of Leisure Research*, 17, 241-250.

Fodness, D. (1994), Measuring Tourist Motivation, *European Journal of Marketing*, 21, 555-581.

Hollender, J. W. (1977), Motivational Dimensions of the Camping Experience, *Journal of Leisure Research*, 9, 133-141.

Hurst, F. (1994), En Route Surveys, in: J. R. B. Ritchie and C. R. Goeldner (Eds.), *Travel, Tourism and Hospitality Research: A Handbook for Managers and Researchers*, 2nd Edn., John Wiley and Sons Inc, New York, pp. 453-471.

Iso Ahola, S. E. (1980), *The Social Psychology of Leisure and Recreation*, W. C .Brown Company, Iowa.

Knopp, T .B., G. Ballman and L. C. Merriam (1979), Toward a More Direct Measure of River User Preferences, *Journal of Leisure Research*, 11, 317-326.

Leisure Consultants (1992), *Activity Holidays: The Growth Market in Tourism*, Leisure Consultants, London.

Lumsdon, L (1996a*), Cycling Opportunities: Making the Most of the National Cycle Network*.

Lumsdon, L. (1996b), Cycle Tourism in Britain, D27-D32.(Abstract).

Lumsdon, L. (1998), Evaluating The Tourism Potential of the National Cycling Network, Environmental Paper Series, 1, 28-36.(Abstract).

Manfredo, M. J., B. L. Driver and M. A. Tarrant (1996), Measuring Leisure Motivation: A Meta-Analysis of the Recreation Experience Preference Scales, *Journal of Leisure Research*, 28, 188-213.

Mansfeld, Y. (1992), From Motivation to Actual Travel, *Annals of Tourism Research*, 19, 399-419.

Markland, D. and Hardy, L. (1997), On the Factoral and Construct Validity of the Intrinsic Motivation Inventory, Conceptual and Operational Concerns, *Research Quarterly for Exercise and Sport*, 18,1, 20-32.

Mason, J. (1996), *Qualitative Researching*, Sage, London.

Maslow, A. H. (1943), A Theory of Human Motivation, in: V. H. Vroom and E. L. Deci (Eds.) *Management and Motivation*, Penguin Books, London.

Masters, K. S., B. M. Ogles and J. A. Jolton (1993), The Development of an Instrument to Measure Motivation for Marathon Running: The Motivations of Marathoners Scales (MOMS), *Research Quarterly for Exercise and Sport*, 64, 134-143.

Maykut, P. and R. Morehouse (1994*), Beginning Qualitative Research: A Philosophical and Practical Guide*, Falmer Press, London.

Miles, M. B. and A. M. Huberman (1994), *Qualitative Data Analysis*, Sage Publications, London.

Murray, H. A. (1938), *Explorations in Personality*, Oxford University Press, New York.

Parrinello, G. L. (1993), Motivation and Anticipation in Post-Industrial Tourism, *Annals of Tourism Research*, 21, 233-249.

Pearce, P. L. (1982), The Social Psychology of Tourist Behaviour, *International Series in Experimental Social Psychology*, 13, Pergamon Press.

Pearce, P. L. (1991), Dreamworld: A report on public reactions to Dreamworld and proposed developments at Dreamworld, (Abstract)

Pearce, P. L. (1993), Fundamentals of tourist motivation, in: D. G. Pearce and R. W. Butler (Eds.), *Tourism Research: Critiques & Challenges*, Routledge, U.K, pp. 113-134.

Pearce, P. L. and M. L. Caltabiano (1983), Inferring Travel Motivation from Travelers' Experiences, *Journal of Travel Research*, 22, 16-20.

Plog, S. C. (1994), Developing and Using Psychographics in Tourism Research, in: J. R. B. Ritchie and C. R. Goeldner (Eds.), *Travel, Tourism and Hospitality Research: A Handbook for Managers and Researchers*, 2nd Edn., John Wiley & Sons Inc, New York, pp. 209-218.

Polovitz Nickerson, N. and G. D. Ellis (1991), Traveler Types and Activation Theory: A Comparison of Two Models, *Journal of Travel Research*, Winter, 26-31.

Ragheb, M. G. and R. L. Tate (1993), *A behavioural model of leisure participation, based on leisure attitude, motivation and satisfaction*, Leisure Studies, 12, 61-70.

Ritchie, B. (1997), Why Pedal? An Examination of Bicycle Tourists' Motivations in the South Island of New Zealand, 51-58.(Abstract)

Ruskin, H. and B. Shamir (1984), Motivation as a Factor Affecting Males' Participation in Physical Activity During Leisure Time, *Loisir et Societe*, 7, 141-161.

Ryan, C. (1998), The Travel Career Path: An Appraisal, *Annals of Tourism Research*, 25, 936-957.

Ryan, C. and Glendon, I. (1998), Application of Leisure Motivation Scale to Tourism, *Annals of Tourism Research*, 25,1,169-185.

Saabye Simonsen, P. and B. Jorgensen (1998), Cycling Tourism: Environmental and Economical Sustainability? (UnPub)

Sato, I. (1988), Bosozoku: Flow in Japanese Motorcycle Gangs, in: M. Csikszentmihalyi (Ed.), *Optimal Experience: Psychological Studies of Flow in Consciousness*, Cambridge University Press, Cambridge, pp. 92-117.

Smith, D. H. and J. Macaulay (1980), *Participation in Social and Political Activities*, Jossey Bass, San Francisco.

Smith, D. H. and N. Theberge (1987), *Why People Recreate, an Overview of Research*, Life Enhancement Publications, Champaign, Illinois.

Stewart, W. P. and E. H. Carpenter (1989), Solitude at the Grand Canyon: An Application of Expectancy Theory, *Journal of Leisure Research*, 21, 4-17.

Sustrans, (1997), The Tourism Potential of the National Cycle Network Routes (Abstract).

Swarbrooke, J. and S. Horner (1999), *Consumer Behaviour in Tourism*, Butterworth Heinemann, Oxford.

Thomas, D. W. and F. B. Butts (1998), Assessing Leisure Motivators and Satisfaction of International Elderhostel Participants, *Journal of Travel and Tourism Marketing*, 7, 31-38.

Tinsley, H. E. A., T. C. Barrett and R. A. Kass (1977), Leisure Activities and Need Satisfaction, *Journal of Leisure Research*, 9, 110-120.

Tinsley, H. E. A. and R. A. Kass (1978), Leisure Activities and Need Satisfaction: A Replication and Extension, *Journal of Leisure Research*, 10, 191-202.

Tinsley, H. E. A. and R. A. Kass (1979), The Latent Structure of the Need Satisfying Properties of Leisure Activities, *Journal of Leisure Research*, 11, 278-291.

Urry, J. (1990), *The Tourist Gaze*, Sage, London.

Wann, D. L., M. P. Schrader and A. M. Wilson (1999), Sport Fan Motivation: Questionnaire Validation, Comparisons by Sport , and Relationship to Athletic Motivation, *Journal of Sport Behaviour*, 22, 114-137.

Ward, J. C. (1997), *Puzzles, Choirs and Archives: Perspectives on Crossing the Quantitative - Qualitative Methodological Divide*, XXIV, 148 (Abstract)

Weissinger, E. and D. L. Bandalos (1995), Development, Reliability and Validity of a Scale to Measure Intrinsic Motivation in Leisure, *Journal of Leisure Research*, 27, 379-400.

Winiarski, R. (1988), *The Questionnaire of Tourist Motivation (QTM): Construction and Psychometric Characteristics*, Problemy Turystyki, 11, 50-60.

Zins, A. H. (1998), Leisure Traveller Choice Models of Theme Hotels Using Psychographics, *Journal of Travel Research*, 36, 3-15.

The 'New Tourist' as anthropologist

Jim Butcher

Canterbury Christ Church College, UK

Abstract

This paper identifies a 'New Tourist' (Poon, 1993); a tourist who seeks selfhood through experiencing other cultures. These other cultures are often seen as embodying a sense of spiritual depth which modern tourists perceive to be missing from their own lives in western, relatively affluent societies. In this way, the view of 'culture' held by the New Tourist is one shaped by a particular historical experience within the west.

Culture as a concept is widely contested and fraught with difficulty. One discipline within which the analysis of culture is central is anthropology. Generations of anthropologists have focused on uncovering the forces within particular societies that cohere them. The New Tourist is often seen as intent on gaining an understanding of the host society's culture, and through this, discovering something about themselves. In this respect they are a little like anthropologists.

This paper identifies a distinctly anthropological view of culture which is mirrored in the broader discussion of New Tourism today. The roots of this anthropological outlook are briefly traced through an exposition of the main theoretical developments of Franz Boas at the turn of the century and Levi Strauss in the post war period. The paper takes a critical stance, arguing that the anthropological conception of culture can be one sidedly relativistic - difference is assumed as a methodological starting point whilst common aspirations and desires between host and tourist are rarely examined.

What is the New Tourism?

In recent years a plethora of new forms of tourism have emerged, including alternative tourism, eco tourism, nature tourism and responsible tourism. Whilst there is little agreement as to the precise meaning or emphasis of these terms (Mowforth and Munt, 1998, p.102-105), they do share an important negative assumption - they are counter-posed to a conception of Mass Tourism as problematic, destructive of the environment and insensitive to cultural differences. Perhaps the term that comes closest to encapsulating these new trends within the discourse is the 'New Tourism' (Poon, 1993, p.3). Poon advocates the New Tourism in the face of 'a crisis of mass tourism ... that has brought social, cultural, economic and environmental havoc in its wake', and adds that 'it is mass tourism practices that must be radically changed to bring in the new' (1993, p.3). Hence New Tourism paints a grim picture of its Other, modern Mass Tourism.

Of course it is important to put the New Tourism in context. The WTO forecasts that such forms of tourism are unlikely to exceed 10% of the total (WTO, 1995). In both the developed and developing worlds, New Tourism is peripheral. But perhaps to view New Tourism empirically is to miss the point. The rise in codes of conduct (Mason and Mowforth, 1995), critical guides promoting ethical tourism (titles such as The Good Tourist, The Green Tourist Guide, Community Tourism Directory etc.) and the increase in campaign and NGO activity around the issues illustrates that the New Tourism is a prominent moral agenda within the debates on tourism. Even large companies have sought to identify themselves with the environmental and cultural critique of mass tourism.[1]

It is conceivable that the outlook of New Tourism owes as much to what Dann describes as 'a situation of perceived normlessness and meaninglessness in the origin (tourist generating) country' (Dann, 1981, pp.187-211) as it does to the actual destructive potential of tourism. For the alienated western tourist, profoundly disillusioned with modernity, tourism becomes a search for a different culture perceived to be more authentic, more human (MacCannell, 1992). In this way, disillusionment with western culture fuels the search for a spiritual centre in the Other's culture (Cohen, 1972).

A key emphasis within the advocacy of New Tourism, then, is on culture. Mass Tourism is held to have had a destructive impact on host culture, whilst the New Tourism seeks to address this through a more ethical approach. This paper will look at the conception of 'culture' within the discourse. It will be argued that a distinctly one sided, anthropological perspective of culture is prevalent; one which carries with it conservative, anti-developmental assumptions.

The New Tourist as anthropologist

New Tourism is a little like amateur anthropology. Just as the anthropological study of tourism emerged with concerns over cultural contact between hosts and guests (Nash and Smith, 1991, p.13), New Tourism has reflected growing misgivings with mass tourism (Poon, 1993). Both anthropologists and New Tourists are interested in learning about the culture of the host. Both may also seek to minimise their own impact on the hosts society - anthropologists seek to 'blend in' in order to avoid eliciting behaviour different from the norm, and New Tourists may be wary of their own capacity to damage the indigenous culture. Also, neither are satisfied with staged aspects of the hosts culture (MacCannell, 1976) - both seek to go beyond that, potentially into the 'backstage' (Goffman, 1959) world of the host society.

There is then a shared emphasis on, and guarded approach to, cultural contact. Yet culture is a contested concept, subject to different meanings and emphases (Williams, 1987). However, it seems that the method of the anthropologist and the outlook of the New Tourist share a common understanding of culture. The anthropologist prioritises the study of cultural difference - their subject is the culture of the Other. The New Tourist seeks out cultural difference with a sense of awe. Both, for academic and aesthetic reasons respectively, focus on culture as *difference*. Whilst there has been a growing quantity of research into the anthropology of tourism (Nash and Smith, 1991, p.15) since Valene Smith edited Hosts and Guests (1977), the conception of culture as *cultures* has remained unexamined.

Tourism as anthropology

According to Nash and Smith (1991, p.13) '... anthropologists draw on a transcultural perspective that embraces all of the cultures of mankind'. They ' ... specialise in the study of the dynamics of human cultures and cross cultural communication.'(Nash, 1996, p.11). Both of these quotations refer to the study of *cultures* rather than culture. The methodological starting point of the tourism anthropologist is, then, *difference*, as is that of much literature in the field of tourism impacts generally. The concept of acculturation, for example, has as its starting point the formal counter position of two separate cultures. One culture encounters another, and there is an interaction between the two. This is codified in the definition of acculturation given by the Social Science Research Council: 'culture change that is initiated by the conjunction of *two or more cultural systems*' (Nash, 1996, p.26) (my italics). Clearly, if we begin with different 'cultural systems' then common strands of culture may be overlooked.

In the light of this it is worth reminding ourselves that historically two strands of culture are discernible: universal or human culture, and culture as cultural difference. For the former, rooted in the Enlightenment conception of human progress, culture embodies a common human project of social development. For the latter, originating in the Romantic reaction to Enlightenment rationalism, culture expresses human difference.

In the field of tourism anthropology, there are rarely allusions to a common human culture. A common position is that of Nunez, who describes the consequences of acculturation as being 'when two cultures come into contact of any duration, each becomes somewhat like the other through a process of borrowing' (Nunez, 1989, p.266). The result of acculturation is a process of mediation between the two cultures. This can result in resistance to the dominant culture by the more fragile, domination of the latter by the former, or a process of hybridisation may occur, through which cultures borrow from each other. Such hybridisation can be seen as a creative process (MacCannell, 1992, pp.3-4), but the relationship is often seen as fraught with problems, even encapsulating 'cultural imperialism' (Nash, 1996 / Turner and Ash, 1975, p.129).

For another author, the level of impact arising from the meeting of host and tourist results from the 'interaction between the nature of the change agent and the inherent strength and ability of the host culture to withstand, and absorb, the change generators whilst retaining its own integrity' (Ryan, 1991, p.148). The tourists are the change agent, an exogenous variable to be withstood, and culture has its own 'integrity', viewed in much of the literature as virtuous in and of itself.

With regard to the formal counter position of different cultures in the above and many other formulations, it is worth thinking about how far one could take such an approach. Does acculturation take place when British tourists go to France, or when residents of the city travel out to the country? In fact, the problematisation of the meeting of cultures usually comes to the fore in relation to '... culture contact and culture change, particularly where the contact has involved a more powerful, more developed Europe and North America and the less powerful, less developed world of countries such as those in most of Africa or Latin America' (Nash, 1996, p. 27). The principal cultural divide is, then, between the developed and developing worlds.

Of course, tourism is not always seen as destructive in relation to host culture. It is sometimes seen as a positive factor when it *reinforces* a cultural practice. On the Greek island of Crete, tourism is seen as holding out the hope of sustaining traditional textile production, if cultural tourism can attract tourists (New Tourists?) interested in buying such traditional goods (Richards, 1998). On a similar theme, referring to the impact of tourism on the Masai, MacCannell argues that, through tourism, 'the assimilation of primitive elements into the modern world would allow primitives to adapt and coexist and earn a living just by 'being themselves', permitting them to avoid the kind of work in factories and as agricultural labourers that changes their lives forever' (MacCannell, 1992, p.19). Masai culture can be sustained, not destroyed, by commoditisation. It is worthy of note that there is an underlying 'anti-change' assumption here. Presumably those Masai who have assimilated into 'work in factories' have ceased to 'be themselves' and are the worse for it.

It is notable that arguments both for and against tourism development often emphasise maintaining cultural difference as a goal. The integrity of culture is deemed worthy as an end in itself (Tickell, 1994, p.ix-x). Where cultural change is discussed, it is as a result of acculturation, through the formal interaction of different cultures.

Such an approach undoubtedly has its merits in helping to identify potential tensions arising from tourism and much research has been carried out highlighting these. Undoubtedly even small numbers of tourists can have a considerable impact in an area where infrastructure is poor, and where the tourists stand out as being conspicuously wealthy compared to their hosts. However, the assumption of the *primacy* of cultural difference has become an unhelpful dogma within much of the discourse. The formal counter position of cultures, host and tourist, negates approaching the issue from the perspective of *commonality*. That the host and tourist may share common needs, desires and aspirations with regard to development is less commonly considered. Not least of these may be the aspiration to join the growing, but very limited, ranks of the world's tourists, an aspiration only achievable in the context of economic growth and cultural change. For example, much has been written about the problems associated with tourism development in Goa. However, residents further down the coast from the main tourist developments have expressed a desire to see tourism develop more widely in their direction. Many expressed the view that revenues from tourism, and consequent economic development, may enable their children to travel, just like the tourists.(Le Divillec, 1997). Some of the hosts desired *equality* above a defence of their culture.

This paper will go on to chart some key developments in the conceptualisation of culture within anthropology this century, and illuminate some of the limitations of the concept in relation to the contemporary tourism debates.

The anthropological roots of cultures

It was at the turn of the century that culture became the central object of study of anthropologists. Franz Boas is probably the most significant figure in this process, in that he, more than any other single figure, shifted the focus of anthropology away from race as a biological category ' ...through his almost ceaseless articulation of the concept of culture' (Degler, 1991, p.61). Boas was largely responsible for challenging the racist logic of social evolutionary thinkers, who held that the fact that some cultures had undergone industrial development and others not, some to the formation of nation states and others not, was the product of differential creative abilities of different peoples.

Yet Boas' riposte was not to argue that the creative aspects of humanity were common to all, but to relativise development and creativity itself. For Boas, whilst culture carried no connotation of inferiority or superiority, it explained the persistence of material inequality. As Stocking (1982, pp.265-66) noted, ironically 'culture',

> *'provided a functionally equivalent substitute for the older idea of race temperament. It explained similar phenomena, but it did so in strictly non biological terms, and indeed its full efficacy as an explanatory concept depended on the rejection of the inheritance of acquired characteristics ...All that was necessary to make the adjustment ... was the substitution of a word. For 'race' read 'culture' or 'civilisation', for 'racial heredity' read 'cultural heritage' and the change had taken place.*

Stocking's argument is that whilst culture emerged in opposition to race, it also carried similar assumptions with regard to human creativity - to assert that biology structured the individual was less tenable, but substitute 'culture' for race and similar conservative assumptions remain if we accept, as most anthropological accounts do, a functionalist conception of culture. It is this aspect of the cultural discourse, widely evident today within the discourse on tourism, which remains largely unchallenged.

The Boasian conception of culture is evidenced clearly in the following, related during a visit to the Arctic to study the Eskimos:

> *'I often ask myself what advantages our 'good society' possesses over that of 'savages'. The more I see of their customs, the more I realise that we have no right to look down on them. Where amongst our people would you find such hospitality? ... We have no right to blame them for their forms and superstitions which may seem ridiculous to us. We 'highly educated' people are much worse, relatively speaking ... As a thinking person, for me the most important result of this trip lies in the strengthening of my point of view that the idea of a 'cultured' person is merely relative and that a persons worth should be judged by his Herzensbildung.'* (Boas, 1982, p148)

Boas view of the Eskimos mirrors that of many advocates of New Tourism. 'We' are no better than 'them'. In fact, 'we' may think that 'they' are actually better off than us. Indeed, New Tourists, disaffected from their own culture, locate their spiritual centre in the host, usually less developed, country (Cohen, 1972). Such an attitude reflects a distinct disillusionment within modern societies (which are also tourism generating societies), intensely critical of aspects of their modernity such as technology ('taking over the world'), industry ('pollution'), genetics ('eugenics?') etc. It is not the object of this paper to comment on the validity of the broader sociological critique of modernity, but to suggest that in the context of the tourist - host encounter we may end up superimposing categories borne of western disillusionment onto societies that have none of the benefits of modern societies (such as technology, industry, modern genetically based medicine etc.) and want them.

Boas was concerned with *cultures* rather than *culture*; his work stood in opposition to the universalistic Enlightenment conception of human culture. The Enlightenment influenced writers understood culture as a universal rather than a particular concept. J.S. Mill for example wrote of different cultures, but in the context of 'the culture of the human being' (Mill, p.75). This view held that there was such a thing as societal progress - societies could become more 'civilised'. Many have criticised such a view as Eurocentric, which indeed it was. However, the Enlightenment conception of culture upheld the possibility and desirability of political and material equality. In relativising culture, and humanity itself, progress towards equality is contradicted by an acceptance and defence of human difference.

The primacy of cultural difference is a key legacy of anthropology inherited by much writing, within different disciplines, on tourism. It provides a methodological starting point that takes difference as the defining aspect of peoples and societies. Morally, this starting point is often justified through a sense of injustice at past and present cultural domination, or 'cultural imperialism' within which defence of difference becomes seen as a counter to domination. Anthropologists, like New Tourists, tend to 'take the side of the Other'. Such an approach is in many senses admirable. Yet it is important to view cultural difference within the context of broader human culture. Otherwise, in countering *cultural* domination, the *material* inequality that characterises different societies and shapes 'culture' ironically can be reinforced through a rejection of development as culturally inappropriate. If wants are 'culturally derived ... [and can] ... vary greatly from one society to another' (Nash, 1996, p.126) why should we see material inequality as anything other than a product of cultural difference?

Levi Strauss and the New Tourist

Levi - Strauss, probably the most influential and certainly the most controversial anthropologist in the post war period, developed a perspective on culture that is key to understanding the outlook of the New Tourist.

Levi - Strauss' post war anthropology shares many of the themes of Boas' work. He expressed a similar conception of culture - cultures, for Levi Strauss, are all about difference - 'us' and 'them', 'self' and 'other'. They impose upon us modes of thinking from which we cannot escape. The 'other culture' remains, then, incomprehensible. Culture is also rooted in the past; it defines 'who we are' by 'where we have come from'. For Levi Strauss: 'We must accept the fact that each society has made a certain choice, within the range of existing human possibilities and that the various choices cannot be compared to each other' (1955, p.385). Moreover, it is 'impossible' to deduce any 'moral or philosophical criterion by which to decide the respective values of the choices which have led each civilisation to prefer certain ways of life and thought while rejecting others' (1981, p.636)

There is an important nuance in the view of the 'Other' in Levi Strauss work. Levi Strauss held that 'primitive' cultures were, in fact, a stripped down version of modern ones, without the trappings of modern consumerism. Hence in the context of a widespread disillusionment with modernity, articulated by Levi Strauss (and evident in many contemporary writings on tourism), the developed world has much to learn from its less developed counterpart. Or, if as MacCannell asserts, 'advanced capitalism is accomplishing the destruction of nature and the human spirit' (1992, p.18), then perhaps a more basic sense of 'who we are', akin to the tourist trying to 'discover the real me', can be gleaned from societies less advanced and more free from the perceived fetters of modernity.

Levi Strauss does suggest a way out of the dilemma - a solution that chimes with many of the micro solutions evident in the New Tourism discourse. He argues that the ideal situation would be one where 'communication had become adequate for mutual stimulation by remote partners, yet was not so frequent or so rapid as to endanger the indispensable obstacles between individual and groups or to reduce them to the point where overly facile exchanges might equalise and nullify their diversity' (1987, p.24). Levi Strauss calls on international institutions to see the 'necessity of preserving the diversity of cultures in a world threatened by monotony and uniformity' (1978, p.362). This is a rallying cry that institutions and NGOs have certainly heeded since the 1970s, when Levi Strauss wrote this. A host of NGOs, as well as national and supranational initiatives have firmly established cultural preservation as a worthy goal, and codes of conduct and carrying capacities have become a part of a new etiquette around the discussion of host-tourist relations.

The understanding of culture, or cultures, in the writings of Levi - Strauss mirrors the contemporary debate over tourism. Civilisation, or a common standard of culture, 'is the destroyer of those old particularisms, which had the honour of creating the aesthetic and spiritual values that make life worthwhile' (1978, p.360). Levi Strauss' sentiment may be reassuring to New Tourists, who seek a sense of wonderment in the face of diversity - a diversity they may freely claim not to comprehend. But for societies struggling against poverty there is little time for aesthetic contemplation. The elevation of the primitive in Levi Strauss' writing and in the worldview of the New Tourist can easily cross over into an aestheticisation of drudgery.

In essence, Boas laid the basis for the understanding of culture as its plural, 'cultures'. Levi - Strauss' disillusionment with modern culture led him to seek spiritual value in 'primitive' culture. Both themes are paralleled in New Tourism discourse. Moreover, they have implications for how the New Tourism conceptualises development and the tourist experience respectively.

(i) Implications for Development

This can be usefully illustrated by comparing the commonplace perception of large, Mass Tourism developments as being destructive of the host culture in comparison to small scale, 'eco' or 'alternative' tourism. For example, one anthropologist compares favourably the way Sherpas in Nepal have maintained their reciprocal community based social arrangements in the light of tourism development, compared to the 'impersonal' development in Mijas on the Costa del Sol (Nash, 1996, p.35). The development of market mechanisms on the Costas are thus seen as negative from a human perspective, perceived as having destroyed an old cohesive community. This is a sentiment shared by some New Tourists, for whom Spanish coastal developments represent the excesses of mass tourism and mass tourists. The Nepalese Sherpas, on the other hand, are seen as having avoided 'cultural levelling' and maintained their sense of community.

Undoubtedly there is a kernel of truth in this. However, the citizens of Mijas are much better off than the Nepalese Sherpas. Many are able to engage in leisure travel, so in this sense can engage in a relationship with the tourist based to a greater extent on equality than the Sherpas can. For many younger Spaniards, the development of tourism has opened up new opportunities to meet with and relate to a broader section of society than previous generations.

Jurdao (1996, pp.34-35) and others may bemoan the changes to community, but perhaps we should see this as an inevitable price to pay. Community can be seen as an enabling concept - a level of social organisation that enables attitudes of reciprocity and tolerance to develop, as people are linked by their closeness and commonality of goals. Yet community can also be divisive. It can be an expression of 'small town' lack of ambition, a bind on younger generations who aspire to a broader sense of themselves in the world. The latter impulse is why travel itself has been so appealing throughout history - it expresses one's ability to go further, experience more, to learn more and to overcome limits. In this sense it is linked to a universal idea of human progress, not a particular culture. The counter position of community and reciprocity to travel can express a profound conservatism.

(ii) The Tourist Experience

For the New Tourist, host and guest are defined by difference, the negotiation of which is a fraught affair. The author takes the view that the host-tourist encounter is less problematic than Poon's (1993) New Tourist and much of the anthropological literature suggests. The tourist encounter is more of a *conduit* for inequality, rather than the cause. It brings together, face to face, peoples divided by unequal access to society's resources and opportunities. The New Tourist collapses the act of tourism itself into these unequal relationships that exist between countries, and comes to see inter-personal conduct itself as part of the problem, as well as the solution. How we behave and consume become the subject of debate, rather than the unequal *context* in which we relate to one another. A large dose of personal guilt for the New Tourist is the result; a guilt that can only be assuaged through 'ethical tourism' practices.

The perceived need to negotiate cultural difference has fuelled a fraught, angst riven debate. I would contend that the trend towards codes of conduct and guarded behaviour implicit in New Tourism can denigrate the tourist experience itself. Young, independent travellers, striking out and learning for themselves, are confronted with a plethora of well meaning advice, codes of conduct and moral regulation. Some environmentalists even suggest it would be better to avoid the risks and holiday closer to home (Jones, 1996). Yet an important aspect of independent travel is the sense of personal autonomy and freedom - there is much to be said for trusting oneself and learning from one's own mistakes in the transition from youth to adulthood (Gmelch, 1997). Moreover, the assumption of the primacy of difference colours the way we see the host. Conditions of relative poverty can be rationalised, and even celebrated, in cultural terms.

This paper has argued that the 'New Tourist' exhibits a distinctly anthropological outlook, and that this outlook carries its own limiting assumptions. Probably a starker summary of the argument is evident in the following anecdote: A young St Lucian waitress dresses in traditional costume because this is how she thinks the tourist has envisioned their host. The tourist asks earnestly about the local way of life, because this is the sort of thing a thinking tourist should do. In the context of such role playing, it is very difficult to discover empathy or commonality. The student traveller concerned was studying at University. The young woman was saving hard in order to travel, and hopefully study abroad. Only after a few drinks, and a loosening of cultural mores did they uncover their common aspirations. Material inequality between North and South, not a fetishised 'culture', set the two apart. The thrill of travel is that, one individual to another, barriers can be stripped away and real friendships made. The New Tourism seems intent on erecting new barriers based on a notion of a decentred, self limiting tourist, who is too busy gazing at the other's culture to empathise with them as an individual. Ultimately, the conclusion of anthropological outlook is that if you look for otherness, you will find it. You can wonder at it, and wonderful it often is. But an over sensitivity borne of a contemplative tourist gaze can equally be a barrier to unrestrained, open communication.

Endnotes

1. For example, British Airways sponsored a recent publication, 'the Green Travel Guide' (Earthscan, 1998) which was implicitly critical of the growth of tourism - ironically, a growth facilitated by BA, Europe's largest airline.

References

Boas, F. correspondence cited in Stocking, G. (1982), *Race, Culture and Evolution: Essays in the History of Anthropology*, University of Chicago Press, Chicago.

Cohen, E. (1972), 'Towards a Sociology of International Tourism', *Social Research*, No.39, pp. 164-182.

Dann, G. (1981), 'Tourism Motivations: an Appraisal', *Annals of Tourism Research*, 8 (2): 187-211.

Degler, C. N. (1991), *In Search of Human Nature: the Decline and Revival of Darwinism in American Social Thought*, Oxford University Press, Oxford.

Gmelch, G. (1997), 'Crossing Cultures: Student Travel and Personal Development', *International Journal of Inter-Cultural Relations*, Vol.21, No.4, pp. 475-490.

Goffman, I. (1959), *The Presentation of Self in Everyday Life*, Penguin, Harmondsworth.

Jones, J. (1996), *Green World*, March.

Jurdao, T. in Nash, D. (1996), *Anthropology of Tourism*, Pergamon, Oxford.

Le Divillec, G. (1997), Director of Worldwrite charity, promoting cultural exchanges and development research campaigner, personal conversation.

Levi-Strauss, C. (1955), *Tristes Tropiques*, Penguin, Harmondsworth.

Levi-Strauss, C. (1981), *The Naked Man*, translated by J. and D. Weightman, Harper Row, London (originally published in 1971)

Levi-Strauss, C. (1987), *The View From Afar*, translated by Joachim Neugroschel and Phoebe Hoss, Penguin, Harmondsworth, originally published in 1983.

Levi-Strauss, C. (1978), *Structural Anthropology, Vol. 2*, Penguin, Harmondsworth, translated, originally published 1973.

MacCannell, D. (1992), *Empty Meeting Grounds*, Routledge, London.

MacCannell, D. (1976), *The Tourist*, MacMillan, London.

Mason, P. and Mowforth, M. (1995), *Codes of Conduct in Tourism*, Occasional Papers in Geography, No. 1, University of Plymouth.

Mill, J. S. cited in Williams, R. (1958), *Culture and Society*, Chatto and Windus, London, p.74-75.

Mowforth, M. and Munt, I. (1998), *Tourism and Sustainability – New Tourism in the Third World*, Routledge, London.

Nash, D. (1996), *Anthropology of Tourism*, Pergamon, Oxford.

Nunez, T. 'Touristic Studies in Anthropological Perspective', in Smith (1989)(ed), *Hosts and Guests: the Anthropology of Tourism* (2nd ed), University of Pennsylvania Press, Penn.

Poon, A. (1993), *Tourism, Technology and Competitive Strategies*, CAB International, Wallingford.

Richards, G. (1998), *Developing and Marketing Crafts Tourism*, ATLAS, Tilburg.

Ryan, C. (1991), *Recreational Tourism, A Social Science Perspective*, Routledge, London.

Smith, V. (1977), (ed), *Hosts and Guests: the Anthropology of Tourism*, University of Pennsylvania Press, Philadelphia.

Smith, V. and Nash, D. (1991), 'Anthropology and Tourism', in *Annals of Tourism Research*, Vol.18, pp. 12-25.

Stocking, G. (1982), *Race, Culture and Evolution; Essays in the History of Anthropology*, University of Chicago Press, Chicago.

Tickell, C. (1994), Foreword in Cater, E. and Lowman, G. (eds) *Ecotourism: A Sustainable Option*, Wiley, Chichester.

Turner, L. and Ash, J. (1975), *The Golden Hordes: International Tourism and the Pleasure Periphery*, Constable, London.

Williams, R. (1987), *Keywords*, Fontana, London.

WTO (1995), *Tourism Trends*, Vol.1, WTO.

Tourism satisfaction and service evaluation

Sandra Carey and John Y Gountas

University of Ballarat, Australia

Introduction

Tourists' satisfaction and how it is achieved is a much debated issue yet there is little relatively little research specifically focusing on the psychological aspects that contribute towards the end state of product satisfaction. This is the case for the majority of academic and industry specific research. Most research is concerned with assessing the product and service levels from the provider end rather than the consumer's perception. Other tourism researchers agree that it is an area that needs more attention, (Swarbrooke, 1999, Seaton and Bennett, 1996, Lumsden, 1997, Ryan, 1997).

Ryan (1997) argues that 'The attitudes, expectations and perceptions of the holidaymaker are significant variables in setting goals, influencing behaviour and determining final satisfaction.'' Ryan proposes that any study of tourist behaviour needs to address, amongst others, the following considerations:

- The perceived importance of the activity in terms of self-development, self-enhancement, ego, meeting perceived roles, and responding to perceived requirements of significant others;

- The importance of the activity being evaluated not only by need, but also by expected outcomes. Thus, questions relating to perceptions of both need and outcome need to be considered;

- The intervening variables such as the skill brought to the recreational activity by the participant are also important. Skill may be a function of innate ability, experience and learning; and,

- Other intervening variables that might include the presence of significant other individuals or groups, and the importance attached to their presence or absence.

The degree to which the participant adjusts expectations, experiences cognitive dissonance, and engages in displacement activities and the role of these in determining final satisfaction if initial expectations are not met within any given situation.

These highlight the individuality of the consumer and the effect of psychological aspects such as the perception of expectations and outcomes, attitudes towards self-development, self-enhancement and relationships with others. These issues do not specify personality type/orientation and how that may influence perceived satisfaction levels nor do they allude to the effect of temporal factors during the consumption of the service. It is, surely, also important to understand how the expectations were formed i.e. from the individual's knowledge and imagination, or through external sources be they word of mouth, the tour organiser, or other media.

All of these may be affected by or relate to both cognitive and affective dissonance leading to an incongruent relationship between perceived need and performance. Frew and Shaw (1999) discuss the issue of personality types and environmental congruence in their work based on Holland's theory of personality and propose that it would appear 'if the perception of a tourist attraction is that it has a congruent environment for certain types of people, then there will be interest among people of those types to visit that environment'. If this is true then the implication is that it is dangerous to ignore or minimise the relationship between personality and satisfaction levels. As Frew and Shaw point out 'the more an environmental pattern resembles a personality pattern, the more a person will find the environment reinforcing and satisfying.

Conditions of satisfaction

Csikszentimihalyi (1998) developed the theory of 'flow', which is concerned, with the experience of complete involvement with the activity undertaken. If this state can be achieved the result would be complete congruence between perceived need and performance indicating a state of complete satisfaction with the experience. There are seven indicators used to assess the frequency and occurrence of flow:

- The perception that personal skills and challenges posed by an activity are in balance;

- The centring of attention;

- The loss of self-consciousness;

- An unambiguous feedback to a person's actions;

- Feelings of control over actions and environment;

- A momentary loss of anxiety and constraint; and,

- Feelings of enjoyment or pleasure.

These indicators imply a sense of total harmony between physiological needs, senses, intellect and actions. The concept of flow is a useful framework in the context of the holiday, even though it seems unlikely that the human condition can reach this state for any prolonged period of time.

If it is reached at all, it is likely to be fleeting and unsustainable over the duration of a holiday. However, the tourist may be subconsciously hoping and expecting to achieve this heightened state, possibly with very little effort on their part. Anyone who has worked for a travel organiser will have anecdotes of holidaymakers' often unreasonably high expectations of the product and service purchased.

Although the likelihood of any single holiday having sufficient attributes is small the concept of flow may provide some indicators of possibly important aspects of what a holiday should provide for people, albeit only for some moments. In this context we need to consider the necessary conditions which need to be in place for 'flow' to be possible during a holiday.

Csikszentimihalyi (1998) proposed that for the flow experience to exist there are four main prerequisite conditions:

- Participation is voluntary;

- The benefits of participation in an activity are perceived to derive from factors intrinsic to participation in an activity;

- A facilitative level of arousal is experienced during the participation in the activity; and,

- There is a psychological commitment to the activity in which they are participating.

The reality of the average holiday is that there is a degree of individual compromise necessary to fit with travelling companions. This is necessary to a greater or lesser degree according to the life stage or stages of the participants but may result in lack of total engagement with the activity. For example, it is common for people travelling with small children to make such concessions that they are no longer striving to satisfy their personal preferences. Then it may be said that that participation is only partially voluntary, that benefits are derived from others' satisfaction i.e. the children's and that arousal and psychological commitment are low.

The overall level of satisfaction will, therefore, be strongly linked to the individual's motivation to travel and the harmonisation of that motivation with their personality and its intrinsic preferences.

Motivation and satisfaction

Mill and Morrison (1985) stated 'Motivation occurs when an individual wants to satisfy a need'. This would suggest that needs develop and motivation is the force that attempts to restore balance to the individual by finding the means with which to satisfy the need. In other words an effort to reduce tension caused by an unsatisfied need. In researching tourists' satisfaction it is useful to understand how motivation actually occurs and how those needs may be satisfied.

Schiffman and Kanuk (1997) describe motivation as 'the driving force within individuals that impels them to action. This driving force is produced by a state of tension, which exists as a result of an unfulfilled need.'

Schiffman and Kanuk (1997) consider that needs and goals are constantly changing and will never be completely fulfilled. The change is triggered by a multitude of factors such as personal circumstances, age, previous experience etc. and because of this human activity never ceases. The analogy of physical hunger is used to illustrate the impermanence of needs' satisfaction. That is that new needs will always emerge and that these may change or develop according to past experiences and learning. This may be applied to many people in their travel experiences.

Indeed, Moscardo and Pearce (1996) referred to a 'travel career ladder' which charted the development of tastes, aspirations, interests, and activities over time. The assumption being that most people will start their 'travel career' cautiously and broaden their horizons as they gain experience and confidence. What satisfied them initially will not continue to do so ad infinitum.

Clearly, consumers' needs, wants, tastes develop during the course of their lifetime as experience, and knowledge is developed. In travel terms it is easy to cite holidaymakers who repeatedly visit the same destination to dispute the hypothesis that needs are constantly changing.

However, it could be argued that whilst the name of the destination may remain the same the *actual* product may change dramatically in a relatively short time. So, perhaps, new needs in the same consumers are being satisfied.

Wilkie (1994) acknowledged that consumers are motivated both by internal and external forces. This raises the question as to how much 'need' within the individual is innate or created through external influences such as other people, social pressure and media. Schiffman and Kanuk (1997) believe that motive arousal may be caused by physiological, emotional, cognitive and environmental factors either independently or in combination.

Need, in consumer terms, is often more *perceived* than *actual*. Obviously, this depends on one's subjective definition of need but if it is taken to mean necessity it may be said that travel and holidays are really luxury items. On the other hand, if we adopt the notion that human beings develop over a long period of time, in many different and unpredictable ways, then it becomes obvious that past wants/desires/dreams become necessities. The evolutionary idea of conceiving motivation as a moving target has the ability to explain the manifold and variable motives that consumers express. Although many motives may be due to innate genetical programming, we need to explore the perspective that motives are learned predispositions and change/evolve according to environmental factors e.g. cultural values, social class, economic, educational and life-cycle stages.

Focusing on the learning aspects of motivation it becomes possible to understand the variety of motives as well as the inability to arrive at a universal theory of what motivation is.

Maslow's (1965) well known assumption of a hierarchy of needs, differentiates between levels of needs and shows a distinction between *physiological* needs in survival terms and *higher* level needs which may not impact on survival but are perceived to be necessary for quality of life. The repeat holidaymaker, described earlier, may be simply expressing a greater need for safety and security primarily but also wanting to experience other things that relate to the higher level of needs.

A possible reason why the higher level needs may not manifest themselves as priorities may be due to lack of experience and development in dealing with new intellectual, emotional and social situations. These constraints may be prohibitive to moving up the 'travel career ladder.' However, this may not mean that the perceived level of satisfaction with the experience is of a lower quality but is simply different.

Beard and Ragheb (1983) derived four classifications of motivation from Maslow's (1965) work:

(a) The intellectual component; the extent to which individuals seek mental activities such as learning;

(b) The social component; the extent to which leisure is seen as a social and inter-personal need;

(c) The competence/mastery component; the extent to which the individual is driven to use leisure, for example, as a means of achievement, challenge, competition etc; and,

(d) The stimulus avoidance; the extent to which individuals use leisure as a means to escape and avoid over stimulation or social contact. The main motivation is to wind down.

This classification would be more effective if it also considered the myriad range of emotional needs, conscious and sub-conscious goals such as feeling good, feeling happy, fulfilment, fun/joy, elation etc.

The aspirational needs of opinion leaders should also be included in the categories of the intellectual, emotional, material and imaginative domains. Referring to the need to achieve balance and redress surfeits and deficits in one's everyday life could broaden stimulus avoidance.

Experience, sophistication and satisfaction

The individual may have more than one of the above motivators at any time but, perhaps, be aware of one representing the most pressing need. In addition, there may be a combination of needs to be satisfied sequentially e.g. stimulus avoidance may be priority with intellectual and mastery needs in second and third place and social needs in fourth.

Again, the order is likely to change at different times in one's life. Indeed, the change in priorities may alter in a very short period of time giving the opportunity for the same travel experience to satisfy a variety of components.

Ryan (1997b) proposed three alternative hypotheses:

(a) *More experienced tourists derive more and better satisfaction than the less experienced because they are further up the travel ladder, that is, they are prompted by qualitatively different needs.*

In his appraisal of the 'Travel Career Ladder' Ryan states 'Those going abroad for the first time may prefer the security of the package tour, but in time will opt for independent ones as they become more experienced'. To cite the U.K. case the demand for both independent and package holiday arrangements is increasing. Most operators are aware of the move towards a desire for more flexible 'independent' arrangements and are addressing this as part of their segmentation strategy. However, there is no concrete research that has documented the conversion rate from package to truly independent holidays and the reasons for why this may occur. Indeed, many experienced tourists continue to use the services of the package holiday operators as they offer a convenient solution to time constraints and accessibility issues.

This does not necessarily mean that they have not ascended their personal 'Travel Career Ladder'.

The suggestion that experience will change behaviour may not be accurate. The issue may simply be that some people enjoy/need more of the same or very similar experiences because they are stuck in a particular stage/mode of living. It could be argued that some consumers are either inner or outer directed or tradition oriented (1993). This is likely to lead to a different order 'Travel Career Ladder' according to personal and environmental characteristics. Due to the dynamic nature of tourism, there are new interactions between consumers and products which form new experiences that do not fit in to any existing typologies or career ladders. Tourism is a tool that fosters self-growth and development that is used by consumers lower down the ladder in learning to become more competent in deriving more and better satisfaction.

(b) *What is important is the need of the moment; it is immaterial whether it is a social need or one of intellect (self actualisation). Satisfaction is derived from the perceived meeting of that need and the different levels of satisfaction between more or less experienced holiday makers is simply that the more experienced are more able to meet their needs. Both the experienced and inexperienced are motivated by the same needs.*

This hypothesis does not clarify whether the more experienced have become so due to material resources, personal preferences, (affective, intellectual needs and many more). There is a need to identify and quantify much more effectively the differences between the various needs and the derived satisfaction levels.

(c) *Both experienced and inexperienced tourists are motivated by the same needs but the more experienced holiday makers are simply, through experience, more able to meet those needs. However, it is recognised that qualitative differences do exist, that, for example, there are differences between life enhancing experiences and others that are needs of convenience.*

Again, personal circumstances and personality differences are likely to affect the *degree* of need in both the life-enhancing driven needs and those of convenience in a fundamental way. This means that the whole 'bundle' of any individual's needs may be subtly and/or significantly different from another's.

Murray (1943) developed a classification system that divided needs into psychological and physiological with more than forty needs fitting into the two categories. Murray believed that needs would vary independently and not in a sequential, predictable fashion that was implied by Maslow. Although this system does not further distinguish between affective and cognitive factors, it does allow that the individual may experience different needs at different times on different levels of personal development and circumstances.

According to Pearce, (1982) 'Some of the novel features pertaining to tourist motivation are that tourists select a time and place for their behaviour often well in advance of the event, that the behaviour is episodic across the life-span, influenced by one's close relationships, that satisfaction may result in the behaviour being repeated or a new form of holiday attempted, and that there is a constantly evolving interplay between how well tourist motivation is understood and what is provided to satisfy this motivation.' In the behaviourists' view, any behaviour that is successful and rewarding is likely to be repeated. Therefore, the habitual buying behaviour can be explained in terms of past experiences and satisfaction levels. It is likely that in addition to the fact the place and time of behaviour is selected in advance, the duration of consumption will affect perceived satisfaction levels. In addition, some consideration should be given to the stage in the experience that the dissatisfaction, if it did, occurred.

The experience of travel is, probably, a quality of lifestyle issue rather than truly essential. Krippendorf (1993) cited results of a German study on tourists' motivation (Starnberg: Studienkreis fur Tourismus, 1987) which asked 'What were the main reasons for your 1986 (main) holiday journey? A list of thirty reasons was presented and the response frequency noted.

The five most frequently given reasons were:

1.   To switch off, relax - 66%;

2.   To get away from everyday life, have a change of scene - 59%;

3.   To recover strength - 49%;

4.   To experience nature - 47%; and,

5.   To have time for one another – 42%.

The above survey revealed a mixture of motives which broadly fell into physiological needs e.g. 'to eat well;' psychological needs e.g. 'to be with other people, to have company;' intellectual needs e.g. 'To broaden one's horizons, do something for one's culture and education.' There were many similarities between this study and the results of the focus groups conducted by Carey and Gountas in 1998. Clearly, the motives mentioned do not relate to what other researchers, (Maslow, 1965; Murray, 1943) regarded as essential needs e.g. survival, safety, but the new *transformed motives* have become/are perceived as essential for continuation of life.

Mayo and Jarvis (1981) considered that motivation is the driving force behind behaviour. They believed that motivation is guided by a number of factors- learning and perception, group and cultural influences and that it is related to the individual's personality. On the other hand, behaviour is not linked to the above a priori factors because there is not enough evidence to support this hypothesis. According To Ehrenberg, (1988) ATR (Awareness, Trial, and Repetition) theory on Repeat Buying Behaviour, consumers buy because they simply have tried it and found it satisfactory that makes them buy/try the brand/product again. Past experiences and availability of the product (opportunity to trial) is the hypothesised reason for the doing something rather than motivation. However, Ehrenberg (1988) does not comment on the reasons for trying this brand as opposed to any other brand and why the consumer became more aware of that brand and not the other competing ones.

There seems a reasonable argument to suggest that there are many intervening causal factors for particular behaviours and ensuing satisfactions. We can follow this line of argument with the means-ends theory and expectations to outcomes and performance.

McIntosh and Goeldner (1986) identified four categories of motivators: Physical, Cultural (material and immaterial aspects), Interpersonal, and Status/Prestige.

This recognises the complexity of needs and desires that an individual will seek to satisfy. This is further complicated by the individual's state constantly changing. The balance of needs will certainly vary at different times according to specific circumstances.

Some of the causes for change in the individual's motivation such as personal life stage were mentioned earlier. It is likely that there will also be some change due to maturity of the market. For example, with long haul travel becoming more common place and operators actively targeting different markets thereby offering greater variety of holiday types, the status and prestige factors may be less significant than they were ten years ago. It seems reasonable to predict that other factors such as self-development and education may become more important.

Push and pull factors

It is interesting that escape from normal life is consistently cited a strong motivator for travel. Dann (1976), using a sociological perspective, considered that anomie and ego enhancement were important and these are among the seven 'Push' factors identified by Crompton (1979). The other 'Push' factors are exploration, relaxation, and facilitation of social interaction, prestige, and regression.

Crompton (1979) also identified two 'Pull' factors, which are education and novelty. During the 1998 focus group research, (Carey and Gountas, 1999), the participants consistently claimed that they were initially motivated by the 'Push' factors but found the 'Pull' factors to provide the 'value added' satisfaction with the holiday and have longer lasting effects.

Iso-Ahola (1990) theorised that leisure needs change in several respects and that there may be a change from *before* to *after* the participation. This may occur especially if the perceived 'Push' factors are very strong and urgent in nature. The 'Pull' factors may be more appreciated after the event when there has been time for reflection. If this is the case, the 'Pull' factors may become part of the next decision making process and start to merge with the 'Push.'

Another reason for the 'Push' factors appearing to be stronger in the initial decision making process may be the distinction between specific and non-specific motivation (1990). Specific motivation in travel would be uniquely satisfied by the experience, e.g. Dann's (1976) concept of escape from 'anomie.'

However, non-specific motivation such as 'Pull' factors may be satisfied by other means (non-tourism offerings/products and services), and perhaps this indicates, that they are not perceived as so urgently in need of instant gratification. Therefore one may legitimately argue that, Dann's (1976) suggested motives of "anomie, and ego enhancement", are very generalised sociological concepts, which could be used as the universal motives to explain just about everything that consumers do in all aspects of consumption. Clearly this is a very difficult hypothesis to prove either way.

Furthermore Howard and Sheth (1969) refer to more than one motive being operative at any one time; a personal hierarchy of motives dominating at any one time leading to 'divergent reaction at different points in time by the same respondent to the same stimuli.' This view is rather compatible with Murray's classification (1943).

Crompton (1979) mentions the possibility that social tensions may mean that true motivations for travel or any activity may be concealed. For example, it is commonly acknowledged that some forms of travel have a prestigious element (Swarbrooke, 1999; Sharpley, 1996; Krippendorf, 1993), etc. but many holidaymakers would be reluctant to overtly express this. Similarly, they may feel a need to elaborate simple motives to avoid unfavourable value judgements.

Very few researchers have written about differences in motivation between the genders. Ryan (1997b) conducted research that suggests that there are gender differences in motivation, flow, and holiday experiences. Many of these seem to be related to the differences frequently found in women's and men's lifestyles and social responsibilities. Ryan found that women were more likely to express a need 'to avoid hustle and bustle' 'to relax physically' 'to be in a calm atmosphere' 'increase knowledge' and 'discover new things' more than men.

In the holiday party composition these findings could have implications for men's satisfaction with the holiday experience as it is well known amongst tour operators that women are much more likely to make crucial decisions relating to destination choice etc. than men. Frew and

Shaw (1999) have discussed the surprising lack of studies that consider the interactive relationship between personality, gender, and tourism.

To understand satisfaction and how it may be derived it is necessary to examine how and why needs develop in the first instance. Perceived needs have a basis in the consumers cultural backgrounds which may be defined as 'The sum total of learned beliefs, values and customs that serve to direct the consumer behaviour of members of a particular society' (Schiffman and Kanuk, 1997). However, the various cultural values that exist in all forms of social interaction, according to Fiske (1991) can be represented in terms of four fundamentally different rule systems: Communal sharing, authority ranking, equality matching, and market pricing. Fiske (1991) suggests that an individual person's life can manifest different values as fundamental as one moves from domain to domain (from family to corporation to religious institution, for example).

Where one particular system operates, a particular set of social values develop and similar personal values manifest in the individual's life. Therefore, we need to look at the manifested values and motives of the individual tourists in the context of their own culture and then to refine its differences in relation to other cultural contexts and the hypothesised universal rule systems.

Beliefs and attitudes

The belief and value components refer to the accumulated feelings and priorities that individuals have about 'things' and possessions. (Loudon and Della Bitta, 1993). Beliefs and attitudes may be enduring and hard to change.

Loudon and Della Bitta (1993) consider that three basic belief types influence the consumer:

- Central beliefs that form the core of a person's cognitive structure;

- Derived beliefs that result from central beliefs; and,

- Central-free beliefs that are separate and apart from other beliefs in the consumer's cognitive structure.

An example of how this works for tourism products may be that the consumer has the central belief that only well organised package holidays will be satisfactory, the derived belief may be that tour operators are the only point of purchase for such holidays and the central-free belief may be that, for example, Thomson Holidays will provide the best experience.

There is usually a distinction made between values and attitudes. Theodoroson and Theodoroson (1969) postulated 'an attitude is an orientation towards certain objects (including persons, others and oneself) or situations. Therefore attitudes may change over a period of time as they are influenced by changes in circumstances and experience levels.

Rokeach (1973) considered that values are more stable over a period than attitudes because they are more central to an individual's cognitive system. Yet many of the values used in his work clearly belong more to the affective domain than the cognitive. Therefore, values have two components, the cognitive and the affective preferences part, which need to be considered in the understanding of how they may affect tourist's behaviour.

Feelings are not always enduring but are sometimes more difficult to understand and change than reason as they often have root in one's childhood and socialisation. Feelings may be so embedded in the individual's character that they are not easily identified, recognised or understood. For consumer behaviour in tourism, the affective domain may cause illogical resistance and cognitive dissonance towards certain destinations, people and product types that potentially impact on perceived satisfaction.

Perception and satisfaction

Perception may be described as 'how we see the world around us. Two individuals may be subject to the same stimuli under the same apparent conditions, but how each person recognises them, selects them, organises them, and interprets them is a highly individual process based on each person's own needs, values and expectations.' 'Perception is the process by which an individual selects, organises and interprets stimuli into a meaningful and coherent picture of the world' (Schiffman and Kanuk, 1997).

'A motivated person is ready to act. How that person acts is influenced by his or her *perception* of the situation. In the same situation, two people with the same motivation may act quite differently based on how they perceive conditions' (Kotler, 1994).

These two, similar views focus on the individual's processing and organisation of values, needs etc. However, in many purchasing situations and almost always in travel and tourism decisions there is usually more than one person involved in the experience. Consumer Behaviour studies mostly focus on individuals but satisfaction levels and perception of a situation are likely to be influenced not only by our personal evaluation but also by those who are closely participating in our experience.

The literature frequently discusses the impact of groups on the *decision* to buy rather than the level of influence on satisfaction during product involvement. Studies of group behaviour support the view that behaviour may change according to the dynamics of group interaction. Group interaction and relationships will certainly affect our perceived reality.

Antonides and van Raaij (1998) propose the possibility of 'objective reality' but point out that 'a lot of perceptual differences exist between people.' They refer to four types of reality:

1.   The objective reality of people, products and brands;

2.   The reality as constructed and represented in advertisements, usage instructions, information given out by consumer organisations and information from other sources;

3.   The reality of other consumers, their experiences and judgements; and,

4,   The subjective reality (perception) of consumers.

It could be argued that subjective reality is the culmination of the first three factors and that no individual can truly decide on the supposedly 'objective reality' as each of us constructs our own realities and is motivated by our own personal drivers. For instance, the tour or trip organisers' may have a different set of 'objective' criteria from the consumer's which are based on an entirely different set of needs.

It may be in the supplier's interest to set lower level objective criteria for satisfaction assessment than those formulated by the consumer. Many tour operators are currently trying to 'educate' the consumer into having more realistic expectations against cost through their marketing activities.

Perception is partly developed through the senses; visual, auditory, olfactory, tactile and taste. This presents a difficulty for tourism experiences as many components are without any tangible form, particularly at the time of purchase. According to Antonides and van Raaij (1998) perception has four main determinants. These are:

1. *Prior knowledge* - the level of prior knowledge will affect perception of the product. It seems less likely that someone who has significant prior knowledge of a holiday will potentially have the same degree of surprise at the reality than the person who has very limited or no prior knowledge at all, although this may be contingent on how the prior knowledge was acquired;

2. *Orientation* -the orientation of the consumer will affect their reaction to the product and their perception of its quality. This may be also be discussed in terms of congruency with environment (Frew and Shaw,1999);

3. *Situation* - situational conditions affect perception. For example, a first time visitor to an underdeveloped or a culturally unfamiliar destination may suffer psychological discomfort that may affect their perception and product satisfaction. This aspect may change with familiarisation; and,

4. *Cognitive style* -this will be very influential in determining the level of importance that individuals will attach to certain aspects of their environment and the benefits that they derive from an experience. Cognition may be described as a personality characteristic and importance attached to levels of satisfaction/dissatisfaction will be affected by this characteristic.

Tourist typologies

As previously mentioned there is insufficient research on tourist consumer behaviour that relates to actual experience changes in behaviour, perceived satisfaction that is integrated with underpinning consumer behaviour theory.

The main attempts to categorise tourists have resulted in a number of typologies that tend to focus on whether tourists can be described as tourists or travellers (Swarbrooke, 1999; Sharpley, 1996). Characterising tourists may help to predict preferences and attitudes and therefore understand expectation and satisfaction levels.

It has been suggest that tourist typologies are useful (Swarbrooke, 1999) as they:

- Represent an attempt to increase our knowledge of consumer behaviour in tourism;

- Can help marketers make important decisions on product development;

- May form the basis of market segmentation techniques; and,

- Might potentially help to predict future trends in tourist behaviour.

Existing typologies have a tendency to focus on what a tourist is seen to be doing in behavioural terms at a particular point in time and forming assumptions on that basis only. However, there is little attention given to behaviour over a period of time and very little reference to life circumstances at the moment of observation. There seems to be an implicit assumption amongst some researchers (Swarbrooke and Horner, 1999; Sharpley, 1996) that the 'tourist' is likely to be less discerning about the product and less realistic about expectations, possibly insensitive and ignorant. These assumptions are made without understanding the individual and there is no hard evidence to support these judgements.

The existing typologies do not usually consider the life-long personal development of the holidaymaker, exposure to a range of product offerings and how these may affect their tastes, decision making, attitudes and satisfaction levels at each and every point in time.

The possibility that tourists/travellers/holidaymaker may adopt different personas during the course of their trip has been explored in this paper, and the way in which a tourist would classify themselves for tourism purposes may be inconsistent with other consumer decisions. Within the short space of a year it is possible for someone to holiday at a 'mass' beach resort in Europe, take a cultural city break, visit an 'exotic' destination and participate in adventure or nature activities using basic accommodation.

It could be argued that these typologies are simply 'snapshots' of the individual at the moment of observation or survey. They are not likely to be very revealing for commercial application nor are they likely to be useful as predictors of satisfaction, nor useful in predicting future behaviour. Perhaps the limitations are due to the research structures which, in each case, are quite inflexible and neither allow for free association or expression, nor build a long term coherent picture of the individual's personality and the environmental context that they live.

Conclusion

To date, most hypotheses for tourists' motivation and choices have been somewhat inadequate. There is room for much more research of a longitudinal nature that examines both changes in individual behaviour as well as the enduring preferences over the period of a 'travel career'. Research would benefit by embracing a multidisciplinary approach that incorporates the social-cultural context. In fact, most of the large tour operators are moving towards developing product lines that could potentially cater for an individual's needs from childhood to old age. There is also an increasing tendency towards guiding the consumer's choice by offering advice on where to go and what to do according to lifestyle and motivational criteria. These strategies seem to acknowledge the varying needs of individuals over a longer period. They also share common characteristics with other industries such as car, retail etc. in the move towards product modification and tailoring to individual requirements.

The distance between purchase and participation and the fact that a travel experience is longer lasting than many other high-involvement purchases probably contributes to potential reality distortion. . There is a case for tourism academics to reconsider assumptions and perceived wisdom in categorising individuals. The authors believe that the following variables should be the subjects of further study in tourist/consumer satisfaction:

1. Personality orientation/type and congruency with destination/holiday types/product choices;

2. The temporal aspects of satisfaction/dissatisfaction;

3. The level of significance attributed to the unsatisfying aspects of the experience;

4. The adoption of different persona during the course of consumption and the relationship to satisfaction levels; and,

5. The relationship with personal motives and outcomes to perceived satisfaction levels.

The authors propose that the understanding of the relevance of these variables is essential to the pertinent understanding of tourism satisfaction and service evaluation.

References

Antonides, G. and Van Raaj, W. F. (1998), *Consumer Behaviour, A European Perspective*, Wiley, Chichester.

Beard, J. G. and Ragheb, M. G. (1983), 'Measuring leisure motivation', *Journal of Leisure Research*, vol. 15 (3): 219-228.

Carey, S., Gountas, Y. (1999), Changing attitudes to 'mass tourism' products-The UK outbound market perspective, *The Journal of Vacation Marketing*, Vol 6 (1): 69 –75.

Crompton, J. (1979), 'Motivations for pleasure vacation', *Annals of Tourism Research*, vol.6, pp. 408 – 24.

Csikszentimihalyi, M. and Csikszentimihalyi, I. (1998), Introduction to Part IV, *in Optimal Experience: psychological studies in flow consciousness,* Csikszentimihalyi, M. ed. Cambridge University Press, Cambridge, pp. 251 –265.

Dann, G.(1976), Anomie, ego-enhancement and tourism, *Annals of Tourism Research*, vol.4, pp.184-94.

Ehrenberg, A. S. C. (1988), *Repeat Buying Behaviour*, Charles, Grittings and Co. UK.

Fiske, A. P. (1991), *Structures of social life: The four elementary forms of human relations*, Free Press, New York.

Frew, E. A., Shaw, R. N. (1999), The relationship between personality, gender and tourism behaviour, *Tourism Management*, 20, pp193 – 202.

Howard, J. and Sheth, J. (1969), '*The Theory of Buyer Behaviour*' John Wiley and Sons, New York.

Iso-Ahola, S. and Weissenger, E. (1990), Perceptions of boredom in leisure: conceptualisation, reliability, and validity in the leisure boredom scale, *Journal of Leisure Research*, vol.22 no.1, pp 1-17.

Kotler, P. (1994*), Marketing Management Analysis, Planning, Implementation and Control*, USA, Prentice Hall.

Krippendorf, J. (1993), *The Holiday Makers*, 5th ed., Oxford, UK, Butterworth Heinemann.

Loudon, D. and Della Bitta, A. (1993), *Consumer Behaviour, Concepts and Applications*, McGraw-Hill, Inc. USA.

Lumsden, L. (1997), *Tourism Marketing*, International Thomson Business Press, London.

Maslow, A. H. (1965), *Eupsychian Management*, Homewood, IL, USA.

Mayo, E., Jarvis, L. (1981), *The Psychology of Leisure Travel*, CBI Publishing Co Boston, Mass, USA,

McIntosh, R. W., Goeldner, C. R., (1986), *Tourism, Principles, Practices, Philosophies*, 5th Ed., Wiley, USA,

Mill, R. C. Morrison, A. M (1985), *The Tourist System*, Prentice Hall Englewood Cliffs, NJ, USA.

Moscardo, E. and Pearce, P., Log, C., O'leary, J. (1996), 'Understanding vacation destination choice through travel motivation and activities.' *Journal of Vacation Marketing*, vol.2 (2): 109-22.

Murray, H. A. (1943), *Manual of Thematic Apperception Tests*, Harvard University Press, USA.

Pearce, P. (1982), '*The Social Psychology of Tourist Behaviour*,' Pergamon Press, Oxford.

Rokeach, M. (1973), *The Nature of Human Values*, New York, NY Free Press, USA.

Ryan, C. (1997), *Researching Tourist Satisfaction*, Routledge, London, UK.

Ryan, C. (1997b), *The Tourist Experience*, Cassell, London.

Schiffman, L. and Kanuk, L. (1997), *Consumer Behaviour*, Prentice Hall, USA.

Seaton, A. and Bennett, M. (1996), *Marketing Tourism Products*, Thomson Business Press, London.

Sharpley, R. (1996), *Tourism, Tourists and Society*, Elm, Huntingdon.

Swarbrooke, J. and Horner, C. (1999), *Consumer Behaviour in Tourism* Butterworth-Heinemann, Oxford.

Theodoroson and Theodoroson (1969), *A Modern Dictionary of Sociology*, Cromwell, New York, USA.

Wilkie, W. (1994), *Consumer Behaviour*, Wiley, USA.

Post-modern tourist typologies: Case study from Flores, Indonesia

Stroma Cole

Buckinghamshire Chilterns University College, UK

Abstract

Tourists are a key stakeholder in tourism and thus the need to understand the tourist is fundamental in achieving tourism that is more sustainable (and ethical). According to some writers (Kripendorf 1987, Poon 1993), tourists are becoming more discerning and responsible in their travel options and behaviour. It is anticipated that changes in tourists as consumers will in turn change demand and lead to better provision by the intermediaries. Understanding tourist motivation and behaviour is important both in business and academic circles. This paper assesses the usefulness of the commonly cited tourist typologies (Cohen 1974, Smith 1977) and examines critical elements that so far have not been incorporated.

Pre and post experience interviews were carried out with tourists. This was part of a long-term ethnographic study of "ethnic" tourism in the interior of Flores, Indonesia. Interviews were carried out in Labuhan Bajo, a tiny port that has seen extensive tourism development in recent years. Situated on the Western tip of Flores it as an emergent diving centre and gateway to Komodo National Park.

The semi-structured interviews were used to analyse motivations, behaviour, spending patterns, understanding and adaptability to local norms. They also revealed the importance of new channels of distribution and the importance of local (rather than international) intermediaries.

My findings lead me to call into question the present tourist typologies. My data show them to be out-dated and inaccurate in reference to immersion and adaptability to local norms. This paper maintains that tourist's level of knowledge, their experiences and sources of information are critical in their motivation and behaviour and should be incorporated into tourist typologies. The post-modern traveller may intend to be more discerning, but ignorance, even among the best-educated elite travellers, is still the major obstacle to more sensitive, sustainable and equitable forms of tourism.

Introduction

The categorisation of tourists into types and the creation of tourist typologies serves two purposes in tourism. The industry categorises tourists into segments that share certain common interests for marketing purposes. Academics have attempted a variety of ways to categorise tourists for analytical purposes. Both the industry and academics have used tourist typologies as heuristic devices to bring about deeper understanding of tourists so that it is possible to understand, explain and predict their behaviour. As Laws (1995) suggests, understanding tourist's choices and behaviour is crucial in determining the management and development of destination facilities. Knowledge of the market demand is an essential aspect of tourism planning (Gunn 1984).

If such planning is to embrace the principles of sustainability, knowledge of tourists needs go beyond life style data and psychographics. As pointed out by Mananec and Zins (1994), life style data convey little information about tourists' behaviour while abroad. From the multitude of tourists typologies that have been developed (Boyd identified 90 types of tourist' types - in Fennell 1999:54) the most often quoted, and the only ones to deal with tourist behaviour, are Cohen's (1974) and Smith's (1978).

Cohen (1974) considers the key to understanding tourist behaviour is whether or not the tourist is institutionalised. His framework has been used to understand the impact of different tourists as, according to Cohen, the uninstitutionalised 'drifters' and 'explores' have a more profound understanding of the hosts and their culture. Cohen (1979) classified his typology as an interactional model that deals with the extent and manner of contact between the tourists and local people (Mo et al 1993).

Smith's (1978) typology built on Cohen's and from his four types Smith developed seven. Her typology linked tourist numbers or frequency with adaptation to local norms. Tourist behaviour and in particular how far tourists adapt to local norms is an important factor in the level of negative socio-cultural impacts and especially the level of social conflict. Understanding this aspect of tourists can thus be considered crucial for the sustainability of a destination. This paper examines these typologies in the light of empirical research from Flores, Eastern Indonesia. It discusses the relevance of these typologies and assesses their usefulness for the development of responsible tourism. Poon (1993) claims a new type of tourist (in opposition to an old type), Wood (1991) claims a new breed. Others claim post-industrial tourists (Moscardo and Pearce 1999) and post-modern tourists (Urry 1996). This paper examines how far this plethora of typologies explains tourists and tourism in a specific location.

Research setting and methods

This research forms part of a larger, long-term, ethnographic study that has been investigating cultural tourism development on Flores, Eastern Indonesia. Flores is part of a string of islands that lie East of Bali called Nusa Tenggara. It is a long (250 miles), narrow (as little as 30 miles in places), volcanic island, that has two renowned, attractions that bring tourists to Flores. In the centre of the island lies Mount Keli Mutu, a volcano with three different coloured lakes at its peak. The village at its base, Moni, has seen considerable development. Off the western tip of Flores, lies the Komodo National Park, its gateway, the tiny port of Labuhan Bajo, has expanded rapidly through tourism. A small number of tourists come to the island for its "ethnic" villages and their ikat weavings. A further, smaller minority, cross Flores en route to other islands without being attracted by any of these attractions. Due to the geography and road conditions on the island nearly all tourists follow a well-worn route either east or west across the island.

The villages at the centre of the study lie in the Ngada region, which is situated between Labuhan Bajo to the west and Keli Mutu to the East. Tourists started visiting the villages in the 1980's in very small numbers, since when numbers have increased continuously. The most popular village, Bena, received 9000 visitors in 1997 (Tourist Department statistics 1998). This examination of tourists should be understood in the context of the wider study. As the focus of the study was the villagers in two villages that receive tourists, it is their attitudes and opinions of the tourists that have remained central to the researcher. For example, impolite behaviour is the opinion of the villagers, and not necessarily the researcher.

The tourist research was undertaken to understand the tourists that visited the villages. The villagers wanted to know why the tourists came, that is their motivation, levels of satisfaction and spending patterns. The researcher was also interested in the level of cultural understanding before and after the visits and the tourists' behaviour in the villages. As will become clear from the findings other important information elicited included: method of transport, use of guides, use of guide books and the amount of time spent in villages. The research was carried out in a number of different ways over a period of eight months between July 1998 and February 1999.

Semi-structured interviews

Informal semi-structured interviews were carried out with tourists in Labuhan Bajo, the western gateway to Flores, to gather pre-experience information from tourists who were heading east; and post experience information from tourists who had visited the villages and were heading west. Similar interviews were held with tourists in the town local to the villages where tourists would overnight before and after a village visit. This enabled the researcher to interview the same tourists both pre and post-experience to attempt to discover if the visit had met with expectations.

Observation

Observation was made of tourist behaviour, clothing, time spent in the village, purchases of souvenirs and interaction with villagers on a daily basis. This was done by the researcher and with help from a villager using a tick box chart. The natural shape of the villages and housing allows for most tourists to be in sight of the researcher sitting with the villagers on their terraces. Although there is no doubt that the presence of the researcher had some effect on tourist behaviour, the arguments presented here are the result of a variety of research methods. Thus any bias due to the researchers presence is not considered significant to the overall findings.

Visitors books

All villages keep visitors books that tourists complete with name, country of origin, age, profession and comments. Clearly some tourist do not take these books seriously, (some, for example, fill in silly names, tourist for their profession and the moon for country of origin) and many filled in the comment section before even walking around the village. However, I placed an additional book at the entrance and explained that I was carrying out research and would welcome comments. A number of common themes could be identified from these comments.

Under-cover observation and questioning

The researcher posed as a tourist and therefore did not admit to being able to speak the local language, know about the local culture and joined groups of tourists to elicit their opinions as one of them. This was considered important to be able to join in freely with tourist talk and not be constantly used as a source of information that happened as soon as tourists knew that I had useful knowledge.

Findings

In attempting a critique of Cohen (1974), Smith (1978) and others tourist typologies the problem of the indiciple of tourism (Tribe 1997) emerges. Here the lack of a common vocabulary presents an immediate challenge. Both Cohen and Smith use explorer as one of their categories but where as Smith's is "almost akin to anthropologists...easily accommodating to local norms" (1978:9), Cohen's explorers still seek the protection of their environmental bubble and do not become fully integrated with the host society.

A small minority of tourists might be said to fit into Cohen's drifter category. They tried to avoid contact with other tourists by making their way to one of the villages alone and avoiding Bena, due to its prominence in guidebooks ("therefore it must be touristy"). However these off-beat tourists, as Smith would term them, did not necessarily adapt well to local norms as Smith's typology suggests. In terms of numbers, tourism in Ngada villages varies from village to village. However, this has as much to do with transport arrangements and which guide they use as to the intensity of visitation. Some tourists visit several villages. As Smiths typology does not specify numbers or more importantly ratios of tourists to locals it is difficult to use her typology or critique her theory on tourist numbers and the relationship with adaptation to local; norms.

The findings from this research suggest that there are a variety of types of tourists that visit the villages of Ngada, and would confirm that some tourists adapt better to local norms than others. However, there are important reasons underlying this adaptation irrespective of where the tourists would fit on Smith's typology. The findings suggest the most important factors underlying tourists' adaptation were experience and sources of knowledge.

Experience

The most important experience that affected how tourists behaved and adapted to local norms was travel experience in less developed countries, but especially other 'cultural village' visits in Indonesia. A clear difference in expectation and adaptability existed between tourists heading east and tourists heading west. Those heading west had usually just arrived in Indonesia (from Australia) and Flores was one of the first islands they had visited. Tourists heading east had often visited other similar villages in North Sumatra or Sulawesi. They were more able to adapt, as they were familiar with many cultural values, for example dress code, that exist in common between such villages. The westward tourists frequently showed more interest, and spent more time in the villages, but had little idea of appropriate dress and behaviour.

Sources of knowledge

The second most important factor in tourist's appropriate behaviour was their source(s) of knowledge about the village's culture and how to behave. Tourists find out about the villages of Ngada from a number of sources: other tourists, guide books, local guides, driver guides, and tour guides. The difference in adaptation to local norms was frequently a function of which source of knowledge the tourists had. As has been noted very few tourists came alone, those that did used a guide book. Some of these "off-beat tourists" adapted well, but many did not. Several of these tourists were described by villagers as impolite and offensive both in terms of their clothing, by not accepting ritual food, and not sharing cigarettes while smoking and trying to interact with locals.

The source of knowledge these tourists had was limited to guide books and in nearly all cases this was one of the lonely planet guides[1] which give little or no space to discussing issues of responsible behaviour. As Abram (2000) notes, guide books often provide visitor's chief means of making sense of a host country and he claims that the Rough Guides try hard to foster environmentally responsible behaviour among readers. However as he points out, many readers look little further than the listings section. There is no space given to culturally responsible behaviour specific to the villages of Flores in any relevant edition of Lonely Planet Guides; so a tourist that has this as their sole source of knowledge can be said to be behaving incorrectly out of ignorance.

Many independent tourists use local guides to travel to the villages. These guides are based in the local town, Bajawa, and find tourists in the town's guesthouses and restaurants, where they offer tourists tours, including visits to a number of local villages. The guides will generally bring together between four and ten tourists to share a minibus for such a tour. These tourists could be said to fit into Smith's 'unusual tourists', but many of them adapt better than the aforementioned group. Their behaviour is to a certain extent directed by the guides. Guides told tourists that the villages did not like tourists showing one another affection in the villages. Further when ritual food is offered they will whisper "take a token offering of food, and pretend, otherwise the hosts will be offended". Unfortunately the guides do not have the confidence to direct the tourists in respect to their clothing and this aspect of offensive behaviour was frequently observed amongst this group. Some tourists had expected the guides to inform them about clothing as they had experienced this in other villages and were surprised that the guides had failed to relay this information.

Most of the tourists chose to use a local guide because it was more convenient. They could be called "semi soft back-packers" as they took reasonably reliable local busses between towns but used guides with private transport rather than infrequent open trucks to visit the villages. Some chose to use guides because of the information they expected to gain. Satisfaction was a factor of the guide's language and interpersonal skills, as the tourists had no way of checking the accuracy of the guide's narratives.

An increasing proportion of tourists visit the villages with driver-guides. Many of these drivers have limited language skills, but know the tourist route across Flores. They are based at the island's gateways and work for local travel agents. In Labuhan Bajo, the western gateway, a number of travel offices exist. Staff from these semi-professional travel agents meet every plane and boat that arrives, and offer a variety of travel services. "Soft back-packers", tired of slow uncomfortable Indonesian bus journeys cease to fit Smith's category of "off beat travellers" and would be better suited in her 'incipient mass' category. Since 1995, the proportion of independent tourists hiring a car and driver, to take them across Flores, has risen from perhaps 20 to 50%.[2] Tourists were sometimes embarrassed about their use of private vehicles, and gave reasons such as feeling unwell or running out of visa time;[3] However, others were not and just said that it was a cheap and convenient way to travel. Clearly situational factors will not only determine a tourist's role on different trips as Mo *et al* (1993) pointed out, but these can change from one day to another. As use of public transport has been a key feature in categorising tourists in the literature, especially for identifying back-packers (see Goodwin 1999, Hampton 1997), this, like other categories and typologies appear dysfunctional in this case.

Smith's 'elite travellers' used pre-arranged services and facilities, and Cohen's 'individual mass' tourists make major arrangements through travel intermediaries. In both cases one assumes these are international intermediaries contacted in tourist' generating regions. However, the use of local intermediaries is not discussed although these stakeholders can play an important part in influencing the tourists' behaviour. A considerable difference existed between tourists with local guides and driver-guides. As noted, the former provided valuable information which enabled the tourists to act in a less offensive way. In contrast the driver guides did not accompany the tourists as they walked around the villages, and provided little if any information for the tourists. In terms of behaviour these tourists resembled those that made their way to the villages independently. However, in groups they behaved in other ways considered inappropriate such as holding hands, kissing or carrying one another.

The villagers receive increasing numbers of three types of tourists travelling as part of pre-arranged groups. The first type of group tourist, travel by air-conditioned coach, bemoan the lack of post cards for sale and spend the least amount of time in the village. They travel with a guide, often from another area of Indonesia, with little knowledge of the village's culture. This new type of tourist was generally older than the other tourists. They wore more clothes, were less inclined to show one another physical affection in public, and never stayed long enough to sit down let alone be offered food (and therefore could not refuse it). It can not be said that they adapted least well, although they adapted little their behaviour was generally inoffensive. As they were often high spenders the villagers of Bena complained less about this group than others.

A second type of group traveller to visit the villages were Australian School groups. These tourists were on study tours and do not fit into general tourist typologies. Their teachers were interested in the culture of Indonesia, which the students were studying, and they clearly had enough knowledge to behave responsibly. The final type of group tourists that visited the villages were those travelling with special interest western tour operators, travelling with a western tour leader and a local guide. These tourists were interested in the culture of the villages and were prepared to adapt to local norms. Sensitive Western tour leaders acted not only as educators but also as disciplinarians: for example not allowing their tourists to wear inappropriate clothing, give sweets to the local children or take photographs without asking. These tourists resembled Hughes (1995) post-industrial tourists "likely to be sensitive to impacts its members have on the host population and be concerned with behaving responsibly in ethnic contact situations" (Moscardo and Pearce 1999:419)

Ignorance and arrogance

Tourists adaptation, or not, has so far been identified as a factor of knowledge and experience. Various different types of tourists have been identified that lacked the knowledge of cultural norms necessary to behave in a responsible manner. Although this lack of knowledge or experience was identified as the major factor hindering responsible behaviour it was not the only factor. As well as knowledge willingness to make the required effort is also a factor. It was noted, particularly among long-term (over 3 months) eastward heading tourists, who had the knowledge but not the will to change their behaviour. They were often tired of making the effort, and were essentially worn out and bored from their travels. These tourists would sit or lie around the village waiting for their travelling companions. The positions they took up were easily read by the villagers as uninterested, and the villagers would ask, " Why do they come?" The tourists were bored with constant greetings and had stopped responding. Villagers were aware that the tourists were weary of the constant "hello mister" that every gang of children shout as one crosses the archipelago. But when an adult said good morning in Indonesian, or even attempting English, they found it offensive when tourists did not respond. "Why are they so arrogant?"[4], villagers would ask me.

This arrogance appears to be linked with self-interest and an individualistic morality that has increased with the cultural shift in Western society in the past twenty years or so. As a result of self-interest and placing ego's needs at the centre arrogance appeared to be an increasingly common characteristic of the young tourists in the late 1990's. This may be linked to the age of these tourists, increasing numbers of which are teenage gap-year travellers.

Levels of interest

There was considerable variation in the level of interest shown by tourists in the culture of Ngada villages. At one extreme the more or less disinterested, "sheep-like" tourists that followed their flock from one Lonely Planet recommended site to another. At the other extreme were tourists that spent the longest time in the villages, quizzed their guides on cultural details and attempted to get 'back-stage' (MacCannell 1973).

The traditional houses of Ngada are central to the society's social organisation and ritual life, but also a key aspect of the villages as a tourist attraction. Due to the houses' construction, with a fairly public open terrace, main living room, and kitchen come inner sacred room at the back of the house; MacCannells back stage metaphor is especially apt. During eight months fieldwork only two tourists ever entered an inner sacred room - true back stage!. Only a handful of tourists got further than the terrace. However, the experience of visiting the village was authentic enough for most. The findings support the view of Dann (1996) Urry (1990) and Cohen (1995) that the postmodern tourist is less concerned with authenticity as long as the visit is an enjoyable one. For many the village was a backdrop for conversation with other tourists. It appeared in many cases that social interaction with their own kind was more important than the authenticity of the setting.

There is also evidence that tourists thought that the villages were contrived for tourism, that they were constructed stages for them to play on. " A Living museum" was an expression used by many tourists in describing the villages. They did not realise that in this case they were experiencing the villagers' reality. The villages were not created or kept for tourism as many tourists supposed. In all but one village, Bena, nothing is presented for tourists except the production and sale of ikats that are only partially made for tourist consumption.

Conclusions

In the findings from this research there appears to be a merging of tourist types. Though the Lonely Planet survival kit series emphasises the individual, adventurous approach to travel in contrast to the easy package tour, many users of these guidebooks took locally packaged tours. As other research has indicated "back-packers are increasingly demanding more up market facilities" (Goodwin 1999:12) such as private Western toilets. Further evidence for the merging of tourist types came from interviews carried out at Labuhan Bajo that revealed back-packers taking up diving. Diving has been considered an up-market elite form of special interest tourism, but as the regional head of tourism pointed out back-packers are trying it out. As the post-modern tourist searches for "new activities, sensations and stimulations" (Urry 1990) they mix a day or two of elite activity with days of hard travel on local buses. As Urry (1996) notes in his ten characteristics of the post-modern tourist "no sustained distinction can be drawn between the insightful traveller and the mere tourist". The distinction, according to Urry is a modern one, which post modern culture dissolves.

Poon (1993) noted the existence of hybrid tourists but she also claimed that: they want to be in charge and not to follow, that they have understanding and are better informed, and know how to behave rather than having a 'west is best' attitude. Trans-Flores tourists were following a well-worn trail. Some admitted that they only came to the villages "because that was what everyone else was doing". Although many would claim understanding of the local culture, rather than superiority, the majority were not well enough informed to travel without causing offence.

Although tourist types have merged I would not agree that "the post-tourist renders tourist typologies meaningless" (Sharpley 1994:88). Placing tourists into types, as pointed out by Shaw and Williams (1994) "provides a platform from which to explore the relationships between tourist consumption and destination areas" (in Mc Minn and Cater 1998:697). The categories identified above were descriptive but have analytical merit in that they highlight which tourists causes more, or less, offence and helps to identify some of the reasons why.

From the findings it appears that little relationship exists between Smith's tourist types and their adaptation to local norms and that previous experience and sources of knowledge are more important factors in determining responsible tourist behaviour. Mc Minn and Cater (1998) identify three different types of tourists and relate them to the impacts of tourism in Belize. Although their categories bear no resemblance of those found on Flores, they reach an important conclusion. namely that better comprehension of tourism processes at the local level requires the disaggregation of tourists. Their typology allowed "a better understanding of what impacts are attributable to each group and more importantly enables a means of addressing the problems of targeting the appropriate group" (Mc Minn and Cater 1998:697).

As has been pointed out much of the offensive behaviour of tourists was the result of ignorance, a point made by Kripendorf (1987:45) and in order to overcome this they need to know how to behave appropriately. The role of the individual tourist in promoting sustainable tourism is, according to Inskeep, to "travel in a sensitive manner, refraining from inappropriate behaviour which negatively affects the community" (1991:466). This raises the question, how can the tourists be sensitive if they are unaware of what locals consider culturally degrading and offensive?

Cater (1997) notes "tourists need to be properly informed about the character of their destination and how to behave". Through the findings of this study it was possible to identify that an increased number of tourists that behaved in the most inappropriate ways were those using driver-guides. If these tourists are to receive the information they require about local etiquette it needs to be disseminated via these important local intermediaries.

The lack and type of clothing worn by tourists was the inappropriate behaviour most bemoaned by the locals and also an area that the local guides felt unable to broach with tourists. Codes of conduct displayed in the local guesthouses would be a way of targeting this information to tourists. The local guides felt they would be able to point out such a code if it was prominently displayed in the guesthouses.

According to Cooper et al (1993:24), Cohen's typology "forms a framework for management practice". From the findings from this study I would suggest that socially responsible management require more specific, locally generated, typologies. Post- modern tourists can not be usefully understood with the global typologies that have dominated the tourism literature for the past twenty years. Understanding of tourists must be sought at the local level where it is believed tourist typologies still have their place for the analysis of tourist behaviour.

Endnotes

1. The amount of space given to the region depends on whether the guide book is for all South East Asia or for Indonesia.

2. Exact numbers are unknown, these estimates come from local guides and the Tourist Department. The steep increase will be in part due to the very favourable exchange rate since the economic collapse of Indonesia in 1997.

3. Tourists are only issued with two months visa at a time.

4. Kenapa mereka sombong?

References

Abram, D. (2000), Guide books turn travellers into package tourists, a debate. *In Focus* No.34 pp5.

Cater, E. (1997), Ecotourism in the 3rd world, in France, L. (Ed) *The Earthscan reader in sustainable tourism*. Earthscan publications, London.

Cohen, E. (1974), Who is a tourist A conceptual classification. *Sociological review* 22: pp 527-555.

Cohen, E. (1995), Contemporary tourism trends and challenges: sustainable authenticity or contrived post modernity? In Butler, R. and Pearce, D. (Eds.) *Changes in tourism: people, places and process*. Routledge, London.

Cooper et.al. (1993), *Tourism principles and practice*, Longman, Harlow.

Dann, G. (1996), *The language of tourism A sociological perspective*. CABI, Oxford.

Fennell, D. (1999) *Ecotourism an Introduction* Routledge, London.

Goodwin, H. (1999), Backpackers good, package tourists Bad?, *In Focus* No.31pp12-13.

Gunn, C. (1984) *Tourism Planning,* 3rd ed. Taylor Francis, Washington.

Hampton, M. (1997*) Unpacking the rucksack: A new analysis of backpacker tourism in South East Asia.* In Nuryanti, W. (Ed) Tourism and heritage management. Gadjah Mada University Press Yogyakarta.

Hughes, G. (1995) The cultural constraints of sustainable tourism. *Tourism Management* 16 pp49-60.

Inskeep, E. (1991) *Tourism Planning: an integrated and sustainable development approach*. Van Nostrand Reinhold New York.

Kripendorf, J. (1987), *The Holiday Makers*, Butterworth-Heinemann, Oxford.

Mac Cannell, D. (1973), Staged authenticity: arrangements of social space in tourist settings *American journal of sociology* 79 pp589-603.

Mc Minn, S and Cater, E. (1998), Tourist Typology Observations from Belize. *Annals of Tourism Research* 25(3) pp 675-699.

Mananec and Zins (1994), Tourist behaviour and the new European life style typology, in Williams T (Ed.*) Global tourism: The next decade*. Butterworth- Heinemann, Oxford.

Mo, C. et. al (1993), Testing an international tourist role typology *Annals of Tourism Research* 20(2) pp319-335.

Moscardo and Pearce (1999), Understanding Ethnic tourists. *Annals of Tourism Research* 26(2) pp416-434.

Poon, A. (1993), *Tourism, technology and competitive strategies*, CABI Oxford.

Tribe, J. (1997), The indiscipline of tourism. *Annals of Tourism Research* 24(3)pp638-657.

Sharpley, R. (1994), *Tourism, tourists and society*, Elm, Cambridgeshire.

Shaw, G. and Williams, A. M. (1994), *Critical issues in tourism: A geographical perspective.* Blackwell, Oxford.

Smith, V. (1978), Introduction, tourism and leisure a theoretical overview in Smith, V. (Ed). *Hosts and guests. The anthropology of tourism.* Blackwell, Oxford.

Wood, K. (1991), How to be a good tourist. *Observer* 31/3/91.

Urry, J. (1990), *The tourist gaze: leisure and travel in contemporary societies.* Sage, London.

Urry, J. (1996), Post modern society and contemporary tourism. In Nuryanti, W. (Ed) *Tourism and culture Global civilisation in Change.* Gadjah Mada University Press Yogyakarta.

Overseas holiday hotels for the elderly: Total bliss or total institution?

Graham Dann

University of Luton, UK

Introduction

Situated on a hill overlooking a popular resort on the island of Mallorca stands a rectangular white building which has all the appearances of a small hospital*. In reality, it is a three-star hotel bearing the fictitious name of *La Paloma Blanca*. The property, which is exclusive to a well-known UK tour operator, is open all year to predominantly British visitors. From November to February, when package rates are at their lowest, it is mainly patronised by senior tourists, most of whom are accommodated on an all-inclusive basis. Those aged fifty years or more also frequent the hotel during the summer months. However, at that time of year they tend to find themselves outnumbered by younger couples with children*.

The following account is based on a one week sojourn at the beginning of December 1997, occasional visits during the summers of 1998 and 1999, and discussions with guests between October-December 1998[1]. Methods employed include a mixture of participant observation, unobtrusive measures, conversation sampling and interviews (cf., Ryan, 1995).

The principal object of this ethnographic inquiry is to gauge the goodness of fit between the qualities of a total institution and all-inclusive holidays for the elderly. While retirees typically face declines in income, autonomy and status in the society of origin, the compensatory freedom they seek elsewhere is often illusory. To this end, the general hypothesis is that the discrimination and social exclusion experienced by those no longer gainfully employed on account of their age in the home environment are somehow carried over into the holiday setting. Indeed, they may be simply exchanging one form of social control for another. The idea that an increasing loss of liberty at home represents an ideal condition for travel has already been explored (Dann, 1997). So too has the argument that the tourism industry subsequently utilises a language of social control in order to manipulate its clientele at the destination (Dann, 1996). What is new in the current investigation is its theoretical grounding, the localisation of such an exercise in normative compliance and its manifestation among a particularly disadvantaged age group.

Erving Goffman (1973), more than any other social theorist, is accredited with developing the notion of a total institution within a dramaturgical perspective. According to him, a total institution is 'a place of residence and work where a large number of like-situated individuals, cut off from the wider society for an appreciable period of time, together lead an enclosed, formally administered round of life' (p.11). Goffman then goes on to distinguish five principal types of total institution, examples of which can be found in orphanages, concentration camps, army barracks, monasteries and mental hospitals - the last mentioned providing the locus of his research and the abbreviated title of his book, *Asylums*. Although all these types have some overlaps and common characteristics, the first probably comes closest to all-inclusive hotels for the elderly since it refers to 'institutions established to care for persons felt to be incapable and harmless' and comprises such places as 'homes for the blind, aged, orphaned and indigent' (p.16).

Later, Goffman identifies a number of behavioural attributes associated with such institutions. Those most germane to the present inquiry include :

(a)   sleeping and playing in the same place under the same single authority

(b)   submission to an overall rational plan which is tightly scheduled

(c)   a division between staff and inmates

(d)   wearing of uniform

(e)   requirement of permission to carry out special activities

(f)   prevalence of rules

(g)   seeking of petty privileges

(h)   adopting a system of secondary adjustment.

Clearly, work is usually absent from a vacational setting, but so too is employment far removed from other total institutions cited by Goffman, such as homes for particular categories of persons, hospitals and sanitoria. The more pertinent idea, therefore, seems to be the experiencing of most activities under the same roof or within the same compound. As for the notion of an hotel being a place of residence for an appreciable period of time, at first sight that quality appears to be somewhat at odds with reality. Yet, on reflection, it should be acknowledged that many elderly holiday makers spend considerable periods away from their regular homes, as much as six months in some cases, sufficient to challenge the customary definition of legal domicile for purposes of taxation and residence. Then there are the possibilities of free entry and exit which operate in an hotel but not in most total institutions. However, and as will be shown, even in the former situation, suasive forces are at work which tend to discourage egress and ingress for individuals. In their stead are scheduled and organised outside collective pursuits, while many are encouraged to remain inside the property in order to avail themselves of the all-inclusive benefits for which they have paid. Weightman (1987) refers to these external processes under the name of "encapsulation", while Cohen (1972) has described the internal scenario in terms of an "environmental bubble" - a haven of safety and familiarity protecting the client from foreign dangers that lurk beyond the boundaries of the hotel as a home-away-from-home. Perhaps that is one reason why tour representatives, in their introductory talks to elderly holiday makers, stress the risks associated with venturing out alone, the perils of public transport, exposure to local criminals, and so on.

In most other respects there is a much closer goodness of fit between an all-inclusive hotel for the elderly and several of the total institutional qualities highlighted by Goffman. They are described from the field-notes in the ethnographic present, along with brief commentaries, under the following headings : admission procedures, command structure, queuing, inmate awareness, working the system, spatial disorientation and attitudes to time.

Admission procedures

Reference has already been made to the clinical features of *La Paloma Blanca*. The admission procedures tend to substantiate this impression. On entry, guests typically join a queue waiting to be registered at the reception area. Here they surrender their identities by handing over their passports. In return they are allocated rooms. At this point, all-inclusive customers have plastic bracelets affixed to their wrists similar to those applied to hospital patients*. The bands have expiry dates on them and are generally worn on and off the premises until departure*. They are colour coded according to the amount of alcoholic intake permitted for their wearers*. Children have green, teenagers white and adults purple*. These bracelets call to mind electronic tagging devices* familiar to all those from the UK, a country deemed by one commentator (Davies, 2000) to be subject to the greatest surveillance on earth. Surrounding the new entrants are interns in undifferentiated holiday attire. Their collective stares focusing on the novice arrivals indicate the expectation that soon the freshly admitted will be joining them. Some of the habitues are chatting in small sedentary groups. Others form part of a much larger assembly watching a Sky-television channel* that relays sports programmes and weather forecasts from the motherland. A few are in wheel chairs*. Some hobble round with the aid of walking sticks. Much younger tour representatives in company livery are in attendance supervising the smooth transition from the outer to the inner world. Their neat dress, healthy demeanour and lingo reinforce distinctions between staff and inmates. Orderlies, in the form of bellboys, carry cases of possessions to identical quarters.

All the plain, carpet-less rooms are small, dark and cell-like, bearing only numbers on the doors. They contain the bare essentials : twin beds with a single blanket on each, a wardrobe and a little chest of drawers. There are no mirrors or distinguishing pictures on the walls. Nor is there any television or radio to maintain independent contact with the outside world. In winter months, an unadjustable, centrally-controlled radiator heats to the point of near suffocation. A tiny bathroom contains only one roll of toilet paper and a miniscule bar of soap. These two items constitute basic rations, as is soon to be discovered. Indeed, after a single day's use, when the slither of lather has all but disappeared and no replacement is forthcoming from the cleaner the following day, an attempt is made to procure an additional morsel from the front desk. Gone are the receptionists solely on hand for yesterday's admissions. In their place stands a large unsmiling woman. To the Oliver-Twist-like request for more, she merely barks out in the tone and volume of a sergeant major that there is just one complimentary piece *issued* on arrival and that it is to be used for emergencies only.

Unless guests wish to venture into foreign territory for extra supplies, the implication is that they must join the remainder of their unwashed compatriots. Olfactory confirmation of this shared plight is subsequently confirmed by the surrounding old people's home odour created by lack of opportunity for personal hygiene. Ancillary observation of the clothes worn by clientele indicates that many garments are well used, decidedly un-chic and have a likely charity shop provenance. Some of the women's dress tops and men's opened casual shirts bear food and drink stains*. Those unfashionably wearing socks with their sandals* have apparently been doing so without the necessary change for quite a while judging from the accompanying smell*.

Command structure

Order is brought to the holiday environment through a varied command structure that operates in several ways and on different levels. Before departure, members of the vacation group are issued with a resort guide[2] which includes such information about the island as its history, scenery, handicrafts, food and drink, sights, and so on. However, the booklet also contains several prescriptions and proscriptions under the guise of advice.

For example, among "tips for a safe holiday", the text counsels adults to be careful : 'do not sit on the balcony rail or wall...do not lean over balconies', watch out for doors without stickers and toughened glass, 'follow the pool rules', 'do not swim after dark or after drinking alcohol', 'do not dive into the pool when there are NO DIVING signs' (capitals in original), 'obey all flag systems and warning signs' (p. 3). But there are many other cases of behavioural guidance. For instance : 'we recommend that you do not drink the tap water' (p.25), 'we...do not recommend the hiring of mopeds in this country' (p.28). There are also instructions which are more explicit:

'On the last day of the holiday customers have to vacate their rooms by 1100 and 1200 noon. The coach pick up time for your return flight will be displayed on the...notice-board. You MUST ensure that ALL luggage and belongings ARE placed on the transfer coach, as a charge will be made for the return of any items left behind' (pp. 69, 70; capitals in original).

Throughout the discourse a dependency is established between the client and the company. In the case of loss or theft, for example, the holiday services executive must be informed in order that (s)he may accompany the victim to the police station (p.24). The executive must also be asked to identify the best local dishes available (p.14). The company's presence is even required to teach some spicey (sic) words in Spanish to their proteges who have got the listed expressions "word perfect" (p. 29). In fact, and as management points out in italicised script on page 5, since *'the guide sets out to suggest a whole range of ideas'*, clients are advised to *'carry this booklet around with you during your stay.'* Additional information, it is intimated, *'can be found on... notice-boards'.*

It is this last revelation that pinpoints the customary channel for top-down communication between management and clientele. Some notices are purely informational, for example those supplying the names of entertainers*, along with brief descriptions of their acts*. However, others of this genre, in addition to providing factual data, also indicate that they represent the desired option. For instance, details of excursions* latently suggest that door-to-door travel in a private coach with a guide and in the company of fellow vacationers is infinitely preferable to, and indeed far safer than, taking public transport by oneself, facing the hazards of strange places, foreign language difficulties, obscure timetables and possible exposure to crime.

As the level of social control increases, so too does the language of the notices evolve through various constraining moods, the culmination of which are the "hortatory" and "minatory" (Dann, 1999). For instance, a sign by the hotel swimming pool admonishes that sun beds cannot be reserved by simply placing towels upon them*, a message presumably delivered to forestall unspoken inmate conflict. Another sign by the restaurant indicates that guests must be dressed appropriately, that is to say, not attired in wet clothes or beachwear*. However, the most stringent of these written commands seem to be those enforcing a divide and rule strategy between all-inclusive and half-board patrons. The former can, for example, obtain free water and ice cream in the dining room*. All-inclusive guests, provided they are wearing their wristbands, are, by means of a sign proclaiming 'Sun Centre Customers Only', also served drinks at a separate point at the bar while others must pay, a distinction reflected in the comparative length of the two queues*. However, and even after waiting for a considerable time, the all-inclusives are limited by another notice to particular varieties of alcoholic beverages. Indeed, only one type of cocktail is on offer to them on any given day, a point not missed by a half-board couple in the following overheard conversation:

'Look at that blue drink that lady's got.'

'That's the blue lagoon.'

'Yes, but that's the only one they're allowed to have.'

'How do you mean?'

'Haven't you seen the notice? It states what drink they're to have each day.'

However, commands are not restricted to the written variety. Oral instructions from representatives to clients are evident throughout the holiday. Beginning with arrival at the airport when passengers are first assembled in groups by responding to company placards announcing specific resorts, and continuing on to the coach bearing them to their final destination, a monologue of advice, suggestions and orders is issued to a necessarily captive audience. The most important of these utterances, judging from its emphasis and repetition, is the need for guests to attend the "welcome meeting"* the following day. The stick for lack of compliance is an implied ostracism due to a mixture of culpable ignorance and rejection of national camaraderie. The carrot is the free drink on offer*, the initiation into what Nash (1970) has termed an "alcoholic assembly".

Other verbal orders can be issued throughout the course of the vacation, either on a one-to-one basis between client and representative, or in groups, as, for example, by couriers on outings or by entertainment leaders. An interesting case of the latter occurs during the nightly sessions when many guests gather in the lounge after their evening meal. Typically, these programmes begin in a low key mode, as illustrated by the following recorded excerpt from the winter stay:

Hello everybody. My name is Malcolm[3]. I'm your resident pianist here at La
Paloma Blanca. *I hope you're going to join in better than the lot we had last
week*

(a line probably borrowed from popular septuagenarian TV personality, Bruce Forsythe)

After playing selections from *Hello Dolly*, *Oh Danny Boy* and (significantly) *The Green,
Green Grass of Home*, which are received in silence, Malcolm continues, 'Come and join in
if you know it. If you don't, just hum.' Again nobody displays much interest and the pianist
exits stage left to subdued clapping. Later, and after he has unsuccessfully attempted to
realise audience participation, the tempo increases with the introduction of some dance
numbers by a colleague. Scant enthusiasm is shown towards a waltz to *Away in a Manger* or
a quick step to *Jingle Bells* and *Gloria in Excelsis Deo* in spite of the compere's 'Let's have
some dancing to make you feel real Christmassy.'

However, on another occasion, when line dancing is on offer, a far more explicit
constraining discourse of the leader evokes greater audience response:

Let's have you all...Come on you line dancers, don't sit and hide. We're going to do the
Cowboy Strut. We'll teach you the steps. Don't worry. Why are you hiding? Doing a
protest? Come on ladies, come on. If you've never tried line dancing before and never had a
go, now's your opportunity.

After eight couples have moved into the dance arena, leaving approximately 100 persons still
watching, the leader directs her attention to the converted:

*OK line dancers...a big "hee haw". Four toe taps : 1, 2, 3, 4. Looking for dog
muck, horse muck. You're getting into your third week you lot, you know. Come
on, this is supposed to be enjoyable.*

Later, she tries again to involve the sedentary uncommitted:

Our next dance is the Honky Tonk Stomp. *Let's have a few more of you up.
Everyone in the line give me a "hee haw". Everyone in the audience give me a
"saddle up cowboy". It's just like Piccadilly Circus - excellent !*

In this particular instance participation in the line dancing may be more appealing than, say,
joining in the songs since, in addition to the former being a familiar routine for retirees at
home, its command structure, being that more explicit, indicates the expectation of the
message giver for corresponding role behaviour in the addressee. However, and in a total
institutional context, willingness to take part may also be linked to the volume of the
imperative and the realisation that shouted orders may produce greater compliance than
softer spoken versions. In this connection, it is noteworthy that the more successful
entertainment leaders tend to make full use of the auditory potential of their microphones*. It
is additionally quite apparent that the more authoritarian and abusive* the command, the
greater the likelihood of its being observed. Thus, the reference to "you lot" and the use of
other verbal degradations establishes a pattern of super-ordination and subordination between
the entertainer and the audience, one which further reinforces the expectation of compliance.

That such perceived superiority on the part of the company representatives is second nature to them may be gauged from the description of their charges as "scum" or "pond life"[4].

Queuing

From line dancing and standing in line at the all-inclusive bar it is but one step to queuing on other occasions. The elderly in the UK are perhaps even more accustomed than their younger compatriots to waiting in serried ranks for every kind of so-called "service". Admittedly, some lines have been partially eliminated by online communication, for example shopping and banking, but these and other types of line avoidance are not particularly evident among retirees. In fact, and if anything, they are more salient among the aged. For years they have had the message instilled into them that queuing is synonymous with orderliness and that its opposite - the disorder of an unruly mob - is distinctly un-British. Indeed, so ingrained is the habit of standing in line that in 1994 the UK Parliament repealed the 1937 *London Passengers Act* (which had empowered bus and Underground inspectors to despatch queue jumpers to the courts), for the simple reason that in almost sixty years of the bylaw's existence there had not been a single conviction (Moore, 1994). Hotels catering to senior tourists can take advantage of this successful socialisation process. Furthermore, they can link such compliance to their command structure both implicitly and explicitly. *La Paloma Blanca* is no exception to this general observation.

At meal times, for instance, especially before dinner, dozens of guests can be seen waiting patiently for the portals of the dining room to open at 6.30pm. In surrounding Mallorca, where restaurants are entered by simply pushing the door, the idea of standing in line is quite anathema. At *La Paloma Blanca*, by contrast, the practice is as *de rigueur* as waiting for a Salvation Army soup kitchen to open. Woe betide anyone who jumps the queue. Such a deviant would be considered to have broken the bounds of decency, if not a national unwritten moral code.

Once inside the eatery, where buffet meals are standard fare, again it is necessary to queue. Now most of the food goes cold while persons wait to pick up their plates behind those who dither over their selections. In fact, and unless individuals pile all their courses on to the one and the same dish, they will have to stand in line at least three times during the length of a single meal.

Indeed, interns must queue for most activities, whether it is waiting for a tour bus to take them on an excursion, waiting for the coach to take them back to the airport, waiting for their tea and biscuits on afternoons*, waiting by the phone in order to call home* or simply standing in line to read a notice whose content implies that there are further queues ahead.

Inmate awareness

Goffman frequently alludes to a sharp division that exists between staff and inmates in total institutions. Among the subordinate latter it yields a sort of "we" feeling or shared identity that derives from belonging to an "in group" (Cooley, 1929) whose sentiments are reinforced by being contrasted with the "them" of an "out group". In the case of *La Paloma Blanca*, there are several indications that the elderly are aware of their common plight and that they see themselves as having opposite interests to their custodians - the tour group representatives.

These views are evident in the following scenario. Two elderly couples are sitting outside sharing their breakfast with a few stray cats. Another group enters in walking attire. The first set in sing-song voice chants, 'we know where you're going, we know where you're going.' The second responds, 'Morning you happy campers.' The greeting is clearly a reference to the heavily organised world of holiday camps, begun in the English resort of Skegness by Billy Butlin in 1936 (Ward and Hardy, 1986 in Urry, 1990, p.36) and surviving in the more up-market versions of Club Mediterranee and Center Parcs. The elderly in Mallorca would probably have experienced the first variant as children when redcoats would have addressed them in such a manner. Today, the pre WWII term "holiday camp" has been removed because of its subsequent association with a concentration camp (Urry, 1990, p.37). Yet the mentality evidently persists and the 'Morning happy campers' seems an appropriate response to the childlike mantra familiar enough to those who in days gone by used to thus taunt their classmates about to engage in illicit activity. One therefore has an exchange where the first group assumes the role of rule keeper and the second that of rule breaker or enforcer (the last two being one and the same in a total institution).

By way of immediate confirmation, a member of the sedentary group notices that a hiker has the name of the tour company emblazoned on his rucksack. She calls out, 'You don't have to wear it on your back. It's not in the regulations.' In another not entirely unrelated incident one person is overheard confessing to a friend, 'I'll have to suss out this telephone thing.' And the reply, in the form of a question - 'Did it say anything on the form?' A situation is therefore soon reached where so clearly accepted is the subordinate identity of the holidaymaker that the form, the rule book and the list of regulations can produce desired results without even the presence of the enforcing agent in the person of the company representative. They operate, as it were, *in loco parentis*.

Working the system

In *Asylums*, Goffman refers to a system of secondary adjustments that inmates create in a total institution as a means of alleviating their oppressive condition. In prisons, for example, inmates can exchange favours with wardens, just as they can stash away their hoards of such valued items as cigarettes and chocolates for subsequent consumption or trade. Camp guards can also be bribed to mete out more lenient treatment to those in custody. The list is endless.

In *La Paloma Blanca*, too, there is some evidence of working the system and, where it is missing, there is potential for so doing. Clearly there is both an opportunity and a need for acquiring additional quantities of soap. There are also *de facto* instances of long term repeat winter visitors tipping maids* and buying them presents* in order to have an otherwise absent room service in the form of fruit, tea and coffee*. Since the rooms themselves have no self-catering facilities, and given that all meals and snacks must be taken in public, the idea of having a staff member, however lowly, actually serving a diminished status elderly guest must be considered an absolute luxury by the latter.

On another occasion, however, and at the end of the "welcome meeting", a man tries to tip the representative and the offer is firmly refused*. The major difference here, apart from one of status between the rep and the maid, is that the second act is in the open, and no official, however virtuous or corrupt in private, can afford to make a public display of a *sub rosa* activity.

Finally, accommodation to the inmate situation can be better endured through joking behaviour and mock role reversal. One example, which must have many analogues, is a guest in the restaurant trying to mimic the behaviour of a waiter. He stands up, takes a serviette from him and, with a flourish, pretends to be opening a bottle of wine for an elderly diner similar to himself. Momentary confusion ensues but order is restored via the laughter of other holidaymakers who demonstrate solidarity with their colleague against the system.

Spatial disorientation

As regards the spatial disorientation experienced by the interns of this total institution, so accustomed are many to being transported in a cocoon-like mode to and from their vacational abode and to spending most of their intervening days within the compound, that the knowledge of their surrounds is extremely limited and often quite inaccurate. This lack of awareness about the host society is hardly surprising given the fact that there are constant reminders of national identity - the omnipresence of the Union Jack* both inside and outside the establishment, UK television programmes*, the ritual of afternoon tea*, music quizzes featuring such numbers as *Doing the Lambeth Walk* and *On Mother Kelly's Doorstep*, bingo*, whist drives*, and so on. One instance of a sense of Britishness intruding into the restricted perception of the local environment is provided by an old gentleman who refers to *The Willows* as '...a nice little English bar; the food's English and they speak English'*. He indicates that it is in Torrenova, whereas in reality it is in Palma Nova, in completely the opposite direction*. Some of his fellow guests do not even know the whereabouts of the hotel in which they are staying, let alone the location of other places of interest*.

Attitudes to time

Attitudes to time are also interesting. Indeed, it is worth asking with Ryan (1997), whether these senior tourists are having the time *of* their lives, time *for* their lives or are simply doing time. Certainly, the retirees in *La Paloma Blanca* like their activities to be *on* time - meal times, excursion times, arrival times, departure times - and they queue accordingly in anticipation of opening time. A few also appear quite upset when the schedule is disrupted and other time-tabled events become adversely affected. When half-day trips, like the one to the Caves of Drach, for instance, return two hours late, the consequence is a forfeited lunch customarily taken at 1pm precisely*. Similar concern is expressed by those missing their dinner on account of a delayed flight and by those thinking (incorrectly) that they will lose their evening meal when they join an organised trip to the nearby night club of Son Amar*. The latter are also worried about re-entering the hotel after midnight when they fear that the doors will be locked*.

Conclusion

This brief account of admission procedures, command structure, queuing, inmate awareness, working the system, spatial disorientation and attitudes to time only gives a partial idea of some of the forces which operate in a typical overseas hotel catering to the elderly. Certainly, there is much more that could have been included under additional categories, but it will need to be postponed to another occasion.

Nevertheless, the indicators of total institutional existence that have been examined reinforce the central message - that a Goffmanesque model provides a useful paradigm for understanding the attitudes and behaviour of those who seek escape from an alienated existence at home, only to have it replaced by a system of social control that builds on those very foundations. That such an interpretation is not unilateral or resort specific may be gauged from a recent paper by Cheong and Miller (2000), in which they argue most convincingly that tourists, far from being free *agents*, are controlled *targets* of the industry. Basing themselves on the ideas of Foucault, they maintain that the power of knowledge, discourse and the "inspecting gaze" displayed by those in charge of such institutions as schools, clinics, asylums, prisons and even gender relationships, is analogous to that exercised in tourism by the creators of images, brochures and guidebooks, travel agents, brokers such as hoteliers, employees, guides, vendors, government officials and market researchers, and even local people themselves. In their words:

> All tourists are captive to a wide variety of agents...The package tour is the extreme case of constrained movement, the self-guided tour the least. In the setting of the former, tourists can find themselves quite literally imprisoned on buses and boats, and in enclave resorts...Brokers as agents in a variety of guises constrain their movements, behaviours and even thoughts (p.381).

> (They)...employ strategies that entail education, instruction, persuasion, advice, interpretation, surveillance and coercion...They influence what tourists can and cannot do, where they can go and cannot go, and what they select and reject (p. 383). Foucauldian power is omnipresent in tourism (p. 386).

Clearly, Cheong and Miller (2000) are right in emphasising that such control is ubiquitous. By corollary, they are also correct in suggesting that it is graduated according to level of confinement and type of tourist, the zenith of which is surely the all-inclusive resort frequented by some of the most powerless members of society - the aged.

Why, then, do the elderly continue to patronise places such as *La Paloma Blanca*? Why are there instances of repeat visits to this and other Mallorcan hotels, up to as many as twenty-six times in one case*? Does the vacational environment provide familiarity, safety, camaraderie and the opportunity to mingle with others (Ryan, 1995)? Is not this a situation of total bliss rather than of total institution? The inmates seem happy enough - they laugh, they chat, they play, or simply sit and watch. Even so, and although they may give the outward impression of having a good time, their new condition perhaps represents only a temporary respite, a marginal improvement on the drudgery of their daily excluded existence under an ideology of *Cool Britannia*. Their smiles may simply indicate that they have been offered and grasped an alternative - a fantasy. They, consequently, appear to respond favourably to the words of the tour representative as they listen to her for the last time on the bus conveying them to the airport for their return home:

Have you all enjoyed your holiday then? If you're suffering from holiday blues, you know the best way to get over them? As soon as you get back, book another...holiday[5]. If you didn't see everything, why not come back to Mallorca - the island of Dreams?

Endnotes

1. The visits and discussions form part of the far more extensive field-notes of Hazel Andrews who has been researching tourists in Mallorca for her doctorate. Those excerpts relating to *La Paloma Blanca* are asterisked, reproduced with her permission and gratefully acknowledged. Although their interpretation is one's own, thanks are also due to Hazel Andrews for her comments on an earlier draft of this paper.

2. This reference is not supplied in order to preserve anonymity.

3. Also fictitious

4. An expression used by a representative in the course of casual conversation*.

5. The name of the company appears just before this noun and is omitted for reasons of confidentiality.

References

Cheong, S-M., and Miller, M. (2000), Power and tourism : A Foucauldian observation, *Annals of Tourism Research*, 27, pp. 371-390.

Cohen, E. (1972), Toward a sociology of international tourism, *Social Research*, 39, pp. 164-182.

Cooley, C. (1929), *Social Organisation*, Scribner's, New York.

Dann, G. (1996), *The Language of Tourism : A Sociolinguistic Perspective*, CAB International, Wallingford.

Dann, G. (1997), Tourist behaviour as controlled freedom, in Bushell, R. (Editor), *Tourism Research. Building a Better Industry*, Bureau of Tourism Research, Canberra, pp. 244-254.

Dann, G. (1999), Noticing notices : Tourism to order, paper presented to the International Academy for the Study of Tourism, Hotel Esplanade, Zagreb, 28 June to 2 July.

Davies, S. (2000), *Counterblast : The Death of Privacy*, (documentary), BBC 2 Television, 1930-2000, 7 February.

Goffman, E. (1973), *Asylums. Essays on the Social Situation of Mental Patients and Other Inmates*, Pelican, London.

Moore, T. (1994), End of the line for the queue?, *Weekend Telegraph*, 28 September - 4 October.

Nash, D. (1970), *A Community in Limbo. An Anthropological Study of an American Community Abroad*, Indiana University Press, Bloomington.

Ryan, C. (1995), Learning about tourists from conversations : the over 55's in Majorca, *Tourism Management*, 16, (3), pp. 207-216.

Ryan, C. (1997), 'The time of our lives' or time for our lives : An examination of time in holidaying, in Ryan, C. (Editor), *The Tourist Experience. A New Introduction*, Casell, London, pp. 194-205.

Urry, J. (1990), *The Tourist Gaze. Leisure and travel in Contemporary Societies*, Sage, London.

Ward, M. and Hardy, D. (1986), *Goodnight Campers! The History of the British Holiday Camp*, Mansell, London.

Weightman, B. (1987), Third World tour landscapes, *Annals of Tourism Research*, 14, pp. 227-239.

The social and economic impacts of gambling in South Africa

Cyril Francis and Berendien Lubbe

University of Pretoria, Pretoria

Abstract

With the institution of the New Gambling Legislation in South Africa, and the opening of 41 new casinos, the gambling environment is becoming very competitive. Established casinos, in the previously "zoned" homelands, are losing their stronghold on gambling as a result of easier entrance to the market and even Sun International, themselves so previously favoured, have to apply for the right to offer gambling facilities.

Gambling can have many different types of impacts on society: political impacts, economical impacts and sociological impacts. The biggest impact that gambling has on society, however, is in the form of social and economic impacts. Gambling has become a leisure activity in which people participate voluntarily by personal choice. It has become a rapidly developing acceptable form of leisure-time entertainment.

It is important to identify those areas on which the social impacts of gambling will be most felt. There are moral reasons for opposing gambling. Many believe that one, gambling negatively affects mans relationship with God. Two, gambling makes man more dependant on chance than on working for a living. Three, the relationship between labour and reward becomes completely distorted. Four, gambling has a negative effect on the gambler's family. And five, gambling impacts negatively on society in general in that it discourages people to work and also facilitates the increase in crime and other "social" evils, such as addiction, waste, prejudice and temptation.

It is important, however, to remember that it is human nature to take risk and to rely on chance once in a while. Prohibition of gambling is therefore unlikely to be successful and it is important to identify the real social dangers of gambling so that they may be controlled and curbed to the greatest extent possible.

The economic impact of gambling on a country is as important as its social impacts, and shows more potential for having positive effects than social impacts do. Economic impacts include:

- The effect of gambling on personal savings. Gambling detrimentally affects the willingness of people to save money. It is a leisure time activity that provides entertainment and in return expects the payment of money. Of course, it is not a forgone conclusion that gamblers would save the money if they did not gamble with it. They could just as easily spend the money on something else.

- Gambling generates employment and income. As with any business, gambling organisations wish to secure profits. In order to do this people are employed to perform services and other duties. Income is circulated throughout the community. The employment and income effects of gambling can be both direct or indirect.

- Gambling impacts on economic growth. The legalisation of gambling formalises an industry which employs people, pays salaries, contributes to the community, pays taxes, etc. It therefore also contributes to the economic well-being and growth of a country.

- Gambling can also draw tourists and benefit the tourism industry as well as offer a source of tax and revenue to the government. Consumer spending and behaviour also changes if gambling is legalised, they now have something new and different to spend their money on.

Finally, this paper would also like to draw a profile of the typical South African gambler.

Introduction

Overview

South Africa is on the threshold of an exciting new gaming dispensation that will provide significant benefits for the country and its people. This is as a result of the introduction of the new National Gambling Act no. 33 of 1996. *Act No. 33 of 1996,* became part of the South African legislation in Cape Town on the 3 July 1996. The main aim was to "make provision for the regulation and co-ordination of certain matters relating to casinos, gambling and wagering; for the purpose of making provision for the promotion of uniform norms and standards applying generally throughout the Republic; making provision for the establishment of the National Gambling Board; and making provision for matters connected therewith" (National Gambling Act, 1996: 2). The new legislation and gaming policy, must however ensure the transparent allocation of all new casino licences.

The "apartheid" regime of the past and all its gaming legislation, resulted in the establishment of a number of casinos in the former Transkei, Bophutaswana, Venda and Ciskei (TBVC states). This in turn created a monopoly, whereby Sun International (SA) opened 17 casinos in these states, of which only 4 were considered to be tourist resorts (Partnership 1994: 1). The rest principally catered for casual gambling, with limited facilities. During the period 1979 to 1992, Sun International (SA) turned over millions, with Sun City and the Wild Coast Sun as the two key resorts. Gambling contributed 80% of the total profits while accommodation, food and beverage and others accounted for the remaining 20%. During the latter years, however, the situation changed tremendously, especially at Sun City. Currently, at Sun City, accommodation contributes 80% of the profits and food and beverage, gambling and others contribute 20%.

With the introduction of the new gambling legislation, the gaming environment in South Africa is becoming very competitive. Sun International (SA) as a licence holder of 17 casinos was granted a temporary concession to operate all its casinos until the end of May 1999. In 1997, due to the pressure of other temporary casinos in the various provinces, Sun International (SA) decided to close down 4 casinos in the North-West Province and 4 in the Eastern Cape. This involved the selling of the operation as well as the casino licences, giving the new owners the opportunity to operate casinos beyond the May 1999 deadline that had been imposed on Sun International (SA) by the national gambling legislation. (Business Day: 1997). This is an indication of how competitive the market has currently become.

The new legislation prescribed that a maximum of 41 casino licenses be issued in South Africa within the next five years, and to be distributed amongst the 9 provinces according to the following table.

Table 1   Casino licences allocated per province

Province	Number of Licenses
Gauteng	6
Western Cape	5
Kwa-Zulu Natal	5
Eastern Cape	5
North West	5
Free State	4
Mpumalanga	4
Northern Province	3
Northern Cape	3

Source: National Gambling Act 1996: 14

Objectives of the gambling licence process

Black empowerment

It is clear that applicants who are representative of a multi-cultural South Africa, will have a better chance for a successful bid. The empowerment of blacks will have to be reflected in the composition of management and will also be emphasised in employee selection and training. Sun International (SA) realised the importance of this objective and has forged strong alliances with national and provincial partners, recognising the principles of black economic empowerment and the participation of historically disadvantaged people and communities.

Contribution to the Reconstruction and Development Program (RDP)

The Reconstruction and Development program is a top priority of the government especially in the field of education and human resource development. Within the current structure, very few "people of colour" fill supervisory and management positions within the South African gaming industry. Many foreigners are appointed in top positions due to their qualifications and expertise. A major gap is to be filled in South Africa.

Social upliftment

Communities in close proximity of gambling operations must benefit from the proceeds and profits of such organisations, invested in appropriate housing, education and other facilities.

City Sun in the North West province for example, part of Sun International (SA), has for many years operated as an oasis in the desert. It is surrounded by poverty, inadequate housing, lack of transport and facilities, and non-existing schooling opportunities. Yet, most of the employees stem from these areas and have to return to these surroundings after a days work in a glitzy and glamorous workplace.

Realisation of tourism potential

It has been proven globally, that gambling has a very small impact on tourism. It is an activity that hardly attracts foreign visitors. The only foreigners attracted to South African casinos are the real "junkets" from the east, who are prepared to spend in excess of R 150 000 per trip. Especially at the resort casinos, such as Sun City and the Wild Coast casino (Admiral Leisure World LTD. : 1997).

Economic development of the region

Economic development, social upliftment and the RDP initiatives should go hand in hand. Licenses will be granted in areas where development and infrastructure could cause considerable economic growth. Development should be monitored to ensure that leakages are limited and real benefits are transferred to the people of the region.

The criteria for the granting of new licences

The Lotteries and Gambling Board, under the auspices of Prof. Nic Wiehahn, made key recommendations to the government for the granting of casino licences:

Two types of licences must be issued:

- Type A: World class resort and convention centre with unlimited gaming facilities and a invest cost of at least R 250 million. Existing casinos that falls into this category are the Wild Coast Sun, Sun City and the Carousel.

- Type B: Casino / entertainment facility with limited gaming and a invest cost of at least R 100 million. Current examples include places like Morula Sun, Tlhabane Sun and Mdantsane Sun.

- Companies or consortiums applying must be financially sound and have an impeccable track record;

- A meaningful black empowerment at all levels and therefore applicants must state the following:

  - the percentage of black equity;

  - the number and identity of black participants; and

  - their programme must ensure broad black participation, training and skills provisioning, management positions and Board participation.

- Licences should afford reasonable exclusivity for 10 years, to vindicate serious investment;

- Non-refundable application fees will attract only serious bidders. Application fees are calculated as a percentage of the investment cost , with a minimum of R 1,5 million;

- Temporary licenses are being granted during construction, which will ensure immediate state and provincial revenues;

- A 10% gaming tax and 5% RDP tax should levied, with a meaningful portion accruing to the provinces (The Partnership, 1994 : 3).

Economic impacts of gambling

In the past 30 years, gaming has evolved internationally from an illegal activity to a major growth industry. In various jurisdictions throughout the world, a wide variety of gaming industries have been created for the purpose of stimulating tourism, bolstering regional and local economies, creating jobs and employment opportunities and generating revenue taxes for the government.

Despite all these benefits, most government leaders throughout the world remain sceptical about the overall economic and social benefits of gambling on society in general.

In South Africa, it has been agreed by the government that the gaming industry ought to be organised and regulated in such as way as to promote the interest of the country as a whole, and to secure the goals of the tourism gear policy.

Size of the industry

It is estimated that the gaming industry contributed approximately R 10,56 billion to the country's economy. Table 2 outlines the various components that make up the figure.

Table 2   Gaming market of South Africa

Breakdown of Market	Income (in R Billions)
Casinos	4
Limited stakes	2,8
Horse racing	1
Fah-fee	1,2
Lotteries	1,5
Total	10,56

Source: Admiral Leisure World LTD. : 1997

Of the R 4 billion, it is estimated that 47% will be spent in Gauteng, 16% in the Western Cape, 13% in Kwa-Zulu Natal, 6 in the Eastern Cape, 5% in the Free State, 5% in Mpumalanga, 5% in the North West, 3% in the Northern Province and 1% in the Northern Cape (Finansies en Tegniek : 1996).

Macro economic impacts

Gambling lends itself towards a substantial source of income for governments all over the world. With the legalisation of gambling in South Africa, the government already has its sights on about R 4,5 billion in taxes, calculated at 14% (Bloom and Theron, 1995 : 16). However, Joubert (Bloom and Theron, 1995 : 16) argues that by the end of this year, the figure could escalate to about R 9 billion. This represents a 100% increase in 5 years, with an average rise of about 20% per annum.

Based on the aforementioned figures, it is clear that the Gauteng province will receive the largest portion of the income, due to its 47% cut of the total gambling contribution in the country. In Gauteng, for the period January to December 1999, the gross gaming revenue amounted to R 2,3 billion and the authority collected R 176 800 000 in taxes (Gauteng Gambling Board : 1999). This causes a tremendous problem for the gambling authorities, as they have to ensure the even distribution of this income throughout the nine provinces. Therefore an in-depth investigation is required to determine the location and characteristics of existing casinos in relation to new casinos coming up.

Micro economic impacts

The investigation of the Wiehahn Commission pertaining to gambling in South Africa, recommended the granting of 41 casino licenses throughout the nine provinces. This, however, does not include the existing 17 Sun International (SA) casinos throughout the country. The commission therefore ruled that Sun International should give up 10 of its existing licences.

According to the new legislation, all casino complexes should comprise of a number of facilities to cater for the needs and desires of a vast array of people. Taking this into consideration, provinces are in line to generate vast amounts of revenue from direct taxes, municipal rates and taxes and also value added taxes.

Feasibility studies to ascertain the sustainability of 41 casinos in South Africa is another point of concern. With the current bidding process, it has become clear that vast financial investments are being made to develop the various casinos in the country. With the bidding process for the 6 Gauteng licences, 23 applications were submitted with the lowest financial investment for development amounting to R 650 000 000 (Admiral Leisure World LTD. : 1997). These are large financial investments and the failure of such ventures will result in great losses for the developers, management companies, employees and communities.

Economic development opportunities for communities

The new gambling legislation aims to develop most of the casinos in close proximity to the majority of people in the country. According to Bloom and Theron (1995), casino developments to the year 2000 will amount to investments in excess of R 10 billion. This investment potential promises great benefits to local communities. However, the licensing board should exercise strict control in this regard to ensure that casino companies fulfil their social responsibility. This should be in the form of educational programs, the stimulation of local businesses and the development of additional tourism attractions and facilities. To curb the outflow of developmental funds, licensing authorities should compel casino licence holders to commit to reinvestment (Bloom and Theron, 1995 : 52).

As the much needed developments take place within communities, there are also fears that existing retail businesses may suffer as local communities redistribute some of their spending away from other household goods in favour of gambling. The decline in business activities can also be ascribed to the decline in turnover due to high interest rates, decline in household income and a decline in the business cycle of the country (Mpumalana Gaming Board : 1999).

A successfully managed casino development should make a meaningful contribution to the social and economic upliftment of the local communities, discourage rural-urban migration and work towards the creation of new resources for social upliftment and family development.

Broader economic impacts of gambling

The following economic impacts are evident:

- Gambling negatively impacts on personal savings. Gambling detrimentally affects the willingness op people to save money, which is an important factor for stabilising a country's economy. It is a leisure time activity that provides entertainment as well as monetary returns in some cases. From figure 11 it is clearly evident that 25% of all gamblers never win and 59% seldomly wins. Also indicating that 47% of these gamblers never win more than R 500 as outlined in figure 12. Thus, indicating that gamblers are always at risk of losing all their money and the possibility of accumulating huge debts are very real. The whole process flows from the concept that casinos can last much longer than the gambler, and before you know it, the gambler has lost all his/her money. Of course, it is not a foregone conclusion that gamblers would save their money if they did not gamble it. The money could just as easily be spent on household goods.

- A decline in disposable income does not equal a decline in gambling activities. Gambling is one of the few industries that do not feel the pinch of a declining disposable income in such a tremendous way. People would rather gamble with their last R 100,00 in the hope of doubling it, rather than to securely invest it. This statement is very true, considering the results in figure 6 stating that 28,2% of all gamblers earn a monthly disposable income of R 0 - R 1000,00. 64,6% of all gamblers earn between R 0 - R 5000,00. Outlining that the biggest contributor to this figure is represented by the lower income groupings.

- The new legislation is also geared to increase potential tourism income. The economic impact from new licences granted will also reflect income generated from support facilities such as accommodation, food and beverage outlets and conference facilities. The casino requirements for new licences include:

  - at least a 4 star hotel;

  - conference and entertainment facilities;

  - sporting facilities.

It is estimated that 1000 extra beds would be needed in Gauteng to accommodate the potential casino traffic. As very few international tourists are attracted by local gambling, it is more the local tourism market that would frequent these casinos.

- The casino industry is a very labour intensive industry and requires many employees, usually from areas within the parameters of the development. The communities will benefit from the direct as well as indirect employment. According to the Wiehahn Commission report, the average income per year for casino employees is estimated at R 35 000,00 including benefits. Which in real terms is slightly higher than the average wage in the hospitality industry (Wiehahn Report : 1995).

- The development of casinos also improves the local infrastructure in terms of buildings, roads, parking and facilities.

- The negative aspects of casino development causes land speculation, causing property values to increase. The increase is due to the demand for property, and causes the local community to get displaced which is a negative effect. Further more, many high paying management positions are filled by people from outside the local community, leaving the local people to fill all the lower paying jobs with minimum wage restrictions. This does not bring much money into the local community.

The social impacts of gambling

Gambling in South Africa has flourished against all odds since the first legislation on gaming was enacted 200 years ago. Gambling in the early days was not for recreation. Many newly created millionaires on the diamond and gold fields played deadly earnest games and saw their fortunes wiped out after prolonged card games.

Although gambling legislation dates back to 1789, to the times of the Dutch East India Company, hard gambling originated on the mines. The discovery of diamonds attracted many inveterate gamblers to South Africa. The early diggers in Kimberley gambled with cards, billiards, dominoes and dice, with stakes of thousands of pounds at a time. Where Kimberley left off, Johannesburg took over. Early Johannesburg hotels catered firstly for the gamblers needs, before seeing to the comfort of the guests.

In the reign of Paul Kruger, most forms of gambling were outlawed, but the "rising tide of the gambling spirit" could not be curbed. Dog racing was banned in 1949 followed by the banning of the Rhodesian Sweepstakes some years later. However, with the new dispensation South Africans will be able to do openly what they often did furtively.

In South Africa, it has been agreed by Cabinet that the gaming industry ought to be organised and regulated in such a way as to promote the interests of the country as a whole, and in particular to secure the RDP (Reconstruction and Development Program) goals of:

- Reducing poverty;

- Generating economic growth;

- Advantaging the least advantaged;

- Encouraging appropriate new investment.

"The liberalisation in the world and the rapid growth of sophisticated gaming types and facilities have provided increasing accessibility to (and availability of) an unprecedented number of gambling opportunities. Gambling has become a great national pastime and entertainment" (Government Report: 1996). As legalised gambling has increased rapidly since 1996 so has the awareness of its social implications. Certain of the provinces have reacted by instituting research projects into aspects such as compulsive or pathological gambling in order to determine the correct measures to be taken to curb or minimise problem gambling.

The social implications of gambling are much more difficult to measure than the economic implications since many of the possible impacts of gambling, such as on the work ethic of a society, are difficult to measure. Furthermore, the availability of statistics to substantiate claims of an increase in crime as a result of gambling are practically non-existent. This makes the identification of the social impacts of gambling based on valid national research very difficult.

The social impacts of gambling can be viewed from a positive and a negative perspective. The positive impacts of gambling are mainly socio-economic and are increased employment, expansion of the tourism industry, promotion of small business, creation of facilities and improvement of infrastructure. These impacts have been discussed under the section on economic impacts. In the South African context a major benefit of the legalisation of gambling has been the equity participation by previously disadvantaged people. Black empowerment is strongly illustrated in the development of the Soweto Casino development project. This is the only project which is both wholly owned and fully directed towards the previously disadvantaged communities. All shareholding, with the exception of that of the financier, is in the hands of black South Africans. Further to this 12,5% of the shareholding has been reserved for a trust fund for the upliftment of the local community, particularly disadvantaged children of the area of the proposed development.

Despite the positive impacts of gambling, government remains concerned about the effects of gambling on society at large. Researchers have concluded that "gambling is becoming more and more acceptable to the broader society. Attitudes based on religious grounds are more difficult to change while those which are based on purely social grounds (that is, the problem of addiction to gambling, the safety and security of the gambler's family, and, the proliferation of crime and other social evils) are more easily changed provided, first, strict control and efficient regulation of gambling can be imposed, and second, on-going research with a view to remedial steps can be introduced (Government report 1996:55).

The negative impacts of gambling can be broadly identified as follows:

- Disintegration of the family structure;

- Moral decay;

- An increase in crime;

- Compulsive behaviour;

- Nonconformism;

- Underage gambling and alcohol consumption;

- Gambling by low-income individuals;

Disintegration of the family structure

The family structure undergoes tremendous pressure if financial difficulties occur, and more so if these financial difficulties have been brought about by people spending their household resources on gambling. In a study conducted by the Mpumulanga Gambling Board it was found that almost 27% of households reported that money for household necessities was diverted to gambling. Figure 1 provides an indication of the sources of displacement of household expenditure in favour of casino gambling. It was found that R1 out of every R3 gambled at the casinos was the result of dissaving. A fairly substantial substitution took place within the entertainment industry itself (19,8% of patrons reported transference from other entertainment as a source of their gambling money).

Figure 1   Sources of displacement of household expenditure in favour of casino gambling

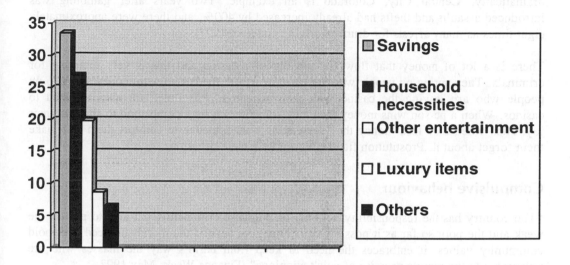

Source: Mpumalanga Gaming Board: 1999

Moral decay

It can be argued that there are moral reasons for opposing gambling because:

- Gambling negatively affects mans relationship with God (certain religions prohibit gambling);

- Gambling makes man more dependant on chance than on working for a living, it discourages people to work;

- The relationship between labour and reward becomes distorted;

- Gambling has a negative effect on the gambler's family. In the University of Pretoria's study it was found that approximately 46% of respondents were unmarried and 47% married (refer to figure);

- Gambling may lead to prostitution, unfaithfulness, alcoholism and avariciousness;

- Gambling facilitates the increase in crime and other social ills such as addiction, waste, prejudice and temptation.

An increase in crime

South Africa has a tremendously high crime rate. An increase in the number of casinos geographically dispersed throughout the country would probably introduce a Mafia element (the more casinos, the greater the scope of Mafia tactics). Crime rates will also increase dramatically. Central City, Colorado is an example. Two years after gambling was introduced assaults and thefts had already increased by 400%, and there were approximately eight times as many arrests for drunken driving (Internet:1997).

There is a lot of money that flows in and out of a casino and this is very tempting for criminals. They spring on people who are on their way to the casino with money and also on people who are leaving the casino with their winnings. Prostitutes are also attracted to casinos. When a person wins money then they sometimes want a companion to share in their joy. Also when they lose money they sometimes want someone to comfort them and make them forget about it. Prostitution fits the bill on both these occasions.

Compulsive behaviour

"The country has the responsibility not only to minimise criminality, but also to protect the weak and the poor so far as it possibly can. This goes beyond the moralistic need to uphold community values; it embraces the need to keep from harm's way the masses who are vulnerable to the remote promise of quick winnings" (Finance Week: May 1992).

It is widely recognised that gambling can be addictive in nature and brings about pathological gamblers, namely problem gamblers, compulsive gamblers and probable compulsive gamblers. Problem gamblers are people who get themselves into serious trouble due to gambling. Compulsive gamblers are people who have been clinically diagnosed as having a compulsion to gamble. Probable compulsive gamblers are those people who have not been clinically diagnosed, but have the behaviour and potential to become compulsive gamblers. These people not only constitute a moral dilemma for the community, but also for the casino itself. They are also people who commit crimes such as fraud, forgery or embezzlement to support their gambling activities.

Compulsive gamblers cannot help themselves from spending their life's earnings in the quest and belief that their luck will turn and they could become millionaires. Casino owners use the term " gambler's ruin", referring to the fact that many gamblers do actually beat the machines but cannot outlast them.

The government realises that communities should be protected against the dangers of gambling and stipulates in the National Gambling Authority (NGA), as part of their general policy underlying gambling that " society and the economy shall be protected against over-stimulation and the latent demand for gambling". Many individual casinos also contribute towards rehabilitation programmes for habitual gamblers or only allow such gamblers to challenge the machines for limited spending.

Nonconformism

Many, especially white South Africans, flocked to "Sin City" (Sun City) in the "apartheid" years for some "forbidden fun and pleasure". It was driven by feelings of rebelliousness and daringness. The artificial environment caused by the apartheid system together with the origin of the South African gambling system caused such behaviour.

Two models for gambling exist: the European model and the American model. European gambling is managed as a form of entertainment, Monte Carlo being a good example. Visitors expect entertainment value for their money's worth. In America, gambling initially grew through Mafia involvement and Las Vegas became an "artificial" resort where many social ills became evident. South African gambling tends towards the American model and has also spawned all the inherent "social ills" that accompany gambling. Only 3 of the 17 Sun International (SA) casinos are classified as resort casinos (Partnership : 1994).

Underage gambling and alcohol consumption

The legal age for gambling and alcohol consumption in South Africa is 18 years. Many teenagers enter casinos illegally and are able to gamble and purchase alcoholic drinks. The issue of underage gambling is of concern to provincial governments since teenagers become very creative in obtaining the money required for gambling which leads to crime.

Gambling by low-income individuals

One of the biggest concerns is the gambling practised by low-income individuals. In a study undertaken by the University of Pretoria's Department of Tourism Management it was found that approximately 28% of all respondents have a disposable income of less than R1000 per month. These individuals tend to gamble all their money away and are then not able to support their families. This can cause problems as severe as homelessness. (Refer to figure 9).

Profile of the typical South African gambler

According to the questionnaires completed at various casinos, it is possible to profile the typical South African gambler.

Demographically, the following results were obtained: Men in the age range 18 to 30 would be the group most likely to gamble. Men represented 64,8% as opposed to 35,2% of women. Their marital status is either single or married, but very few have children. In most instances they originate from the Gauteng area, mainly Pretoria followed by Midrand and Johannesburg. There are slightly more English speaking gamblers than Afrikaans who challenge the slot machines. Of the native languages spoken, Sotho is most commonly used.

Their occupations vary from the business sector, to education, to the unemployed. The business sector makes up 49,4% , referring to figure 13. 28,2% of all the respondents receive a monthly disposal income of between R 0 - R 1000,00. Interesting to note is that those who have R 5001 - R 7000 to their disposal, represented only 8,2% of the respondents

(Figure 6). It confirms the theory, highlighted in the economic impacts of gambling, that the less you have to spend the more likely you are to gamble instead of investing it.

Assessing their gambling activities, it seems as if the frequency of visits to a casino varies tremendously. The highest percentage 21,6% was noted in the "once a year" category, but 15,9% of them frequented the casino "at least once a week" (Figure 7). This makes it difficult to conclude frequency. Almost all respondents arrive by private car, as this gives them flexibility, and is also important for Sun City to note, as adequate parking should be available.

Per visit approximately R 50 - R300 is spent (40,2%). Quite a high percentage 18,4% spends less than R 50 and only 11,5% spends more than a R 1000,00. Only 12,5% of this expenditure is by credit card as most gambling seems to be cash trading. Very few people actually win on a regular basis, but keep returning to play the odds. Most of the visitors will have a meal (fast foods) and a few drinks and then proceed to the slot machines. Roulette seems to be the preferred table game. From responses it seems evident that new casinos in Gauteng will definitely adversely influence the traffic flow to the entertainment centre at Sun City as most of their visitors are captured in Gauteng. Although the Wild Coast Sun was the second choice of casino for many, it is clearly aimed at a different market.

Conclusion

Taking into consideration the literature study and the results from the research done, it is quite difficult to exactly profile the typical South African gambler. However, there is a strong correlation between some of the results and the social and economic impacts as outlined in the study.

From the study it is clear that many of the respondents see gambling as a "game of chance". Thus, clearly indicating that gamblers are putting themselves at risk, with the possibility of losing considerable amounts of money. It should also be noted that gambling revenues increase during periods of economic downswing.

Gambling has a negative impact on personal savings. This is substantiated by the result obtained in the study where it was shown that most of the respondents have a disposable income of between R0 and R1000. In the study conducted by the Mpumulanga Gambling Board it was concluded that there is a displacement of household expenditure in favour of gaming. R1 out of every R3 was a result of dissaving. A fairly substantial substitution took place within the entertainment industry itself where 19,8% of patrons reported transference from other entertainment as a source of their gambling money. No less than 26,9% of households reported that money for household necessities were diverted to gambling (see figure 1). This indicates the pressure that is placed on the stability within the household and family structure. This can also be an indication of problem gambling.

While one of the objectives of the new gambling legislation is to increase tourism potential in South Africa, it is evident from the results of the study that most patrons are South Africans. Only 14,2% are shown to be from foreign countries. The current casino structure shows only three casinos that can be classified as casino resorts in South Africa. Therefore it can be concluded that foreigners do not primarily visit the country for gambling purposes. It appears that most foreign visitors are the gambling "junkets" from the Asian countries.

There is very little research on the social and economic impacts in South Africa, particularly on a national level. This study can be regarded as an initial research foundation that could lead to further research on aspects such as the impact of gambling on crime, compulsive gambling and alcohol abuse.

Appendix

Figure 1   Age

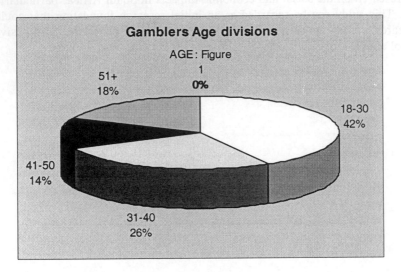

Figure 2   Gender

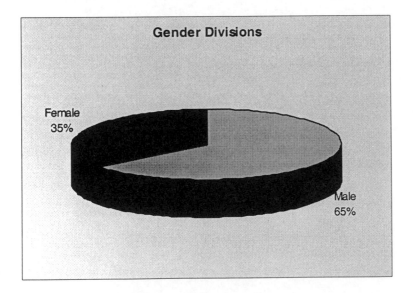

Figure 3   Marital Status

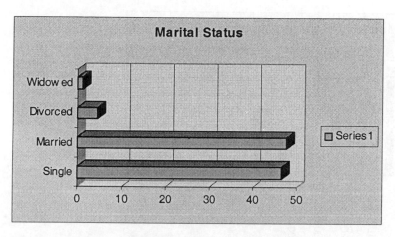

Figure 4   Number of Dependents

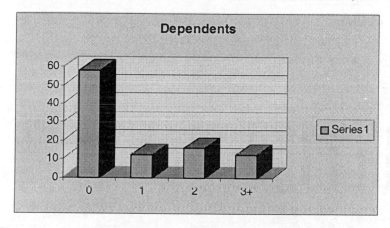

Figure 5   Language Preferences

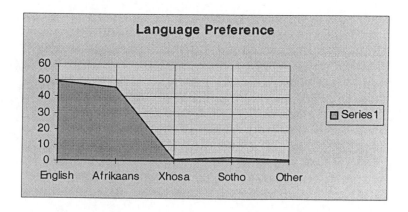

Figure 6   Monthly Disposable Income

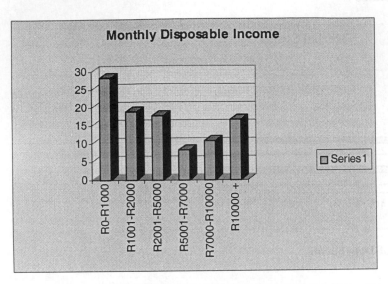

Figure 7   Frequency of Visits

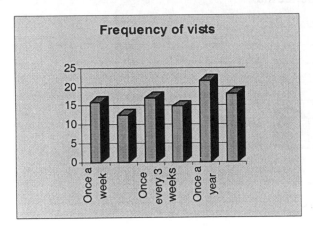

Figure 8   Transport

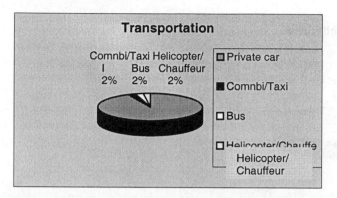

Figure 9   Money Spent Per Visit

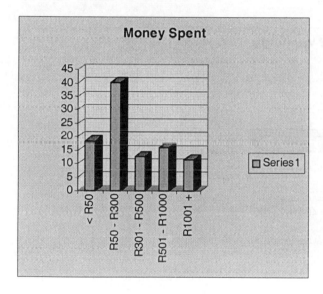

Figure 10   Other Activities

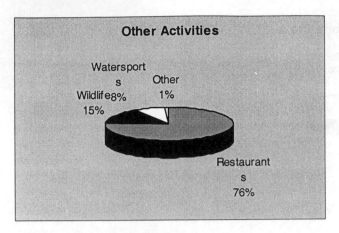

Figure 11   Frequency of Winning

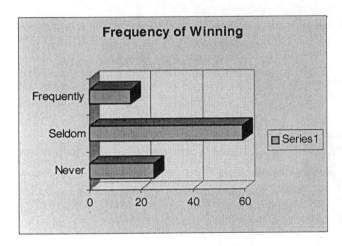

Figure 12   Largest amount ever won

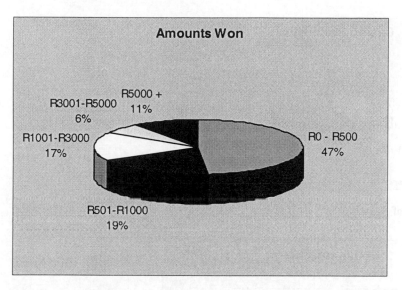

Figure 13   Occupations

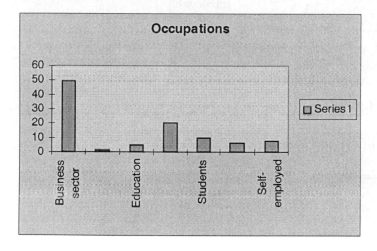

Figure 14   Casino Preferences

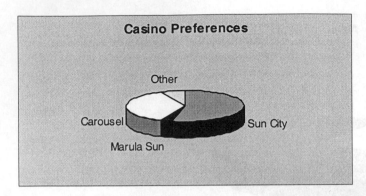

Figure 15   Length of Stay

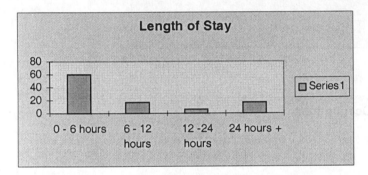

Figure 16   Use of Credit Cards

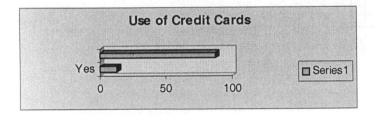

References

Admiral Leisure World Ltd. (1997), *Soweto Casino Bid.* 13 June.

Anonymous. (1996), *Dobbelbedryf dalk nie so rooskleurig nie.* Finansies and Tegniek. Page 24. 31 May.

Anonymous. (1992), *Last Gamble.* Finance Week. Page 25. 21 – 27 May.

Bloom, J. Z. and Theron, E. (1996), *Die ekonomiese voordele versus die sosiale koste van dobbelary.* Tydskrif van studies van ekonomie en ekonometrie. Pages 47 – 71. University of Pretoria: Pretoria.

Anonymous. (1997), *Casino cutbacks at Sun International.* 1 February.

Gauteng Gaming Board. (1999), *Statistics on gaming revenues.* JHB.

Internet. (1997), Gambling in South Africa.

Lotteries and Gambling Board. (1996), *Main report on Gambling in the Republic of South Africa.* Government Printers: Pretoria.

Mpumalanga Gaming Board. (1999), *Economic impact study.* Government Printers: White River. Mpumalanga.

Parliament. (1996), *The National Gambling Act. No; 33 of 1996.* Government Gazette. Cape Town.

The Partnership. (1994), *The Casino Industry in South Africa : Key considerations with regard to the new gaming policy and casino licence allocation.* Sandton. JHB.

Wiehahn Commission. (1995), *Wiehahn Report on gambling in South Africa.* Cape Town.

The impact of airlines on student's travel preferences

Frederick A Frost and Tekle Shanka

Curtin University of Technology, Australia

Abstract

A significant degree of research has been conducted in forms of international travel. However, a growing segment has not received the attention it deserves - the student market. Student travellers account for a significant portion of the market and this research explores aspects of the decision making process used in identifying potential destinations. A total of 1230 students attending a university in Perth, Western Australia were surveyed in an attempt to determine who made or influenced the decision process. The students were from Australia, Singapore, Malaysia, Hong Kong, Indonesia with smaller numbers from Europe, Africa and America.

The research concluded that family and friends were the dominant influences with travel agents and airlines playing an almost insignificant role. There is clearly a significant opportunity for the two groups to become more involved in what is a high involvement decision process.

Introduction

Students represent a potentially viable segment of international travel. The changing demographics of international travel would indicate that students represent a growing proportion of international travellers. It has been pointed out that measurement of this segment is difficult (Bywater, 1993). The segment's importance is often masked by other consideration such as students travelling in groups or with family (McGehee et. Al., 1996). There is also a perception of students representing the less profitable market associated with working holiday, backpacking, youth hostels and in general low budget travel. The position is further confused by organisations representing youth hostels opening up their membership to families which might suggest a decline in one of their traditional markets - students. However, recent research shows that far from being insignificant, student travel was estimated to constitute 20 percent of all international travellers. The Federation of International Youth Travel Organisations (FIYTO) has also estimated that its members annually account for four million airline tickets, five million train tickets, ten million travellers and 30 million overnight stays (Bywater, 1993).

The growth in the study of international tourism demand parallels the growth in demand itself with 80 studies over the past three decades (Crouch, 1994). Student travel, however has not captured any significant attention over the period.

Nevertheless, recent studies suggest that student travel to international destinations is a significant market segment. Chadee and Cutler (1996), Sung and Hsu (1996), Hsu and Sung (1997), and Frost and Shanka (1998) reiterate that despite the substantial size of the student segment of the international travel industry, little is known about the characteristics of this portion of the industry.

Waitt (1996) in his study of Korean students to Australia noted that the 20-29 year-old age cohort is that growing most rapidly and suggested that the most important inhibiting factor, too little information, be addressed. Cho (1996) writes that the potential of the Korean youth market has shown that younger Koreans such as honeymooners, young office women and students travelling as backpackers with the secondary aim of improving their English are rapidly emerging as the growth area of the tourism market. Frost and Shanka (1998), Shanka and Musca (1998) and Musca and Shanka (1998) reiterate that the uniqueness of the international student market has significant marketing implications for travel and tourism marketers.

Students travel to other countries either during their holiday breaks or as a revitalisation after a few years of study towards their degrees and spend a few nights at the destination. Regardless of when they take their holidays, they contribute to growth in tourism. They tend to stay a few nights in their destination, spend a fair amount of money in the destination and would further recommend the destination to their friends. Sung and Hsu (1996) in their study of international students' travel in the U.S. indicated that about 76 percent of those responded were likely to stay up to six nights in their destinations.

The concept of image has received increased attention by tourism researchers, industry practitioners and destination marketers. Image differentiates tourist destinations from each other and is an integral and influential part of the traveller's decision process. Several definitions of image suggest that it has both cognitive and affective components: Image is the sum of beliefs, ideas and impressions that people have of a place or destination (Kotler, Haider and Rein, 1993; Mok and Armstrong, 1994; Ahmed, 1996; Frost and Shanka, 1998). Dobni and Zinkham (1990) concluded that image is a perceptual phenomenon that formed through consumers reasoned and emotion interpretation and it has both cognitive (beliefs) and affective (feeling) components.

An extensive literature review of tourism destination image measurement revealed that the image construct has been limited to studies dealing with its perceptual or cognitive component, where objective attributes or features of destinations were used as a basis for measuring destination images (Echtner and Ritchie, 1993; Waitt, 1996; Ross 1998). Most destination image studies in travel and tourism usually deal with large-scale environments (i.e. city, state, region or country) that are not directly perceivable. Russel and Snodgrass (1987) proposed an effective space structure to better understand how people assess environments or places. This technique was shown by Baloglu and Brinberg (1997) to be applicable to places that are not perceived directly. In this study we are using country destinations as used by Baloglu and Brinberg (1997.

This study

The objective of this research is to investigate the stakeholder's involvements in student travel arrangements. The study involves students studying business courses at a University in Perth, Western Australia. The sample includes local (Australian) students as well as overseas based students attending courses on the Perth campus. In addition students studying at 'off-shore' locations in Malaysia, Singapore and Hong Kong are included.

This study does not include the travel arrangements made by students as part of their studies. Rather, it has to do with travel associated with holidays and vacations.

Methodology

Students in the faculty of commerce comprise of Australian citizens, those qualifying for Australian residency status and international students with student visas. In addition students studying at remote campuses in Hong Kong, Malaysia and Singapore were included. The sample comprised 1230 students in total.

All participants were asked to complete an 18 item questionnaire covering the following issues:

- Participants demographics

- Destination and purposes of visits

- Details of stay

- Funding issues

- Factors that influenced their choice and mode of destination and travel

- Details on stakeholder involvements

- Promotional considerations

- Choice of airfare

The study was completed during tutorials and yielded a high response rate (98%). Overseas students represent approximately 30 percent of the Perth business student cohort.

Discussion of results

A total of 1217 responses were received yielding a response rate of 99%. The sample represented approximately 20 percent of the total faculty population.

The ratio of male to female was approximately 2:1 and approximately one third indicated their country of residence to be Australia. The bulk of the students were in their second or third year of study. Of the valid responses 157 stated that they had not taken an overseas holiday in the past two years, hence their input was not considered. A summary of their profiles is shown in Table 1 and of their holiday history in Table 2.

Table 1   Profile of Respondents

Gender	Frequency	Percent
Male	791	65
Female	426	35
Total	1217	100
Usual country of Residence		
Australia	426	35.0
Hong Kong	136	11.2
Indonesia	83	6.8
Malaysia	238	19.6
Singapore	304	25.0
Other	30	0.4
Total	1217	100.0
Year of Study		
First Year	113	9.3
Second Year	306	25.2
Third Year	777	63.9
Honours/above	21	1.6
Total	1217	100.00

Table 2   Holiday Profile

Last time overseas holiday taken prior to study		
	Frequency	Percent
Less than 6 months	319	26.2
6-12 months	302	24.8
13-18 months	123	10.1
19-24 months	88	7.3
> 24 months	228	18.8
Did not take overseas holiday	157	12.9

Recognising that any such trip may well involve more than one destination, the respondents were asked to nominate a prime country destination. These results are shown in Table 3. Indonesia was the most visited destination, probably due to the holiday destination, Bali, with Singapore in second place.

Table 3   Destination Choice

Destination	Frequency	Percent
Australia	108	8.9
Hong Kong	105	9.9
Singapore	134	12.6
Thailand	78	7.4
Indonesia	150	14.2
Malaysia	109	10.3
Other-Asia	94	8.9
U.S.A	83	7.8
Europe	77	7.3
U.K.	49	4.6
Other	73	6.9

The survey revealed significant findings in terms of funding and promotional considerations. Details are shown in Table 4. In relation to promotion, two questions were posed. The first, "How did you learn about the destination?", and the second, "Who influenced you in choosing that destination?". These results are shown in Table 5.

Table 4   How did respondent learn about destination?

	Frequency	Percent
Through friends/word of mouth	404	38.1
Travel agent	69	6.5
Airline	34	3.2
Internet	22	2.1
Tourism promotion centre	45	4.2
Prior experience	296	27.9
Other	190	17.9
Total	1060	100.00

Table 5   Who influenced the decision?

	Frequency	Percentage
Own decision	350	33.0
Family	432	40.8
Friends	165	15.6
Travel Agent	46	4.3
Airline	30	2.8
Other	37	3.5
Total	1060	100.0

The dominant elements in terms of the first question were friends and word of mouth along with prior experience. Together these two elements accounted for 66% of all responses. The professional infrastructural elements, airlines, travel agents and tourism centres had a relatively low impact.

Also, the major influencing factors were dominated by the individual along with family and friends. Again, the airlines and travel agents played a very minor role.

To complete the understanding of influencing factors, funding was considered in terms of who funded the trip. The results are shown in Table 6.

Table 6   Who mainly funded the holiday?

	Frequency	Percentage
Self	405	38.2
Family	594	56.1
Friends	16	1.5
Other	45	
Total	1060	100

Clearly the fact that others finance the trip to a significant degree raises a number of issues. The standard of the trip is likely to be higher if additional funding is made available. The presence of others, particularly family, might also ensure a higher class of travel. In addition this situation would have an impact on the promotional strategy used by tour operators.

In terms of the airlines used, all of those nominated provide full services in the region. All sectors are inter-linked by the carriers and all provide services directly or through partners to all major destinations.

The international airlines nominated by the students are shown in Figure 7.

Table 7   International airlines nominated by students

Airlines	Frequency	Percent
Singapore Airlines	276	26.1
Qantas	212	20.2
Malaysian Airlines	180	17
Cathy Pacific	106	10
British Airways	65	6.2
Garuda-Indonesia	39	3.6
Other	179	16.9
Total	1060	

This research would indicate that the actual operator and their distributors play a minor role in the students choice process. The choice of airline appears to be a secondary consideration to the choice of destination. Given that the overall decision is a high involvement decision, it would appear important for the airline to ensure that it's offering be considered early in the decision process. This research also indicates that the promotional messages need to be communicated to other parties involved in the decision process. For example it has been shown that parents, relatives and friends are often the key to initiating or supporting the process. Thus they must be considered in terms of the overall strategy.

Similarly, the role of the travel agent needs to be reconsidered. What is their role? From this research it appears to be passive - again they do not appear to be part of the influencing process. One can conclude that they are merely processing a previously made decision.

The wide range of factors that could potentially influence the choice of airline needs to be considered. Effectively once the conceptual approval stage in the model (Figure 1) has been reached, it is too late to influence the decision. Therefore, the airline needs to examine more fully the various influences. For example the parents and family of the student traveller are themselves targeted by airlines using loyalty programs, safety considerations, in-flight comfort appeals (The Singapore Girl). In a large measure prior experiences of this group will play a significant role in the decision process. The concept needs to be extended to include the student traveller.

Figure 1   Selection of Travel Destination - Influences on the Decision Process

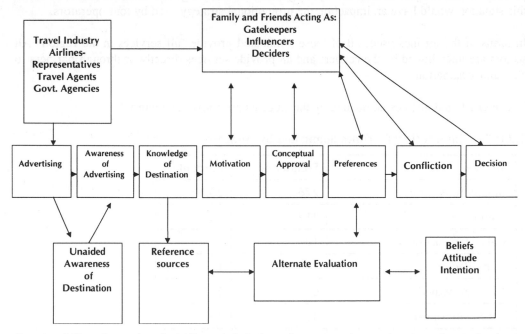

Certain airlines have already indicated their intention to pay increasing attention to business-class travel. However, if the economy component is important, the student segment is certainly a viable option. This research has highlighted the role of the family in funding the trip. In many instances the student may be accompanied by others. This all points to an ability to search for value rather than price.

Preliminary focus group sessions with students who formed part of this research indicated that they were not aware of airline directed promotion. This may again be due to the fact that airlines are targeting the more mature market segments.

The traditional airlines, through deregulation are now being challenged by a number of new players in the Australasian region. Companies such as Virgin Atlantic are set to compete both internationally and domestically within the region.

Summary and conclusions

The image of student travel must be reassessed. The youth hostel-backpacker image of yesteryear has been replaced with a more brand aware, more affluent student traveller. The motivation to travel is also changing. The concepts of globalisation and internationalisation are having major impacts of selection criteria used by businesses today. International experience is now a requirement more often than not. Universities are offering international programs with students travelling to various national campuses as part of the education process.

The segment is sufficiently large to necessitate a dedicated approach by the airlines. The unique nature of the decision making process and the influences involved must be taken into account if this segment is to be handled meaningfully. The numbers suggest that this could be a viable exercise.

References

Ahmed, Z.U. (1996), The need for the identification of the constituents of a destination's tourist image: a promotion segmentation perspective, *Journal of Professional Services Marketing*. 14 (1): 37-60.

Baloglu, S., and D. Brinberg (1997), Affective Images of Tourism Destinations *Journal of Travel Research* 35 (4): 11-15.

Bywater, M. (1993), Market Segments in the Youth and Student Travel Market. *EIU Travel and Tourism Analyst* (3): 35-50.

Chadee, D. D. and Cutler, J. (1996), Insights into International Travel by Students, *Journal of Travel Research* 35 (2): 75-80. Fall 1996.

Cho, B-H, (1996), An Analysis of the Korean youth tourist market in Australia, *Australian Journal of Hospitality Management*. (Spring). 3 (2): 15-25.

Clarke, J. (1992). A Marketing Spotlight on the Youth four S's Consumer, *Tourism Management*. 321-27 September.

Crouch, G. I. (1994), "The study of international tourism demand: a survey of practice", *Journal of Travel Research*, (Spring), pp. 41-55.

Dobni, D. and G. M. Zinkham (1990), In Search of Brand Image: A Foundation Analysis. *Advances in Consumer Research*. (17):110-119.

Echtner, C.M. and I.R. Brent Ritchie (1993), The Measurement Of Destination Image; An Empirical Assessment *Journal of Travel Research*. (31):3-13. Spring.

Frost, F. A. and Shanka, T. (1998), The perception of Ethiopia as a tourist destination: an Australian perspective, Proceedings of *The Fourth Asia Pacific Tourism Association Conference*. Series A. August 18-21, 1998. Tanyang, Chung-Buk, Korea. Pp 60-88.

Hsu, C. H. C. and Sung, S. (1997), Travel behaviours of international students at a Midwestern University, *Journal of Travel Research*. (Summer). Pp 59-65.

Kotler, P., Haider, D. H. and I. Rein (1993), *Marketing Places: Attracting Investment, Industry and Tourism to Cities, States and Nations*. New York: The Free Press.

McGehee, N. G., Loker-Murphy, L. and Uysal, M. (1996), The Australian international pleasure travel market: motivations from a gendered perspective, *The Journal of Tourism Studies*. May. 7 (1): 45-57.

Mok, C. and Armstrong, R. W. (1994), Perception of Australia as a holiday destination: a case of Hong Kong and Taiwanese tourists, *Australian Journal of Hospitality Management*. (July). 1 (2): 25-28.

Musca, J. and Shanka, T. (1998), "Travel industry-why aren't we marketing to international students?", proceedings of the *New Zealand Tourism and Hospitality Research Conference*, Akaroa, New Zealand, (December 3-6), vol. 1.

Ross, G. F. (1998), *The Psychology of Tourism*, 2nd edition, Melbourne. Hospitality Press.

Russel, J. A. and Snodgrass, J. (1987), Emotion and Environment, in *Handbook of Environmental Psychology*. Eds D. Stockols and I. Altman. New York: John Wiley and Sons, 245-280.

Shanka, T. and Musca, J. (1998), "An exploratory study of international students' involvement in domestic tourism - a West Australian case ", *Proceedings of the 1998 Australia and New Zealand Marketing Academy Conference*, Dunedin, New Zealand. (29 Nov-3 Dec).

Sung, S. and Hsu. C. H. C. (1996), "International students' travel characteristics: an exploratory study", *Journal of Travel and Tourism Marketing*, 5 (3): 277-283.

Waitt, G. (1996), "Korean students' assessment of Australia as a holiday destination", *Australian Geographer*, 27(2): 249-269.

Personality and values as variables for segmenting the tourism market

John Y Gountas, Sandra Carey and Peter Oppenheim

University of Ballarat, Australia

Abstract

The aims of this paper are to identify and discuss the relevant concepts related to Tourists/Travellers Values and Personality; to analyse and discuss the validity and reliability of the various theories on values and personality; to develop an argument for the usage of a new tourism personality typology with the concomitant values/preferences for each personality type; and explain the methodology of the empirical research and report the data findings.

The paper concludes with a discussion on the way forward using this research instrument to identify more clearly other psychological characteristics such as attitudes, values, motives and learning styles for tourism segmentation purposes.

Introduction

The reason *why* it is worthwhile pursuing studies on segmentation has not changed in essence for many years. Due to the intense competition currently facing both destinations and tourism principals (tour operators, accommodation providers, transport companies, destination, attractions etc.) it has become even more crucial to understand tourists' underlying reasons for their choices and decision making processes (psychographic characteristics) more accurately. For accurate segmentation, it is not sufficient to know what the tourists' behaviour is in relation to their Life Cycle stages, geodemographics and behavioural characteristics. The key questions of why tourists choose a destination or type of holiday are possible to answer by looking at the internal psychological factors which should also be correlated with the external situational factors. The market intelligence gained by providing more insightful answers to the questions of how tourists make decisions and what are the influences and processes would clearly be invaluable for most aspects of marketing e.g. product development, segmentation and target marketing, promotions and competitive differentiation (Gountas and Gountas 2000).

The main methods generally used to segment tourism consumer demand are geodemograhic characteristics, psychographic, behavioural and destination product attributes. No single method, in isolation, has the potential to predict accurately what tourism consumers will or will not purchase. Each method has its strengths and weaknesses and is, therefore, more appropriate for different applications as some of the criteria within each segmentation method have greater relevance given different circumstances.

The overall explanation for any type of tourism activity is more likely to be influenced by all the previously mentioned methods and most likely if a hybrid segmentation method is used. For example, marketing research has shown that older, as opposed to younger consumers, tend to go bowling more frequently (Hisrich and Peters, 1974); Marriott hotels operate a number of brands based on the income and purpose of visit by a variety of market segments, e.g. Short -stay (Fairfield Inns), apartment type of accommodation for extended stays (Residence Inns), and many other types of brands for the budget traveller, the business person and the leisure/vacation type of guests (Schiffman and Kanuk, 1997).

Tourism segmentation tends to be more on the basis of geodemographic, behavioural and destination product characteristics which are concerned with questions of who travels, where they go, what they do and so on. These are essential characteristics because they describe what the consumers want. However, geodemographics does not give any accurate insights into *why* certain tourism products and activities are chosen. Psychographics, on the other hand, describes the inner-psychological characteristics of the consumers and provide a better understanding of the reasons why they prefer one product/service to another. In the tourism literature a large number of tourism typologies are a mixture, hybrid type of segmentation, i.e. of psychographic and other segmentation methods (Hawes 1979, Klenosky, Genger, Mulvey 1993,Waryszack, Kim 1994).

Value based segmentation methods

Human values tend to be small in number, relatively stable over time (Rokeach 1979) and serve as the yardsticks or criteria for consumers' behaviour (Williams 1968). They also tend to be the precursor of motives, attitudes and behavioural outcomes (Kamakura, Novak 1992), because they are higher cognitive constructs that organise other psychological constructs into a hierarchical order.

Pizam and Calantone state 'Psychologists believe that a person's standard behaviour is influenced by his/hers values' and have proposed a conceptual framework in the shape of a pyramid with values at the top, followed successively by interests, attitudes, beliefs and opinions at the bottom of the pyramid (Pizam, Calantone 1987). They define values as 'a class of beliefs shared by the members of a society or sub-society, concerning what is desirable or 'good' or what ought to be and what is undesirable or 'bad.'

Other social scientists suggest that values are more central than attitudes and precede motives, therefore more appropriate variables for understanding consumer's inner world (Rokeach 1973). However, the issue of identifying the values which consumers hold is far from straight forward. Most consumers have more than one value to guide their actions in terms of overall life style, purchasing brands/services and dealing with specific issues either social, professional or/and personal. The motives, attitudes and actions will therefore be different according to the situation and the degree of relevance of the values guiding the consumers' behaviour. A segmentation approach that includes a plurality of values has been proposed to be a more effective way of understanding the consumer's behaviour, (Tetlock 1986, Valette-Florence 1986).

Rokeach (1973) developed the RVS (Rokeach Value Survey) instrument, which is one of the most frequently used instruments for measuring values. The RVS contains 18 Terminal, meaning end state of being as well as a life long achievement; and 18 Instrumental values, which are the means, and methods of achieving the end results, goals and terminal values.

According to Rokeach, there is a hierarchical order based on the importance each value has as a guiding principal in the consumer's lives. Rokeach identified the personal and social preferences. The personal preferences are those which exist as a result of the individual's personality but the socially derived preferences are those influenced by the social context and environment within which the individual lives or lived in previously.

Values are usually defined as being terminal or instrumental (Engel 1993, Wilkie 1994, Pitts and Woodside 1986). RVS consists of eighteen instrumental values (or desirable modes of conduct) and nineteen terminal values (or desirable states of existence) that are ranked according to their level of importance as guiding principles in the individual's life (Rokeach 1973). The eighteen instrumental values are descriptively ambitious, broad-minded, capable, cheerful, clean, courageous, forgiving, helpful, honest, imaginative, independent, intellectual, logical, loving, obedient, polite, responsible and self-controlled.

The terminal values are a comfortable life, an exciting life, a sense of accomplishment, a world of peace, a world of beauty, equality, family security, freedom, happiness, inner harmony, mature love, national security, pleasure, salvation, self-respect, social recognition, true friendship and wisdom.

Most of these values may be associated with motivation to travel but some of them may vary according to the situation and personal perception of the condition. For example, excitement, imagination, beauty, happiness are all very subjective and affective by nature. They do not depend on cognition for their existence and do not allow for the possibility that values may be compromised and/or modified by experience and resources.

Rokeach (1973) posited that values are more stable over time than attitudes as they are more central to the individual's cognitive system. This implies that individuals will evaluate their values using rational thought processes. However, many researchers have proposed different personality types that influence thought processes and regardless of which classification seems more plausible to a reviewer, it is unlikely that anyone would deny that differences exist.

Therefore, it is logical that different personalities will evaluate their different values using a variety of cognitive and affective measures or perhaps not at all. If the individual acts more on their affective system, values and attitudes may be harder to change.

Feelings are not always enduring but are sometimes more difficult to understand and influence than reason as they often have root in one's childhood and socialisation. Feelings may be so imbedded in the individual's character that they are not easily identified, recognised, or understood. For consumer behaviour in tourism, the affective domain may cause illogical resistance to certain destinations, people, and product types. Frew and Shaw (1999) have referred to this as lack of congruence with the environment that is rooted in the personality. They also found that gender difference is influential in leisure activities and behaviour. Values may be subject to impression management in the consumption of products and services with aspirational appeal, therefore, they could be very weak predictors for brand specific and product category choices which may result in inconsistency. Also, some individuals lack clarity about the existence of values and how they can be related to their buyer behaviour.

Many studies have used the RVS instrument to describe the value structure of populations, (Inglehart 1985; Rokeach 1973, 1979; Rokeach and Ball-Rokeach 1989); to explain the value hierarchies and systems amongst different groups (Becker and Connor 1981; Pitts and Woodside 1983; Tetlock 1986; Toler 1975). However there is a distinct lack of specific studies that relate to the application of the RVS as a segmentation tool attempting to predict what the relationship is between values and brand/holiday choices.

Mitchell (1983) is credited for the development of VALS, meaning values and lifestyles, which is a copyrighted, syndicated lifestyle study research tool. It took into account Maslow's need hierarchy, Riesman's (1961) ideas of the inner, outer and tradition oriented consumers and overlaid demographic characteristics to develop clusters and segments of American people according to their attitudes, wants, needs, beliefs and resources.

The VALS 2 framework developed eight clusters of lifestyle segments, which are considered representative and appropriate for marketing applications for the whole of the USA market. An international version comparing the lifestyles of the UK, Germany, France, Sweden and Italy was published which produced similar lifestyle segments in all of these developed countries (Mitchell, 1983). Mitchell (1983) attempted 'to put the thinking of those trying to understand the trends of our times in the marketplace, economically, politically, sociologically and humanly.'

In doing so, Mitchell identified three basic categories/origins of consumer values:

- Need driven –this means that consumer behaviour is driven by need more than by values, attitudes and preferences.

- Outer directed -most people fall into this category buying with awareness and consideration of social opinion and pressure.

- Inner directed- these people are able to listen to their personal needs more than those influenced by their peer group or society in general.

These categories may be said to be personality related and influential in shaping the consumer's attitude towards products and their providers. For tourism products, values may be significant in expectancy formation.

We must remember that an American in the context of the American consumer base developed VALS and VALS2. However, the categories were translated into European terms (Engel et al, 1993) which embraced different cultural characteristics.

The list of Values (LOV) is another well-known research instrument developed by Kahle (1983). It is a shorter modified version of the RVS Terminal values, and has only nine values that relate to the more personal daily-life roles and events. Unlike the RVS it does not assume a hierarchy/ranking order and respondents can choose any values, which are then analysed to clusters and segments.

The main difference between the LOV and RVS is that the nine LOV values can be generalised across all the major aspects of consumer's life and roles (Beatty et al. 1985). They are closely related to the terminal values, which are likely to influence the product category (Howard 1977), as opposed to instrumental values which guide choices among brands and situation-specific contexts (Pitts, Wong, and Whalen, 1991).

A number of studies have been reported using Values and specifically the LOV typology in the tourism industry acknowledging that values alone are not reliable enough but they need to be integrated with destination attributes, demographics and other psychological constructs (Madgrigal and Kahle 1994; Pitts and Woodside 1986, Dalen 1989; Muller 1991).

The most important caveat for application is an estimation of the size of the segment to ensure a statistically worthwhile sample for targeting. VALS is generally considered a useful tool but is not considered to be as accurate as Kahle, Beatty and Homers' (1986) List of Values or LOV.

Kahle, Beatty and Homers' (1986) List of Values (LOV) uses a scale to measure importance attached to aspects such as security, accomplishment, a sense of belonging, excitement, fun and enjoyment, self fulfilment, being well respected and warm relationships with others. As mentioned these were developed from RVS terminal values. When used in combination with methods such as demographic segmentation, LOV has been found more successful in predicting consumer behaviour than VALS (Engel et al 1993). LOV values can be divided into internal and external orientation and consumers with an internal locus of control are much more individualistic. Those with an external locus of control will be more concerned with their social group and its approval.

Rokeach (1973) stated that 'Personal values are intricately related to one's attitudes and behaviour. Whereas values represent abstract ideals, positive or negative that are not tied to any specific object or situation.' It is worth considering the possibility that holiday or travel behaviour may differ from the 'normal.'

As mentioned, a main motivator for travel is frequently identified as a need 'to get away from it all' or have a completely different experience. These motivations do not usually arise in the purchase and consumption of more tangible goods.

Tourist specific typologies

Being away from one's usual environment can be a liberating experience which may include the temporary suspension of normal values and attitudes particularly if one is usually concerned with peer and public opinion. There have been many cases of 'out of character' behaviour by tourists which is contradictory to their regular, accepted social mores. Therefore, it is possible that the liberating effect of being away from home may sometimes confound otherwise reliable measures of consumer behaviour. It may also lead to unrealistic and unreasonable expectations of the product offering.

Holiday habits and behaviour were examined, amongst other consumer behaviours, to arrive at the criteria for classification (Cohen, 1972). The main drivers of Principle, Status, and Action will be fundamental in influencing choices in destinations, types of holidays and activities embraced during the holiday experience. It is also reasonable to assume that the different drivers will result in different criteria for expectation and its satisfaction, also that different drivers will apply to different personalities. It follows that beliefs, values, attitudes, and personality affect expectations by contributing towards them. Expectations affect buying behaviour and perceptions of satisfaction levels.

Behavioural studies in tourism tend to be limited in depth and breadth and do not embrace consumer behaviour theory that is applied to most other situations. Neither do they pay enough attention to the personality of the tourist or traveller.

Much of the existing debate focuses on whether a holidaymaker is a 'tourist' or a 'traveller' with a value judgement in favour of the 'traveller.' Sharpley (1996) wrote 'The term traveller is usually applied to someone who is travelling/touring for an extended period of time, particularly on a limited budget. It contains a spirit of freedom, adventure, and individuality. The word tourist on the other hand, is frequently used in a rather derogatory sense to describe those who participate in mass package tourism.' This seems to suggest a supposed inherent difference between personality and chosen mode of travel, yet there is generally limited discussion about the reasons behind the choices.

Some tourist typologies most frequently discussed are:

Plog (1974)- Plog tried to link personality traits to tourist behaviour and divided tourists into Psychocentrics at one end of a continuum and Allocentrics at the other. Psychocentrics were considered insular and less adventurous, preferring the 'safe' and familiar. Allocentrics at the other extreme were considered outward looking, risk taking adventurers. Frew and Shaw (1999) discussed the debate amongst many academics that Plog's theory is flawed and may be useful as a description but not as an explanation.

Cohen (1973) identified four types of tourists the organised mass, the individual mass, the explorer, and the drifter. These categorise people according to their taste in destinations and activities. Cohen discusses attitudes towards safety and new experiences, but does not relate his work to outcomes; his research is mostly based on informal observation (Lowyck et al, 1992).

Perreault, Darden and Darden used a postal questionnaire to survey 2000 households (Lowyck et al, 1992). The questionnaire comprised three parts 1) questions about holiday behaviour, 2) questions about socio-economic characteristics and 3) questions about activities during leisure time and holidays. A Likert scale was used to assess the extent to which respondents agreed or disagreed with a statement. From this five types of tourist were identified, Budget travellers, Adventurers, Homebodies, Vacationers and Moderates.

These types were formed based on the respondents' predisposition towards safety, adventure and activity levels but it did not address the reason for choices or perceived levels of satisfaction. As with the previous methods, there is little consideration of the personal factors that influence choices.

In 1989 American Express commissioned research that surveyed more than 4000 travellers, again five groups were identified –Adventurers, Worriers, Dreamers, Economisers and Indulgers (Lowyck et al, 1992).

Personality characteristics were attributed to these categories but again there is no consideration for the possibility that an individual may fit into more than one category at the same time and express different needs and motivations according to changes in circumstances.

Yiannakis and Gibson (1992) researched tourists' preferences using demographics, benefits/attributes, and psychographic characteristics. They identified a number of personality types and related those to the cause of behaviour in product consumption.

Personality based segmentation

Jung's (1971) work on personality types was developed over a period of time starting in the early twentieth century. Jung postulated the existence of four personality types or orientation, Thinking, Feeling, Intuitive and Sensation Seeking. He stated that each type has distinct characteristics and displays a propensity towards either extraversion or introversion.

Jung described the basic drivers of the four types thus:

> *The Thinking Type* is oriented by what they think and simply cannot adapt to a situation that they are unable to understand intellectually.

> *The Intuitive Type* is concerned with possibilities; they do not concern themselves with ideas, reactions or reality.

> *The Sensation Seeking Type* is concerned with a simple perception of concrete reality, without thinking about it or taking feeling values into account.

> *The Feeling Type* is guided in everything by how they feel. They concern themselves with whether a thing is pleasant or unpleasant, they orient themselves by their feeling impressions.

Jung considered that this predominantly one sidedness is balanced or compensated by an unconscious counter-position. This indicates that a particular type might display a secondary tendency towards another type, for example the Intuitive type may show less dominant but a significant level of characteristics normally associated with the Thinking type.

According to Kiersey and Bates (1984) Jung believed that 'people are different in fundamental ways even though they all have the same multitude of instincts (archetypes) to drive from within.' This suggests stability in the personality types, which is due to innate temperament.

At the same time that Jung was researching personality types other researchers such as Adickes, Spranger, Krethschmer and Adler were examining the possibility of dividing personality types into four major groups. The notion of four personality types is not new as it is recorded in accounts of the works of the ancient Greeks.

Jung's general personality types are rather broad but the hypothesis has been tested in more recent years. In the 1950s Myers and Briggs devised the Myers-Briggs Type Indicator (MBTI) (Kiersey and Bates 1984). MBTI is a tool that identifies sixteen main patterns of activity, which fall into the theory of four temperaments. The Myers-Briggs Type Indicator is currently used in industry for personality assessment purposes and has been applied successfully to leisure activities (McGuiggan 1996).

McGuiggan's research adapted the MBTI inventory to suit leisure preferences and concluded that personality types are better explanatory variables for issues like planning, follow through, variety, people and pace of activities. Demographics, on the other hand, indicated a stronger correlation for household tasks, team sports and modernity (Gountas and Gountas, 2000). These findings support the view of others that personality is useful in predicting consumer behaviour in leisure and tourism activities (Holbrook and Hirschman 1982, Frew and Shaw 1999,).

Research methodology

The new research reported and discussed in this paper is part of a bigger ongoing survey. Whilst the methodology remains the same it is the intention to test new samples of tourism consumers in order to identify seasonal characteristics of the same variables at each stage of the research. The incremental stage-by-stage approach of studying the consumers personality types all year around enables us to build a larger and more detailed picture of each personality type in different tourism situations. As previously reported the authors adopted the Jungian personality types theory and the MBTI inventory as a basis for the conceptualisation of the consumers as a whole person (Gountas and Gountas 2000). The exploratory tests and refinements have been made in the context of tourism preferences as well as expressions of personality characteristics including values.

The exploratory work led to the hypothesis of the four the four types: *Thinking/logically* oriented, *Sensing/materially* oriented, *Feeling/affectively* oriented and *Perceptive/intuitively* oriented. The authors believe that the concepts of extraversion and introversion are not valid for the purpose of defining personality and the extensive research on the issue is inconclusive. It is suggested that the attention given by Jung to extraversion and introversion can be explained as common practice in his time. The MBTI additions of Perceiving and Judging have no sound foundation as to why they should be separate orientations. The original four types postulated by the ancient Greeks were much easier to work with, understand and identify.

The initial research was conducted through a series of depth interviews and focus groups with normal subjects who have participated in travel of all ages and social, economic and educational levels.

The four orientations, their motivations and preferences were tested and retested through a number of inventories that emerged from the literature review and the field -work. A clearer list of items emerged which indicated that there are distinct characteristics between each of the orientations differentiating consumers in terms of how they see the world and they behave.

A testable hypothesis emerged about the correlation between the existence of the four orientations and the actual activity/holiday preferences. A self-completion questionnaire was constructed in 1998 and tested on a sample of holiday- makers in the Greek Ionian Islands.

The results tentatively supported the hypothesis of the four reformulated orientations, but the sampling method and the administration of the survey needed to change to improve the rate of responses and level of representativeness. A new and shorter, 50-item inventory/questionnaire was developed and pilot tested with a sample of the actual travelling consumers. The results were deemed reliable enough to justify a larger survey (Gountas and Gountas 2000).

Survey 1

A leading UK charter airline, Air 2000, is collaborating with the ongoing survey. The questionnaire consists of 50 questions about the 4 orientations and 12 questions regarding the satisfaction levels for the airline purposes, using a five point Likert scale.

In the first survey, three thousand questionnaires were distributed amongst in-bound and out-bound sectors of flights from 11 UK airports to a variety of European and long haul destinations. Nearly eight hundred questionnaires were returned and from that seven hundred and sixty were fully completed and suitable for factor analysis. This survey was conducted in November/December 1999. It is recognised that seasonality may affect the nature and motivation of tourists, which is another critical reason for the survey to be repeated at different times of the year. The results of the first survey are shown below.

Table 1   Factor Analysis/Findings for Survey 1

Salient oblique loadings		Av.ICR	Alpha Value
Factor 1			
.80 (30)	I like order in my life		
.74 (29)	I like certainty/facts in life	.59	.74
.51 (31)	I am a realistic person	.50	.75
.46 (28)	I value material possessions	.40	.73
.45 (26)	I am a practical person	.37	.75
.41 (36)	I am a logical person	.36	.77
Factor 2			
.74 (48)	I make mountains out of molehills		
.73 (49)	My heart rules my head	.47	.64
.59 (50)	It's important to spend time daydreaming	.35	.62
.55 (47)	I depend on other people	.33	.66
Factor 3			
.86 (44)	I often put other people first		
.83 (43)	I am sensitive to others	.65	.79
.70 (42)	I like to mix with other people	.50	.75
Factor 4			
.81 (39)	I am very interested in new inventions, discoveries, future		
.63 (37)	I prefer to understand the meaning of how and why things are	.51	.68
.63 (41)	I am an ideas person	.38	.65
.57 (38)	I am very objective	.39	.72
.46 (40)	I think before I act	.34	.72
Factor 5			
.67 (33)	I am a doer		
.60 (32)	I am self sufficient	.50	.67
.60 (27)	The pleasures of food/eating are important	.26	.52
.54 (34)	I am confident about my feelings	.30	.63
.45 (25)	I am down to earth	.28	.66
.43 (26)	I am a practical person	.31	.73
.41 (31)	I am a realistic person	.33	.77

(Gountas and Gountas 2000)

Although four personality orientations with distinct value preferences were hypothesised through the exploratory research, five factors emerged from the analysis. The findings of factors 2 and 3 were hypothesised as being one factor. Factor 2 seems to be relevant for the general/personal life issues and factor 3 is more related to the working environment and therefore the splits are due to the appropriateness of behaviour by the same orientation for different issues. All other factors predicted are strongly supported by the findings.

Factor 1 - Sensing/materially oriented

This orientation seems to value the material world, is pragmatic, likes order and certainty and considers itself pragmatic in its decision/choices. The preferred holiday/leisure activities would, most likely, include the enjoyment of all tangible/material attributes, the natural world that can be experienced primarily with the senses.

Factor 2 - The feelings/affective oriented

The issues relating to emotional and feelings driven experiences would be of primary importance. People and issues regarding the ego enhancement are the centre of the activities. Action and direct experiential exploration of the world is the medium of making sense of their lives.

Factor 3 - The perceptive/intuitives

The ability to perceive the external world through their intuition gives them a distinct perspective of the objective and subjective world.

The are likely to be interested in the destinations whereby they can imagine past civilisations, as well as experience new possibilities for interaction with the host and other travelling populations.

Factor 4 - Thinking/logical

The main emphasis is on the understanding of how things work, what is best way to deal with any situation and learning about the new cultures, places and people. Mind is the driving force and using logical/rational thinking is the process. The dominant values are likely to be the intellectual interests, exposure to novel ideas, situations and understanding how the system/society/specific artefacts work. The secondary values are likely to be interested in are the materialistic, pleasures of the senses, feelings and imagination *(Gountas and Gountas 2000)*.

Survey 2

The second survey, which took place in February 2000, produced 490 useable questionnaires. The sample was drawn from ten different flights to the USA, Caribbean, Austria, Italy, France, Switzerland and Cyprus. The U.K. departure points were Manchester, Stanstead, Newcastle, Gatwick, Glasgow, Bristol, Birmingham and Dublin in Ireland.

The return rate of the questionnaire was 20-30% on average for each flight. Overall the sample size is large enough to be representative of the winter tourism consumers market and has covered all the regions of the U.K. airports. The same procedure of administering the questionnaires on board the inbound and outbound flights was followed as in the first study/survey in November 1999.

Table 2   Findings for Survey 2

	Factor Loadings
Factor 1	
Q39 In general, I'm interested in inventions/new things/the future	.737
Q37 In general, I prefer understanding/meaning/how things work	.711
Q41 I am an ideas person	.700
Q38 In general, I'm an objective person	.571
Q45 In general, I have very good imagination	.526
Q40 In general, I think before I act	.495
Factor 2	
Q32 In general, I'm self-sufficient	.759
Q34 In general, I'm confident with my feelings/emotions	.683
Q35 In general, I value experience more than ideas	.655
Q33 In general, I'm a doer/action person	.554
Q47 In general, I depend on other people	-.492
Q31 In general, I am a realistic person	.448
Factor 3a	
Q43 In general, I'm sensitive to other people	.815
Q44 In general, I often put other people first	.780
Q42 In general, I like to mix with others	.517
Q46 In general, I'm very perceptive	.433
Q26 In general, I see myself as a practical person	.420
Factor 3b	
Q49 In general, my heart rules my head	.778
Q48 In general, I make mountains out of molehills	.638
Q50 In general, it's important to daydream	.627
Q47 In general, I depend on other people	.429
Q26 In general, I see myself as a practical person	-.398
Q25 In general, I see myself as down to earth	-.319
Factor 4a	
Q30 In general, I like order in my life	.815
Q29 In general, I like facts/certainties	.790
Q28 In general, I value material possessions	.467
Factor 4b	
Q27 In general, I see food/eating as a very important pleasure	.736
Q28 In general, I value material possessions	.417
Q42 In general, I like to mix with others	.412
Q40 In general, I think before I act	-.308

(Extraction method: Principal Component Analysis. Rotation Method: Varimax with Kaiser Normalisation. Rotation converged in eight iterations.)

Discussion of findings

The results and the factors of the second survey (winter tourism consumer market) are consistent with the first survey (November 1999, end of summer season tourism consumer market).

The factors 3a, and 3b are the same orientation, perceptive/intuitive as factors 2 and 3 in the first survey/study. The split of the same orientation into the two separate factors is probably due to the different modes behaviour for working and general/personal life. The same explanation applies to the split of factor 4 into 4a and 4b. The interesting finding is that the factors are almost identical in the variables they contain. The alpha values are very high and therefore very valid, because they are less likely to be due to pure chance.

The Bivariate Correlations of the individual items are highly significant and support the inter-correlation within each factor reported above. The majority, except a small number 15%, of the hypothesised items for each orientation and the ones that came out in the factor analysis have Pearson correlations of .132-.548; and the significance levels (2-tailed), are all .000, except a few items with significance of: .003 and .004.

This finding is much more useful in describing in a bivariate mode the nature of all the possible relationships and therefore adds more support to the hypothesised relationships of the orientations with the specific variable correlations. The validity (internal, construct, external and statistical) of the instrument is supported based on the two different tests (factor and bivariate correlations) and the two independent studies.

The research findings are robust enough to support the hypothesis of the four distinct personality orientations. The different values and preferences of each orientation are distinct but not exclusive. Each orientation has a stronger preference towards a cluster of values/preferences and is differentiated by the degree of the preference from the other orientations. The motives and attitudes of each orientation are somewhat, by degree, different from the other orientations. Within each, there are many differences according to the socio-economic, cultural and other demographic characteristics.

Consumers are not the same; they are different with similar overall tendencies/preferences towards themselves, the environment and other people. This paper provided empirical evidence, which supports this point.

The next stage of the research is to carry out another survey during the summer season, June-September, 2000, using the same instrument and sampling method. The research questions that need to be studied in detail are the specific attitudes, motives, learning styles and behavioural preferences for each factor/orientation separately. The study will be continued in the U.K. and Australia to test the cross cultural impacts on the results. The study so far has identified the existence of the main orientations at the general level. The variations within each orientation are potentially many, and therefore another level of conceptualisation with more detailed picture of all the psychological constructs is needed to explain and organise these variations in the tourism consumers behaviour.

References

Beatty, S. E., Kahle, L. R., Homer, P., Misra, S. (1985), 'Alternative Measurement Approaches to Consumer Values: The List of Values and the Rokeach Value Survey', *Psychology and Marketing*, 2 (Fall), pp 181 -200.

Becker, B. W., Connor, P. E. (1981), 'Personal Values of the Heavy User of Mass Media' *Journal of Advertising Research*, 21, October, pp 37-43.

Cohen, E. (1972), 'Towards a Sociology of International Tourism', *Social Research*, 39, pp 164-182.

Cohen, E. (1973), 'Nomads From Affluence: Notes On The Phenomenon of Drifter Travel' *International Journal of Comparative Sociology*, Vol. 14 89 - 103.

Dalen, E. (1989), 'Research into Values and Consumer Trends in Norway, *Tourism Management*, 10 (3): 183-186.

Engel, J. F., Blackwell, R. D., Miniard, P. W. (1993), *Consumer Behaviour*, Dryden Press, London.

Frew, E. A., Shaw, R. N. (1999), 'The relationship between personality, gender and tourism behaviour', *Tourism Management*, 20, pp 193-202.

Gountas, Y., Gountas, S. (2000), 'A New Psychographic Segmentation method using Jungian MBTI Variables in Tourism Industry, Second Symposium on the Consumer Psychology of Tourism, Hospitality and Leisure (CPTHL), Vienna.

Hawes, D. K., (1979), 'Satisfaction Derived From Leisure Time Pursuits: An Exploratory Nation-wide Survey, *Journal of Leisure Research*, Vol. 10 247 - 264.

Hisrich, R. R., Peters, M. P. (1974), 'Selecting the Superior Segmentation Correlate' *Journal of Marketing*, 38, pp 60-63.

Holbrook, M. B. and Hirschman, E. C. (1982), The experiential aspects of consumption: consumer fantasies, feelings, and fun. *Journal of Consumer Research*, 9, (Sept), pp. 140.

Howard, J. (1977), *Consumer Behaviour: application of theory*, Wiley, New York.

Inglehart, R. (1985), 'Aggregate Stability and Individual-level Flux in Mass Belief Systems: The Level of Analysis Paradox' *American Political Science Review*, 79 (March), pp 97-116.

Jung, C. G. (1971), 'Psychological Types' (German Publication), the translated version *'The Collected Works'* eds. Reid, H. Fordham, Adler, G. Revised by Hull, R. F. C., Routledge and Kegan, London.

Kahle, L. R. (1983), *'Social Values and Social Change: Adaptation to Life in America'*. New York, Praeger.

Kahle, L. R., Beatty, G. E.and Homer, P. (1986), 'Alternative Measurement Approaches to Consumer Values: The List of Values (LOV) and Life Styles (VALS), *Journal of Consumer Research*, Vol. 13 Dec. 405 - 409.

Kamakura, W. A., Novak, T. P. (1992), 'Value System Segmentation: Exploring the Meaning of LOV, *Journal of Consumer Research*, Vol. 19 119 - 132.

Kiersey, D. Bates, M. (1984), *Please Understand Me*, Prometheus Nemesis Book Company, USA.

Klenosky, D. B., Gengler, C. E., Mulvey, M. S. (1993), 'Understanding the Factors Influencing Ski Destination Choice: A Means-End Analytic *Approach' Journal of Leisure Research*, Vol. 25 362 - 379.

Lowyck, E., Van Langenhove, L., Bollaert, (1992), L 'Typologies of Tourist Roles' in (eds) Johnson, P. Thomas, B *Choice and Demand in Tourism*, Mansell Publishing, London.

Madrigal, R. Kahle, L. R. (1994), 'Predicting Vacation Activity Preferences on the Basis of Value-System Segmentation', *Journal of Travel Research*, Vol. 32 (3): 22-28.

McGuiggan, R. L. (1996), *The relationship between personality, as measured by the MBTI, and leisure preferences*. Ph.D. diss., Macquarie University, Australia.

Mitchell, A. (1983), *'Nine American Lifestyles: Who are we and where are we going?'* MacMillan, New York.

Muller, T. E. (1991), 'Using Personal Values to Define Segments in an International Tourism Market', International *Marketing Review*, Vol.8, 57 - 70.

Pitts, R. E. Woodside, A. G. (1983), 'Personal value influences on consumer product class and brand preferences' *The Journal of Social Psychology*, (58) pp 193-198.

Pitts, R. E. Woodside, A. G. (1986), 'Personal Values and Travel Decisions' *Journal of Travel Research*, Vol.25, summer 20 - 25.

Pitts, R. E., Wong, J. K., Whalen, J. D. (1991), 'Consumers Evaluative Structures' In 'Two Ethical Situations: A means-end approach' *Journal of Business Research*, 22, pp 119-130.

Pizam, A. Calantone, R. (1987), 'Beyond Psychographics- Values As Determinants of Tourist Behaviour' *International Journal of Hospitality Management*, Vol.6, (3) 177 -181.

Plog, S. (1974), 'Why Destination Areas Rise And Fall In Popularity', *The Cornell Hotel and Restaurant Administration Quarterly*, Vol. 14 (4): 55-58.

Riesman, D., Glazer, N., Denney, R. (1961), *The Lonely Crowd*, Yale University Press, USA,

Rokeach, M., Ball-Rokeach, S. J. (1989), 'Stability and Change in American Value Priorities, 1968-1981' *American Psychologist*, Vol. 44 (May) 775-784.

Rokeach, M. (1979), 'From Individual to Institutional Values: With Special Reference to the Values of Science' in *Understanding Human Values: Individual and Societal*, New York, The Free Press, pp 47-70.

Rokeach, M. (1973), *'The Nature of Human Values'*, NY Free Press, USA.

Schiffman, L. G., Kanuk, L. L. (1997) ,*Consumer Behaviour*, Prentice Hall, London.

Sharpley, R. (1996), *Tourism, Tourists and Society*, Elm Huntingdon, U.K.

Tetlock, P. (1986), 'A Value Pluralism Model of Ideological Reasoning', *Journal of Personality and Social Psychology*, Vol. 50 (4): 819-827.

Toler, C. (1975), 'The Personal Values of Alcoholics and Addicts', *Journal of Clinical Psychology*, 31, July, pp 554-557.

Valette-Florence, P. (1986), 'Les Demarches de styles de vie: concept champs d'investigations et problemes actuals.' Recherche et Applications en Marketing, (1): 94-109.

Waryszak, R. Z., Kim, H. (1994), 'Psychographic Segmentation of Tourists as a Predictor of their Travel Behaviour: An exploratory study of Korean Tourists to Australia, *Journal of Hospitality and Leisure Marketing*, vol. 2 (4): 5-19.

Wilkie, D. (1994), *Consumer Behaviour*, Prentice Hall, London.

Williams, R. M. (1968), *'Values in International Encyclopedia of the Social Sciences*, Ed. E Sills, New York, McMillan, pp 203-207.

Yiannakis, A., Gibson, H. (1992), 'Roles Tourists Play' *Annals of Tourism Research*, Vol. 19, 287-303.

Sport tourism and the transition to professional Rugby Union in New Zealand. The spatial dimension of tourism associated with the Otago Highlanders, Southern New Zealand

James Higham

University of Otago, New Zealand

Tom Hinch

University of Alberta, Canada

Abstract

This paper applies two dimensions of the theoretical framework proposed by Hinch and Higham (2000, in press) to the transition from amateur to professional rugby in New Zealand. Specifically under this framework, sport tourism is described in terms of three dimensions: (1) The motivational dimension of sport, (2) The spatial dimension associated with travel flows and (3) The temporal dimension associated with travel. Three themes are proposed within each dimension which provide a framework for systematically examining relationships within sport tourism that to date have received little academic attention. For the purpose of this paper the relationship between two of these dimensions will be explored; they being the spatial dimension of tourism and the sport dimension as characterised by the development of professional Super 12 rugby.

Interviews were conducted with representatives from provincial Rugby Unions, Local Government Economic Development Units (EDUs) and Regional Tourism Organisations (RTOs) within the Otago Highlanders franchise region. The analysis of data confirms that the introduction of the Super 12 in 1996 has had various effects upon the spatial dimensions of tourism within the Highlanders region. All three themes within the spatial dimension of sport tourism identified by Hinch and Higham (2000, in press); location, region and landscape, have been implicated in the development of professional rugby. Each of these themes are examined and discussed.

Introduction

The essence of tourism lies in its spatial, temporal and motivational dimensions. These dimensions are repeated in the multitude of definitions of tourism that are found in the literature. Almost all of these definitions are explicit about the spatial nature of tourism associated with the *"travel of non-residents"* (Murphy, 1985, p.9). While less explicit attention is paid to its temporal context, there is almost always an implicit assumption that tourism requires a *"temporary stay away from home"* (Leiper, 1981, p.74). Considerably less consistency is found in the third dimension which relates to trip purpose or motivation to travel. Although popular definitions of tourism often focus on pleasure as the primary motivation or purpose of travel, a wide range of other motivations have also been suggested (World Tourism Organisation 1981). The common element is the existence of this dimension, not the specific motivation or trip purpose associated with it. In fact, it is within this dimension that many of the sub-fields of the study of tourism find their genesis. One such sub-field is sport tourism which is defined as *sport motivated travel away from the home environment for a limited time where sport is characterised by unique rule sets, competition related to physical prowess, and a ludic or playful nature* (Hinch and Higham 2000, in press).

Figure 1 provides a graphic representation of the sport tourism research framework used in this study. Each of the three dimensions encompasses a range of themes or elements. Due to space constraints, this paper reports on one set of relationships within this framework; that is the relationships between sport as a motivation for travel and the spatial dimension of tourism. It is our contention that recent changes to rugby union in New Zealand have had substantive impacts on the spatial characteristics of travel relating to Rugby Super 12. Fundamental changes to the sport dimension of the framework are manifest in 1) new rules, 2) the emergence of different player skill sets with a coexistent change in the nature of the competition, and, 3) the further commodification of the sport through professionalisation. The nature of the resulting spatial impacts can be found in the areas of the development of locations hosting Super 12 matches, the development of regional destination imagery associated with the Highlanders franchise and the development of the sport tourism landscape.

Figure 1   Framework for Sport Tourism Research

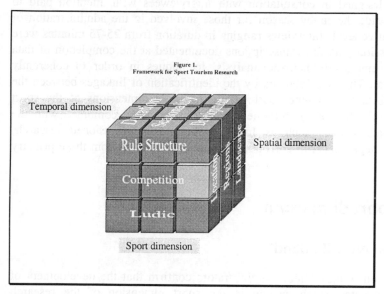

Figure 1.
Framework for Sport Tourism Research

Methods

In order to achieve an insight into the tourism implications of Rugby Super 12 within the Highlanders region, a qualitative research methodology was developed. The collection of data via semi structured interviews was adopted to allow the detailed investigation of changes to Rugby Super 12 spectatorship driven by the professionalisation of Rugby Union and the development of Rugby Super 12. Qualitative methods were required as the researchers sought to achieve specific and detailed responses from a range of respondents, rather than eliciting responses from a standard format for comparison between respondents (Banister, Burman, Parker, Taylor and Tindall, 1996). This research was designed to explore relationships within and between professional groups with a depth of detail that could only be achieved through qualitative methods. Semi-structured interviews were considered appropriate due to the need for flexibility based on the positions and comments of the respective interviewees.

The selection of interviewees considered the need for insight into changes to both the sport and tourism dimensions of the framework as they apply within the study area. The criteria for the selection of interviewees extended to the need for experienced administrators within their respective fields to comment accurately on the changes that had taken place during the period under review. This necessitated the selection of sport and tourism administrators with experience in their respective positions and fields dating to 1996, the inaugural year of the Rugby Super 12 competition.

Semi-structured interviews were conducted with rugby administrators in each of the three member rugby unions within the Otago Highlanders franchise (North Otago, Otago and Southland). Economic development staff and Regional Tourism Organisation staff at Local Government offices (Tourism Waitaki, Dunedin City Council and Invercargill City Council) were also interviewed in order to shed light on the tourism potential that Rugby Super 12 offers. Eleven interviewees from these organisations were selected and contacted. An interview schedule was designed in consultation with interviewees with attention paid to conducting interviews outside the rugby season for those involved in the administration of the sport at the representative level. Interviews ranging in duration from 25-75 minutes were tape recorded with permission, and full transcriptions documented at the completion of data collection. Data analysis employed 'thematic analysis' techniques in order to coherently organise interview material. This was followed by the identification of linkages between the responses of interviewees and the themes outlined in the three dimensions of the sport tourism research framework (Figure 1). Interview transcriptions were combined with the analysis of secondary data sources such as Industry Reports, commissioned research, newspaper articles and strategic plans, to corroborate the results derived from these primary methods.

Changes to the sport dimension

Professional rugby in New Zealand

Interview transcriptions from Rugby Union administrators confirm that the development of Rugby Super 12 has generated much change in the sport dimension of the research framework (Figure 1). Each of the three themes illustrated on the sport dimension have been extensively modified in the process of creating a professional Rugby Union competition (Table 1). The rule structure of Rugby Super 12, for example, has been altered with the stated aim of promoting the entertainment value of rugby (Otago Rugby Football Union 1998). The consequence has been the adoption of a faster style of rugby, a move encouraged by new substitution rules and an extended half-time interval. New lineout rules have been introduced to reduce the territorial advantages of kicking the ball and promote attacking play with the ball in hand. Restart and dead ball rules have also been introduced to maximise 'ball in play' time during the 80 minutes of the match. These rule changes are enforced by professional referees who, under the directions of SANZAR, have been instructed to minimise stoppages of play. The effect has been to encourage and reward skilful running play, which is attractive to spectators.

Table 1   Changes to the sport dimension of professional Super 12 Rugby Union

Rule structure
1. New rules designed to speed up play (e.g. substitution rules and extend half time breaks).
2. New rules to encourage attacking play and the maintenance of possession (e.g. lineout rules).
3. New rules to promote 'ball in play' time (e.g. dead ball and restart rules).
4. Professional referees and touch judges directed to facilitate continuous play.
5. SANZAR directive on rule interpretation to minimise stoppages of play (e.g. advantage rule).
6. Disciplinary rules introduced to eliminate illegal play.
7. Development of a judicial system designed to reduce foul play.

Competition
1. Points system developed to reward try scoring and guarantee 80 minutes of intense play.
2. The involvement of international rather than domestic teams.
3. Amalgamation of twenty-seven provincial teams into five regional franchises.
4. Drafting introduced to ensure that only the most talented players are selected to play Super 12.
5. Audio networked referees and touch judges
6. The scheduling of pre-season warm-up games to ensure a high level of early season performance.
7. The entertainment packaging of Super 12 to act as a vehicle for its branding and promotion.

Ludic nature
1. Professional players with greater attention paid to fitness, skill base and match preparation.
2. Professional management teams travelling in association with players.
3. Enhanced public liaison through school visits, advertising, competitions and arrangements for young fans and disabled children to meet the players.
4. Creation of five franchise headquarters each representing professional regional teams.
5. Required standard of stadium facilities to act as headquarters for a Super 12 franchise. SANZAR/NZRFU have power to revoke or modify franchise status.
6. Need for floodlighting, seating capacity and television production facilities to host professional, globally televised sport.

The nature of provincial rugby **competition** has also changed through the development of Rugby Super 12. Most obviously, the competition has involved the amalgamation of twenty-seven provincial unions into five Super 12 regions (with possible implications for associated travel patterns). The competition points system has changed. Teams earn points for winning, but they also earn bonus points by (a) scoring four or more tries during the game and/or (b) by losing by a margin of seven points or less. The result has been to promote an open and attacking style of play (Otago Rugby Football Union 1998). Bonus points have, in some cases, allowed teams to qualify for the semi-finals over rival teams who have recorded more wins, but failed to gain bonus points. This is the ultimate reward for attacking play and a fact that has effectively changed the skill set required of players at this level of sport (Southland Rugby Union 1998). This also ensures that teams still have much to play for in the last quarter of the game even if the overall result is beyond doubt. The outcome appears to be a new rugby philosophy for many teams in which risk taking and flair have been promoted over conservative styles of play. The international nature of the competition is also an important development in professional rugby as it has widened the appeal of Rugby Super 12. Other competition developments include the creation of regional teams, the implementation of a player draft system (to ensure the involvement of only the most skilled players) and audio-networked referees and touch judges to make them audible to television commentators and viewers.

The **ludic** nature of professional rugby was also seen to have changed with the advent of Rugby Super 12. While the essential elements of play remain, the players involved are contracted to Rugby Super 12 as professionals over the months of February – May (inclusive) and paid accordingly. This, according to Loy *et al.* (1989), represents an intriguing junction for the concepts of work and leisure or business and play, generally considered to exist only in distinction to each other. As a consequence, the players are also contracted to undertake fitness training (December - January), play preseason warm up matches (January - February), and meet public liaison, school visit and advertising commitments. School children have greater access to players and the public image of rugby and rugby players has changed commensurate with the professionalisation of the code (North Otago Rugby Union 1998). These changes have increased the profile of rugby through its commodification, widened its spectator appeal and made it far more competitive in terms of the discretionary leisure dollar (Otago Rugby Football Union 1998). This being so, it seems likely that changes to the sport dimension will have held implications for the spatial (eg distances people will travel to attend matches) and temporal (eg length of stay at the destination) dimensions illustrated on Figure 1. The following section explores these avenues of inquiry within the spatial dimension.

The spatial dimension of tourism in southern New Zealand

Interviewees confirmed that, from their perspective the transition to professional rugby and the development of Super 12 had implications for tourism within the region. Many of these changes relate to changing spatial patterns of tourism within the Highlanders franchise area. While the authors recognise the close relationship between the spatial and temporal elements of tourism, this paper focuses on the spatial elements of changes associated with travel into and within the Highlanders region.

The three spatial elements of tourism identified in Figure 1 were considered by interviewees to have been moderated by the development of the professional Super 12 competition (Table 2). Various aspects of change within the spatial dimension were identified by interviewees. Location, in the context of the research framework, describes the possibility that Rugby Super 12 may have affected patterns of travel into locations hosting Super 12 games (be they pre-season or regular season fixtures). That the success of Rugby Super 12 had extended distance decay travel patterns associated with rugby spectatorship achieved a general consensus. The North Otago Rugby Union (1998), for example, identified that *"an astronomical number of people make the trip to Dunedin* (from Oamaru) *to watch the Highlanders in the Super 12, but they don't come to watch a local game of rugby"*. The focus on entertainment value was generally considered to attract people from further afield to be spectators at Rugby Super 12 games.

Table 2   Changes to the spatial dimensions of tourism in the Highlanders Super 12 franchise region

Location
1. Extension of distance decay travel patterns.
2. Creation of new rugby spectator markets travelling to the central location to watch rugby.
3. Designation of five Super 12 franchise headquarters which are central locations for travel flows.
4. Travel into the central location associated with the status of professional teams as groups of tourists
5. Intra- and inter-region tourism patterns associated with travel of supporters to the central location
6. Potential to redistribute international travel flows within southern New Zealand into the host city.
7. Development of secondary locations competing to host pre-season warm-up matches.

Region
1. Creates a regional differentiation of the New Zealand tourism product in the minds of domestic and international travellers.
2. Carisbrook has become and icon for southern New Zealand with implications for the movement of travellers in the southern macro region
3. Greater international traveller awareness of distinct regional identities, values and lifestyles, history and heritage.
4. Promotion of urban tourism destination status for franchise headquarters
5. Television promotion of tourist attractions and activities within the region (packaging of sport for a television audience).
6. Break down of provincial parochialism within the region

Landscape
1. *Physical*: Development of locations such as Carisbrook (Dunedin), Homestead Stadium (Invercargill) and Centennial Park (Oamaru) will implications for the sport tourism landscape within the region.
2. *Cultural*: The image associated with rugby has changed from one of brute strength and aggression to speed, skill and tactics with implications for the cultural landscape
3. Improved spectator experience through the development of a safer, cleaner facilities and enhanced viewing experience with implications for perceptions of the sport landscape.
4. *Social*: Development of night sport and associated entertainment packaging has transformed the social landscape Super 12 has become a social as well as a sporting occasion.

This suggests that new markets for rugby spectatorship have been created through careful modification of the sport dimension (Figure 1). However, the tourism benefits for host locations were found to extend beyond expanded flows of travel into the central location. Host cities were considered to also benefit from the secondary travel motivations of 'new rugby markets'. *"A lot of people travel, particularly to Dunedin, do a bit of shopping, or, if they have relatives, stay with them... it is a big family day out and sometimes they make a whole weekend of it"* (North Otago Rugby Union, 1998).

It transpires that central locations hosting Rugby Super 12 games in the second half of the regular season benefit additionally from the increased likelihood of inter-regional tourism associated with the Rugby Super 12 competition. Teams that remain in contention for the semi-final play-offs receive increased domestic support as the competition advances (due to the involvement of teams from three different countries). It transpires that *"Carisbrook gets such good numbers of people into the ground because it attracts spectators from the wider region... and from one region to another as you get through towards the end of the season"* (North Otago Rugby Union, 1998). Both North Otago Rugby Union (1998) and Tourism Waitaki (1998) staff in Oamaru reported travel flows into Dunedin from as far north as Christchurch (part of the rival Canterbury Crusaders region) during the 1998 Rugby Super 12 season when both teams remained in contention for the semi-finals).

Indeed Tourism Dunedin and the Economic Development Unit (Dunedin City Council, 1998) speculate on the potential for Rugby Super 12 to redistribute international visitors in Southern New Zealand into the primary location. They submit that Rugby Super 12 in itself is perhaps insufficient to attract international tourism, but may act as a secondary motivation to travel. If so, the consequences may include some modification of the spatial aspects of travel itineraries to include travel to the Rugby Super 12 location. Any such itinerary change is unlikely to occur in the absence of wider tourist activity during the visit to the Rugby Super 12 location. It seems that Rugby Super 12 may be an important secondary motivation that may act to 'tip the scales' during the travel and destination decision-making processes, while also perhaps influencing travel itinerary planning.

To a certain degree these tourism benefits extend to secondary and tertiary locations. Interviews revealed that *"some people travel to every single game... even the pre-season games in places such as Queenstown"* (North Otago Rugby Union 1998). This raises the spectre of competition between locations within the region, primary, secondary and third tier centres, to host Super 12 matches and harness the tourism potential that they offer. This has certainly been recognised by the North Otago Rugby Union which has succeeded in hosting one pre-season match involving the Otago Highlanders in both 1998 and 1999. *"On February 14, 1999, against the ACT Brumbies, we're expecting the crowd to be bulging at the seams... there are a few alterations going on at present with a view to that"* (North Otago Rugby Union 1998).

The second element illustrated on the spatial dimension (Figure 1) is titled **region** in order to convey the potential for sport and, in this case Rugby Super 12, to act as a vehicle for region differentiation. In discussing this possibility, interviewees identified that the Highlanders brand serves as a vehicle for regional differentiation that operates on both domestic and international travel markets. *"The Highlanders brand reflects the terrain, the Scottish heritage and the values of the region: honesty, integrity and hard work...it is very much reflective of what we are all about* (Otago Rugby Football Union 1998). This, according to the Dunedin Council's Economic Development Unit *"translates into actual value for tourism"* (Dunedin City Council, 1998). The branding of the Highlanders represents a vehicle for regional tourism differentiation and the promotion of a regional tourism product. This is confirmed by Laidlaw (1998) who states that *"towns and regions are identifying with their team...as an expression of the town's own brand identity"*.

The result, in all probability, has been a greater traveller awareness of the distinct regional identities, values and lifestyles, history and heritage of Southern New Zealand. If this is so, then Rugby Super 12 contributes to the tourism industry in several ways. One, clearly, is to promote awareness of the tourism resources of the southern macro-region. Its wider contribution extends to regional differentiation of the New Zealand tourism product and its potential role in tourism promotion. The contribution of Rugby Super 12 to urban destination status and the promotion of cities as tourist destinations is also considered in this theme. Indeed several interviewees identified the strong link between Otago Rugby and the tertiary educational institution of Otago University (Otago Rugby Football Union, 1998; Southland Rugby Union, 1998). These linkages clearly benefit tourism and non-tourism avenues of economic development within the Highlanders region.

The geographical concept of **landscape** represents the third spatial element in the research framework. This element incorporates aspects of change to the sporting landscape arising from the development of sport. In the case of the Super 12 three fundamental aspects of change to the landscape were identified through data collection. First, the physical landscape, and tourist perceptions of it, has changed with the advent of Rugby Super 12. The sporting resources of Southern New Zealand have traditionally centred on the alpine region of Central Otago and the international tourist resort of Queenstown (Higham, E., 1994). The sporting resources of this area focus in winter upon skiing, and extend to adventure activities associated with mountain, lake and river resources. Tramping (hiking), climbing, parapenting, rafting, jetboating and fishing are some of the outstanding natural sporting resources of the interior region. The unbalanced distribution of natural resources for sport within the Highlanders franchise has been redressed to some degree by the development of sporting ('built' rather than natural) facilities in the coastal region. Rugby Super 12 has, in the case of the franchise headquarters, necessitated the development of stadium facilities to meet international standards. The potential tourism benefits of Rugby Super 12 have also acted to stimulate stadium development in secondary and third tier locations such as Invercargill (Homestead Stadium) and Oamaru (Centennial Park). These developments have brought significant change to the sporting landscape, in physical terms.

The landscape theme within the spatial dimension extends from the physical to the cultural and social landscapes. The former describes the change that Rugby Super 12 has heralded for the culture associated with Rugby Union in New Zealand. Rugby Union has traditionally been a male dominated sporting code. Many literary (Macdonald 1996) and photographic (Bush 1997) contributions on this subject record the minor role that women played in this sport throughout all but the last years of the twentieth century. The advent of Rugby Super 12 has coincided with and perhaps contributed to a change in the culture associated with Rugby Union. Female involvement in rugby, which once involved little more than washing players' uniforms, now extends to playing, coaching, team management, medical and administrative involvement as well as spectatorship. A clear link between the physical and cultural aspects of this theme emerged during data collection. The Otago Rugby Football Union (1998), for example, states that *"the redevelopment of stadium facilities has really facilitated the family and the female involvement"*.

The social linkages between players and public provides another aspect of change arising from professional Rugby Super 12. Changes to the social landscape have taken place at two levels. First, rugby has been largely transformed from a purely sporting occasion into an entertainment product. While it seems that for some Rugby Super 12 remains a sporting occasion, for others, the entertainment packaging associated with Rugby Super 12 has made it a social experience. It emerges that *"the product is still rugby but the extra 6000 spectators are coming to see the fireworks and the bands and the hoopla"* (Otago Rugby Football Union 1998). A preponderance of young people in certain sections of the stadium (Carisbrook) has been a feature of Rugby Super 12. For these people Rugby Super 12 has become a feature of the social landscape.

Secondly, Rugby Super 12 and the development of professional rugby have resulted in a new philosophy regarding the importance of links between players and public. This philosophy has resulted in young people becoming stakeholders in Rugby Union. Indeed 'ownership' of the team, in much the same way as it is described by Hornby (1997) in reference to England Premier Football fanship, has become a feature of Rugby Super 12. The North Otago Rugby Union (1998) recognises this point by commenting that *"our plans are to have the Highlanders here (Oamaru) for a 2-3 day camp, to be available to the town itself, the people and the schools"*. In doing so, the Otago Highlanders have contributed to changes in the social and cultural landscape, with developmental implications for the future of sport and tourism.

Conclusion

Much debate surrounds the changes brought upon New Zealand rugby since the advent of professionalism in 1995. There is little doubt that the Super 12 has been a success in terms of spectatorship, entertainment and profile. Laidlaw (1998) confirms that with the colour and drama of professional rugby, the *"spectator catchment has widened"*. From this scene arises a variety of factors that affect flows of tourists into and across the regional tourism landscape. This article explores the spatial dimension of tourism in the Highlanders Super 12 franchise. The interpretation of interview transcripts supports the conclusion that Super 12 has affected tourism in all three spatial themes. The travel motivations associated with Rugby Super 12 were found to have changed significantly through the professionalisation and commodification of the sport. This has affected spatial travel patterns in terms of extending distance decay thresholds, while also extending the demographic profile of rugby spectators. Rugby Super 12 acts as a vehicle for regional differentiation and the development of sporting facilities has held implications for the tourism landscape. This qualitative programme of research supports the notion that the introduction of Rugby Super 12 has had various implications for the spatial elements of tourism identified in Figure 1. The logical extension of this work is quantitative studies that will provide more definitive measures of these impacts.

Acknowledgements

The authors acknowledge the willing participation of sport and tourism administrators from the following Rugby Unions and Local Government Organisations: Otago Rugby Football Union, Southland Rugby Union, North Otago Rugby Union, Dunedin City Council Economic Development Unit, Tourism Dunedin, Southland Economic Development Unit, Tourism Waitaki and Invercargill City Council. The authors also acknowledge Richard Mitchell (Centre for Tourism, University of Otago) for the production of Figure 1.

References

Bale, J. (1982), *Sport and Place: A Geography of Sport in England, Scotland and Wales*. C. Hurst and Company, London.

Banister, P., Burman, E., Parker, I., Taylor, M. and Tindall, C. (1996), *Qualitative Methods in Psychology: A Research Guide*. Open University Press. Philadelphia. U.S.A.

Bush, P. (1986), *The Game for All New Zealand*. Moa Publications, Auckland, New Zealand.

Fitzimmons, P. (1996),*The Rugby War*. Sydney, N.S.W. Harper Sports.

Garmise, M. (ed.), (1987), *Proceedings of the International Seminar and Workshop on Outdoor Education, Recreation and Sport Tourism*. Emmanuel Gill Publishing, Israel.

Glyptis, S. (1991), Sport and tourism. *Progress in Tourism, Recreation and Hospitality Management*. Vol. Belhaven, London.

Hall, C. M. (1992), Adventure, sport and health tourism, in Weiler, B. and Hall, C.M. *Special Interest Tourism*, Belhaven Press, London, 141-158.

Hall, C. M. (1997), Recent progress in sport tourism in New Zealand, *Tourism Recreation Research*. 22 (2): 63.

Higham, E. (1996), *The regional structure of tourism in Southern New Zealand*.

Unpublished Masters Thesis (Commerce), University of Otago. Dunedin, New Zealand.

Higham, J. E. S. (1996). The Bledisloe Cup: Quantifying the direct economic benefits of event tourism, with ramifications for a city in economic transition. *Festival Management and Event Tourism*. 4(3/4):107-116.

Hinch, T. D. and Higham, J. E. S. (2000), Sport Tourism: A framework for research *International Journal of Tourism Research* (in press).

Hornby, N. (1992), *Fever Pitch*. Victor Gollancz Ltd. London.

Kurtzman, J. and Zauhar, J. (1995), Tourism Sport International Council, *Annals of Tourism Research*, 22 (3): 707-708.

Kurtzman, J. and Zauhar, J. (1997), Wave in time: the sports tourism phenomena, *Journal of Sport Tourism*, 4 (2): 5-20,

http://www.mcb.co.uk/journals/jst/archive/vol14no2/welcome.html. (28 May 1998).

Labrie, P. (1988), The long term tourism and economic impact of major sports events, in *Tourism Research: Expanding Boundaries,* Travel and Tourism Research Association,

Nineteenth Annual Conference, Montreal, Quebec, Canada. 19-23 June 1988, Bureau of Economic and Business Research, Graduate School of Business, University of Utah, Salt Lake City, 103-105.

Laidlaw, C. (1998), Rugby's Rip van Winkle awakes. *Otago Daily Times*. 28.10.98. p. 9.

Lawson, R., Thyne, M. and Young, T. (1997), *New Zealand Holidays: A Travel Lifestyle Study*. Marketing Department, University of Otago, Dunedin, New Zealand.

Leiper, N. (1981), Towards a cohesive curriculum in tourism: the case for a distinct discipline, *Annals of Tourism Research,* 8, 1, 69-74.

Leiper, N. (1990), Tourist attraction systems, *Annals of Tourism Research,* 17: 367-384.

Loy, J. W., McPherson, B. D., and Kenyon, G. (1989), *Sport and Social Systems*. Addison-Wesley, Reading, MA.

Macdonald, F. (1996), *The Game of Our Lives*. Penguin Books (NZ) Ltd. Auckland, New Zealand.

McPherson, B. D., Curtis, J. E. and Loy, J. W. (1989), *The Social Significance of Sport*. Human Kinetics, Champaign, Illinois.

Murphy, P. (1985), *Tourism: A Community Approach*, Methuen, New York and London.

Nogawa, H., Yamaguchi, Y., and Hagi, Y. (1996), An empirical research study on Japanese sport tourism in sport-for-all events: case studies of a single-night event and a multiple-night event, *Journal of Travel Research,* 35 (2): 46-54.

NZRFU 1998a. *History of the Super 12.*

http://www.nzrugby.com/nzrfu/Pages/Super12/s12histf.htm

NZRFU (1998b), NZRFU *brand values and positioning articulation*. Unpublished report. NZRFU. Wellington, New Zealand.

Okrant, M. J. (1988), Sporting events: an untapped market share for travel and tourism, in *Tourism Research: Expanding Boundaries*, Travel and Tourism Research Association, Nineteenth Annual Conference, Montreal, Quebec, Canada. 19-23 June 1988, Bureau of Economic and Business Research, Graduate School of Business, University of Utah, Salt Lake City, 91.

Redmond, G. (1991), Changing styles of sports tourism: Industry/consumer interactions in Canada, the USA and Europe, in M.T. Sinclair & M.J. Stabler (eds.), *The Tourism Industry: An International Analysis*, CAB International, Wallingford, Oxon.

Rooney, J. F. (1988), Mega-sports events as tourist attractions: a geographical analysis, in *Tourism Research: Expanding Boundaries*, Travel and Tourism Research Association,

Nineteenth Annual Conference, Montreal, Quebec, Canada, June 19-23, (1988), Bureau of Economic and Business Research, Graduate School of Business, University of Utah, Salt Lake City, 93-99.

Southland Economic Development Unit (1998*), Economic Impact Report: Highlanders versus Golden Cats Rugby match*. 28 March 1998. Unpublished report. Invercargill, New Zealand.

Standeven, J. and De Knop, P. (1998), *Sport Tourism*. Human Kinetics, USA.

Stevens, T. and van den Broek, M. (1997), Sport and tourism- natural partners in strategies for tourism development. *Tourism Recreation Research*. 22 (2): 1-3.

STIC Research Unit, (1995), Sports tourism categories revisited, *Journal of Sport Tourism*, 2, 3.

Weed, M. E., and Bull, C. J. (1997a), Integrating sport and tourism: a review of regional policies in England, *Progress in Tourism and Hospitality Research,* 3: 129-148.

Whitson, D. and Macintosh, D. (1996), The global circus: international sport, tourism, and the marketing of cities, *Journal of Sport and Social Issues*. 20 (3): 278-295.

World Tourism Organisation, (1981), *Technical Handbook on the Collection and Presentation of Domestic and International Tourism Statistics,* WTO.

Zurn, M. (1973), Tourism and motor activity of Cracow inhabitants, *International Review of Sport Sociology*. 1 (8): 79-94.

The motivations of trekkers in the Annapurna area of Nepal - an environmental link?

Andrew Holden

University of Luton, UK

John Sparrowhawk

University of North London, UK

Introduction

The Annapurna area of Nepal covers an area of 7000 km^2 and contains an outstanding array of both biological and cultural diversity (Gurung and De Coursey, 1994). This diversity includes 474 species of birds, 101 species of mammals and 1226 species of plants (Banskota and Sherma, 1998). The rare fauna in the area includes the snow leopard *(Panthera uncia)*, musk deer *(Moschus rnoschifrrus)*, blue sheep *(Pseudois nayaur)*, and the red panda *(Ailurus fulgens)* (Bajracharya, 1993). The area also contains the spectacular mountain scenery of the Annapurna mountain range and interesting geomorphologic features, such as the Kali Gandaki river valley, which is the world's deepest, cutting an 1824 metre chasm between the summits of Annapurna 1 (8091 metres) and Dhaulagiri (8151 metres) (Gurung and De Coursey, 1994).

It is the rich cultural and biological diversity of the area that has made it attractive to the growing numbers of tourists who go trekking. The growth in tourism to Nepal has been rapid, rising from 6,179 in 1962 (when official records began) to 393,613 in 1996 (Department of Tourism, 1997). International tourism is important for strengthening the national economy, earning foreign exchange and creating extra demand in the economy for goods and services, subsequently creating employment opportunities. Until 1949, Nepal was closed to the outside world and the economic development of Nepal is subsequently a central priority for the country. The combination of isolation, an over-dependency upon Sino-Indian trade, a lack of raw materials and an upwardly spiralling population have contributed to making Nepal into one of the world's poorest nations (Sparrowhawk and Holden, 1999).

Besides contributing to national wealth creation in Nepal, tourism is also an important means of aiding regional development. The areas of the country that have developed mountain trekking tourism, notably the Annapurna area and the Solu-Khumbu area which includes Everest, are wealthier than those areas of the country that have not developed tourism. As well as inter-regional differences, intra-regional differences also exist, with villages that accommodate trekkers and are situated on the main trekking routes being wealthier than those that are not (Rogers and Aitchison, 1998). The number of trekkers who go to the Annapurna area is now over 40000 per annum. With the accompanying support staffs that support the trekkers, especially in organised groups, the total number of visitors per annum can be estimated to be approximately 80000 (Gurung and De Coursey, 1994).

Although the arrival of tourism has brought undoubted economic benefits to the Annapurna area, its development has also brought environmental problems and placed pressure on the natural resources of the area. The traditional material used for the construction of housing and for cooking has been wood. Whilst a balance existed between the needs of local people and the use of forest resources, the addition of extra trekkers into the area, has meant this use has become unsustainable. The demand of trekkers for food and often-hot showers every day means that extra demand is being placed upon forest resources, and deforestation has become a major environmental problem. Additional environmental problems have also been created by problems of disposing of the human sewage and toilet paper generated by trekkers. Where toilet facilities exist, they have been historically located too close to the streams, and pollution of the water supply for local people is a major concern. Also, the importation of bottled water and other food imports with plastic wrapping means that littering and waste disposal are issues of concern in the Annapurna area.

Although many of the environmental problems are associated with the trekkers, little is understood about the motivations of the trekkers, and the reasons why they trek in Nepal. Consequently, the rest of this paper is concerned with reporting the results of interviews with 156 trekkers in the Annapurna area, about their motivations for trekking. The subsequent discussion is based upon what the results infer about how trekkers interact with the environment and the possible implications for environmental management of the area.

Motivation studies in tourism

Allusions to why people decide to take certain actions had, up to the beginning of the twentieth century, belonged to the domain of philosophers. For example, the 'realists', believed that human behaviour was directed by pain avoidance and pleasure seeking, known as the concept of hedonism (Gross, 1992). Alternatively, the 'rationalists' believed that reason determined what people do and therefore people were responsible for their own actions, making a concept of motivation unnecessary.

With the advancement of biology as a science and the development of Darwin's theories of evolution at the end of the last century, motivation began to be analysed using scientific as opposed to philosophical principles, and the discipline of psychology emerged based upon a scientific approach to understanding behaviour. However nearly a century later, despite various attempts to produce theories of motivation, there still remains no universally agreed theoretical approach by psychologists to understanding motivation (Atkinson *et al.*, 1983; Gross, 1992; and Davidoff, 1994). Unsurprisingly, there is no agreed theoretical approach to understanding leisure and tourism motivation, as Fondness (1994:559) comments: 'A widely accepted integrated theory of the needs and personal goals driving these reasons given for travel and the benefits sought from it is however lacking'.

Any researcher examining the motivations of tourists is therefore reliant upon the adoption of techniques that are used within other disciplines such as social psychology. One application that permits a multi-variate and dynamic analysis of motivations is the 'travel ladder', proposed by Pearce (1988) who suggests that people have 'careers' in tourism, just as at work. Just as in a work career a travel career is both consciously determined and purposeful, although an important difference is that a career in tourism is more likely to be intrinsically motivated than a work career, which is likely to be extrinsically motivated. The basis of the 'travel career' is that motivations for participating in tourism are dynamic, and will change with age, life cycle stages, and the influence of other people. Additionally, past tourism experiences are likely to influence future behaviour.

Methodology

The survey work was conducted during 1999, in the Annapurna area, with 156 trekkers being interviewed. The surveys were carried out in the two main trekking and lodging areas of Ghorepani and Tatopani, which are 'honey pot' areas, for trekkers who are walking the popular 'Jomosom Trail' and the 'Annapurna Circuit'. Interviews were carried out at random, based upon the use of a self-complete questionnaire, and also involved unstructured discussions with trekkers about their motivations and attitudes to the environment of Annapurna. Interviewees were asked about the importance of 22 motivations to explain why they were trekking. The 22 motivations were based upon the work of previous leisure and tourism researchers including Pearce (1988). For each motivation, the attached importance was noted on a Likert scale, ranging from 5 (very important) to 1 (very unimportant).

Results

The demographic characteristics of the trekkers, shown in Table 1, suggest that trekkers are more likely to be male than female although this difference is marginal. The results also reveal, perhaps as would be expected given the energetic nature of trekking in the mountains and the fairly basic conditions of accommodation in the Annapurna area, the distribution of trekkers ages is skewed towards a younger profile. In this case 68 per cent of the sample was under 35 years of age and 83 per cent was under the age of 45 years.

Table 1   Gender and Age characteristics

Gender	Male	Female
Percentage	54	46
Age group (percentage figure of total)		
< 16 years	2.6	0
16-24	11.0	11.0
25-34	23.2	20.0
35-44	7.7	7.1
45-54	5.2	4.5
55-64	3.2	2.6
65 +	1.3	0.6

To aid the analysis of the twenty-two motivations included in the survey, they were separated into groups that are loosely based upon the work of Pearce (1988). The groups are in order of ascendancy; 'relaxation', 'thrills', 'relationships', 'self-esteem and development', and 'fulfilment'. Five motivations were included in the 'relaxation' group as shown in Table 2.

Table 2   The ratings of importance of the needs associated with relaxation (all figures are expressed in percentages)

Motivation	Very Important	Important	Neither important or unimportant	Unimportant	Very important
To relax mentally	37.0	33.8	16.9	5.8	6.5
To enjoy nature	68.6	28.2	3.2	0	0
To relax physically	10.3	23.2	32.9	16.8	16.8
To be in a calm atmosphere	34.8	43.2	16.1	3.2	2.6
To have a change from my daily routine	45.8	34.8	11.0	4.5	3.9

The results highlight the trekkers' needs for change, enjoyment of nature, mental relaxation and calm. It is suggested that the expressed motivations represent a desire for escapism from the pressures of the home environments that trekkers originate from. The majority of the trekkers are from economically developed countries, in which the common view is held, that people have increasingly stressful lifestyles. Implicit in the results is a health dimension within the motivation to trek. The desire to improve one's physical health has historically been an important motivatory factor for undertaking travel. In this case, the mental health dimension is emphasised with physical relaxation being important to only 35 per cent of the sample, perhaps a reflection of the sedentary nature of a post-modem western lifestyle. The results also point to a high positive correlation between the enjoyment of nature and the achievement of mental relaxation.

The next category of motivations examined the extent to which thrills and excitement were important motivatory factors for participation in trekking as is shown in Table 3.

Table 3   The ratings of importance of the needs associated with thrills and excitement (all figures are expressed in percentages)

Motivation	Very Important	Important	Neither important or unimportant	Unimportant	Very important
To feel excited	19.9	35.9	30.8	11.5	1.9
To feel stimulated	30.3	36.8	22.6	9.0	1.3
To feel a sense of 'freedom'	30.3	38.1	18.1	8.4	5.2
To place myself in risky situations	4.5	17.3	19.9	21.2	37.2

The desire for risk is not of importance in motivating the majority of the trekkers. This is a significant difference in comparison with other types of mountain tourists, such as downhill skiers and mountaineers, for whom the risk associated with the activity is likely to be an important motivatory factor. However, a sense of freedom and the need for stimulation are important to the majority of the trekkers. Given that risk is of little importance for motivating the majority of the trekkers, it is therefore probable, that the need for stimulation and a sense of freedom are associated with the environmental surroundings rather with the actual physical activity of trekking.

The levels of importance that the trekkers attach to social interaction are shown in Table 4.

Table 4   The ratings of importance of the needs associated with social interaction (all figures are expressed in percentages)

Motivation	Very Important	Important	Neither important or unimportant	Unimportant	Very important
To develop close friendships	5.8	20.8	41.6	17.5	14.3
To spend time with loved ones	14.9	20.8	26.6	13.0	24.7
To meet a new boyfriend/ girlfriend	0	0.6	13.0	11.7	74.7
To have a good time with friends	22.6	41.3	20.6	7.7	7.7
To make new friends	8.4	32.3	31.6	15.5	12.3

The results emphasise the importance of friendship through trekking with the most important social need being attached to having a good time with friends. The results probably reflect the nature of the trekking market, which is predominantly composed of couples, friends and groups, rather than families or single people.

The next set of needs related to those associated with self-esteem and development. The responses to these needs are shown in Table 5.

Table 5   The ratings of importance of the needs associated with self-esteem and development (all figures are expressed in percentages)

Motivation	Very Important	Important	Neither important or unimportant	Unimportant	Very important
To be in a competitive atmosphere	1.3	5.2	14.8	14.2	64.5
To challenge my abilities	23.2	36.1	20.6	11.6	8.4
To impress friends at home by saying I am going trekking in Nepal to get fit	5.1	10.9	21.8	16.0	46.2
To get fit	17.9	42.9	24.4	5.1	9.6
To feel a sense of control over the natural environment	3.2	10.3	27.1	16.1	43.2

Based upon the responses to the statement, 'To impress friends at home by saying I am going trekking in Nepal', it would seem that trekkers place little importance upon gaining esteem from others. More emphasis seems to be placed upon their own development through challenging their abilities and getting fit. The need for competition, or a feeling of domination and control over the environment, is low in importance for the majority of the trekkers.

The last set of needs deals with those associated with fulfilment as is shown in Table 6.

Table 6   The ratings of importance of the needs associated with fulfilment (all figures are expressed in percentages)

Motivation	Very Important	Important	Neither important or unimportant	Unimportant	Very important
To increase my knowledge of the natural environment	19.9	41.0	30.1	5.1	3.8
To feel a sense of solitude	10.9	29.5	34.0	12.8	12.8
Too feel close to nature	43.6	42.9	9.6	2.6	1.3

The results stress the importance of nature as a central theme of the experience for the majority of the trekkers. For 86 per cent of the sample it was important to feel close to nature and for 60 per cent it was important to increase their knowledge of the natural environment.

Discussion

The results emphasise that the environment of the Annapurna area plays a central role in motivating people to trek there, in the sense that it both directly and indirectly, plays a part in meeting their expressed needs. This is not perhaps surprising as the promotional images of the Annapurna area are of its physical and cultural environments. The results also suggest that unlike other groups of mountain tourists such as downhill skiers and mountaineers, trekkers place emphasis on 'being' in the environment, rather than using the environment as a setting for a physical activity to provide stimulation. It would seem that for the majority of the trekkers, the quality of the environment of the Annapurna area offers an opportunity for mental recuperation and stimulation, and critically a place where a change from the routine of everyday life can be achieved.

In the informal discussions with trekkers it also became evident that there was an awareness and concern amongst trekkers over the impact of tourism in the area. Yet, few were aware of the code of conduct aimed at trekkers which had been developed to try to address environmental concerns, even though the code was printed on the back of the trekking permit which is required to gain admittance to the Annapurna area. This was particularly the case for people trekking in groups, many of whom never saw their permits, as the tour guides administered these.

The future planning and environmental management of the Annapurna area is the key factor to ensuring its sustainability and securing an improvement in the well being of the people who inhabit the area. A key part of achieving sustainability will be through modifying aspects of tourist behaviour that are harmful to the environment. The encouraging aspect of the results of this research, is that given that trekkers seem to value the environment for providing the focus of their experience, there exists a real opportunity to educate tourists and to get them to modify aspects of their behaviour which are environmentally harmful. However to achieve this will require raising levels of awareness of the issues. In terms of the future development of the area, there also exists an opportunity to gain the economic benefits of tourism, whilst continuing to attract a type of tourist who places an emphasis on environmental conservation and respect of the local culture. The future of Annapurna should not be jeopardised by the old-fashioned, yet still common notion, that success in tourism is measured by an increasing number of visitor arrivals. Instead careful strategic planning for the area is required, which as well as including land-use and carrying capacity measures, needs to consider marketing and the type of tourist that is compatible with the environmental surroundings of the area. In this sense, the motivational research of tourists has a part to play not only in strategic business decisions, but also in strategic environmental decisions.

References

Atkinson, L. R. and Atkinson, C. R. and Hilgard, R. E. (1983), *Introduction to Psychology,* 8th Edition, Harcourt Brace Jovanich, New York.

Bajracharya, S. B. (1993), *Obtaining Ecological Balance: Contemporary Local Resource Management Practices in the Annapurna Mid-Hill Zone,* Bangkok, AIT.

Banskota, K. and Sharina, B. (1998), Understanding Sustainability in Mountain Tourism: Case Study of Nepal, in East, P., Luger K., Inmann, K (eds) *Sustainability in Mountain Tourism: Perspectives for the Himalayan Countries,* Book Faith India, Delhi, pp 111-146.

Davidoff, L. L. (1994), *Introduction to Psychology,* 3rd edition, McGraw-Hill Book Company, New York.

Department of Tourism (1997), *Nepal Tourism Statistics,* Ministry of Tourism and Civil Aviation, Kathmandu.

Fodness, D. (1994), 'Measuring tourist motivation', *Annals of Tourism Research, 21,* (3), pp 555-581.

Gross, D. R. (1992), *Psychology: The Science of Mind and Behaviour,* 2nd edition, Hodder and Stoughton, London.

Grirung, C. P. and De Coursey, M. (1994), 'The Annapurna Conservation Area Project: a Pioneering Example of Sustainable Tourism' in Cater, E. and Lowman, 0. (eds.) *Ecotourism: A Sustainable Option,* John Wiley and Sons, Chichester, ChI 1, pp 177-194.

Pearce, P. L. (1988), The Ulysses Factor.' Evaluating Visitors in Tourist Settings, Springer-Verlag, New York.

Rogers, P. and Aitchison, J. (1998), *Towards Sustainable Tourism in the Everest Region of Nepal,* IUCN Nepal, Kathmandu.

Sparrowhawk, J. and Holden, A. (1999), 'Human Development; The Role of Tourism Based NGOs in Nepal', *Tourism Recreation Research,* pp 37-44.

The tourist gaze and its games of truth: An elaboration of 'the governmentality' of Foucault via Urry

Keith Hollinshead

University of Luton, UK

Abstract

Following Hollinshead's (1999) dialectical inspection of Foucauldian thought and of the extension of Foucauldian ideas on the power of surveillance (*le regard*) to tourism and travel --- an inspection brought about in response to recent unenquiring commentaries of and about Urry's deft treatment of Foucault's eye - of - power in his much discussed book The Tourist Gaze --- this paper offers further elaboration on the relevance of Foucault's ideas about the manner in which tourism and travel may be seen to constitute a juridical space in which various institutions (and individuals within them) act with micro - fascist or everyday forms of power, judgment, and authority to quietly and frequently unsuspectingly consolidate the dominance of held institutional truths. To that end, the paper provides a further distillation of Foucault's insights on the governmentality of things for tourism/travel in order to help catalyse a portfolio of future research agendas on the objectifying discourse and praxis within the industry. Thereafter, the paper provides an interpretive indexation of what Urry conceivably covered when he attempts to channel Foucauldian notions into the study of tourism/travel via 'the tourist gaze'. Overall, this follow - up paper seeks to encourage the various influential 'practitioners' of everyday tourism studies and everyday tourism management to be more alert to the small but cumulatively huge biases they systematically honour in what they say and do, and thereby in what they themselves continue to become as they help make some peoples, pasts, and places dominant, and coterminously as they frustrate the potential of other populations, other histories, and other locales --- that is, while they grow or stagnate day - by - day on the job.

Introduction

Recently, Hollinshead (1999) provided a useful examination of the French litero - philosophical term *le regard*. He sought to provide a searching examination of Foucault's insights into the eye - of - authority which acts through the institutions, the organisations, and the agencies that act powerfully in tourism management and development and also in tourism research. In probing Foucault's observations on 'surveillance', on 'power - knowledge', and on 'will - to - power', within the *dispostif* (i.e., the governing apparatus) of such institutions/organisations/agencies, Hollinshead attempted to show how 'quiet' and seemingly 'smalltime' but ultimately significant and essentialising powers of judgement and governance may so frequently be caught up within the authoritative mix which constitutes the totalising discourse and the objectifying praxis of those institutions as certain preferred visions of heritage, of society, and of the world are normalised and may be universal through tourism management and/or travel research. Through this distillation of the Foucauldian concept of surveillance, Hollinshead attempted to extend Urry's (1990) earlier adroit translation of the French humanistic construction of *le regard* by revealing how the person who works in tourism management/development (and also the individual who travels) may be seen to be *homo docilis*, that is, someone who not only engages in the petty and the quotidian governance of the world and in the related objectification of its social, cultural, natural, and geographical milieux, but becomes an individual who administrates himself/herself, and thereby disciplines himself/herself through the scopic drive (i.e., the outlooks of surveillance) which he/she supports in his/her everyday work in and across tourism. Thus Hollinshead's (1999) work was an endeavour to sharpen up what could be seen to be the somewhat blunt and unelaborate Foucauldian insights which Urry (1990) had provided in his important text.

One may argue, however, that Hollinshead's (1999) observations were also insufficiently translative for the maturing field of Tourism Studies, and the dictates of available journal space seem to have reduced the degree to which he was able to provide penetrative transcriptions of Foucauldian ideas on normalisation of and through universalised vision and on the objectification of and through totalised talk and practice to tourism studies. Such matters of the everyday dominance and subjugation of peoples, places, and pasts warrants much fuller scrutiny, and much more pointed ferriage of Foucault's constructions into tourism studies. This current paper attempts that conceptual conveyability: it seeks to elaborate further upon Foucault's ideas on the way the scopic drive of institutions in tourism cumulatively totalises the world (something which indeed occurs in all other fields of human endeavour, according to Foucault's theses on the *governmentality* of things) as the so called agents - of - normalcy of those institutions suspectingly (but more powerfully, *unsuspectingly*) indulge in their petty games of truth and participate in their micro - power privilege - making.

This elaboration is built around the provision of two key exhibits. The first, Table 1, constitutes an attempt to show how and where Foucauldian critique can be brought more concertedly into tourism studies, not so much as a fresh bureau of investigative approaches, but more as a re - tooling or re - empowering of the existing conceptual work of the work of Shames and Glover (1989), of Fjellman (1992), of Richter (1994), of Edwards (1996), of Hall (1996), and of others on matters of tourism management and development. The purpose of Table 1 is then to show that Foucauldian insight into the surveillance of organisations and agencies is not merely some vague, esoteric, and acutely philosophical pursuit of little operational value to tourism management and development, but it is a highly luminous and richly catalytic way in which the day to day governance of tourism and travel can be made thinkable and practicable. It is an attempt to show that there are all kinds of readily observable thoughts and conscious and subconscious intentions behind and within the *governmentality* (or, rather, the governmentalities) of tourism, where that which governs "is not just a [removed] power needing to be tamed or a [supreme] authority needing to be legitimised. It is an [everyday] activity and [ubiquitous] art which concerns all [who manage/develop/research] and which touches each [who manage/develop/research]" (Burchell, Gordon, and Miller 1991: x). Table 1 thereby aims to reveal how "there is a parcel of [governing] thought in even the crassest and most obtuse parts of the social reality" (Burchell, Gordon, and Miller 1991: x) of managed tourism, developed travel, and/or the researched trade in either.

Thereafter, Table 2 comprises the endeavour to inspect how much of Foucault's insight into 'governmental rationality' was indeed captured by Urry (1990) in his highly praised work *The Tourist Gaze*. This second exhibit attempts to outline what Urry himself meant when he adapted Foucault's construction of the magisterial gaze of organisations specifically for tourism and travel: viz., what indeed did Urry have in mind by the term the tourist gaze, per se? Table 2 thereby uncovers the ways in which Urry delineated the tourist gaze as that set of disciplinary techniques by which the nature and the practice of the governance of tourism/travel is carried out. This second exhibit thus seeks to clarify and highlight what Urry proffers as the principal characteristics of the microphysics of the power that is the tourist gaze - something that Urry did not himself do accessibly: rather, it is something which has to be painstakingly deconstructed from his important 1990 work. Let us now examine these two tables.

The governmentality of tourism: Forum as a Foucauldian juridical space

In his assessment of how a Foucaudlian approach in tourism studies could conceivably compare with the research agendas of various contemporary investigators of tourism/travel, Hollinshead (1999) examined Foucault's work from the point of view of the following twelve illustrative and suggestive (rather than comprehensive) outlooks:

- the *relations of power;*

- the *normalising consequences* of the exercise of power;

- the *ubiquitous illusory projections* of tourism;

- the *closed fields of knowledge* of tourism;

- the *political apparatus* of tourism;

- the *rhetoric of tradition* in tourism;

- *individual action* in the management/administration of tourism;

- the *seductive properties of* the *semiotics* of tourism;

- invisible sites of *mediated coercion*;

- *transformative political events*;

- the *disjunctive temporalities* of dominant/suppressed populations; and,

- the creation/invention of *'totalised' objects*.

These twelve outlooks, or Foucauldian issue arenas, are now more substantively inspected in Table 1. First, the work of an exemplary *established tourism studies researcher* who is already conducting research in that or a like arena is cited, and then the evidential relevance of Foucault's own line of attack (as translated for tourism studies) is given for that said issue arena. Thereby, the table suggests that Foucauldian forms of critique of governmentality could fruitfully be deployed in tourism studies to pry into:

For issue arena 1: *Relations of Power*

- the making visible of the privilege - bestowing networks of various management/development practices in tourism (which are all too frequently hidden/unsuspected);

For issue arena 2: *Normalising Consequences*

- the making visible of the invented nature of notions of society which are exhibited in tourism (whereby those promoted notions of societal place/societal identity are not so much 'given' as 'made' in discourse and praxis);

For issue arena 3: *Ubiquitous Illusory Projections*

- the making visible of the everyday essentialising power of tourism articulations of people/places/pasts (where so much of the industry's powers of representation and objectification is illusory);

For issue arena 4: *Closed Fields Of Knowledge*

- the making visible of the huge potential for the projection of culturally violent storylines through the discursive suppressions and in-service subjugations of tourism and travel (particularly where are only narrow pre - selected range of storylines is articulated through the entrepreneurial talk or through the commodifed deeds of industry practitioners);

For issue arena 5: *Political Apparatus*

- the making visible of the opaque appartuses of administration and of prejudgement or pre - suppression by which tourism narratives and tourism services are normalised (and on which the promotions and actions of the industry are regularly platformed);

For issue arena 6: *Rhetoric Of Tradition*

- the making visible of the potential role of tourism as an important source of transformative knowledge - production about peoples/places/pasts (not just as a channel of externally derived narrative about things);

For issue arena 7: *Individual Action*

- the making visible of the need for institutions to regularly critique the games of truth they may be indulging in (and of the need for individuals within those agencies/organisations to more concertedly self - examine the character of their own will - to - power);

For issue arena 8: *Seductive Properties Of Semiotics*

- the making visible of the infinite number of alternative styles of interpretation and contested articulations of difference/interest which invisibly lies within the language(s) of tourism (and which variously relate to the rise or fall of different 'doxa' ['doxa' - holding populations] in a given territory);

For issue arena 9: *Mediated Coercion*

- the making visible of tourism/travel as an important site of juridical space where all sorts of judgments/prejudgments are made or exercised which render some populations dominant and others suppressed (and where all sorts of privileges are bestowed upon the same constructions of culture/history/geography/nature vis - a - vis other conceptualisations of culture/history/geography/nature);

For issue arena 10: *Transformative Political Events*

- the making visible of subtle changes in rationality across different economic, different cultural, different political, and different other contexts across the world of tourism/travel (particularly where seemingly imperceptible transformations of meaning are involved);

For issue arena 11: *Disjunctive Temporalities*

- the making visible of the incohesive affiliations of local, mobilising, and diffuse populations within states (and the mapping of those changes in the profile and juxtaposition of those disjunctive temporalities overtime, as occasioned through developments in or of tourism); and,

For issue arena 12: *'Totalised' Objects*

- the making visible of the manner in which things have been inappropriately essentialised or indecently subjectified through tourism (and of the way in which certain natural or cultural phenomenon have become appropriated via false totalisations or false naturalisations).

Table 1
The Governmentality of Tourism: The Distinct and Comparative Contribution of Foucault's Eye-of-Power Research Approaches

A Suggested Portfolio of Potential Research Lines

Key:

- *Issue Arena* = Sample problem area in international tourism where Foucauldian thought conceivably applies;

O *Representative Researcher* = Sample Tourism Studies investigator currently already at work in that issue arena/research domain, conceivably;

- *Foucauldian Critique* = The intellectual specificity of Foucault --- the evidential realm - of - possibility for a Foucauldian research agenda to be further developed on this (particular) issue agenda/domain.

- *Issue Arena 1* = Power at Work in Tourism Management and Development: The Relations of Power

O *Representative Researcher* = Shames and Glover have studied the cultural tunnel vision of managers in tourism who work (particularly in developing nations) with die-hard management notions as if culture did not matter [1>1]; they have focused upon the ethnocentrisms that routinely exist in the management of tourism as a disjointed array of largely Western management principles that are borrowed from the non - service industries of the urban - industrial, metropolitan West [1>2]. They have noted that such 'Western' managers have not recently been trained to deal with 'wholes' (as do many non - Western/local/indigenous populations), and their heavily programmatic and fragmentary approaches unwittingly interrupt local cycles and host cultural systems by focusing too narrowly on piecemeal 'things' to be managed [1>3].

- Foucauldian Critique = Foucault's insights on the way mainstream truths (i.e., here, ethnocentric understanding) are produced and transmitted in an immensely diffuse fashion [1>4] are of considerable relevance here. They would enrich the work of Shames and Glover by enabling the researchers to more clearly see the world of networks that that those ethnocentric notions are transmitted through as the identified power relations intermingle with other types of relations (of production/kinship/family/et cetera) [1>5]. Thus, the Foucauldian approach enables researchers and managers to more clearly see management/development practices as they really are --- as what people really do [1>6] -- and what they really privilege. Thus Foucault's philosophical examination of management and development praxis at work enables people not so much to see what is hidden, but to make visible those relations, actions and deeds that are 'visible' everyday, but which tend to go unexamined [1>7].

- *Issue Arena 2* = Power as Normalising Discourse: Power as Deep Disciplines

O *Representative Researcher* = Recently, Sofield has produced a rather interesting study of Anuha Island Resort in the Solomons, where (as did Shames and Glover, above) he examined the problems which arise in tourism development out of inter - cultural misunderstanding and/or insensitivity to local value systems [2>1]. Sofield's conclusion (in this examination of a so-called failed development) was that, in this instance, the traditional values of Melanesian society clashed with the value systems of the modernising, monetary economy: "it emphasised the fact that if a tourism development lacks the support of the resident community then its sustainability will be jeopardised" [2>2].

- *Foucauldian Critique* = Such studies on the clash of under - recognised 'values' at play can be much enriched by Foucauldian lines of critique, particularly where Foucault advances the old Durkheimian judgement that ' society' is itself a given (or rather dominant) system of thoroughly - entrenched disciplinary forces [2>3]. Hence disciplinary power is that power/knowledge which makes certain norms prescriptive but not necessarily noticed within the given institution/realm/society --- and which does not act as a monolithic force within that institution/realm/society, but rather as a passive, capillary form of truth - in - circulation [2>4]. Hence, Foucauldian analyses tend to view the exercise of power as a game [*jeux de pouvoir*] in which 'the language' of that power/knowledge (i.e., of those prescriptive 'values') lie structurally very deeply within the given institution/realm/society [2>5]. Hence, for Foucault, the capillary power of organisations or of populations goes (or rather commences) much deeper than one generally suspects deep down in that society, and its true dominations and solidities perhaps occur and re-occur where one does not expect them [2>6]. For a brilliant attempt to apply Foucault's evidential 'Western' discursive model of knowledge and power at work in a distant, South Pacific society, refer to Lindstrom's examination of the local discursive orders of Tanna society, in Vanuatu [2>7].

- *Issue Arena 3* = Illusory Objects and Illusory Unities: The Power-Produced 'Thing' C The Power-Produced 'Other'

O *Representative Researcher* = In Selwyn's long - overdue edited examination of the manufacture of myths in and through tourism, Edwards has perceptively written on the manner in which external experiences/external populations are appropriated through the manufacture and sale of postcards in tourism: she notes how 'the capture' of certain images are domesticated through such souvenir - production as the experiences/the judgements/the norms of the observer's/the manufacturer's/the seller's own identities are self - affirmed, and as significant or serviceable others are thereby 'created' [3>1]. To Edwards, the manufacture of such exotic visions (as souvenirs), is part and parcel of the central motivating forces of the tourism process, itself --- a process which consistently and cumulatively conspires "to create and sustain tourist desire and fantasy" [3>2]. While the production of the exotic may be combined with a genuine *desire* 'to know', such manufactured exoticism is highly self - referential act which reifies certain culturally formed images as observed realities --- or rather as, 'objects'. Under this process, fragmentary images are essentialised as the physical object depicted becomes indistinguishable from its symbolic/metaphorical meaning: the symbol becomes reality, as the romanticised Other is thereby produced [3 > 3].

• *Foucauldian Critique* = In drawing substantively from Sturrock [3 > 4], Edwards acknowledges the high relevance of Foucault (and also of Lacan) to such self - referentiality in the everyday essentialising acts of tourism projection: she acknowledges that the appropriated realities she writes about in tourism are strongly reflective, and perhaps primordially associated, with the play of desire, and thereby with the quotidian force of Foucauldian knowledge and power [3 > 5]. Thus, in the projections and the representations of tourism, everyday players of all sorts concretise and/or historicise false objects as natural objects [3 > 6], and, under such Foucauldian forms of objectification by the dominant, we should learn to recognise the objects/things/peoples depicted are largely correlatives of (at the general level) coding acts of self-validation, and (at the specific level) perhaps of the ethnocentric or essentialising acts of other - making. The production and the reproduction of such seemingly natural objects is highly illusory, therefore: to Foucault, it is the everyday exercise of normalised power - knowledge which projectively manufactures impressions of unity and constancy for things and for populations [3 > 7]. Such is the Foucauldian governance of Others --- yet also the Foucauldian governance of Self: refer in the glossary for this paper to *practique de soi*, to *rapport a soi* and to self regulation [self-regulation].

• *Issue Arena 4* = Closed Fields of Knowledge

O *Representative Researcher* = In 1992 Stephen Fjellman produced a powerful study of the Disney Corporation's supreme techno - corporate control over the narratives it appropriates and reprojects at Walt Disney World [4 > 1]. The text details how the Corporation (and its bedfellow companies), work in close harmony --- largely through the exercise of cross - referential marketing activities [4 > 2], the clever 'emplotment' of stories, and the brilliant technological conveyance of those re-aligned realities [4 > 3]. Fjellman's insight - loaded examination of 'Disneytalk' and of the Corporation's control over commodity aesthetics --- where the desires of visitors to Walt Disney World are increasingly regulated by the Disney companies own preferred commodity forms --- is a fascinating study of cultural control and of the decontextualisation of things in the marketplace: he alarmingly shows how that cultural control requires the invention and the dissemination of narratives as well as vigilance against counter - narratives [4 > 4], and how it involves the annihilation of history, geography, politics, language, the present, et cetera [4 > 5].

• *Foucauldian Critique* = While the acknowledged influences upon Fjellman are many, such as Baudrillard, Gramsci, Huxley, Jameson, and F.J. Turner [4 > 6], his inspection of the marketplace power by which the Disney Corporation is able to insinuate its own characters, its own stories, and its own image into the consciousness of millions of visitors could have been pungently enriched via the use of Foucauldian critique --- yet Foucault does not appear in the work's index. Fundamentally, Fjellman's longitudinal study of the entrepreneurial violence and the intense commodification through which the Disney Corporations act to rob visitors of their interpretive autonomy, is a sustained critique of the manner in which culture and the commodity form became dialectically intertwined [4 > 8]. Indeed, Fjellman could have platformed the whole of his analysis of the commodity aesthetics of Walt Disney World as an analysis on and of Foucauldian 'truth' --- where truth is seen to be that "ensemble of ordered procedures for the production, regulation, distribution, circulation and functioning of statements [on that appropriated history, geography, et cetera]" [4 > 8]. Thus Fjellman's treatment of the derivation/manufacture of Disney narratives almost constitutes a very rare Foucauldian study of knowledge - production (*connaissances* [4 > 9]) in tourism studies, i.e., a study of how narrative - makers in tourism function in their day - to - day networking, and their day - to - day suppression of counter - truths [4 > 10].

• *Issue 5* = The Political Apparatus: *Dispositifs* of Policy and Power

O *Representative Researcher* = C.M. Hall is a researcher interested in the policy debates over definitions of place which crop up in tourism. He considers that even though the scale and scope of tourism at local/regional/national/international levels give the field enormous political importance, tourism has rarely received serious examination from political scientists. Indeed, Hall considers that the technical - rational and managerialist outlooks which currently predominate in tourism research and teaching preclude substantive questioning of matters of power and policy in tourism [5 > 1], and the norms and ideologies which dominant groups operate within or under are grossly under - investigated [5 > 2]. Studies of the political dimensions or the power structures of tourism have thereby been inclined to be incidental to social, economic, or environmental considerations in tourism research [5 > 3].

• *Foucauldian Critique* = A research agenda along Foucauldian lines --- prying into the apparatuses (*dispositifs*) of power [5 > 4] --- would clearly be very welcome in tourism studies by Hall, and also by Matthews who has long bemoaned the lack of research into the power structures the policy battles and the political confrontations of tourism [5 > 5]. Such a research agenda would examine how the so called tourism system 'produces' its discourse and its praxis, and thereby privileges some visions of development and possibility in tourism, yet represses others. Hence, the *dispositif* of tourism would be not so much the administrative apparatus through which tourism is administered, but the normalising body of discourse, political propositions, institutions, laws, and policy statements which together constitute the network which binds 'the industry' together as an accumulated phenomenon, or as an aggregate mix of 'utterances' [5 > 6]. In Deleuze's view, the *dispositif* of tourism (or any public matter) comprises "an abstract machine immanent to the entire social field [of that administered or institutionised subject]" [5 > 7]; and within the sometimes diffuse heterogenous multiplicity of each *dispositif* of such power - knowledge lie micro - *dispositifs* [5 > 8].

• *Issue 6* = The Rhetoric of Tradition in Tourism

O *Representative Researcher* = In his fascinating study of the spectacular ritual of 'the land dive' of South Pentecost in Vanuatu --- the forerunner of bungee jumping [6 > 1] --- de Burlo reveals how the local Sa people have manipulated the tradition of the event to support their own outlook on the world [6 > 2]. Thus de Burlo positions the land dive as "a potent cultural text for the Sa about themselves, their values and beliefs" [6 > 3], and he shows how esoteric knowledge about the tradition comprises the basis of political competition on South Pentecost [6>4], where secret or unshared knowledge forms the heart of the pervasive Melanesian concept of power [6>5].

- *Foucauldian Critique* = No doubt there are many populations around the world who currently manipulate major sacred events or customary traditions to benefit one population (and its worldview) over another. And Foucauldian insight into the role structures which produce knowledge - statements and which regulate subsequent transformations of interpretations [6>6] can clearly be of considerable value in describing how new structures of 'knowledge' came into being under the pressures or the exigencies of tourism. Such a line of enquiry would compose a study of the rhetorical value of the contesting 'knowledge'/'statements'/'interpretations' of the events, the traditions, and the drawcards of tourism --- viz., of the Foucauldian grammaticality of the industry [6>7].

- *Issue 7* = Individual Action in Management/Administration/Development

O *Representative Researcher* = In an interesting but somewhat uneven account as to how tourism can readily pollute the given cultural environment, White and Kanahale trace the efforts of companies in Hawai'i to incorporate cultural parameters into their mission statements [7>1]. White and Kanahale report that while the drafting of the mission statements themselves is not an unduly arduous task, the succeeding task --- that of getting the said mission statements internalised --- appears to be much more difficult [7>2]. Such inspections of individual action vis - a - vis group norms or agency policy are extremely rare in tourism studies, however.

- *Foucauldian Critique* = Such matters of implementation and internalisation are the stuff of Foucault's lines of investigation into the interiority of knowledges/statements/truths. What persistently interested Foucault was the degree of awareness which individuals within institutions/organisations/agencies held of the way in which they themselves were applying that body's rules/truths/presuppositions [7>3]. Are individuals within organisations alert to their own will - to - power as they help make decisions [7>4]? Hence what continually intrigued Foucault was the extent to which an individual working within an institution or representing an agency actually held due self - analysis of his/her own aesthetic - of - existence cum aesthetic of power: does he/she 'self - govern'? [7>5]. Does he/she train the self by the self? [7>6].

- *Issue 8* = Discourse as Ingrained Political Seduction

O *Representative Researcher* = Dann is an active member of the International Academy for the Study of Tourism and a semiotician who has lately produced the first sizeable sociolinguistic inquiry into tourism [8>1]. In his examination of the content of promotional literature produced by and within the tourism industry, Dann has inspected the heuristic and semantic content of the symbols and codes of the projectivity of peoples, places, and pasts, and he has concluded that the practitioners and clients of tourism participate in a special discourse --- viz., in a language of tourism by which millions of people are either seduced into becoming tourists or are otherwise seduced into adopting particular attitudes about visitable populations, sites, and heritages. Readers should note that some experts on 'discourse' would not call the overt promotional material and language of tourism 'discourse', *ipsissima verba*, because so much of that articulation is consciously delivered and knowingly or intentionally 'engineered'. Macdonnell would consider such promotion to exist naturally and be the constituted or enshrined literature of the industry rather than being the unconscious vehicle of normalisation and/or seduction [8>2]. Hollinshead would also hold back from calling such designed promotion 'discourse', per se, since it largely contains formulated or preformulated projections rather than literature [8>4] rather than 'unformulated thematics [8>3]; he would call that polished or re - polished articulation public - professional literature [8>4] rather than discourse, itself. Nonetheless, Dann's work on the registers of the language of tourism (such as the registers of *ol' talk, spasprech, gastrolingo, and greenspeak)* is a most useful initial analysis of the force of the seductive in the networked compositionality in and of tourism.

• *Foucauldian Critique* = Foucault does not appear in the index of Dann's painstaking, pioneering, work. Hopefully, Dann has only just begun his critique of the register of talk and text in tourism, and can bring much more Foucauldian insight into his turn - of - the century examinations of the properties of the articulations of tourism. It would thereby be notably useful if Dann could bring a stronger orientation to the political densities which are implicitly rather than explicitly contained in the literature of tourism. Hence, what are the embedded but scarcely suspected importunations of and within the language of tourism (?); what are the intrinsic permissions (?) and the tacit prohibitions (?) of that talk and text? [8>5]. What deeply hidden and quietly chastising/quietly silencing/quietly violenc(e) - ing cultural warrants can Dann unmask politically the capillary cultural warrants of the talk and text of tourism? [8>6]. Hopefully, Dann and others can then add a decent measure of Foucauldian 'enterology' to that research agenda, and can genuinely inspect the 'enterography' of each institutional language (therefore, of the 'discourse'!) examined.

• *Issue 9* = Power - Knowledge as Invisible Site of Mediated Coercion

O *Representative Researcher* = In the early 1990s, Harrison produced a serviceable study of the social, cultural, and environmental ramifications of the explosive growth of tourism in the less developed nations of the world [9>1]. In the work, Harrison appeared to be notably interested in the economic ties and the marketplace relationships which have increasingly typified the so - called modernisation of 'developing' countries [9>2], especially the substantial role of transnational companies in concert with the state on matters of investment, development, and legislation in and of tourism. Indeed, in Harrison's edited text, Sinclair, Alizadeh, and Onunga note that the ties between multinational companies and host governments are often concealed and the mix and range of contractual and other relationships is often significantly under - suspected: hence "if foreign firms pose a high level of bargaining power, they may not need to engage in direct investments to obtain advantageous relationships with the host country" [9>4].

• *Foucauldian Critique* = Foucault was, of course, highly interested in how institutions mediate regimes of activity. What intrigued Foucault was the exercise of political power through the mediation of institutions "which look as if they have nothing in common with the political power [of governing states/governing agencies/governing entities], as if they are independent of it, while they are not" [9>5]. Under Foucauldian analysis, universities just do not just disseminate knowledge, they keep certain social classes in power; under Foucauldian analysis, agencies of care in psychiatry and health do not just dispense medical knowledge, they support the political status quo in and of the realm of medicine [9>6]. And by extension, Foucauldian analysis might take the investigations of Harrison/Sinclair, et al., to further levels of critique by exposing the massive (?) degree to which multinational institutions appear to be neutral and independent of governments around the world, yet are actually highly instrumental in controlling the sorts of information and intelligence with which those governments have to or actually do work. One might find that in developing countries and in operational scenarios in tourism management -- as Foucauldian investigators have uncovered in other spheres of human activity -- that political power sweeps much wider and deeper than one suspects: in Foucault's own words, "there are centers and invisible, little - known points of support: [the true solidarity of such interfusive power - knowledge] is perhaps where one doesn't expect it" [9>7]. Henceforward, under Foucauldian critique in tourism, the goal will not be to examine the predictable place where such institutional influence will be exercised (as in the Sinclair, Alizadeh and Onunga study of contractual matters in Kenya within Harrison), but those scarcely suspected sites (i.e., those unfamiliar and enigmatic points of activity, places, and forms where such dominant power - knowledge is at work.

• *Issue 10 =* Transformative Political Events: Imperceptible Social and Psychic 'Utterances'

O *Representative Researchers =* Richter has long been interested in the major political issues which affect decision-making on tourism at subnational, national, and international levels. Like Hall, and like Matthews above (see point 5), she is rather concerned about the neglect political scientists have shown towards the industry [10>1]. Richter is especially bothered about the lacuna of scrutiny which exists over the pace of development and the nature of the control of political development in tourism. Drawing from Peck and Lepie [10>2], she suggests that the impacts of tourism are cyclical phenomena which bring about the least disturbance to community values whenever 'political power' is reasonably evenly distributed. And in this respect Richter has turned her attention to the special events in and of tourism development around the world. Taking insight from Lin and Patnaik [10>3], Richter suggests that many major events in tourism development --- particularly 'Worlds - Fair' - type mega - events --- characteristically cause intensive political problems because they are typically and narrowly elitist initiatives which are designed/constructed/promoted at extraordinary speed, and without due concern for those others local individuals who are caught in the resultant inflationary spiral and housing squeeze [10>4). But Richter is unable to make broadscale assessments of and about the character of political action on and around special events in tourism because the political science inspection of occasions and occurrences are still rare as yet, and only lately emergent [10>5].

• *Foucauldian Critique =* No doubt Richter would be pleased if a plethora of researchers in tourism undertook Foucauldian inspections of the large and small events of tourism, where those 'happenings' are seen or found to be significantly reformative incidents or significantly deformative episodes. Foucauldian research tends to privilege such restructuring moments, however large or small they may be, and he terms them 'transformations' [10>6]. In understanding the power which lies within institutions and within particular arenas, Foucault is inclined to search for "the set of necessary and sufficient transformations" which occasion the change from one form of epistemology (or from one form of held rationality) to another [10>7]. What Foucault was always keen to identify was not the isolated but highly visible event itself --- or, elsewhere, the natural object --- but the concealed discourse and the concealed practice that helped bring it out, and which might themselves be altered by its tectonic appearance [10>8]. And for Foucault, the value of the event that must be deciphered within its *petits recits*, i.e., in its seemingly imperceptible properties of meaning. To Foucault, the sign of transformation and the sign of history does not consist in the essence of the event itself, nor in the apparent and immediate consciousness of its perpetrating actors or its involved agents, but in its force as a spectacle --- i.e., as a narrative which imbues social and psychic identification, or as a 'locus' of social utterance. See Bhabha's writings on the Foucauldian notion of everyday enunciative or epochal 'events' [10>9].

• *Issue 11* = The Disjunctive Temporalities of Dominant and Suppressed Populations

O *Representative Researcher* = Hollinshead has lately endeavoured to translate Bhabha's [11>1] writings on the ambivalences in and by which so many populations are culturally engaged within states/nations/territories today as pre - given ethnic traits and national identities are increasingly the focus of complex antagonistic negotiation and affiliative disjuncture [11>2]. What Hollinshead has endeavoured to do is to point out that while tourism --- fundamentally the business of 'difference', par excellence --- can learn prodigiously from Bhabha's intelligences on contemporary/postcolonial strategies of cultural representation, Bhabha can himself learn much about the sense of disorientation and disturbance that halfway/in - between/interstitial populations feel towards imposed straitjacket representations of national culture from tourism and the ubiquitous but dynamic projections of peoplehood it deals in. To Hollinshead, tourism practitioners and tourism studies researchers can learn much from Bhabha about the ambiguous and hybrid locations in which so many previously suppressed or newly emergent populations find themselves nowadays, but Bhabha can reciprocally enrich his own interpretations on and about the new polarities of 'Self' and 'Other' and of 'East' and 'West' by observing the performative invention of culture and the performative creation of identity in tourism today [11].

• *Foucauldian Critique* = For too long, perhaps, tourism has dealt in people - as - one representations of populations. Hollinshead's efforts to translate the thinking of Bhabha on the restlessness of postcolonial cultural identity is a clear expression of the view that the representations of tourism have tended to be for too 'horizontal' and much too 'homogenous'. And Bhabha has admittedly borrowed much of his own ideas on the articulation of culture/ethnicity/identity from Foucault: 'the great contribution of Foucault's ... work is to suggest that people emerge in the modern state as a perpetual movement of 'the marginal integration of individuals' [where that state or nation is increasingly involved in the battle to unite the disjunctive affiliations of resident, mobile, and diasparic populations] [11>4]. But Bhabha's borrowing of insights from Foucault is no lame debt. Indeed, Bhabha finds Foucault to be rather too historicist in his colouration of culture and ethnicity [11>5]. Foucault's writings on power/right/truth might constitute (for matters of cultural and national definition) a most praiseworthy contemporary and Nietzschean critique of relations - of - truth as relations - of - force [11 > 6]. But Bhabha deems Foucault's understanding of the social and psychic character of culture identification to be far too Eurocentric: to Bhabha, the differences which Foucault spots are too rigidly framed in an architecture of understanding which suggests that competing identifications are contemporaneous - in - time, and synchronous - in sense [11 > 7]. Foucault's own comprehension of difference/alterity/otherness is rather too fixed for Bhabha, and does not readily reflect the discontinuous historical nature and the transgressive character of so many late, honest - to - self, representations of people [11 > 8; 11 > 9].

• *Issue 12* = The Creation/Invention of 'Totalised' Objects

O *Representative Researcher* = Morris is a cultural studies expert whose investigations (on how all manner of things became economically appropriated) frequently take her into the domain of tourism studies. Fundamentally, Morris inquires into the powers which corporations/institutions/agencies harness as a productive, positive capacity to act [12 > 1], and into the contexts in which cultural representations/iconological significations are articulated (that is, how they are 'made', 'unmade', and 'remade') [12 > 2]. In the realm of tourism, Morris has examined 'the life' of tourist sought images [12 > 3]. Hence the film Crocodile Dundee is positioned by her as a productive commodity, which help project Australia as a fascinating international destination [12 > 4], the Sydney (Telecommunications) Tower is positioned as a monument to that nation's viewable human-technological and economic - imperial progress [12 > 5], and the Aboriginal people of the dry continent are positioned as an appropriated object of the dominant white male narrative of becoming which fuels Australian tourism [12 > 6]. What especially concerns Morris is who has the authority (i.e., the inherited or the claimed or the assumed authority) to invoke various objects as natural/authentic/axiomatic objects representative of a people, a place, or a past [12 > 7].

• *Foucauldian Critique* = Much of Foucault's writing and commentary pivots on the false objectification of things. He warns that we must stop focussing our gaze upon supposedly natural objects [12 > 8], for no thing is always so governed [12 > 9] --- such is the pervasive illusion of the apparently 'natural object' [12 > 9]. And such is the false unity of objective history, where the joints all fit together seamlessly [12 > 10]. To Foucault, each and every culture is only a chaos of false precision --- a mishmash of rigorously over - interpreted and over - unified practices [12 > 11]. It was Foucault's view that natural objects are only 'natural' for the forms of discourse and praxis which so objectify it --- and that would have been true, for tourism as for any realm of signification or domain of knowing. Thus the incorporation of a Foucauldian perspective in tourism studies, and in the projectivity of tourism management/promotion, would instruct tourists/travellers/visitors about the illusory character of all culture: "what is made, the object, is explained by what went into its making at each moment of history" [12 > 12].

References for Exhibit 1

1>1 Shames and Glover 1989:xv	2>1 Sofield 1996:176
1>2 Shames and Glover 1989; 16	2>2 Sofield 1996:200
1>3 Shames and Glover 1989:24	2>3 Morris and Patton 1979:66
1>4 Morris and Patton 1979:46	2>4 Morris and Patton 1979:47
1>5 Morris and Patton 1979:55	2>5 Foucault 1994:541-2
1>6 Veyne 1997:156	2>6 Chomsky and Foucault 1997:130
1>7 Davidson 1997:2	2>7 Lindstrom 1990

3>1 Edwards 1996:201	4>1 Fjellman 1992
3>2 Edwards 1996:197	4>2 Hollinshead 1998/A
3>3 Edwards 1996:200-1	4>3 Hollinshead 1998/B
3>4 Sturrock 1979	4>4 Fjellman 1992:8
3>5 Edwards 1996:199	4>5 Fjellman 1992:24
3>6 Veyne 1997/A:159	4>6 Hollinshead 1998/B
3>7 Veyne 1997/A:160	4>7 Fjellman 1992:9
	4>8 Morris and Patton 1979:47
	4>9 Davidson 1997:7
	4>10 Macdonnel 1986:3

5>1 Hall 1996:19	6>1 Lindstrom 1993:138
5>2 Hall 1996:14	6>2 de Burlo 1996:255
5>3 Hall 1996:196	6>3 de Burlo 1996:263
5>4 Morris and Patton 1979:52	6>4 de Burlo 1996:269
5>5 Matthews 1975:195	6>5 Tonkinson 1982
5>6 Davidson 1997:11	6>6 Davidson 1997:11
5>7 Deleuze 1997:184	6>7 Chomsky and Foucault 1997:119
5>8 Deleuze 1997:184	

7>1 White and Kanahele 1989:53	8>1 Dann 1996
7>2 White and Kanahele 1989:57	8>2 Macdonell 1986:6
7>3 Veyne 1997/A:154	8>3 Hollinshead 1993:672
7>4 Veyne 1997/A:158	8>4 Hollinshead 1993:678
7>5 Foucault 1997:234	8>5 Chomsky and Foucault 1997:128
7>6 Foucault 1997:235	8>6 Chomsky and Foucault 1997:130

9>1 Harrison 1992	10>1 Richter 1983
9>2 Harrison 1992:31	10>2 Peck and Lepie 1978
9>3 Harrison 1992:32	10>3 Lin and Patniak 1982
9>4 Sinclair, Alizadeh and Onunga 1992:47	10>4 Richter 1994:223
9>5 Chomsky and Foucault 1997:130	10>5 Richter 1994:229
9>6 Sinclair, Alizadeh and Onunga 1997:130	10>6 Davidson 1997:11
	10>7 Foucault 1969
9>7 Chamsky and Foucault 1997:130	10>8 Veyne 1997/A:149-150
	10>9 Bhabha 1994:242-3

11>1 Bhabha 1994:2	12>1 Morris 1997:40
11>2 Hollinshead 1998/C	12>2 Morris 1997:44-45
11>3 Hollinshead 1998/D	12>3 Morris 1996:182
11>4 Bhabha 1994:150-1	12>4 Morris 1996:182
11>5 Bhabha 1994:151	12>5 Morris 1996:183
11>6 Deleuze 1997:188	12>6 Morris 1996:188-9
11>7 Bhabha 1994:243	12>7 Morris 1997:50-51
11>8 Bhabha 1994:195-6	12>8 Veyne 1997/A:149-50
11>9 Hollinshead 1998/D	12>9 Veyne 1997/A:150
	12>10 Veyne 1997/A:159
	12>11 Veyne 1997/B:228
	12>1 Veyne 1997/A: 160-1

The deployment of such research agendas in and across the microphysics and macrophysics of power as exercised in and through tourism, would conceivably unearth a litany of previously unsuspected (or, at least, severely under-inspected) instances of how certain usages of power --- i.e., of power - knowledge formations --- held an almost absolute capacity to muzzle and regulate individuals. Such research agendas into the order of things in tourism and travel would constitute an examination of the games of truth which inevitably lie here and there within the tourism industry and which inevitably crop up round and across the travel - trade (as they appear to do in almost all other domains). It should be realised, though, that such Foucauldian manifestations of truth (i.e., such encountered power relations) are always to some extent potentially reversible (Morris and Patton 1979). Consonantly, under Foucauldian thought, the suppressed need not always be suppressed, particularly if they learn to appreciate the degree to which they may have been blindly participating in discourse and praxis which sustains their own very suppression.

The dimensions of the tourist gaze: Urry's translation of Foucault's scopic drive

Having attempted to clarify how Foucauldian lines of critique into practical philosophy could productively be deployed in tourism/travel to probe the held rationalities which determine the order of things in and across the industry, it is now propitious to examine the degree to which Urry (1990) faithfully built Foucauldian outlooks into his own construction of 'the tourist gaze'. Now clearly, since Foucault did not himself pass judgement on the nature or profile of any industry as globally tentacular as the tourism industry, Urry's effort ought not so much be sincerely transcribed Foucauldian ideas *exactly* or *literally* to the industry, but rather in terms of the degree to which his concept 'the tourist gaze' perhaps does creditable service as an extension of Foucauldian *logique* into the domain of tourism and travel in the spirit of Foucault's clinical gaze and magisterial gaze (Merquior 1989). In this respect, Urry's endeavour to relocate Foucauldian discursive model of knowledge and of power across service settings (from the conglomerate profiles of the medical service and the prison service to the disparate - cum - linear profiles of the tourism industry) conceivably matches in kind Lindstrom's (1990) thoughtful and earnest attempt to relocate Foucauldian thought away from Foucault's own visual theoretical targets in open cosmopolitan Western Europe to the removed apography and closely contained island culture of the South Pacific.

In Hollinshead (1999), a brief critique was given of Urry's deployment of the term "the tourist gaze' via the use of six broad questions:

- What is the fundamental nature of the tourist gaze?

- What do 'gazers' principally do in tourism and travel?

- What do 'gazers' also do in tourism and tourism and travel?

- Why (else) is the tourist gaze important?

- What are the consequences of the tourist gaze?

- What other features or tangential trends of the tourist gaze are significant?

Table 2: The Character Of The Tourist Gaze: A Synthesis of and About Urry's Concept, Interpreted by Hollinshead

Common Elements/Features of the Tourist Gaze As Identified by Urry (1994 And 1992/B)

What is the Fundamental Nature of the Tourist Gaze?

1 = The Institutional Ways - of - Seeing in Tourism The tourist gaze is the systematic and socially organised ways in which things are seen in and through tourism [[172]]. The tourist gaze is the ways tourists collectively tend to perceive things, and the way in which 'professional' experts in tourism help construct and develop those outlooks. The tourist gaze loosely approximates to the clinical gaze which Foucault maintains exists within medicine [1]: there are, however, not one but many different tourist gazes in tourism [[173]] --- there is not just one scopic regime across the industry [[180]].

2 = The Highly Visual Nature of Knowing Peoples, Places, And Pasts According to Foucault, tourism has always involved spectacle [86]. The tourist gaze of the contemporary mood builds upon that by making a show, marvel, or an intensively visual 'display' out of all manner of sites, settings, and scenes [93]: such is the spectacle-isation of 'place' in and through tourism]156]. While much of the force of the tourist gaze in the twentieth century has been captured in and for the photography of peoples and places [140], *flânerie* is the quintessential form of turn of the century gazing, where the *flâneur* (after Benjamin 1973; Wolff 1985) is the contemporary hero who is able to travel, to arrive, to gaze, to move on, to be anonymous, to thrive in the liminal zone of tourist places [135;138]. Under *flânerie*, the strolling *flâneur*/flâneuse becomes part of the scene being gazed upon [149 - 150].

3 = The Revelation of the Tourist Gaze In Urry's view, the tourist gaze helps us understand other societies by revealing the normal practices of 'host' or 'gazed upon' populations which might otherwise remain opaque [2]. It can help us get to know those societies by identifying and displaying what they consider to be 'deviant' [2], and it can also help us to comprehend them by seeing what those societies select as being worthy of being incorporated within their own illuminated/viewable 'gaze' [2]. Overtime, many things and themes are selectively and performatively reified through being seen by or within a particular tourist gaze, and they thereby become normalised for the society under view [2].

4 = The Unconscious Force of the Tourist Gaze The tourist gaze acts as a sort of *habitus* (after Bourdieu 1984) by which people learn to see, label, and classify things [88]. This power to identify and know peoples, places, and pasts operates below the level of individual consciousness [88]. It is inscribed within the discourse and the practices of tourists and of the institutions which direct/influence/regulate tourism and travel. It becomes a sovereign and empirical power [[175]].

5 = The Diverse Sorts of Tourist Gaze Urry maintains that there is no single tourist gaze, as such: it varies by society, by social group, and by historical period [1]; in particular, the tourist gaze tends to differ considerably as 'generation', 'gender', and 'ethnicity' interact with class [140]. The nature of a given tourist gaze is therefore a highly contextual and intersubjective matter: being conceived and constructed through visions of apparent 'difference', it depends what a particular observing (or normalising!) society deems as being essentially or intrinsically 'unusual' about the people/place/past in question [2].

What Do 'Gazers' Principally do in Tourism and Travel?

6 = Tourist Gazers are very Strongly Predisposed to Seeking Fun and/or Pleasure The Tourist Gaze is put forward by Urry as a book about pleasure, and he describes it as a text about what people desire when they are free from the imperatives which arise in the usual place of work and residence [1]. Thus, the work details the pleasurable experiences people wish to indulge in or they travel and when they are free of life's quotidian domestic calls. Hence, tourist gazers are inclined to seek to find 'fun' of some sort as they explore the environment with interest and curiosity, and if the gazed are post - tourists (after Feifer 1985), they will delight in the endless availability of 'different' pursuits of each place, they will revel in the multitude of choice amongst the available experiences, and they will view the whole postmodern practice of travel and touring as an infinite and endeavoring 'game' which proffers multiple 'readings' and rarely demands pure authenticity to things [100]. These so called post - tourists will also rejoice in the seemingly perpetual opportunity to 'gaze', in and of itself [100]. To Urry, tourism is the paradigm case for imaginative pleasure - seeking in the contemporary world [13]. Under the postmodern and post - tourist impulses of the tourist gaze, holidays and vacations "have become less to do with the reinforcing of collective memories and experiences and more to do with [the gain of] immediate pleasure" [102].

7 = Tourist Gazers are very Strongly Predisposed to the Consumption of Things Urry suggests that tourist gazes exult in the opportunity to consume goods and services which "are in some sense unnecessary" [1]. But they do not just consume material things, and also are keen to consume favoured 'peoples' encountered, favoured 'landscapes' witnessed, and favoured 'histories' observed, in memoriam [[175]]. Some of the more recent modern and postmodern sites of visitation (such as the macro - shopping centres of our age) are seen by Urry to be temples of consumerism [143]. He cites Fiske (1989:17) who has investigated the sensuous consumption of images (rather than the consumption of commodities, per se) by youths at such massive developments [152].

8 = Tourist Gazers are Strongly Predisposed to Seeking Different/Revered/Cherished Things as Determined by Their Own Cultural Preferences and Ethnocentrisms When 'gazers' indulge in their observations of peoples, places, and pasts as they travel, their 'gaze' is inclined to be framed by culturally specific notions of what is unusual/extraordinary/worth viewing [66]. And when gazers consume items, images, or ideas, their purchase, use, or consecration of the said 'object' also tends to be highly 'culturally' determined. Accordingly, different groups of tourists will have quite different variations in or of expectancy in the given contextual setting [69]. To repeat, there is not just one, single, uniform tourist gaze, there are many -- interpretively.

9 = Tourist Gazers are Strongly Predisposed to Appropriating Other People, Other Places, and Other Pasts Tourists gazers are quite prone to appropriating the sites and sights they observe. Sometimes this appropriation may be relatively innocuous, when visitors want to indulge in the countryside or otherwise 'personally capture' the ordinary countryside (rather than delighting in provided/pre - captured visions of the rural landscape) [99]. Under such an appropriation of the environment, nature is so frequently relegated to being a perceptual sensation [[179]]. In other circumstances, the appropriative demands of visitors can be much more dictatorial --- particularly where historic sites have to be cleaned up and/or reauthenticated in terms of some tourist group or travel - trade notion of what the relevant 'true tradition' was (i.e., ought - to - have - been/ought - to - be) [155]. Under such latter circumstances, it is the gazing tourists themselves, or the image - makers and place - makers of the industry who assume the right to authorise populations, settings, inheritances [135]: and that they so often do unwittingly.

10 = Tourist Gazers are Strongly Predisposed Towards Pursuits which Industrialise and Commodify Things As the tourist gaze is established over a place or subject, there is a tendency for the popularity of that phenomenon to become industrially organised overtime [39]. Many objects become heavily commercialised clichés of their former/original selves, and here Urry cites Shield's (1990) work on the two honeymoon capitals of Niagara Falls and Gretna Green, both of which have now conceivably became over - projected places whose signifiers are now empty of meaning [10 - 11]. Hence, tourist gazers can rapidly commodify all sorts of 'different'/'unusual'/'special' places, and the particular gaze of 'professionals' working in leisure/recreation/tourism convert nature into becoming an 'outdoor recreation resource' as they seek to organise, manipulate, and control the physical environment serviceably [[181; 183]].

What do 'Gazers' also Commonly do in Tourism and Travel?

11 = Tourist Gazers are Drawn Towards Projections and Promotions Which Selectively Celebrate Sites and Sights Urry maintains that tourist gazers are prone to 'experiencing' the exceptional and the remarkable, where those non-ordinary objects may be seen to be (i) unique phenomenona; (ii) pedigree versions of particular significations; (iii) unfamiliar aspects of the familiar; (iv) the ordinary aspects of life, in unusual contexts; (v) familiar activities in unusual settings; et cetera [12]. Sometimes the effort to develop or reinvent places in accordance with a dominant 'preferred vision' causes difficulties. In England, tourists are denied access to much of Lancaster Castle and its historic dungeons because the site is currently still used as a prison --- something ironically deemed to be inappropriate under the tourist gaze! [117 - 118]. In Chester, the tourist gaze has occasioned some tough selectivity decisions: Urry cites Stamp's (1987) commentary on the difficult priority - making that arose when one set of heritage enthusiasts wanted to enlarge the site of a Roman amphitheatre/diva which would involve the demolition of a listed Georgian house, and only raised the wrath of a competing local conservation group who objected to the axiomatic predominance of the 'Roman' theming of Chester [111]. Such contestations over matters of heritage and conservation are bound to occur under and around the tourist gaze: Urry registers Samuel's (1987) point that the National Trusts 1.5 million members make it "the largest mass organisation" in the United Kingdom [110].

While people may appropriate the physical environment (viz.: its sites and sights) also through acts of stewardship, acts of exploitation, and acts of scientisation, tourist gazers appropriate the physical environment through acts of visual consumption [[178]] as those sites and sights are translated into objects of 'desire' [[174]].

12 = Tourist Gazers are Drawn Towards Projections and Promotions Which Substantively Reduce the Horizontal and Vertical 'Aura' of the Culture, The History, and The Heritage of Peoples and Places Urry argues that under the postmodern mood or condition, the established horizontal boundaries between things frequently dissolve --- where those things had hitherto been contained with different institutional or normative spheres [84]. And with each horizontal sphere of culture, the established aura of things also frequently became similarly de-differentiated where previous vertical differentions of 'high' from 'low' cultural forms dissolve [84]. Under the anti-auratic discourse of the postmodern predicament, the horizontal and the vertical distinctiveness of things breaks down, each imploding into the other --- a process which frequently involves considerable 'spectacle' and 'play'. With television performing a central role in this anti-auratic de-differentiation, many cultural forms are no longer seen to be original and unique to particular horizontal spheres or vertical realms of life, but are borne mechanically and electronically as the old distinctions and the received unities of aesthetic/artistic/cultural life are challenged. Under the anti-hierarchical mood of postmodernity, old originalities, old uniqueness, and old singularities are negated or contravened by de-differentiated forms of culture which emphasise pastiche, collage, and allegory over and above ordered orthodoxy. Commerce, spectacle and culture become indissolubly intertwined under these postmodern and electronic counteractions [85] and --- after Baudrillard (1985) and Eco (1986) --- the world of the traveller becomes much more hyper-real where "the fake seems more real than the real [85]. Under this de-differentiated spirit of spectacle, the media is heavily involved in the simulation of things, as 'expression' and 'style' increasingly count over and above 'the correct or the foundational order of things' [87 - 91]. Hence the electronic media have an enormously enlarged power in the representation of people's lives and inheritances, generating a kind of institutional voyeurism amongst people at home and people who travel [91]. One outcome of all of this pastiche and parotic treatment of culture/being/identity is --- after Jameson (1985) and Featherstone (1987) --- the cultivation of a form of calculating hedonism in which the old trajectories of history and heritage become eerily 'lost' [92]. This bewilderment of our received historical sense thereby gives rise to the prevalence of the media - induced --- or rather the media-reduced --- three-minute culture of the postmodern moment [92; 101 - 2]. Elsewhere, Fjellman (1992) has termed this media and electronic commodified decontextualisation and de - differentiation of inheritances as 'culture redux'.

13 = Tourist Gazers are Drawn Towards Projections and Promotions Which Re-Mould Or Re-Fabricate Material, Physical, and Notional Things in Terms of New Interpretations of Being, Identity, and Celebrity In the Tourist Gaze Urry suggests the contemporary culture market mixes up the 'grid' (i.e., the received classifications of things) and the 'group' (i.e., the boundaries which distinguish the inner from the outer in and of things) [91]. As previously distinct and perhaps privileged systems of information about things succumb to more generally available systems of information [91], new complex processes of production and consumption appear. And these socially-organised and market-driven processes are rather inventive in terms of the material objects or physical features they project as being 'extra - ordinary' and therefore worthy of being viewed under the tourist gaze [101]. Consonantly, people are fed and now demand ever new forms of out - of - the - ordinary experiences, such as "'Eastenders' holiday breaks run by Islington Council in London, football weekend breaks organised in Liverpool, the Leprosy Museum in Bergen, the Japanese Death Railway in Burma, the Gestapo headquarters in Berlin, and 'boring tours' in Sydney" [102]. Urry considers that it is almost possible to construct a postmodern tourist site around each and every kind of object [102]. Even the decaying industrial backwater of Glasgow has been turned into a dynamic growth area attractive to tourists --- "a preferred object of the gaze of many tourists" [156]. Such is the transformation of Glasgow via the gaze of tourism, whereby the city is reinvented through the combination of economic restructuring, social change, policy intervention, and cultural re - evaluation which there constitute the gaze [156]. Urry muses that if seedy Glasgow can indeed be remanufactured as a tourist/post - tourist gaze, there are no limits to what can be reinvented under the reinventions of ocularcentrism in tourism as the world is materially and symbolically remade [156]. Such is the mysterious and dramatic power [156] of the tourist gaze to re - envision and re - present whole and even seemingly 'spent' places [116].

14 = Tourist Gazers are Drawn Towards Projections and Promotions Which Re - Mould or Re - Fabricate 'Other', 'Removed', or 'Exotic' Populations in Terms of Some New Notion of 'Difference'/'Uniqueness'/'Celebrity' In The Tourist Gaze Urry argues that the new modes of visual perception which drive so much contemporary tourism are not just targeted upon material and physical entities, and the tourist gaze has been decidedly influential in the redesignation or the refabrication of 'other' or 'distant' populations as people worthy of being celebrated. In such fashions, a number of ethnic groups have come to be constructed or reconstructed under the tourist gaze as a lead part of the 'attraction' of some places [143]. In Britain this has notably occurred with the highlighting of the culture and heritage of Asian peoples where they are positioned as being exotically different in places like Bradford and Birmingham [144].

15 = Tourist Gazers are Drawn Towards Projections and Promotions Which are Highly Semiotic and/or Pungently Significatory In his loosely Foucauldian study of the systematic ways in which things and people are 'seen' in and through tourism, Urry notes the rising importance of the consumption of themes and images of and about things in the tourism of the late twentieth century [152]. What increasingly counts, in his view, under the tourist gaze is how places are 'marked'/'signified'/'represented'. Either that making of the 'real' or the 'invented' celebrity may be conducted via a 'sign' or it may be carried out metonymically via "the substitution of some feature or effect or cause of the phenomenon for the phenomenon itself" [129]. Hence, "the ex - miner, now employed at the former coalmine to show tourists around, is a metonym for structural change in the economy from one based on heavy industry to one based on services" [129]. Under this acute representation, the fame of the idea/the sign/the object becomes its meaning under the new celebrity agenda of the tourist gaze. And --- to recap --- there has been a massive broadening of the kind of features/objects/phenomena deemed worthy of being so signified [129]. It is the understood mark or the noted sign which now gives attribution to 'the different'/'the unique'/'the authentic' --- and which thereby designates the preferred 'authenticity' being newly or correctively articulated. Such is the fresh placemaking projectivity of the tourist gaze according to Urry, where in Canada --- after McKay (1988) --- maritimicity is a new and "peculiar petit - bourgeois rhetoric of lobster pots, grizzled fisherman wharves, and schooners... a Golden Age mythology in [Nova Scotia], a region that has become economically dependent on tourism". And it is also visible at the award - winning tourist development of Coronation Street in Manchester where --- after Goodwin (1989) --- following a visit to the Street's famous Rover's Return public house, gazing tourists then develop their photographs to consume "a representation of a representation of a representation" [145].

Why (Else) is the Tourist Gaze Important?

16 = The Tourist Gaze Helps Render People/Travellers/Tourism More Self-Indulgent In The Tourist Gaze Urry suggests that the tourists who cruise about and gaze over the world are partly encouraged so to do via the rising power of self - actualisation in and across society --- particularity in the U.S.A. [93]. Drawing from Ehrenreich (1983), he notes the increased influence of 'the myth of me', and for the transformations of identity and being which have cultivated a moral climate where irresponsibility, isolationist detachment, and self - indulgence are increasingly praised virtues [93]. The generation of such self - sufficient and self - regarding outlooks on life under the postmodern moment have indeed helped reconfigure travel patterns and tourism profiles, according to Urry. Taking from Mercer (1983:84), he notes how the pursuit of travel and tourism --- as of other arenas of being - confirming pleasure and identity - bestowing desire --- nowadays demands increasingly that the individual is wholesomely and unabashedly involved in the cultural happenings or leisure pursuits they participate in [101]. And Urry notes that, under the tourist gaze, such self indulgent practices frequently necessitate "the energetic breaking of mild taboos that operate on various forms of consumption, such as eating or drinking to excess, spending money recklessly, wearing outrageous clothes, keeping wildly different time patterns, and so on" [101]. Consonantly --- after White (1987:10) --- the imperative is on 'action, participation, and fun', where 'living' museums replace dead ones! [130].

17 = The Tourist Gaze Helps Render the World More Idealist Under the postmodern mood of so much late - twentieth century tourism, Urry notes that despite the imperative upon tourists and travellers to directly indulge in sought experiences themselves --- see the immediate previous point --- much of the gaze of tourism, per se, is expended not in real scenes or at 'real' settings, but is absorbed or internalised from representations of the view/the wonder/the culture in question [86]. What counts is not just the fact that the value of the encounter is 'signified', *ipso facto* --- see point 15 above --- but that so many of the representations on which tourists gaze are idealist [86]. Hence it is not necessary for tourists to actually physically travel to the cultural showcase or to the natural wonder to sense or envision the celebrity or the difference in and of that place themselves [86]. Accordingly, tourists can gaze over and about 'peoples', and 'pasts' from postcards, from guidebooks, and from television programmes, and the idealised impressions they intimately become acquainted with in this fashion may frequently outlast the 'real' impressions they subsequently gather in situ [86].

18 = The Tourist Gaze Helps Render the World More Romantic Urry believes that romanticism has been heavily involved in the emergence and development of mass tourism [16 - 39], and he repeatedly notes the importance of romanticism as an invented and variable pleasure under the tourist gaze [46]. To Urry --- borrowing from Walter (1982) --- the romanticism of the gaze is that effort to sacralise nature or to proselytise the virtue of 'peoples', 'places', and 'pasts' to others [46]; and it is a practice of whimsical *fantasque* and pastoralisation which all places and nations now give in to [46 - 47]. Yet, to Urry, the tourist gaze has its most virulent romanticist roots in Great Britain where its seventeenth century 'disease of nostalgia [nowadays] seems to have become an epidemic" [105] --- in the 'quaint, old country' [48; and 109].

19 = The Tourist Gaze Helps Render the World More Illusory In The Tourist Gaze, Urry maintains that tourists choose to visit places out of a sense of anticipation that they will find pleasure/immersion/reward there [3]. To Urry, tourists build up that sanguine expectancy about places having absorbed the constructions of films, television programmes, videos, magazines, books, et cetera, each of which help construct and reinforce particular fantasies which the gazing tourists daydream about [3]. But, frequently, the visions put before potential tourist are not just idealist (see point 17 above), they are illusory, building up a projection of the place that is far removed from manifest 'reality'. Accordingly, the potential tourist, and then the gazing tourist, are "directed to features of landscape and townscape which separate them off from [less savory/less pleasant] everyday experience [3]. And frequently, the tourism industry for and within a place advances a particular epoch as the age by which that place should best be encountered, thereby privileged some features of local vernacular history over others --- after Lynch {1973) [126]. To Wright (1985:20) --- cited by Urry [126] --- this illusory signification can occur on a vast scale and is often totalised in scope: to him it constitutes the "abstract and artificial aestheticisation of the ordinary and the old".

20 = The Tourist Gaze Helps Render People More Submissive to the Constant New Ecstasies of Travel and Celebrity As tourism now enbloats to become the largest industry in the world, Urry considers it is critical to study the tourist gaze because of its propensity to act as an immense tidal wave engulfing peoples, places, and pasts [156]. To Urry, the tourist gaze is an immense social, political, economic, cultural, and human - geographic force which promises all manner of new ecstatic experiences, and noteworthy associations with, celebrity for people. Under the postmodern mood of ceaseless representation, an enlarging array of tourist professionals conspire to develop and reproduce ever - new creatively - imagined objects of the tourist gaze [3] to which potential and existing tourists increasingly wish to stroll by, to gaze upon, to participate in, and to succumb to as they take their own place in the worldwide community of dreaming travellers [149-50]. In each place, it is the imaginative, fabricating, and calculating alliance of, perhaps, the conservationists and the developers who work together to ensnare the vulnerable, desire - seeking, tourists [127]. And, once captured, it is that gazing tourist who so frequently help sublimely corroborate such visions, and who help performatively validate such schemed constructions.

What Are the Consequences of the Tourist Gaze?

21 = The Transformation of Peoples and Places At the outset of The Tourist Gaze, Urry states that one of his main purposes is to identify the consequences of the gaze on the places which are its object (explicitly), and one may assume also on the peoples which are its object (implicitly) [1]. In the seven chapters of this 1990 work, he then reveals how the gaze itself has changed over the decades as new ways of seeing are cultivated [4], and as post - tourism takes its hold [49; 100 -2]. But the work is more directly a work which gives testimony to the ways in which the gaze has influenced the living, the being, and the identities of tourist locales which --- wherever they are in the world -- have (after Culler (1981:127) "unsung armies of semioticians, the tourists [and all]… fanning out in search of signs of Frenchness, typical Italian behaviour, exemplery Oriental scenes, typical American thruways, traditional English pubs, [whatever}… ." Perhaps Urry's chief conclusion is that the tourist gaze has helped make the people of the many locales so much more aware, confident, and articulate about their 'real' or 'imaginary' inheritances, but it has made the locales where they reside that little bit more agitated and inconstant as city leaders/state administrations/national planners feverishly question the received history and the assumed natural history of their designated territory to uncover projectable 'difference' and promotable 'singularity' [156].

Such are the transformations of the day - by - day gaze toward, and the quest for, the distinctive essence of a population and for the unique selling points of a place.

22 = The Universalisation of Traits and Tastes Despite the perpetual ongoing search for the essences of peoples and the unique qualities of places (see immediate point, previously), Urry notes that the tourist gaze actually helps collapse the boundaries between places as ever wider reaches of the globe fall under the surveillance of travellers [156]. In Urry's view, the media have clearly been pivotal in helping produce the generalisations of the tourist gaze, playing a large contemporary role in structuring fashion and taste [19]. And certain middle class groups have also worked to the same universalising ends in fashion and taste, constantly devising ever - new and conspicuous cultural patterns under the tourist gaze, and also gaining heightened prestige from the in vogue cultural capital they deal in. For instance, in Great Britain, this middle - class driven universalisation in, by, and of tourism has taken the shape of a vernacular and heritage - based restyling of both the urban and the rural landscape, according to Urry [135]. And such universalisations by and through the tourist gaze have flowered under the increased confusions of tourism and other 'conventional' activities such as shopping, sport, leisure, and education.

23 = The Democratisation of Peoples and Places The third significant consequence of the tourist gaze which one may ascertain from Urry, is that the twentieth century's ocularcentrism in and through tourism has helped democratise peoples and places [156]. Much of this democratising force comes with the postmodern impulses in and behind the tourist gaze, for postmodern culture is anti - auratic and involves the de - differentiation of things [84]. As grid and group change so rapidly, it is harder for the priviligentia to hang on to their hold over cultural resources and over societal esteem, and (borrowing from Bourdieu (1984:317)) the new bourgeoisie that crop up in and alongside tourism are inclined to score lowly in terms of both grid and group. Furthermore, the widening of the range of objects considered worthy of being conserved/protected/highlighted under the tourist gaze gives rise to a steady flow of new/alternative/vernacular narratives as emergent feminist/ethnic/other storylines are freshly legitimated [130]. And the nascent appeal of the ordinary under the tourist gaze is also egalitarian/libertarian/populist in its reflexivities [130] --- as is the capacity of people to photograph all forms of human experience: the camera is an archetypal tool of democratised experience --- after Barthes (1981:34) --- and is nowadays available to each and every amateur - travelling - semiotician [139].

24 = The Internationalisation of Traits and Tastes The fourth consequence of the tourist gaze, as identified in this critique of Urry's 1990 work, stems from the internationalising forces that accompany the gaze. Urry notes that tourism itself has internationalised: "every potential object of the tourist gaze now has to compete internationally, and this had led to substantial changes in just what is [deemed to be] extraordinary, and what is [considered to be] internationally ordinary [39]. Perhaps the point is best explicated here by re - registering Parry's (1983:192-3) poignant words --- as cited by Urry: "The holidaymaker of the 1930s had no choice and was prepared to take a chance. If he [sic!] lived in a mill town, at least all his neighbours would have suffered from the same 'poor week'. Not so his counterparts in the 1970s. He wanted sun --- and if half of the street was to come back from Mabella or Torremolinos with burned backs, peeling noses and queasy stomachs, he wasn't going to be left out". [39]. Such is the unquenchable thirst of tourists, and the competitiveness of peoples and places in global travel today: "In the middle ages, people were tourists because of their religion, whereas now they are tourists because tourism is their religion" (Dr. Robert Runcie, Archbishop of Canterbury --- cited by Urry) [Foreward Quotations].

25 = The Creative and Empowered Vision of Individuals The final significant consequence of the tourist gaze --- as encountered in Urry's text --- stems from the fact that the act and art of observing other peoples and different places inherently informs travellers of and about the world [140]. As tourists anticipate distant or foreign climes, they intrinsically learn how to daydream beyond the confines of their own domesticity, and they have increased opportunity to participate in the world's communities --- even though it may be increasingly a communitas of consumers [149]. Yet, Urry does not think that all who regularly travel and gaze are axiomatically liberated and enriched. Under the hyper - realities of the tourist gaze, what is 'real' and what is 'fake' and what is 'authentic' and 'unauthentic' is increasingly hard to discern [146]. And when an all - powerful force like the Disney Corporation is involved, there may actually be less geography (and by extension, less history, less nature, et cetera) available to be seen and understood [147]. Clearly, the tourist gaze can considerably empower one and all: but it can also close down the available and accessible interpretations.

What Other Features of Tangential Trends of the Tourist Gaze are Significant?

26 = The Tourist Gaze is Increasingly Ubiquitous Urry argues that as the tourist gaze universalises (see point 22 above) its discourse and praxis, and its high accent on the visual, becomes apparent is an ever - widening mix of locations. All manner of new locales are invaded by the felt necessity to render 'other'/'different'/'unique' experiences of and about the world systematic and pleasureable. Urry suggests that the expansion of the gaze is now well noted in the postmodernization of museums, where people are no longer "only interested in seeing either great works of art or artefacts from very distinct historical periods [130]. And there has been a large change in the character of museums, too: "no longer are visitors expected to stand in awe of the exhibits" --- interactivity with the exhibitry and accessibility of it are now *de rigeur* [130; 132]. The increasing ubiquity of the tourist gaze within museums is also indicated by the new sorts of objects being exhibited/projected/communicated, and all manner of previously unlikely phenomena are now tourized through the gaze such as 'pencil museums', 'chemical industry museums', 'prisoner - of - war museums', 'dental museums', 'shoe museums', *ad infinitum* [134].

27 = The Tourist Gaze is Increasingly Varied in its Reach In his coverage of the development of mass tourism at the start of The Tourist Gaze, Urry notes that the development of mass tourism was formerly part and parcel of the separation of work and leisure which typified nineteenth century social development, where both work and leisure were characterised by being progressively and distinctively rationalised [16 - 39]. Urry maintains that in Britain, his main research setting, the appearance of mass tourism at the end of that century was merely a confirmation of this divorce of work from leisure: "tourism came to be systematised and organised. It was the antithesis of work and of education and learning " [153]. But the postmodern and postindustrial consolidation of the tourist gaze, and the liberalisation of travel and personal nobility, have begun to challenge the establish separation of leisure/travel/tourism from work, from education, and from learning, as the consumptive and pleasure - seeking imperatives of identity and of travelling extend their reach into other previously 'alien' zones of living and being. Hence, by the late twentieth century, Urry notes "that [an individual's] holidays are not so straightforwardly contrasted with education and learning as in the past" [154], and idiosyncratic interpretive sites like the

Sellafield Nuclear Processing Plant can draw in 150,000 visitors each year, while the former Trusthouse Forte were able to cultivate important new 'extended patronage' or 'visit enrichment' markets by programming an extensive portfolio of tuitionary 'breaks' at its various hotels [154].

28 = The Tourist Gaze is Increasingly Interfused with Other Discourses and Practices This third 'tangential trend' is perhaps an extension of points 26 and 27, above. As the scope and reach of the tourist gaze enbroadens, and as it becomes interlaced with a host of other social previously 'different' practices (see point 22, above), it is becoming difficult to determine what is specifically 'tourism' and what is specifically 'culture' [102]. As group and grid alter, what is 'pleasure' and what is 'pain' seems to change: "Pleasure was associated with being away from the place in which one worked and from the boring and monotonous pari of work, especially of industrial production. Now, however, such a division is much less clear - cut. Pleasures can be enjoyed in very many places, not at all concentrated at the seaside [or other tourist 'play' - site]" [102]. Consonantly, under the commodifications and the de - differentiations of the tourist gaze, pleasure and pain can be experienced at all sorts of locales, alike, and are not so situationally or contextually dependent upon particular geo - physical settings. Perhaps this interfusion of tourism with culture and with other aspects of life is best highlighted, again, with regard to the penetration of the tourist gaze into museums. Urry considers that it is now increasingly problematic to determine what is a museum and what is some other social or productive institution [131]. Many shops now look like museums [131]. Many factories are past workplaces and part gazing - zones [131]. Many pubs are just as much sites for the cultivation of local nostalgia/atmosphere/identity as they are sites of refreshment [132]. And many shopping malls are purposefully designed as public sites of and for *flânerie*, as they are designed spaces for business and enterprise [148 - 150]. And so the dramatic admixing of the discourse and praxis of leisure and travel with the discourse and praxis of work and entrepreneurialism goes on.

29 = The Tourist Gaze is Increasingly Aesthetic Under the Post - Fordist mood, and under the postmodern predicament, Urry considers that 'consumption' is now a more important force across society than is 'production' [14]. Clearly, to him, the tourist gaze is a complex human activity which not only is associated with the aestheticisation of consumption, but it yields a mix of decontextualising discourse and praxis which cross - cuts the old divisions between 'consumption' and 'production' --- see points 26 to 18, above. In Urry's view, vacation settings, travel sites, and holiday centres are prototype locales for the demonstrable aestheticisation of life in so many of its domains [14]. And, by his account, the new 'service' and 'intellectual' classes in Western metropolitan society have been highly ostentacious in displaying 'aesthetic - ascetic' preferences and in legitimating 'aesthetic - ascetic' (i.e., natural - wild) travel/leisure pursuits, both at the expense of the bourgeois liking for 'sumptuous' things [89] --- after Bourdieu (1984). Thus, to Urry, the aesthetic can be both the marker for the gaze, and the nucleus of the gaze.

30 = The Tourist Gaze is Increasingly Culturist (and Evidences the Triumph of Culture over Nature) The final characteristic feature or element of the tourist gaze --- as read in and from Urry's fast translation of Foucauldian panopticism to the demesne of contemporary tourism and travel --- concerns the effects of the enduring regard today for spectacle, *ipso facto*. This current and persevering call for the display of and for the inspection of revered and celebrated things -- particularly for the history and heritage of places -- is an ardent example of the attractivity of seemingly 'raw' and/or 'invented' nostalgia about peoples and places [93 - 4]. To Urry, this imperative for signs of nostalgia here, there and everywhere is highly symptomatic of the depthless world of the tourist gaze where 'the fake' appears to be more real than 'the real' [85]. The call for display and spectacle *ad nauseam* is reflective of a new world of hyper - real travel, indeed of hyper - real living, where --- after Eco (1986) --- there is little of worth that is 'original', and where valued things comprise a copy of things, or a text upon a text [85]. After Lash (1990:15), this new flaccidity of reality is a world of constant signification (resignification?): while modernism had conceived of such representations as being problematic, the new condition of postmodernism perhaps problematises reality [85]. And all this preference for spectacle, display, and representation prioritises 'culture' over nature [94]. Nature itself loses out as being raw and uncooked --- an uncivilised, tasteless, animalistic thing --- after Bourdieu (1984). It is postmodern culture which brings civility of a sort that is seemingly appropriate to desire and seemingly appropriate to consume. As the eye is privileged over other senses, ocular experiences tend to predominate: nature only becomes important when it has been 'seen' [[174]]. But it then tends to be significant not for its intrinsic 'naturalness', but for its serviceable value as 'landscape', per se, [[179]].

Key:

Numbers in single square brackets [ ] refer to pages in Urry 1990; numbers in double square brackets [[ ]] refer to pages in Urry 1992/B.

In the light of the absence of Urry's own clean, clear, and comprehensive explanation of what indeed he felt constituted 'the tourist gaze', Table 2 has now been composed as an interpretation of what Urry appears to have built into his composite concept. Table 2 therefore consists of a refinement of the points already registered in Hollinshead (1999), and it details pointed references to both Urry (1990) and to his valuable follow - up piece of work in the American Behavioural Scientist, two years later (Urry 1992).

So, indeed, what does Urry conceivably imply "the tourist gaze" consists of or? While Hollinshead's (1999) comments may be taken to be an *a priori* summary of the Urry construction (i.e., an *a priori* introduction to or condensation of Table 2 of this later, follow - up paper), an attempt will be made here in this appositional paper to register the cardinal components of the early-1990s Urry conceptualisation. A close reading of Urry (1990) and of Urry (1992) suggests that "the tourist gaze" is a theoretical construction which embraces the following interacting imperatives --- where the numbers 1 to 30 refer to the thirty "common - elements" as given in Table 2:

(A) *An Institutional Way of Perceiving Things*

   (i.e., a highly scopic regime)

   = 1 2 6 9 11 12 13 21 22 28

(B) *A Spectacle Producing Force*

   (i.e., a highly ocularcentric marvel-making regime)

   = 2 6 11 12 13 14 23 26 30

(C) A Pungently Contemporary Mood

(i.e., a vogueish regime)

= 2 6 12 21 22 24 28

(D) A Cool/Anonymous/Liminal/Unengaged But Empowering Outlook On The World

(i.e., a superficial, uninvolving regime)

= 2 7 16 19 24 25

(E) A Revelatory Power Of/About Culture And Inheritance

(i.e., an admixed regime which exposes interestingly yet highly selectively as it recombines with other forces in and of culture)

= 3 28 30

(F) A Highly Dramatic And Reproductive Performative Force

(i.e., a regime which makes and manufactures as it makes manifest)

= 3 12 13 14 19 21 22

(G) A Self - Celebratory Mood of Unification

(i.e., a self-congratulatory/rallying regime)

= 3 8 25

(H) A Normalising/Universalising/Mainstreaming/Power

(i.e., a concretising and privilege-bestowing regime)

= 3 5 8 9 11 12 14 15 19 22 24

(I) An Unconscious Will - To - Truth

(i.e., an unsuspected/under-suspected regime of compilation to place and position things in relation to ones own felt world-order)

= 4 9

(J) An Impulse To Self - Actualise And See, Know, And Talk Of And About The World And Also 'Be' There In

(i.e., a regime of inquiry and articulation)

= 4 16 21 24 25 26

(K) *An Impulse To Be Supreme/Superior In And Across The World*

(i.e., a regime of heightened and comparative pride)

= 4 9

(L) *An Ethos Of Difference And Celebrated 'Specialness'*

(i.e., a regime of imagined distinctness and exhibited uniqueness)

= 5 6 8 10 11 14 15 17 21

(M) *A Celebration Of Pleasure And Fun*

(i.e., a hedonistic regime of self-indulged immersion in that which is desired --- of animated *joie de vivre* and play)

= 6 7 9 11 12 16 18 19 20 26 27 30

(N) *A Spirit Of Freedom And Mobility*

(i.e., a regime of liberation to be, to travel, to see)

= 6 12 17 20 23 24 25

(O) *A Spirit Of Escape From Responsibilities And Care*

(i.e., a regime of liberation from domesticity)

= 6 16 20 21

(P) *A Celebration Of Choice In/Of Life*

(i.e., a regime of profusion)

= 6

(Q) *An Experiential Mood Of Novelty - Seeking encounters*

(i.e., a regime of infective [but generally superficial] sensation)

= 6 13 17 23 16

(R) *A Compulsion To Consume*

(i.e., a regime of owned experience/possessed object/marketplace-captured-entity)

= 7 8 10 12 13 14 16 22 27 28 29 30

(S)   *An Impulse To Appropriate 'The Other'*

(i.e., a regime of cultural conquest)

= 9 11 13 14 16 18 19 24 27 30

(T)   *An Industralising Outlook On/Over The World*

(i.e., a regime predicated upon productivist/developmentalist/progressivist notions)

= 10 13

(21) *A Utilitarian/Re-Valuation Of The Natural/Inherited World*

(i.e., a regime which harnesses that which is serviceable)

= 30

(V)   *A Professionialised Outlook*

(i.e., a regime of conspiracist, banausic profanities)

= 7 10 17 20 27

(W) *A Falsifying Order Generally Shorn Of Traditional Value Or Embedded Worth*

(i.e., a regime of decorous, expedient 'value' and mediated 'myth' ... a regime of 'fantasque')

= 10 14 15 17 18 19 30

(X)   *A Highly Inventive And Hyper-Real Projectivity*

(i.e., a regime of heightened creativity and inflationary fanciful fecundity)

= 11 12 13 14 19 20 21 30

(Y)   *An Essentialising Framework*

(i.e., a regime which invents and bestows imagined pedigrees on peoples, places, and/or pasts)

= 11 14 15 19 21 22 30

(Z)   *A Portrayal Of The 'Elevated' Ordinary*

(i.e., a regime which triumphalises the assumed simple, customary, or prosaic)

= 11 13 15 19 22 23 30

(AA)An Anti - Auratic Temper

(i.e., a de-differentiating regime which can disarticulate received differences in and of things)

= 12 13 23 24 26 27 28

(BB)A Mediated World Of Massified Consciousness

(i.e., a regime of mechanised/electronic kinematics)

= 12 17 20 21 27

(CC) A Potently Postmodern And Implosive Spirit

(i.e., a regime of accelerating abandonment which casually replaces the received, the foundational, and the established with the new, the ephemeral, and the hybrid)

= 12 13 14 20 21 22 23 24 26 27 30

(DD)A Fleeting, Transitional Re - Envisionment Of Culture And Community

(i.e., a regime of reduced and decontextualised understanding)

= 12 13 17 18 19 20 21 22 27 28 30

(EE) A Compulsively Semiotic World - Order

(i.e., a regime of constant signification and directive representation)

= 13 15 17 19 21 23 30

(FF) A Place - Making Power

(i.e., a regime which manufactures local identity, and which generally engenders a highly-inventive sense of place)

= 13 14 15 19 21 22 26 28

(GG)A Romantic Affectation About Self And Of Quaint Nostalgia Over/About The World

(i.e., a regime of whimsical allure and sentimental attachment towards the seemingly 'pastoral' world)

= 18 28

(HH) *A Sentiment Which Selectively Sacralises Nature As Being Bounteous And Wonderful*

(i.e., a regime of mild [but generally not informed] awe of and about nature which anthropomorphises and reculturalises it, or otherwise which denaturalises it)

= 6 18 30

(II) *A Submissive Temper*

(i.e., a regime which promotes ease and passivity in the getting of experience and the gain of sensation)

= 20

(JJ) *A Democratising/Popularising Power*

(i.e., a regime which reflects an egalitarian spirit, or which otherwise conjures one up ubiquitously across the world)

= 23 26

(KK) *An Internationalising Mood*

(i.e., a regime which privileges the global connectivity and ecumenical reach of things)

= 24 25

(LL) *An Aestheticisation Of Life*

(i.e., a regime which accentuates the creative, artistic, atmospheric, and sumptuous merit in and of objects/ideas/places --- though not necessarily in terms of received/orthodox/conventional differentiations)

= 29

Discussion: Re-regarding the gaze of and across the panorama of tourism and travel

Clearly then, Urry does not envision the gaze as being one single or constant thing. The close scrutiny of *The Tourist Gaze* which lead to the interpretive production of Table 2 suggests that to Urry:

The plurality of tourist gazes

there are many sometimes distinct and sometimes interfusive 'sub - gazes' rather than one all purpose magisterial *le regard* in tourism and travel;

The historicity of tourist gazes

the gaze (or other, these gazes) may change considerably over time;

The complexities and counter-complexities of the imperatives behind tourist gazes

there may sometimes be internal disjunction between the imperatives behind any such sub -
gazes (where for instance, (AA) "the pressure through the tourist gaze to build up an anti-
auratic temper", may lie in tension with (LL) "the pressure to aestheticise life", and where
(I) "the highly activated drive towards an unconscious will - to - truth" may work with some
disaccord against other 'passive' or submissive tempers [such as II]).

Such is but the complexity of human outlooks on life being and identity: such is merely
reflective of the richer rational/irrational/arational make up of the dance (or rather, the
dances) of our depolarising and yet repolarising lives. No one should expect that the realm of
life we label 'tourism' or 'travel' should be anymore fathomable or anymore classifiable,
than the intricacies of 'life' itself. This deconstruction of Urry's tourist gaze therefore seems
to tell us that in tourism and travel, tourists, travel programmers, and leisure managers *are*
all driven by a litany of different (sometimes conflictive) imperatives, and that they also
coterminously *drive* a litany of different (sometimes conflictive) imperatives.

And obviously, the deconstruction given in Table 2 is only one person's studied
interpretation of what Urry inferred, implied, or was indicative about in his undefined term
'the tourist gaze! No doubt some readers may find that the deconstruction offered is not
sufficiently 'vision - based' vis - a - vis being 'imagination - based', per se. No doubt some
astute social economists will insist that the above deconstruction does not reflect the degree
to which Urry views 'the tourist gaze' as being largely a middle class imposition on and over
the world. No doubt there are other readers of Urry elsewhere (especially those well versed
in the Urry within Lash and Urry 1994) who would insist that the deconstruction of Table 2
is insufficiently reflexive with Urry's strongly held views about the accelerating mobility of
organised capitalism and citizenship whereby the tourist gaze is conceivably seen to be a
highly representative cultural, geographic, economic, political, and psychic sense of 'social
flow' across space, place, and territory. No doubt others would state that the above
deconstruction makes an insufficient effort to distinguish what Urry was stating about the
nature of 'the tourist gaze' in his post - industrialising hinterland of Northern England (viz.,
which is perhaps the strong and contained econo - geographical space cum psycho -
structural axis of *The Tourist Gaze*) as compared to what Urry was ever attempting to
uncover in terms of the character of the tourist gaze *in a more generalised form* elsewhere
around the globe. And no doubt there are specialists of 'time' out there who would maintain
that the fast deconstruction of Table 2 does not adequately capture what Urry was stating (or
implying) about the subtle ways in which 'the tourist gaze" mirrors rich recent changes in
social temporality. And so on, et cetera.

Ladies and gentlemen of tourism and travel out there, promoters and consumers of tourism
and travel out there alike, travel - makers and tour - takers out there, you are each invited to
critique further what Urry claimed to have found under his sociologists eye - glass, and
whether those who 'work' and 'play' or who 'manage' and 'desire' in arenas of tourism and
travel are highly regulated, are highly coercive, and are highly professionalised individuals
acting within some form of Foucauldian 'carceral society' (Miller 1993: 212; Morris and

Patton 1979: 117). So, pick up the pen … step up to the keyboard … give us your views about the supposed dominance-bestowing and privilege-manufacturing magisterialities in and across these so called juridical space of tourism and travel. We do need a continuously serving 'jury' observing vigilantly over such vital matters of being, knowing, living, and making. Give out your verdict: give forth your views. Look out, for the sake of the world we tourise! Look out, for the selves we variously empower and contain!

References

Barthes, R. (1981), *Camera Lucida*. New York. Hill and Wang.

Baudrillard, J. (1985), The Ecstacy of Communication. In H.Foster, ed. *Postmodern Culture*. London. Pluto. pp. 126 - 134.

Benjamin, W. (1973), The Work of Art in the Age of Mechanical Reproduction. In W. Benjamin. *Illuminations*. London. Fontane. pp. 219 - 54.

Bhabha, H. (1994), *The Location of Culture*. London. Routledge.

Bourdieu, P. (1984), *Distinction*. London. Routledge and Kegan Paul.

Bourdieu, P. (1984), *La Plaisir de Savoir*. Le Monde. June 27.

Burchell, G., C. Gordon, and P. Miller. (1991), *The Foucault Effect: Studies in Governmentality*. Chicago. University of Chicago Press.

Culler, J. (1981), Semiotics of Tourism. *American Journal of Semiotics*. 1. 127 - 40.

Dann, G. (1996), *The Language of Tourism - A Sociolinguistic Perspective*. Wallingford, Oxford. CAB International.

Davidson, A. I., ed. (1997), *Foucault and His Interlocators*. Chicago. University of Chicago Press.

de Burlo, C. (1996), Cultural Resistance and Ethnic Tourism on South Pentecost, Vanuatu. In R. Butler and T. Hinch, ed. *Tourism and Indigenous Peoples*. London. International Thomson Business Press. pp. 255-277.

Deleuze, G. (1997), Desire and Pleasure. In A.I.Davidson, ed. *Foucault and His Interlocators*. Chicago. University of Chicago Press. pp. 183 - 194.

Eco, U. (1986), *Travels in Hyper - Reality*. London. Picador.

Edwards, E. (1996), Postcards: Greetings from Another World. In T. Selwyn, ed. *The Tourist Image: Myths and Myth Making in Tourism*. Chichester. John Wiley. pp. 197 - 222.

Ehreneich, B. (1989), *Fear of Falling*. New York. Pantheon.

Featherstone, M. (1987), Consumer Culture, Symbolic Power and Universalism. In G. Stauth and G. Zubaida, eds. *Mass Culture, Popular Culture, and Social Life in the Middle East*. Frankfurt. Campus. pp. 17 - 46.

Feifer, M. (1985), *Going Places*. London. Macmillan.

Fjellman, S. M. (1992), *Vinyl Leaves: Walt Disney World and America*. Boulder. Westview Press.

Foucault, M. (1969), *Linguistique et Sciences Sociales. Dits et écrits, 1954 - 1988*. D. Defert and F. Ewald with Jacques Lagrange, eds. (4 vols.). 1:823 - 24. Paris. 1994.

Foucault, M. (1994), *La Philosophie Analytique de la Politique. Dits et écrits, 1954 - 1988*. 1978. ed. D. Defert and F. Ewald with J. Lagrange. Paris. 4 vols. 3:540-542.

Foucault, M. and Chomsky, N. (1997), Human Nature: Justice versus Power. In A.I.Davidson, ed. *Foucault and his Interlocators*. Chicago. University Chicago Press. pp. 107 - 145.

Foucault, M. (1997), Writing the Self. Translated by Ann Hobart. In A. I. Davidson, ed. *Foucault and his Interloctors*. Chicago. University of Chicago. pp. 234 - 247.

Goodwin, A. (1989), Nothing Like the Real Thing. *New Statesman and Society*. 12th August.

Hall, C. M. (1996), *Tourism and Politics: Policy, Power and Place*. Chichester. John Wiley.

Harrison, D. (1992), *Tourism and the Less Developed Countries*. London. Belhaven Press.

Hollinshead, K. (1993), *The Truth about Texas: A Naturalistic Study of the Construction of Heritage*. Unpublished Doctoral Dissertation. Dept. of Recreation, Park, and Tourism Sciences. Texas A and M University. College Station, Texas, U.S.A.

Hollinshead, K. (1998/A), Cross - referential Marketing across Walt Disney's World: Corporate Power and the Imagineering of Nation and Culture. *Tourism Analysis*. 23 pgs.

Hollinshead, K. (1998/B), Disney and Commodity Aesthetics: A Critique of Fjellman's Analysis of 'Distory' and the 'Historicide' of the Past. *Current Issues in Tourism*. 54 pgs.

Hollinshead, K. (1998/C), Tourism, Hybridity, and Ambiguity: The Relevance of Bhabha's 'Third Space' Cultures. *Journal of Leisure Research*. Special Issue on Race, Ethnicity and Leisure.

Hollinshead, K. (1998/D), Tourism and the Restless Peoples: A Dialectical Inspection of Bhabha's Halfway Populations. *Tourism, Culture and Communication*. 1:1.

Hollinshead, K. (1999), Surveillance of the Worlds of Tourism: Foucault and the Eye - of - Power. *Tourism Management*. 20. 7-23.

Jameson, F. (1985), Postmodernism and Consumer Culture. In H. Foster, ed. *Postmodern Culture*. London. Pluto. pp. 111 - 25.

Lash, S. (1990), *Sociology of Postmodernism*. London. Routledge.

Lash, S. and Urry, J. (1994), *Economics of Signs and Space*. London. Sage.

Lin, S. G. and Patnaik, N. (1982), Migrant Labour at Asiad '82 Construction Sites in New Delhi. *Bulletin of Concerned Asian Scholars*. 14(3). July -Sept. 23 -31.

Lindstrom, L. (1990), *Knowledge and Power in a South Pacific Society*. Washington. Smithsonian Institution Press.

Lynch, K. (1973), *What Time is This Place?* Cambridge, Ma. M.I.T. Press.

Macdonnell, D. (1986), *Theories of Discourse*. Oxford. Basil Blackwell.

Matthews, H. G. (1975), International Tourism and Political Science Research. *Annals of Tourism Research*. 2:4. 195 - 203.

McKay, I. (1988), Twilight at Peggy's Cove: Towards a Genealogy of 'Maritinicity' in Nova Scotia. *Borderlines*. Summer. 29 -37.

Mercer, C. (1983), A Poverty of Desire: Pleasure and Popular Politics. In T.Bennett, ed. *Formations of Pleasure*. London. Routledge and Kegan Paul. pp. 84 - 101.

Merquior, J. G. (1985), *Foucault*. London. Fontana Press.

Miller, J. (1993), *The Passion of Michel Foucault*. New York. Doubleday.

Morris, M. and P. Patton, eds. (1979), *Michel Foucault: Power, Truth, Strategy*. Sydney. Feral Publications.

Morris, M. (1996), Life as a Tourist Object in Australia. In M - F. Lanfant, J.B. Allock, and E.M. Bruner, eds. *International Tourism: Identity and Change*. London. Sage. pp. 177 - 191.

Morris, M. (1997), A Question of Cultural Studies. In A. McRobbie, ed. *Back to Reality?: Social Experience and Cultural Studies*. A. McRobbie, ed. Manchester. Manchester University Press. pp. 36 - 57.

Parry, K. (1983), Resorts on the Lancashire Coast. Newton Abbot, Devon. David and Charles.

Peck, J. B. and A. S. Lepie. (1978), Tourism and Development in Three North Carolina Coastal Towns. In V. L. Smith, ed. *Hosts and Guests*. Oxford, England. Basil Blackwell.

Richter, L.K. (1983), Tourism and Political Science: A Case of Not So Benign Neglect. *Annals of Tourism Research* (Special Issue on Political Science). Oct. - Dec.

Richter, L.K. (1994), The Political Dimensions of Tourism. In J. R. B.Ritchie and C. R. Goeldner, eds. *Travel, Tourism, and Hospitality Research: A Handbook for Managers and Researchers*. New York. John Wiley.

Shames, G. W. and W. G. Glover. (1989), *World Class Service*. Yarmouth, Maine. Intercultural Press, Inc.

Shields, R (1990), *Places on the Margin*. London. Routledge.

Sinclair, M. T., P. Alizadeh, and E. A. A. Onunga. (1992), The Structure of International Tourism and Tourism Development in Kenya. In D. Harrison, ed. *Tourism and the Less Developed Countries*. London. Belhaven. pp. 47 - 63.

Sofield, T. H .B. (1996), Anuha Island Resort, Soloman Islands: A Case Study of Failure. In R. Butler and T. Hinch, eds. *Tourism and Indigenous Peoples*. London. International Thomson Business Press. pp. 176 - 202.

Sturrock, J. (1979), *Structuralism and Since*. Oxford. Oxford University Press.

Tonkinson, R. (1982), Kastam in Melanesia: Introduction. *Mankind*. 13.4. 302 - 15.

Urry, J. (1990), *The Tourist Gaze: Leisure and Travel in Contemporary Society*. London. Sage.

Urry., J. (1992/B), The Tourist Gaze 'Revisited'. *American Behavioural Scientist*. 36. 2. (November) 172-186.

Veyne, P. (1997/A), Foucault Revolutionises History. In A. I. Davidson, ed. *Foucault and his Interloctors*. Chicago. The University of Chicago Press. pp. 146 - 182.

Veyne, P. (1997/B), The Final Foucault and His Ethics. In *Foucault and his Interlocators*. A. I. Davidson, ed. Chicago. The University of Chicago Press. pp. 225 - 233.

Walter, J. (1982), Social Limits to Tourism. *Leisure Studies*. 1. 195 - 304.

White, H. (1978), *Topics of Discourse: Essays in Cultural Criticism*. Baltimore, Maryland. The Johns Hopkins University.

White, M. and G.S. Kanahele (1989), Tourism: Keeper of the Culture. In G. W. Shames and W. G. Glover, eds. *World Class Service*. Yarmouth, Maine. Intercultural Press. pp. 51 - 59.

Wolff, J. (1985), The Invisible Flâneuse: Women and the Literature of Modernity. *Theory, Culture and Society*. 2. 37 - 48.

Wright, P. (1985), *On Living in an Old Country*. London. Verso.

Social and cultural impacts of tourism and the tourist motivation: Turkish Republic of Northern Cyprus (TRNC) as a case study

Şöhret Başaran Howells

East Devon College, UK

Introduction

The impact of tourism is identified by Pearce (1992) as the most common theme to emerge in the review of tourism research, with varying emphasis being given to economic, social, cultural and environmental issues depending on the background of the writers concerned. Geographers usually emphasise tourism's spatial structures, sociologists and anthropologists highlighting social relationships with respect to tourism and economists emphasising economic attributes. Apart from these, emphasis shifts from one tourism impact to another depending on the stages of development of tourism, region under consideration and time. However, whenever impacts of tourism are mentioned, the economic benefits seem to be the main point emphasised by most authors and researchers. As Pizam and Milman (1984) point out, tourism is not exclusively an economic activity, but it also involves social, cultural, political and environmental aspects. A similar scenario is drawn by Liu, Sheldon and Var (1987), who state that non-economic impacts tend to be negative on the whole, since tourism disrupts social and environmental systems at destinations. It is emphasised by Lindberg and Johnson (1997), that the exclusion of these negative non-economic impacts however, lead to the overestimation of the net social benefits of tourism. Travis (1980), however, suggests that the undesirable impacts of tourism can be anticipated and handled. This can be achieved by monitoring the social, economic and other various effects of tourism development and, if necessary by adjusting and regulating through feedback systems. Similarly, Mathieson and Wall (1982) mention that, when books and articles are searched, it is observed that, in contrast to the economic effects, social and cultural impacts are usually portrayed in the literature in a negative light. Only recently has research challenged the validity of the belief that tourism promotes understanding between people of different nationalities and cultures. On the other hand, Travis (1982) states that, until recently there has been a lack of adequate academic attention to the economic disbenefits of tourism, and the costs and benefits in the environmental and socio-cultural realms. Similarly, Duffield (1982) points out that the social impact of tourism is largely *"under-researched"* (p.249), and compared with studies of its physical and economic impact, social impacts assessment has come late to the agenda.

It can be concluded that, whilst most researchers analysed the economic and environmental impacts of tourism, social and cultural impacts were only briefly touched upon and require further exploration. Travis (1982) refers to Loukissas (1977) who states that one of the main reasons for this could be that although it is easier to measure and quantify the economic impacts of tourism, social and cultural effects of tourism are relatively more difficult to quantify. Similarly, Inskeep (1994) mentions that, although socio-cultural impacts are major considerations in developing tourism in any place, they are more difficult to measure than economic or environmental impacts. Duffield (1982) argues that in essence, there exists within tourism a basic economic and social contradiction: that is, a tourism industry which has been adopted as a tool for regional development, employment and as an income generator, often depends on the maintenance of the social, cultural and environmental characteristics of the society it is meant to change. He adds that,

> *"as a result, there is tension between the forces of economic convergence represented in the use of tourism as a tool for regional development and the cultural and environmental ossification which the industry itself tends to demand of its product"* (p.252).

The above background information on impacts of tourism encouraged the author to carry out further research to decide on the scope of her study, which developed into a Ph.D. thesis. An in-depth literature review has been carried out on economic, environmental and social and cultural impacts of tourism. However, although politics have always been a major issue in the development of tourism in Cyprus, it has intentionally been omitted, since it does not constitute a topic of interest to the author, and she would like to consider it as a "given" determinant. The analysis carried out on economic and environmental impacts have not been included in this paper, since they are not in the scope of the thesis. However, a brief discussion of the social and cultural impacts of tourism and tourist motivation, leading to the selection of the scope of this study is emphasised below.

Social and cultural impacts of tourism and tourist motivation

Social and cultural impacts of tourism are defined by Pizam and Milman (1984, p:11) as *"the ways in which tourism is contributing to changes in value systems, individual behaviour, family relationships, collective lifestyles, moral conduct, creative expressions, traditional ceremonies and community organisation"*. Social impacts are said to involve more immediate changes in the social structure of the community, whereas the cultural impacts focus on the longer-term changes in a society's norms and standards, which will show itself gradually in a community's social relationships and artefacts (Murphy, 1985). Pearce (1995) and Travis (1982), refer to Lundgren (1972), who emphasised that *"the social impact of tourism will vary according to the differences between the visitors and the visited, whether in terms of numbers, race, culture, or social outlook"*. Travis (1982) suggests that one cannot see cultural impacts, simply in monolithic terms of the "host culture" and the "visitor culture" since there may be several host cultures, as well as several tourist cultures represented at one place, at one point in time. He also adds that the critical determinants of the cultural impacts depends on the stage of social, economic and political development of the society hosting tourism, and whether its relationship is primarily with international tourists from a society at a different stage of development, or primarily with domestic tourists from the same society. All the above facts make it difficult to measure and analyse social and cultural impacts. Moreover, in order to assess cultural impacts which concentrate on longer term changes in a society, longitudinal studies are deemed necessary. Many studies relating to the social and cultural impacts of tourism were initially concentrating on social and cultural costs, but subsequent research has tended to be more balanced, acknowledging also the advantages and disadvantages which the expansion of tourism can bring to different societies and communities (Pearce, 1992).

Tourist motivation, on the other hand, though neglected for a long time (Holden, 1999), has gained importance especially over the last decade. One of the earlier reasons for emphasising the importance of tourist motivation came from marketers and promoters of tourism, who realised that it enables the identification of market segmentation and target marketing which is essential in the extremely competitive tourist travel market (Shaw and Williams, 1994). However, another importance, which is mostly neglected, is that motivation links to the impact of destination areas (Crompton, 1979).

Scope and aims of the study

Studies on social and cultural impacts of tourism have been very limited. Moreover, these studies usually concentrated on a single aspect such as language, or emphasised negative impacts until recently. This may be due to the difficulty in measuring social and cultural change, often necessitating longitudinal studies. Finally, as yet, any direct relevant search on motivation and its link to the socio-cultural impacts have not been discovered, although numerous research exist which links to the economic and environmental impacts. As it is suggested by Parrinello (1993), perhaps motivation should not only be analysed as a broad topic on its own, but should be studied within a narrower framework but along wider interdisciplinary lines of inquiry. These difficulties and limitations turned into a challenge and shaped the scope of the study, concentrating on scrutinising the tourist motivation and its links to socio-cultural impacts in this thesis. This may have important implications as to how to motivate, promote and develop loyalty amongst the "social and cultural friendly" tourists which may help to shape the socio-cultural change in a positive way and minimise its negative impacts (see Figure 1).

Figure 1   Broad Conceptual Framework of the Study

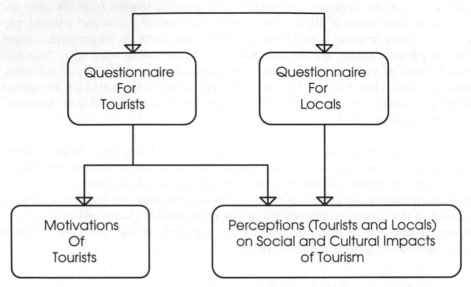

The main aims of the study can be summarised as: exploring the social and cultural impacts of tourism from the perceptions of visitors and local residents, and identifying the role of motivation in the social and cultural impacts exerted in TRNC (Turkish Republic of Northern Cyprus). It was also an intention to investigate the implications as to how to motivate, promote and develop loyalty amongst the "social and cultural friendly" tourists which may help to shape the socio-cultural change in a positive way and minimise its negative impacts. A causal relationship is not strictly being tested since it is very difficult to rule out alternative explanations.

These broad aims can be subdivided into a number of more explicit aims. These are:

- To analyse the motivations of visitors to TRNC;

- To analyse the motivations of first-time visitors;

- To analyse the motivations of the repeat visitors;

- To compare the motivations of first-time and repeat visitors;

- To analyse the role of nationality on motivations of first-time and repeat visitors;

- To develop a "cultural friendly" visitor profile;

- To explore the perceptions of the repeat visitors and local residents on social and cultural impacts of tourism;

- To compare the change observed by repeat visitors and local residents on predetermined social and cultural variables of: traffic accidents, crime, clothing habits, eating habits, language, religious beliefs and practices and sexual behaviour;

- To compare the role of nationality on perceptions of repeat visitors about social and cultural change;

- To compare the role of differences between the local residents of the two settlements, such as gender, age, education level and tourism related jobs on perceptions about social and cultural change; and

- To analyse the reasons stated by repeat visitors and local residents on social and cultural change, and explore the direct and indirect role of tourism in this change.

In order to achieve the aims stated above, two separate questionnaires were prepared to investigate the motivations of the first-time and repeat visitors, and the perceptions of repeat visitors and local residents on social and cultural impacts of tourism.

Case study: selection criteria and methodology

In order to analyse the perceptions of tourists on social and cultural impacts of tourism and the role of motivation in TRNC, Girne (Kyrenia) region was selected as a case study area. On the other hand, in order to analyse the perceptions of local residents on social and cultural impacts of tourism, two different villages are chosen. One of these villages, Karaoğlanoğlu is situated at the northern cost of the island along the Girne (Kyrenia) range, near to tourists and tourism activities. The other village, Ortaköy is situated inland, near Lefkoşa (Nicosia), the capital city, where virtually no tourism activity takes place and almost no tourists visit (see Figure 2).

Figure 2   Location of the Villages/Towns and Region Chosen for the Case Study

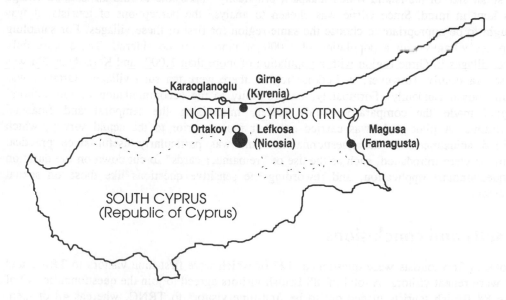

This study can also be considered as a "comparison" with a "longitudinal" dimension (Yin, 1984). The case of TRNC can be considered a comparison since two different villages will be compared using the same measure of the same variables to find out if any difference with relation to perceptions on social and cultural change exists. Moreover, although the same group will not be analysed through time, at least for the purposes of this thesis, these groups will be asked to comment as to the socio-cultural change over the last twenty years. Therefore, it also carries the implications of a longitudinal study (Dixon, Bouma and Atkinson, 1987). Likewise, the tourists from three different nationalities, namely Turkish, British and German who have been visiting North Cyprus on repeated occasions will be asked to comment as to their perceptions of change in social and cultural aspects over time. One point needs to be emphasised here. Throughout this paper, the terms "North Cyprus" and "TRNC" (Turkish Republic of Northern Cyprus) will be used interchangeably.

The reasons for the choice of the region of Girne (Kyrenia) and the villages of Ortaköy and Karaoğlanoğlu for the case study can be summarised as follows. Tourists visiting TRNC are concentrated mainly in two regions, Girne (Kyrenia) and Maðusa (Famagusta). Girne has been chosen as the case study region since it has the largest number of bed capacity with 4,997 as compared to Mağusa, which has a bed capacity of 2,396 as of 1995 (Statistical Yearbook, 1995). Another reason for choosing Girne was its proximity to the parents' house of the author in Lefkoşa, where she stayed during her field study. However, the fact that not all tourists stay at hotel establishments, some prefer to stay with family and friends, is acknowledged, and special attention has been given to choice of samples and collection of data from the intended sample. The reasons behind the selection of the above named villages are as follows. For comparison purposes, it was decided to choose two villages/towns for the study. One of these would be from an area with proximity to tourists, so that local residents have the maximum possibility of contact with the tourists. The other would be from an area far away from tourist accommodation establishments and has virtually no attractions appealing to the tourists. This would ensure the minimum contact with tourists and might be helpful to explore the role of tourists in the perceived social and cultural change. However, the small size of the island which makes it practically impossible to find an isolated village was kept in mind. Since Girne was chosen to analyse the perceptions of tourists, it was thought to be appropriate to choose the same region for first of these villages. For sampling purposes villages with a population of 1,000 or more were considered. There were only three villages in Girne region with a population of more than 1,000, and Karaoğlanoğlu was chosen randomly. However, in Lefkoşa region, there were ten such villages. Ortaköy was again chosen randomly. Fortunately, its proximity to the accommodation of the authors' parents made the comparative study easier, minimising the temporal and financial constraints. A pilot study was carried out four months prior to the actual survey, which enabled adjustments to the questionnaires. This was particularly useful since practical solutions were introduced, such as the use of "remainder cards" to cut down on the duration of questionnaire application, and rewording the sensitive questions like those on sexual behaviour.

Results and conclusions

A total of 266 tourists were questioned, 123 of which were first-time visitors to TRNC and 143 were repeat visitors. A total of 88 British visitors agreed to join the questionnaire. 40 of these 88 British tourists turned out to be first-time visitors to TRNC, whereas 48 of them were repeat visitors. On the other hand, of the 100 Turkish tourists who consented to join the questionnaire, 48 of the Turkish tourists were first-time visitors to TRNC, whereas 52 of them were repeat visitors to TRNC. Finally, 78 German tourists participated, 35 of which were first-time visitors. On the other hand, a total of 208 Turkish-Cypriots were questioned. 112 of these were from Ortaköy, a village near the capital city Lefkoşa, which is far away from tourists establishments. The rest, 96 of them were from Karaoğlanoğlu, a village near to several tourist establishments and the touristic area of Girne, which is a major city on the north coast. The results obtained from the study and the conclusions arrived at are summarised below.

Comparison of the perceptions of repeat visitors and local residents on social and cultural impacts

This section is comprised of comparisons of the perceptions of the repeat visitors and the local residents on a set of predetermined social and cultural variables which are: traffic accidents, crime, clothing habits, eating habits, language, religious beliefs and practices and sexual behaviour. Comparison of the stated above variables with respect to the type of change has been possible since similar questioning techniques were used for both sets of respondents. However, difficulties have been encountered when reasons for change were analysed. This was primarily due to the different types of questioning techniques used for repeat visitors and local residents. The details of this are discussed in the related sections below. It should be noted here that, some aspects were discussed with only one set of respondents, therefore comparison was not possible. Specifically, change in hospitality was only asked to the repeat visitors but not to the local residents since it would not be relevant. On the other hand, changes in the taste of music of the Turkish Cypriot youth and gambling were only asked to the local residents. The reason behind this is that, unless they have very close contacts with the Turkish Cypriot youth, visitors are unlikely to comment as to changes in taste of music, and gambling habits, while other aspects such as change in clothing habits are more likely to be observed. In these comparisons when deemed necessary differences between the repeat visitors with respect to nationality and differences between the villages of Ortaköy and Karaoğlanoğlu will be emphasised. Other times, these differences will be omitted for simplicity and to facilitate the comparison of results.

Amongst repeat visitors, changes in clothing habits have been reported by 23.1% of Turkish, 22.2% of British but by none of the Germans. This may be due to the fact that German visitors due to their accommodation type have the minimum contact, hence the least observation. However, all of the local residents questioned stated that there is a visible change in the clothing habits of the youth. It can be concluded that there is a consensus that the clothing habits are changing. It is agreed by a considerable percentage of both repeat visitors and local residents that clothing is becoming less conservative and more "sporty" (see Table 1).

Table 1   Perceptions on Type of Change in Clothing Habits: Comparison of Visitors and Local Visitors

Change in Clothing (%)	Repeat Visitors		Local Residents
	Turkish	British	Ortaköy & Karaoğlanoğlu
Less Conservative (or sexy)	44.4	16.6	63.9
"Sporty"	55.6	83.3	12.5

Nationality differences were not significant when the perceptions on change in eating habits were considered. Similarly there were no significant differences given between the two villages. Overall, 38.1% of repeat visitors and all of the local residents reported some sort of change in eating habits. When the results relating to the type of change were analysed, it was difficult to categorise both sets of data under exactly the same categorisation. However, in general there was an agreement that "junk food", fast food or ready made food replaced home-made or traditional food, and there were more of the less traditional food such as pizza as opposed to traditional dishes (see Table 2).

Table 2   Perceptions on Type of Change in Eating Habits: Comparison of Visitors and Local Residents

Change in Eating (%)	Repeat Visitors	Local Residents
"Junk", Fast food (i.e.: kebabs), Ready-made	53.27	28.9
Less Traditional (i.e.: Burgers, Pizza)	12.6	69.2

It is agreed by 95.2% of repeat visitors regardless of nationality and all of the local residents under question regardless of residency, that there was a dramatic increase in the level of traffic accidents. Both of these groups entered into long discussions as to the reasons for increases in traffic accidents. Although there were some differences as to the reasons for such an increase, the common determinants were stated as speed, lack of maintenance and road signs (see Table 3). Moreover, both groups perceived youngsters as the major cause for traffic accidents. It should be noted that the lack of road signs constituted a major handicap for the repeat visitors, however, this was considered as a minor problem by the local residents. This can be due to the fact that local residents are familiar with the roads, but not the visitors. Therefore, local residents feel less need of road signs as compared to the visitors.

Table 3   Reasons for Increase in Level of Traffic Accidents: Perceptions of Repeat Visitors and Local Residents

Reasons for traffic Accidents (%)	Repeat Visitors	Local Residents
Speed/Dangerous driving	100	77
Lack of Maintenance and Road signs	100	10.1

Regardless of their nationality, 14.26% of repeat visitors perceived an increase in crime like theft and robbery, while all of the local residents questioned reported an increase. However, there was a consensus that the increase in such crime was not directed towards the tourists. This is especially evident by the fact that, German repeat visitors have not observed any change in crime level, while all of the local residents reported increase (see Table 4).

Table 4   Perceived Increase in the Level of Crime: Comparison of Visitors and Local Residents

Change in	Repeat Visitors			Local Residents
CRIME LEVEL (%)	Turkish	British	German	Ortaköy & Karaoğlanoğlu
Increased	20.5	14.8	0	100
Not Changed	79.5	85.2	100	100

Perceptions of change in sexual behaviour was analysed from several different aspects such as marriage with foreigners and approval of pre-marital sex in the case of local residents. However, only one aspect, that of the main change in sexual behaviour was analysed in the case of the repeat visitors, therefore only one aspect was comparable. It should be noted here that, actually the compared variable is slightly different in each case. In the case of repeat visitors, to become less conservative in attitude especially in the public was reported. On the other hand, in the case of the local residents, tolerance to pre-marital sex was the question. Still, it is decided that these two variables are converged and analysed as a single aspect to enable comparison (see Table 5).

Table 5   Perceived Change in Sexual Behaviour: Comparison of Visitors and Local Residents

Change in Sexual Behaviour (%)	Repeat Visitors			Local Residents
	Turkish	British	German	Ortaköy & Karaoğlanoğlu
Less Conservative/Tolerant to pre-marital sex	25.6	18.5	0	52.5
Not Changed/Not tolerant	74.4	81.5	100	47.5

As was the case with change in sexual behaviour, various aspects related to religion, ranging from belief in God and visitation of the Mosque have been scrutinised in the case of local residents. However, only a single aspect, that of perceived change in religious practices have been asked to the repeat visitors. The results are indicative that it was only the Turkish repeat visitors who have perceived decrease in religious practices, such as visiting the mosque. This may be due to the fact that British and German repeat visitors, due to their different religion and less contact with the local residents are less likely to differentiate such change. When the local resident answers were analysed, although mosques have been visited for various reasons like burial ceremonies and tourist guiding, majority believed that religious practices were disappearing especially amongst the young generation, while a minority claimed that there was a revival of religious practices (see Table 6).

Table 6   Perceived Change in Religious Practices: Comparison of Visitors and Local Residents

Change in Religious Practices (%)	Repeat Visitors (Turkish)	Local Residents
Decreasing Religious Practices	9.5	88
Revival of Religious Practices	0	12
No Perceived Change	90.5	0

Finally, changes in the language have been interpreted by the repeat visitors and the local residents. Turkish repeat visitors talked about changes in the Turkish language of the Turkish Cypriots, while the German repeat visitors mentioned the improvement in the level of foreign languages spoken. However, it is natural that British and German repeat visitors would be unlikely to comment on the changes of the Turkish language unless they speak it themselves. The perceptions of the local residents concentrated on changes in the Turkish of especially the youth. Amongst various changes, there was an agreement by both sets of groups that the Turkish language of the Turkish Cypriot youth was becoming more like the Turkish of mainland Turks (See table 7).

Table 7   Perceived Change in Language: Comparison of Visitors and Local Residents

Change in Language (%)	Repeat Visitors			Local Residents
	Turkish	British	German	Ortaköy & Karaoğlanoğlu
Change in Turkish towards that in mainland Turkey/better	28.2	0	0	70.7
Improvement in German usage	0	0	33.3	0
No perceived change	0	100	66.7	0
Other	0	0		29.3

The above comparisons show that there was an agreement by both groups of respondents that there was at least some perceived change in clothing habits, eating habits, level of traffic accidents and crime, sexual behaviour and religious practices and the language of the Turkish Cypriots. In most of the cases there was a consensus as to the type of change taking place. However, in all aspects it was the local residents who made the most detailed observations. Moreover, in some aspects such as religious practices and the language, nationality of the repeat visitors seemed to play a role in the perceptions.

Reasons for change

The reasons for change have not been directly questioned in the case of the repeat visitors. However, the results are indicative that increase in traffic accidents are blamed on youth, relaxed sexual behaviour mainly on TV, and change in eating habits and the language on the visitors. On the other hand, the local residents were given a multiple choice of reasons for change in various social and cultural aspects. These were education, television, travelling abroad, economic conditions and tourists. Results are indicative that not all change can be attributed to tourism. The main reasons for change in various social and cultural changes are summarised as follows. Media seems to be an important factor in changes in taste of music, clothing habits and language, while economic conditions seem to be the main reason for changes in, sexual behaviour, increase in crime, gambling and language. Finally, tourism seems to be having some impact, at least indirectly on eating habits, sexual behaviour, increase in crime, gambling and language. Although religious values and practices were scrutinised, any change and its reasons could not be determined due to open ended questions which led to extremely vague and long answers. Tourism's impact seemed to show variations according to residents of Ortaköy and Karaoğlanoğlu in these variables, which enabled to differentiate the implicit impact.

Motivation of visitors

It is stated by various authors such as Krippendorf (1987), Ryan (1997) and Jefferson and Lickerish (1991), that the main motivation for travel are determined by factors ranging from good climatic conditions to price and political situation. It is a known fact that TRNC has guaranteed sunshine (Statistical Yearbook, 1995), has a very rich history and people are said to be very friendly (Volkan, 1980). Due to the high inflation and devaluation rates the prices are reasonably low compared to most European countries (Kýbrýs, 8 June 1997). Ryan (1997) also state that price, inflation in the host generating countries and rate of exchange as important economic factors as key demand determinants. Food and cuisine, on the other hand, are what the Turkish Cypriots are proud of (Volkan, 1980). Therefore these variable are included in the questionnaire for the repeat visitors as well as the first-time visitors.

For the first-time visitors, amongst the reasons for going to TRNC, good climatic conditions with guaranteed sunshine seems to be the most important factor. 91% of those questioned consider the climate as the most important factor to motivate them to go to TRNC. The other important factors in order of importance are richness of history and culture, reasonable prices and people/hospitality with 38.5%, 36.9% and 28.7% respectively. Apart from climate, the other factors carry more or less the same importance in arriving at a decision about where to go.

When the reasons for visiting TRNC by repeat visitors were scrutinised, the most important motivation for the Turkish repeat visitors is climate which is stated by all of those questioned. This is followed by ease of travel and people/hospitality with 78.4% and 54.9% of the cases respectively. Similarly, for the British repeat visitors climate seems to be the most important motivation with 97.9% of the cases, followed by food and history/culture, both with 41.7% of the cases. People/hospitality, despite expectations appear to have lesser importance with 31.3% of the cases. A very different scenario appears for the repeat German visitors. The main motivation is history and culture with 93% of the cases. This is followed by good climatic conditions with 76.7% of the cases. People and hospitality holds the third position with 60.5% of the cases.

It can be concluded that motivations of first-time and repeat visitors show slight variations. Although all visitors are motivated by suitability of the climate, Turkish repeat visitors give more emphasis to ease of travel, followed by hospitality as compared to the first-time Turkish visitors, who give more emphasis to hospitality followed by history and culture. However, British repeat visitors emphasise the importance of history and culture as much as the first-time British visitors. The importance shown to hospitality is somehow replaced by another cultural aspect, food by the repeat British visitors. On the other hand, both first-time and repeat German visitors give priority to the history and culture, and hospitality becomes a very important motivator for the repeat visitors, which was not the case for first-time German visitors. Overall, the importance given to climate, history and culture seems to increase for the repeat visitors, while importance of hospitality is maintained the same.

Implications for repeat visits: is there a "social and cultural friendly" tourist?

After scrutinising various differences such as nationality, age, gender and the historical and cultural places visited a "Cultural friendly" tourist profile is drawn. In general, the "Cultural friendly" visitor likes visiting many number of historical places, has higher average age, is likely to be found most amongst Germans followed by the British, does not show any differences with respect to gender and is likely to become a repeat visitor. It is also concluded that, due to their close contacts with the local people, and sharing the same language, Turkish repeat visitors are more likely to perceive and create social and cultural impacts. However, contact and language limitations are indicative that British visitors are less likely to perceive or create such impacts, and the German visitors the least. The next question to ask is: are these so called cultural friendly visitors less likely to exert negative social and cultural impact? The implications are in that direction. Let us hope that future will ascertain this issue.

Conclusion

This paper has analysed the variations in motivations of first-time and repeat visitors to TRNC. Overall, the importance given to climate, history and culture seems to increase for the repeat visitors, while importance of hospitality is maintained. Apart from this a "Social and cultural friendly" visitor profile is arrived at, who likes visiting many number of historical places, has high average age, is likely to be found most amongst Germans followed by British and is likely to become a repeat visitors. When the perceptions of repeat visitors and local residents are joined together, it can be concluded that: there is an obvious increase in traffic accidents; there is a dramatic shift from listening to British pop music to Turkish pop; clothing seems to be getting less conservative and sporty; home made food is replaced by burgers and pizza; sexual behaviour becoming less conservative; there is a decrease in religiousness and practice of religion in general; although there seems to be some increase in petty theft, crime seems to be no threat to the visitors; there is a rise in gambling; and a change in the accent towards the Turkish mainland accent and better knowledge of the German language. It can be concluded from this analysis that the social and cultural impacts of tourism has been minimal in TRNC as yet. One may have the impression that when people were asked for the reasons for change, tourism does not seem to be very important. However, it actually is in two ways. First, there seems to be a rise in inverse tourism (travelling abroad), second economic conditions and income seems to be getting better. It should be kept in mind that these are likely to be the result of tourism. These indirect influences can be recognised when eating habits and restaurants were discussed. However, it is difficult to pinpoint these indirect influences without further research.

References

Crompton, J. L. (1979), "Motivations for Pleasure Vacation", *Annals of Tourism Research,* 6 (4): 408-424.

Dixon, B. R., Bouma, G. D. and Atkinson, G. B. (1987), A Handbook of Social Science Research, Oxford University Press, Oxford.

Duffield, B. S. (1982), "Tourism: the Measurement of Economic and Social Impact", *Tourism Management,* 3 (4). 248-255.

Holden, A. (1999), "Understanding Skiers' Motivation Using Pearce's 'Travel Career' Construct", *Annals of Tourism Research,* 26 (2): 435-438.

Inskeep, E. (ed.) (1994), National and Regional Tourism Planning: Methodologies and Case Studies, Routledge, London.

Jefferson, A. and Lickerish, L. (1991), Marketing Tourism: A Practical Guide, (2nd ed.) Longman, Essex.

Kýbrýs (Newspaper), 8 June, 1997.

Krippendorf, J. (1987), The Holidaymakers, Routledge, London.

Lindberg, K. and Johnson, R. L. (1997), "The Economic Values of Tourism's Social Impacts", *Annals of Tourism,* 24 (1): 90-116.

Liu, J., Sheldon, P. and Var, T. (1987), "A Cross-national Approach to Determining Resident Perceptions of the Impact of Tourism on the Environment", *Annals of Tourism Research,* 14, pp.17-37.

Mathieson A., and Wall, G. (1982), Tourism: Economic, Physical and Social Impacts, Longman, New York.

Murphy, P. E. (1985), Tourism: A Community Approach, Methuen, New York.

Parrinello, G. L. (1993), "Motivation and Anticipation in Post-industrial Tourism", *Annals of Tourism Research,* 20, pp. 233-249.

Pearce, D. (1995), Tourism Today: A Geographical Analysis, Longman-Wiley, New York.

Pearce, D. (1992), Tourist Development, (2nd. ed.), Longman Group Ltd., New York.

Pizam, A. and Milman, A. (1984), "Social Impacts of Tourism", *UNEP Industry and Environment,* 1.7 (1): 11-14.

Ryan, C. (1997), The Tourist Experience: A New Approach, Cassell, London.

Shaw, G. and Williams, A. M. (1994), Critical Issues in Tourism: A Geographical Perspective, Blackwell Publications, Oxford.

Travis, A. S. (1982), "Managing the Environmental and Cultural Impacts of Tourism and Leisure Development", *Tourism Management,* 3 (4): 256-262.

Travis, A. S. (1980), "Tourism Development and Regional Planning in East Mediterranean Countries", *International Journal of Tourism Management*, 1 (4): 207-218.

TRNC Statistical Yearbook (İstatistik Yilliği) (1995), State Planning Organisation, Statistics and Research Department, Lefkoşa.

Volkan, D. V. (M.D) (1980), Cyprus-War and Adaptation: A Psychoanalytic History of Two Ethnic Groups in Conflict, University Press of Virginia, Charlottesville.

Yin, R. K. (1984), Case Study Research: Design and Methods, Sage Publications, London.

Holidays and homosexuals: A constrained choice?

Howard L Hughes

Manchester Metropolitan University, UK

Introduction

World Tourism Organisation: 'Global Code of Ethics' 1999:

Article 7: 'the prospect of direct and personal access to the discovery and enjoyment of the planet's resources constitutes a right equally open to all the world's inhabitants... The universal right to tourism must be regarded as the corollary of the right to rest and leisure... guaranteed by the Universal Declaration of Human Rights 1948 article 24'.

Article 8: 'tourists and visitors should benefit.. from the liberty to move within their countries and from one state to another in accordance with... the Universal Declaration of Human Rights 1948 article 13'.

There is considerable interest in targeting gay men[1] as a market segment for tourism. They are regarded as a high-income group with few dependants and with a lifestyle that is highly leisure-focused. The propensity to go on holiday is considered to be high. 'With more leisure and disposable income than the average person, gays have been represented as the marketing department's dream consumer' (MAPS 1998: 5). Various surveys report an above average proportion of gays as being in ABC1 social groups, earning above average incomes and being more likely than others to have additional holidays (Clark 1997; MAPS 1998). Similar claims are made for gay men in other countries such as the USA with them taking more overseas trips than other US travellers (Jefferies 1999, Wood 1999). It is relatively uncontentious that few gay men have children and therefore discretionary incomes are likely to be higher than other people of a similar age. Gays are also often characterised as being free-thinking and at the 'cutting edge' of life and as individualistic and style-conscious.

In this paper it is argued that the gay market is not an easily identifiable one but that for many gay men the holiday does perform a vital function related to identity. It is suggested that there are a number of features relating to homosexuality which might influence the choice of holiday and of destination in such a way as to make the process different from that of other people. The final part of the paper reports on a small-scale initial study of gay men with the aim of identifying some of the key issues in holiday choice.

A market segment?

It is not too certain that gay men are a viable market segment. Problems arise as it is not easy to define homosexuality or being gay. There is a common assumption that the homosexual is defined by sexual activity. There is though a distinction between homosexual activity and homosexual orientation; the former is probably more widespread than is the latter. Some men may occasionally have same-sex sex but may not identify as gay and they may have opposite-sex partners or spouses; others may identify as gay but not have sexual activity. Sexuality is a very fluid concept and being homosexual is ultimately a self-defined category. (That is not the same as saying that a person chooses to be homosexual). The social (and legal) censure of homosexual acts means that many will choose not to be open about defining themselves as homosexual. The invisibility of the gay population creates difficulties in ascertaining the exact size and composition of the gay population. It is relatively easy to segment markets by geography or demographics but not so by sexuality (MAPS 1998).

Fugate (1993) refers to the four criteria - identifiable, sufficient, stable and accessible - and concludes that the segment is not viable. Pritchard and Morgan (1996) consider that 'it is widely recognised that it (the gay market) includes a potentially large market of upscale, well-educated professionals' (p12) and these characteristics and others such as 'an entertainment menu' distinguishes them from the mainstream. There is a fundamental problem with this however in that these are identified as distinguishing characteristics through surveys. Being homosexual is a characteristic that many people will not admit to and will conceal. The distinguishing characteristics are no than more a reflection of the readership of certain magazines and the likelihood of response to surveys! The respondents are self-selecting. The reality is that it is unwise to assume that gays are anything else but a mirror of the rest of society in terms of age, class, ethnicity and income. There are dangers in regarding the gay market as an homogeneous entity exclusively identified by sexual orientation. There are great differences within it defined by demographic, attitudinal and ideological factors (MAPS 1998). There are many niches within the market and the distinctions are increasing so that the gay market is fragmenting making it less identifiable. There is no such thing as a typical homosexual though there may well a certain identifiable segment within that overall classification: 'out', young, fashion conscious, etc and it may at that 'sub-segment' that products are targeted.

In terms of sufficiency the estimates of numbers vary widely but there could well be a sizeable gay and lesbian population - perhaps 10% of the population. Not all of these are open about their sexuality and therefore cannot be targeted as part of the market. The experience of some companies that have ventured into the market does though point to sufficiency in some cases.

Pritchard and Morgan (1996) regard the market as being accessible as being one that can be reached in an economical way. The market can be reached through the many gay publications as well as through straight media. The market is accessible too in the sense that a high proportion are allegedly urban dwellers. For many reasons there are undoubtedly a number of obvious concentrations of gay people in places such as London, Brighton and Manchester. Achieving brand loyalty may be a matter of targeted advertising in gay media and or sponsorship of gay events. It is believed that the market shows a high degree of brand loyalty and relies heavily on word of mouth recommendations (Wood 1999). Direct marketing is also regarded as being particularly effective.

Fugate (1993) is less optimistic and fears that specialised advertising would need to be developed which would not be economical for such a relatively small market. There is a view too that the sexual content of many gay magazines and papers may inhibit the willingness of firms to place advertisements in them. In addition advertisers of 'straight' or 'mainstream' products may be unwilling to target gay market because of fears of backlash from regular purchasers. It is possible that there may be a gay backlash: gays themselves may resent being targeted and regard it as patronising or as an undesirable exploitation of sexuality for commercial purposes (Field 1995). Penaloza (1996) accepts that targeting of the gay and lesbian markets does at least serve to legitimise them as individuals though this is not adequate in itself.

When referring to the final criterion of stability, Fugate (1993) comments on the possibility of individuals moving into and out of the segment and the ultimate extreme when gays become fully integrated into society and no one considers them to be a distinct segment!

It also needs to recognised that it is difficult, if not undesirable, to segment most products according to sexuality. For most goods and services, gays will purchase the same products as anyone else - washing machines, cat food, pens, petrol, etc - and will not need to be targeted. It is conceivable however that gays may be responsive and loyal to mainstream producers who promote their products in gay media or represent gay life in advertisements, etc. Nonetheless there are certain products that may be reasonably targeted at the gay market - in particular those relating to leisure activity as it is within this sphere that gays find much of their identity and wish to be with like-minded people. This will be the case for bars, clubs and restaurants and also for holidays in the sense of destinations chosen but also possibly in the choice of intermediary (travel agent, tour operator), etc.

Holidays

In the holiday market there is already evidence of products being developed and targeted at the gay market. There is a view that there are clearly identifiable market needs for this segment which are not met by the more general provision of tourist products. There is a small number of specialist tour operators such as the long-established Sensations and the more recent Respect. Mainstream operators have entered the market also but tentatively: Going Places launched Travel Unlimited in 1998 as a call centre booking operation. There are also a number of places that are identified as gay-friendly destinations such as Brighton, Blackpool and Manchester in the UK and foreign destinations such as Sitges, Ibiza town, Gran Canaria, New York and Amsterdam. A casual glance at the gay press and its holiday advertisements suggests that gay men are interested very largely in sun, sea, sand and sex when on holiday. There are few obvious holidays devoted to 'special-interest' tourism: heritage, arts, sport, ethnic tourism, adventure, safari, etc. unless 'special-interest' is defined to include sex (Weiler and Hall 1992). There are clear sexual images in advertisements and brochures as well as advice as to where casual sex encounters occur.

The apparent pre-occupation with sex may seem no more than a reflection of the popular perception of gay life generally. Much of the 'gay scene' - the gay leisure space - appears to be directed towards the pursuit of casual sex. The popular image of promiscuity amongst homosexuals is, however, clearly a mis-representation of the reality of the lives of most homosexual men. It is likely that the majority of gay men do not frequent the 'gay scene'. Many gay men find the 'scene' to be over-commercialised and youth oriented as well as a symbol of undesirable ghettoisation. Holidays for gay men are, though, rather more than 'sex-tourism' and may be more usefully interpreted in terms of their contribution to the process of establishing identity. 'The holiday... is likely to make a very significant contribution to the creation and validation of identity for many gay men' (Hughes 1997: 7). Being away from home gives an opportunity to be gay in a way that many people cannot experience at home or in work. The nature of society has been such that it has been difficult for gay men to be open about their sexuality. Discrimination against gays has encouraged them to find their identity in the leisure sphere. The significance of the holiday may be even more important for gay men than it is for many others in providing an opportunity, over an extended and continuous period of time, to be oneself.

Clift and Forrest (1999) not surprisingly discovered that rest and relaxation, comfort and good food, and sunshine were important factors in choosing a holiday. This is probably no different from the average holidaymaker but, in addition, survey respondents did consider it important to socialise with gay men and to access gay culture and venues ('fairly' or 'very important' to 76.8% and 80.2% respectively).

There are undoubtedly market activities geared towards this market segment. The London Tourist Board (LTB) launched a major campaign in USA in 1998 which was aimed at gays aged 30-50 in New York, Washington and San Francisco. It currently operates a 'pink' phone line giving information on bars and clubs, cafes and restaurants and shops and stores. The British Tourist Authority (BTA) launched a campaign in 1999 aimed at the UK travel trade in order to raise their awareness of the potential of this market (Jefferies 1999). It is felt that there is great potential for encouraging overseas visitors to the UK and the BTA has published a number of brochures aimed at this gay market. In one it claims that 'Britain has a vibrant gay and lesbian culture and community just waiting to welcome you' (BTA 1999). BTA and LTB research shows that gays are as interested in the mainstream attractions of Britain as are other travellers; they probably eat out more and visit the theatre more. They are interested in visiting a gay-friendly destination, not necessarily a gay destination and not necessarily wanting to stay in gay hotels.

These campaigns are not without their opponents however. Manchester, through its agency Marketing Manchester, launched a promotion (1999) to establish the city as 'one of the world's gay capitals'. The particular purpose was to attract US gay visitors to the city. Reactions were not obviously homophobic but included comments such as this from the chair of the Civic Society: 'we need to be tolerant of all sorts of people but we have to get the balance right. The decision to highlight the city's gay image is misleading and... could alienate other visitors Manchester wants to attract' (quoted Daily Telegraph 24 July 1999). He felt that the unique heritage of the city should have been given precedence in any tourism campaign. A prominent city councillor also expressed the view that 'the priority is to market Manchester as a family-friendly city and a place for new business. We welcome any spending tourists but gay tourism is not our priority' (quoted Manchester Metro News 14 August 1999). Not all gays welcome the idea of their gay space being promoted as part of the tourist product.

Even in Amsterdam there have been problems. The city is well known for its liberal attitudes to drugs and sex and alternative lifestyles and has a reputation for being particularly tolerant of homosexuality. There are a number of distinct gay leisure clusters in the city that are strongly associated with tourism. The city is identified by gays worldwide as a centre for gay life and is perceived as a gay-friendly place where gay life-styles go unremarked (Hughes 1998). Despite this, a tourist board campaign aimed at the US gay market in 1992 was not repeated largely because of reactions amongst the tourist trade in the city. It was considered to project an undesirable image which would alienate other visitors to the city. Gay tourism remains a 'hidden aspect of Amsterdam's tourism' (Hughes 1998: 177). Amsterdam is a popular destination for gay tourists from the UK. Nearly half of gay men in a 1996 survey had visited Amsterdam during the previous five years (Clift and Forrest 1999) and visitors from Great Britain and Ireland make up just over 20% of all gay visitors to the city (Hughes 1998).

Inhibitors

Despite the eagerness of many in tourism to capitalise on the gay market there remain a number of practical issues that serve to inhibit gay tourism. It has already been noted how much of the imagery of holidays is (understandably) heterosexual and often family-oriented. That in itself may reduce the willingness of gays to use the services of the major inclusive tour operators. The difficulties associated with being openly gay are not removed by being on holiday but by being on holiday with similar others and in gay-friendly locations. Travelling and staying with heterosexuals may not be popular.

There is also some evidence of discrimination in hotel accommodation. Jones (1996) undertook a 'mystery-shopper' type of study of a number of (320) hotels in the USA. He found that in responses to enquiries for bookings 'significantly fewer requests were granted to the same-sex couple than to the opposite-sex couple' (Jones 1996: 155). This was most evident for the smaller, bed and breakfast, hotel. It was conjectured that this might be due to personal prejudice or to a fear of same-sex couples being more conspicuous. A much smaller (and non-academic) survey conducted by a national newspaper showed similar discrimination in the UK. A gay couple were refused bookings or required to sleep in separate beds by three out of ten hotels contacted in the small ad-hoc survey (Tuck 1998). The newspaper also referred to a Stonewall report which indicated that 17% of gay people had been made to feel unwelcome because of their sexuality when staying in a hotel. There is further anecdotal evidence of gay people being given a twin room rather than a double (Clark 1997). The manager of a Birmingham hotel has stated that they 'would never knowingly let a double room to two males but would... offer them a room with twin beds'. The policy was introduced after complaints from other guests in the past (Skinner 1995). An obvious explanation for much of this is prejudice though there is also some fuzziness in the law as it relates to men. The Sexual Offences Act 1967 which legalised sexual acts between (adult) men did so only if they were 'in private'. It is arguable that a hotel is a public place. It is not altogether surprising that gays seek out gay-friendly accommodation and tour operators as well as gay-friendly destinations.

The choice of holiday destination may be constrained by the fact that in certain countries homosexual relations are illegal and in others subject to severe social censure. Homosexual acts were reported by Amnesty International (1997) as being illegal in over seventy countries including many Caribbean countries, many middle-eastern countries, the countries of the Indian sub-continent and five states of the USA. Laws relating to public decency or public order (as in China) may also be applied to demonstrations of affection. Punishments in some Islamic countries can be particularly severe. Laws are not, however, always applied and often gay tourists are tolerated. Nonetheless the proscription of same-sex acts can give out signals to potential tourists.

The legality of same-sex relationships does not guarantee tolerance of course. Despite the legalisation of homosexual acts (consenting adults in private) since 1967 in Britain, for instance, much prejudice, social disapproval and inequality of legal rights remains. The appeal of Amsterdam to two visitors from England (1996) was that 'we did something we've never done before.. We walked down the street holding hands' (quoted in Hughes 1998: 168). The choice of destination may well therefore be limited to those places where gays are openly tolerated and where it is known that hostile reaction will be minimised.

It is common for persons who are HIV positive to be refused long stay visas or immigration status in many countries of the world. Any HIV positive person wishing to holiday in the USA however will be denied entry (Alcorn 1999). Any HIV person, gay or straight, who wishes to holiday in the USA therefore faces a problem. Being open about status to immigration officials runs the risk of entry being denied. Not disclosing status may not be advisable as many HIV positive people will be taking medication which may be identified at immigration. An alternative is to send on medication to a 'safe address' (Alcorn 1996). An added problem for an HIV positive person is that travel insurance usually excludes claims arising from HIV infection.

A number of studies, unconcerned with gay men particularly, have identified similar inhibitors to destination choice and also to holiday or leisure participation. A study of the Afro-Caribbean community in the UK suggested that their holiday profile differed considerably from that of the white population (Stephenson 1998). Travel, for this community, has overtones of exploitation - the transatlantic slave system - and of economic necessity - the migration to industrial societies and is regarded as having been a mechanism for oppressing the Afro-Caribbean community. The holiday was regarded as a western white activity and for the African-Caribbean community travel was most often friends and relatives-based visits to the Caribbean. There was evidence too that domestic tourism based on the countryside was not undertaken often. Again it was associated with a white concept of ruralness and heritage.

Travel was also inhibited by perceptions of rejection and exclusion. There was a fear that presence in rural areas would be conspicuous and would arouse antagonism. At the least, the prospect of being the object of the residents' and other tourists' 'gaze' was sufficient to confine leisure activities to familiar urban areas. Travel to many parts of Europe was also considered undesirable in view of perceived strong racist feelings in some countries. There is a fear too of harassment at borders by customs and immigration officials.

This may be analogous with the situation of gay men. Holidays are something that are associated with 'others' - at least in terms of images and marketing strategies - and presence in a place may give rise to adverse reactions from others. 'All tourists transform the space they occupy, but in the case of gay tourists, transformation is the consequence of a group of people who are marginalised in society. The transformation thus has the potential for alienating other tourists' (Hughes 1998: 164). Knowledge of the adverse tourist and locals' gaze may be sufficient to limit destination choice considerably.

Destination choice may therefore be a much more constrained process than it is for heterosexual tourists. The choice of destination is a complex process that is explained in many ways that include the interaction between the destination attributes and the tourist's motives and values and time and income constraints. A convenient framework for analysing this is that of 'tourism opportunity sets'. Um and Crompton (1990, 1992) categorise beliefs about a destinations into facilitators and inhibitors: respectively beliefs about attributes that help satisfy motives for travel or that are not harmonious with motives. The choice decision initially is from within an 'awareness set' or 'perceived set' of destinations, a possibility range of which, all could potentially be considered (Stabler 1991). This is restricted to a 'consideration set' or 'evoked set' as a range that is actually considered though there may also be a more manageable 'decision set' of those from which the final choice is made. Um and Crompton (1992) suggested that facilitators were important at the early stages of the choice process but that 'at the final stage it is inhibitors which prevail' (p24). Initially the positive attributes of a destinations guide the determination of the evoked set but there is a strong negative influence that acts to discard destinations at the decision or choice stage.

Some initial findings

In order to illuminate these issues a limited study was undertaken of gay men during the early part of 2000. The aim was to identify influences on holiday destination choice and to determine the extent to which the sort of constraints mentioned above might have arisen in the process. The study was a pilot prior to refinement of the interview schedule and interviews with a greater number of informants. The information was gathered through semi-structured interviews conducted with an opportunistic sample of gay men. They were interviewed in a number of bars in the Gay Village of Manchester. The interview schedule focused on whether or not the gay men sought out gay space as a holiday destination, whether their holiday activities were similar to home activities, whether the extent of 'gayness' altered on holiday, the range of destinations considered and actually visited and identification of gay-friendly countries and towns. The schedule was 'neutral' and was designed so as not to deliberately lead to emergence of 'inhibitors'. In the pilot, ten men were interviewed and initially asked to refer to the last holiday taken though the discussion considered earlier holidays as appropriate. The informants ranged in age from 26 to 63 years old.

Given that this was a 'pilot ' based on a small number of informants, the results are presented as points that emerged, without any attempt to indicate frequency of occurrence or influence of the issue raised.

destinations:

- preference for visiting destinations that are gay-friendly

- loyalty to a small number of places

- repeat visits because of familiarity with its gay-friendliness and sizable gay tourist numbers

- networks of friends established in holiday places; certainty that the network would be present year after year was part of attraction of a destination

- relatively small community of gay men meant that holidaymakers were well known to bar and club managers and this added to destination attractiveness and the return visit

- reliance on personal recommendation and networks for destination and accommodation choice

- a number of countries were perceived as not being gay-friendly

accommodation, tour operators, etc:

- stopped from taking someone back to the hotel room (Spain)

- refused a double bed (Derbyshire)

- apartments popular as giving more privacy and sense of community

- commonly used mainstream tour operators and travel agents with a rapport frequently established with a regular travel agent. Some tour operators (or at least individual employees) identified as being particularly gay-helpful

- 'ripped-off' when dealing with one 'gay' travel agent

- where individual travel arrangements were made this was usually because of the type of holiday, such as long-haul or camping, rather than because of any problem with tour operators

- at the destination:

- gay bars and clubs were frequented more than others

- some felt less 'comfortable' in some gay spaces and facilities (such as beaches) than in general ones

general feelings:

- 'funny looks' from others

- solte voce comments about gays

- unease at being in social situation where macho heterosexual men dominated, especially in large numbers; perceived as a possible threat

- self-conscious in public places and behaviour - conversation, tone of voice and gesture - modified as a result

- restrained behaviour even in gay destinations especially after incidents which demonstrated limits of tolerance

- complaints received about non-sexual matters (such as excessive noise) were perceived to arise because of sexuality

- liberal image of some places had more to do with money than genuine toleration

Conclusions

There is optimism amongst many tourist boards, tour operators, travel agents and hoteliers that gay men constitute a particularly productive market segment to target. There is a perception of gays as being a high-income, low-dependent, leisure-centric segment.

It is clear however that giving meaning to homosexuals as a viable market segment is problematic. The very concept of sexuality is a fluid one and, in addition, there are strong reasons for believing that homosexuality is often concealed. The apparently identifiable gay segment may amount to no more than a particular sub-segment of all gay men. For many gay men however the holiday does provide one element of the gay space that is a necessary part of establishing identity. An a priori consideration of the nature of homosexuality and of acceptance of that by society suggests that there may well be constraints in the holiday decision process. The awareness (perceived) sets and consideration (evoked) sets may be more limited than for others.

The points to emerge from the limited study undertaken would suggest that in many ways this is so. These will be utilised in developing the interview schedule for the full study which will be based on interviews with a larger number of informants.

note: [1] the discussion is limited to male homosexuals for ease of analysis.

References

Alcorn, K. (1999), *'AIDS reference manual'* 22nd ed. London: NAM Publications.

Amnesty International UK (1997*), 'Breaking the silence: human rights violations based on sexual orientation'* London: AIUK.

British Tourist Authority (1999), *'Britain: you don't know the half of it'* London: BTA.

Clark, S. (1997), 'Glad to be gay?' *Caterer and Hotelkeeper* (5th June). 62-63.

Clift, S. and Forrest, S. (1999), 'Gay men and tourism: destinations and holiday motivations' *Tourism Management* 20 () 615-625.

Field, N. (1995), *'Over the rainbow: money, class and homophobia'* London: Pluto Press

Fugate, D. (1993), 'Evaluating the US male homosexual and lesbian population as a viable target market segment' *Journal of Consumer Marketing* 10 (4): 46-57.

Hughes, H. (1997), 'Holidays and homosexual identity' *Tourism Management* 18 (4): 3-7.

Hughes, H. (1998), 'Sexuality, tourism and space: the case of gay visitors to Amsterdam' in D Tyler, Y Guerrier and M Robertson (eds) *'Managing tourism in cities'* Wiley. 163-178.

Jefferies, T. (1999), 'Trade told to target overseas gay market' *Travel Weekly* (1st November). 28.

Jones, D. (1996), 'Discrimination against same-sex couples in hotel reservation policies' in D. Wardlow, (ed) *'Gays, lesbians and consumer behaviour: theory, practice and research issues in marketing'* New York: Harrington Park Press. 153-159.

MAPS (1998), *'The pink pound 1998: strategic market report'* London: Market Assessment Publications Ltd.

Penaloza, L. (1996), 'We're here, we're queer and we're going shopping! A critical perspective on the accommodation of gays and lesbians in the US marketplace' in D Wardlow (ed) *'Gays, lesbians and consumer behaviour: theory, practice and research issues in marketing'* New York: Harrington Park Press. 9-41.

Pritchard, A. and Morgan, N. (1996), 'The gay consumer: a meaningful market segment?' *Journal of Targeting*, Measurement and Analysis for Marketing 6 (1): 9-20.

Skinner, T. (1995), 'Gay couple denied room in top hotel' the *Pink Paper* (24th November).

Stabler, M. (1991), 'Modelling the tourism industry: a new approach' in T Sinclair and M Stabler (eds) *'The tourism industry: an international analysis'* Wallingford: CAB International. 15-43.

Stephenson, M. (1998), 'The perceptions of Manchester's Afro-Caribbean community concerning tourism access and participation'; unpublished PhD thesis, Department of Hospitality and Tourism Management, Manchester Metropolitan University.

Tuck, A. (1998), 'Book a double room? Not if you're gay, sir' *Independent on Sunday* (8th February). 5.

Um, S. and Crompton, J. (1990), 'Attitude determinants in tourism destination choice' *Annals of Tourism Research* 17 (): 432-448.

Um, S. and Crompton, J. (1992), 'The role of perceived inhibitors and facilitators in pleasure travel destination decisions' *Journal of Travel Research* (Winter) 18-25.

Wood. L, (1999), 'Think pink! Attracting the pink pound' *Insights* (January) A107-A110.

Classifying the health tourism consumer

Philippa Hunter-Jones

Manchester Metropolitan University, UK

Introduction

Historically research suggests that health and tourism have enjoyed a symbiotic relationship (Wightman and Wall, 1985). The aim of this paper is to review one of the most commonly reported areas of this relationship, the health tourism product. This product, whilst in vogue in recent years, especially among the tourism community (see for example Goodrich and Goodrich, 1987 and 1991; Becheri, 1989; Hall, 1992; Horner and Swarbrooke, 1998), is not new and exactly what it constitutes is unclear. The term implies a product designed to impact in some manner upon a person's health. Yet much of the debate to date has tended to portray the product as little more than an expression of societal status with distinctions between travel for health purposes or simply for recreational purposes often blurred. That said, both purposes of travel do themselves contribute to health given the long established and frequently quoted World Health Organisation (WHO) definition of health as covering both physical and psychological well being (WHO, 1946).

Witt and Witt (1989) argue that from a UK perspective, there is a distinct lack of published material available formally confirming the existence of a health tourism product. The problem is not simply confined to the local scene with reviews of the international scene confirming it to be the case elsewhere also. This paper will provide a broad overview of the debate to date before focusing specifically upon reviewing the health tourism consumer. It will attempt to define and classify such a consumer by considering both a historical and contemporary perspective. Through this review the case will be made that the true health tourism consumer extends far beyond the narrow 'spa' consumer which literature most commonly associates it with and instead underpins forms of tourism activity which are related not only to recreational activities but also medical consumption.

The health tourism product - the debate so far

Definitions and evolution

Most authors writing about health tourism make some attempt to profile an evolution of the product. That said, historically literature has systematically failed to comprehensively define the product with much of the work published relying often upon superficial distinctions between *health tourism*: "the provision of health facilities utilising the natural resources of the country, in particular mineral water and climate" (International Union of Official Tourist Organisations, 1973 p 7), *spa tourism*: "a place in which scientifically approved deposits of therapeutic substances may be used and in which the necessary spa facilities exist" (Kaul, 1985 p 140), and, more recently, *health-care tourism*: "the attempt on the part of a tourist facility (e.g. hotel) or destination (e.g. Baden, Switzerland) to attract tourists by deliberately promoting its health-care services and facilities, in addition to its regular tourist amenities" (Goodrich and Goodrich, 1991 p 107). Such services are often taken to include medical examinations, special diets, acupuncture, injections and special medical treatments.

These definitions provide only a narrow understanding of a highly complex relationship and take little account of the deeper sense of health and well being travel has long been recognised as offering. Pilgrimage tourism for example, one of the earliest documented forms of holiday taking provides clear evidence that the origins of travel were to a degree founded in a belief that such an activity contributed to health and well-being. Reporting on *El Camino Frances,* a long distance footpath thought to be one of the oldest pilgrimage routes in the western world, at its' height of popularity during the eleventh and twelfth centuries, Raju (1994) suggests improving spiritual health and repaying the wrongs of present day life ready for the next to have been central motives, relevant not only to this pilgrimage but also to other such sacred journeys. Not everyone agrees with such pious sentiments however, for as Morgan and Pritchard (1998, p 9) sceptically argue

> *"In undertaking the pilgrimage, the tourist temporarily visits an unfamiliar location. At that location he or she worships at the feet of various tourist 'shrines' and as a result of this recreational process the tourist is emotionally uplifted and spiritually refreshed. Alienation has been mediated – at least for another year!"*

Despite such cynicism, works covering these periods and the more recent 'tourism pilgrimages' of the eighteenth and nineteenth centuries, commonly referred to as the Grand Tour, seldom dispute the search for spiritual and psychological health and well-being travel of this nature sought. Discussing the European Grand Tour for example, Towner (1996) focuses upon the educational and cultural significance of such travel suggesting that "the idea of travel for health was part of a more general leisured-class concern for its mental and physical welfare which linked spas, seaside resorts and 'healthier climates' with other cultural forms of touring" (Towner, 1996 p 102). Yet even given this clear relationship, 'tourism pilgrimages', sacred or secular, are seldom overtly linked to a review of the health tourism product.

Literature more commonly linked with such a product has tended to focus upon the taking of waters at mineral spas and hot springs which has occurred since Roman times (see Wightman and Wall, 1985; Gilbert and Weerdt, 1991; Bacon, 1997) and the 'taking to the waters' by the elite of seventeenth century Europe. Hembry (1990), for example, notes the tradition of affluent ancient Romans and English who visited Bath to both bathe in the warm springs and mineral waters and take of the water for its supposed health benefits. Editing a text on the rise and fall of British coastal resorts, Shaw and Williams (1997) suggest the original growth in seaside resort popularity to be a by-product of the perception that sea-water offered some health enhancing qualities - a far cry from contemporary opinion! That said, the true contribution of taking mineral waters to cure ailments such as rheumatism, skin infections and poor digestion has never gained widespread recognition or acceptance. The medical fraternity in particular are sceptical of any claims that such activities in any way improve health. Nevertheless given the existence of such relationships it is perhaps not surprising to see a reference to health related tourism in most general tourism texts, with many citing the history and development of this type of industry as an important and integral factor in the evolution of tourism (see for example Burkart and Medlik, 1981; Wightman and Wall, 1985; Holloway, 1998; Cooper et al., 1998).

Supply

Published research on what could be classified as the supply of health tourism facilities is scarce. Much of the literature concerns itself only with the narrow definitions of health tourism, particularly spa tourism, and is inevitably limited by this approach. Even countries with an established traditional industry offer limited published material (the Italian tourism service, for example, provides a range of brochure and guide material). Academic research, where it does exist, has tended to concentrate upon the type of facilities on offer (see Bywater, 1990; Bacon, 1997) and locations offering health-tourism facilities (see Goodrich and Goodrich, 1991; Gilbert and Weerdt, 1991). Hall (1992) considers both, identifying two distinct, yet related parts of the sector, the health resort in which the emphasis is on improving overall health and fitness, and the spa resort which is specifically targeted at providing medical services to clients suffering from a range of diseases. This is also one of the few occasions that the medical and recreational product are distinguished between. Locations in Europe and North America are listed with supplementary references provided. That said, no attempt is made to provide an international map of health tourism locations or facilities world wide, although the work is not alone in this shortfall. Dominant within this and other literature is the significance of the European industry (notably Western Europe) and North America, although marked differences in focus between continents can be identified.

Gilbert and Weerdt (1991) examine the *health-care* tourism products of the principal countries of Western Europe tabling the product on offer country by country. Three groups of health care products are identified: the classical health-care product; the specialised health-care product; the remise en forme product (developed by the French in the 1970s). Collectively, such products include medical check-ups, special diets, vitamin-complex treatments, herbal remedies, hydrotherapy, balneotherapy. Also investigating *health-care* tourism and providing an American perspective, Goodrich and Goodrich (1991) report typical facilities, closely aligned to Gilbert and Weerdt (1991) and argue that "these services will spread as we enjoy higher incomes, devote more time to leisure/recreational activities, and seek longer, healthier lives" (p 108). It is questionable whether in fact health-care tourism may distort the true health tourism product. Such facilities have little locational association and could be offered anywhere in the world, far removed from the original health spa product reliant in part upon specific mineral waters for patronage.

From a European perspective marked differences in provision are apparent with Germany and Italy in particular having a formalised, relatively well developed *health-care* tourism industry "....followed closely by France, Switzerland and Austria, Spain, Portugal and Greece.......mainly geared to the home market...... Relatively smaller participants in decreasing order of importance are Finland, UK, Sweden, Belgium and The Netherlands". (Gilbert and Weerdt, 1991 p 8). Bywater (1990) provides a detailed account of *Spas and Health Resorts in the EC*, reviewing key features of the industry country by country. The relationship between tourism and medicine is questioned, although without clear conclusion and again it is suggested that the medical fraternity across Europe are deeply divided in their attitudes towards the true contribution of health tourism. Statistics for German, Italian and French resorts are presented with differing attitudes to the industry used to explain the variances arising.

Goodrich and Goodrich (1991) add Hungary and the USA to the list of health destinations arguing that many cities and resorts in these countries have grown up around thermal springs and concomitant health facilities. Hungary also features in the work of Horner and Swarbrooke (1998) who suggest that the health-tourism product provides a tool for the regional development of such destinations. North America, particularly Canada, is covered by Wightman and Wall (1985), and South America, notably Mexico, by Williams et al., (1996). The popular health resorts of the Caribbean such as Cuba, Jamaica and St Lucia are the focus of empirical research by Goodrich (1994). Further afield, the growing health tourism industry in Israel is detailed by Bar-On (1989) and Niv (1989), both of whom illustrate how the product has evolved in recent years into a *'health-cure'* industry. Closer to home considerable confusion exists as to the UK health tourism position with few indicators confirming that such a concept is recognised at all. Bacon (1997) profiling *The Rise of the German and the demise of the English Spa Industry* acknowledges specifically a spa industry in the UK and goes on to explain business success and failure here by reference to a model of political and economic factors impacting on the development of spa resorts. Product planning, regulation, investment and quality control are proposed to be the way forward for the UK. Yet such actions will only be of value if the concept itself gains credibility as an industry worthy of encouragement and support as is the case in other regions of the world.

One example of a location where this has happened is in the spa town of Saratoga Springs in New York State (see Swanner, 1988). Following a thorough study of the Spa by the Saratoga Springs Commission, the New York State authority placed Saratoga Spa under medical supervision for the first time in 1932. Through legislation, money was appropriated to develop the spa for medical purposes. Designation was founded solely on a scientific study which had investigated the various health attributes the mineral waters offered and concluded that they could provide a source of health and well-being for the population of New York State and beyond. Research programmes into the health attributes of the spa began in 1932 with an investigation into the effects of the waters upon blood pressure. Such investigations were conducted over a period of approximately twenty years. In the initial stages, the development of the spa was encouraged by the Jewish community, many of whom had emigrated from Europe where spa therapy enjoyed an established tradition. Through its early development the medical attributes of the Spa were not promoted in isolation for the attitude during this era (the 1930s and 1940s) was one of making a spa a place of all around therapy:

> *"In addition to the qualities bestowed by nature, spas usually have amenities provided by man for utilising the natural therapeutic agents found in the area. .....drink halls, fountains and bath houses......facilities for physical exercise such as gradual walks, golf courses, tennis courts and the like.......a spa is a place where all forms of treatment, spa therapy, rest, exercise, diet and recreation, may be integrated and tailored to the needs of the individual"* (Swanner, 1988, p 13).

The design and layout of the Springs even today, during a period of decline, still clearly shows the original integration of the mineral waters, recreation and entertainment facilities deemed necessary for health and well-being.

The health tourism consumer

Given the limited recognition of what constitutes the health tourism product it is perhaps not surprising to discover that there is no definitive account of the health tourism consumer. Empirical studies have been few and far between with statistics available providing an incomplete picture. Gilbert and Weerdt (1991) account for such 'sketchy statistics' by suggesting that the health tourism industry is in the initial phase of product development, a somewhat bizarre claim given the historical association of the product with the earliest forms of tourism. Where findings have been published the objectivity, validity and reliability of the research methods employed are often vague and imprecise with much of the empirical data requiring verification. Furthermore, there is no comprehensive study covering both the national and international health tourism market, a necessary review given the transnational nature of the tourism industry. The availability of published statistics instead reflects the significance of the industry to particular destinations.

The thrust of what constitutes the narrowly defined health tourism consumer is generally determined by reference to characteristics, nationality and motivations. The characteristics of the health tourist are documented by Goodrich and Goodrich (1991); Viceriat (1984); Becheri (1989); Cornell Hotel and Restaurant Administration Quarterly (CHRAQ) (1993) although even taken collectively the picture is still incomplete, complicated further by the subtle differences existing in the products being questioned. Nationality is a feature of the work of Mesplier-Pinet (1990) and Gilbert and Weerdt (1991). Motivations are covered by Gilbert and Weerdt (1991); Goodrich and Goodrich (1991); Becheri (1989); Goodrich (1994); Hall (1992).

Characteristics

Basing their conclusions upon a sample of 206 respondents, Goodrich and Goodrich (1991) profile the *health traveller* as:

- Average age, 39;

- Average educational level, bachelor's degree;

- Average annual household income, $41,000;

- average number of persons in family, 4;

- Mrried, 146 (71%);

- Sngle, 60 (29%); and

- Number who used health facilities at destinations, 21 (10%).

Viceriat (1984) presents the results of a survey of the international clientele for *health-care products* at the resort of Abano. Key findings indicate the main market to be 40-60 year olds (50% over 55), female (59%), professional or middle and higher management with the majority enjoying high incomes. Becheri (1989) argues that the *health tourism market* is made up of two distinct groups. First, the average customer: an independent, self-employed professional or a high level manager, 35, 40 to 50 years of age, who has achieved economic success in life, and who now turns their thoughts to the restoration of their body. Second, a thermal spring patient, on average older and often a low career achiever. Becheri (1989) favours the second group as they are found to exhibit a certain habit towards repetitive treatment generally on an annual basis.

CHRAQ (1993) details the international scene reporting the alleged first comprehensive study of *spa goers*. The study, conducted by Health Fitness Dynamics, a spa consulting group, in conjunction with Innova, surveyed nearly 2,000 spa users in 1992 at 27 US spas. Key findings suggest the typical spa consumer to be most likely a woman (75%), married in her mid forties, engaged in a professional career with a total annual household income typically exceeding $100,000. Most interested in visiting with a friend two to four times a week and having little interest in visiting a spa with a family or group. Visiting on average five times during the preceding two years as a respite from a hectic life-style and influenced in their choice by word of mouth, print media and travel agents. Definitions of what constituted a spa for this survey were not provided although would have been particularly helpful in interpreting these results.

Nationalities

In terms of nationalities frequenting thermal resorts, Mesplier-Pinet (1990) places Italy and West Germany as leaders in spa consumption, 2% and 2.5% of the population respectively. This confirms earlier work by Gilbert and Weerdt (1991) who suggested that in 1986 in Italy and West Germany, approximately 2-3% of the population visited spa facilities compared to 1-2% in France, Switzerland and Austria. The remaining Western European countries were suggested to account for less than 1% of the total health spa population. Why this is so is seldom considered but likely to be related, in part at least, to the natural resources and facilities available.

Motivations

Why people participate in health tourism is complex. Gilbert and Weerdt (1991) suggest that "the motivation of those demanding health care will vary from genuine preventive health-care to a more narcissistic beauty health-care" (p 7). In their empirical study of health tourism, Goodrich and Goodrich (1991) established that none of the research sample had used the criterion of *health-care facilities at the destination* as the main reason for destination selection. Instead, more traditional reasons such as cost and variety of attractions were used. Becheri (1989) focuses more specifically upon classifying reasons for participation. Four categories emerge as a result:

- People looking for relaxation and convalescence;

- People wishing to 'delay' their own ageing;

- Short break weekend market; and

- Illness prevention.

To Gilbert and Weerdt (1991) such categories provide only a crude indicator of motivations. More likely to be of significance in these authors opinions are social environment and age, a theme also picked up by Goodrich (1994). Goodrich (1994) argues that wealthy Europeans have viewed going to the spa as a regular part of their social activity, and a part of their everyday culture since early times, a habit which has become more fashionable in North America in recent times. This work links health tourism with élitism. Earlier work by Goodrich and Goodrich (1991) focused upon a different perspective namely the growing health conscious nature of contemporary society. The authors argued that the future development of the product lies in targeting people on the basis of their health, promoting preventative health care and methods of combating present afflictions such as obesity. This was to an extent covered also within the work of Becheri (1989) who found an increasing reliance today upon accessory treatments such as fitness programmes and physiotherapy in health tourism areas. Gilbert and Weerdt (1991) extend this work by suggesting that three distinct groups of consumers attending health resorts can be distinguished: medical patients; excursionists, tourists. To Becheri (1989) such groups illustrate the transition from "thermalism" to "thermal spring tourism" to "health tourism" by means of a corresponding evolution where the 'patient' has increasingly become also a tourist. Whilst this may well be the case, as Hall (1992) points out there is currently a lack of longitudinal data to fully support this hypothesis.

A future direction for the health tourism debate

Much of the literature to date has focused upon health alongside recreational consumption. Adopting such a perspective has inevitably led to a narrow review of the subject and left a considerable gap in health tourism consumer research. One of the most glaring omissions in the debate so far has been the failure to consider health tourism consumption by people experiencing various forms of ill health. Little academic research currently exists in this area but some understanding of the significance of such tourism participation can be gained from a number of non-academic papers including the work of Monette (1988), Englefield (1999),

Mackie and Brattle (1999) and Kingsman (1995). On each occasion, holiday taking is discussed as one part of the work but not necessarily as the main issue under consideration. What is significant about these works is that they show clearly a form of tourism consumption which is directly inter-linked with health issues yet which so far has gained little, if any, recognition as contributing to a health tourism product or consumer.

Providing an autobiographical account of living with a partner with Acquired Immune Deficiency Syndrome (AIDS), Monette (1988) illustrates well the changing significance of holiday taking to someone coping with terminal illness. In the pre and early diagnosis stages of illness, participation in holiday taking is found to be a positive activity providing a means of escaping from the paramount reality of living with a terminal illness. During the later stages of illness the focus changes away from participation to holiday taking as a subject, a reference point, a comforting and safe area of conversation within the minefield of terminal illness. On a similar theme, reviewing respite care for those living with Human Immunodeficiency Virus (HIV) and AIDS, Englefield (1999) focuses upon the potential benefits of staying at one of two health farms for the HIV positive, Bethany Trust and Sussex Beacon respite care home. Bethany, situated in Devon and suggested to be the first 'health farm' of its kind in Europe, offers "visitors.....a chance to recharge their batteries and take stock of the way their lives are changing" (Englefield, 1999 p 22). Recreational activities such as walking and cycling are encouraged in an unstructured manner supported by group discussions in the evenings. Sussex Beacon, a hospice and nursing home with an increasing emphasis upon respite care, focuses upon improving quality of life issues for people with HIV/AIDS. Designed to be a relaxing environment offering both medicinal and psychological support ".....visitors to the centre gain both physical and mental strength in this supportive atmosphere as the stresses and strains of HIV living gradually ebb away" (Englefield, 1999 p 22). The treatment and rehabilitation provided whilst at the 'farms' and the contribution to psychological well-being is very much the focus of analysis.

Mackie and Brattle (1999) consider tourism consumption for someone living with Multiple Sclerosis (MS). Diagnosed at twenty three with MS, Carole Mackie provides an account of the first ten years of her life following diagnosis. All aspects of living are detailed with one of the main coping strategies she employed built around holiday taking. Recounting a significant three month holiday in Australia, key health benefits attributed to holiday taking she summarises as:

> *"Over the weeks the tingling in my arms and legs had eased away; I hadn't even noticed until I realised that I had not felt ill for a long time. As my visit went into the third month (...) I found I had the energy to enjoy going out for meals, shopping trips and exploring. We went walking in the bush and even go-karting. I was glowing with health. ....it's amazing what a tan can do for you...."*
> (Mackie and Brattle, 1999 p 119-120).

Such benefits are referred to on a number of occasions throughout the text and as with Monette (1988) and Englefield (1999) are built primarily around psychological health and well-being.

Kingsman (1995) details an activity programme for people in remission from various forms of cancer which is supported by the Chaucer Hospital, Canterbury. Started in February

1994, 'The Odyssey Programme' is described as an outdoor holiday experience, designed specifically to enhance the quality of life of people in remission from cancer. Geared at patients who have completed a course of treatment, Kingsman (1995) suggests the principal purpose of the break to include "......helping the participants to rediscover the richness of being – to move on from a time of introspection and despair to the next stage of their lives" (p 1). Referral to the Programme is through a medical oncologist with preliminary evaluation results indicating that the Programme to that date (1995) "...(had) achieved its objective of fostering a more positive self-image and a greater sense of self-worth in very many of them (i.e. participants)" (p 1). More recent analysis of the Programme suggests that such success continues to be the case (Lyster, 1999).

Having reviewed the direction of much of the health tourism debate so far it is evident that none of these or other such cases to date have been readily acknowledged as contributing to such a product. Yet each singles out holiday taking as a significant activity undertaken at a time of ill health. In the case of Englefield (1999) and Kingsman (1995), holiday taking is a deliberate strategy employed to combat illness, whilst for Monette (1988) and Mackie and Brattle (1999) the relationship is much more subtle and indirect. Even given this the positive benefits of travel are referred to on at least six different occasions by these authors. Probably the most common theme in each of these cases is the emphasis and contribution to psychological health and well-being holiday taking can foster. Such benefits themselves may well outweigh any physical benefits travel may offer. The problem, however, does not end here as there is a further consumer who has remained largely neglected in the debate so far, the carer. In an upbeat report focusing upon the provision of short break holidays as a support for care in the community, Weightman (1996) argues that carers may be just as in need of a holiday as those they care for. Some of the very real problems carers face in actually taking full advantage of holiday opportunities available to them are highlighted and overwhelming evidence presented to suggest that carers can experience very real psychological health benefits from holidays, provided such opportunities are well planned, provided for and thought through. Each of these consumers constitute a health tourist. It is time for the debate to widen and for industry and academics alike to research and plan for the needs of all health tourism consumers in the future.

Summary

This paper has reviewed the health tourism product, past and present. Definitions have been considered and the limited scope of the subject to date highlighted. In particular the paper has argued that, taken from both a national and international perspective, the coverage of a health tourism consumer is at best sketchy. This is due in part to a lack of conceptual research, frameworks, philosophy and paradigms within published literature to date. To extend the debate the paper has attempted to segment two different types of health tourism consumer distinguishing between the traditional recreational consumer and the largely neglected medical consumer. That said no claims have been made that holiday taking offers any measurable medical benefits but rather that it does provide instead varying opportunities to seek spiritual and psychological health and well-being not only for the healthy and wealthy in society but also for those exposed to varying forms of ill health. Little research currently exists in this area. The scope for future work, particularly of an empirical nature, is considerable.

References

Bacon, W. (1997), The Rise of the German and the Demise of the English Spa Industry: A Critical Analysis of Business Success and Failure. *Leisure Studies*. 16 (3): 173-187.

Bar-On, R. (1989), Cost-Benefit Considerations for Spa Treatments, Illustrated by the Dead Sea, Israel. *Revue de Tourisme*. 44 (4): 12-15.

Becheri, E. (1989), From Thermalism to Health Tourism. *Revue de Tourisme*. 44 (4): 15-19.

Burkart, A. J. and Medlik, S. (1981) *Tourism. Past, Present and Future*. 2nd Edn. Oxford: Heinemann.

Bywater, M. (1990), Financial Services/Leisure Industries. Spas and Health Resorts in the EC. *EIU Travel and Tourism Analyst*. No 6, pp 52-67.

Cooper, C. P. Fletcher, J. Wanhill, S. Gilbert, D. and Shepherd. R. (1998*), Tourism. Principles and Practice*. 2nd Edn. London: Addison Wesley Longman Ltd.

Cornell Hotel and Restaurant Administration Quarterly (CHRAQ) (1993), Who Goes to Spas? *Cornell Hotel and Restaurant Administration Quarterly*. 34 (5): 13.

Englefield, N. (1999), Health Farms for the HIV Positive? *Axiom*. 11 February, p 22.

Gilbert, D. C. and Van De Weerdt, M. (1991), The Health Care Tourism Product in Western Europe. *Revue de Tourisme*. 46 (2): 5-10.

Goodrich, J. N. and Goodrich, G. E. (1987) Health-Care Tourism - An Exploratory Study. *Tourism Management*. 8 (3): 217-222.

Goodrich, J. N. and Goodrich, G. E. (1991), Health-Care Tourism reprinted in Medlik, S. (ed) *Managing Tourism*. Oxford: Butterworth-Heinemann, pp 108-114.

Goodrich, J. N. (1994), Health Tourism: A New Positioning Strategy for Tourist Destinations. in Uysal, M. (ed) *Global Tourist Behaviour*. London: Haworth Press, pp 227-238.

Hall, C. M. (1992), Adventure, Sport and Health Tourism in Weiler, B. and Hall, C. M. (eds) *Special Interest Tourism*. London: Belhaven Press, pp 141-158

Hembry, P. M. (1990), *The English Spa, 1560-1815: A Social History*. London: Athlone Press.

Holloway, J. C. (1998), *The Business of Tourism*. 5th Edn. Essex: Addison Wesley Longman Ltd.

Horner, S. and Swarbrooke, J. (1998), The Health Tourism Market. *Insights*. The Tourism Marketing Intelligence Service. London: BTA/ETB.

International Union of Official Tourist Organisations (IUOTO) (1973), *Health Tourism*. United Nations: Geneva.

Kaul, R. N. (1985), *The Dynamics of Tourism*. New Delhi: Sterling Publishers Private Limited.

Kingsman, J. (1995), Odyssey Enhances the Quality of Life for People with Cancer. *BMI Bulletin*, June, p 10.

Lyster, C. (1999), Telephone Interview with Author and other Communications, September.

Mackie, C. and Brattle, S. (1999*), Me and My Shadow. Learning to Live With Multiple Sclerosis*. London: Aurum Press Limited.

Mesplier-Pinet, J. (1990), Thermalisme et Curistes: Les Contraintes. *Revue de Tourisme*. 45 (2): 10-17.

Monette, P. (1988), *Borrowed Time. An AIDS Memoir*. London: Abacus.

Morgan, N. and Pritchard, A. (1998), *Tourism Promotion and Power. Creating Images, Creating Identities*. Chichester: John Wiley and Sons.

Niv, A. (1989), Health Tourism in Israel: A Developing Industry. *Revue de Tourisme*. 44 (4): 30-32.

Raju, A. (1994), *The Way of St James: Spain*. Cumbria, England: Cicerone Press.

Shaw, G. and Williams, A. (eds) (1997), *The Rise and Fall of British Coastal Resorts. Cultural and Economic Perspectives*. London: Mansell.

Swanner, G. M. (1988), *Saratoga Queen of Spas*. New York: North Country Books, Inc.

Towner, J. (1996), *An Historical Geography of Recreation and Tourism in the Western World 1540 - 1940*. Chichester: John Wiley and Sons.

Viceriat, P. (1984), Un Thermalisme a la Francaise? Espaces, No 67, April, pp 5-7 in Gilbert, D.C. and Van De Weerdt, M. (1991) The Health Care Tourism Product in Western Europe. *Revue de Tourisme*. Vol 2, pp 5-10.

Weightman, G. (1996), A Real Break. A Guidebook for Good Practice in the Provision of Short-Term Breaks as a Support for Care in the Community.
http://www.doh.gov.uk/pub/docs/doh/realbrea.pdf

Wightman, D. and Wall, G. (1985), The Spa Experience at Radium Hot Springs. *Annals of Tourism Research*. 12 (3): 393-416.

Williams, P. W. Andestad, G. Pollock, A. and Dossa, K. B. (1996), Health Spa Travel Markets: Mexican Long-Haul Pleasure Travellers. *Journal of Vacation Marketing*. 3 (1): 11-31.

Witt, C. and Witt, S. F. (1989), Does Health Tourism Exist in the UK? *Revue de Tourisme*. 44 (3): 26-30.

World Health Organisation (WHO) (1946) *Constitution*. Geneva: WHO.

The contribution of frontcountry tourist recreation towards increased crowding and dissatisfaction in New Zealand's natural environments

G Kearsley, S Russell and R Mitchell

University of Otago, New Zealand

Introduction

The demand for natural areas where outdoor recreation can take place has been increasing rapidly for some time. In New Zealand a threefold increase in tourism over the past two decades, to 1.7 million visitors a year, has put pressure on resources that were traditionally utilised by domestic recreationists. The clean green image of New Zealand and the reputation of its natural environments has brought an influx of international recreationists so that those natural resources are coming under increased pressure. This increase in recreational demand has come to threaten the very resources upon which it is based, and has brought associated problems, both for visitors and managers. Crowding has become the most serious of these, affecting the very nature of the outdoor recreation experience itself (Kearsley 1996, 1997; Kearsley, Coughlan, Higham, Higham and Thyne 1998).

Crowding in outdoor recreational environments has become a growing focus of research in recent years (e.g. Shelby et al 1989; Vaske et al, 1980; Ditton et al, 1993) and many of the factors that influence perceptions of crowding have been identified. Among them, the personal characteristics of visitors, the characteristics of others encountered and situational variables are considered most significant. The personal characteristics of visitors that have been found to influence perceptions of crowding include motivations for outdoor recreation, preferences and expectations of contacts, experience levels and attitudes towards management.

This paper is concerned with the motives of users of the back country, their perceptions of crowding and wilderness and the extent to which they might be displaced in the future. These perceptions are compared with similar information from the first part of a study of front country users, that is, those who use easily accessible natural areas for periods of less than a day. In particular, the aim is to see whether or not such users, who are by far the majority, numerically, are likely to graduate to back country use. If, as is suspected, they are, then back country pressures will be greatly magnified as natural environments are obliged to absorb not just a growing visitor market, but also a growing market share.

Back country use

Because of the nature of backcountry recreation, precise participation figures for the domestic population are hard to come by, but the various local and regional studies that are available show little sign of a major shift in the profile of backcountry users. The Life In New Zealand survey (1991) shows that only two percent report tramping as an activity, although since the relevant question asked for participation in the previous four weeks only, this may under-represent overall participation. There is no documentary evidence to suggest that there has been any great fluctuation in that figure over a considerable period of time, and there has been little change over a ten-year period. However, in the longer term, a present trend towards increased tramping activity among the elderly could lead to a 75 percent increase in activity by 2051, leading to nearly 105 000 participants in a four week period. Natural increase and present patterns of immigration, then, are likely to lead to an increase in use of the backcountry for the foreseeable future.

Domestic New Zealanders are not the only users of this rich and diverse recreational resource; international tourists have also become major visitors to the backcountry (Higham 1996; Higham and Kearsley 1994). In 1975 New Zealand had only 250 000 international tourists; they tended to be Australians and to patronise scheduled coach tours and few left the highways and scenic highlights, so few were to be found in the backcountry. Even in 1982, when visitor numbers had begun to grow towards the half million mark, a study of Fiordland National Park, by far the country's largest, showed that overseas backcountry users were a minority, overwhelmingly Australian (Kearsley 1982; Higham and Kearsley 1994; Kearsley and Higham 1997). By 1985, the number of tourists had reached half a million, with a much greater range of nationalities and a high level of demand for adventure experiences, such as white water rafting and bungy jumping. It was at this point that a significant tourist presence could be recognised in remoter natural areas. The present total of visitors is one and a half million, many of whom use the Conservation Estate, especially the more popular walking tracks and scenic destinations. In 1987, New Zealand's then ten National Parks received a total of three million visits; 70 percent of the visitors to Mount Cook, for example, were from overseas.

The most complete study of the volume of international tourist use of conservation lands is that of Duncan and Davison (1991). It revealed that in 1990/1 inbound tourists represented 45 percent of the 100,000 trampers on the 32 tracks reviewed. The presence of international trampers also proved to be heavily concentrated on a restricted number of tracks. Sixty-five percent of all tramping use by overseas visitors took place on just five tracks – Abel Tasman, Milford, Routeburn, Kepler and Lake Waikaremoana; 85 percent of all use was based on just 11 tracks. Overseas tourists were the majority of guided walkers as well. In all, 23,800 visitors made 43,200 tramps. Germans, Swiss and other Europeans were most likely to have made repeat tramps. The number of trampers was forecast to reach 104,000 by 2000, with 125,300 trips being made. The use of the frontcountry through short walks was estimated at 489,700 for half to one-hour walks and 69,200 for half to one-day walks. These were forecast to double in each case.

The 1995/6 International Visitor Survey shows that 33 percent of international visitors took a bush walk or tramp of more than half an hour, but less than half a day and that 29 per cent took a short bush walk of less than half an hour (NZTB 1997). Twelve percent walked for between half and a whole day, while seven per cent took part in full scale tramping that lasted for several days. These figures are up from the 1992/3 survey which recorded 30 percent taking a walk of less than half a day, seven percent walking between half and all of a day, with four percent tramping. In other words, the proportion of trampers has nearly doubled, even as the total market has grown by some 50 percent. As stated above, the key question that this paper helps to answer is whether the very large numbers of short duration users of the front country will evolve to become users of the back country also. If this should be the case, then a sensitive environment, already at capacity in social terms, will be over-run by a very much larger user population than it has currently seen. Since those new users are particularly likely to come from the overseas tourist market, the potential for growth is great, with profound consequences for the satisfaction of the host community and thus the community's acceptance of tourism.

Methods

This paper utilises data collected as part of a sequence of questionnaire surveys conducted by the Centre for Tourism, University of Otago, as part of a larger study into the issues of recreational use, facilities, motivations, perception of crowding, and constraints associated with the use of New Zealand's natural environment.

In the first study a total of 1603 surveys were distributed at various back country sites throughout the South Island of New Zealand during the 1995/96 tramping season, as part of a larger national survey. Questionnaires were distributed on tramping tracks, at huts and at selected Department of Conservation Offices and Visitor Information Centres (Kearsley, Coughlan, Higham and Thyne 1998). In the second and more recent study, a total of 1469 surveys were distributed at various front country sites throughout the South Island of New Zealand during a two week period in February 1999. The questionnaires were distributed at car parks and entrances to day tracks within the Department of Conservation's territory. Out of the 1603 surveys distributed in the back country, 781 were returned giving a response rate of 48.7 percent, while in the front country, 623 were returned giving a response rate of 42 percent

Both Front and Back country questionnaires were designed to assess the nature and extent of crowding and displacement in natural environments as perceived by overseas and domestic recreationists. This was accomplished by ascertaining the following:

- Use of New Zealand's natural and wilderness environments, especially walking tracks.

- Satisfaction with recreation experiences.

- Perceptions of modifications to the natural environment by human impact.

- Displacement to alternative locations and experiences by perceived crowding and impact.

- For the Front country, possible displacement into the Back country by perceived crowding and impact.

- Satisfaction with alternative locations (Back country only)

- Resentment with displacement and adoption of mitigating strategies

- Willingness to accept management procedures for mitigation.

Sample characteristics

Of the 656 completed and useable returned Front Country surveys, 396 (60%) were from non New Zealand residents, while 255 (39%) were from New Zealand residents, with the balance not defining their country of residence. In the back country survey non New Zealand residents only provided 48 percent of the responses, with New Zealanders higher at 51 percent. Table 1 outlines the country of residence for the international visitors in each sample.

Travelling groups were similar for both surveys. The commonest was 'with partner' and the second highest group was 'with friends'. For the third highest group, respondents to the front country survey cited 'family' and the back country quoted 'single'. Similarly the number of people travelling together was similar between the two studies with most travelling in groups of two. Female front country survey respondents were slightly in the majority at 53 percent, whereas they were 48 percent of back country respondents. This is not typical of most previous, smaller, surveys (Booth and Peebles 1995) where males tended to dominate, especially in the back country.

Table 1   Country of Residence

Country	Front country		Back country	
	Frequency	Percent	Frequency	Percent
New Zealand	255	39	399	
Australia	43	7	57	7
UK/Ireland	107	16	64	8
West Europe	100	15	142	18
East Europe	1	0	0	0
Nordic Europe	6	1	4	1
North America	96	15	81	10
Japan	22	3	6	1
Asia	8	1	1	0
Other Asia	6	1	1	0
Other	7	11	16	2
No Response	5	1	10	1
Total	656	100	781	100

The largest age group for both the Front and Back country were between 25-34 years old (front country 25%; back country 35%). However, the overall age of respondents from the front country was generally older, Table 2.

Table 2   Age Groups

Age	Front country		Back country	
	(n)	**%**	**(n)**	**%**
15-19	7	1	67	9
20-24	46	7	145	19
25-34	163	25	267	34
35-44	103	16	130	17
45-54	106	16	115	15
55-64	129	20	38	5
64+	93	14	11	1

Motivations for front and back country use

Respondents were presented with a series of possible motives for visiting the front country; they also had the opportunity to add their own if they wished. These are compared, Table 3, with the similar, but slightly smaller, set of motives that were recorded for using back country environments (Kearsley and Higham 1997).

Clearly, both samples have very similar motivational structures, with the main motivations being virtually identical. The three most important were *scenic beauty and naturalness*, *to enjoy the outdoors* and *to experience wilderness/untouched nature*. These were similarly strong and ranked; the main differences between the samples were the position of *to face the challenges of nature* and *to achieve personal goals*, which were seen as more important by the back country sample, perhaps understandably, given the nature of the experience. By contrast, front country users were slightly more inclined to favour both *exercise* and *relaxing with others* and a desire to *learn about NZ flora and fauna*. In spite of these very small differences, however, the similarities between the two samples are very strong. In other words, they are seeking similar experiences, even though at different levels of involvement.

Table 3   **Motivations for front and back country use**

	Front country (n=656)				Back country (n=781)			
	Mean*	Rank	Dom	Int	Mean*	Rank	Dom	Int
Scenic beauty/naturalness	4.75	1	4.66	4.80	4.75	1	4.68	4.83
Enjoy outdoors	4.46	2	4.5	4.42	4.65	2	4.66	4.64
Wilderness/untouched nature	4.08	3	3.94	4.15	4.25	3	4.17	4.33
Exercise	3.71	4	3.93	3.57	3.76	5=	3.94	3.58
Get away	3.62	5	3.77	3.55	3.77	4	3.95	3.58
Relax with others	3.56	6	3.87	3.37	3.36	7	3.71	2.98
Learn about N.Z. flora/fauna	3.39	3.54	7	3.43	3.61	3.28	9	3.17
Different experience	3.42	8	3.32	3.47	3.24	10	3.15	3.33
Challenge of nature	3.17	9	3.05	3.23	3.76	5=	3.75	3.79
Solitude	3.01	10	2.79	3.13	2.98	11	2.97	3.00
Personal goals	2.69	11	2.86	2.58	3.34	8	3.52	3.16
Excitement	2.67	12	2.66	2.67	N/A	N/A		
Face new challenges	2.64	13	2.71	2.59	N/A	N/A		
Build on skills	2.46	14	2.53	2.42	N/A	N/A		
Educate family	2.08	15	2.37	1.91	N/A	N/A		
Meet people	2.04	16	1.97	2.07	2.37	6	2.36	2.37

Note: On a scale of 1-5, where 5 is *extremely important*
Dom: Domestic; Int: International

Perceptions of wilderness

The urge to experience wilderness, however that might be personally defined (Kearsley, Kliskey, Higham and Higham 1997), is a significant motivator for both samples, and, to a great extent, both samples encountered wilderness conditions. Less than 5 percent of respondents (4.5 percent of front country and 2.6 percent of back country responses) indicated that they did not experience wilderness at all. While the remainder indicated that they experienced some degree of wilderness less than 10 percent experienced *pure wilderness* (9 percent and 9.2 percent, respectively). Whether this relates to different perceptions and expectations, or different environments, or both, is at present unclear. Not surprisingly, though, the back country sample believed that they had experienced a slightly purer wilderness environment than the front country users, although differences are not great with means of 3.32 and 3.45, and medians of 3 and 4, respectively. These are on a five point scale where five was pure wilderness and one not at all wild.

Around three out of four respondents in both samples had expected to encounter wilderness, while a similar number said they had experienced it. Over 90 percent of those who had expected wilderness from both samples also said they had experienced wilderness conditions to some degree. Few are finding absolute wilderness, but most are finding some. In general, front country users are finding rather less and to a lesser degree than are back country users and this raises the important question of whether, having sampled wilderness, will front country users then attempt to seek it further in the back country?

Table 4   Expectation and experience of wilderness

	Front country	Back country
Expected wilderness	73.9	70.7
Experienced wilderness	75.0	72.0
Expected and experienced wilderness	93.6	91.0

It might seem quite odd that front country users should expect and find wilderness conditions in trips that are often quite close to roads or lakeshores and certainly substantially less than a day's walk away. Part of the explanation lies in the fact that the strict conditions governing the management of New Zealand's National Parks, in particular, mean that the Conservation Estate is relatively wild land immediately it is entered. The only facilities permitted are tracks, a few simple overnight huts, minimal signage and the occasional walkway and bridge. These are consistent with the expectations of wilderness held by the majority of users of the Conservation Estate and certainly with those of the New Zealand public (Kliskey and Kearsley 1993; Kearsley *et al* 1997), so that, for many, wilderness begins the instant the Conservation Estate is entered.

Perceptions of crowding

That crowding is a serious issue in the back country had already been established by a number of studies (Kearsley and O'Neill 1994; Kearsley 1997, Kearsley *et al* 1998). A similar series of questions was posed to front country users. In the first of these, respondents were asked to assess the overall extent to which they had felt crowded during their visit, using a scale developed by Shelby *et al* (1989) and used elsewhere in New Zealand (Kearsley and O'Neill; 1994 Kearsley *et al* 1997). As can be seen, the patterns are broadly similar, but with a tendency for front country users to feel slightly less crowded, Table 5.

Table 5   The overall extent of crowding, per cent

	Back country	Front country
Not at all crowded	30	40
2	16	18
3	15	13
Slightly crowded	16	15
5	7	5
Moderately crowded	9	7
7	4	3
8	1	1
Extremely crowded	2	1

Over half of the front country sample experienced little or no crowding; neither sample saw extreme crowding to any great extent. Nearly a quarter of the back country sample experienced moderate crowding or more, the comparable figure for the front country was half that, at 12 percent. However, in both samples, the degree of crowding varied substantially during the experience. In the back country, for example, scenic points and overnight huts were the principal areas of crowding. While these figures indicate that that crowding is emerging as a significant management problem, it has little impact, as yet, on overall satisfaction, Table 6, although the effect is considerably stronger in the case of the back country. This may in part be because, with many trampers relying on overnight huts, it is impossible to escape crowding, whereas in the shorter and less constrained front country experience, it is possible to avoid potential crowding at the time when it is experienced.

Table 6   The extent to which crowding affected enjoyment, per cent

	Back country	Front country
Not at all	24	66
2	23	20
Moderately	40	10
4	12	2
Extremely	2	1

A considerable amount of information on numbers encountered and the extent to which this met with expectations and wishes was also collected for each sample. While it is not the purpose of this paper to discuss those figures in detail, they confirm the pattern of a reasonable degree of crowding for both samples, with the situation more critical at present in the back country.

In detail, as crowding perception rose, so too did dissatisfaction and consequent displacement behaviour (Anderson and Brown 1984; Neilson and Endo 1977 Kuentzel and Heberlein 1992). One of the first reactions, in both samples, was to became dissatisfied with the location (15 percent in the back country and 10 percent in the front), often leading to a decision to go elsewhere another time (18 percent and 12 percent, respectively). In the case of the front country sample, it is particularly significant that more than a half of those who said that they would go elsewhere said that they would seek out somewhere more remote the next time. Thus, at a very minimum, some six percent of the overall front country sample are contemplating more remote locations for their next experience. Although this may not sound much as a proportion, in absolute terms, and compared with the size of the total back country user population, this is a very significant figure.

In each case there was some evidence of product shift; that is to say, the user had re-evaluated and re-interpreted their previous perception of the location (Shelby, Bregenzer and Johnson 1988). Some 22 percent of the back country sample reported this, whereas only eight percent of front country users had made such a perceptual change. In other words, it seems likely that the front country users experienced what they expected to a greater extent than did the back country sample. In the latter case, a significant factor was the degree of sophistication of track and facilities on the 'Great Walks' where a great deal of overseas use is concentrated. For many overseas visitors, the numbers of people and degree of development are not at all what they expected, and not really commensurate with the wilderness that they hoped to encounter.

In both samples, significant numbers said that they would take some future action, or were already taking action, to avoid crowds. In the back country 35 percent said that they were or would. In the main, they would camp to avoid huts and adjust their daily departure times, either sooner or later, to avoid others (Kearsley *et al* 1998), along with a variety of other avoidance strategies. Rather fewer (16 percent) of the front country sample indicated similar action. Of these, 22 percent said that they started early in the day, but 16 percent said that they had or would venture 'deeper into the unknown', and this confirms the earlier suspicion that front country users plan to enter the back country, or are already doing so to some extent.

Conclusion

Compared with the past, a wider population is using the Conservation Estate, in terms of age, gender and nationality. It is no longer the largely exclusive preserve of young, well-educated New Zealand males. There is no doubt that there are growing visitor pressures; those associated with increased numbers have been outlined in this paper. The back country is already experiencing significant crowding problems, especially on the Great Walks, where international visitors are especially to be found. Visitor numbers are increasing, and there are significant signs of displacement to more remote locations. In terms of the back country, this implies greater pressure on fragile and presently untouched environments and greater safety risks for relatively inexperienced users who may be tempted to go further than their abilities permit. In the front country, this implies a possible turn to back country environments and experiences. If this should happen, then the most likely receptors are the more accessible and safe locations, namely those that are already under the most pressure. It is hard not to imagine that this will create a domino effect of further back country displacement.

This somewhat preliminary paper suggests that there is already some propensity for front country users to graduate to back country experiences and overnight tramping. As stated, the percentages appear to be small, but the numbers are large; the front country user population is many times larger than the back. Subsequent work will use more detailed information from this, and from larger surveys, to quantify the extent to which these trends are apparent and to explore associated issues. The front country sample, for example, is currently being expanded, while the back country sample will be replicated in 2001, after a five-year interval. The relevance of this work remains in the fact that more than 50 percent of a growing international visitor market are front country users, but only seven percent, at most, use the back country. Indeed, that proportion has risen considerable since the early 1990s, and, since the Asian financial crisis, there has been a considerable growth in the market share of precisely those countries that are most likely to use the back country, namely Australians, Europeans, British and North Americans. It seems almost inevitable that back country pressures will increase dramatically even if these trends do not continue.

References

Anderson, D. and Brown, P. (1984), The displacement process in recreation. *Journal of Leisure Research* 6 (1): 61-73.

Booth, K. and Peebles, C. (1995), Patterns of use. In Devlin, P. J., Corbett, R. A. and Peebles, C. J. *Outdoor Recreation in New Zealand*. Wellington: Department of Conservation and Lincoln University.

Ditton, R. B., Fedler A. J., and Graefe A. R. (1983), Factors Contributing to Perceptions of Recreational Crowding, *Leisure Sciences*. 5 (4) 273-288.

Duncan, J. and Davison J. (1991), *Review of the Capacity of Selected Tramping Tracks to Cater for Projected Increases in Overseas Trampers,* New Zealand Tourism Board, Wellington.

Higham, J. E. S. (1996), Wilderness perceptions of international visitors to New Zealand: The perceptual approach to the management of international tourists visiting wilderness areas within New Zealand's conservation estate. Unpublished PhD Thesis. University of Otago, Dunedin, New Zealand.

Higham, J. E. S. and Kearsley, G. W. (1994), Wilderness Perception and its implications for the management of the impacts of international tourism on natural areas in New Zealand. In *Tourism Down-under: A Tourism Research Conference, 6-9 December, 1994* (pp.505-529). Palmerston North: Department of Management Systems, Massey University.

Kearsley, G. W. (1982), *Visitor Survey of Fiordland National Park.* Lands and Survey Department. Wellington, New Zealand.

Kearsley, G. W. (1996), The Impacts of Tourism in New Zealand's Back Country Culture, in Robinson M., Evans N. and Callaghan P. (eds). *Tourism and Cultural Change*, University of Northumbria Press (1996) 135-146.

Kearsley, G. W. (1997), Perceptions of Social and Physical Impacts upon New Zealand's Back Country Environments, in Opperman M. (ed) *Pacific Rim Tourism*, (1997) CABI Wallingford, 156-166.

Kearsley, G. W. and Higham, J. E. (1997), Wilderness and backcountry motivations and satisfaction in New Zealand's natural areas and conservation estate. *Australian Leisure*. 8(1):30-34.

Kearsley, G. W., Coughlan, D. P., Higham, J. E. and Thyne, M. (1998), Impacts of tourist use on the recreational back country. *Research Paper Number 1. Centre for Tourism, University of Otago. Dunedin, New Zealand.*

Kearsley G. W., Kliskey A. D., Higham, J. E .S. and Higham E. C. (1997), Different People, Different Times: Different Wildernesses?, in Higham J. E. S. and Kearsley G. W.

(eds) *Trails in the Third Millennium* Centre for Tourism and the International Geographical Union, University of Otago 197-214.

Kearsley, G. W. and O'Neill, D. (1994), Crowding, Satisfaction and Displacement: The Consequences of the Growing Tourist Use of Southern New Zealand's Conservation Estate. In Ryan C. (ed) *Tourism Down Under*, Massey University, Palmerston North, New Zealand, 171-184.

Kliskey, A. and Kearsley, G. W. (1993), Mapping Multiple Perceptions of Wilderness in North West Nelson, New Zealand: A Geographic Information Systems Approach *Applied Geography*, 13, 203-223.

Kuentzel, W. F. and T. A. Heberlein. (1992), Cognitive and Behavioural Adaptations to Perceived Crowding: A Panel Study of Coping and Displacement. *Journal of Leisure Research*. 24 (4): 377-393.

Nelson, J. M. and Endo, R. (1977), Where have all the purists gone? An empirical examination of the displacement hypothesis. *Western Sociological Review* 8 (1): 61-75.

New Zealand Tourism Board (1997), *International Visitor Survey 1995/6*, NZTB, Wellington.

Russell, D. and Wilson, N. (1991), *Life in New Zealand Survey Commission Report*, University of Otago, Dunedin, New Zealand.

Shelby, B., Bregenzer, N. S. and Johnson, R. (1988), Displacement and Product Shift: Empirical Evidence From Oregon Rivers. *Journal of Leisure Research*. 20 (4): 274-288.

Shelby, B., Vaske, J. J. and Heberlein, T. (1989), Comparative analysis of crowding in multiple locations: results from fifteen years of research. *Leisure Sciences* 11 (4): 269-261.

Vaske, J. J., Donnelly, M. P., Heberlein, T. A. and Shelby, B. (1980), Perceptions Of Crowding And Resource Quality By Early And More Recent Visitors, *Leisure Sciences*. 3 (4): 367-381.

Destination avoidance

Rob Lawson and Maree Thyne

University of Otago, New Zealand

Introduction

Miron and Lo (1997) say "research on consumer behaviour commonly envisages destination choice as a two step process: (1) delineate the search set, and (2) evaluate the choices there in." Not all researchers would support this hierarchical view as an accurate representation of how consumers actually work when making choices about destination alternatives but for the purposes of this paper it is a convenient classification to explain the context of this research. Miron and Lo proceed to say that much of the work relates to the second step and in doing so it concentrates on the chosen alternatives. The objective of this paper is to provide more information about why consumers may choose to avoid particular destinations. In doing so, it contributes in part to our understanding of how different choice sets are defined and may directly complement the work of Sonmez and Graefe (1998a, 1998b) who analysed risk factors in general, and terrorism in particular, in connection with destination choice.

The motivation behind this research came from previously conducted work on the social impacts of tourism in New Zealand (Lawson et al, 1998; Thyne and Lawson, 1998 and Williams and Lawson, forthcoming). This work had focused on residents' perceptions of tourism and its impacts. Qualitative parts of these studies had suggested that some New Zealanders felt their travel patterns were being affected by the growth of inbound tourism into New Zealand, so that they now avoided particular destinations within the country. A comprehensive travel lifestyle survey was developed to measure the travel motivations and behaviour of a random sample of New Zealanders and questions were included about destination avoidance to see if this could be limited to particular travel lifestyles. This paper records the results that identify the destinations within and outside of New Zealand that people identified as wishing to avoid and reasons behind such avoidance.

Background and literature

Previous research relating directly to this topic is sparse, though there are significantly more studies that relate to destination image and choice which provide an overall umbrella for the study. Broadly speaking, this existing work can be divided into several strands. Firstly, there is research dealing with the formation and measurement of destination images (for example, Echtner and Ritchie 1993; Bagloglu and McCleary 1999; MacKay and Fesenmaier 1997 and Walmsley and Young 1998).

A second strand includes investigations into images held for particular destinations. For example Langlois et al (1999) looked at images of Poland held by potential UK visitors; Choi et al (1999) investigated images held of Hong Kong as a tourist destination and Embacher and Buttle (1989) did similar research looking at Austria. Some studies, for example Haati and Yuvas (1983), Haati (1986), Driscoll and Lawson (1994), Baloglu and Brindberg (1997) have looked at several destinations at once, on a comparative basis.

A third set of literature has looked at individual variables that may affect destination images and affect the question of whether the destinations are considered as available options. Much of this work deals with familiarity and knowledge (for example, Milman and Pizam, 1995) or distance and market access (Johnson and Messmer 1991; Zimmer et al 1995 and McKercher 1998). As noted above a variation in this area is provided by Sonmez and Graefe (1998a and 1998b) who looked at the dimensions of risk that people perceived to be associated with destinations and the personal characteristics that influence how risk is assessed. The dimensions of risk identified by Sonmez and Graefe seem highly correlated and if reduced to a few underlying concepts they seem to emphasise psychological risk and the risk of unmet satisfaction, physical safety, and political risk.

Thinking in terms of "risk" implies some, however remote, possibility that the particular destination might avail itself as an option. It implies a continuum of acceptance that is in some ways at odds with studies in the general area of consumer behaviour that have made use of the idea of limited sets that the consumer might hold when making decisions. These sets are an integral part of the seminal paper by Woodside and Lysonski (1989) that describes a general mode of destination awareness and choice. It is proposed that alternatives of which people are aware, be classified into one of three basic sets by consumers. The evoked set refers to that group of alternatives that are evaluated as meeting the basic criteria established by the consumer and from which the choice will be made. The next set (inert) is a group of options neither excluded nor specifically included by the tourist. People are conscious of this group as possible alternatives but do not bring them into the evoked set for evaluation. The final group is the "inept set". These are alternatives that are consciously rejected by the tourist as options. Court and Lupton (1997) use this classification to segment tourists in relation to the images they held of New Mexico as a destination and discuss the subsequent strategies that might be used to serve the adopters (evoked set) or inactives (inert set).

Sometimes destination sets are also divided on the basis of availability to the individual so that a separate group are defined as those that fail on the basis of price or distance but would be acceptable on other attributes available. Since marketers would normally regard price and location as attributes of the product, these may be regarded as simply a special form of the inept set, which is the specific focus of this study. No previous research has been identified which has attempted to research the inept set in quite the method employed in this study. Woodside and Lysonski (1989) do provide some description of how people might characterise a destination within the inept set as opposed to other sets, but they do not offer research results that help to define the important dimensions people use for including destinations in the inept set.

Method

Personal in-depth interviews were conducted with twelve residents in Dunedin, that were randomly contacted by telephone. Interviews gathered information on the respondent's last holiday; alternatives considered and the process of choosing. Part of the interview covered places the respondent would not visit (in the inept set) and the reasons associated with it. From this, a list of 10 reasons was developed for people avoiding New Zealand destinations and a list of 12 reasons why they might avoid various overseas destinations (see Table one). Seven of these were identical and related to crowding, cost or danger. Further discussion on these items is offered in the first part of the results section to follow.

Table 1   Reasons for Avoiding Particular Destinations

New Zealand Destinations	Overseas Destinations
Too many people from other countries	Too many people from other countries
Too many people from New Zealand	Too many people from New Zealand
Overall it is too crowded	Overall it is too crowded
Too expensive to travel there	Too expensive to travel there
Too expensive to stay there	Too expensive to stay there
Too expensive to shop there	Too expensive to shop there
Too expensive to participate in any of the activities there	Too expensive to participate in any of the activities there
It is dangerous to go there	
It is not a family place	It is dangerous to go there
It is too family orientated	I disagree, politically with what is happening there
	It is very different from New Zealand (in its lifestyle/culture and customs)
	Language difficulties make it too difficult to communicate with people there
	I want the money I spend to stay in New Zealand

These items were included in a comprehensive survey of travel behaviour questions that was mailed to a randomly generated sample of 3586 New Zealanders. Prize draw incentives were used to encourage the response rate and a total of 1703 usable responses were obtained (47.5 %). The full survey included over 200 questions relating to travel motivations, expenditure, accommodation, transport, booking and payment behaviour, information search and activities undertaken, as well as the avoidance data. The holiday information was used to generate travel lifestyle segments (see Lawson et al, 1999). The avoidance questions were split nationally and internationally. Respondents were asked to name any destination that they would choose not to visit within New Zealand and not to visit overseas. They were then asked to rate the reasons given in Table one on a five-point importance scale, as to why they would not visit that destination. They were also offered the opportunity to add and rate items not captured in the scale.

The sample was checked against census statistics and was found to be slightly older than the full population and also it contained an under-representation of Maori and Pacific Island

New Zealand groups. Neither of these is unusual for mail surveys in New Zealand. Geographic and income distributions were good.

Results

Destinations avoided

Of all the respondents, 812 identified a New Zealand destination that they would avoid and 1174 respondents chose to name an overseas destination to which they would not travel. The most frequently mentioned options are listed in Tables two and three below.

Table 2   New Zealand Destinations Avoided

	Number of respondents	Percentage of respondents
Queenstown	161	19.8
Rotorua	95	11.7
Auckland	98	12.1
Wellington	20	2.3
Mt. Maunganui	33	4.1
Taupo	37	4.2
Coromandel	20	2.3

Table 3   Overseas Destinations Avoided

	Number of respondents	Percentage of respondents
Africa	63	5.4
Asia	103	8.8
USA	33	2.8
Middle East	115	9.8
South America	30	2.6
Papua New Guinea	39	3.3
India	88	7.5
Japan	25	2.1
China	25	2.1
South Africa	26	2.2
Russia	38	3.2
Eastern Europe	46	3.9

Tables two and three show all those destinations identified with a frequency count of at least twenty responses. It is admitted that this cut off is somewhat arbitrary, but sufficient responses were required to calculate the mean importance ratings of the avoidance reasons for each destination. The next highest frequency in the New Zealand data was only 13 and had a much larger standard deviation in the rating scales. Therefore, it was considered unreliable to take any destination with fewer responses. The New Zealand observations are all specific locations that are clearly identifiable. Responses to the overseas question are more general. Most are identified by specific countries but they do vary up to whole continents. This is an interesting observation that given a free response the whole of Asia or Africa can be placed in the inept set without recognising the variation within these continents.

Reasons for avoidance

A simple examination of the means for the avoidance reasons shows that for the New Zealand destinations overall crowding and expense were the most important reasons for avoidance. While for the overseas destinations the perception of physical danger was the most important reason followed by concerns over different languages and political issues.

One issue that arose in the section of the survey that allowed people to name other reasons, was that of climate. Climate (or weather) had not been referred to as an issue at all in the preliminary qualitative sessions, but it was mentioned by 53 people as an avoidance reason in the survey. Unfortunately, most did not complete the rest of the question by filling out the importance rating evaluation, so this could not be incorporated into the multidimensional scaling described below. In retrospect, this was probably a weakness of completing all the qualitative work for the questionnaire construction in the local community of Dunedin. Dunedin has a temperate climate similar to the UK, Northern France or Germany while places like Auckland are a full 10° latitude further north. It is known that some residents have perceptions of the South Island as a cold place. However, it should be noted that other research on destination images (e.g. Baloglu and Brindberg 1997) has not identified climate as a relevant dimension in destination images.

In order to help understand the multidimensional scaling analysis that positions the avoided destinations in their perceptual space, the importance rating data were factor analysed across all the destinations. Quite clearly, several of the items listen in Table one are related to each other. For example, the four expense variables were all separately suggested, but it is perhaps unlikely that in many instances they are highly correlated in the consumer's mind. Likewise, a wish to avoid tourists from other countries is different to a wish to avoid New Zealanders and both may be different to a dislike of general overcrowding. Avoiding overseas nationalities seems to be a manifestation of xenophobia, whereas avoiding New Zealanders is perhaps the complete opposite and either or none may be related to crowding. Exploratory factor analysis was undertaken to clarify these interrelationships and to determine if a good underlying structure could be found amongst these avoidance reasons.

Using principle component extraction and a varimax rotation, a three-factor solution to the New Zealand destination was generated. This was using the default eigenvalue of 1.0 and the scree plot also indicated that the three factor solution was appropriate. The solution captured 66.7% of the variance. The rotated solution is presented below showing all factor loadings above 0.3. It is seen that no variables cross-loaded at all.

Table 4   Rotated Factor Solution - New Zealand Destinations

Avoidance reason	Factor 1	Factor 2	Factor 3
Too many people from other countries		.739	
Too many people from New Zealand		.842	
Overall it is too crowded		.720	
Too expensive to travel there	.760		
Too expensive to stay there	.909		
Too expensive to shop there	.900		
Too expensive to participate in any of the activities there	.890		
It is dangerous to go there			.836
It is not a family place			.787
It is too family orientated			.555

This is an equivocal factor solution that suggests three clear dimensions relating to people and crowding, costs, and the character and safety of the destination. One would have expected the last two variables to show an inverse relationship, but the last item is also the one with the lowest communality and thus is not best captured in the solution.

The factor analysis on the reasons for avoiding overseas destinations also produces a very clear solution. The default extraction produced a four factor solution, explaining 70.3% of the variance. In this case the scree test was less clear and indicated that three factors might be more appropriate.

Table 5   Rotated Factor Solution – Overseas Destinations

Avoidance reason	Factor 1	Factor 2	Factor 3	Factor 4
Too many people from other countries			.764	
Too many people from New Zealand			.821	
Overall it is too crowded	.317	.349	.478	
Too expensive to travel there	.884			
Too expensive to stay there	.908			
Too expensive to shop there	.819			
Too expensive to participate in any of the activities there	.867			
It is dangerous to go there				.808
Disagree with politics				.812
Different from New Zealand		.853		
Language difficulties		.848		
Money to stay in New Zealand		.502		

In this solution, the crowding reason crossloads on three factors as compared to the New Zealand data where it is clearly identified with the first two variables. This difference can be understood if the different population environments are considered. In the context of New Zealand, with its low population base, crowding is more usually associated directly with tourism and therefore the variable should load with the first two variables. In the context of the overseas destinations, the countries where crowding is noted as more important are those with larger populations, for example China, India, the U.S.A. and Japan. The cost factor remains the same as in the New Zealand solution, while politics and physical danger go together in factor 4 and finally factor 2 is concerned with cultural difference. Again the last variable in the table is the one that is not especially well captured in the solution. This item was proposed, not as a generic reason for avoiding overseas travel, but as a discriminating variable that would recognise acceptable "trading partners", where it would or would not be acceptable to substitute for a New Zealand holiday. In this context it was surprising that it was not linked to the fourth factor and avoided due to unfavourable political views.

Perceptual mapping of the inept sets

The Alscal procedure in SPSS was used to generate perceptual maps of the destinations using the mean scores for each destination on each avoidance reason. Both the New Zealand destinations and the overseas destinations were trialled over two, three and four dimensional solutions. The stress and RSQ fit statistics both suggested that in each case the optimal solution was likely to be the three dimensional one.

Figure 1   Perceptual Map of Avoided New Zealand Destinations

Perceptual Map of Avoided New Zealand Destinations

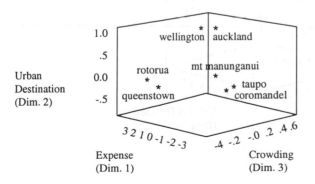

Stress = 0.02146   RSQ = .99796

The three dimensions in this analysis follow the three dimensions described in the factor analysis. Dimension one is concerned with cost and both Queenstown and Rotorua are associated with this dimension. These are both developed tourist resorts, with an extensive tourism infrastructure that caters for a large number of international visitors to New Zealand. Previous work on the economic and social impacts of tourism in New Zealand has suggested that Queenstown, in particular, is seen as an expensive option as a holiday destination by local New Zealanders (Cossens 1994, Lawson et al 1998). Dimension two seems to be associated with the urban nature of the destination and its safety and suitability for family holidays. Auckland and Wellington are positioned separately from the others on this dimension. Mt Maunganui, Taupo and Coromandel are all popular domestic destinations. The former is a seaside resort close to the town of Tauranga. The Coromandel is a scenic peninsula between Tauranga and Auckland, with many small bays that are excellent for swimming, snorkelling, boating and fishing. Taupo is in the centre of the North Island, on the edge of New Zealand's largest inland lake and is another popular fishing and boating resort. The third dimension that distinguishes these resorts is the one associated with crowding. This is a seasonal problem at many popular New Zealand domestic destinations since the main holiday period is condensed into a tight period of three or four weeks around Christmas and the New Year.

Figure 2   Perceptual Map of Avoided Overseas Destinations

Perceptual Map of Avoided Overseas Destinations

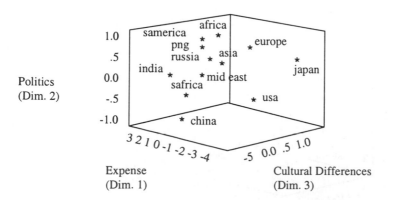

Stress = 0.04215   RSQ = .99175

This perceptual map is not as easy to interpret as the New Zealand data. Dimension one seems to be associated with the cost factor identified earlier. Japan is positioned especially strong on this dimension and cost was seen as the most important inhibiting factor in not considering Japan as a destination. Conversely Papua New Guinea is easily accessible from New Zealand and figures at the other end of this dimension along with South Africa. Despite the distance to South Africa, there are some well developed connections to New Zealand and recent growth in tourism between the two countries has been based largely around Southern Hemisphere rugby competitions.

Dimension two proved difficult to interpret. It shows the USA, China and to some extent South Africa positioned away from the rest of the destinations. Ultimately the only variable where this pattern occurs is the disapproval of politics, which was more highly rated in all three of these places. In the factor analysis, this variable was clearly linked to perceptions of physical danger but this does not emerge in the multidimensional scaling. As mentioned earlier, physical danger and safety are the most important overall variables for nearly all destinations avoided and therefore it is perhaps not a surprise that they do not emerge as important in the relative positioning of the destinations. Without a lot of variance it does not assume much influence in the MDS solution. In this survey, China is rated as safer than many of the destinations at the other end of dimension two and so it is difficult to associate with politics in this solution.

The third dimension relates to the cultural difference factor identified in the factor solution. This places China, India and Asia generally (excluding Japan) well away from the USA and Europe. A logical interpretation of this is that the cultural difference relates to first versus third world status, as opposed to values and customs.

Discussion and conclusions

This research has described examples from the inept sets of destinations held by a sample of New Zealanders for both domestic and international travel. Inept sets for the two seem based on slightly different dimensions, though in both cases cost and access are important considerations. The New Zealand domestic analysis is easily understood and seems very logical. Besides cost, the other important dimensions are (1) other tourists present and associated crowding and (2) the character of the destination and its suitability for family holidays. All the places mentioned in the domestic part of the survey, are precise locations with distinct images. A feature of the international responses was the tendency to name whole countries or continents in the free response section. This changes the level of analysis somewhat and it could be one of the issues that makes interpretation of the dimensions more difficult. Obviously respondents have some very simple stereotypes in their minds when considering this question and in one word are prepared to dismiss large sections of the earth as potential destinations. The most important reason is some perceived threat of physical danger for a country or area to be included in the inept set but beyond this costs, politics and culture are important.

The dimensions that underlie the image maps of the inept sets have obvious similarities with the risk dimensions listed by Sonmez and Graefe (1998) in their analysis of risk types and avoidance of different regions. For example, we commented that the culture dimension seems to be related to first versus third world status. This is clearly a similar idea to ideas on equipment, finance and health that are part of Sonmez and Graefe's solution. Our initial respondents did not suggest a need to break physical danger into specific issues like health, terrorism and crime, but these are clearly present in both analyses, as is political risk. Sonmez and Graefe also have dimensions that relate to not achieving satisfaction, both personally and socially. Consumer behaviour literature does link satisfaction to perceived value for money and subsequently to costs, so again there is some concordance with their suggestions.

Although this study enabled people to choose a destination in their own inept sets and was therefore restricted only to material related to these sets, the dimensions on which they were asked to judge were predetermined from the qualitative research. A suggestion for future research is to look at inept sets using personal construct theory (see Walmsley and Jenkins, 1993; Walmsley and Young, 1998). Application of personal construct theory in the context of general destination images, seems to produce affective dimensions similar to those described by Baloglu and Brindberg (1997) in their specific study of affective dimensions in Mediterranean countries. The dimensions in this study (and Sonmez and Graefe) can be characterised as much more cognitive in nature. This distinction, if confirmed, could be analogous to work in the general area of satisfaction and dissatisfaction, that suggests different factors contribute to the constructs in the general way of two factor theory. That is, we would expect the inept set to be governed by a different set of dimensions from the evoked set. These dimensions would be related to features that cause dissatisfaction if they fail to perform and that, like functional attributes of products, they may be characterised as largely cognitive in nature. Personal construct approaches would offer a different, but systematic, way of analysing images associated with inept sets.

References

Baloglu, S. and Brinberg, D. (1997), Affective Images of Tourism Destinations, *Journal of Travel Research,* 35 (4): 11-15.

Baloglu, S. and McCleary, K. W. (1999), A Model of Destination Image Formation, *Annals of Tourism Research,* 25 (4): 868-895.

Choi W. M., Chan A. and Wu J. (1999), A Qualitative and Quantitative Assessment of Hong Kong's Image as a Tourist Destination, *Tourism Management,* 20, pp 361-365.

Cossens, J. (1994), *The Application of Branding and Positioning to Destination Marketing: A Study of the Relationship between Destination Image and Destination Position using Multidimensional Scaling,* PhD Dissertation, University of Otago, Dunedin, New Zealand.

Court, B. and Lupton, R. A. (1997), Customer Portfolio Development: Modeling Destination Adopters, Inactives, and Rejecters, *Journal of Travel Research,* 36 (1): 35-43.

Dadgostar, B. and Isotalo, R. M. (1992), Factors Affecting Time Spent by Near-home Tourists in City Destinations, *Journal of Travel Research,* 31 (2): pp 34-37.

Driscoll, A., Lawson, R. W. and Niven, B. (1994), Consistency Between Two Alternative Measures of Perception, *Annals of Tourism Research*, vol 21 (3): 499-511.

Echtner C. M. and Ritchie, J. R. B. (1993), The Measurement of Destination Image: An Empirical Assessment, *Journal of Travel Research,* 31 (4): 3-13.

Embacher, J. and Buttle, F. (1989), A Repertory Grid of Austria's Image as a Summer Vacation Destination, *Journal of Travel Research,* 27 (3): 3-7.

Haati, A. J. and Yuvas, U. (1983), Tourist's Perceptions of Finland and Selected European Countries as Travel Destinations, *European Journal of Marketing,* 17 (2): 34-43.

Haati, A. J. (1986), Finland's Competitive Position as a Destination, *Annals of Tourism Research,* 13, pp 11-35.

Johnson, R. R. and Messmer, D. J. (1991), The Effect of Advertising on Hierarchical Stages in Vacation Destination Choice, *Journal of Advertising Research,* December, pp 18-24.

Langlois, S. M., Theodore, J. and Ineson, E. M. (1999), Poland: In-bound Tourism from the UK, *Tourism Management, 20,* pp 461-469.

Lawson, R. W., Merret, T., Williams, J. and Cossens, J. (1998), Residents' Attitudes to Tourism in Ten New Zealand Towns, *Tourism Management,* 19 (3): 247-256.

Lawson, R., Thyne, M., Young, T., and Juric, B. (1999), Developing Travel Lifestyles: A New Zealand Example, in Pizam, A. and Y. Mansfeld *Consumer Behaviour in Travel and Tourism,* The Haworth Hospitality Press, New York.

MacKay, K. J. and Fesenmaier, D. R. (1997), Pictorial Element of Destination Image Formation, *Annals of Tourism Research,* 24 (3): 537-565.

McKercher, B. (1998), The Effect of Market Access on Destination Choice, *Journal of Travel Research,* 37. (August), pp 39-47.

Milman, A. (1993), Maximising the Value of Focus Group Research: Qualitative Analysis of Consumer's Destination Choice, *Journal of Travel Research,* 32 (2): 61-64.

Milman, A. and Pizam, A. (1995), The Role of Awareness and Familiarity with a Destination: The Central Florida Case, *Journal of Travel Research,* 33 (3): 21-27.

Miron, J. R. and Lo L. (1997), A Selection Bias Approach to Destination Choice, *Geographical Analysis,* 29 (2): April, 145-168.

Sonmez, S. F and Graefe A. R. (1998), Determining Future Travel Behaviour From Past Travel Experience and Perceptions of Risk and Safety, *Journal of Travel Research,* 37 (2): 171-177.

Sonmez, S. F. and Graefe, A. R. (1998), Influence of Terrorism Risk on Foreign Tourism Decisions, *Annals of Tourism Research,* 25 (1): 112-144.

Thyne, M. and Lawson, R. (1998), Attitude Segmentation of Residents with regard to Tourism, *New Zealand Tourism and Hospitality Research Conference 1998*, Akaroa, New Zealand, Lincoln University, Canterbury, New Zealand.

Walmsley, D. J. and Jenkins, J. M. (1993), Appraisive Images of Tourist Areas: An Application of Personal Constructs, *Australian Geographer*, 24, pp 1-13.

Walmsley, D. J and Young M. (1998), Evaluative Images and Tourism: The Use of Personal Constructs to Describe the Structure of Destination Images, *Journal of Travel Research* 36 (3): 65-69.

Williams, J., and Lawson, R. (Forthcoming), Community Issues and Resident Opinions of Tourism in New Zealand. *Annals of Tourism Research*.

Woodside, A. G. and Lysonski, S. (1989), A General Model of Traveller Destination Choice, *Journal of Travel Research,* 27 (4): 8-14.

Zimmer, Z., Brayley, R. E. and Searle, M. S. (1995), Whether to Go and Where to Go: Identification of Important Influences on Seniors' Decisions to Travel, *Journal of Travel Research,* 33 (3):3-10.

Consumption of the countryside at the turn of the millennium: A post-modern desert of experience or valuable link in the chain of 'real', lived identities, day visitors to the Peak Park have their say

Scott McCabe

University of Derby, UK

Abstract

This paper explores some of the myths about the tourist consumption experience at the turn of the millennium. We are increasingly being told that tourism is changing both from the point of view of the 'new' tourist (Poon: 1993), and from the point of view of the tourist industry that must respond by commoditising and sanitising tourism experiences as 'products' (cf: Urry, 1990; MacCannell, 1992). Although Selwyn (1996) argues that tourists can seek a variety of experiences from different (or for that matter the same) actual trip(s) there appears to be an assumption in the literature that tourists blindly go about failing to achieve 'authentic' experiences in destinations. Selwyn attributes this partially to a lack of knowledge on behalf of the tourist (and the anthropologist - pointedly), but also partly because tourist consumers are supposed to be concerned with authenticity in the face of a lack of meaning and social structure associated with the post-modern condition.

This paper makes problematic the meta-theoretical approach to the explanation of the meaning of tourist experiences, with a phenomenological study of day visitor behaviour in the Peak National Park. It is contended that, whilst for longer vacations or distances away from home, a lack of knowledge may make authentic experiences more of an issue, for the day visitors in this study, the Peak Park represents a connection to real, lived identities through individual 'heritages' or geneologies that can be understood as authentic and meaningful on an individual level. Although the frame of consumption may be classified as post-modern, the site of experience can serve as a conduit for authentic individual experiences based upon the working up of identities associated with the past or the countryside, which at face value bear little representation to the indicators of post-modern existence. Whilst visitors want to experience the Park as a representation of a 'by-gone' era (perhaps underlining a post-modern planning orientation), the knowledge of this by visitors does not appear to lessen the value or the nature of the experience themselves. This paper seeks to address these issues as well as discussing the methodology underpinning the research.

Introduction

This paper seeks to draw attention to a recurrent issue within the social sciences generally and also within theories about tourism in particular. As such this conference affords a good opportunity to re-address these issues and to hopefully provide some suggestions for further study. In essence the issue addressed within the paper is that of the consumption of tourism at the turn of the millennium, and the nature of that consumption. There are a wide variety of literatures that seek to address different aspects of the consumption of tourism 'products', including, Sociology, Consumer Behaviour and Marketing, Psychology, and Cultural Geography. These different aspects are primarily concerned with the nature of the consumption experience to the consumer herself, or the ways in which goods, services and ideas are bought and experienced. This paper is concerned with the sociological analysis of tourism which is characterised by two methodological approaches. These methodologies can be broadly grouped as positivist, quantitative approaches on the one hand, and more interpretive approaches on the other. The former approach takes as its starting point the consumer as rational individual, who, although constrained by societal and situational factors, is free to make choices that can be modelled, hypothesised, measured and tested with quantitative tools of analysis. The latter tends to look for broad structures within society and interpret trends and general behaviour to social theories. What tends to be disregarded within these two approaches is a concern for the 'actual' experience-of-behaviour of ordinary citizens within society in a more detailed sense. Although there are many studies that have used qualitative methods and lengthy time spent interviewing tourists or as participant, or non-participant observations of behaviour, there are few studies in tourism that try to understand the meaning of behaviour to tourists themselves. This paper begins with an analysis of the foundational theories that have formed current thinking about tourist behaviour, before going on to assert the relevance of tourists accounts of their own actions as a valid way of understanding the meaning of tourism at the turn of the millennium.

The post-modern desert of tourism experience

Early analyses in the sociology of tourism suggested that the tourist was seeking something different, 'the other' (Bourdieu, 1964). This 'other' was later characterised as the obviously false, playfully inauthentic experience denied in the rigorously structured meaningless factory production system (Boorstin, 1964), or the centre out there, a semi-religious state of self-fulfilment and engagement with an activity (Turner, 1973). Thought shifted with the work of MacCannell who challenged Boorstin's analysis to suggest that tourist's were seeking some authentic experience from tourism as a response to the meaningless and insignificance of everyday life. Cohen (1988) in his review of the traditions of the sociology of tourism put it succinctly:

"...The resulting inauthenticity of tourist experiences is hence, not a consequence of the tourist's superficial desire for the spurious and illusory, as Boorstin argued, but rather a structural consequence of the development of tourism." (Cohen, 1988: 34).

MacCannell however, going on to ascribe authenticity-seeking as a basic value, suggested that such a quest is the concern of every tourist. His otherwise widely accepted argument was criticised because of the 'dynamic' and 'negotiable' elements of the search for authentic experiences from tourism (Cohen, 1988: 36/7). In the post-modern era, the quest for authenticity of experiences appears to be less important as tourists become more 'knowing' and 'complicit' in the production of spuriously framed experiences. For example, Urry (1988, 1990) talks of holiday making as being 'post-modern' in post-industrial societies. Mass tourism is explained by Urry as the organised, and socially-constructed opposite to work. Tourism of this sort has become a central feature of consumer culture. Urry argues that the 'post-(mass) tourist' does not have to leave the house to experience all the 'framed' experiences of tourism, as (s)he can watch them on T.V. The post- tourist can move easily between 'high' culture and 'pleasure principle' to gain the benefits of the both types of experience. The world is a stage and the post-tourist 'gazes' upon tourism places and people, and is able to play a multitude of games. On aspect of those games are that the post-tourist 'knows' that they are a tourist, that there are multiple texts framing such experiences and no single authentic experience. Drawing heavily on Foucault, Urry says that what we now consume are not products but signs or images, and identities are constructed through the exchange of sign values. Although attempts are made to dominate through the assignation of single, univocal meaning to signifiers, the images are taken in the spirit of the spectacle, and that:

"This world of spectacle is one in which there is nothing which is original, no real meaning, everything is a copy, or text upon a text. It is a depthless world of networks of information and communication in which information has no end-purpose in meaning." (Urry, 1988: 39).

Cohen and Taylor (1992, 2nd ed), talk of the experiences of holidays as 'escape attempts' from everyday life. They define everyday life as a mixture of 'chained activities', which render collective life predictable, and escape attempts aim to use these as a precondition of freedom. Reality is formed of multiple life worlds and 'escapes' are achieved when the individual suspends self-consciousness and can get an adequate opportunity for self-expression, this is where he really lives. The life-worlds that Cohen and Taylor document are; sex, gambling, holidays, sport, games, drugs, and therapy. Assertions of authenticity may turn out to be organised deceptions and typical of this is the fantasy escape messages of consumer culture. They provide enticing images to the consumer of escape from monotony and do not provide any means of empowerment to make the trip possible. Leisure features heavily in Cohen and Taylor's argument as they see that it is in leisure that the chained activities of everyday life threaten to engulf consciousness with their denial of freedom. Instead of being satisfied with our consumption of market goods we (consumers) are left wanting, dissatisfied and psychologically left with sensations of: incompleteness; arbitrariness; fragmentation; and indifference. Modernity represents a great poetic age, where through the release of energy through constant change and upheaval the poetry of our involvement with an activity could mitigate against the effects of mundane work and bureaucracy.

Selwyn (1996) argues that the search for the 'other' in tourist experiences is conceived around a world which is more structured, whole and authentic, although not all tourists are searching for the same authenticity. Selwyn makes the distinction between 'hot' and 'cool' authenticity. In the former the quest for the 'other' is described as being authentically social (1996:21), in that the 'other' derives from an imagined world, pre-modern, where the locals are friendly. In the latter the quest of the tourist is a quest for knowledge – although the validity of this knowledge may be drawn into question – and as such, the 'observer' is centrally placed to differentiate between the knowledge of the anthropologist and that of the tourist in the 'high street' (1996: 26/7). Only in this way will the bridge between the narratives of the tourists and the people who live in tourist destinations, and the 'observers' of post-modern tourism activity be created.

However, in all this the tourist experience as the search for authenticity and structure is based on assumptions of alienation, which Selwyn argues is out-dated and of limited explanatory power (1996: 3);

> *"Following the absolute triumph of consumerism, individuals have become, in the penetrating words of Baudrillard (1988) 'no more than monitoring screens'.....'monitoring screens' cannot feel alienated."* (Selwyn, 1996: 3/4).

In all the 'sexiness' of post-modern thinking, and there is without doubt a great deal of merit in such approaches to the development of understandings about tourism experiences, there are few authors that challenge this apocalytic view of experience and meaning. It is simply arrogant to assert that firstly, the 'individual' is the basic unit of existence in society. Individuals do not exist in a vacuum of social influence even if traditional notions of society are breaking down. Secondly, not all tourism is about consumption, although much of the tourism experience is widely held to be packaged and organised and sanitised, and therefore, commodised. Some tourism is about 'gazing', and so Urry claims this is part of the commodification process, however, some tourism is about sensing and experiencing bodily, hedonically, and not easily connected to consumption in any way. Thirdly, it is not possible to argue that experience of any kind is not imbued with meaning of some kind by the people doing the experience. Whether or not that meaning is 'real' as Urry argues, is difficult to ascertain. However, we must proceed from the idea that meaning is 'real' enough to the individual, whether that presupposes an authentic experience or not is a debate that shall be returned to later. Let us begin to think of an alternative approach to the study of tourism experience.

A link to Tourist experience

Gottlieb (1982), argued for an 'emic' view of authenticity, bemoaning Cohen's and MacCannell's view that tourist experience can be 'meaningless', or based on 'false consciousness'. Gottlieb proposed instead that research should

"...proceed(s) from the premise that what the vacationer experiences is real, valid and fulfilling, no matter how 'superficial' it may seem to the social scientist." (Gottlieb, 1982: 167).

Rojek's phenomenological sociology of leisure (1995) is also concerned with how people construct meaning and negotiate social interaction. The approach is oriented around the methodological standpoint of the naïve or native actor; in other words, it attempts to make sense of the world by using the constructs and categories used by individuals themselves in daily life. Rojek defines 'everyday life' as residual, what is left over after the distinct, superior and structured activities have been singled out (health system, police, judiciary). What is left over is the raw substance of everyday human existence, simple but rich. It is not the expression of conscious choice in lifestyle terms, rather, everyday life is incidental to conscious lifestyle and unavoidable. Everyday life is the relatively minor background discourse in a state of tension with the foreground. Rojek proposes that we must proclaim the knowledge and creativity of modern consumers in making leisure choices, and so consumption and leisure practice should be studied at the level of the micro-politic rather than the macro, where leisure is seen in terms of freedom, not class domination.

Despite the fact that leisure has been conceived as myth, deception, empty time-filling activity, and control in the critical sociology of leisure, the weekend remains an immensely popular attraction in our time budgets, in fact Rojek argues that we live for leisure, we are engaged and our emotions and interests are stretched to the full. Rojek asks a pertinent question:

"Are we to grandly attribute false consciousness to them? Must we insist that they are poor drabs who confuse the vulgar pleasures of patriarchal capitalism with real freedom?" (Rojek, 1995: 127).

It is without doubt that critical sociology has exaggerated claims of repression, yet Rojek claims that there are still four sources of dissatisfaction in modern life; mortality, inequality, change and myth. The major criticism of this latter, macro perspective is that it appears to have no basis in everyday life experiences of ordinary people, and is nothing really to do with personal meanings.

Dann (1999), whilst talking of the distinction between notions of 'traveller' and 'tourist' within travel writing, discusses some of these debates about the academic discussion on the nature of tourist experiences. Through being able to disregard aspects of space and time, the travel writer is able to connect with the 'anti-tourist' (165, after MacCannell, 1989) in all of us. The distinction has sparked off a debate about the authenticity of tourist experiences and whether we seek contrived or genuine experience, it has helped define tourism as, for example 'sacred' journey (Graburn, 1989), or as play (Lett, 1983). The tension that is formed when tourists meet other tourists is called 'tourist angst' by MacCannell (1989), who assumes that tourists seek to distance themselves from their fellows. Tressider (1999) has argued that the tourist landscapes of national parks represent a sacred space to tourists, creating a means of reference to allow us to find roots away from the 'horrors' of rootlessness in the post-modern culture (1999, 144). And so, another way of approaching the subject of the nature and meaning of tourist experiences is to talk the role of the naïve actor and assume that there is meaning inherent in the activity of the tourist. However, I propose that there are methods of drawing a link between the two opposing views, to suggest that ties to the meta-narratives can be identified in the everyday talk of tourists about their experiences, and in the next section I want to discuss how social representations can be used to reveal practical accomplishments of social identities that demonstrate these links.

The social construction of identity in talk

In this paper I want to describe how the method of understanding 'accounts' (Scott and Lyman, 1968) can be applied to the issue of social representation. This mode of analysis draws on the tradition within psychology and social psychology of discourse analysis. This approach is not concerned with the discovery of psychological universals but the social contexts within which talk in constructed (Potter and Wetherell, 1987; Edwards and Potter: 1992). In other words this paper seeks to demonstrate the ways in which members construct notions of their own identities through the formulations of accounts for their behaviour. Due to considerations of space, this paper seeks to present data from one interview in order to show in more detail the range of accounts that each individual uses to construct identity.

In recent years the study of identity has shifted away from being conceived as a purely cognitive process underpinning human action, towards the notion of identity construction being a social accomplishment of interaction (Potter and Wetherell: 1987). In this way all manner of 'psychological' subject areas such as 'blame', 'perception', 'causal reasoning' can be analysed, not for the underlying mental processes that may be occasioned in their construction, but for the discursive practices in their construction themselves (Edwards and Potter, 1992; Edwards, 1994). The notion of 'identity' being a social, interactional, accomplishment has been conceived in terms of the 'self' for some time (Goffman, 1959). Goffman drew upon the contextual nature of social life to develop the theory that people create and sustain social roles, or 'identities', in a dramaturgical production of everyday life. This theatre of everyday life was understood to be created for, and directed towards, others in society, that made the direct link between the 'self' and society. Everyone, all the time, is playing some role, more or less consciously, and this role is the self we would like to be. Sometimes we come to believe we are the people in the role. This type of cynicism/conviction can also be reversed (especially shamanism for example). There are personal 'fronts' which are the expressive equipment's used to act out performances and these are standardised and fixed. Examples of fronts include sex, age, race, clothes, facial expressions, gestures. Through the performance of a routine using a front, claims are made upon an audience, abstract claims, and therefore the performance becomes socialised, modified to fit social expectations of society associated with that role. Performers offer their observers an impression that is idealised in different ways. In the context of performance the "front region" (Goffman, 1959: 110) refers to the place where the performance is given. The fixed sign equipment in such a place has been termed the "setting" (110). The front region is the place of the direct encounter. The "backstage" or "back region" (114) is the private place where clothes or equipment can be hidden, scrutinised for flaws or adjusted. The performer can relax here and drop his/her front, forego speaking his/her lines and step out of character. The back region will be adjacent (but concealed from the audience), to the front region.

As such, notions of identities become fluid, as individuals slip between negotiated selves according to the demands of the interactional setting. Goffman later developed the idea of an interactional order for 'self'-production in social encounters (1979). These interactional relationships Goffman called 'footings', consisting of five levels of roles or identities produced in interaction.

The links between phenomenological thought, the interactional order, society and the self has been made eloquently recently by Malone (1997). Malone draws a thread through Schutz's descriptions of the Lebenswelt (Schutz and Luckmann, 1973), ethnomethodology and its concerns with the accomplishments of everyday life (cf: Heritage, 1984), Goffmans interaction order (Goffman, 1959) and the conversation analytic Programme of Sacks that sought to formalise a rigorous method of handling the events of everyday interaction as sociological data (Sacks, 1972). In this way Malone constructs the basis for the identification of the presentation of self in everyday talk through the reconceptualisation of information, meaning and intention within conversational data (Malone, 1997: 144).

> *"In the interaction order, information, intention, and meaning are dependent on the twin demands of self-presentation and sense-making so there are no simple signs. All information transmission between people must be treated as potentially complex."* (Malone, 1997: 145).

Self presentation is understood to be an endless social accomplishment (after Garfinkel: 1967), reflexively created and recreated in the interaction order that prioritises self-presentation and the making of common sense in interaction. In this way:

> *"...meaning is not something that social scientists attribute to interaction. It is the constitutive property of interaction which is necessary for it to continue."* (Malone, 1997: 147).

Shared meaning is a shared agreement not of substance but of method, rationality is a method acceptable without discussion (Garfinkel, 1967). Gubrium (1993) argues for a cautious naturalism, in that the agent or member is a practitioner of everyday life and is therein engaged in a production of meaning in the local setting of activity and the overall products of the enterprise. Gubrium refers to this as the embeddedness (99) of the social construction process;

> *"...stressing the formal and informal organisational parameters of meaning that impinge on the agent or, putting it in reverse order, that provide the agent with interpretive resources. The agent's constructive activity is embedded in a context of interpretation."* (Gubrium, 1993: 99).

It is this ordinary practical quality of constructive agency that allows one to methodologically tolerate the tension between culture and nature, and so features of everyday life are treatable as natural even if they are constructed, members' projects take things for granted and as immutable (ibid: 100).

In studies of identity this naturalism, or attention to the cultural context of an interactional situation, allows for the analysis of how social actors orient towards and manage performed identities. In such a framework, the analysis of previously under-researched data, such as broadcast and media interactions can become the subjects of scrutiny for the identity work that they reveal on behalf of the participants, such as the case of the Panorama interview between Martin Bashir and the late, Diana, Princess of Wales (Abell and Stokoe, 1999).

The analysis that follows intends to demonstrate how members draw upon social discourses of leisure and tourism consumer behaviour in their experiences that can be derived from a close attention to the detail of the interview narratives. The intention here is not to provide a full analysis but to describe in some detail the identity work achieved by the accounting of experiences in one instance in greater detail.

Accounts of experiences and what they reveal about identity

Experiential accounts can serve to establish warranted identity claims on behalf of the participants in the interview setting. The analysis that follows was presented previously at the first international conference on consumption and representation in Plymouth, September 1999. Names have been changed in order to protect the speakers anonymity.

In extract 1, Don talks about the 'clubs' reasons for going to the Peak District and also personal experiences that differentiate his walking activities from those of the club. The interview was undertaken whilst on an organised ramble with a walking group from Nottinghamshire. The extract begins with the interviewers question asking for an account of Don's history of his involvement in walking in the Peak District.

Extract 1. Don

(SM)   When was the first time you came to the Peak District do you think?

(D)   *Well that would have been the Autumn of '68, when I first started walking, because the Peak District itself has always been the club's stomping ground, sometimes slip over into Staffordshire, and Yorkshire and so on.*

(SM)   Is that the only reason you come to the Peak district because it's where the club sort of goes?

(D)   *Well no, you come with the club, and the club has it's own regular programme once a fortnight all year through, but, er yes, it's on your doorstep. I get off to Wales, I've done gold hunting in Wales.*

(SM)   Gold hunting, yes?

(D)   *And in fact only last summer I did the fourteen three thousands at one go, at about the third attempt, although I did that the unofficial way, North to South, because it's more practical.*

(SM)   Goodness me

(D)   *I mean I've seen Wales from an early point in time because I mean*

> *it'd be about 1970 one of the club members used to have a section,*
> *used to go away at bank holidays and a guy took me, a guy called Eric*
> *Stokes, he's now dead and buried, got cancer, poor bloke, er, he took*
> *me out to er near Capel Curig, and I rather liked the mountains, took*
> *to the mountains.*

In Don's reply to the interviewers question, we are offered an 'explanatory' account of Don's first visit to the Peak District, indicated by Don's use of the word 'because'. This extract is interesting for a number of reasons. The first being that Don accounts, in the way that he gives a reason, for something that happened long ago, for which no justification is needed. This is understood as Don's natural orientation to the production of an account for his behaviour. His first visit to the Park was in the Autumn of '68 (1.2) when he first started walking. The explanatory use of because (at line 1.3) is heard as giving a reason why he came to the Peak Park, 'because' he came with the club and the club's 'stomping ground' (line 1.4) had always been the Park.

The interviewer poses a direct question asking for Don to account for his visits (line 1.6/7). Don's reply is equivocal and requires detailed examination. We first notice that Don changes the subject from first to second person in his turn from lines 1.8 - 1.10. Don first disagrees with the interviewers suggestion that the only reason Don comes to the Park is on trips with the club, by saying "well, no..." (line 1.8), which can be heard as a discourse marker. His use of the second person from here to say first that "...you come with the club..." (line 1.8) and then to talk about the clubs programme is followed by a formulation; "...but, er, yes, it's on your doorstep." (line 1.9/10). Malone (1997) argues that this device of shifting between 'footings' is a signal of the type of identities that are being drawn upon. Don, when talking about 'you' to describe in effect 'his' coming with the club works to declare a role that is associated with a type of activity. Since we were both participating in this activity at the time of the interview, his use of the pronoun 'you' at this stage could be interpreted to mean him and me. Yet the quality of the turn here has the effect of meaning 'all of us' (Malone: 1997: 45), rather than in the specific instance of the walkers (interviewer and interviewee) themselves. Although Malone signals that the use of the second person singular is always ambiguous in English since there is no distinction between how many 'yous' are referred to, the hearer is not always the recipient, the 'direct target' of the speakers words (Malone: 1997: 68). In the instance of extract 1, Don can be heard to use the word 'you' as meaning 'people like us' (ibid: 68, from a discussion of Sacks' work on the topic). In other words Don is heard to invoke the second person plural. Even more ambiguous however, Don is heard as saying people like us in the sense that 'we' are all on the walk with 'the club', which has its own agenda, his talk has the effect of de-personalising the talk as if to say that the choice of place of the walks is not his. Don comes with the club because he is a member, and the club comes to the Peak Park because it is on 'your doorstep' (line 1.10). Here we can hear that whilst Don is heard as constructing 'the club' as the decision making body, he still formulates an account for why the club comes to the Peak Park. This interpretation gains currency when we discuss the nature of the shift in pronoun construction to the first person singular as being significant, in that it serves to distance Don's own personal preferences in terms of choices of places from the those undertaken by the club in the Peak Park. Don's turn at line 1.10; 'I get off to Wales, I've done gold hunting in Wales'. Goffman (1979) agues that changes in footing imply a change in the alignments of speaker and recipient and the management of the talk. Don is heard to refer to two different roles or selves, in that he talks about his role in the club in terms of people like us and his separate, solitary walking experiences in Wales. And further, his turn from lines 1.12 - 1.14 are oriented to his, not insignificant, recent walking achievements. From this hearing we can get a sense that the reason 'it is on your doorstep' is not a positive factor for Don, the fact that the club goes there because the Peak has always been the clubs 'stomping ground' and 'it is on your doorstep' serves to account for the club's activities in the Park.

However, Don constructs his own, personal activities in terms of other places with actual differences from the Peak Park. We can hear evidence that Don draws on a discourse that serves to present an identity of what we might call a 'serious walker' throughout the extract, with the use of such formulations as 'stomping ground', 'get(ing) off to Wales', and 'the fourteen three thousands'. In Don's final turn of extract 1, lines 1.16 - 1.21, we hear another account that explains how Don got interested in walking in Wales that he ends with the words; "...and I rather liked the mountains, took to the mountains."

We get a sense of what Don personally likes here as opposed to what his actual behaviour in the setting of the interview indicates (we are on a gentle walk around the Derbyshire Dales). In this case, it is probably the clearest hearing of a construction of a particular identity in this data, perhaps because of the nature of interview setting. Don can be heard to be doing two different types of identity work in this extract. He constructs his own identity as 'serious walker' through stories of his own exploits in the first person, and constructs his role as a club member, justifying their visits to the Park using the second person formulation.

In extract 2, (Don's first response of the interview) he begins to talk of the extent of his walking. Don constructs a chronology of his involvement with the group that again uses a different footing in that Don started coming with 'them' (2.5).

Extract 2

(SM)   And you've been with the Rambling club since 1968 when you left school?

(D)   *The Autumn of 1968, went round the corner and had a chat*
with the guy who was then the editor of the Notts free
press, and I started coming with them, and I've been with
them ever since and a couple of years after that we had a
camping group started camping with them, and then after I
got a camera, which I don't carry so much now, except when
I'm up in the highlands back-packing, but yes, I've given
Derbyshire a good walking, still plenty of little nook and
crannies to find, occasionally go over into what's now
Greater Manchester and Staffordshire and down into
Leicestershire and so on, and before now I've actually gone
over into Lincolnshire and actually walked and seen a ship
at sea.

This construction has the effect of portraying Don's progression first from being an outsider of the social scene of the 'club', then to membership and integration into the society of the club 'I've been with them ever since' (2.5/5) and then his role within the club when he changes footing to 'we' had a camping club at line 2.6. His construction first of him and them as distinct, through to the construction that confers membership charts Don's development in terms of his social identity as member of the club. He then reverts to his personal identity as what we termed 'serious walker' as he says at lines 2.9/10 that; "...but yes, I've given Derbyshire a good walking...".

A little later in the interview Don says that he usually goes to Scotland each year (extract 3.3 - 3.7) and again constructs the vocabulary of the 'serious walker', as when he says he sleeps in the 'bothies' (Line 3.6).

Extract 3

(SM)   What is it about them that you prefer, those areas, Kinder and all that?

(D)   *Just like the roughness the ruggedness, I usually get off to*
        Scotland on my own at least once a year for about a
        fortnight, and I'll go out and do two, three, occasionally
        four day trips, back-packing, using the bothies, which are
        equivalent of a mountain hut.

(SM)   Yes

(D)   *Er, you see originally I was a civil servant for almost*
        twenty seven years and so there is a big element of escapism
        in it, originally it was exercise to come in the club and
        after that I wanted to er, spread my wings, go a bit further
        afield, and I started doing that when I was 19, I walked the
        Pennine Way, southwards to home, er, the following year I
        did Offa's Dyke, North to South, so on,

In extract 3 we have an example where Don provides an account for his behaviour that is not specifically formulated in response to a request in terms of a why? type question, but which, with careful attention to the detail of the talk, can be analysed in terms of its identity production work. In talking about the yearly trips to Scotland, Don begins a new turn with the phrase, "you see..." (3.9), and this alerts us to the possible forthcoming 'account', it serves as a discourse marker. Don then explains that he was a civil servant for 27 years (a fact that might 'explain' any type of errant behaviour!); "...and so there is a big element of escapism in it, originally it was exercise to come in the club..." (lines 3.10/11). Don is oriented to answering a question, what it is that he likes about Kinder Scout and other places (lines 3.1/2). He constructs an account at line 3.3/4, and turns the topic to his visits to Scotland, as examples of this 'roughness' and 'ruggedness' and being on his own. Don's turn at line 3.10 beginning "so there..." could be reconstructed as 'I go to Scotland on my own each year because I want to escape'. Don can be heard to construct his role in work as requiring that he 'get away' on his own to Scotland, as distinct to the more social element of exercising provided as an account for originally joining the club (3.11/12). Don is heard to construct both a social membership identity as well as an identity that is partly formed by his response to his work role and also partly formed by his own desire to escape to isolation. His formulation of his institutional identity is placed in distinction to his identity as 'loner' through his construction of his account for his behaviour of going off on his own, 'spread my wings' (3.12). This behaviour of being on his own doing intrepid walks enhances our interpretation of Don's identity as 'serious walker' as is the talk in extract 4.

In extract 4 Don, when asked how he chooses a route or a place to go, Don replies that; "...oh just look at a map...and look for a clod of mountains to go and knock off..." (lines 4.6/7), and later on in the extract talk of how few there are left to 'knock off' for him (4.11 - 4.15). These terms refer to a 'discourse' of serious walking (Potter and Wetherell: 1994).

Extract 4

(SM)   How do you choose to do a route or a, go to a different place you know, is it?

(D)   *With the club?*

(SM)   No, on your own?

(D)   *On my own, oh just look at a map and sort of, you know,*
get some large scale maps and look for a clod of mountains
to go and knock off, certainly it was that way when I was
younger, perhaps a little bit more calculated about it now
finding my routes and so on.

(SM)   Done all the ones that are worth knocking off, have you?

(D)   *Yes, basically, there's not many, there's Cluny Forest,*
that's going down into the Kyle of Lochelm (?) that's a big
long ridge, and there's still this stuff out in Noidart
there's a couple of big ones out there I want to do, that
sort of thing.

This discourse is not lightly used, Don validates his liking for the countryside, and so also his current preference for leisure activity type, and also travel behaviour in terms of his self-identity. This is most evident in extract 5, where Don gives reasons for his preferred activities based on his personal biographical, or genealogical, heritage.

Extract 5

(SM)   Is that part of the attraction?

(D)   *Part of it, yes. I mean I am not married, I'm single live on*
my own, have done for about seventeen years now, but,
possibly I like the countryside because my mother and my
fathers side of the family were farming people off the Welsh
Borders originally, but then my Grandfather came over to
Nottinghamshire, and had his last farm just outside Sutton-
in-Ashfield, and in fact from my very teens, to leaving

school I used to go and help out on a farm where my uncle
worked and I liked that, used to come back with arms prickled
from hay-making and straw, and things like that, you know
and splatters of shit when you're mucking out stalls and
that, but I always used to enjoy it, so I think perhaps,
I enjoy it because that's where my roots lie.

In our analysis we could argue that Don is accounting for his behaviour in terms of his childhood experiences, he offers us reasons for liking what he likes based on the historical fact of his lineage as 'farming people' (5.5). In extract 5, the conversation with Don had turned to his visiting remote places on his own, and the interviewers question at line 5.1 is a leading question asking if being alone is part of the attraction of visiting places like the Scottish mountains. Don at first talks about the fact that he lives on his own, and then shifts the topic to say that he possibly likes the countryside; "...because my mother and my fathers side of the family were farming people off the Welsh Borders originally..." (5.4 - 5.6). This use of the statement 'because' is heard as a 'justificatory' account that may have several interpretations as to the type of work it serves Don. Firstly, Don can be heard to offer a reason for liking the countryside that is based on an account of his early socialisation. He likes the countryside because he comes from a line of country folk, who moved over to Nottinghamshire (5.6/7), and he used to go and work on the farm where his uncle worked (5.8/10), which he liked, and at the end of the extract Don reiterates using a formulation; "...so I think perhaps I enjoy it because that's where my roots lie." (lines 5.13/14). This last formulation of the turn, in a sense can be heard to discount the interpretation that Don's reasons are grounded in his childhood experiences, and instead almost infer that Don's reasons for liking the countryside are more 'naturalistic'. In this we mean that Don formulates his reason, 'where my roots lie' as if he had no choice in the matter, other than to completely abandon what he considers is his heritage as a 'country folk'. This abandonment is clearly not acceptable. It also signifies that Don identifies himself as belonging to a classification of people that may be similar in lay terms to class structures, as 'country folk' who are opposed to 'town folk'.

Discussion

In the interview with Don we can hear that there are accounts for behaviour that signify that Don is working to present himself to the interviewer in a certain way that may be at odds with the situation in which the interview takes place. Don is from the town, he was a civil servant, he is a senior member of a rambling club, and he is on a gentle ramble as the setting for our interview. Yet it was noted how Don accounts for his walking behaviour away from the Peak Park, in his construction of his walking experiences. His experiences in the Park are embedded in his social role within the rambling club. This is a role that is bound up in the notion of membership in a club hierarchy, due to his length of service in the club, since 1968. However, Don's social identity as member of the club walking in the Peak National Park is constructed by means of the invocation of a personal identity.

It was claimed that Don constructs a personal identity of a 'serious walker', in that he is experienced and competent and can draw upon the terminology of the 'knowledged' expert. It is since Don is at pains to establish his personal (separate from club) experiences and account for these activities that enable us to hear the identity work Don undertakes in the interview to establish himself as a 'serious walker', as complementary to his club identity. In other words, the individual identity formulations serve to legitimise Don's role in the club, together with his length of membership. Don draws on changes in 'footing' (Goffman: 1979, Malone: 1997) to differentiate these different identities from each other, legitimise his consumer experiences and account for his behaviour.

Members account for their day visit behaviour using formulations of accounts for behaviour that present some notion of their identities through stories of past lived experiences. This is accomplished in some cases when members construct accounts of their behaviour that denote levels of 'involvement' in either activity or place. In the extracts above we claimed that Don presented himself as a 'serious walker' through the use of specialised vocabulary and accounts of stories of behaviour. We further claimed that Don drew on formulations of his childhood experiences and lineage to account for his interest in the countryside, and subsequent consumer behaviour. Accounting for behaviour through the recollection of childhood memories that can be associated with the Peak Park itself, or a similar type of countryside, day visit experience or activity type serves to facilitate the production of identity work. It may be possible to hypothesise or reasonably assume that childhood experiences, in what Berger and Luckman term 'primary socialisation', define and shape individuals' everyday reality in adulthood (1966).

In extract 6, we noted that Don associates his love of the countryside to his 'roots' being from farming people. Here we can hear that Don is accounting for his general interest in the activity and countryside places as a social identity as well as being place-specific, as though denoting that there are 'types' of background, upbringing or social heritage that are specific to places. This also infers that places in terms of 'town' and 'countryside' are repositories of different realities, each imbued with certain meanings. Country people are different from town people, there are perhaps country 'ways' that may be represent social identity characteristics for Don that make them different people from town, or city folk. Don seems to suggest that the countryside has meaning for him in that he sees the countryside as a part of his personal identity.

Prior experiences then, serve to enable participants to construct notions of self and identity in what are essentially, consumed/consumer environments. Identity production in conversational interviews is understood as 'fluid', responsive to the interactional setting (Abell and Stokoe: 1999). When Don legitimises his current behaviour in terms of his childhood experiences, he is in effect drawing upon an identity as child within a cultural, and historical setting as if to relegate the notion of choice in the current activity. In other words, he could be heard as saying that he is drawn to this activity because it is part of his 'nature'. In terms of the earlier debate about the authenticity of tourism experiences, it must be made clear that not all tourists will share the same experiences and meanings as Don. However, I claim that all tourists do attach meaning to their experiences of tourism, which can be authentic or inauthentic, recognised as such or not by the actors, depending on knowledge and level of involvement with a place, activity or people. The search for the 'other' in this case seems to be inverted into a search, not for the 'self' but for the means to express a meaning for participation in tourism through the invocation of 'self'. In the same way that we may assume that Don's reasons for going to Scotland on his own to 'escape' from work, is not an 'escape' for the 'other' but an attempt to demonstrate identity work. It serves the purpose of saying 'I'm a civil servant, but I'm also more than that – I like to do this'. Don's experiences are authentically his, rich in meaning about his personal selves, his experiences shape him, in the same way that he shapes his experiences.

Interview material such as this is a rich source of data that can help us to understand more fully the processes of identity production and meaning and interpretation of individuals' tourism and leisure experiences. Members draw on social roles to legitimise their behaviour and warrant their activity as they account for their behaviour within situational, cultural contexts. They account for behaviour simultaneously as they describe consumption experiences, which are themselves rich in identity formulations. Therefore consumption is embedded within identity production and analyses of interview data using such notions as changes in footing and the discursive approach to data generally can further our understanding of the nature of tourism and leisure experiences.

References

Abell, J. and Stokoe, E. H (1999), Constructing culturally situated identities in Princess Diana's 'Panorama' interview. *Forthcoming in the British Journal of Social Psychology.*

Antaki, C. and Widdicombe, S. (1997), (eds). *Identities in Talk.* London. sage.

Berger, P. L. and Luckmann, T. (1966), *The Social Construction of Reality.* London. Penguin.

Boorstin, D. (1964), *The Image: A Guide to Pseudo Events in American Society.* New York. Harper.

Cohen, E. (1988), Traditions in the Qualitative Sociology of Tourism. *Annals of Tourism Research,* 15: 29-46.

Cohen, S. and Taylor, L. (1992), (2nd Ed). *Escape Attempts.* London. Routledge.

Czarniawska – Joerges, B. (1992), *Exploring complex Organisations: a cultural perspective.* Newbury park, CA. Sage.

Dann, G. (1999), Writing out the tourist in space and time. *Annals of Tourism Research,* 26, 1 pp 159-187.

Edwards, D. and Potter, J. (1992), *Discursive psychology.* London. Sage.

Edwards, D. (1994), Discursive psychology: illustrations and some methodological issues. In *La psicologia discorsiva: Presentazione ed alaine questioni metodologiche. Rassegna di Psicologia.* 11 (3): 9-40.

Garfinkel, H. (1967), *Studies in Ethnomethodology.* Englewood Cliffs, N.J. Prentice-Hall.

Goffman, E. (1959), *The Presentation of Self in Everyday Life.* London. Penguin.

Goffman, E. (1979), Footing. *Semiotica.* 25: 1-29.

Gottleib, A. (1982), American's Vacations. *Annals of Tourism Research,* 9: 165-187.

Graburn, N. H. H. (1977), (1989 second edition). Tourism: the sacred journey. In V. Smith (ed). *Hosts and Guests. The anthropology of tourism.* Philadelphia: University of Pennsylvania. Press. 21-36.

Gubrium, J. F. (1993), For a Cautious Naturalism In Holstein. J.A., and G. Miller (eds) *Reconsidering Social Constructionism. Debates in Social Problems Theory.* N.Y. Aldine de Gruyter.

Heritage, J. (1984), *Garfinkel and Ethnomethodology.* Cambridge. Polity Press.

Heritage, J. (1991), Intention, Meaning and Strategy: Observations on Constraints on Interaction Analysis. *Research on Language and Social Interaction,* 24: 311 - 332.

Lett, J. W. (1983), Ludic and Liminoid Aspects of Charter Yacht Tourism in the Caribbean. *Annals of tourism research.* 10: 35-56.

MacCannell, D. (1976 (1989)), *The Tourist: A New Theory of the Leisure Class.* London. Macmillan.

MacCannell, D. (1992) *Empty Meeting Grounds: the tourist papers.* New York, Dubleday.

Malone, M. J. (1997), *Worlds of Talk: the presentation of self in everyday conversation.* Cambridge. Polity Press.

Potter, J. and Wetherell, M. (1987), *Discourse and social psychology: Beyond attitudes and behaviour.* London. Sage.

Potter, J, and Wetherell, M. (1994), Analysing Discourse. In Bryman. A, and R.G. Burgess (eds) *Analysing Qualitative Data.* London. Routledge.

Rojek, C. (1995), *Decentring Leisure: Rethinking Leisure theory.* London. Sage.

Sacks, H. (1972), An Initial Investigation of the usability of conversational data for doing sociology. In D. Sudnow (ed) *Studies in Social Interaction.* New York. Free Press.

Selwyn, T. (1996), Introduction, in Selwyn, T (ed) *The tourist Image: Myths and Myth Making in Tourism.* John Wiley, New York: 1-31.

Schegloff, E. A. (1997), Whose Text? Whose Context? *Discourse and Society,* 8 (2): 165-187.

Schutz, A. (1972 {1938)), *The Phenomenology of the Social World,* London. Heinemann.

Schutz, A. and Luckmann, T. (1973), *The Structures of the Life-World.* Evanston, Ill. Northwestern University Press.

Tressider, R. (1999), Tourism and sacred landscapes, In Crouch, D. (ed). *Leisure/tourism Geographies: practices and geographical knowledge*. London, Routledge.

Urry, J. (1988), Cultural Change in Contemporary Holiday Making. *Theory, Culture and Society*, 5: 35-55.

Urry, J. (1990), *The Tourist Gaze, Leisure and Travel in Contemporary Societies*. London. Sage.

Wetherell, M. (1998), Positioning and Interpretive Repertoires: Conversation Analysis and Post-Structuralism in Dialogue, *Discourse and Society*, 9 (3): 387-412.

Datascapes

Alan Machin

Leeds Metropolitan University, UK

Introduction

The educational nature of tourism has been recognised for many years, but has not received much attention in considerations of tourism management during the last two decades. Historians were earliest in the field. Bates (1911) and Parks (1951) wrote of touring in the seventeenth century as a means of education. Hibbert (1969) and Towner (1981, 1994) discussed the importance of Grand Tour in education and cultural life. Graburn (1989) hinted at an educational role writing that tourism is amongst the means that people have to "add meaning and embellishment to their lives". Berlyne (1968) saw the role as psychological, with clear educative implications: "Human exploratory behaviour is behaviour whose principle function is to change the stimulus field and to introduce stimulus elements that were not previously accessible". Other writers on environmental psychology and spatial behaviour, fields of study with implications for education, include Ittelson et al (1974), Walter (1988), Walmsley and Lewis (1993) and Golledge and Stimson (1997) and Crouch (1999). Discussions of the sociology of tourism by MacCannell (1976), Turner and Ash (1976), Krippendorf (1987), Urry (1990), Ryan (1997) and others are well-known, as are the collections of papers from previous *Tourism and Culture* conferences.

Educational writers have a long perspective, though usually writing about educational excursions rather than tourism *per se,* such as Reynolds (1901) and Fairgrieve (1926), Boulding (1956), Dilke (1965) and Parker and Meldrum (1973). Educational tourism as a marketing opportunity, often categorised as special interest tourism, has featured in Weiler and Hall (1992), Smith and Jenner (1997) and Cooper (1998), the latter two largely concerning language teaching. Other recent authors have linked tourism as education to the goals of sustainability and eco-friendly tourism: Laarman and Durst (1987), Mowforth and Munt (1998), and Fennell (1999). Read (1980), writing after the growth in tourism and the rise in environment fears on the 1960s and 70s, called for 'REAL' travel which should be Rewarding, Enriching, Adventuresome and a Learning experience. It is worth making the point that while good quality is not always guaranteed, all travel arguably involves some kind of gain. Prentice (1996,1997) and Beeho and Prentice (1997) have discussed the experiential effects of cultural and landscape tourism. Gartner (1993, 1997) has written about destination images, how people perceive them, and the implications as part of a management process. Dann (1996, 1997) connected tourism experiences with message formation through the management and acquisition of linguistic judgements. These are further steps towards general understanding of the influence of tourism on knowledge.

This paper aims to examine the tourist environment and propose some theoretical ideas which will be of practical use in planning sustainable, community-sensitive forms of tourism. Its perspective is geographical and historical, with approaches from communication theory. The general position is taken that all forms of travel and tourism (cf Read, 1980) provide travellers with a range of experiences which are 'educational' in the broadest sense. They all supply some level of new knowledge, and help to develop ideas, viewpoints and skills through encounters in places different from the norm. To agree this point might require a definition of education which is not confined to its institutional modes. What is sometimes called vicarious education is included, as is self-education, through hobbies and interests pursued privately. The distinction may be made between didactic modes (teacher or author driven) and heuristic modes, which are driven by the individual's wish to find out things.

Tourism's origins

A consideration of tourism's origins is always useful as a reminder of what its early significance was. Ancient travel was rarely for leisure reasons. Few people in Greece or Rome had either the freedom or the motivation to travel for what we would term touristic reasons. Whole life spans would be spent within a comparatively short distance of home unless armed service, trade or government missions demanded it. For those who travelled in such occupations the world would have been met with little foreknowledge, education and any mass media input being lacking (Leed, 1991). Reports and rumour would have dominated life. New landscapes and people must have had an amazingly powerful effect on the traveller, a feature understood by leaders who exercised control through fortresses and temples which were functionally *and* symbolically effective.

Secular leaders travelled out from their castles to wield their power. The 'progresses' of medieval monarchs, supported by the ritual of court and the pageant, were travelling shows of sovereignty radiating from a central place. The pilgrimages of the faithful during the same period had them travelling towards a central place where the rituals of belief were practised at highly symbolic places (Feifer 1985, Coleman and Elsner, 1995). Much of tourism's beginnings came from those journeys which refreshed the soul and informed the mind.

The Grand Tour was the activity which established the recognisably leisure element in major modes of travel. It has been well described and examined by several writers (Pimlott 1947, Hibbert 1969, Towner 1981) who have traced its start as an exercise of educational experience and its culmination as fashionable leisure pursuit. Through its influence the architecture, art, philosophies and practices of Italian, French and Greek cities were fed back into British landscape and life (Towner, 1994). At the same time, the media influence was growing as printing spread through books and journals.

To take but one example: the magnificent Piece Hall in Halifax, functionally a cloth warehouse and market building, was modelled after classical designs on the principles of Vitruvius. A giant open square overlooked by colonnaded galleries in Yorkshire stone, the building is more Italian than English. The committee of merchants who oversaw its opening in 1779 wanted to impress, so chose highly prestigious styles familiar in the Mediterranean but certainly not in the West Riding of Yorkshire. Builders' pattern books supplied the technical information, but the comprehension of the effect must have been come from someone travelling on the Grand Tour. In turn, the business travellers and local weavers who sold cloth in the hall each Saturday must have been given a clear message that here was a well-informed and cultured community.

While health was the prominent reason for visits to spas and resorts, they were made most popular for their socialising and entertainment. The encounters with people and places also fed new experiences into individual and the collective memories, vicarious education of many forms. The social histories (Walton, 1983; Parry, 1983; Stafford and Yates, 1985: Blume, 1992) amongst many others have born witness.

Too little coverage has been given to tourism based on formal education, yet the market is large, if so far poorly researched (Smith and Jenner, 1997; Cooper, 1999). Kalinowski and Weiler (1992) make reference to the Grand Tour and one or two historically interesting examples, but without any attempt at a full survey. Such a study remains to be done, but the present writer has covered some of the ground (Machin, 1997).

There have been a number of strands of development. Field teaching in botany, geology and geography can be traced back a century or two: in fact applied botanical instruction started in the seventeenth century. It was the nineteenth century which, in Europe and the United States at least, saw the growth of earth sciences fieldwork, and also the use of the countryside for teaching personal skills (Machin, 1997). This was almost institutionalised in the twentieth in the curricula of pioneering schools like Gordonstoun, of movements like Outward Bound (James, 1997) and field and adventure centres (Parker and Meldrum, 1973).

Alongside these ran 'non-tourist' movements such as the Scouts and Guides, stemming from the same motivation of improving perceived weaknesses in knowledge, skills and attitudes by using the challenges offered by the environment (Rosenthal, 1986). Young peoples' activities like these built up forms of specialised tourism. Adventuring in the open air was encouraged as well by popular fiction by writers like Arthur Ransome in the *Swallows and Amazons* books (Townsend, 1983) and Garry Hogg (for example, *Explorers Awheel,* Hogg 1938), whose stories set out accessible role models and locations for the increasingly mobile and affluent young. Ransome's stories bridged the gap between fantasies of exploration and the realities of holidays, virtually creating the concept of family adventure tourism.

The outdoor interests of society in the eighteenth and nineteenth centuries became the special-interest tourism of the 1970s onwards. Painting, photography, botany, local history and topography were subjects for weekend breaks and longer in programmes like *Leisure Learning,* introduced in 1975 by Ind Coope Hotels and successful for twenty five years. Many other single-centre or multi-centre programmes have been put on the market. In many ways the efforts of the Victorian self-improvement societies, translated into the adult education movement (Kelly, 1970) and the Workers' Educational Association (Stocks, 1953) has reached a new leisure market where three-star food and accommodation and good quality, entertaining education go together as it did for the Grand Tourists.

Didacticism and heuristicism

The two modes of educational communication referred to above, didactic and heuristic, have played historic parts in varying ratios ever since people have travelled the world. The existence and distribution of forms of communication media have partly been responsible, as has the organisational form of the journeying undertaken.

Those on pilgrimage or the Grand Tour made many of their advances in knowledge thanks to their individual encounters with other people and places. A religious leader might have addressed the pilgrims at stages on the route, but most of their discoveries came from scenes and events. The main communication *en masse* would have been through the language of architecture: the monuments, temples, basilica and churches such as Stonehenge in England, St Peters in Rome, Borobodur in Java and the Medicine Wheel near Calgary in Canada. The iconography of such places has been well described (see Anderson 1971, Lavin 1990, Josephy 1995, Grabsky 1999). The associated site rituals added to the rehearsals of belief that they were created for. Often, the surrounding landscape, as times strange, wonderful and impressive in its unfamiliarity, continued and reinforced the experiences. Recent work has drawn together many ideas about landscape narratives (Potteiger and Purinton, 1998).

The Grand Tour started with clear educational objectives. After courtiers like Ffynes Morrison and Sir Philip Sydney pioneered the practice, it became common for wealthy fathers to send their sons off to Europe to learn about culture, society and politics (Hibbert, 1969). A tutor would usually be sent with them. As time went on the socialising and entertainment element began to dominate the itineraries (Towner, 1981). Dutiful sons might make their obligatory tour of Roman architecture from a carriage within a few hours (Hibbert, 1969). The fashion for European touring came to a temporary end with the French Revolution and Napoleonic wars, but the principle of genteel exploration was transferred to parts of Britain formerly ignored - Wales, the north of England, the Lake District and Scotland (Trench, 1990). It added to the fashion which had already begun of visiting country houses: within the ruling class something akin to visiting friends and relatives.

A butler in a great house might show the visitor around (Tinniswood, 1989). In the British Museum during the eighteenth century a uniformed doorkeeper (often apparently rather condescending) could be booked to do a similar service (Hudson, 1987). Guidebooks to houses came towards the end of the nineteenth century, the pioneering work being that of town or route guides (Vaughan, 1974) often sold in the new railway station kiosks to those enduring long journeys.

It was revolutionary France which took a new view of museum communication by labelling pictures in the Louvre for the benefit of all citizens (Hudson, 1987). Museums and art galleries slowly improved their labels, but labels they would stay until more modern times brought ideas of attractive interpretive panels explaining wider significances. Yet while these are fairly modern, the principle of special shows and displays to interpret great events and places is quite old. Drawing on ideas from the theatre and (most likely) church painting, there were successful attempts from the 1780s onwards to operate permanent showplaces open to fee-paying visitors. These included the audio-visual theatre of the *Eidophusikon* by de Loutherbourg (Klingender, 1947), the many panoramas and dioramas opened from the nineteenth century onwards (Cook 1963, Comment 1999), some of which are still in use. One show placed its audience in a ship-like structure. Slowly-unwinding canvases moved past them to left and right, painted to represent the scenes encountered in a journey down the Rhine (Hyde, 1988). Another, just prior to the First World War, used a railway carriage: back-projected films just behind the windows showed a railway journey (Coe, 1981). Fixed cinema shows and travelling panorama shows were common in fairs and exhibitions early in the last century. In London over the centuries all kinds of this type of attraction were to be found, variously educational or misleading in turn (Altick, 1978).

All of these facilities and experiences mixed the didactic and the heuristic in various ways. The level of educational impact depended on both variables in the equation - the host and guest, or in communications terms the transmitter and the receiver. As the range of attractions increased and more people gained access to them, what communication methods were employed were often broadened in order to deal with numbers and needs. Most of the changes came with the media boom of the late nineteenth century onwards, and especially the twentieth. The new media - sound recording, film, graphic booklets especially - were utilised in attractions almost as soon as they were introduced. Graphic display techniques were largely confined to trade shows and international expositions until after World War II, the art-conscious 1960s having a major influence. By the end of the twentieth century commercialism, the popularity of visiting, and the availability of so many media techniques, has often made the visitor experience one of communication rather than ambience.

It also appears to have moved the much of the initiative from the communicator to the audience. The control of the messages supplied is still in the hands of the interpreters, but they operate under the influence of values which are often imposed externally (Machin, 2000). The visitor does not arrive as a "blank sheet of paper" on which the interpreter can write anything, but as the holder of a set of experiences, knowledge and opinions derived over many years.

Visitors are receipt of four primary groupings or channels of information: person-to-person and person-to-environment contacts; the extension of these through travel and tourism; the mass media and finally formal education (see an earlier expression of this idea in Machin, 1989). They are not mutually exclusive but build up, each on the one before, the stated order being that in which they are encountered from birth onwards. In tourism, these channels allow the visitor to exert more of his or her own choice in the messages received from attractions. This gives their own experience at the attraction a stronger heuristic ("discovery") element than the more didactic ("instructed") mode.

Interpretation of environments

Walmsley and Lewis (1993), Golledge and Stimson (1997) and Holt-Jensen (1999) have reviewed the extensive literature underlying ideas in behavioural geography. It is worthwhile drawing out here some of the main strands of thought in order to come to a consideration of new ideas.

Everyone who travelled interpreted the environment in the sense of trying to understand it. Early thinkers tended to 'explain' it according to their own philosophical views -religious or secular. Some, like Bacon drew lessons about scientific observation. Rousseau thought of it as an ideal place to educate children (Pollard, 1956), Wordsworth perceived a setting full of lessons about man's place in nature. Thoreau also believed it could teach through its potential for contemplation and introspection (Pepper, 1996). Political writers observed the coming of the industrial world and founded dozens of social movements on its revelations.

Mid-twentieth century studies took rather more analytical views. The art critic Panofsky (1939) described the iconography of painting as the symbolic communication of ideas, helping to pave the way for a number of authors developing communication theories. Gerbner (1956) introduced a key concept. This was the idea that when one person communicates information about an event or object to another, the recipient can only construct an approximating idea of what it is from that information, with three factors controlling the variability of the received message. These are the *creative* nature of the communication process; the *context* in which the communication takes place, and the *open* nature of human communication. The distinction between reality and communicated image is a fundamental one in media studies, education and tourism.

The relationship between human beings and perceptions of their environments was investigated by anthropologists including Tuan (1977) and Walter (1988) and urban researchers such as Lynch (1960) and Cullen (1961). Tuan traced the significance of environmental feature and concepts for pre-industrial communities, Walter for urban ones. Early societies needed to be sophisticated in reading landscapes (and seascapes for fishing and navigation). Theirs was a practical, often subsistence need, and often a religious one too, rather than a concern for the design of living spaces.

Lynch's book *The Image of the City* has been continuously in print for forty years and examines the ways in which twentieth century people make sense of townscapes by reference to a range of features. Lynch also saw the urban fabric as a storehouse of community knowledge. His work was pioneering in the way it identified a typology of significant elements in the townscape. Lynch divided it into points, nodes, paths, districts and landmarks. These were 'learnt' and recognised by the inhabitants in order to find their way around and to relate to the urban functions.

Cullen was interested in urban design and his work was full of analysis of form. His most influential work (Cullen, 1961) contained proposals for improving the South Bank of the Thames. The most notable concept in his work was that of "serial vision". A visitor moving through a town reads a succession of scenes as if they were a narrative. Good town planning, argued Cullen, depended on understanding and working to this idea in order to supply a rewarding experience. Implied in the development of Cullen's idea are many others useful to the study of tourists and their destinations. Chief among them is the notion that environments communicate messages to be read like a book or newspaper. Writing in the early sixties, Cullen's preoccupation was with the aesthetics of urban space and form, in which by clearing, rebuilding or adding new the planner could produce a better living space. Like most ideas in the modernist school, this kind of functionality could sweep away the senses of time, place and character that a landscape grown by accretion would have acquired. Globalised styles could destroy meaningful ambiences.

During those same years concerns for the countryside were bringing forward new approaches which in the 1970s would begin to rescue town identities. The first concerns were for environmental interpretation as a tool for visitor management and education about the outdoors. In the USA, Tilden's *Interpreting Our Heritage* (1957) laid the foundations by turning into a strategic approach techniques which had been developed separately over many years. The ideas spread with varying speed, in Britain coming to prominence in the 1970s with the parallel growth of heritage centres and much improved museum and gallery interpretive planning. Some tourism text books now incorporate the subject (Holloway 1998), and yet it is missing from most, with the exception of a number of works on tourism and the environment and some on tourism and culture. One example of omission: the useful papers on the future of tourism (Theobald, 1998) omit it, even in the chapter dealing with socio-cultural contacts (Swinglehurst, 1998).

Soon after Tilden's work appeared, Holton considered the ways in which students experience environmental reality (Holton, 1965). Holton's interest was in the teaching of science in the classroom, but as Ittelson et al (1974) discussed his seven modes apply very well to knowledge of places. He listed seven modes:

1. Experiential, directly and in full contact

2. Didactic, as in a lecture room

3. Depicted, as through pictures, films etc

4. Analogous, through models or animations

5. Condensed coded, through speech, writing etc

6. Metasymbolic, in the language of direct abstraction in physics, maths, etc

7. Intuitive, direct apperception of complex realities in their entirety

Those working in the field of environmental interpretation might suggest that mode seven, 'intuitive', is less to do with communication and more with the human mind interpreting the information it has received by other means.

Holton's approach raises an important principle. The normal view of communication processes is to consider them via their individual media - film, TV, books, theatre and so on. The tendency is to concentrate on the producers of messages - film directors, TV producers, book authors and theatre writers and directors. This diverts attention from the crucial fact that the audiences for these media are not exclusively influenced by just one, but by a very wide spectrum of other media, and indeed, by people encountered on a one-to-one basis, and by formal education.

The tourist is an "audience", recipient to 'messages' decoded from environments of natural and man-made landscapes. Some of these perceived messages read only what the visitor makes of them. English hedgerows were planted as practical arrangements in farming, and not as statements for visitors. Yet their field patterns are read as identity statements: they remind the visitor that they are in rural England, a place with a history and a changing present situation. Knowledgeable people can also read in the botanical assemblies of the hedgerows information about how old they are, and in their sinuous curves perhaps their origins in the ox-ploughed fields of the Middle Ages. Architectural language is often more explicit. A medieval cathedral is likely to share with a nineteenth-century town hall a whole set of statements about power and values within its style and decoration. Decoding these statements has to be done using the cultural keys which are accumulated through person-to-person contact, the media and education.

Holton's approach was student-centred. Understanding tourism in terms of cultural outcomes requires a similar orientation to his in which the tourist is seen at the receiving end of a series of primary channels of discovery: one-to-one contact, the extension of that which is travel and tourism; the indirect contacts of the mass media, and finally formal education. This order is the order in which they are encountered from babyhood. Formal education is, in life terms, usually the most transient, even though it is the most intensive. The channels are not exclusive, but work in combinations. The travel and tourism channel adds to the one-to-one contact channel as an extension of that channel's activity. The mass media channel also adds to the one-to-one channel and extends it. The travel and tourism channel sometimes combines with the mass media channel, as when, for example, an individual travels to a cinema. The educational channel uses all of the others at different times.

New theory

The tourist experience can be examined in terms of the information that environments contain. Tourists enter indoor and outdoor information domains as they travel. The data to which they are exposed is both that which was created deliberately by senders or transmitters (writers, designers, speakers etc) and the wider range which can be interpreted, but was not created as 'language' – a field of flowers, a scattering of rubbish or the sight of a storm at sea. Of course even these can be considered symbolic creations by man or supernatural power. Throwing litter might be a symbolic gesture against society, but as a statement it would not fit many definitions of language (Sapir 1921, Chomsky 1957) but would fit others (Webster 1961) and would certainly fit definitions of communication (Hockett, 1960) and semiotics (see Crystal, 1987, pp399-403). And it would be ascribed a meaning by an observer.

Environments are not only made up of primary data, however. They also contain devices which store data and which must be opened first - for example, books, CD-Roms and videos, as well as the bookcases, filing cabinets and electronic equipment which house them. These can all be considered as *datastores*.

The environments also contain devices and means to access information held elsewhere, such as telephones, web terminals, radios and television sets. These can be considered to be *access points*.

People also encounter other people within environments. One-to-one meetings, casual or arranged, might happen anywhere. There are places which are designed to encourage encounters, however, such as town squares, coffee houses, legislatures, religious buildings and cybercafes. These might be termed *venues*. There are also *showcases*, constructions or assemblages intended to communicate ideas, information, values and opinions directly to observers and visitors. Examples include monuments, temples, display gardens, museums, zoological collections, theatres and exhibition halls.

Many datascape units fulfil multiple functions: a cathedral is itself a statement, it stores other forms of data within it, and it is a venue for people to share ideas. Other units (*disseminators*) can perform all of those functions and also have an additional primary function, namely to actively disseminate data. Examples are radio and TV stations, and printing works and publishers.

Environments can be analysed in terms of these attributes, and such can be termed *datascapes*. The terms *data rich* and *data poor* are used to describe environments according to the amount of symbolic data they contain. Table 1 shows a classification of six levels of data environment with description and examples. Increasing numbers of information components like access points, datastores, showcases and disseminators are found at higher levels.

Table 1   Data levels

Data Level	Description	Examples	Plus Level	Temporary additions
1	Seascape, sandy desert, empty sky	Open ocean Empty desert quarter	1+	and/or vehicle, some wildlife and/or people, ales
2	Landscape without man-made features but with clear variation in natural features	Mountain range Grassland	2+	With much wildlife and/or human activity including vehicles
3	Largely rural landscape as (2) but with some man-made features: buildings or other items	Open country Farmland	3+	With wildlife, farm animals, humans, active vehicles
4	Largely man-made landscape ('townscape') with distinctive areas of open space with grass, trees, water	Townscape: e.g. Canberra, Australia	4+	With wildlife, human activity, active vehicles
5	Almost entirely man-made landscape, heavily built up, few or no organic features	Cityscape: e.g. area of Arc de Triomphe, Paris	5+	Busy with people, traffic, events
6	Heavily built-up landscape with many language features: billboards, advertising signs, lights	City centre: e.g. Times Square, Manhattan;	6+	Very heavy human and vehicle activity, events

The most important information in the environment might be the "navigation" data. Lynch (1960) included landmarks as one of his list of distinguishing features in cities. Other writers have developed concepts based on mental maps (Moore and Golledge 1976, Gibson 1979) for navigating and interpreting environments.

This concept can be extended. There is a constant systematic relationship between people and places which goes further than *acting* - it sustains *being*. All living things are part of the ecological system within which they exist. Knowledge about that system is needed to enable them to function. The essential information is geographical, historical and managerial. Geography tells of resources and opportunities. History records experiences, which unlock the ability to use the resources and to predict the outcomes of actions. Management information drawn from experience stores knowledge on the procedures available and which are appropriate for situations as they arise. The information is partly in the central nervous system and partly distributed around in the environment. This is the *datascape*.

Every landscape feature presents data which observers decode to enable them to fix themselves in time, place and cultures. The observer (not only in a visual sense but in all senses) locates himself/herself geographically like any navigator. He/she also fixes his/herself historically with features being recognised (crudely or sophisticatedly according to knowledge) as belonging to particular ages or times, giving a measure of how long has elapsed since then, and therefore indicating how things might have changed.

Highly variable levels of knowledge about geography and history mean that some observers see features with detailed recognition of time's passage, others virtually none. Some see only distinctions of old/new for history, near/far for geography. Nevertheless the varying levels of information constantly, and perhaps unconsciously, remind the individual who they are, where they are and when they are. The act of perception and interpretation of a feature gives a measurement of its geographical position relative to the observer. It also gives a historical position, being both of the same time as the observer, but also of its own time. The time gap is also measurable within the limits of the observer's knowledge. It helps to give a necessary historical sense, the sense of time which goes with sense of place. Similarly, there is a sense of character, of cultural identity, from the interpretation of the culture represented by the feature, and how different it might be from that of the observer.

An example might help to explain the point. A twenty-first century Japanese visitor stands looking at the Eiffel Tower. The evocation of place is powerfully French, indeed Parisian and 'not Japan'. There is clearly a difference in architecture and engineering which denotes first the nineteenth century origins of the tower and second of the modern age in which such towers would be space-age needles of steel. The Tower is 'not of today'. Recognising the industrial nature of 'France then' is a reminder to our knowledgeable observer of 'Japan then' and the difference. It is also a reminder of the comparative nature of 'France now' and 'Japan now'.

Perceptions of the environment like these can be visual, auditory, tactile, olfactory and occasionally gustatory (such as the taste of salt on the lips near the sea). They allow measurements of distance and direction in a number of senses. Using a term borrowed from mathematics, they might be called *vectors*, having measurable direction and dimension. Environments contain virtually infinite data - or vectors - which an observer will either ignore or absorb, and if absorbed will then interpret in their own way.

This is to see landscapes in terms of data, and people within it must represent "data" themselves by their appearance, body language, clothing, actions and language. Animals present further data for other creatures to interpret and interrelate. Human beings move around the landscape. They encounter other people, other places, and also sources of more data stored in specialised forms. The destinations that attract visitors do so for their inherent qualities which have to be perceived and interpreted before they can be used. The management of these qualities, the supplementing of them with further information, and the management of their inter-relationships, is essential for quality, meaningful tourism.

Conclusion

The approach of behavioural geography, linked with that of general communication theory, can offer new insights into the significance of tourism and its management. The proposals above suggest a new theoretical framework for tourism research.

References

Altick, R. D. (1978), *Shows Of London, The*, Boston, Ma, Harvard University Press.

Anderson, M. D. (1971), *History And Imagery In British Churches*, London, John Murray.

Bates, E. S. (1911), *Touring In 1600: A Study In The Development Of Travel As A Means Of Education*, Boston, Houghton-Mifflin.

Beeho, A. and Prentice, R. (1997), *Conceptualising The Experiences of Heritage Tourists*, Journal of Tourism Management 18: 2 75-87.

Berlyne, D. E. (1968), *New Directions In Motivation Theory*, Anthropology and Human Behaviour, Washington DC, Anthropological Society of Washington.

Blume, M. (1992), *Cote D'Azur: Inventing The French Riviera*, London, Thames and Hudson.

Boulding, K. (1956), *Image, The: Knowledge In Life And Society*, Ann Arbor, University of Michigan Press.

Buzard, J. (1993), *Beaten Track, The: European Tourism, Literature & the Ways to Culture*, Oxford, Clarendon Press.

Chomsky, A. N. (1957), *Synactic Structures*, The Hague, Mouton.

Coe, B. (1981), *History Of Movie Photography, The*, London, Ash and Grant.

Coleman, S. and Elsner, J. (1995), *Pilgrimage: Past And Present In World Religions*, London, British Museum Press.

Comment, B. (1999), *Panorama, The*, London, Reaktion.

Cook, O. (1963), *Movement In Two Directions*, London, Hutchinson.

Cooper, C. (1999) *European School Travel Market, The*, Travel and Tourism Analyst 5: 89-105.

Crouch, D (ed) (1999) *Leisure/Tourism Geographies*, London, Routledge.

Crystal, D (1987) *Cambridge Encyclopedia of Language*, Cambridge, Cambridge University Press.

Cullen, G. (1961), *Townscape*, London, Architectural Press.

Dann, G. M. S. (1996), *Language of Tourism, The*, Wallingford, CAB International.

Dann, G. M. S. (1997), *The Green Green Grass Of Home: Nature And Nurture In Rural England*, Tourism Development and Growth: The Challenge of Sustainability, London, Routledge.

Dilke, M. (1965), *Field Studies For Schools*, London, Rivingtons.

Fairgrieve, J. (1926), *Geography In School*, London, University of London Press.

Feifer, M. (1985), *Going Places*, London, Macmillan.

Fennell, D. A. (1999), *Ecotourism: An Introduction*, London, Routledge.

Gartner, W. C. (1993), Image Formation Process, *Journal of Tourism Marketing* 3 (2/3): 191-215.

Gartner, W. (1997), *Image and Sustainable Tourism Systems*, Tourism, Development and Growth, London, Routledge.

Gerbner, G. (1956), *Towards A General Model Of Communication*, Audio Visual Communication Review 4.

Gibson, J. J. (1979), *Ecological Approach To Visual Perception, The*, Boston, Houghton Mifflin.

Golledge, R. G. and Stimson, R. J. (1997), *Spatial Behaviour: A Geographic Perspective*, Guilford Press, New York.

Grabsky, P. (1999), *Lost Temple Of Java, The*, London, Orion.

Graburn, N. (1989), *Tourism: The Sacred Journey*, Hosts and Guests: The Anthropology of Tourism, Philadephia, University of Pennsylvania Press.

Hibbert, C. (1969), *Grand Tour, The*, London, Weidenfeld and Nicholson.

Hockett, C. F. (1960), *The Origin Of Speech*, Scientific American 203 Sept.

Hogg, G. (1938), *Explorers Awheel*, London, Thomas Nelson.

Holloway, J. C. (1998), *Business of Tourism, The*, London, Pitman.

Holt-Jensen, A. (1999), *Geography: History And Concepts - A Students' Guide*, London, Sage.

Hudson, K. (1987), *Museums of Influence*, Cambridge, Cambridge.

Hyde, R. (1988), *Panoramania!*, London, Trefoil.

Ittelson, W. H. et al (1974), *Introduction To Environmental Psychology, An*, New York, Holt, Rinehart and Winston.

James, D. (ed) (1957), *Outward Bound*, London, Routledge and Kegan Paul.

Josephy, A. M. (1995), *500 Nations*, London, Hutchinson.

Kalinowski, K. M. and Weiler, B.(1992), *Educational Travel*, Special Interest Tourism, New York, Wiley.

Kelly, T. (1970), *History Of Adult Education In Great Britain, A: From The Middle Ages To The Twentieth Century*, Liverpool, Liverpool University Press.

Klingender, F. (1947), *Art And The Industrial Revolution*, [revised edition], St Albans, Paladin.

Krippendorf, J. (1987), *Holiday Makers, The*, London, Heinemann.

Laarman, J. G. and Durst, P. B. (1987), *Nature Travel And Tropical Forests*, quoted in Ecotourism: An Introduction, London, Routledge.

Lavin, M. A. (1990), *Place Of Narrative, The: Mural Decoration In Italian Churches*, , Chicago, University Of Chicago Press.

Leed, E. J. (1991), *Mind Of The Traveller, The: From Gilgamesh To Global Tourism*, New York.

Lynch, K. (1960), *Image Of The City, The*, An Introduction To Environmental Psychology p15, New York, Holt, Rinehart and Winston.

MacCannell, D. (1976), Tourist, The: A New Theory of the Leisure Class, London, Macmillan.

Machin, A. (1989), Social Helix, The: Visitor Interpretation As A Tool For Social Development, Heritage Interpretation Vol2, London, Belhaven.

Machin, A. (1997), Tourism And The Information Society, Leeds, LMU/School of Hospitality & Tourism.

Machin, A. (2000), Tourism As Education: Components For A Management System, , CHME Research Conference, Work in Progress Paper.

Mathieson, A. and Wall, G. (1982) *Tourism: Economic, Physical and Social Impacts*, Harlow, Longman.

Moore, G. T. and Golledge R. G. (1976), *Environmental Knowing*, Stroudsberg, Dowden, Hutchinson and Ross.

Mowforth, M. and Munt, I. (1998), *Tourism And Sustainability: New Tourism In The Third World*, London, Routledge.

Panofsky, E. (1939), *Studies In Iconology: Humanistic Themes In The Art Of The Renaissance*, Oxford, Oxford University Press.

Parker, T. and Meldrum, K. (1973), *Outdoor Education*, London, J. M. Dent.

Parks, G. B. (1951), *Travel As Education*, The Seventeenth Century: Studies In The History of English Thought and Literature From Bacon To Pope, London, Oxford University Press.

Parry, K. (1983), *Resorts of the Lancashire Coast, The*, Newton Abbott, David and Charles.

Pepper, D. (1996), *Modern Environmentalism: An Introduction*, London, Routledge.

Pimlott, J. A. R. (1947), *Englishman's Holiday, The*, Hassocks, Harvester.

Pollard, H. M. (1956), *Pioneers Of Popular Education*, London, John Murray.

Potteiger, M. and Purinton, J. (1998), *Landscape Narratives: Design Practices For Telling Stories*, New York, John Wiley & Sons.

Prentice, R. (1996), *Tourism As Experience: Tourists As Consumers. Insight And Enlightenment*, Inaugural Lecture, Edinburgh, Queen Margaret's College.

Prentice, R. (1997), *Culture And Landscape Tourism: Facilitating Meaning*, Tourism, Development and Growth: The Challenge of Sustainability, London, Routledge.

Read, S. E. (1980), *A Prime Force In The Expansion Of Tourism In The Next Decade: Special Interest Travel,* Special Interest Tourism, London, Belhaven.

Reynolds, J. B. (1901), *Class Excursions In England And Wales*, Geography (Oct).

Rosenthal, M. (1986), *Character Factory, The*, London, Collins.

Ryan, C. (1997), *Tourist Experience, The*, London, Cassell.

Sapir, E. (1921), *Language*, New York, Harcourt, Brace.

Smith, C. and Jenner, P. (1997), *Educational Tourism*, Travel and Tourism Intelligence 97:3 60-75.

Stafford, F. and Yates, N. (1985), *Later Kentish Seaside, The*, Gloucester, Alan Sutton/Kent Archives Office.

Stocks, M. (1953). *Workers' Educational Association, The: The First Fifty Years*, London, George Allen and Unwin.

Swinglehurst, E. (1998), *Face To Face: The Socio-Cultural Impacts Of Tourism*, Global Tourism: The Next Decade, Oxford, Butterworth Heinemann.

Theobald, W. F. (ed) (1998), *Global Tourism: The Next Decade*, Oxford, Butterworth Heinemann.

Tilden, F. (1957), *Interpreting Our Heritage*, Chapel Hill, University of North Carolina.

Tinniswood, A. (1989), *History of Country House Visiting, A: Five Centuries of Tourism Taste*, Oxford, Basil Blackwell.

Towner, J. (1981), *Grand Tour, The: A Key Phase In The History Of Tourism*, Annals of Tourism Research 12 (3): 297-333

Towner, J. (1994), *Historical Geography Of Recreation And Tourism, An*, London, Belhaven.

Townsend, J. R. (1983), *Written for Children*, Harmondsworth, Kestrel.

Trench, R. (1990), *Travellers in Britain*, London, Aurum.

Tuan, Y. F. (1977), *Space And Place: The Perspective Of Experience*, Minneapolis, University of Minneapolis.

Turner, L. and Ash, J. (1976), *Golden Hordes, The: International Tourism And The Pleasure Periphery*, London, Constable.

Urry, J. (1990), *Tourist Gaze, The*, London, Sage.

Vaughan, J. (1974), *The English Guide Book, c1780 - 1870: An Illustrated History*, Newton Abbot, David and Charles.

Walmsley, D. D. and Lewis, G. J. (1993*), People And Environment: Behavioural Approaches In Human Geography*, Harlow, Longman Scientific.

Walter, E. V. (1988), Placeways: A Theory Of The Human Environment, Chapel Hill, Ca, University of North Carolina.

Walton, J. (1983), *English Seaside Resort, The: A Social History 1750-1914*, Leicester University Press, Leicester.

Webster, (1961), *Webster's Third New International Dictionary*, New York, Merriam-Webster.

Weiler, Betty, and Hall, C. M. (1992), *Special Interest Tourism*, Chichester, Belhaven/John Wiley.

Walkway users, activity patterns, issues of conflict and management dimensions: An urban based case study from New Zealand

Peter Mason

University of Luton, UK

Sarah Leberman and Shirley Barnett

Massey University, New Zealand

Abstract

This paper presents findings from field research conducted during 1999 concerned with the recreational and tourist use of the Manawatu Riverside Walkway and Bridle Track (MRWBT), Palmerston North, New Zealand. The aims of the research were to investigate the type of activities engaged in on the MRWBT and to identify any user issues. The main research instrument was a questionnaire survey and 683 completed questionnaires were received, providing a response rate of 68.3%.

One of the key findings of the field research was that whilst both men and women used the MRWTB, women users were more common. In terms of the demographic characteristics, both younger and older groups used the walkway. A high proportion of students used the walkway, and also those in professional occupations. The predominant activity taking place on the MRWBT was walking, followed by biking and running. Exercise, fitness and health was the primary reason for participating in all three activities, followed by leisure and pleasure. Dog-walking and the natural environment were also seen as important reasons for walkers, whereas a means of access was a prime reason for bikers. Most of the walkway users lived within three kilometres of the MRWBT, suggesting that the resource is linked to the local neighbourhood and has more of a local recreation use rather than a significant tourist use. A number of issues of conflict between user groups were identified and these are discussed. Management implications of the field research findings are also presented and the paper sets the MRWTB findings within the context of other research on trails, greenways and walkways conducted in the United States of America, United Kingdom and New Zealand.

Introduction

This paper discusses findings of research conducted in 1999 concerned with users of the Manawatu Riverside Walkway and Bridle Track (MRWBT) located in Palmerston North, New Zealand (see Figure 1). The main aims of the research were to investigate the demographics of walkway users, their locational characteristics and the activity patterns of these users.

Figure 1   Map of New Zealand

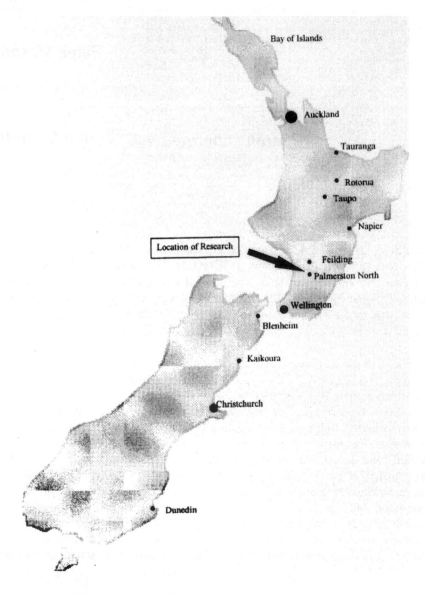

The impetus for this research came from the Palmerston North City Council (PNCC). In addition to the aims stated above, PNCC were interested in identifying any issues that users associated with the MRWBT. The Council provided support in the form of staff time, equipment and resources for the printing, distribution, collection and processing of the questionnaires, as well as the provision of a room and facilities for the focus groups, which followed on from the questionnaire survey. They also offered to fund the publication of the research findings in the form of a report.

Walkway research

This section of the paper discusses two main areas of research literature on walkways. First, walkways, trails, recreational greenways, tracks or routes are discussed in terms of demographics, locational characteristics and activity patterns. Second, research relating to user conflict on trails is presented.

The importance of urban and semi-urban outdoor recreation opportunities was identified as early as the 1960s in the United States in the Outdoor Recreation Resources Review Commission's report (Moore and Ross, 1998). The 1991 'Trails for All Americans' report more specifically included the "vision that there should be a trail within 15 minutes of every American" (cited in Moore and Ross, 1998, p.76).

Moore and Ross (1998) provided definitions for different trail types and recreational greenways. The North American term which best describes the MRWBT, is a "recreational greenway", in that it "is a linear open space that contains a trail" following along a natural corridor (Moore and Ross, p.70). Research by Furuseth and Altman (1991) considered the socio-economic, demographic and locational characteristics of greenway users on the Capital Area Greenway System in Raleigh, North Carolina. The primary aim of their research was to gain an understanding of who the greenway users were, as well as to consider the distance people travelled to use the greenway. They argued that it is important for managers to understand the characteristics and attitudes of users in order to make appropriate decisions with respect to maintaining and developing greenways. The findings suggested that more women than men used the greenway and that the predominant user age group was between 25-44 years. They also indicated that greenway users are generally employed, well-educated, and have above average income.. There also appeared to be "distance decay" (Furuseth and Altman, 1991, p.330) amongst the users of the greenway – few of the users of a greenway travel a great distance to use it. This suggested that greenways serve more localised neighbourhoods rather than whole communities.

Research was conducted in the Mount Rogers National Recreation Area in Virginia by Mowen, Graefe and Williams (1998), to ascertain the determinants for trail user diversity. Mowen et al's (1998) research was based on work, which suggested that there was more diversity than homogeneity in user characteristics across trails, and in particular rail trails. They focused on activity type and trail type, in an attempt to assist managers in marketing their recreation resources. Their findings suggested that the type of activity engaged in best-determined socio-demographic characteristics, visit patterns and visitor attitudes.

The benefits of trails to users and the wider community are highlighted by Moore and Ross (1998). They emphasised five main benefits including outdoor recreation, alternative transportation, economic benefits, open space protection and sense of place. Outdoor recreation, and in particular, activities such as walking and biking are seen as important in fostering a healthy lifestyle. As in the United States of America (Moore and Ross, 1998), walking for pleasure was rated the most popular physical activity by New Zealanders in 1998 (Hillary Commission, 1998). Short walks were more popular than long walks (over 30 minutes), with biking ranked sixth out of the top ten physical activities (Hillary Commission, 1998). In many developed countries, alternative forms of transport are encouraged by local government, a move associated with the increasing levels of traffic congestion and pollution. Trails if well managed can provide these access routes, as well as opportunities for protecting natural spaces. Where trails and walkways provide for opportunities to interact with other people and are regarded as an important part of a town's or region's make-up, a strong sense of place may be associated with them. Some trails may also contribute to the economic development of an area if they attract extra visitors to the area.

In the New Zealand context the terms "recreational greenway" or "trail" are not commonly used. Instead, walkways are classified either as, walks, tracks or routes. Walks are generally well developed and suitable for families. Tracks are well-defined walking tracks suitable for people of good average physical fitness. Routes are lightly marked routes for use only be well equipped and experienced backpackers (New Zealand Walkway Commission, 1984). The Walkways Act was introduced in 1975, which had as its main objective to provide:

> *"walking tracks over public and private land so that the people of New Zealand shall have safe, unimpeded foot access to the countryside for the benefit of physical recreation as well as for the enjoyment of the outdoor environment and the natural and pastoral beauty and historical and cultural qualities of the area they pass through"* (cited in the New Zealand Walkway Commission, 1984, p.4).

The initial focus of the Walkways Act 1975, which was managed by the New Zealand Walkway Commission, was to establish long distance walking tracks similar to those found in the United States of America (e.g. the Appalachian Trail) or in the United Kingdom (e.g. the Pennine Way). However, fifteen years after its inception the New Zealand Walkways Commission was disbanded and with this went its responsibility for the nation wide administration of the walkway system (Balfour, 1990). In addition, most of the walkways established by 1990 were close to urban centres, rather than the long-distance walkways that were originally envisaged (New Zealand Walkway Commission, 1984; Balfour, 1990).

Following the disbanding of the New Zealand Walkways Commission, the New Zealand Walkways Act 1975 was repealed and the New Zealand Walkways Act 1990 introduced. The management of current walkways and the development of new walkways was taken over by the Department of Conservation and the New Zealand Conservation Authority Walkways Committee. By the mid 1990's there were over 150 walkways spread throughout the country and these offer a variety of opportunities for outdoor recreation. Many of these walkways are close to urban centres and are popular for family outings (Department of Conservation, 1993).

The urban focus of walkways was further developed with the establishment of the KiwiWalks concept that was launched in December 1997 with the aim of combining fun and fitness. "The KiwiWalks brand is being given to free community walks of an hour or less, that are suitable for most ages and fitness levels, and reasonably accessible to people wearing leisure footwear" Hillary Commission, 1997, np). A further requirement of KiwiWalks is that they are maintained and information about them is provided. In general, this takes place via the regional sport trusts and local councils.

The following section discusses the issue of user conflict identified by research literature into walkways. Moore and Ross (1998) suggested that user conflict is a key issue in relation to greenways and trails which may be precipitated by crowding and poor track design. Research undertaken in the United Kingdom by Banister, Groome and Pawson (1992) sought to identify what use level of recreation resources might be acceptable, in order to address the issue of crowding. Their research was based on a canal towing path and considered the conflict between walkers, anglers and cyclists. The findings suggested that there was conflict between cyclists and other users, but also that there was a considerable amount of tolerance. Furthermore, there also appeared to be no clear relationship between user density and degree of conflict. In other words, an increase in the total volume of users did not necessarily lead to more conflict. The authors, therefore, concluded that it was possible to have multiple-use tracks depending on the physical characteristics of the track, as well as the range of activities undertaken and the actual level of use by different recreational users (Banister et al, 1992). However, they did note that "account would need to be taken of anglers who, often taking part in competitive sport, are particularly sensitive to increased levels of activity by both land- and water-based users" (Banister et al, 1992, p.158).

Moore, Scott and Graefe (1998) considered user conflict on a paved greenway trail in Cleveland Ohio. The focus of their research was on conflict between four different recreation groups, walkers, runners, bicyclists and in-line skaters. The methodology involved both on-site contact as well as a mail follow-up survey. The findings suggested that there was conflict between users, which in most cases was asymmetrical. This meant that cyclists were disliked more by walkers than vice versa. Most conflict was attributed to the speed of cyclists and in-line skaters, and their behaviour. Moore et al (1998) concluded that the management implications of their findings were in terms of the impacts of a given activity on other recreationalists and the impacts of other recreationalists on that given activity.

In his synthesis of a number of USA-based studies, Moore (1994) also noted the issue of conflict on multi-use tracks. Whilst the focus of his report was on conflict, he did suggest that further research was needed on the characteristics of trail users, their length of stay, activities, time of use and spatial distribution of use.

As with some of the research conducted in the United Kingdom and the United States of America, user conflict has been noted in several walkway studies undertaken in New Zealand. Horn (1994) in her Christchurch-based study focussing on mountain biking, indicated that conflict between different recreation user groups was perceived as real conflict for those involved. She found an asymmetrical relationship where bikers were disliked more by trampers (hikers) than vice versa. Horn suggested that one reason for conflict is that bikers are 'activity focused' (1994, p.137) while walkers are more likely to be 'location focused' (1994, p.138). Horn also claimed walkers felt less in control of their experience and hence felt threatened by bikers.

Coughlan (1996) also investigated the relationship between mountain bikers and trampers in the greater Dunedin region and reported similar findings to Horn (1994). Coughlan, however, reported that the perceived conflict between the different user groups was greater than the actual conflicts. He suggested that both mountain bikers and walkers/trampers appreciate the natural environment and wish to conserve it as much as possible. In his study walkers/trampers accepted that mountain bikers needed areas to recreate in and that sharing was an option. He pointed to increased understanding between user groups, information and education as tools for reducing conflict between the groups.

The study setting

The Manawatu region is characterised by its low, rolling plains and is bounded by the Ruahine and Tararua Ranges in the East and the Tasman Sea in the West. Palmerston North, with approximately 75,000 people is the major city of the region. It houses Massey University, the Universal College of Learning (previously Manawatu Polytechnic), the International Pacific College and a number of government research centres.

The Manawatu Riverside Walkway and Bridle Track (MRWBT) is located at the southern end of Palmerston North and runs for 9.6km along the Manawatu River (see Figure 2). It follows the edge of the stopbank (a raised bank to prevent flooding) for most of its length, passing through the riverside environment, parks and reserves and is adjacent to residential areas. People have walked beside the Manawatu River for many years, but it was not until 1962 that the Manawatu Pony Club cut a track through vegetation adjacent to the river for use by horse riders and walkers. In 1981 the Palmerston North City Council adopted a greater role in the development of the MRWBT developing a Draft Management Plan in 1983 (Palmerston North City Council, 1983). This plan was updated in 1988, to include a statement of goals and objectives (Palmerston North City Council, 1988).

The mission statement adopted for the MRWBT in 1988 was "to recognise the significance of the Manawatu River and its associated open space in providing recreational opportunities and to maintain a walkway and bridle track" (Palmerston North City Council, 1988, p.2). Five key management areas were identified in the 1988 plan – track development, landscape character, planting strategies, river system protection works, and the use and promotion of the walkway (Palmerston North City Council, 1988).

Figure 2　Manawatu River Walkway and Bridle Track

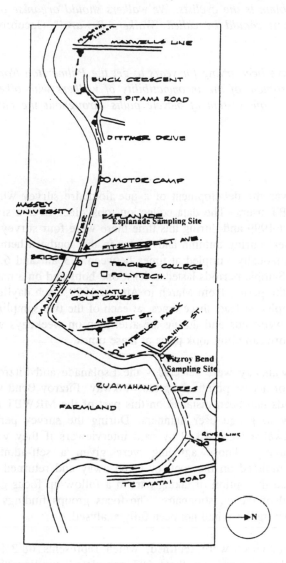

To gauge user numbers hidden pressure pads were installed at two sites along the MRWBT in 1996. The figures collected indicated a dramatic rise in user numbers at the Esplanade (see Figure 2) from 47,229 in 1996 to 161,278 in 1998 and from 3,591 in 1996 to 34,000 in 1998 at Buick Park (A. Middleton, personal communication, 13 November, 1998). These numbers, however, provided no indication of the demographics of the users, their locational characteristics or their activity patterns, so these areas became the focus for this research. During the research period there were letters in the local newspaper suggesting that conflict was a problem on the MRWBT. The following exerts highlight the points made:

"A recent letter . . . .stated that there is no problem with trailbikes on the walkway. I agree. The problem is the cyclists. We walkers should organise our own lobby group. Perhaps it should be called 'Walkers Beware'" (Jacobsen, 1999).

"Many in the community have been trying for years to get the Palmerston North City Council to take the problem of the incompatibility of walkers with bikers seriously, and to provide a safe system of bicycle paths throughout the city" (Morris, 1999).

Methods

The first stage of the research was the development of a questionnaire survey which was distributed to a sample of MRWBT users. The data collection took place over a six-month period between March and August 1999 and during this time there were four survey periods coinciding with the end of summer, during autumn and winter in the southern hemisphere. All days of the week were systematically sampled at times between 7.30am and 6.30pm – the hours of daylight in the area. Sample periods lasted at least one hour and on a number of occasions for two hours. During the period from March to August 1999, each daylight hour of every day of the week was sampled at least three times, at each of the two sampling sites. As anecdotal evidence suggested weekends and during the afternoon on weekdays were the busiest times on the walkways, more sampling took place at these times.

Two sampling points along the walkway were selected – the Esplanade and Fitzroy Bend (see Figure 2), as these were major access points along the walkway. Fitzroy Bend was also selected as no hidden pressure pads had been installed on this part of the MRWBT and this research provided an opportunity to gauge user numbers. During the survey periods all walkway users over the age of twelve were asked by paid interviewers if they would be willing to participate in the survey. Those agreeing were given a self-administered questionnaire, which could be completed on the spot, or taken away and returned using a pre-paid envelope. Participants had the option of taking part in a follow-up focus group by signalling their interest at the end of the questionnaire. The focus groups findings are not reported here, as at the time of writing these had not been fully analysed.

A total of 683 completed questionnaires were returned, which represents 68.3% of the questionnaires distributed to walkway users. Of these 683 completed questionnaires 415 came from the Esplanade and 268 from Fitzroy Bend.

Questionnaire results

Demographics

There were 683 respondents to the questionnaire, 341 males and 342 females. At the Esplanade 57% of the participants were male and 42% female. These figures were almost reversed for Fitzroy Bend, where 40% of the participants were male and 60% were female. Table 1 shows the age groups of the respondents.

Table 1   Age of Respondents

Age Class (years)	Percentage of Respondents Esplanade	Percentage of Respondents Fitzroy Bend
12-14	5%	2%
15-19	16%	3%
20-29	21%	23%
30-39	17%	18%
40-49	16%	22%
50-59	18%	17%
> 60	7%	14%

The occupational categories used in the questionnaire were based on the New Zealand census. The highest percentages were found for students and professionals. There was also a fairly high non-response rate to this question, with 12% at the Esplanade and 17% at Fitzroy Bend as can be seen in Table 2.

Table 2   Occupation of Respondents

Occupation Classes	Percentage of Respondents Esplanade	Percentage of Respondents Fitzroy Bend
Student	39%	14%
Professionals	21%	25%
No Response	12%	17%
Legislators, Administrators and Managers	6%	8%
Technicians and Associate Professionals	6%	3%
Retired	4%	10%
House Person	4%	6%
Service and Sales Workers	3%	6%
Clerks	2%	3%
Trade Workers	2%	6%
Elementary Occupations	1%	3%

Locational characteristics

90% of the respondents came from Palmerston North, with the majority living within 3 kilometres of the walkway, as is illustrated in Figure 3.

Figure 3   Residential Location of Respondents

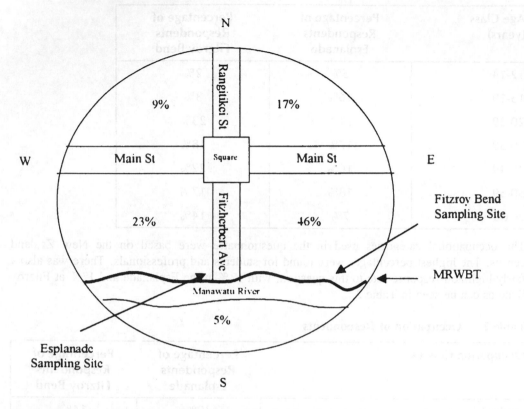

The walkway itself was used for most of its 9.6 km length. However, the segment up to Dittmer Drive at the MRWBT's western end was less frequented than other segments, this is illustrated in Figure 4.

Figure 4   Stylised MRWBT Map Indicating Use

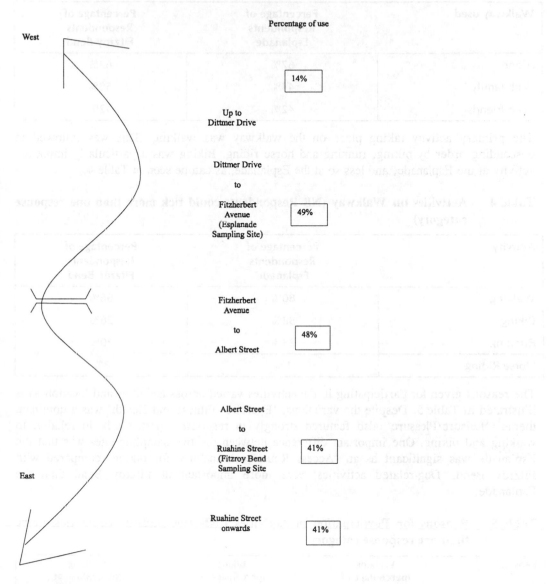

Percentage of use

West

14%

Up to
Dittmer Drive

Dittmer Drive

to

Fitzherbert
Avenue
(Esplanade
Sampling Site)   49%

Fitzherbert
Avenue

to   48%

Albert Street

Albert Street

to

Ruahine Street   41%
(Fitzroy Bend
Sampling Site

East

Ruahine Street
onwards   41%

Activity patterns

The predominant use of the walkway was by individuals who were alone. This was followed by usage with family and then with friends (see Table 3). Only a small proportion (4% at the Esplanade and 1% at Fitzroy Bend) used the walkway with clubs.

Table 3 Walkway use with (NB Respondents could tick more than one response category)

Walkway used	Percentage of Respondents Esplanade	Percentage of Respondents Fitzroy Bend
Alone	67%	63%
With family	44%	58%
With friends	42%	42%

The primary activity taking place on the walkway was walking. This was followed in descending order by biking, running and horse riding. Biking was a particularly important activity at the Esplanade, and less so at the Esplanade, as can be seen in Table 4.

Table 4   Activities on Walkway (NB Respondents could tick more than one response category)

Activity	Percentage of Respondents Esplanade	Percentage of Respondents Fitzroy Bend
Walking	80%	96%
Biking	58%	28%
Running	23%	20%
Horse Riding	1%	3%

The reasons given for participating in the activities varied across activities and location as is illustrated in Table 5. Despite the variations, 'Exercise, Fitness and Health' was a dominant theme. 'Leisure/Pleasure' also featured strongly in responses, particularly in relation to walking and biking. One important difference between the two sampling sites was that the Esplanade was significant as an 'Access Route', particularly for biking, compared with Fitzroy Bend. Dog-related activities were more important at Fitzroy Bend than the Esplanade.

Table 5   Reasons for Participation in Activities ((NB Respondents could tick more than one response category

Reasons	Walking (percentage of respondents) Esplanade (n=271)	Fitz Bend (n=259)	Biking (percentage of respondents) Esplanade (n=197)	Fitz Bend (n=76)	Running (percentage of respondents) Esplanade (n=77)	Fitz Bend (n=53)
Exercise Fitness and Health	44%	43%	32%	50%	81%	91%
Leisure Pleasure	43%	25%	23%	43%	6%	1%
Dog related activities	15%	43%	1%	18%		
Nature Environs	11%	15%				
Access Route	10%	1%	57%	8%		
Social	8%	5%	2%	8%		

Table 6 shows that the frequency patterns of the three main activities varied both between activities and locations. However, 'once a week' was high for all activities, as was 'once a month'. Significant differences between sites were found for biking, which took place twice a day at the Esplanade for 33% of the respondents and for only 1% at Fitzroy Bend. In contrast, biking at Fitzroy Bend occurred once a month for 45% of the participants and for 13% at the Esplanade.

Table 6   Frequency of Activity (NB Respondents could tick more than one response category)

Frequency	Walking (percentage of respondents)		Biking (percentage of respondents)		Running (percentage of respondents)	
	Esplanade	Fitz Bend	Esplanade	Fitz Bend	Esplanade	Fitz Bend
1/day	13%	23%	19%	3%	19%	13%
2/day	7%	7%	33%	1%	6%	0%
1/week	27%	17%	13%	22%	25%	26%
2/week	7%	14%	9%	11%	13%	15%
3/week	13%	15%	11%	7%	20%	15%
1/month	28%	18%	13%	45%	7%	21%

The majority of the participants indicated that they spent between either up to 30 minutes or between 30 minutes and one hour participating in their activity. The main differentiation was between locations, where participants at Fitzroy Bend spent between 30 minutes and an hour doing their chosen activity, whereas at the Esplanade up to 30 minutes was the preferred time frame.

The preferred time for participating in walking and biking was in the afternoon between two and five o'clock. Running tended to take place later between five and seven o'clock in the evening. There was little differentiation between the two locations as can be seen in Table 7.

Table 7   Preferred Time for Activity (NB Respondents could tick more than one response category)

Time	Walking (percentage of respondents)		Biking (percentage of respondents)		Running (percentage of respondents)	
	Esplanade	Fitz Bend	Esplanade	Fitz Bend	Esplanade	Fitz Bend
Before 8am	17%	13%	37%	8%	22%	28%
8-12pm	25%	34%	43%	17%	18%	34%
12-2pm	17%	17%	18%	13%	8%	11%
2-5pm	46%	48%	51%	43%	26%	19%
5-7pm	39%	35%	36%	34%	45%	32%
After 7pm	13%	8%	8%	4%	16%	8%

All three activities were undertaken predominantly during the weekend. However, running also took place on weekdays and biking was more frequent at the Esplanade on weekdays. Participant responses indicated that there was little seasonal variation in activity participation. However, the southern autumn (March through May) was a period when all recorded activities took place. The southern summer (December through February) was an important period for walking and the spring (September through November) for biking and running.

Respondents' awareness of information on the walkway was the same at both locations, but low at 34%. The awareness of other users on the walkway was high with 95% of the respondents indicating this at the Esplanade and 97% at Fitzroy Bend. Related to this awareness, is the issue of conflict between user groups, which was mentioned by a number of users. This was identified as existing between walkers and bikers, bikers and dog walkers as well as between walkers and dog walkers.

Other comments

A number of themes emerged from the 'any other comments' section at the end of the questionnaire. The main theme was that the walkway was regarded as a quality facility in Palmerston North. It was also noted that the walkway needed to be maintained and protected, with 'rubbish' and 'dogs' being mentioned frequently as issues to be dealt with.

Safety was identified in two contexts. There were those respondents who indicated that some areas were less safe than others along the walkway. Other respondents, however, indicated that they felt the walkway was a safe open space.

Suggestions were made for improving the walkway. These included providing rubbish bins, doggy 'doo' bins and toilets. Better access was also sought for push chairs and this linked to improving the surface, which at present becomes very muddy when wet. More trees and sign posting were also mentioned, as well as the addition of BBQ areas.

Discussion

The findings from the MRWBT suggest a number of similarities with previously published work on greenways and walkways, but also some important differences.

Demographics

In terms of demographics overall there were almost equal numbers of female and male users of the MRWBT, with more women than men using the walkway at the Fitzroy Bend area. The most common age group was the 20-29 years category, followed by the 30–59 years categories. The 20-29 age range is to be expected given the high number of students living in Palmerston North. These demographic findings are similar to the study by Furuseth and Altman (1991), who found that the predominant age group of greenway users was between 25-44 years, with more female than male users. The users at the Fitzroy Bend area tended to be older than users at the Esplanade, which may be due to the higher percentage of retired people living close to this area.

When considering the occupations of the MRWBT users the highest percentages were for professionals and students. The majority of users were employed in paid work, with only 10% of the users indicating that they were either retired or working in the home. Furuseth and Altman (1991) also reported that walkway users tended to be employed and well educated.

Locational characteristics

The majority of the MRWBT users lived both in Palmerston North and within 3 kilometres of the walkway. This would tend to support the research of Furuseth and Altman (1991) who discussed the concept of 'distance decay' where only a few users travel a great distance to the walkway. They also suggested that walkway users tended to be from neighbourhoods rather than from whole communities. Linked to this is the geographical use of the MRWBT, which indicated that users generally resided in the areas of Palmerston North closest to the walkway. This means that users living in the east of Palmerston North used the Fitzroy Bend end more while users from the West, used the Esplanade end. The extreme western end, however, by Dittmer Drive was the least used part (see Figure 3). This may be due to the path actually diverging away from the river and being perceived as being less attractive. This point is illustrated by the following comments:

> *"We would like to be able to walk along the riverside from Dittmer Drive to behind Buick Crescent".*

> *"It would be good if the Council could put some more money and effort into beautifying the river walkway as at present a lot of the track is not particularly attractive such as by Dittmer Drive/Maxwell's line. It could be very attractive with trees and it would increase the use of this area by families and groups for picnicking etc".*

Activity patterns

As with other walkway research (Banister et al, 1992; Furuseth and Altman, 1991; Moore et al, 1998; Mowen et al, 1998) a variety of activities took place on the MRWBT. The most common activity was walking, followed by biking and running. Interestingly, most users participated in activities on their own, which would suggest that users may use their walkway time as 'time out'. Whilst different reasons were given for pursuing the activities the key factor appeared to be 'Exercise, Fitness and Health', followed by 'Leisure/Pleasure' for all of the activities. The following comments highlight these factors:

> *"The walkway is a great asset to Palmerston North. I deeply appreciate being able to exercise and relax while walking beside the river".*

> *"It is a source of great pleasure for all including the quite elderly. Handy to town its something to enjoy."*

Other reasons featuring strongly for walking were 'Dog Related Activities', followed by 'Nature/Environment', 'Social (family/friends)' and as an 'Access Route'. The 'Dog Related Activities' were more important at Fitzroy Bend than the Esplanade. The importance attached to this reason is exemplified by the following statement:

> *"It is an excellent facility for dog owners in this city to have an area where dogs can really exercise and owners can spend quality time with their animals. Over the last 6-7 years I have noticed an increasingly positive aspect as dogs become socialised. There used to be some dog fights but these have decreased a lot over the last 2-3 years. I don't know of any fights. This is a result of allowing dogs freedom in this area".*

Interestingly, the 'Nature/Environment' reason was only given by walkers. As one participant observed:

> *"Seriously, it's just a pleasant, natural place to spend time in. That sums up my reason for being there."*

The reason 'Access Route' was very important at the Esplanade site as there are large numbers who use part of the walkway to access the cycle track to Massey University.

Similar factors were identified by Moore and Ross (1998), particularly with respect to the benefits of outdoor recreation, open space protection, a sense of place and the opportunity to provide for alternative transport routes. Some of the comments at the end of some questionnaires illustrated the 'sense of place' theme in particular. These included participant responses on the questionnaire survey such as:

> *"It's great to have a place so close to town to get away from things".*

> *"The walkway is a great asset to Palmerston North".*

> *"I think we are very lucky to have such a peaceful area so close to the city".*

> *"We bought our house to be close to the walkway which indicates how important it is to us".*

The findings regarding preferred times of walkway use were perhaps not surprising, with 'once a week', 'once a month' and 'once a day' being the most common frequencies of activity participation. The figures would suggest that the Fitzroy Bend walkers use the MRWBT more often than those at the Esplanade, as there were higher percentages at Fitzroy Bend for once a day, twice a week and three times a week. Some differentiation did exist amongst activities. Biking was most frequently done twice a day indicating that the walkway was being used as an access route to Massey University. Running was also high in the three times a week category, which is to be expected if people are regular runners, although this did not appear to be linked to club activities.

All activities took place mainly in the afternoon between 2-7pm, with the other most common time being between 8-12pm. The exception to this was running, which was also popular before eight in the morning. Weekends were the most favoured time for using the MRWBT, with all activities taking place then. Running was also important during the week, with biking featuring strongly on weekdays at the Esplanade, probably due to the access to Massey University. Interestingly, there appeared to be little seasonal variation in the use of the walkway during the survey period. As one participant observed:

"I really love the walkway and enjoy it every day whatever the weather."

The theme of user conflict was also a finding of this research. Whilst there were some indications that user conflict did exist and that it would appear to be asymmetrical, there was also evidence of tolerance amongst user groups. These findings would support the research of Banister et al (1992), Horn (1994) and Moore et al (1998). The following comments are representative of the diversity of user opinion on conflict

Conflict between bikers and dog walkers:

"Bikes are a pain for dogs and walkers as they pass at speed and you get startled by bikers coming from behind without warning".

"As a regular biker along the bridle track I often come across people walking their dogs. I have felt unsafe on a number of occasions with big dogs running up and barking at me while the owner seems oblivious. I have nearly run over a dog who wasn't aware of me as he was running after another dog".

Conflict between bikers and walkers:

"Bikes cause a concern as we don't always hear them and they don't seem to slow down".

"With cyclists and walkers using the same track conflict of space does occur especially when going in the same direction".

Conflict between walkers and dog-walkers:

"It's good that people have somewhere to take dogs for a decent walk/run, but some are not controlled and are allowed to run up to and jump at walkers."

"Another area should be designated for use of owners of big and fierce dogs so that others could feel safe and have peace of mind when taking their pleasant stroll."

There were also a number of comments indicating tolerance between different user groups. Two typical examples are provided below:

"I would not like to see the walkway developed any further, as it's OK at the moment for current users as people know there are dogs and bikes on the walkway and make allowances".

"It's good to include bikes and dogs on the walkway".

The findings would suggest that there may be some evidence for Horn's (1994) 'activity focus' and 'location focus' concepts in relation to conflict, particularly at the Fitzroy Bend area of the MRWBT. The contention that walkers tend to be more 'location focused' is supported by the fact that only walkers mentioned that 'Nature/Environment' was a reason for being on the walkway. In contrast to this, 'Exercise, Fitness and Health' was the key reason given for biking, indicating an 'activity focus'. Whilst the reasons were given at both sampling sites, relatively higher percentages were found at Fitzroy Bend.

Implications for management

There appeared to be different users groups at the Esplanade and Fitzroy Bend. The Esplanade users tended to be younger, they took part in all activities, but did this predominantly on their own and there were more male than female users here. The access route to Massey University was seen as an important reason for using the MRWBT. In contrast, Fitzroy Bend users tended to be older who mainly participated in walking and dog-walking, not only on their own, but also with their families and friends and a greater proportion of users were female here. This indicates that there may be a need for different management approaches and strategies.

Some conflict between user groups was identified, particularly by walkers with respect to bikers. This was mainly in relation to the speed at which bikers were perceived to travel by walkers. Both walkers and bikers saw dogs as a potential source of conflict. However, there were significant numbers of users who commented that they were not unhappy with the diversity of user groups.

Overall the findings would suggest that the MRWBT is a valued outdoor recreation resource, which should not only be maintained by the PNCC, but also extended and enhanced. Suggestions by users for improvements to the MRWBT included toilets, separate tracks for walkers and bikers, more planting of trees and resurfacing of the walkway.

This research has provided an understanding of the user characteristics of the MRWBT, as well as their attitudes towards the walkway as a local outdoor recreation resource and the nature and level of user conflict that presently exists. It is clear from the research that the MRWTB is viewed as a highly valued resource and it is hoped that the findings will assist the PNCC in making appropriate decisions with respect to its maintenance, future management and longer term development.

References

Balfour, R. (1990), *A review of trends in walkway use: Selected New Zealand and overseas findings*. Occasional Paper No.3. Lincoln, N.Z.: Department of Parks, Recreation and Tourism.

Banister, C., Groome, D. and Pawson, G. (1992), The shared use debate: A discussion on the joint use of canal towing paths by walkers, anglers and cyclists. *Journal of Environmental Management, 34*, 149-158.

Coughlan, D. (1996), Conflict in the outdoors: Mountain biking - a case study. *Proceedings of Tourism Down Under II: A Tourism research Conference.* Dunedin, 3-6 December, (pp.24-35).

Department of Conservation. (1993), *Draft New Zealand walkways policy*. Wellington, N.Z.: Department of Conservation.

Furuseth, O. J. and Altman, R. E. (1991), Who's on the greenway: Socio-economic, demographic, and locational characteristics of greenway users. *Environmental Management,* 15 (3): 329-336.

Hillary Commission. (1998), Sport facts. *http://hillarysport.org.nz*

Hillary Commission. (1997), KiwiWalks – combining fun and fitness. *Active Communities, November,* (8).

Horn, C. (1994), *Conflict in recreation: The case of mountain-bikers and trampers.* Unpublished MA thesis, Lincoln University, Lincoln.

Jacobsen, W. N. (1999, June 30), Cyclists the problem. *Evening Standard,* p.11.

Moore, R. L. (1994). *Conflicts on Multiple-Use Trails: Synthesis of the Literature and State of the Practice.* (FHWA-PD-94-031). Raleigh, NC: North Carolina State University.

Moore, R. L., Scott, D. and Graefe, A. R. (1998), The effects of activity differences on recreation experiences along a suburban greenway trail. *Journal of Park and Recreation Administration,* 16 (2): 35-53.

Moore, R. L. and Ross, D. T. (1998), Trails and recreational greenways: Corridors of benefits. *Parks and Recreation,* 33 (1): 68-79.

Morris, G. (1999, July 16), A problem for the city council. *Evening Standard,* p.11.

Mowen, A. J., Graefe, A. R. and Williams, D. R. (1998), An assessment of activity and trail type as indicators of trail user diversity. *Journal of Park and Recreation Administration,* 16 (1): 80-96.

New Zealand Walkway Commission. (1984), *New Zealand walkways*. Wellington, N.Z.: New Zealand Walkway Commission c/o Department of Lands and Survey.

Palmerston North City Council. (1983), *Draft management plan – Riverside Walkway and Bridle Track*. Palmerston North: Palmerston North City Council.

Palmerston North City Council. (1988), *Manawatu Riverside Walk and Bridle Track Management plan – A statement of goals and objectives*. Palmerston North: Palmerston North City Council.

Watch this space: Observing patterns of tourist behaviour on a cultural tour

Tove Oliver

Nottingham Trent University, UK

Abstract

This paper presents findings from participant observation conducted during a seven-day escorted cultural 'highlights' tour of Eire. Environmental psychology provides the conceptual basis for this study and for the ongoing doctoral project of which it forms a part, and seeks to understand tour members' experiences of cultural tour routes. This framework has enabled the study of interactions between tourists' spatial behaviour and their touring environments. Participant observation has rarely been used as a part of an academic study on an escorted tour (Quiroga, 1990; Schmidt, 1975; Schuchat, 1983), seldom on a tour of this duration (Gorman, 1979), and never on a tour with a predominantly cultural itinerary within a single destination. This empirical research therefore provides a unique source from this industry segment, whose market is international and unfamiliar with their cultural destination. Analysis of spatial activity on-tour has demonstrated strong cohesion between pre-defined travelling companions, but which is absent *between* affinity groups. This is not inconsistent with motivation studies that have shown social interaction to be supplementary to the acquisition of knowledge on sightseeing tours (Duke and Persia, 1996; Dunn-Ross and Iso-Ahola, 1991; Geva and Goldman, 1991; Quiroga, 1990). However, it questions the exact nature of the social role of tour groups, and could imply that new acquaintances merely replace the function performed by others in 'every day life' (c.f. Schmidt, 1975; Schuchat, 1983). In seeking to understand tour satisfaction, the terms 'group dynamics' and 'group formation' are overly simplistic, and the social interactions performed while touring require greater scrutiny (c.f. Duke and Persia, 1996; Gorman, 1979; Quiroga, 1990). By developing a conceptual structure for observing and analysing tour participants and their settings, this study has found that individual social contexts, notably the size and nature of pre-existing affinities, appear to influence spatial behaviour on tour. The desire for social stability on-tour compensates for the constantly changing, unfamiliar external environment.

Background

This paper forms part of ongoing Ph.D. doctoral research which is seeking to enhance understanding of the dynamic experience of touring from a customer centred perspective by examining the interactions between tourists, touring environments, and cultural destinations, specifically cultural tour routes. One of the main questions posed by this thesis, is the extent to which generic 'types' of tour participant can be identified from their spatial preferences and experiences. This extends previous work indicting that tour participants can be grouped according to their social and environmental preferences, and this can predict the extent of their spatial learning of a destination (Beck and Wood, 1976). This paper discusses this issue, by reference to empirical research recently conducted by this writer. This sought, through participant observation of tour members on a seven-day escorted cultural tour of Eire, to identify the degree to which, if any, patterns of spatial behaviour could be identified. It further aimed to explore whether similar types of *behaviour* might correspond to participants with other similar *characteristics*, such as age, gender, or nationality, or to the nature and size of their pre-determined tour affinities (i.e. travelling companions).

A combination of judgement and convenience-based sampling was used to select a cultural destination from the wide range available. Eire was chosen because it represents a diverse cultural environment that includes both 'high' and 'popular' elements (c.f. Richards, 1996). In addition, selecting a tour consisting of single rather than multiple destinations would delimit the range of potential variables affecting tour participants' behaviour. As a country in rapid economic transition, Eire is especially interesting and may present a conflict between the promotion and expectation of traditional images and the reality experienced by tourists.

Having identified a suitable destination from which the research population, the tour participants, could be sampled, the next stage in the sampling process was to identify the sampling frame from which to select a tour (McDaniel and Gates, 1993). Principal tour operators and product listings offering itineraries to Eire's most visited cultural and natural attractions were identified from promotional literature produced by the National Tourist Office, Bord Failte, national and international operators. The aim was to select a cultural tour of average quality and value that would be representative of the product as a whole, and attract an international market that had not previously experienced this destination directly. For the purpose of this research, product quality was defined by the number and popularity of cultural and scenic attractions included in the overall price, together with the standard of accommodation offered. Many of the tours were geographically confined to the south of the country and displayed similar tour circuit patterns, a feature noted elsewhere (Pearce, 1989). Organised tours provide safety and convenience, and therefore tend to attract people who are visiting culturally and physically unfamiliar environments. It could be assumed, therefore, that these tours would predominantly consist of first-time visitors (Quiroga, 1990). A tour's duration could be another influential factor and it seemed a relatively short itinerary of between four to ten days would be less likely to attract repeat visitors, who may opt for longer and less well known tour routes instead[1].

The scheduled departure, considered to be average in terms of quality and value for money and selected for this study, was a seven-day tour, operated by *Insight*. This included many of Eire's top attractions, such as Dublin, the Wicklow Mountains, Glendalough, Avoca (or

'Ballykissangel'), Waterford and the Crystal Factory, Cork, Blarney Castle, Ring of Kerry, Tralee, the Cliffs of Moher and the Burren, Limerick and Bunratty Folk-park.

The participants included a guide, a driver, this researcher, and thirty-two other tour members: 18% UK; 22% AUS; 67% USA. These figures are consistent with the statistics for escorted coach tour passengers arriving at Dublin Airport in 1998, where 10% UK; 10% Other non-European; 65% USA (Lynch, 1999), and can therefore be considered representative of the total research population in this study

Observing participants

Observational techniques were first employed in leisure research over sixty years ago. Before this, anthropologists used observation to analyse social interactions and cultural differences. The approach became particularly endorsed in cross-cultural research in psychology (Seaton, 1997) and Hall's classic description of how people use space *The Hidden Dimension,* revealed the importance of the spatial dimension in human communication (Hall, 1966).

Behavioural observation generates qualitative descriptions, and the basic tenet of qualitative research is that theory develops from the observation of the actions of those under study (Jorgensen, 1989). However, this implicit and empathetic approach has resulted in a general paucity of standards for methodological procedures and theoretical frameworks for interpreting observations. Much has been done to redress the balance in the field of Environmental Psychology, and the method followed here has been principally developed to assist successful environmental design (e.g. Zeisel, 1990). This focuses upon individuals' uses of space, and the influences that environmental factors have, by observing both behaviours and their physical traces *(ibid).*

In tourism alone, observation consists of a range of techniques including the unstructured, structured, and electronic recording of behaviours. These are most frequently used to evaluate the on-site activities of visitors, but are often directed towards gross physical parameters, such as visitor flow patterns, rather than to understanding the nuances that users of a setting feel (Pearce, 1988). As a methodology, participant observation provides direct experiential and observational access to the insider's 'world of meaning', and the access it provides to emotional phenomena which is normally difficult to investigate is one of its greatest strengths (Jorgensen, 1989). Another principal quality of the method is that it is *dynamic.* The observer gets a glimpse in time of the life of an environment (Zeisel, 1990). The environment of the coach tour is complex, presenting internal and external space, which coexist and rapidly change. Furthermore, a complicated mix of motivations and experiences can evolve throughout the tour and influence participants' behaviours (Quiroga, 1990).

Observing behaviour in context

To guide the observations, a structure was developed which replaced the complex reality of the observed situation with a simpler version (Zeisel, 1990).

Contexts and settings

Contexts can consist of situations or cultural affinities that influence the way individuals perceive environments. One of the challenges for environmental psychology is to identify the meanings that people attribute to physical and social environments from their reactions (Zeisel, 1990). In particular settings, such interpretation may depend on the options provided, but reference to sensory impacts can assist in defining peoples' relationships to their physical and social environments. For example, coach windows act as *screens* that selectively separate and connect, enabling a visual link, but a tactile separation with the external environment. The *shape* of a setting, such as the seating positioned in the corners of a coach can be more easily seen as separate to the rest of the coach (c.f. *ibid*). The *size* of a coach environment relative to the number of passengers on-board has a considerable affect on passengers' comfort. One of the key *social* contexts influencing tour participants' personal experience of the tour is their travelling companionship status (Quiroga, 1990).

Actors and actions

The subjects of observations are individuals or 'actors' who perform roles. They can be noted for characteristics or affiliations that are similar or different to other actors, such as nationality, gender, age, social affinities, and travelling companions. Although the observer may be unable to identify these features accurately, paradoxically clues from the intentional displays of self-image can sometimes be used to infer associations. In touring environments, name tags, flags, pins, badges, slogans, and brand names are used to express individuality, to enable others to identify them more easily, or to express group membership (Zeisel, 1990). Observing the photographic activities of tour members can be particularly useful in revealing individuals' motives for ensuring tour satisfaction. For example, taking group photographs in the early stages of a tour can be used as a mechanism to develop social interaction (Markwell, 1997). Since sight-seeing forms the main activity of a tour itinerary and this is mainly experienced from on-board a coach, in-tour seating arrangements will be pivotal in the identification of participants' adaptive behaviour to their environment which aims to secure their satisfaction.

Analysis and discussion

The purpose of the analysis was primarily to understand the social and physical meanings underlying participants' spatial behaviour by focusing on change and consistency in their seating preferences. No seat rotation policy was in operation on the departure selected, and as visibility of the route is central to the production of a satisfying experience of a sightseeing tour, this would have a significant effect on participants' seating preferences. The observations made by this writer indicated that the desire to share the experience with companions also influenced seating patterns. Analysis therefore focused on participants' social contexts (i.e. pre-existing travelling companions and the new affinities that developed on-tour), the roles they performed, and opportunities presented by the physical setting of the coach interior (c.f. Gorman, 1979).

Fifteen distinct seating behaviour patterns were observed during the seven-day tour, and are listed below.

Table 1

Seating preference	Participants
Near to travelling companion(s) (i.e. next to, or immediately in front, across from, or behind)	1,2; 3,4,5,6; 8,9; 10,11; 12,13; 14,15,16; 18,19,20,21; 22,23,24; 25,26; 27,28; 29,30; 31,32
Mobile (i.e. move throughout front, middle, and rear sections of coach)	1,2; 8,9; 14,15,16
Sedentary (i.e. remain in the same *general* location, either front, middle, or rear section of coach, except for up to one day spent in front seat)	3,4,5,6; 7; 17; 19,20,21,22; 22,23,24; 27,28; 33
Near to **compatriots**	29,30; 31,32
Same seat (except for up to one day occupying front seat)	10; 11; 12,13; 18/19; 26/27; 29,30; 31,32
Alone (i.e. adjacent seat unoccupied)	7; 10,11; 17; 18,19; 29,30; 31,32; 33
Same seat in **corner**	29,30
Back row	29,30; 31
Alternate positions with travelling companions	3,4,5,6; 8,9; 14,15,16; 20,21; 22,23,24
Separate from travelling companion(s) after a few days	1,2; 8,9; 27,28
Move to **rear** of coach the day after sitting in front seat	8,9; 14,15,16
Seats selected for optimum **view**	3,4,5,6; 32
Seat selected for optimum **leg**-room	13
Aisle seat only	7; 11; 13; 18
Front seat at least once	1,2; 7; 8,9; 12,13; 14,15,16; 17; 22,23,24; 27,28; 25,26

Three distinct pre-formed affinity groupings were identified from the thirty-three tour members, and are shown below.

Table 2

Social context (pre-formed affinities)	Participants
Single (i.e. travelling unaccompanied)	7; 17; 33
Pair (i.e. married couple, friends, or family members)	1,2; 8,9; 10,11; 12,13; 18,19; 20,21; 27,28; 25,26; 29,30; 31,32
Group (i.e. 3-4 family members or friends)	3,4,5,6; 14,15,16; 18,19,20,21; 22,23,24

The data was collected in the form of daily seating plans supplemented by notes and photographs that recorded the behaviour its physical traces, set within the conceptual structure (outlined above). This needed to be summarised, to identify whether patterns or trends in tour members' spatial behaviour existed. Due to the volume and range of potentially significant information that had been assembled, the initial analytical procedures followed those used in the analysis of *quantitative* data (Bryman and Cramer, 1997). Frequency distribution tables enabled the calculation of the number of cases in each category, or, the relative frequency with which participants had exhibited particular behaviour patterns during the tour. These distributions were generated with the aid of SPSS for Windows (Release 9.0). The most significant finding is the high percentage (94%) of tour members' who consistently preferred to sit in proximity to their travelling companions (i.e. either *directly* next to, across the aisle, in front or behind). *All* accompanied tour members (i.e. all but two of the participants) behaved in this manner for *the duration* of the tour. However, it is also striking that 47% of tour members chose to sit alone (i.e. with an unoccupied seat immediately adjacent to them). With a 67% load factor[2], a high proportion of unoccupied seating was available on this tour, potentially facilitating a wide range of spatial behaviours. Optimum levels of physical and psychological comfort will be sought from the opportunities that an environment presents. The tendency by about half of the participants to sit near to companions, but retain a degree of personal space, may indicate that personal security is more important than sociability or the desire to share the tour experience (c.f. Gorman, 1979; Reisinger and Waryszak, 1994). It is interesting to note that a pair of seats was unoccupied on three occasions, suggesting that the spatial opportunities presented by this environment and the optimum comfort levels had been satisfied.

Other significant findings included the predominantly sedentary behaviour of participants, where 41% preferred to sit in the same approximate location (i.e. front, middle, or rear of the coach) compared to 22% who sat in more than one section of the coach. A further 38% occupied the *same seat* for the duration of the tour except when in a front seat position. A total of 56% spent up to one day in the front of the coach, demonstrating the value placed upon this optimum viewing position. Nonetheless, the desire to obtain a good view never overrode that to be near travelling companions, who would invariably occupy adjacent seats on the same day. A concern for 'fairness' and communal behaviour was exhibited by the behaviour of 19% of the tour members who deliberately chose to sit in the rear section of the coach the day after they had sat in the front seats. The desire to appear equal to others in the party was shown by Participant 8 who, following a day in the front with his wife (Participant 9) commented, 'we'll be at the back today'. When asked if the view was much better from the front he replied, 'sure, but the views from the rest of the coach are good!'

Conformity is a theme that is also borne out by travelling companions' reciprocal behaviour where for example, 44% of the total group regularly exchanged seating positions with companions. There were either physical or medical explanations where this behaviour was not in evidence, for example Participant 13 required extra leg-room and Participant 26 had a severe visual impairment. Alternatively, travelling companions remained alone in separate seats, and thus negated the need to exchange seats. Perhaps surprisingly, those who sat alone did not always prefer window seats and 13% remained in aisle seats, seeming to favour the extra leg-room and views through the front windscreen of the coach.

The second part of the analysis considered participants and the frequency of their spatial behaviours in relation to social context, in particular whether members were travelling alone, as a pair, or in a group. This aimed to determine whether pre-formed affinities had significantly affected participants' spatial behaviour. These affinities were thought to represent independent variables that may influence seating preferences. The distribution frequencies are in themselves interesting: 44% of tour members were travelling as a part of a group; 57% were in a pairs, and 6% travelled alone. These figures are consistent with those found by other researchers and therefore seem likely to be representative (e.g. (Gorman, 1979). The relatively low proportion of single travellers again supports the view that meeting people is not a major motivation for selecting cultural tours from this particular industry segment, unlike those specialising in the singles/youth niche markets (Schuchat, 1983). This is reinforced by the behaviour of the accompanied participants *all* of whom stayed close to their companions during the tour, rather than choosing to sit with new acquaintances.

Further analysis of participants' spatial activities showed that certain behaviours corresponded with participants' pre-defined social contexts (Figures 1-3). Pairs were more likely to occupy the same seats, and sit apart from their companion at some time during the tour (Figure 2). In contrast, pre-formed groups rarely sat alone, were relatively mobile, and frequently alternated their seating arrangements with other members in their party (Figure 3). This appears to demonstrate the significance of social interactions *between* pre-existing companions rather than new acquaintances, with couples preferring to sit either with each other or alone, and groups having a selection of alternative seating companions. There was one exception to this seen in the seating arrangement of three Australian men, who preferred to sit together on the back seat. Only two of these represented a pre-defined pair. This group referred to themselves as the 'boys at the back'. This naming of a recognised clique corresponds exactly with Gorman's 'back of the bus bunch', and indicates the unity that these members felt (Gorman, 1979). This also seems to support Quirogia's finding that nationality is a significant variable in the formation of cliques (Quiroga, 1990), although it is not certain the extent to which this grouping was gender based. However, this behaviour seems to confirm the idea that tour participants seek new acquaintances to replace the social function performed by those in their home environments. The tendency for pairs to sit in the same seats may further indicate their desire for stability in a changing and unfamiliar environment. Larger groups of travelling companions do not need stability in their surroundings to such an extent, perhaps because their security is provided in numbers.

Figure 1   Single participants
Note: Different shading represents individual participants

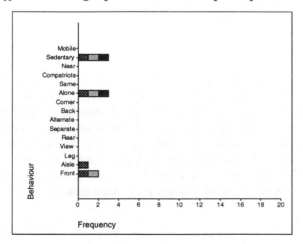

Figure 2   Participants in pairs

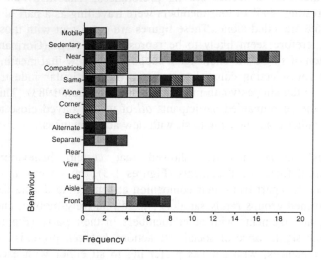

Figure 3   Participants in groups

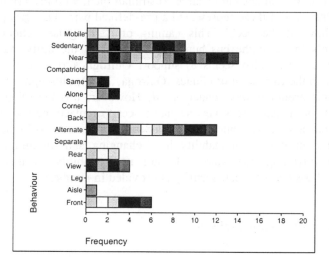

Conclusion

The escorted tour group serves multiple functions for its' members. These can be physical, psychological, economic and social in nature (Mayo and Jarvis, 1981; Schmidt, 1975). A person joins a group to satisfy certain requirements, yet the group may fulfil different needs for each member. The knowledge that the organised tours facilitate safety and interpersonal relations, and that these are positively valued by participants, is quite well documented (Duke and Persia, 1996; Quiroga, 1990; Schmidt, 1975; Yang, 1995). However, exactly how the tour environment satisfies these needs, whether by providing 'safe strangers', or because a group provides safety in strange places, has not been made clear (Schuchat, 1983).

This paper has presented an analysis of the interactions observed between tourists' spatial behaviour and their touring environments. It poses the idea that tour participants adapt to their unfamiliar destinations by spatial and social mechanisms to ensure their security. Although the notion of intra-group descriptive 'types' based on tourists' spatial preferences has not been supported, it would appear that pre-defined social contexts *do* influence in-tour behaviour patterns (c.f. Beck and Wood, 1976; Swarbrooke and Horner, 1999). The modern organised cultural tour is characterised by its rapid pace and changing environments, presenting a kaleidoscope of images that are ephemeral and sometimes indistinct. This environment imposes demands on tourists, particularly those who are experiencing it for the first-time. In contrast, touring companions provide stability, and new acquaintances afford the opportunity to replace the absent primary relations from more familiar environments. These can fulfil a great social need and, in turn, help to secure a satisfying experience (Gorman, 1979).

Endnotes

1. Participant observation Globus, Cosmos 1997.

2. Where a minimum break-even load factor could as little 37%, i.e. 18 passengers (Globus company policy).

References

Beck, R., and Wood, D. (1976), Comparative developmental analysis of individual and aggregated cognitive maps of London. In G. Moore and R. Golledge (Editors), *Environmental Knowing*, New York, John Wiley.

Bryman, A., and Cramer, D. (1997), *Quantitative Data Analysis with SPSS for Windows: A guide for Social Scientists*, London, Routledge.

Duke, C. R., and Persia, M. A. (1996), Consumer-defined dimensions for the escorted tour industry segment: expectations, satisfactions, and importance. *Journal of Travel and Tourism Marketing*, 5, (1/2), pp.77-99.

Dunn-Ross, E. L., and Iso-Ahola, S. (1991), Sightseeing tourists' motivation and satisfaction. *Annals of Tourism Research*, 18, (2), pp.226-237.

Geva, A., and Goldman, A. (1991), Satisfaction measurement in guided tours. *Annals of Tourism Research*, 18, pp.177-185.

Gorman, B. (1979), Seven days, five countries. The making of a group. *Urban Life*, 7, (4), pp.469-491

Hall, E. T. (1966), *The Hidden Dimension. Man's use of space public and private*, London, The Bodley Head Ltd.

Jorgensen, D. L. (1989), *Participant Observation. A methodology for human studies* London, Sage Publications.

Lynch, V. (veronica.lynch@dublin.aer-rianta.ie) (1999), *Aer-Rianta passenger statistics* 1998. 20 September. Email to: Tove Oliver (tove.oliver@ntu.ac.uk).

Markwell, K. W. (1997), Dimensions of photography in a nature-based tour. *Annals of Tourism Research*, 24, (1), pp.131-155.

Mayo, E. J., and Jarvis, L. P. (1981*), The Psychology of Leisure and Travel. Effective marketing and selling of travel services*, Boston, MA, CBI Publishing Company.

McDaniel, C., and Gates, R. (1993), *Contemporary Marketing Research*, St. Paul, Minneapolis, West Publishing Company.

Pearce, D. G. (1992), *Tourist Travel Patterns and Regional Impacts: issues and examples from New Zealand*. Paper presented at the Spatial Implications of Tourism, University of Grongen.

Pearce, P. L. (1988), *The Ulysses Factor. Evaluating visitors in tourist settings*, New York, Springer-Verlag.

Quiroga, I. (1990), Characteristics of package tours in Europe. *Annals of Tourism Research*, 17, pp.185-207.

Reisinger, Y., and Waryszak, R. (1994), Japanese tourists' perceptions of their tour guides: Australian experience. *Journal of Vacation Marketing*, 1, (1), pp.28-40.

Richards, G. (1996), *Cultural Tourism in Europe*, Oxon, CAB International.

Schmidt, C. J. (1975), *The Guided Tour: insulated adventure*. Paper presented at the 6th Annual Conference Proceedings of the Travel Association, UK.

Schuchat, M. (1983), Comforts of group tours. *Annals of Tourism Research*, 10, pp.465-477.

Seaton, A. V. (1997), Unobtrusive observational measures as a qualitative extension of visitor surveys at festivals and events: mass observation revisited. *Journal of Travel Research* (Spring), pp.25-30.

Swarbrooke, J., and and Horner, S. (1999), *Consumer Behaviour in Tourism*, Oxford, Butterworth Heinemann.

Yang, M. (1995), *An Exploratory Analysis of the Travel Benefits sought, Travel Satisfaction, Culture Shock, and Image Differences among International Tourists on Bus Tours between Los Angeles and Las Vegas (California, Nevada)*. PhD Thesis, The Pennsylvania State University.

Zeisel, J. (1990) *Inquiry by Design. Tools for environment-behaviour research*, Cambridge, Cambridge University Press.

Tourism in Kenya: Past, present and future challenges

Tom Ondicho

University of Nairobi, Kenya

Abstract

This paper examines the yesterday, today and tomorrow of Kenya's tourism industry. Tourism development in Kenya had witnessed tremendous growth in the early years, and since 1987, became the country's single largest source of foreign exchange earning surpassing the combined earnings from tea and coffee, both traditionally leading foreign exchange earners. Because of its enormous contribution to economic development, Kenya's tourism industry has been exemplified as a success story (Dieke, 1991). However, factors, which have affected Kenya's success in the past decades, may no longer be applicable in today's competitive global tourism industry. Faced with a definite downward trend in visitor arrivals since 1990, there are concerns that the Kenya's tourism industry may have entered a period of permanent decline, which if not checked will eventually kill the goose that lays the golden egg. This paper includes a review of past trends and problems that the industry faces in the present times. The paper concludes with a discussion of the future challenges of Kenya's tourism industry and the steps that are being undertaken to revive the "lost glory" in the industry.

Introduction

The republic of Kenya straddles the equator covering an area of 582, 646 sq. km (224,960 sq. Miles). It borders the Indian Ocean and Somalia to the east, Sudan and Ethiopia to the north, Uganda and Lake Victoria to the west and Tanzania to the south. Being located near to the Indian Ocean it has been a hub of the region for both sea and air traffic.

Diversity and contrast characterise both its people and its geography. Its varied terrain rises from the sea level at the coast to Mt. Kenya (5, 199 metres) to the east of the Great Rift Valley, and Mt. Elgon (4,321) metres to the extreme west. The country is bisected by the Rift Valley that runs through the whole country from north to south. The country has a total population of 28 million people with a rich cultural mix comprising 42 ethnic communities and a scattering of immigrants in the cities. Kenya was British colony up to 1963, when it attained self-rule from Britain.

Due to its varieties in natural tourist attractions, such as wildlife, miles of coastal beaches, a pleasant sunny tropical climate, and its culture and strategic position, Kenya has been a popular tourist destination accounting for about 6% of the total visitors coming to Africa. A rapid growth of tourism in the past three or so decades in conjunction with a strong international demand has yielded high economic returns, stimulated the national economy, created jobs, encouraged investments, and raised the standards of living. It is, therefore, not surprising that tourism in Kenya is considered an economic boon and principle means of economic development.

However, Kenya's tourism industry has been undergoing difficult times in the recent past. Since 1990, the industry has increasingly shown a definite downward trend, ironically, at a time when other African destinations are recording unprecedented increases in tourist arrivals and revenue. The effects of such a trend on the national economy are a source of concern to the tourism industry and government. This paper will review past trends in Kenya's tourism industry and the problems that the industry faces at present. The paper concludes with a discussion of the future challenges and the steps being undertaken to improve Kenya's competitive position.

Tourism in Kenya before 1960s

It has often been stated that tourism in Kenya was instituted during the colonial period as a "European hedonocracy", that is a leisure-oriented activity for which only Europeans were culturally, socially and economically equipped to take part in, and around which they reserved for themselves the right to undertake entrepreneurial activity (Jommo, 1987 quoting Crompton). In the colonial days, tourism was the "hunter" brand of independent adventurers. The hunting expeditions were arranged by a few specialised bush and game trackers also European.

The colonial travellers were mainly settler holidaymakers resident in Africa, some of whom only used Kenya as a convenient stopover to the colonised countries, including Tanzania, Uganda, and Zimbabwe. Up to WWII, the colonial travellers, especially the British and Germans, had been the most important foreign tourism source to Kenya. Guesthouses and hotels appeared in Kenya during the nineteenth century especially in response to the demand for lodging. Most of these facilities were small and operated by individual families, such as Norfolk considered then the best such lodging facility in East Africa.

However, before the colonial period, the East African Coast had long received visitors from Arabia, Persia (now Iran), Greece, and India. However, those who came were not tourists in the true sense of the word, as they mainly comprised of traders and conquerors. Foreign trade brought to Kenya not only flows of capital, but also a flow of investors and traders who upon return to their countries raised curiosity amongst people of their countries about the beauties of Kenya, some of who travelled to Kenya as leisure seekers (Ouma, 1970).

It was not until the 1940s, however, that the foundations were laid for the development of a modern tourism industry. The completion of the Kenya-Uganda Railway in the late 1930s linking Port Bell, Entebbe and Mombasa enhanced internal mobility, which was also available to tourists. The introduction of Boing 707 and jumbo jet aircraft in the late 1950s revolutionised air travel by drastically reducing flight time and doubling carrying capacity.

This technological advance in aircraft engineering accompanied by improved commercial air travel significantly influenced Kenyan tourism. However, during the colonial time tourism development was a *laisse faire* process without appropriate planning. Possibilities of organised tourism were further inhibited by lack of accommodation and transport facilities.

Tourism in Kenya after the 1960s

The year 1965 is often cited as the starting point of Kenya's unprecedented tourism growth, which was primarily influenced by three factors. In 1965, tourism was incorporated into independent Kenya's first National Development Plan 1965-1970 (Kenya, 1965). The plan aimed to strengthen the Kenyan economy in the areas of international trade, investment, and tourism to boost foreign exchange earnings and expand employment opportunities. Since then, tourism has been a permanent feature of all subsequent national development plans.

In the same year, the Kenya Tourist Development Corporation (KTDC), a governmental parastatal within the Ministry of Tourism and Wildlife, was established by an act of parliament, as the state's executive agency in all matters pertaining to tourism development in the country.

A third event was the establishment of privileged policies to facilitate tourism development. One such policy concerned the establishment and maintenance of planned and permanent floral and faunal sanctuaries. The Kenya National Parks Organisation and the game department were formed to deal with various aspects of wildlife management and conservation. The two bodies were merged in 1976 to form the Wildlife Conservation and Management Department under the Ministry of Tourism and Wildlife before being absorbed by the Kenya Wildlife Services (KWS), a government parastatal in 1990 which is the body today charged with the responsibility for developing sustainable wildlife and nature tourism. Another major policy was concern with the training of manpower to take up the various positions in the tourism industry, which resulted the establishment of the Kenya Utalii College in 1974.

A series of promotional campaigns initiated by the government were extremely successful. The success of tourism was evident when the sector became the fastest growing and most important sector of the Kenya's economy. By 1987 tourism had surpassed tea and coffee as the leading single source of foreign exchange earnings for the country. As one of the state's primary exporting industries, tourism has helped support other industries in Kenya such as construction, retail and finance.

Between 1965 and 1988, international tourism arrivals increased at an average of 10% annually, from under a quarter a million in 1970 to 676,900 in 1988 while earnings from tourism rose by more than 1,600% (Kenya, 1991) visitor arrivals between 1989 and 1993 increased by just 5.9 per cent from 642,100 to 679,000 while tourism earnings measured in US dollars fell by 10.2% from US$400 million in 1989 to US$ 359 million in 1993 (Kenya, 1994). After almost picking up in 1994 the industry suffered another slump in 1995 with the number of arrivals declining by 20% from 863,400 in 1994 to 690,500 in 1995 (Kenya, 1996). In the same period, Kenya slipped to the sixth position from 5th as the most popular destination in Africa (Mudasia, 1996, quoting WTO statistics). Due to the Persian Gulf War, economic recession in the USA and Europe, as well as rising insecurity and crime rates, high prices, competition and hotel room oversupply, biting infrastructural shortfalls and lack of foresightedness on the part of tourism planners, tourism then entered an unprecedented decline.

Kenya's tourism profile

The profile of visitors has changed considerably since 1965. At that time about 80 per cent of the visitors were from Europe compared to about 56 per cent today. Foreign visitors from Germany, United Kingdom, America, Switzerland and France formed the greatest percentage between 1983 and 1990, however, since the 1990s other countries in Europe, Africa and Asia are also increasing in importance.

Tourism expenditure patterns have also exhibited a change as tourists now spend more money and time on shopping. In 1986, for example, international tourists spent almost 44% of their budget on lodging and food and 27% on shopping (Ondicho, 2000). By 1990, shopping expenditure accounted for 39%, while spending on accommodation and food decreased to 38%. Inexpensive arts and crafts are some of the most popular items for international visitors.

In terms of purpose of visit, business travel surged ahead of leisure travel due to an increase of international trade and conventions. In 1990, business travel increased by 27.8% while leisure travel increased only by 5.6%.

Problems in Kenya's tourism industry

Tourism has played an important role in the diversification and development of the Kenyan economy. Tourism continues to make the largest contribution to GNP, as well as showing consistent growth at a time when the agricultural sector has shown only limited growth and several of the other leading sectors of the economy have been stagnant.

After decades of tourism growth, Kenya's tourism sector is presently experiencing difficulties that have led to lower arrivals and depressed market conditions. The rapid expansion that brought forth economic benefits has resulted in the deterioration and disorderliness of Kenya's tourism industry. The recent slow growth of Kenya's tourism sector could be attributed to the long-term problems that are inherent in Kenya's economy and society. They are a degraded environment, inadequate infrastructure, safety issues and negative publicity.

Deteriorated environment

Banking on past growth, tourist accommodation facilities have continued to increase with the construction of new beach hotels and game lodges. However, most of the constructions have been ad hoc responses to the increased volume of tourist traffic, and have been concerned primarily with the short-term increase in coastal hotel capacities. Richards (1980) has coined the term *unplanned ribbon development* to describe the haphazard hotel development on the Kenyan coast. Other environmental problems include: ecological disruption to animal breeding and feeding by uncontrolled access to game parks, congestion in beach resorts and game parks especially during the peak season, visual pollution resulting from haphazard high-rise hotel buildings at beach resorts, water pollution due to discharge of sewerage effluent into beach and rivers, litter, traffic fumes and overcrowding. To a large degree these problems have been caused by the too rapid increase in tourist arrivals, which puts pressure on infrastructure and the environment.

Inadequate infrastructure

The development of infrastructure services - covering public utilities, amenities, transport, communications and energy services - cannot meet the demand. Traffic in Nairobi has adversely affected the average length of tourist stay, room rates and incomes of hundreds of shops and restaurants, which depend on earning from tourism. Many tourists bypass Nairobi and fly direct to Mombasa in the coast.

In addition, the construction of public utilities has slipped so far behind that it may take as long as five years before they can meet demand. For instance, in Nairobi, daily power cuts and failure to replace damaged telephone cables in time are a major problem. Due to the insufficient infrastructure, international investors in tourism are seeking alternative places in Africa for their investments.

In order to improve the infrastructure and service, the Kenyan government has taken some positive steps, which include the privatisation of the Kenya Power Company and the on-going privatisation of the telecommunication sector are expected to improve delivery of the services. The El Nino road recovery programme being sponsored by the World Bank, which includes some major projects to build new roads in Nairobi and expand others to cope with the increasing traffic, are expected to ease transport problems. Meanwhile plans are underway to privatise water supply and sewage disposal sub sectors.

Safety issue

The deteriorating security situation is another concern for tourists to Kenya. Kenya has experienced some amount of political unrest since the 1990s. What started as an agitation for political reform degenerated into a wave of violence, which first started in 1992 before resurfacing again in 1997 and 1998, and the subsequent media coverage it received both locally and internationally had a profound impact on Kenya's tourism industry. Though the political unrest was instrumental in arousing the nation and drawing the world's attention to the magnitude of problems facing Kenyans, and the need for immediate action, it served to cause an image problem in the eyes of potential tourists.

The impact was heightened in 1998 with the simultaneous terrorist bombing of the USA embassy in Nairobi and Dar es Salaam, which resulted in the US government issuing a travel warning urging Americans to "exercise caution" (Hughes, 1998) in travelling to Kenya and to leave if they felt unsafe, affected arrivals from the USA.

The crime rate in Kenya, especially carjacking, armed robbery, thugery, mugging and other types of violent crime have been on the increase in the 1990s. Though the government has been making all possible efforts to curb crime, these efforts are yet to bear fruit.

Negative image

Negative publicity in Kenya's tourism markets is another problem that the industry is facing. For instance, the emergence of AIDS in Kenya has coincided with deteriorating security and infrastructure, and an escalating number of road accidents all of which have received extensive media coverage both locally and internationally. The "image problem" has not only served to scare away potential tourists but has also led into Kenya being categorised as a "high risk tourism destination" in the country's major markets.

Competition

Kenya is currently facing stiff competition from other African destinations especially Zimbabwe, Botswana, Tanzania, Uganda and South Africa. The fall of apartheid in South Africa, for instance, and the rise of Mandela as one of the greatest statesmen in recent times together with its vast wildlife resources have added appeal to international tourists wishing to tour Africa.

Future challenges

In the light of these problems, Kenya's tourism industry has been the subject of extensive analysis by both the private sector and government. In particular, Kenya's ability to compete with other emerging African destinations such as South Africa is being examined, and its future is being discussed actively in industry circles. It is acknowledged that the good days of yester years are long gone while the number of visitor arrivals has fallen since the 1990, there are many who think believe that the visitor industry has entered a stage of permanent decline. In order to understand Kenya's tourism development, therefore, it might be helpful to review the concept of a destination's lifecycle.

Destination life cycle

Historically, resorts have tended to undergo an economic life cycle of development, maturation and decline, which may cover 50-75 years. This lifecycle can apply to both the overall resort destination as well as to a specific resort. Each resort area can be said to be at a different stage and consequently faces different problems.

In the first or "exploration" stage of the life cycle, the destination is generally unknown, tourist facilities are lacking, air accessibility is limited, and only a small number of tourists visit.

In the second or "development stage" most major outbound markets become aware of the destination, international tourist class facilities become available, air accessibility improves, and the number of visitors increases. During this second stage, government and residents tend to welcome tourism because of its contribution to the local economy, but the development is spontaneous and uncoordinated. Towards the end of this stage, the number of visitors increases sharply. At the same time, the original developers are replaced by new, outside investors and local residents begin to lose control to absentee owners.

During the third or "maturity" stage, the destination receives a large number of tourists and the industry's services and roles become more formalised. Hostels generally have full occupancy, but there is only occasional reinvestment. Frequently, there is a loss of local decision-making power and control over the industry as many of the hotels, airlines, and other tourism services become affiliated with international corporations. Residents may develop hostile attitudes toward visitors, often as a result of competition over the use of resources.

In the fourth or "Decline" stage, the destination has a well established image but is no longer popular; planning controls are established too late, the destination is over commercialised, the environment spoiled, and there is little sign of self renewal or reinvestment.

While the destination cycle may apply differently in actual experience for each area, it can serve as a useful framework in understanding the yesterday, today and tomorrow of Kenya's tourism industry. Both the public and private sectors are determined that this destination life cycle need not apply to Kenya, and steps are being taken to ensure a better future of the industry.

Competitive analysis

It is obvious that if Kenya is to remain competitive, it must continuously examine what other destinations have to offer and to work on improving its products. In terms of the market, there are differences in preferences between the various market niches. For example, among European visitors, Kenya has strongest competition from South Africa, Tanzania, Uganda and Zimbabwe.

Market analysis

The immediate challenge facing Kenya is to widen the range of tourists both in terms of geographical origins and the type of activities they seek. This requires an understanding of the changing demographic and preferences of today's travellers. For example, in the next century most tourists are likely to be old people aged over 55 years. The preferences of this ageing population will likely move toward specific types of holidays such as cruises and resort vacations and less active recreational activities. There is therefore urgent need to develop new attractions and resorts to meet the ever-changing tastes and preferences of different tourism markets or segments.

Repeater market

Another important trend is the increasing number of repeat visitors especially to resorts. In Kenya, repeaters constitute about 40% of the total visitor market, and this has affected the planning of new resorts and the modification of existing ones. What is important to keep in mind is that repeat visitors are different from first-time visitors, they spend less, and Kenya should look for alternative activities for repeaters.

Product analysis

Kenya projects the image of a tropical destination which offers both beach and safari holidays. However, these are not enough in today's competitive resort environment. Part of the "image" projected includes Kenya's wildlife resources. It is clear that if tourism in Kenya is to succeed there is need to develop and promote new attractions and activities. In order to compete effectively, however, the industry is currently re-examining its tourism attractions and services.

Price and value relationship

Another consideration is price as related to value. Europeans are generally price- conscious and expect good value for the amount paid for a vacation. Other markets are also price conscious and seek out less expensive hotels which offer value for price. A growing trend is the increasing demand for five star hotels. In the past, Kenya has tended to overbuild medium priced hotels as a result of miscalculating the size of this market, resulting in low occupancies and low profitability. In the last few years it has become evident that Kenya must offer a balance in the type of accommodation to compete.

Conclusion

For Kenya, tourism has undergone very rapid transformations over the years culminating in the present decline in arrivals. The question that has arisen is whether as a mature destination, Kenya's decline will continue as more and more tourists seek newer destinations. Whether Kenya will succeed in repositioning itself is an important question. It is clear that Kenya's tourism industry cannot remain the same year after year, but will need to adjust to the interests of different tourist groups. The kind of attractions, accommodations and activities which are popular today may not be popular tomorrow, and it is important that Kenya adjusts quickly to these markets. To prevent further decline, Kenya needs to undertake a number of strategies.

The Kenyan government has realised the urgency of improving tourism conditions, as the industry is important to the nation's economy. Policies and regulations have been developed to improve the quality of tourism infrastructure and service. It is expected that Kenya's infrastructure network bottlenecks will ease. However, for future success, both the public and private sectors need to put prime focus on policy enforcement. Government departments need to be well co-ordinated in order to attain the objectives and targets. Legal actions are needed for corruption and environmental deterioration.

To maintain a competitive position, a number of issues need to be addressed. First, accommodation capacity expansion needs to be regulated to avoid haphazard development and in order to maintain standards. With tourist demand shifting towards the upper end of the market, what is needed is the creation of five star properties. However, there have been very few firm proposals in the tourist arena from large private investors, and the only initiatives have come from national organisations. The lack of large scale investment is part of the wider stagnation in foreign investment in Kenya, as investors are held back by the country's institutional problems, infrastructural shortfalls, the general instability caused by rising crime levels and insecurity, and by the failure of the government to reduce its budget deficit or to generally restructure the economy significantly. Moreover, the government is has not been honouring its promises in some cases.

In addition, new markets and a new image must be developed to maintain tourism growth. Investment in marketing and promotion activities is, therefore, critical to maintaining the numbers and creating diversified visitor patterns. Promotional efforts have been directed towards an increasing number of long-haul traditional markets, such as continental Europe and North America, and more recently Japan and Pacific Asia in general. Advertising and promotion in major tourist markets is aimed at restoring confidence among tourists that Kenya is a safe and stable destination.

The disadvantage of Kenya as a holiday destination remain ones of distance from most markets, competition and a reputation of offering beach and wildlife holidays, with other attractions. To counter this image, there are many positive features that ought to receive greater publicity, particularly the multicultural nature of the Kenyan society, the hospitality and friendliness of its peoples, the possibilities of visiting rural farms (green or village tourism), interesting landscapes and architecture and the wide range of accommodation. In contrast, the high levels of crime is seen to be a potential problem and the government has been arguing for the need to reduce crime in order to attract foreign investment and tourists.

Despite its attraction and multifaceted character, tourism is not an easy sector to develop. It thrives first in an atmosphere of peace and security. It requires good infrastructure, marketing, market research, interpretation, orientation, and promotion to be successful. It requires infrastructural support from the public sector, good transport and communication networks and public services such as water and electricity supplies. The domestic tourist market also should not be overlooked. The home holidaymakers can be the backbone of the tourism industry and thus help bring prosperity to areas, which could otherwise never know it.

The challenge is for Kenya to maintain a balance within tourism industry development, so that growth will not destroy the environment or cause change that undermines its sense of cultural and historic identity. While it will be years before the results of current efforts will be known, the steps, which are being taken, appear to be in a positive direction.

References

Dieke, P. U. C. (1991), Policies for Tourism development in Kenya, *Annals of Tourism Research* 18, pp. 269-294.

Jommo, R. B. (1987), *Indigenous Enterprise in Kenya's Tourism Industry*, Itineraries Etudes du Development 3, Institut universitaire du Development.

Kenya, Republic of (1965), *National development Plan 1965-1970*, Government Printer, Nairobi.

Ondicho, T. G. (2000), Tourism in Kenya: development, problems and Challenges, in *East Africa Social Science Review*, in press.

Ondicho (1999), *Environmental Challenges and Influences on Tourism: The Case of Kenya's Tourism Industry*, unpublished.

Ouma, J. P. B. M. (1970), *The Evolution of tourism in East Africa 1900-2000*, East African Literature Bureau, Nairobi, Dar es Salaam, Kampala.

Richards, G. (1980), Planning for Future Development of the tourist Sector in Kenya, in T. Pinfold and G. Norcliffe, Eds, Development Planning in Kenya: Essays on the Planning Process and Policy Issues, *Geographical Monograph* 9, pp. 141-156.

Summary, R. M. (1987) Tourism's Contribution to Kenya's Economy, *Annals of Tourism Research* 14, pp.531-40.

Australian tourists and their interest in wildlife based tourism attractions

Chris Ryan

University of Waikato, New Zealand

Introduction

In the year 2000 it is generally recognised that nature based tourism has experienced considerable rates of growth in recent years. In many instances, in the private sector, the supply of such tourist experiences has been motivated by those who hold wildlife dear, believe strongly in a need to protect the environment, and while wishing to retain financial viability, wish to spread educational and conservation messages to their publics. It has also been assumed that those who visit such attractions, especially those based on wildlife, share similar concerns and are motivated by a wish to learn. Such assumptions have been questioned. McKercher (1993) has pointed out that tourists, whether eco-tourists or not, remain tourists seeking escape and relaxation. In a much cited article, Wheeller (1993) argued that eco-tourists are, in reality, ego-tourists, following the latest trend and massaging their egos and guilt by engaging in what may be termed 'edutainment' in a holiday setting. On the other hand, major studies derived from international visitor monitors have labelled tourists as eco- or nature based tourists on the basis of visitor behaviour as measured by visitation to mammal based attractions or national parks (for example see Blamey and Hatch, 1998, Blamey, 1997, Eagles 1992). However such data does not provide insights in motives, and as this author has noted (Ryan, 1997), to impute motive from behaviour alone is an exercise exposed to many difficulties. In one sense the turning of a Millennium offers an excuse (if any is really needed) to examine our basic assumptions in what have emerged as growth sectors within tourism. Can academics and tourism researchers reading the tea leaves of new trends be confident that there really exist new trends, or is it a case that new products meet old needs for escape, seeking something different, but in reality do not lead to new modes of behaviour once the holidaymaker re-enters the daily world of domestic and work life? This chapter sets out some preliminary results from a study into Australians attitudes towards the environment and holiday activities based on wildlife attractions. Does there exist a new sensitivity towards the environment that informs attitudes towards wildlife locations? Do visitors learn something that changes their subsequent behaviours?

The study

The data for this chapter is derived from a study of responses made by 2334 respondents to a postal questionnaire. The chapter solely reviews descriptive data and at the time of writing further work has yet to be completed in terms of a more sophisticated analysis. Nor has any attempt yet been made to locate the work within the wider literature relating to wildlife management and tourism. In short it represents a work in progress. The sample was derived from a mail list of those Australians who had, in the period 1996 to 1998 undertaken a holiday that had involved a visit to Kakadu National Park. This criterion was selected because its location (in the Northern Territory), the nature of the Park as a World Heritage Site and its renowned reputation for birds, reptiles and large mammals like water buffalo represented the type of location to which tourists with an interest in nature based tourism and wild-life would be attracted. Indeed, because of the cost and effort required to reach the Park it can be thought that the sample represents a group with a significant interest in wildlife based tourist attractions. It is not therefore a sample of the wider Australian public. It can be considered to be a sample of active holidaymakers who have at least a modicum of interest in wildlife. The sample was derived from residents of New South Wales, Queensland, Victoria and South Australia as representing the major areas of population.

A total of 7,000 questionnaires were posted with a post-paid envelope that could be used by respondents with a covering letter explaining the purpose of the research. The initial large size meant that a workable sample was derived without a need for follow up procedures, something that in any case the research budget did not permit.

The questionnaire consisted of the following sections

- data on past holiday patterns in the last 12 months;

- a Likert scale requiring people to indicate level of importance of various features of Australia as a holiday destination;

- the New Environmental Paradigm questionnaire;

- statements about wildlife attractions that required a response about the level of agreement with the statement using a 5-point scale;

- a section requiring socio-demographic data; and

- a section eliciting open-ended responses.

The second section used a seven point Likert type scale with the option for non-response for the reasons provided by Ryan and Garland (1999). Simply such an option avoids use of the mid-point of the scale by people who have no knowledge upon which to base an opinion, while the pattern of non-response can be analysed to ascertain whether it is random. If it is not random, then this in itself becomes a source for further investigation. The items were from past studies by Ryan and Huyton (2000a) based on scales derived from physical manifestations of the Beard and Ragheb Leisure Motivation Scale re-located to an Australian context (Beard and Ragheb, 1983). The New Environmental Paradigm was introduced as a recognised measure of environmental awareness that permits cluster analysis. Additionally, because the Scale was used in a prior study by the New South Wales Environment Protection Agency it permitted comparison between samples.

It needs to be emphasised that this chapter does not attempt to report a full analysis of the data. The length and construction of the questionnaire plus the size of sample does not lend itself to a complete report within the permitted space. However, the results illustrate the existence of an ambiguity on the part of visitors to wildlife locations in that while adhering to conservation values they still wish for small group viewing activities. Such viewing runs the risk of negative intrusion effects because of a need for higher numbers of such groups and hence more frequent incursions on wildlife territories in the absence of any limits on numbers of visitors.

The sample characteristics

Of the 2334 respondents 964 were male, 1352 were female and 18 respondents did not provide details of their gender. Sixty-six percent of the sample was married or had a permanent partner. Sixteen percent had a child below the age of ten years, and 13 percent had children between the ages of 11 to 16 years of age. While the sample is biased towards older people this is not uncommon for this type of survey. Nonetheless, with the exception of those under the age of 18, the cell sizes are large enough to permit comparisons to be made. No correcting weighting techniques to account for differences between the sample and the wider Australian population have been undertaken in this analysis. The sample was asked whether they had had a holiday of over 6 or more days away from home the previous year and if so, where. Seventy-six percent of the sample had had such a holiday. Most of those who had not had such a holiday came from the 25 to 39 age group, while only 9 percent of the over 60s had not taken such a holiday. Approximately a quarter of those taking vacations had holidayed overseas in the previous 12 months. It can be concluded that the samples were 'active holidaytakers'. The respondents were also asked to indicate whether in the last 12 months they had visited a tourist attraction based on wildlife, the frequency of such visits, whether they had ever visited such an attraction in the past, and lastly whether they would ever wish to do. They were then presented with a list of potential wildlife tourist attractions. These data are summarised in Table 1.

Table 1   Use of Wildlife based on Tourism Attractions

Attraction	Number who have visited in last 12 months	Mean frequency of visit	Number who have ever visited	Number who would like to visit
A wildlife park	846	1.45	1096	421
A zoo	751	1.44	1192	259
Visiting sites known for bird life	607	1.69	1010	430
Visiting an aquarium	472	1.20	1263	317
Visiting a koala sanctuary	362	1.19	1256	318
Seeing crocodiles in natural surroundings	352	1.24	916	620
Going snorkelling	314	6.65	648	314
Dolphin watch trip	227	1.28	460	1161
A crocodile farm	204	1.08	812	432
Whale watch trip	187	1.14	430	1345
Camel riding	131	1.01	725	554
Going scuba diving	84	4.43	242	648
A shark watch/swim trip	66	1.12	177	609
Swim with dolphins	61	1.07	158	1242
Other wildlife activities	161	1.34	135	122

From Table 1 it can be seen that the most popular attractions are 'managed ones' like wildlife parks, zoos and aquaria. This popularity is evident by two measures, a) the number who have visited such an attraction in the last twelve months, and b) the number who, at any one time, have made such a visit in the past. Additionally it can be seen that passive sightseeing activities are more popular than more active wildlife attractions. Scuba diving or swimming with dolphins are ranked below activities like seeing crocodiles in natural settings or visiting sites known for their bird life, although the latter may require tramping to reach the site. Given the popularity of dolphin sites (Davis et al, 1997, Orams, 1997) it had been thought that these would have ranked more highly, but evidence for their popularity is evidenced in the final column of Table 1. This shows a high desire for future visits to this type of attraction. Given the basis of the sample, the comparatively low ranking of crocodiles might imply either a degradation of memory or a lack of importance being ascribed to this part of the sample's visit to the Northern Territory.

While active pursuits are engaged in by a small proportion of the total sample (for example only 3.6 percent went scuba diving in the previous twelve months), it is noticeable that the frequency with which scuba diving and snorkelling are undertaken is very high. Evidence from the open-ended comments indicates that these activities were very popular among a subset of the sample that lived near the coast. Similarly a large proportion of the sample had made two or more visits to zoos or wildlife parks in the past twelve months (7.1 percent and 7.8 percent respectively). Examining these two groups indicated that the presence of young children appeared to be a factor. In the case of zoos, of those with no children under the age of 10 years, only 33 percent visited a zoo (n=583). On the other hand 44 percent of those with children under the age of 10 (369 respondents had such children) did make such a visit, and indeed 10 percent of these parents had made two or more visits in the past year. Cross-tabulating numbers of visits to zoos and the presence of young children in a family showed a statistical correlation in that $\chi2 = 31.3$, $df=3$, $p=.000$. The same tendency emerged with visits to wildlife parks. Sixty percent of respondents who had children under the age of 10 had visited a Wildlife Park in the previous twelve months, whereas of those without such aged children, only 36 percent had made such a visit.

Table 2   Ratings of Importance of holiday activities and places

Activity/attraction	Mean Score	Standard Deviation	Number	Ryan & Huyton
Visit places that are different to elsewhere	6.16	1.20	2281	6.17
Look at animals in natural settings	5.97	1.31	2292	na
Visit National Parks	5.86	1.41	2289	5.73
Visit Australian 'icons' like Uluru	5.78	1.47	2271	5.90
Visit historic sites	5.57	1.47	2292	na
Just have fun with friends	5.55	1.47	2275	na
Visit family and friends	5.44	1.75	2233	1.89
Experience a vastness of space	5.42	1.70	2281	5.25
Go on outback tour	5.39	1.62	2269	4.25
Just have a quiet time with loved ones	5.37	1.60	2257	na
Meet new friends and interesting people	5.36	1.52	2280	4.99
Learn about animals, birds and plants	5.29	1.60	2270	4.78
Go bush walking	5.20	1.67	2251	4.57
Satisfy a sense of adventure	5.05	1.77	2199	5.04
Have comfortable motel/hotel accommodation	4.84	1.96	2253	4.56
Go swimming	4.75	2.00	2215	na
Go on tours guided by local Aboriginal people	4.58	1.94	2177	4.12
Go to restaurants	4.59	1.85	2266	na
Camp under the stars	4.52	2.02	2196	4.01
View Aboriginal Rock Art	4.36	1.88	2199	4.54
Go to the shows	4.16	1.93	2222	na
Go shopping	3.84	1.90	2225	na
See an Aboriginal Music and Dance Performance	3.84	1.90	2166	3.88
See crocodiles	3.79	1.82	2163	4.00
Go fishing	3.78	2.26	2146	2.02
Go canoeing/kayaking	3.14	1.82	1923	2.34
Sun bathe	3.07	2.10	2108	na
Buy authentic Aboriginal souvenirs	3.04	2.00	2046	3.22
Go dancing at clubs/discos	2.40	1.80	2037	na
Visit casinos and go gambling	2.20	1.77	2033	na
Go hunting	1.85	1.66	1845	0.85

Importance of wildlife based attractions

Table 1 indicates that wild life attractions are popular among visitors, but as an indicator of importance it suffers by not offering any comparative measures. Hence section two of the questionnaire contained, as previously stated, a list of tourist attractions and activities that tourists undertake in Australia. Among the purposes achieved by this list is that it represents a means by which the relative popularity of wildlife attractions can be assessed. The mean scores on a seven-point Likert type scale are shown in Table 2, where seven represents the highest score. Respondents were asked to indicate how important to them as holiday activities. The final column table of Table 4 includes mean scores from, as yet, unpublished research by Ryan and Huyton (2000b) derived from 358 interviews conducted at Alice Springs and Uluru. The commonality of results for many items is significant. From the perspective of wildlife it is worth noting that the current sample score higher on the item 'to learn about animals, birds and plants', implying that while many motivations are similar this sample does have a higher interest in natural things. They also rate bush walking and camping more highly than the Alice Springs/Uluru sample. In the final report it will be possible to provide more comparative data, but at this stage it would appear that this sample tends to have a higher interest in wildlife based attractions than the norm as might be expected from the sample composition and this is specifically demonstrated by the second place ranking gained by the item 'Look at animals in natural settings'.

Scores on the New Environmental Paradigm

The New Environmental Paradigm is a measure of sensitivity to environmental issues. It consists of the first 17 items listed in Table Three. The 18th item, about governments lacking the will to enact appropriate policies, was added in the light of the Howard Government in Australia seeking and gaining an increase in emission targets for Australia at the Kyoto Environmental Conference. Again the Table shows the mean scores and standard deviations for the whole sample. The five-point scale used by the New South Wales Environment Protection Authority (1997) was retained to permit comparisons. The higher the score the more respondents have tended to agree with the statement. Thus respondents tend to strongly agree with the statements that 'When humans interfere with nature it often produces disastrous consequences' (mean = 4.18) and 'Plants and animals have as much right as humans to exist' (4.41) among other statements. They tend to disagree with items like 'The balance of nature is strong enough to cope with the impacts of modern industrial nations' (2.03) implying a view of the fragility of natural systems, which is supported by other indices. Indeed it might be said that the scores indicate a tendency to pessimism although respondents seem to feel that as individuals they can do something even while governments appear to fail to enact the legislation their electorate may wish for.

Having ascertained data on respondents' tourist behaviour, their rating of the different attractions and activities in Australia and their environmental views, the next stage was to assess whether any linkages existed between them with specific reference to wildlife attractions. A first stage was to elicit responses to statements about the way in which wild animals are presented and their responses to those settings. These data are shown in Table Four. A five-point scale was used ranging from 1, 'Disagree strongly' to '5, 'Agree strongly'.

From the table the high rating attributed to dolphins is consistent with research in New Zealand, where New Zealanders also rated dolphin based attractions as one of the leading natural tourist attractions (Ryan, 1999). The difference in ratings as to the fascination that crocodiles and dolphins possess ($t=38.5$, $df = 2276$, $p=0.000$) is also consistent with the thesis advanced by Ryan (1998) that wildlife may be assessed by dimensions of familiarity, awe, comfort and difference. However the main finding from Table 4is that this sample is willing to accept controls on their ability to view animals in natural settings, although there still appears to be a reluctance to see animals in 'animal friendly' zoos. Given the popularity of zoos as an attraction, this implies that many who visit zoos may yet, nonetheless, be critical of them.

Table 3   Scores on the New Environmental Paradigm

Item	NSW 1997	Mean Score	Std Dev	Number NSW
We are approaching the limit of the number of people the earth can support	3.67	3.65	1.09	2325
Humans have the right to modify the natural environment to suit their needs	2.72	2.43	1.19	2312
When humans interfere with nature it often produces disastrous consequences	4.06	4.18	0.93	2324
Human ingenuity will ensure that we do NOT make the earth unliveable	3.01	2.87	1.07	2315
Humans are severely abusing the environment	4.08	4.10	0.95	2318
The earth has plenty of natural resources if we just learn how to develop them	3.76	3.66	1.11	2314
Plants and animals have as much right as humans to exist	4.33	4.41	0.82	2323
The balance of nature is strong enough to cope with the impacts of modern industrial nations	2.30	2.03	0.93	2322
Despite our special abilities humans are still subject to the laws of nature	4.03	4.22	0.70	2321
The so-called 'ecological crisis' facing humankind has been greatly exaggerated	2.50	2.30	1.02	2317
The earth is like a spaceship with very limited room and resources	3.51	3.53	1.07	2270
Humans were meant to rule over the rest of nature	2.27	2.34	1.13	2277
The balance of nature is very delicate and easily upset	3.97	4.19	0.81	2287
Humans will eventually learn enough about how nature works to be able to control it	2.89	2.68	1.01	2279
If things continue on their present course, we will soon experience a major ecological catastrophe	3.78	3.76	0.96	2280
There is a lot that I as an individual can do to help protect the environment	na	3.99	0.81	2284
Australia can no longer afford the luxury of having so many people drive cars to work.	na	3.76	0.94	2280
We know a lot about how human action effects the environment but governments lack the will to enact appropriate policies	na	4.17	0.84	2277

The next step was to identify clusters within the sample based on the New Environmental Paradigm. Five clusters were identified through the use of cluster analysis, and the different mean scores for each of the clusters on the Paradigm items are shown on Table 5. In each case the difference between the clusters was significant at $p < 0.001$. The clusters can be described as:

Table 4   Attitudes towards wildlife

Item	Mean score	Standard Deviation	Number
Dolphins are fascinating creatures	4.62	0.56	2319
I would accept controls on my ability to see wildlife in order to protect natural settings	4.11	0.77	2311
Dolphins are like humans in some ways	4.02	0.84	2311
Access to wild creatures in natural states should be tightly controlled even if it means higher prices for tourists	3.95	0.95	2316
The only way to appreciate wild life is to see it in natural settings	3.83	1.07	2280
Crocodiles are very different to mammals	3.80	0.86	2263
Crocodiles are fascinating creatures	3.79	0.97	2288
I would accept being on a bigger boat/vehicle to see wildlife as it means less trips to intrude on natural behaviours	3.74	0.96	2307
I would prefer being on smaller boats/vehicles as it means a more 'private' view	3.71	0.96	2299
Crocodiles scare me	3.62	1.15	2278
Our need to touch dolphins should not be encouraged	3.41	1.05	2307
I would prefer seeing animals in 'animal friendly zoos' rather than disturb natural settings	3.11	1.06	2304
It is all right to reinforce natural modes of animal behaviour to entertain tourists	2.65	1.05	2292

Cluster One - the Aprés Moi

This title was based on the supposed statement of Louis XV of France, that after him would occur the deluge that was to sweep away the Ancién Regime. This particular cluster agree that the balance of nature is delicate, can be upset (4.2) and that human activity is abusing the environment (4.2). They are pessimistic that humans will learn sufficient about nature to know how to control it (2.3) and tend to agree that the continuation of present policies can only lead to a major ecological catastrophe (3.7). However they have the highest score on the item that humans were meant to rule over the rest of nature, albeit this is not a strong view (3.2), but equally they have, for this sample, a low score that by their own actions they could help the environment (3.8). They feel that government has no will to enact appropriate policies (4.2).

This group numbered 398 and formed 18.3 per cent of the sample.

Cluster two - the optimists

Numbering 345 (15.9 percent of the sample) this group had the lowest scores relating to a perception of reaching the limits of the earth's resources (2.8), the highest score that indicated a belief that human ingenuity could solve the problems (3.7), and that the earth has plenty of natural resources should we learn how to develop them (4.1). They also had the lowest score on the item about a lack of government will to enact appropriate policies (3.5). They also tended to disagree with the statement that Australia could no longer afford the luxury of having so many people drive to work (2.9).

Cluster three - the 'very concerned'

For the '*Very Concerned*', the crisis is now! The earth's natural balance is delicate (4.7), human action is abusing the environment (4.7), the ecological crisis has not been exaggerated (1.5), the limits of the earth's resources are being approached (4.3) and governments seem blind to the need to enact legislation (4.6). Nonetheless this group feel that individuals can do something about the environment (4.1). The group numbered 647, that is 29.8 percent of the sample and thus is the largest individual sub-group.

Cluster four - the 'less pessimistic'

This group shares many of the same views of the previous group, but not to the same extent. It too believes that balance of nature is delicate (4.3), and that should things continue there could be a catastrophe (3.9). They also share some features with the first cluster in that like them they have a moderate belief in human ingenuity (3.2 as against the 3.1 of the *Après Moi*). Where this group appears to differ from the *Après Moi* is in the right of humans to modify the natural environment. The *Après Moi* score more highly than the *Less Pessimistic* on items like 'humans have the right to modify the natural environment' (3.3 *cf* 1.9) and 'humans were meant to rule over the rest of nature' (3.4 *cf* 1.9). They also believe that the earth has plenty of natural resources if 'we just learn how to develop them' (4.4). This cluster may be said to occupy a space between the *Après Moi* and *The Very Concerned*, and possess a view that human intervention in natural affairs is appropriate. They form 20.3 percent of the sample.

Cluster five - the 'nebulous'

While this group also expresses some pessimistic views about human activity on the natural environment it also scores comparatively low on the item that as an individual there is much that can be done (3.7). Yet they also have the second lowest score on the item about Australia being able to afford current patterns of car driving and are not so ready as others to state that governments lack the will to do enact appropriate policies (3.7) - although such a score cannot be construed as an endorsement of government policies. Apart from the pessimism expressed by this group it is hard to specify the points of distinction from the other groupings, other to say that statistically the differences are significant. As can be seen from Table 7 their scores tend to fall in the mid point of the others. The group accounted for 15.7 percent of the sample.

As stated the next stage was to examine the relationship between the different clusters and their attitudes towards wildlife. Did, for example the '*Optimists*' have different attitudes to those of the '*Very Concerned*', and if so in what direction? An analysis of variance was undertaken for the items in Table Four. The results are shown in Table Six. These show fairly clearly that those who are most worried about the state of the environment tend to appreciate wild animals more and, while agreeing with the statement that animals are best seen in their natural settings, are, in fact, more willing to accept controls on their access to the animals. Indeed, it is interesting to note that the '*Optimists*' are the least likely to view animals in 'animal friendly' zoos. Again, the '*Optimists*' are the least likely to support a move towards larger vehicles for sightseeing on the basis that it may mean fewer sightseeing trips (thereby perhaps removing some stress for the animals). They are also the least concerned about humans touching dolphins.

Table 5   Cluster group Mean Scores

Item	Apres Moi	Optimists	Very Concerned	Less Pessimist	Nebulous
We are approaching the limit of the number of people the earth can support	3.8	2.8	4.3	3.1	3.5
Humans have the right to modify the natural environment to suit their needs	3.3	3.6	1.7	1.9	2.2
When humans interfere with nature it often produces disastrous consequences	4.3	3.4	4.7	4.5	3.4
Human ingenuity will ensure that we do NOT make the earth unliveable	3.1	3.7	2.2	3.2	2.7
Humans are severely abusing the environment	4.2	3.0	4.7	4.3	3.7
The earth has plenty of natural resources if we just learn how to develop them	3.7	4.1	3.0	4.4	3.3
Plants and animals have as much right as humans to exist	4.1	3.7	4.8	4.7	4.3
The balance of nature is strong enough to cope with the impacts of modern industrial nations	2.2	3.0	1.4	2.1	1.9
Despite our special abilities humans are still subject to the laws of nature	4.2	3.9	4.5	4.1	4.0
The so-called 'ecological crisis' facing humankind has been greatly exaggerated	2.5	3.4	1.5	2.4	2.3
The earth is like a spaceship with very limited room and resources	3.8	2.7	4.3	2.8	3.4
Humans were meant to rule over the rest of nature	3.4	3.2	1.6	1.9	2.1
The balance of nature is very delicate and easily upset	4.2	3.4	4.7	4.3	3.9
Humans will eventually learn enough about how nature works to be able to control it	2.3	3.4	2.1	2.9	2.4
If things continue on their present course, we will soon experience a major ecological catastrophe	3.7	2.6	4.4	3.9	3.5
There is a lot that I as an individual can do to help protect the environment	3.8	3.8	4.1	4.2	3.7
Australia can no longer afford the luxury of having so many people drive cars to work.	3.8	2.9	4.2	3.8	3.4
We know a lot about how human action effects the environment but governments lack the will to enact appropriate policies	4.2	3.5	4.6	4.3	3.7
Number in cluster	398	345	647	442	340

It is also interesting that while the '*Aprés Moi*' were distinguished by a feeling that they could perhaps do little as individuals about the environment, they nonetheless would happily accede to policies designed to minimise negative impacts on wildlife.

Table 6   Attitudes towards wildlife by cluster groupings

Item	Apres Moi	Optimists	Very Concerned	Less Pess	Nebolous
Dolphins are fascinating creatures	4.6	4.4	4.7	4.7	4.5
I would accept controls on my ability to see wildlife in order to protect natural settings	4.1	3.7	4.4	4.1	4.0
Dolphins are like humans in some ways	4.0	3.8	4.1	4.2	3.8
Access to wild creatures in natural states should be tightly controlled even if it means higher prices for tourists	3.9	3.5	4.2	4.0	3.7
The only way to appreciate wild life is to see it in natural settings	3.8	3.5	3.9	4.0	3.6
Crocodiles are very different to mammals	3.9	3.8	3.8	3.6	3.7
Crocodiles are fascinating creatures	3.7	3.6	3.9	3.9	3.6
I would accept being on a bigger boat/vehicle to see wildlife as it means less trips to intrude on natural behaviours	3.8	3.5	3.9	3.8	3.6
I would prefer being on smaller boats/vehicles as it means a more 'private' view	3.9	3.7	3.8	3.6	3.6
Crocodiles scare me	3.7	3.6	3.5	3.7	3.6
Our need to touch dolphins should not be encouraged	3.4	3.2	3.6	3.3	3.3
I would prefer seeing animals in 'animal friendly zoos' rather than disturb natural settings	3.2	2.9	3.2	3.2	3.1
It is all right to reinforce natural modes of animal behaviour to entertain tourists	2.9	3.0	2.3	2.6	2.7

Did any relationship exist between the clusters and past holiday behaviours? The only statistically significant relationship that appeared to exist was that the *Optimists* indicated a higher predisposition to visit National Parks ($\chi2 = 15.58$, df=8, p=0.048). It thus appears that no relationship existed between attitudes as measured by the New Environmental Paradigm and actual past or intended predisposition to attend tourist attractions based on nature or wildlife. To further examine this relationship the question arose as to how independent of socio-demographic factors were the identified clusters. It emerged that age, sex and level of education were possible determinants of the cluster. For example the over 60s were over-represented among the '*Optimists*' and the '*Aprés Moi*' while the under-thirties were over-represented among the '*Very Concerned*' and the '*Less Pessimistic*' ($X^2=106.2$, $df = 32$, $p = .000$). Similarly females formed 62 percent of the '*Very Concerned*', but only 40 percent of the *The Optimists* ($X^2=98.0$, $df = 4$, $p = .000$), and level of attained education was also linked with 71 percent of the '*Very Concerned*' comprising of those with graduate or post-graduate qualifications. This 'educational' group formed 56 percent of '*Less Pessimistic*' ($X^2=41.0$, $df = 12$, $p = .017$). The presence or absence of children was not a factor in this instance. If therefore no relationship was found between cluster type based on the New Environmental Paradigm and past holiday activities, but a strong correlation existed between socio-demographic variables and the clusters, then it would follow that no relationship should exist between socio-demographic variables and past holiday activity. However, it had already been noted that visits to zoos and wildlife parks had been affected by whether young children existed in the family. The thesis was thus formulated that on the whole socio-demographic variables would not be a predictor of past holiday activity other than at the margins where threshold affects might operate. For example, it might be thought that age and going scuba diving might be related, but as already noted, scuba diving was a minority choice. This thesis was then examined. Using tests of categorical data and analysis of variance it was found that socio-demographics variables had no statistical relationship with the holiday activities and wildlife attractions listed in Table 1 with one exception. Males tended to have more frequently visited crocodiles in a natural setting that females where $p < 0.05$. The only other factor of importance was the presence of young children in families as previously noted with reference to visits to zoos, wildlife parks and aquariums.

Conclusions

This preliminary analysis leads to the following conclusions:

(a) Wildlife attractions appeal across a wide range of the public. In this sample of people who had visited wildlife attractions in the last three years no relationship was found between frequency of visit and socio-demographic variables like age, gender or level of education. The only factor that did affect the rate of visitation to certain attractions was whether young children existed within a family. Zoos, aquariums and wildlife parks were more likely to be visited if a family contained young children.

(b) While rates of visitation to a natural attraction cannot be predicted on the basis of socio-demographic variables, the sample revealed that wildlife parks, zoos, sites known for bird life and aquariums were among the most frequently visited locations. However a very high potential demand exists for sea mammal based operations in that high levels of desired future visitation was expressed by the sample.

(c) From the responses to the New Environmental Paradigm Scale, a cluster analysis revealed five groups of people. However no relationship was found between cluster membership and rates of visitation to wildlife attractions. On the other hand those visiting wildlife attraction will evidence varying levels of concern with environmental issues, and most visitors will be sensitive to and appreciate messages relating to environmental issues. Also, considering that a high proportion do believe that individual action can be effective, messages that show how individuals can impact upon the environment in positive ways will be appreciated by a large proportion of visitors (e.g. see Aiello, 1998).

(d) A relationship was found between cluster groupings and their attitudes towards wildlife attractions once they were making a visit. For example the most environmentally sensitive were more inclined to accept controls which limited their touching or approaching wild-life. Given that this sub-sample accounts for about 30 percent of the total sample, this is significant. As, with the exception of the 'Optimists', the other groups tend towards a similar position, this means that up to 85 percent of visitors to wildlife attractions may accept controls.

(e) However, the attitudes expressed remain ambiguous. Visitors still wish to have 'private' views and over 66 percent still scored 4 or above on a 5-point scale stating that the only way to appreciate wild life is to see it in natural settings. This compares with 86 percent of the sample expressing agreement or 'strong agreement' with the view that controls on access to wildlife should be used. In short, while many accept the need for some limitation on viewing wildlife, a strong preference continues to see wildlife in a natural setting, in spite of the possible detrimental affects upon animals' behaviour, territories, food gathering and breeding patterns. However, if instructions are specific it is proposed that the majority of people will adhere to those instructions. It can be argued that seeing wildlife in a natural setting is not inconsistent with controls or a means of arranging small party access to wildlife, but the need to manage such encounters becomes obvious.

In turn it might be said that these conclusions give rise to the following pragmatic management implications. These include:

(a) Visitors will generally accept restrictions upon access to wildlife under natural conditions, but the need for such restrictions need to be explained.

(b) There exists an ambiguity on the part of visitors in that they still prefer visits to be undertaken in small groups. In some instances this is preferable in terms of mitigating intrusion upon wildlife, but as numbers of visitors increase this may cause disturbance because of the need for a larger number of visits. Fewer visits in larger groups, which might not approach animals so closely, will be an acceptable alternative to many visitors, but this again implies a requirement to explain reasons for these policies.

(c) Visitor requirements can be satisfied within managed wildlife environments that are perceived to be 'animal friendly' - that is they seek to replicate as far as is possible the natural environment. However, in practice this may impose limitations upon the numbers of any one species within a given area, and this has implications for issues like breeding programs and possibly culling.

(d) Visitors to wildlife attraction tend to visit many such attractions. They will make comparisons between what they see as 'best practice'. Hence it can be hypothesised that any wildlife attraction that does not undertake benchmarking to ensure it adheres to 'best practice' will find high levels of visitor dissatisfaction.

(e) Finally, managed wildlife attractions like zoos are attractive to families with young children. Such sites need to be managed with this in mind and indeed many are.

So, where does this leave us, other than with the point that more research is needed both in terms of completing the analysis of the current dataset and extending research beyond the current phase. This research began with an expectation that wildlife attractions would appeal to specific market segments. There is no evidence to support this. Little correlation was found between environmental awareness and attitudes towards such products. In short perhaps Wheeller (1993) was right. Our eco-tourists remain but tourists oblivious to the motives and behavioural changes academics impute towards categorisations that evolve from scales where visitors agree that they are interested in learning, beauty and conservation. As Mandy Rice Davies stated, albeit in another situation, 'they would say that, wouldn't they!'

Acknowledgements

The financial support of the Wildlife Research Programme of the Co-operative Research Centre for Sustainable Tourism, Gold Coast, Australia, is duly acknowledged. The CRC have also allocated funding for future work. The support of Professor Greg Hill, Northern Territory University is also acknowledged.

References

Aiello, R. (1998), Interpretation and the Marine Tourism Industry, Who needs it? A case study of Great Adventures, *Australia, Journal of Tourism Studies*, 9, (1), pp.51-61.

Beard, J., and Ragheb, M.G. (1983), Measuring Leisure Motivation, *Journal of Leisure Research*, 15, (3), pp.219-228.

Blamey, R. (1995), The Nature of Ecotourism, Occasional Paper No 21, *Bureau of Tourism Research*, Canberra, Commonwealth of Australia.

Blamey, R., and Hatch, D. (1998), Profiles and Motivations of Nature-Based Tourists Visiting Australia, Occasional Paper No 25. *Bureau of Tourism Research*, Canberra, Commonwealth of Australia.

Davis, D., Banks, S., Birtles, A., Valentine, P., and Cuthill, M. (1997), Whale sharks in Ningaloo Marine Park: Managing tourism in an Australian marine protected area, *Tourism Management* 18, (5), pp.259-272.

Eagles, P, F.J. (1992), The Motivations of Canadian Ecotourists, in Weiler, B, (Editor) Ecotourism: Incoprorating the Global Classroom, *Bureau of Tourism Research*, Canberra: Commonwealth of Australia.

Environment Protection Authority New South Wales, (1997), *Who Cares About the Environment in 1997?*, Chatswood, NSW: Environment Protection Authority New South Wales

Mckercher, B. (1993), Some Fundamental Truths About Tourism: Understanding Tourism's Social and Environmental Impacts, *The Journal of Sustainable Tourism*, 1, (1), pp.6-16.

Orams, M.B. (1997), Historical accounts of human-dolphin interaction and recent developments in wild dolphin based tourism in Australasia, *Tourism Management* 18, (5), pp.317-326.

Ryan, C. (1997), *The Tourist Experience - a new approach*, London, Cassell.

Ryan, C. (2000), Tourism and cultural proximity – Maori and Pakeha. Paper submitted to *Annals of Tourism*.

Ryan, C., and Garland, R. (1999), The use of a specific non-response option on Likert type scales, *Tourism Management*, 20, (1), pp.107-115.

Ryan, C., and Huyton, J. (2000a), Aboriginal tourism - a linear structural equations analysis of domestic and international tourist demand, *International Journal of Tourism Research*. 2 (1), pp.15-30.

Ryan, C., and Huyton, J. (2000b), Balanda visitors to Central Australia - their perceptions. Paper submitted to *Annals of Tourism*

Wheeller, B. A. (1993), Sustaining the Ego, *The Journal of Sustainable Tourism*, 1, (2), pp.121-129.

Tourism as a sensory transition: The impact of the process of travelling on the tourist experience

Tom Selanniemi

The Finnish University Network for Tourism Studies, Finland

Abstract

In this paper I will explore how the relation between the tourist and the place visited is affected by the process of travelling drawing on my own fieldwork among Finnish tourists in many Mediterranean tourist destinations, like Athens and Rhodes in Greece and Bodrum in Turkey, as well as Gran Canaria in Spain and Aqaba in Jordan. In some types of recreational mass tourism to beach resorts the local heritage or the spirit of place is of marginal importance. In other types of tourism, like cultural tourism to Athens, the importance of the place is central to the tourist experience and, thus, the journey can be described as a secular pilgrimage. But it seems that in all types of recreational tourism the transition, or even transgression, from home and everyday life into holiday and what could be described as the liminoid space and time is central to the way in which we as tourists experience our environment.

In the paper I, will from an emic perspective, analyse the tourists' experiences and compare cultural tourism to beach tourism in order to cast light on the tourists' own experiences in both types. This analysis casts doubts on what could be called the 'authenticity paradigm' in the anthropology and sociology of tourism. My aim is to show that by understanding the tourist trip as a fourfold transition from home to holiday, a spatial, temporal, mental and sensory transition, it is possible to analyse the experiences of tourists in destinations ranging from beach resorts to cultural attractions without value-laden notions on authenticity or inauthenticity of places or experiences.

Introduction

In this paper I will explore the relation between the tourist and the place visited drawing on my own fieldwork among Finnish tourists in many Mediterranean tourist destinations, like Athens and Rhodes in Greece and Bodrum in Turkey, as well as Gran Canaria in Spain and Aqaba in Jordan. In some types of recreational mass tourism to beach resorts the local heritage or the spirit of place is of marginal importance. In other types of tourism, like cultural tourism to Athens, the importance of the place is central to the tourist experience and, thus, the journey can be described as a secular pilgrimage. But what seems to be in the heart of the tourist experience in not necessarily the place visited itself. More important in the formation of a tourist experience is the fact that in order to be a tourist one has to go through a series of transitions, and that process influences the way we react to stimuli in our holiday surroundings.

Tourism to the Mediterranean region and the Canary Islands has become an integral part of modern Finnish culture, which is indicated by the adoption of special terms into the spoken language. Finns very often refer to their holiday destinations with the concept *"etela"* (=south) without clarifying more exactly what geographical place they are talking about. Common phrases are *"kavimme etelassa lomalla"* (we went to the south on our holiday), *"lahden etelanmatkalle"* (I will go to the south) etc. The concept "etela" is widely used also in tourism marketing, especially in newspaper advertisements, sometimes without any clear indications of where this "south" is.

The difference between the destinations studied as well as the tourists travelling to these destinations comes forth very clearly in the motives for choosing a certain destination. When tourists in my field work destinations were asked why they had chosen this one, only the tourists in Athens (67%) and Aqaba (46%) answered that their main singular motive for choosing the destination was the place's culture or history. For the tourists in the other destinations the culture and history had no importance. Instead, motives that are interchangeable between any tourist destination in the "south", were given as answers to the open question in the questionnaire. The sun and the climate, familiarity of the place and suitability of the flight or date of departure are motives for destination choice that are not related culturally or geographically to any specific location.

The holiday destinations and their Finnish tourists: Two examples

Playa del Ingles

Gran Canaria is an island located just off the Moroccan coast north of the Tropic of Cancer. The island has since the beginning of the 1970's been one of the most popular destinations for Finnish tourists during the winter season. Playa del Ingles in the southern part of the island, together with nearby Maspalomas and Puerto Rico, receive the majority of Finns travelling to Gran Canaria. In 1991 a total of 283.003 Finnish tourists travelled to the Canary Islands by charter planes. During the economic recession the number has decreased.

Playa del Ingles on Gran Canaria is probably one of the best examples of a tourist resort with minimal attributes of local cultural authenticity. In the area of Playa del Ingles and nearby Maspalomas there has never been any local habitation or local culture. The hotels and restaurants were constructed on the sand dunes of Maspalomas, where there was nothing but sand and sea in the early sixties, except for a couple of fishermen's huts. In the early days of tourism to the Canary Islands tourists sometimes took a taxi from Las Palmas to Maspalomas to enjoy the natural scenery and privacy of the place. Nowadays there are about 200.000 beds in the hotels of the area.

The cleanly paved streets of Playa del Ingles are lined with supermarkets, fast food stalls, pubs and restaurants, and, of course, hotels. Alongside these there are several shopping centres or malls in the area of Ingles and Maspalomas. To cater the Finnish tourist, there are Finnish shops, bars, restaurants and nightclubs, like Casa Finlandia with karaoke-singing in Finnish, and Tiffany with Finnish popular music artists performing almost every night. These services, together with the large number of mostly retired Finnish tourists, probably make the Finns feel very much at home in Playa del Ingles. In a way, Playa del Ingles could be described as an *extension of the tourists' home culture* (see Hanefors and Larsson 1989; 1993), the southernmost province of Finland. Similarly and simultaneously with the "little Finland" in Playa del Ingles there exists little Swedens, Englands, Germanies etc.

In one of the diaries I asked the Finnish tourists to write on their holiday, a middle-aged woman from a rural area in Finland expresses the journey to Gran Canaria as a journey to the summer, away from the arctic winter in Finland. The thought of the south as eternal summer, like the summers of childhood when it was always warm and you seemed to have almost unlimited time at your disposal, is clearly present in this diary. Another way of returning to childhood on a trip to the south is expressed by the writer when she writes about the enjoyment of feeling the heat under the bare feet, just the way it was when she was a child (cf. Game 1991, p.177).

The change from the cold countryside of central Finland with hard agricultural labour seem to be absolutely wonderful. She does not express any kind of wish to get into contact with local people, not even to see other ways of life - she and her husband even dine either at the apartment or at the Finnish restaurant Casa Finlandia! These tourists are happy with the "south", where they can do as they please in their own rhythm. The writer expresses almost daily how wonderful the climate and the warmth is.

Rhodes

The island of Rhodes in Greece has been one of the most popular summer destinations for Finnish vacationers since the beginnings of mass tourism from Finland at the end of the sixties. According to the statistics of the Dodecanese branch of the National Tourist Organization of Greece 86.883 Finns spent their holiday on Rhodes in 1989. Finns were the third largest group of tourists on Rhodes by nationality after British and German tourists. From those days the number of Finns travelling abroad on holiday has decreased drastically, but Rhodes still receives about 50.000 Finnish tourists yearly.

The island of Rhodes is located just 20 km off the Turkish coast. It is the largest island in the Dodecanese archipelago and it is about 65 km long and 20 km wide. Rhodes is very rich in history and has a favourable climate - elements that have contributed to the development of one of the most popular tourist destinations in the Mediterranean region. The main historical attractions on the island are the acropolis of Lindos, the archaeological site of Kamiros and, of course, the medieval old town of Rhodes that is included in the UNESCO World Heritage list. Cultural history is, however, not what brings tourists to Rhodes. The attractiveness of the island and especially the town of Rhodes lies in good beach facilities, ample tourist services, a vital night life and, most important (at least for the Finnish tourists), almost secure sunshine during the six months of summer. The tourist influx has been so intense in the town of Rhodes that the northern tip of the town where most of the hotels, restaurants and bars are located, is more resemblant to the tourists' home cultures than anything Greek or Rhodian.

The diaries that some tourists kept for me during their stay on Rhodes, and my observations, confirm that Finnish tourists enjoy the unstructured time usage while on holiday. The tourists do not have to conform to any time-tables, they have the freedom to eat, sleep, drink and do whatever whenever they please - and they use this freedom. The climate - the warm sun - is always mentioned in the diaries, often with at least an implicit comparison to the uncertainty of nice weather in Finland. The sun is clearly the most important entity in the holiday experience. All the rest is depending on the climate, as comes forth in the sections, where people write about rainy days or cold days and the trouble to find anything to do and, consequently, of the frustration about the lack of the thing they came all the way here to enjoy: the sun.

Sensing the "south"

Art historian E.H. Gombrich has written that looking is to seeing what listening is to hearing (Gombrich 1979: 199). This metaphor comes well to hand when analysing the ways tourists look at their touristic environments on beaches, in museums, souvenir shops, etc. Different tourists look at their environment and objects in it in different culturally constructed ways and, consequently, see these things differently. Thus, the same tourist attraction is looked at in different ways and also perceived differently. The Acropolis of Athens, for instance, may for some tourists be seen only as a sight among others, a ruin, and for other tourists it can be seen as the perfection of classical architecture and a symbol of western civilisation - a goal for a secular pilgrimage (Selanniemi 1994a).

The way tourists look at their environment can be roughly dichotomized. The first type of looking could be called *the travelling eye* and the second type *the fastening gaze*. The travelling eye wanders over the landscape or view without fixing on details or objects if they are not special in some way or interesting to the tourist. This type of gaze looks for the impression of a place, not for specific information about a place. The fastening gaze focuses on details, looking for information and observing the objects. It does not wander like the travelling eye, it moves from one object or detail to another. In museums and on archaeological sites the fastening gaze is characteristic of the cultural tourists and the pilgrims, and the travelling eye of the holiday makers (Selanniemi 1994a; 1994b; 1994c; 1996). In the old town of Athens, the Plaka, and especially on the streets with souvenir shops, on the hyperpolished streets of Playa del Ingles, and in the towns of Aqaba, Bodrum and Rhodes, almost all tourists have a travelling eye.

The two ways of looking at objects are related to the different backgrounds of the tourists. In order to be able to read the display in a museum or the ruins e.g. on Acropolis, in Ephesus or Petra, the tourists need some kind of information about what they look at. The speech of the tour guide or the text in the guidebook, if used as the only information, produces mostly the travelling eye -type of looking. The more thorough the preparation for confronting the sight is the more intense the gaze will develop. An education in for instance art history or the history of ancient Greece in the case of the Acropolis gives more significance to the sight in the tourists eyes, and thus produces a gaze interested in details and information: the fastening gaze. (Selanniemi 1994b.)

In Rhodes tourists very often walk around the old town with the travelling eye focusing only on objects for sale on Socratous street. Few tourists stop at the end of Ippoton, one of the best preserved medieval streets of Europe, and if they stop, it is only to take a photo with someone posing in front of the view. In the observation material from Rhodes there is only a few examples of tourists that obviously are aware of the historical importance of the medieval town of Rhodes and come for instance to the Ippoton in order to *see* it. Tourists very often walk through places like the old town of Rhodes, the Acropolis, Ephesus or Petra taking some snapshots with the companion posing in front of the view, and looking at something without really seeing anything, their eyes searching for the closest toilet or (to put it sarcastically) grieving over the loss of one sunny day on the beach (Selanniemi 1994b).

Thus, everything in mass tourism is not about looking at places, or to put it more exactly, to see places. The sense of sight is not exclusive in experiences of the vacation. The tourists seem to enjoy pleasures derived from tactile stimuli of a very basic nature, like heat or the cooling seawater on your skin. These are pleasures we do not necessarily experience or pay attention to in everyday life, or we do not have time to stop to enjoy them. As Pasi Falk (1994, p.2) has written: • the human body as a sensory and sensual being presupposes always (already) its counterpart, the 'sensible' body, that is, a body subsumed to a cultural Order - both symbolic and practical - defining its boundaries and its position in the larger whole (community or society). Maybe the transition from home to the south in suntourism could be understood also as a transgression of the boundaries of the sensible body. The diary of the 52-year-old lady from the countryside of central Finland, alongside with the other diaries included in my material about Finnish tourism to Playa del Ingles (and Rhodes and Bodrum) accentuate the point made by Soile Veijola and Eeva Jokinen (1994) that the tourist• s body is largely absent in studies on tourism. Focusing on the tourist gaze (Urry 1990) or on MacCannell's (1973; 1989) theories based on the primacy of visual stimuli in the tourist experience are not sufficient in analysing this type of suntourism to beach resorts.

The tourist experiences the "south" synesthetically. On different occasions different senses take priority over the others, but the tourist experience is very seldom purely aesthetical as the above mentioned theories largely claim (cf. Jokinen and Veijola 1994). A simple example clarifies this well: Turn on your television set and video unit and play a tape with views from a strange location but turn the volume to zero. Have you experienced anything like this when you have been a tourist? The closest you might get would be touring a place in a fully air-conditioned bus just driving past places never stopping and getting outside the bus. As soon as the bus stops and opens its doors local odours, noise and temperature can be sensed. When you step out you can immediately feel the intense sunshine and heat on your skin (if we pretend that the bus is driving for instance in Rhodes at summertime), you can smell the wonderful odours of the nearby tavern preparing dolmades and moussaka alongside the smell of the neighbouring butcher;s gutter that makes you a bit nauseous. You feel the grip of the souvenir seller, when he directs you into his shop and taste the ouzo he is offering you. After the round-trip you feel hot and dirty on your skin and decide to take a dip in the sea, which feels nicely cooling on the skin. You forget to take a shower after swimming in the sea water, so after a while in the sun you feel much more unpleasant sensations on your skin. After greasing your back (or somebody else has spread lotion on it = more tactile stimuli), you decide to leave the beach and have dinner, where your senses of taste and smell are once more activated. Finally you experience a "bodily communitas" in a nearby disco before returning back to the hotel, alone or with someone.

As the above example shows, we can perceive the slum we are passing by in an air-conditioned bus to be looking dirty and ugly. But only if we open the window and let the smells of gutters enter our noses do we realize how repulsive the place really is. A person who only sees is a sight-seer who does not interact in any other way with the environment. A world sensed by sight is more abstract than a world sensed with other senses also (Tuan 1974). While the local residents live the place the sight-seer merely gazes upon it. As Yi-Fu Tuan writes:

> *The visitor's evaluation of environment is essentially aesthetic. It is an outsiders view. The outsider judges by appearance, by some formal canon of beauty. A special effort is required to empathize with the lives and values of the inhabitants.* (Tuan 1974: 64).

An object or place becomes concrete reality in our minds only when our experience of it is total, that is, we perceive it actively and reflexively with all our senses (Tuan 1977: 18).

The majority of the sociological treatments on tourism have concentrated on this superficial way of perceiving places and objects, namely the gaze. In fact, the term tourist refers mainly to a person who tours different places and looks at sights. This ocularcentrism in tourism theory is probably a result of the distinction between "higher" and • lower• senses in the western philosophical tradition (cf. Falk 1994: 10-11). In the Aristotelian hierarchy of senses sight, hearing and smell were classified as human senses and taste and touch were animal senses (Synnott 1991: 65). Even though we normally think that sense perception is more a physical than a cultural phenomenon the way we interpret and classify our perceptions is culturally patterned. Not even the five senses of the Aristotelian tradition are culturally universal as for instance in some Buddhist cultures the mind is categorized as the sixth sense and among the Hausa in Nigeria there are only two senses, sight and all other senses. (Howes and Classen 1991: 257-258; Classen 1993: 1-3.) Nevertheless, in the sociology of tourism much attention has been given to the nature of sights and attractions and the problematics of authenticity with MacCannell (1973; 1989) in the lead, or to how tourists gaze upon these sights (cf. Urry 1990). The attentions has, thus, been directed towards those types of tourism that have the "highest" Aristotelian human sense, the sight, in its centre and the animal senses, and thus, the body, has been given less attention. It is peculiar to notice then, that the tourism of the educated middle classes where looking at authentic (or perceivedly authentic) sights or cultures with the human sense of sight has been in the focus of scholars who also come from the educated middle class and, most probably, engage themselves in this type of tourism, while the lower middle class/working class mass tourism to sunlust destinations where the Aristotelian animal senses are in the centre have been much neglected or treated with value-laden theory. But, as Walter Ong (1967: 74) argues, the sense of sight can only reveal surfaces but never the real inside which also influences understanding:

If understanding is conceived of by analogy with sight alone ... rather than by analogy also with hearing ... as well as with smell and taste, understanding is ipso facto condemned to dealing with surfaces which have a "beyond" it can never attain to.

During tourist trips our relations to the environment are more physical and sensual than in our everyday lives. This opens the possibility to rediscover aspects of childhood spontaneity and directness. (Curtis and Pajaczkowska 1994: 206-207.) The inherent nostalgia in tourism does not limit itself only to longing for the past and admiration of historical monuments, but it may be more powerful in childlike bodily experiences - like in the example from the diary cited above where the lady walked bare feet in the hot sand which brought back to her the childhood summers with their bodily experiences. A similar observation is made by Jennifer Beer on Japanese tourists:

Tourism permits fanciful engagements with "authentic" times past or elegant futures; in the same manner, it allows tourists to enjoy a nostalgic child-like awareness of the body. (Beer 1993: 229).

According to Orvar Löfgren (1990) behind the Swedish sunlust tourism was a dream of a different land, a dream of turning into a different person by travelling to the sunlust destination - different in the way of being more sensual, more lazy and relaxed and more bodily. This dream of freedom in the different land did not only concern the cliché of excessive sex, food and drink stereotypically connected to sunlust tourism, but Löfgren stresses that especially in the early days of mass tourism the trip to the south offered freedom and a possibility to "unswedish" behaviour - of Swedish behaviour of the kind that is kept uder control in the home country by habits, routines and social control. (Löfgren 1990: 36).

The fourfold transition

A good clue to understanding the phenomenon of mass tourism comes from the anthropological theories on the ritual process, especially the writings on transition rites by van Gennep (1960: 1908) and Turner (1978). In transition rites, of which initiations are a case in point, the ritual subjects go through phases that are called preliminal, liminal, and postliminal. The preliminal is the normal profane state of being, the liminal phase is sacred, anomalous, abnormal and dangerous, and the postliminal is the normal state of things to which the ritual subject re-enters after the transition. The liminal is a state and a process in the transition phase during which the ritual subjects pass a cultural area or zone that has minimal attributes of the states preceding or following the liminal. This "betweenness" has been compared to e.g. death, bisexuality and invisibility. (Turner and Turner 1978.) Nelson Graburn(1989) has, by using Leach's (1982) refinements on van Gennep's and Turner's theories, shown how tourism can be understood as a journey to the sacred in an analogy with transition rites.

The stage in tourism that resembles the liminal stage or phase in rites of passage could be called the *liminoid* or *quasiliminal* in Turner's terms. The liminoid is related to the ritually liminal, but it is not identical with it. The main difference is that the liminoid is *produced and consumed by individuals* and the liminal is believed by the members of society to be of divine origin and is to its nature anonymous. The liminoid is also fragmentary compared to the liminal. Often elements of the liminal have been separated from the whole to act individually in specialized fields like art. (Turner and Turner 1978, p. 253.) In art, popular culture, entertainment and tourism products are made for consumption by individuals and groups that promise to remove the consumer away from the everyday experience. They promise a transition into a stage that resembles the liminal for a limited time-span. The attractiveness of mass tourism lies in the possibility to be transported and transformed for a moment into the liminoid where "everything is possible".

When tourists enter the *liminoid* some changes take place. Normal social time stops in the marginal state of liminality, and it seems to stop also in the liminoid south. People normally confined to the everyday timetables and routines forget the lapse of time and sleep late, eat whenever it suits them, follow no or flexible time schedules, party until they drop and so on. One of the freedoms of the • • • • • • • is that you do not *have* to do anything. (Selanniemi 1996.) Social antistructure or the so called *communitas* - undifferentiated, democratic, direct, and spontaneous social bonds or contacts - is characteristic of liminality. Communitas relieves the individuals from following the common norms. This has to be a temporary state so that society can continue its organised existence.(Turner and Turner 1978, pp. 249-250.)

If the "south" is understood to be a liminoid "play-zone" for the tourists, it becomes obvious that the cultural and geographical location of this pleasure periphery has only marginal importance. In fact, it seems that the more placeless the destination is, the easier it is for the tourist to break away from everyday life. In this liminoid "south" people behave in ways they wouldn't normally do at home. This could be interpreted as a result of the antistructure of the "south" that entices the latent Other in the tourist's self to come forth. On holiday the anti-self that drinks, hooliganises, forgets safe sex etc. or an ideal self that is social, sensitive and creative may take over. These selves may also alternate in the same person.

In Finnish mass tourism to the "south", i.e. the Mediterranean region and the Canary Islands, it seems to be more important *that you travel* than *where you travel*. The chosen destination is of marginal importance as long as it provides the tourist good opportunities to beach life and partying and that there are ample services for the tourist. In this type of tourism tourists travel more to a different state of being than to a different place. In an analogy to the anthropological theories of transition rites, mass tourists can be understood as striving to free themselves for a limited time-span from everyday life both at work and at home. Leaving home and going on a trip seems to be a prerequisite for some people to attain a desired state of relaxation. This is, of course, culturally determined. Only in our western societies has tourism become to such a degree a democratic and common activity that it is seen as a normal way of getting away from everyday for a while. It is positively sanctioned in our culture (cf. Smith 1989.) Thus, people buy time for themselves, their spouses and families, as much as they buy a place to visit, when they walk into a travel agents office to purchase a mass tourism trip to Rhodes or Playa del Ingles for instance. They buy time that is more their own than the time lived in everyday life, where you have to conform to the clock and the rational rhythm of work that do not synchronise with the natural rhythms of the body - and, consequently, this tension between the rhythms add another element of stress to our lives (cf. Adam 1995). The liminoid time of the "south" is like the time of our childhood summers that were always sunny and warm and lasted forever.

In our culture there are numerous examples of strivings towards a non-ordinary bodily state that can not be reduced to a mere satisfaction of needs. The hot sandy beach of the tourist, the luxurious meal of the gastronome, • one more pint for the road• or the endorphine explosion of the keen jogger could be better understood as objects of desire, not means to satisfy needs. With and through them people seek experiences that are different from the ordinary, a non-ordinary state of being. (Selänniemi 1996.) Pasi Falk (1994) makes an interesting remark on that in theories of duality of the cultural dynamics – Durkheim's (1954 [1912]) profane vs. sacred, Bataille's (1962) and Caillois's (1959) everyday life vs. fête, Turner's (1969) structure vs. anti-structure, or Nietzche's (1956) apollonic vs. dionysian and Benedict's (1950) anthropological application thereof - corporeality is granted a special status as an central element of the non-normal state. Falk continues (1994: 58-59):

> The "liminality" (van Gennep) in rituals or the more secular popular festivals includes dancing and singing, eroticism and orgy, intoxication and ecstacy and lack of restraint in general (feasting, drinking, debauchery) - in other words the manifestations of human corporeality in which sensuality and pleasure play a leading part. The articulating of corporeality is a major part of the dual cultural dynamics in which the profane or everyday order is momentarily laid aside and replaced by a sacred or festive order.

This articulating of corporeality may be a result of that our senses may be stimulated and become more sensitive in ritual contexts - either through direct stimulation of some senses or through dumbing the other senses in benefit of the sense that is central to the ritual (Howes and Classen 1991: 278-280), eg. by tying the eyes and blocking the ears to enhance olfactory stimulation. This gives us a clue to understanding the tourist experience in sunlust tourism - and other types of tourism as well. If the sunlust trip can be understood to be a transition, or even a transgression in the Bataillean (1962) sense, to another state of being or to the Turnerian (1978) liminoid and, thus, has some characteristics of a rite of passage (van Gennep 1960 [1908]), one might assume that a sense or some senses are stimulated to a larger extent than in everyday life - and that we as tourists become more sensitive, and also more aware of our senses because we go through such a transition (Selänniemi 1996).

The trip to the south for Finnish sunlust tourists could, thus, be interpreted to be a fourfold transition/transgression. First of all, and naturally, it is a *spatial transition* from home to somewhere else - a journey through space. A journey from place to, in a sense, placelessness (cf. Relph 1986) as the destination is of marginal importance in this type of tourism. Secondly it is a *temporal transition* away from everyday time, the time of work, home, routine, clock, to timelessness where the only time you have to keep is the time of the return bus to the airport at the end of the holiday. These two, the spatiotemporal transitions, make the third transition, the *mental transition* possible. The mental transition is a transgression of our boundaries at home and work, the place and time of everyday life, into the placeless and timeless liminoid "south" where our latent Other may come forth and reveal characteristics that self-control and social control keep hidden in everyday life. Fourth, the transition from home to "south" is a *sensory/sensual transition* as the rite of passage -like features of the trip stimulates our senses at the same time as we are more aware of these stimulations. Thus, the spatiotemporal transition/transgression from home and everyday life to the "south" changes our psychological state, the social order and our bodily state or the way we perceive and experience our surroundings. (Selänniemi 1996.)

Conclusion: The importance of the process of travelling

In Finnish mass tourism to the "south", i.e. the Mediterranean region and the Canary Islands, it seems to be more important *that you travel* than *where you travel*. The chosen destination is of marginal importance as long as it provides the tourist good opportunities to beach life and partying and that there are ample services for the tourist. In this type of tourism tourists travel more to a different state of being than to a different place. In an analogy to the anthropological theories of transition rites, mass tourists can be understood as striving to free themselves for a limited time-span from everyday life both at work and at home. Leaving home and going on a trip (anything from 24-hour cruises to nowhere to longer trips abroad) seems to be a prerequisite for some people to attain a desired state of relaxation. This is, of course, culturally determined. Only in our western societies has tourism become to such a degree a democratic and common activity that it is seen as a normal way of getting away from everyday for a while. It is positively sanctioned in our culture (cf. Smith 1989.) Thus, people buy time for themselves, their spouses and families, as much as they buy a place to visit, when they walk into a travel agents office to purchase a mass tourism trip to Rhodes or Playa del Ingles for instance. They buy time that is more their own than the time lived in everyday life, where you have to conform to the clock and the rational rhythm of work that do not synchronize with the natural rhythms of the body - and, consequently, this tension between the rhythms add another element of stress to our lives (cf. Adam 1995).

But even more important in understanding the experiences of sunlust tourists and probably tourist experiences in any kind of tourism is to realize the significance of the *process of travelling* and the way it may influence the tourist. When trying to analyse why the same tourist returns for the 30th winter in row to Playa del Ingles the ocularcentric theories that stress the quest for authenticity fail to give us guidance. Where in the experiences of the cultural tourist it might be central *what* is gazed and experienced, in sunlust tourism it is more important *how* one experiences. And here the transition in the form of a tourist trip, the process of travelling, becomes central as it is through this transition that experiences that differ from the ordinary ones become possible.

References

Adam, B. (1995), *Timewatch. The Social Analysis of Time*, Polity Press, Cambridge.

Bataille, G. (1962), *Death and Sensuality. A Study of Eroticism and the Taboo*, Walker and Co, New York.

Beer, J. (1993), *Packaged Experiences: Japanese Tours to Southeast Asia*, PhD diss. University of California, Berkeley, Department of Anthropology.

Benedict, R. 1950 (1934), *Patterns of Culture*, Mentor Books, New York.

Caillois, R. (1959), *Man and the Sacred*, The Free Press, Glencoe.

Classen, C. (1993), *Worlds of Sense. Exploring the Senses in History and Across Cultures*, Routledge, London.

Curtis, B. and Pajaczkowska, C. (1994), "Getting there": travel, time and narrative, in Robertson, George et al (Editors) *Travellers Tales. Narratives of Home and Displacement*, Routledge, London.

Durkheim, E. 1954 [1912], *The Elementary Forms of the Religious Life*, Allen and Unwin Ltd, London.

Falk, P. (1994), *The Consuming Body*, SAGE, London.

Game, A. (1991), *Undoing the Social. Towards a Deconstructive Sociology*, Open University Press, Buckingham.

van Gennep, A. 1960 (1908), *The Rites of Passage*, The University of Chicago Press, Chicago.

Gombrich, E. H. (1979), The Museum: Past, Present, and Future, in *Ideals and Idols. Essays on values in history and in art*, Phaidon, Oxford, pp. 189-294.

Graburn, N. H. H. (1989), Tourism: The sacred journey, in Smith, Valene (Editor) *Hosts and Guests. The Anthropology of Tourism* 2d.ed, University of Pennsylvania Press, Philadelphia, pp. 21-36.

Hanefors, M. and Larsson, L. (1989), *Fardledaren: Turismkunskap for frontpersonal*, Liber, Malmo.

Hanefors, M. and Larsson, L. (1993), Video Strategies used by Tour Operators: What is Really Communicated? *Tourism Management*, 14 (1): 27-33.

Howes, D. and Classen, C. (1991), Sounding sensory profiles, in Howes, David (Editor) *The Varieties of Sensory Experience*, University of Toronto Press, Toronto.

Leach, E. R. 1982 (1961), *Rethinking Anthropology*. The Athlone Press, New York.

Löfgren, O. (1990), *Längtan till landet annorlunda. Om turism i historia och nutid.* Gidlunds, Varnamo.

MacCannell, D. (1973), Staged Authenticity. *The American Journal of Sociology*, 79 (3): 589-603.

MacCannell, D. (1989), *The Tourist. A New Theory of the Leisured Class*, Schocken Books, New York.

Nietzsche, F. (1956), *The Birth of Tragedy and The Genealogy of Morals*, Doubleday, New York.

Ong, W. (1967), *The Presence of the World: Some Prolegomena for Cultural and Religious History,* Yale University Press, New Haven.

Relph, E. (1986), *Place and Placelessness*, Pion Ltd, London.

Selanniemi, T. (1994a), *Pakettimatka pyhaan paikkaan - suomalaisturistit Ateenassa* (A Charter Trip to a Sacred Place - Finnish Tourists in Athens), Jyvaskylan yliopisto, etnologian laitos, tutkimuksia 25 (publications of the Dept. of Ethnology at the Univ. of Jyvaskyla (25)), Jyvaskyla.

Selanniemi, T. (1994b), Heritage and the Tourist: From Quick Glimpses to Devotional Visits. Paper presented at the XIIth World Congress of Sociology, RC50 Sociology of Tourism, July 18-23, Bielefeld, Germany.

Selanniemi, T. (1994c), Touristic Reflections on a Marine Venus. An Anthropological Interpretation of Finnish Tourism to Rhodes, *Ethnologica Fennica*, 22, pp.35-42.

Selanniemi, T. (1996), *Matka ikuiseen kesaan. Kulttuuriantropologinen nakokulma suomalaisten etelanmatkailuun* (A Journey to the Eternal Summer. The Anthropology of Finnish Sunlust Tourism), SKS, Helsinki.

Smith, Valene, L. (1989), Introduction, in Smith, Valene (Editor) *Hosts and Guests: The Anthropology of Tourism* 2d.ed., University of Pennsylvania Press, Philadelphia, pp. 1-17.

Synnott, A. (1991), Puzzling over the senses: from Plato to Marx, in Howes, David (Editor), *The Varieties of Sensory Experience*, University of Toronto Press, Toronto.

Tuan, Yi-Fu (1974), *Topophilia. A Study of Environmental Perception, Attitudes, and Values*, Prentice-Hall, New Jersey.

Tuan, Yi-Fu (1977), *Space and Place. The Perspective of Experience*, Edward Arnold Ltd, London.

Turner, V. (1969), *The Ritual Process. Structure and Anti-Structure*, Routledge and Kegan Paul, London.

Turner, V. 1978 (1974), *Dramas, Fields, and Metaphors,* Cornell University Press, London.

Turner, V. and Turner E. (1978), *Image and Pilgrimage in Christian Culture*, Columbia University Press.

Urry, John (1990), *The tourist gaze: leisure and travel in contemporary societies*, SAGE, London.

Veijola, S. and Jokinen, E. (1994), The Body in Tourism. *Theory, Culture and Society*. 11 (1): 125-151.

Waiting by a waterhole: Visitor behaviour in Etosha National Park, northern Namibia

Myra Shackley

Nottingham Trent University, UK

Abstract

Etosha National Park is Namibia's premier ecotourism attraction, with low visitor numbers and an interesting variety of game. Its 78 000 visitors/year must stay inside their vehicles, unless inside a rest camp, but can otherwise choose to spend their days either continually driving around, driving for part of the time and parked near a waterhole for the rest, or parked all day by a waterhole. Most choose the second option (with the exception of photographers who tend to favour the third). Etosha is a semi-desert area and its waterholes attract game, optimising the chances of seeing interesting animals. Some of the park's 35 waterholes are natural artesian springs, others water level or contact springs, some seasonally dry between September-December. Others are permanently closed to reduce grazing pressure and the incidence of anthrax in surrounding areas. The fact that a waterhole is dry, either permanently or temporarily, does not greatly affect whether tourists will visit it since game may still be seen in the vicinity.

Seven waterholes were chosen for a detailed study of visitor behaviour, each around 15km from a restcamp, with a wide field of view and unlimited parking. Observations derived from over 100 hours of observation at waterholes were combined with notes of traffic density and distribution on park roads, and a simple Geographic Information System (GIS) constructed using ArcView software. Results suggest that a new vehicle arrives at a waterhole on average every 8 minutes, with 2.6 cars present at any one time. Most waterholes receive 80-100 cars per day; some do not stop but the average stay is around 10 minutes. The presence of a vehicle acts as an inducement to others (who assume that its occupants must be watching something interesting) until a critical threshold of 12 vehicles is reached, after which vehicles begin to leave as the waterhole is perceived as overcrowded.

Slow driving speeds, large diesel engines and a habit of leaving engines switched on while parked (for air conditioning) generate substantial vehicle emissions. Encouraging visitors to switch off and wait rather than drive on would reduce air pollution and disturbance to animals. Utilising a GIS would enable routes to be planned avoiding congested waterholes and maximising the variety of habitats traversed. Visitors to a waterhole have only a 14% chance of arriving when large or interesting animals are present but if they stay an hour this rises to 44% - suggesting that everything really does come to s/he who waits.

Wildlife watching in Africa

Safari destinations

The word 'safari' is a Swahili term meaning 'journey', and in today's tourism market it is generally applied to wildlife-watching holidays in National Parks, particularly in Africa. The global safari market was estimated by the Ecotourism Society (1997) at between 106-211 million trips, with a growth rate of 10-30%/year, depending on location. Wildlife-watching 'safari' holidays vary in type, but the market is still dominated by sub Saharan Africa (Shackley 1996). Kenya, for example, derives some 80% of its tourism revenues from wildlife tourism (and 34% of its foreign exchange). Maximising visitor enjoyment and minimising the environmental impact of wildlife-watching is therefore of political, economic and environmental significance. Namibia is competing very successfully in the safari tourism market, with evidence to suggest that it is gaining market share at the expense of east African destinations. This is partly on a good reputation for security and stability but principally on the high quality of experience available to visitors in its National Parks (Economist Intelligence Unit 1992). Safaris come in many shapes or form, depending on their cost, means of transport, location and objectives. At the lower end of the market a budget safari, usually involving 8-10 passengers in a minibus may often be purchased as an add-on to a beach holiday in east or south Africa, for example, although there is widespread concern about overcrowding in many National Parks. Many new destinations in Botswana, Zambia, Zimbabwe, South Africa and Namibia are exploring the top end of the market, with products that generally include personalised itineraries and guiding provided by wildlife experts, together with a very high standard of catered accommodation. Popular variations currently include safaris on foot, horse or elephant back or even by canoe in the Okavango area of Botswana. The safari customer is purchasing a remarkable experience, familiar to many from wildlife documentaries, and requires excellent transport, information and guiding. Common complaints about budget safaris include poor driver behaviour and overcrowding in National Parks, particularly those dominated by the packaged safari tour market rather than self-drive visitors whose itineraries can be more flexible.

Tourism in Namibia

Tourism plays a major role in the development of Namibia, contributing an annual N$1.5 billion into its economy. Currently, in excess of half a million tourists a year visit the country and in 1997 tourist arrivals grew by 18% (Ministry of Environment and Tourism data), with most visits motivated by an interest in landscape and environment. Namibia has a long and distinguished history of conservation, starting with the proclamation of Etosha in 1907, and since then more than 20 national parks, game reserves have been designated, occupying a total of 13% of Namibia's land area. Namibia's National Parks have relatively low visitor numbers and are dominated by self-drive tourists rather than packaged tours (Olivier and Olivier 1992). Etosha National Park in northern Namibia is the country's premier ecotourism attraction, occupying an area of some 2 227 000 hectares of mainly savannah grassland surrounding Etosha Pan (Fig.1). It is generally thought to be one of the most spectacular National Parks in southern Africa, because of low visitor numbers with visitors disseminated over a wide area, and the possibility of seeing an interesting variety of game. A typical visitor to Etosha might be taking a 2-week vacation in Namibia, and combining the Park with a visit to the capital (Windhoek), some 300-km south, together with the Namib Desert, Fish River Canyon or Okavango.

Etosha

Visitors to Etosha must stay inside their vehicles and off-road driving is prohibited. Park roads are mainly dusty gravel in moderately good condition, easily travelled by 2-wheel drive vehicles. A speedlimit of 60 kph is in place but infrequently enforced. Etosha has limited visitor accommodation in three self-catering rest camps (Okaukuejo, Halai and Namutoni) which can get very busy. At present the park is receiving c. 78 000 visitors per year, only 1% of whom are day visitors. 50% are from overseas, 15% from RSA and the remainder from Namibia. Visitors have the option of staying in one of the three rest camps or staying outside the park in one of the luxury hotels just outside its perimeter and entering the park either on a self-driving visit or as part of an organised tour. Some visitors stay at game farms outside the park; some visit it as part of a trans-Africa trip from Windhoek to Victoria Falls via the Caprivi Strip. The landscape of Etosha is flat, though varied by different vegetation types. It is punctuated by waterholes that act as major visitor attractions since they present the best possibility of seeing animals. The park is open from dawn to dusk but outside those hours visitors must be within the rest-camp compound. During the day a visitor can either be within a rest camp, waiting at a waterhole or travelling along park roads. The relative simplicity of visitor movements made Etosha a particularly suitable area to consider for a project of this type, preferable to the more heavily-visited national parks of eastern and southern Africa, especially those where out-of-vehicle activities are permitted. Etosha is an all year round destination; October-December are the hottest months with daytime temperatures above 32C and considerable diurnal variations. The park is managed, and regulations enforced, by the Namibia Ministry of Environment and Tourism.

Figure 1   Map of Etosha showing restcamp and waterhole locations

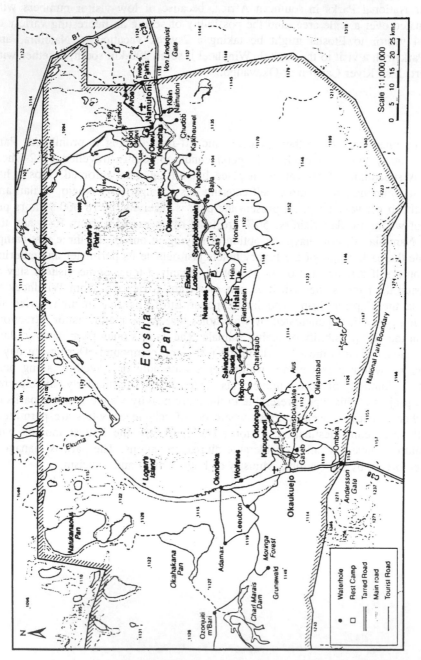

Etosha contains a huge and diverse fauna including 114 species of mammal and 340 species of birds. The animals are typical of southern savannah, including large herds of springbok, Burchells's zebra, gemsbok, blue wildebeest, giraffe and elephants. Numbers vary depending on migration patterns, availability of water and food but there are probably 1500 elephants, 300 black rhino, 2000 giraffe, 4-6000 gemsbok, 1000 lion plus unknown numbers of cheetah and leopard in the Park. After the first summer rains there is plenty of *veldt* water so large herds of springbok, gemsbok, blue wildebeest and Burchells zebra are attracted to the sweet-*grassveld* of the Okondeka plains along west and north west edge of the pan and Grootvlakte (Figure 2). As rainwater pools dry up and pastures fail these large herds split into smaller groups which are drawn to the permanent waterholes around Okaukuejo, before trekking further east to their winter grazing around Gemsbokvlakte (Figure 2). A few days after the summer rains have stopped animals migrate back to the grasslands north and south of Okaukuejo where they stay until April before starting the next migration cycle. These seasonal changes are well publicised and visitors adapt their strategies accordingly, targeting the areas most likely to contain game at the season of visiting.

Figure 2   Map of Etosha with vegetation zones

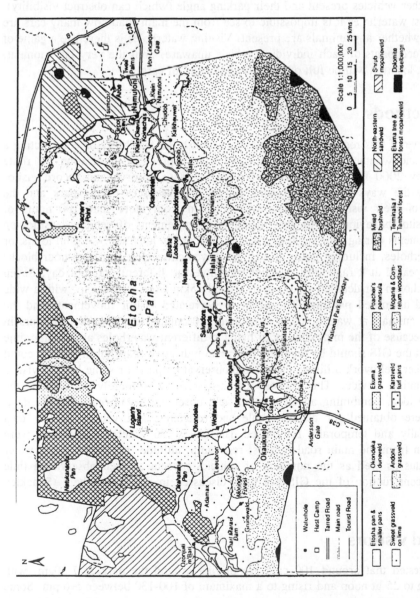

Waterholes

Some of Etosha's 36 waterholes (Figure 2) are natural artesian springs; some are seasonally dry between September-December. Others are permanently closed to reduce grazing pressure and the incidence of anthrax in surrounding areas. The fact that a waterhole is dry, either permanently or temporarily, does not greatly affect whether tourists will visit it since game may still be seen in the vicinity. The park visitor guide gives a summary of the condition and vegetation of each waterhole, together with information about the likelihood of seeing particular animals in its vicinity. Each waterhole is approached from the road and surrounded by a 'parking' area of varied size, permitting visitors to get a clear view of the waterhole without leaving their cars. However, the clarity of the view is obviously related to the numbers of other vehicles present and their parking angle (which can obstruct visibility). In the case of most waterholes it is impossible to see from the main road how many cars are parked, let alone whether any animals are present. Visiting waterholes is therefore a game of chance, with the occupants of each individual vehicle unaware, until the very last moment, whether the target location will be full of animals and/or full of cars.

Research methods

The major objective of this research project was to establish the feasibility of constructing a GIS for Etosha, and whether such a system could have a practical application for route planning (Shackley 2000 in press). A secondary aim was to observe and record visitor behaviour, noting the ways in which visitors utilised the resources of the park and the potential impact of their visits. Field data was obtained from more than 100 hours of observation of visitor behaviour in Etosha, including measurements of vehicle densities on different road segments during four separate visits. Considerable attention was paid to visitor behaviour at waterholes, including notes on vehicle movements being kept in 3-hour blocks of observation repeated at 4 randomly selected waterholes at different times of day. Seven waterholes were chosen for detailed study, each around 15km from a restcamp, with a wide field of view and unlimited parking. The observer correlated visitor movements and the presence of large animals at waterholes in structured 100-minute segments for 50 hours in total. However, because of the impossibility of being at different waterholes at the same time the data utilised in the GIS should be regarded just as an indicative snapshot in time. It could be refined by further fieldwork utilising more fixed observation posts or some kind of visitor tracking and counting device. The purpose of this study was merely to explore the boundaries of the idea, combining an element of field observation with cartographic data. GPS readings were obtained for all waterhole and restcamps and vehicle density data recorded as spatially and temporally referenced data tables. 36 waterhole attributes were noted included km from the main road, nearest rest camp, altitude, vegetation zone, water source, water status as well as the numbers of vehicles present at each observation time (Figure 3). The construction of the GIS has been discussed in detail elsewhere (Shackley 2000 in press).

Vehicles and visitors

Observation suggested that around 100 cars are driving around the park at 7.30am, with numbers dropping to 25 at noon and rising to a maximum of 100-130 between 5-6 pm. Some visitors will have stayed in the park overnight, others will enter on a daily basis, and some may be traversing the park on its main through road. There are no official quotas on the number of vehicles that can enter the Park on a daily basis; the only limit is imposed by the availability of accommodation. Records are kept of the number of vehicles entering and leaving the park each day at both of its gateways. Visitors can choose to spend their days in the Park in one of three ways; continually driving around, driving for part of the time and parked near a waterhole for the rest, or parked all day by a waterhole. Most choose the second option (with the exception of photographers who tend to favour the third). Visitor distribution within the park also depends on recent reported sightings of animals noted in the rest camp visitor books, the time of day (for example there is little traffic around at noon heat when most visitors are in camp), whether the visitor has been to Etosha before (if so s/he may have preferred locations or routines), and the length of stay. People staying for a short time drive the most. Those staying one night at each of the three camps can drive either west-east or east-west, stopping at waterholes as they go. Those visiting on a day trip make a round trip from the park gates to those waterholes which they can reach in the time allocated, and those taking a pre-arranged tour follow the tour operator's routine. Only personal preference and the distance each person is prepared to drive limit the number of waterholes visited in a day, but a trip requires careful planning since the visitor must be back in the rest camp at dusk. Informal interviews suggested that the average visitor drives 100-150km/day. A popular pattern involves an early morning game drive, returning to camp for breakfast, with morning and early-evening drives separated by another return to base during the heat of the day. This is partly to allow for a siesta and partly because of the view (not always accurate) that few animals are to be seen in the noonday sun, when the intense glare of Etosha in any case makes midday photography difficult.

Vehicle densities

Vehicle densities were greatest nearest to a rest camp and least on roads near the boundaries of the tourist area. They were especially low on roads leading to outlying waterholes, which required visitors to drive along the same route in both directions with no option of taking a circular tour (Figure 3). Major management concerns in Etosha include minimising the impact of vehicles on animal and plant communities (from dust, emissions and impact), prohibiting off-road driving, speeding, littering or other adverse impacts (Shackley 1996). A secondary concern is to ensure that the visitor has a high quality of experience, which is related not only to whether they have seen a wide variety of interesting animals but whether they have done so in the absence of too many other visitors. In Etosha it is extremely rare to get more than 12 cars at a waterhole (Figure 3) whereas there are frequent complaints in east African parks about high vehicle concentrations and the way animals have become habituated to tourists' presence and altered their behaviour accordingly. The presence of a vehicle at a waterhole in Etosha seems to act as an inducement for others to stop, hoping that its occupants may be watching something interesting. However, if more than 13 vehicles accumulate some will immediately start to leave and total numbers decline rapidly, as the waterhole is perceived by newcomers to be overcrowded. This can happen even if interesting animals are still present; visitors clearly prefer to make their observations and take their photographs in relative privacy.

Figure 3   'snapshot' of vehicle densities at waterholes

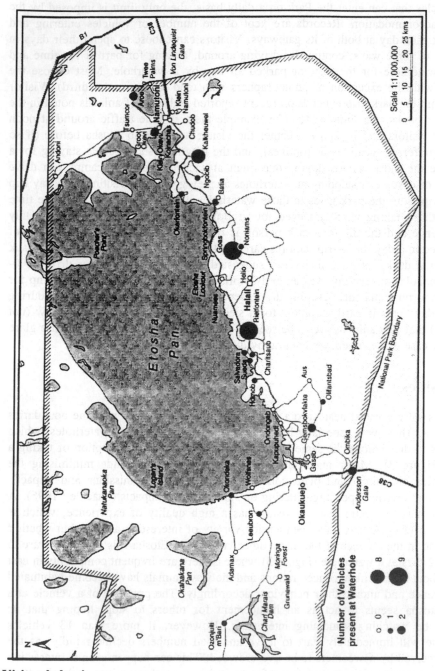

Visitor behaviour

On average a car spends less than 10 minutes waiting by a waterhole. Less than 5% of cars watched in the course of this study waited throughout the 100-minute observation slots. Some drivers' switch off their engines, others leave engines idling. Some will merely 'pass by ' a waterhole even if there are many animals present, others will wait for a long time even if nothing comes. Vehicle emission rates increase sharply at low speeds (as when carefully passing a waterhole) and are also higher with diesel 4WD engines, common in the park. Theoretically, noise and smoking are banned at waterholes but many visitors park and leave their car radios and air-conditioning switched on. Despite the fact that it is forbidden on several occasions visitors were seen to get out of their cars illegally. Vehicle occupants frequently take the opportunity to eat and drink while waiting at waterholes, thus unconsciously mimicking the actions of the animals they are observing. Three patterns were apparent; a relatively short-term wait (generally with engine off), a long-term wait (often an hour or more, also with the engine off) or a short drive-past without pausing, if nothing interesting was to be seen. A new vehicle arrives at a waterhole about every 8 minutes with an average of 2.6 cars present at any one time. Most waterholes receive 8-100 cars per day and on average a car stays 10 minutes. This provides a very substantial quantity of exhaust emissions to those animals visiting the waterhole, which may be separated from the vehicles by only a few metres. Parking with an idling engine not only wastes fuel but also increases both noise pollution and the quantity of exhaust emissions (McInnes 1996 Poloden and Hillman 1996). It seems probable that high levels of hydrocarbon exhaust emissions react with sunlight and nitrous oxides to increase ground-level ozone levels dramatically near waterholes, although no research has been done on the effect of this process on the animal inhabitants. Encouraging visitors to switch off and wait, rather than drive on, would significantly reduce air pollution (Banister and Button 1993) and reduce disturbance to animals.

Visitor distribution

Figure 3 shows a correlation produced by the GIS with the number of vehicles present at waterholes plotted against spatial data including the location of waterholes, roads and rest camps. Other maps plotted from GIS data showed that the highest densities of vehicles were to be observed at waterholes less than 30km (half an hours drive) from a rest camp, with the lowest densities at waterholes furthest away. There was also a correlation between waterholes with high vehicle densities and proximity to the main through-route linking the rest camps. The reason is obvious; visitors are reluctant to drive a long distance out to peripheral waterholes (Andoni or Ozonjuiti, Figure 2) where nothing might be seen, whereas driving to the nearest waterholes permits a quick return to restcamp for comfort breaks or if dusk is approaching. The highest densities of vehicles were also observed, not surprisingly, on roads approaching the rest camps and the main through-routes. Further interrogation of the GIS showed, for example, that the most frequented waterholes were on the Halali-Namutoni road, and it proved possible to utilise the GIS to construct a route avoiding the majority of these (Shackley 2000, in press). The GIS could also be used to construct a route to enable visitors to be selective. For example, it could produce a route helping a determined visitor to get to all the waterholes between Halali and Okaukuejo in a 12-hour period, for example, allowing a 30-minute stop at each. Infinite variations were possible, such as planning routes taking in localities where particular bird species were most common, or traversing a large number of different vegetation zones.

Conclusions

The work forms part of the increasing literature dealing with the spatial analysis of tourist behaviour (e.g. Ashworth and Dietworst 1997) and assumes that the behaviour of visitors to Etosha is not random, but motivated by a desire to optimise game-viewing possibilities and their use of available time. Further spatial modelling of visitor activities must include a discussion of capability constraints and choice orientation (Floor, 1990) utilising time budget analysis. Although in many ways Etosha is not the most 'typical' of African National Parks its particular characteristics (flat topography, low vehicle densities) provided ideal for this project. However, care should be taken before transferring the observation to other parks although it seems likely that there will be many similarities in the ways visitors utilise park resources. There will also be major differences in parks which, for example, are dominated by organised tours rather than self-drive cars, where the itinerary will be determined by the tour operator and the amount of time spent driving or waiting is not up to the discretion of the individual visitors. In order to produce a more accurate picture of visitor movements the research methods used in this pilot study would need to be refined by more observation points generating a more detailed data set. An additional way of counting vehicles would be required, and it would be nice to track the movements of selected vehicles during the course of their visit, combining such an activity with a structured interview with the vehicle's occupants.

In terms of the ways in which visitors utilise park resources preliminary results show a correlation, as expected, between the most frequently used waterholes and their proximity to rest camps. However, this pattern can be altered if, for example, the restcamp visitor book suggests the presence of interesting animal elsewhere, causing visitors to divert from planned routes, or when a route or waterhole is closed for any reason as is occasionally the case. This pilot study showed that it would be perfectly possible to utilise a simple GIS in Etosha to generate different routes to match different visitor requirements. It could be, for example, that a visitor might wish to traverse all the different vegetation zones in the park, or to visit the maximum number of waterholes in a certain time or travelling distance. It is also theoretically feasible to present travellers with different recommended routes on entry to the park, which would reduce the likelihood that they followed the same direction, thus minimising waterhole congestion or the chance of seeing too many other vehicles. The GIS could also be used for 'what if' scenarios, for example to construct a recommended route avoiding all dry waterholes, or if an area of park or roads off-limits for any reason. This project was not concerned with management implications (such as the cost of installing and upgrading such a GIS or the feasibility of distributing such routes to travellers) but the work did established that the construction of such a system is very cheap. It could be installed, upgraded and maintained at park headquarters and it is even feasible to imagine the scale versions for installation in future generations of cars with in-built navigational computers.

One implication of the work derived from visitor observation is the desirability of introducing a regulation preventing engine idling, which would considerably reduce pollution and disturbance.

In a lighter vein; observation suggested that visitors to a waterhole have only a 14% chance of arriving when large or especially interesting animals (lion, cheetah, leopard, elephant, rhinoceros or giraffe) are present. However, if they chose to stay an hour the chances of seeing such an animal arriving rise to 44% - suggesting that in this case everything really does come to s/he who waits.

Acknowledgements

I am most grateful to Mike Shand (University of Glasgow) for his work on developing the pilot GIS described in this paper, and drawing the figures. Paul Nathanail, Bob and Margaret Oldroyd also contributed to the research, and fieldwork was financed by an interdisciplinary grant from the Research Development Fund of Nottingham Trent University.

References

Ashworth, G. and Dietvorst, A. (1997), Tourist behaviour and the importance of time-space analysis. pp.164-181 *in Tourism and Spatial Transformation; implications for policy and planning* Oxford; CAB International.

Banister, D. and Button, K. (1993), *Transport, the Environment and Sustainable Development* London; E. and F. N. Spon.

Economist Intelligence Unit (1992), Namibia. *International Tourism Reports* 4 101-114.

McInnes, G.(1996), *Atmospheric Emissions Inventory Guide,* Brussels: European Environment Agency

Olivier, W. and Olivier, S. (1993), *A guide to Namibian Game Parks,* Windhoek: Longman.

Ploden, S. and Hillmann, M. (1996), *Speed Control and Transport Policy.* London: Policy Studies Institute.

Shackley, M. (1996), *Wildlife Tourism* London: International Thomson Business Press.

Shackley, M. (2000, in press), Spatial analysis of visitor behaviour in Etosha National Park, Namibia *Tourism Geographies.*

The consumption of tourism revisited

Richard Sharpley

University of Northumbria, UK

Introduction

Researchers have long been concerned with consumer behaviour within the specific context of tourism. Indeed, the explanation and prediction of tourist-consumer behaviour has been a dominant theme throughout the modern study of tourism. However, much of the research has traditionally adopted a largely uni-dimensional, tourism-centric perspective. That is, many commentators have focused primarily upon the tourism demand process, working within the 'accepted and popular and professional usage...[of consumption]...to refer to an exclusively economic activity' (Campbell 1995: 101). The consumption of tourism has been viewed as a logical, rational process whereby particular needs or wants may be satisfied, in a utilitarian sense, through tourism (Mill and Morrison 1985: 4; also Warde 1992: 17). As a result, much of the literature is concerned with developing models of the tourism demand process (for example, Schmoll 1977; Goodall 1991) or with particular elements of or influences within that process. Thus, extensive research has been undertaken into tourist motivation whilst other more specific issues, such as the influence of values on tourist-consumer decision-making, are also addressed (for example, Pizam and Calantone 1987; Madrigal and Kahle 1994).

In contrast, relatively little attention has been paid until recently to the broader role of tourism as a form of consumption. In other words, tourism has, by and large, been considered in isolation from other forms of consumption in general and from the wider cultural framework within which it occurs in particular. As a result, although the practice of consumption has become a defining cultural element of many (allegedly postmodern) tourism-generating societies (Bocock 1993: 4), the influence of a dominant consumer culture on tourism has been overlooked. At the same time and related, few attempts have been made to apply consumer behaviour theory to the specific context of tourism.

This is not to say that the study of tourism consumption has remained completely divorced from consumer culture theory. Since Urry (1990a) first considered the 'consumption of tourism', a number of commentators have explored the cultural context of tourist-consumer behaviour, in particular the link between tourism and postmodern culture (for example, Urry 1990b; Munt 1994; Pretes 1995). However, the purpose of this paper is to build upon existing knowledge through the application of a specific theory of consumer behaviour – namely, Holt's 'typology of consumption practices' (Holt 1995) – to the consumption of tourism. First, however, it is important to revisit briefly the relationship between tourism and cultural change as a foundation to exploring the influence of consumer culture on tourism consumption.

Tourism, consumption and cultural change

As considered elsewhere (Sharpley 1999), an identifiable relationship has long existed between tourism and the cultural condition of society. To a great extent, this relationship has directly influenced tastes and styles of tourism consumption, reflected in, for example, the emergence of sunbathing in the late 1920s or, more recently, the popularity of individualistic, adventurous forms of tourism. At the same time, however, the nature of the relationship has also changed (Urry 1994). During the nineteenth century, tourism and culture were largely in opposition. Thus, contrasting with 'the bourgeois culture with its concerts, museums, galleries, and so on' (Urry 1994: 234), tourism for the masses was centred upon the rapid development of seaside resorts as places – separated in time and space from the tourist's 'normal' existence – as places of 'ritualised pleasure' (Shields 1991).

Conversely, during the twentieth century, up to the 1970s, the tourism-culture relationship gradually transformed to the extent that tourism practices came to reflect cultural change. In particular, the emergence of a culture based upon mass production/consumption was manifested in the development of mass forms of tourism yet, importantly, tourism as an activity remained separate or differentiated from other social activities and institutions. More recently, however, this differentiation between tourism and other practices has arguably become less apparent. 'Tourism is no longer a differentiated set of social practices with its own and distinct rules, times and spaces' (Urry 1994: 234); rather, it has merged into other places (for example, urban tourism) and other social activities, such as shopping or watching television, that were previously considered separate from tourist places and behaviour. Indeed, it has been suggested that people are tourists most of the time and that tourism has simply become cultural.

Thus, the tourism-culture relationship has evolved through two distinct stages. Firstly, throughout most of its development, tourism has been separated off from other social activities and institutions, reflecting broader distinctions in social class, employment, gender roles and so on. Even tourism itself has been subject to differentiation with, for example, different resorts or activities became associated with different social groups. However, more recently, tourism has now entered a second, 'de-differentiated' (Lash 1990: 11) stage of development, reflecting the emergence of similarly de-differentiated economic, political, social and cultural processes that have been collectively referred to as the condition of postmodernity (Harvey 1990). As a result, it is suggested by some that tourism practices in particular have also become postmodern. Not only has tourism fused with other social activities, representing the 'marriage of different, often intellectual, spheres of activity with tourism' (Munt 1994: 104), but also a variety of 'postmodern tourisms' have also emerged – though no causal relationship between postmodern culture and tourism practices has been established. Nevertheless, such 'postmodern tourisms' include theme parks, heritage tourism and inland-resort/holiday village tourism whilst, in the extreme, it is claimed that tourists themselves have become postmodern – the 'post-tourist' (Feifer 1985; Urry 1990b).

More importantly in the present context, however, is the fact that, for many, postmodernity is epitomised by the emergence of a consumer society. That is, within postmodern societies the practice of consumption has assumed a dominant and significantly more complex role than simple utilitarian need satisfaction. People now consume goods and services for a variety of reasons and purposes, in particular as a means of compensating for the loss, through the process of de-differentiation, of traditional social markers. 'Under modern conditions, work roles in production processes were defined as being central for identity, which is in contrast with consumption patterns of action being posited as central to postmodern identity construction' (Bocock 1993: 79).

This shift from a production-mode to a consumption-mode of consumer culture (Featherstone 1990) is certainly evident within the context of tourism. In recent years the tourism industry, which throughout the 1960s and 1970s produced mass, standardised package forms of tourism produced according to modernist, 'Fordist' principles, has been obliged to become increasingly responsive to the changing needs and demands of the tourist-consumer. However, although it is widely recognised that tourists have assumed the dominant position in the tourism production-consumption process, little attention has been paid to the ways in which consumer culture in general influences or is related to the consumption of tourism in particular. In other words, few attempts have been made to apply the 'new consumer behaviour [which] attempts to understand how consumption relates to the rest of human existence' (Belk 1995: 62) to the specific context of tourism. It is this omission which this paper begins to address.

Tourism and consumer culture

As noted above, a fundamental feature of postmodern culture is that 'consumption, rather than production, becomes dominant, and the commodity attains the total occupation of social life' (Pretes 1995: 2). This has resulted, in part, from a variety of factors and transformations within the wider social and economic system in post-industrial societies that have enabled the practice of consumption to assume a leading role in people's lives. Such factors include the large, widely-available and ever-increasing range of consumer goods and services, the popularity of leisure-shopping, the emergence of consumer groups and consumer legislation, pervasive advertising, greater and faster access to goods and services through the Internet, and 'the impossibility of avoiding making choices in relation to consumer goods' (Lury 1996: 36). In short, the *practice* of consumption has been simplified and facilitated by socio-economic transformations.

However, of equal, if not greater importance, in the emergence of a dominant consumer culture has been the increasing *significance* of consumption. It has long been recognised that commodities, whether goods or services, embrace a meaning beyond their economic exchange or use value (Douglas and Isherwood 1979; Appadurai 1986). 'The utility of goods is always framed by a cultural context, that even the use of the most mundane objects in daily life has cultural meaning...material goods are not only used to do things, but they also have a meaning, and act as meaningful markers of social relationships' (Lury 1996: 11). Indeed, it has been argued that consumption results only from the inherent significance of goods and services, their use value being irrelevant (Baudrillard 1988), although this is disputed by others (Warde 1992: 6). Nevertheless, social lives are patterned or even created by the acquisition and use of things.

To put it another way, consumption in postmodern capitalist societies 'must not be understood as the consumption of use-values, a material utility, but primarily as the consumption of signs' (Featherstone 1991: 85). Typically, this significance of consumption is related to status or identity messages or for establishing distinctions between different social groups (Bourdieu 1986) and, not surprisingly, much contemporary consumer behaviour research is concerned with the symbolism of consumption, with how consumption conveys 'information to us and others about who we are' (Belk 1995: 64).

At the same time, however, a variety of other topics, such as consumption festivals and rituals, the significance of possession, and gift-giving and exchange are all considered ways in which cultural meaning is transferred from goods/services to the individual (McCracken 1986). These all provide a valid theoretical framework for the analysis of the consumption of tourism in particular. For example, tourism has long been utilised as a status symbol, whilst the ritualistic elements of tourism consumption represent 'a kind of social action devoted to the manipulation of cultural meaning for purposes of collective and individual communication' (McCracken 1986: 78). Such actions include the purchase of souvenirs (possession ritual), sending postcards, or the taking and showing of holiday photographs.

Importantly, this multitude of ways in which cultural meaning is transferred through consumption suggests that, generally, 'the act of consuming is a varied and effortful accomplishment underdetermined by the characteristics of the object. A given consumption object...is typically consumed in a variety of ways by different groups of consumers' (Holt 1995:1). Thus, although some individual's consumption practices may be identity or status driven – in the case of tourism, a flight on Concorde or, perhaps, a holiday at an exclusive resort – the same consumption objects may be consumed by others in different ways. Holt suggests four different categories of consumption which, as the following section demonstrates, may be effectively applied to the specific context of tourist-consumer behaviour.

A typology of (tourist) consumption practices

According to Holt (1995), consumer research has traditionally conceptualised consumption practices under two broad headings – the purpose of consumption and the structure of consumption. In terms of purpose, consumers' actions may be ends in themselves (autotelic) or means to an end (instrumental). Structurally, consumption may be focused directly upon the object of consumption (object actions) or, conversely, the objects of consumption may serve as a focal point for interpersonal actions. Thus, within a combination of these two dimensions of consumption practices lie four possible 'metaphors' of consumption:

1.   Autotelic/object actions: *consuming as experience*

2.   Autotelic/interpersonal actions: *consuming as play*

3.   Instrumental/object actions: *consuming as integration*

4.   Instrumental/interpersonal actions: *consuming as classification*.

Each of these represent different ways in which an object of consumption (including tourism) may be consumed:

Consuming tourism as experience

The consumption-as experience perspective, focusing upon the subjective or emotional reactions of consumers to particular consumption objects, draws attention to the ways in which consumers make sense of different objects. As Holbrook and Hirschman (1982: 132) explain, 'this experiential perspective is phenomenological in spirit and regards consumption as a primarily subjective state of consciousness'. Moreover, 'how consumers experience consumption objects is structured by the interpretative framework(s) that they apply to engage the object' (Holt 1995: 3); consumption objects are embedded in a social world which provides the framework for their definition or understanding.

Tourism is no exception to this process. As a form of consumption it is firmly embedded in tourists' social world and the ways in which people experience, or consume, tourism will depend very much on their interpretation of the meaning of tourism within that social world. For example, tourism may be interpreted as a form of sacred consumption (Graburn 1989) – it occurs outside normal (profane) times and places, a 'festive, liminal time when behaviour is different from ordinary work time' (Belk *et al* 1989: 12) and is consumed as a sacred or spiritual experience. Tourists' behaviour will, therefore, be framed by this sacralisation of tourism and may be manifested in different ways. Some for example, may seek the spiritual refreshment of solitary, natural places (Belk *et al* 1989; Urry 1990a); for others, the sacred nature of tourism may be reflected in the collective experience of sites and destinations.

The consumption of tourism is also framed by the experiential aspect of modern consumption as a whole, namely, that 'the consumption experience [is] a phenomenon directed towards the pursuit of fantasies, feelings and fun' (Holbrook and Hirschman 1982: 132). In other words, modern consumption is directed towards the hedonistic pursuit of pleasure which results not from physical (utilitarian) satisfaction but, according to Campbell (1987), from romantic day-dreaming. Thus, tourism represents the consumption of dreams, again an escape to the non-ordinary, the sacred or novel 'other'.

Consuming as play

As a form of consumption that is autotelic and interpersonal, the consuming-as-play perspective suggests that people utilise objects as a resource or focus for interaction with other consumers rather than for the object's experiential characteristics. In other words, from the play perspective, the object of consumption becomes a vehicle for the achievement of broader, interpersonal goals. Thus, in the context of tourism, consuming-as-play does not refer, for example, to the ludic or 'tourist-as-child' (Dann 1996) character of certain tourist experiences, but to the fact that tourism is used as a means of socialising or sharing particular experiences with fellow consumers.

This highlights the fact that, frequently, tourism is a social experience, an element of which is ' to be able to consume particular commodities in the company of others. Part of what people buy is in effect a particular social composition of other consumers' (Urry 1990a: 25).

In this sense, tourism provides the focus for people to socialise or to fulfil a more 'performative, reciprocal' (Holt 1995: 90) role in entertaining each other. Thus, tourism in resorts such as Agia Napa in Cyprus may be consumed not primarily for the attraction of the clubs and bars in the town, but for the communal enjoyment of those facilities and the contribution to the social atmosphere of the resort.

Equally, tourism my be a means of sharing unusual or extraordinary experiences; the communal interaction with the consumption object allows tourists to commune or experience communitas (Arnould and Price 1993), the sense of which may be heightened by the collective sharing of challenging or dangerous experiences. In either case, however, the focus is on the communal, social nature of the consumption experience rather than the object of consumption.

Consuming as integration

According to Holt, consuming-as-integration is an instrumental action through which consumers are able to 'integrate self and object, thereby allowing themselves access to the objects symbolic properties' (Holt 1995: 2). The object becomes a constituent element of their identity through a process of assimilation, either by merging external objects into their self-concept, or by adapting their self-concept to match the socially or institutionally defined identity of the object.

In the tourism context, integration is automatic given the inevitability, as with all services, of tourists' participation in the production of tourism experiences – the inseparability of the production / consumption of tourist services means that the tourist-consumer must integrate into the object of consumption. However, much depends upon the nature or direction of integration desired by the consumer. On the one hand, a tourist who wishes to be identified with a particular destinational culture or type of tourism may adapt his / her self-concept to 'fit' the identity of the destination or tourism-type through a process of assimilation into the local / tourist culture or through personalisation practices (Holt 1995). This may be achieved by utilising local services or travelling independently, or adopting modes of behaviour that are deemed appropriate to particular forms of tourism or travel. On the other hand, certain types of tourism or tourist experience may be integrated into the individual's self-concept in a process of self-extension; for example, Arnould and Price (1993) analyse white-water rafting as one such form of touristic activity that enables personal absorption and integration, providing communitas and personal growth / renewal.

Consuming as classification

As suggested above, consumption practices are most commonly considered a status / identity signifier, a means of achieving social distinction. That is, especially within de-differentiated, postmodern societies, consumers utilise consumption objects to create self-identity and to 'classify themselves in relation to relevant others' (Holt 1995: 10). This process of consuming-as-classification is not, of course, new; in the 1920s, positional consumption (conspicuous consumption) was identified by Veblen (1925) whilst the so-called 'aristocratic model' (Thurot and Thurot 1983) of tourism development points to the inherent and long-held role of tourism as a social classifier.

The role of consumption in identity creation is widely considered in the literature (Bourdieu 1986; Featherstone 1990; Warde 1992), as is its applicability to tourism (Voase 1995; Sharpley 1996). Generally, however, it is interesting to note that, although the consumption of tourism has become increasingly democratised (Urry 1990b), and 'while travel has remained an expression of taste since the eighteenth century, it has never been so widely used as at present' (Munt 1994: 109). In response, the travel industry is developing more specialised, niche products which, though relatively affordable and available to the masses, nevertheless have the aura of status or luxury. Examples of such products include eco- (or 'ego') tourism, all-inclusives and package cruise holidays.

Discussion: Implications of the tourism consumption typology

As suggested in the introduction to this paper, research into the consumption of tourism has typically been tourism centric and uni-dimensional. That is, it has tended to consider tourism largely in isolation from other forms of consumption and from a pervasive consumer culture. As a result, an extensive literature exists on *why* people consume tourism (i.e. tourist motivational studies), but substantially less research has been undertaken into *how* tourism is consumed. In other words, although many commentators have explored the enormous variety of factors that influence participation in tourism, there is less understanding as to how cultural meaning is transferred from the cultural world through the consumption of tourism.

This, in turn, has meant that much of the research into tourism consumption has taken as its starting point either particular types of tourism (each implicitly offering a variety of attributes which yield particular benefits) or particular types of tourists. Thus, the consumption of tourism has been over-simplified through concepts such as sunlust/wanderlust tourists (Gray 1970) and a variety of tourist typologies which typically follow a continuum from mass-charter-package to explorer-independent tourists, or through the linking of particular forms of tourism to particular tourist-consumer types. For example, eco-tourism is usually considered as appealing to the 'good' tourist, whilst any form of non-standardised/packaged holiday is allegedly demanded by the 'new tourist' (Poon 1993). In short, much research into tourist-consumer behaviour has not allowed for the fact that any single tourism product may be consumed in as many ways as there are tourists.

In other words, the consumption of tourism is a hugely complex process; it is 'discretionary, episodic, future oriented, dynamic, socially influenced and evolving' (Pearce 1992: 114). It is also, as argued here, saturated with cultural meaning. Tourist-consumers utilise tourism in a variety of ways to convey cultural messages; as the typology outlined above suggests, particular tourism products can be consumed in a number different ways. Therefore, not only is it unrealistic to attach stereotypical labels to specific types of tourism / tourists, but also by developing a consumer culture of tourism an extra dimension is added to the understanding, knowledge and prediction of tourist-consumer behaviour.

This may be demonstrated by applying the typology of tourist consumption practices to a specific tourist product, namely, adventure tourism. Adventure tourism is considered to be one of the fastest growing sectors of international travel and tourism. For example, it has been estimated that recent growth rates for adventure tour operators is in the region of 13% - 15% per annum whilst, between 1995 and 1999, European adventure trips increased by about 60% (Smith and Jenner 1999). Inevitably there are many forms of 'adventure tourism'; generally it has been divided into 'hard' and 'soft' categories, the former including relatively risky outdoor activities requiring some level of skill on the part of participants, such as sky diving, mountain climbing or kayaking. At the same time, hard adventure tourists usually stay in remote lodges or camps with few amenities. Soft adventure tourism, conversely, combines adventure with comfort, and embraces activities such as hot-air ballooning, cycling or bird-watching (TIA 1997). Nevertheless, adventure tourism is generally defined as 'a trip or travel with the specific purpose of activity participation to explore a new experience, often involving perceived risk or controlled danger associated with personal challenges, in a natural environment or exotic outdoor setting' (adventuretravel.com: 2000).

Given the wide range of activities that comprise adventure tourism, there is likely to be a wide profile of adventure tourists. Nevertheless, if a specific activity, such as white-water rafting trips, is selected, it would normally be assumed that participants would be people would correspond to the characteristics of the 'new' tourist. They would be seeking novelty and adventure but at the same time they would be responsible, aware individuals. According to Smith and Jenner (1999), such tourists are environmentally aware and interested in traditional culture, and they have found to be, typically, younger, single, relatively affluent and challenge-seeking (TIA 1999).

At the same time, however, participants in white-water rafting may consume the experience according to any one (or a combination) of the consumption typologies. That is, the consumption of a white-water rafting experience may be defined as:

- *consuming-as-experience*: the challenge/novelty of the experience is framed by the safety / predictability of normal, profane life. It takes on the aura of a spiritual ritual of personal renewal and discovery combined with the 'pleasure' of pushing to physical limits, of taking on nature and surviving.

- *consuming-as-play*: the communal experience of the trip, facing and overcoming challenges as a team/group, each playing a role in the adventure and celebration of success.

- *consuming-as-integration*: integrating the self into the natural world, respecting the power of nature, or integrating the experience into the self. That is, the adventure is consumed as an extension of the self.

- *consuming-as-classification*: the experience as a marker of social status or identity, by communicating to others through stories or photographs the challenge, danger and success of the experience.

Therefore, although demographically the participants in white-water rafting may be similar, the ways in which they consume the experience may vary considerably. Therefore, in order to attract as wide a market as possible, such tourism experiences need to be designed and marketed in a manner which takes each of the four consumption typologies into account.

More generally, this also suggests that the application of consumer behaviour theory adds an extra dimension to the knowledge and understanding of tourist-consumer behaviour. In an increasingly competitive business world where consumer culture is becoming ever more dominant, such knowledge can only be an advantage to providers of tourist services and experiences. That is, different types of tourism are likely to attract consumers according to recognised demographic and socio-economic factors. However, even within specific consumer groups tourism experiences will be consumed in different ways by different consumers; recognition of and responses to such differences can only lead to competitive advantage. In conclusion, therefore, the application of consumer behaviour theory to the specific context of tourism may significantly increase the level of knowledge and understanding of both why and how tourism is consumed.

References

adventuretravel.com(2000) www.adventuretravel.com

Appadurai, A. (ed.) (1986), *The Social Life of Things*, Cambridge: Cambridge University Press.

Arnould, E. and Price, L. (1993), River Magic: Extraordinary Experience and Extended Service Encounter, *Journal of Consumer Research* 20 (June): 24 45.

Baudrillard, J. (1988), *Selected Writings*, Cambridge: Polity Press.

Belk, R. (1995), Studies in the New Consumer Behaviour, in D. Miller (ed.) *Acknowledging Consumption*, London: Routledge: 58-95.

Belk, R., Wallendorf, M. and Sherry, J. (1989), The Sacred and the Profane in Consumer Behaviour: Theodicy on the Odyssey, *Journal of Consumer Research* 16 (June): 1-38.

Bourdieu, P. (1986), *Distinction: A Social Critique of the Judgement of Taste*, London: Routledge.

Campbell, C. (1995), The Sociology of Consumption, in D. Miller (ed.) *Acknowledging Consumption*, London: Routledge: 96-126.

Campbell, C. (1987), *The Romantic Ethic and the Spirit of Modern Consumerism*, Oxford: Blackwell.

Dann, G. (1996), *The Language of Tourism: a Socio-Linguistic Perspective*, Wallingford: CAB International.

Douglas, M. and Isherwood, B. (1979), *The World of Goods*, London: Allen Lane.

Featherstone, M. (1990), Perspectives on Consumer Culture, *Sociology* 24(1): 5-22.

Featherstone, M. (1991), *Consumer Culture and Postmodernism*, London: Sage Publications.

Feifer, M. (1985), *Going Places*, London: Macmillan.

Goodall, B. (1991), Understanding Holiday Choice, in C. Cooper (ed.) *Progress in Tourism, Recreation and Hospitality Research, Vol 3*, London: Bellahven Press: 58-77.

Graburn, N. (1989), Tourism: The Sacred Journey, in V. Smith (ed.) *Hosts and Guests: the Anthropology of Tourism, 2nd Edition*, Philadelphia: University of Pennsylvania Press: 21-36.

Gray, H. (1970), *International Travel: International Trade*, Lexington: DC Heath.

Harvey, D. (1990), *The Condition of Postmodernity*, Oxford: Blackwell.

Holbrook, M. and Hirschman, E. (1982), The Experiential Aspects of Consumption: Consumer Fantasies, Feelings and Fun, *Journal of Consumer Research* 9: 132-140.

Holt, D. (1995), How Consumers Consume: A Typology of Consumption Practices, *Journal of Consumer Research* 22 (June): 1-16.

Lash, S. (1990), *Sociology of Postmodernism*, London: Routledge.

Lury, C. (1996), *Consumer Culture*, Cambridge: Polity Press.

Madrigal, R. and Kahle, L. (1994), Predicting Vacation Activity Preferences on the Basis of Value-System Segmentation, *Journal of Travel Research* 32 (3): 22-28.

McCracken, G. (1986), Culture and Consumption: A Theoretical Account of the Structure and Movement of the Cultural Meaning of Consumer Goods, *Journal of Consumer Research* 13 (June): 71-84.

Mill, R. and Morrison, A. (1985), *The Tourism System*, New Jersey: Prentice Hall International.

Munt, I. (1994), The 'Other' Postmodern Tourism: Culture, Travel and the New Middle Classes, *Theory, Culture and Society* 11 (3): 101-123.

Pearce, P. (1992), Funamentals of Tourist Motivation, in D. Pearce and R. Butler (ed.) *Tourism Research: Critiques and Challenges*, London: Routledge: 113-134.

Pizam, A. and Calantone, R. (1987), Beyond Psychographics – Values as Determinants of Tourist Behaviour, *International Journal of Hospitality Management* 6(3): 177-181.

Poon, A. (1993), *Tourism, Technology and Competitive Strategies*, Wallingford: CAB International.

Pretes, M. (1995), Postmodern Tourism: The Santa Claus Industry, *Annals of Tourism Research* 22 (1): 1-15.

Schmoll, G. (1977), *Tourism Promotion*, London: Tourism International Press.

Sharpley, R. (1996), Tourism and Consumer Culture in Postmodern Society, in M. Robinson *et al* (ed.) *Tourism and Cultural Change*, Sunderland: Business Education Publishers.

Sharpley, R. (1999), *Tourism, Tourists and Society, 2ⁿᵈ Edition*, Huntingdon: Elm Publications.

Shields, R. (1991), *Places on the Margin: Alternative Geographies of Modernity*, London: Routledge.

Smith, C. and Jenner, P. (1999), The Adventure Travel Market in Europe, *Travel and Tourism Analyst, No 4*.

Thurot, J. and Thurot, G. (1983), The Ideology of Class and Tourism: Confronting the Discourse of Advertising, *Annals of Tourism Research* 10 (1): 173-189.

TIA (1997), *The Adventure Travel Report*, Travel Industry Association of America.

Urry, J. (1990a,) The Consumption of Tourism, *Sociology* 24 (1): 23-35.

Urry, J.(1990b), *The Tourist Gaze*, London: Sage Publications.

Urry, J. (1994), Cultural Change and Contemporary Tourism, *Leisure Studies* 13 (4): 233-238.

Veblen, T. (1925), *The Theory of the Leisure Class: An Economic Study of Institutions,* London: Allen and Unwin.

Voase, R. (1995), *Tourism: The Human Perspective*, London: Hodder and Stoughton.

Warde, A. (1992), Notes on the Relationship between Production and Consumption, in R. Burrows and C. Marsh (ed.) *Consumption and Class*, Basingstoke: Macmillan:15-31.

The international backpacker market in Britain: a market waiting to happen

Richard Shipway

University of Northumbria, UK

Abstract

Backpacker travel continues to be overlooked by both academic and market research and by the tourism industry and tourist boards in Britain, in favour of more traditional tourist types. This paper seeks to establish whether backpacker travel is an under-estimated and under-valued sub-sector of the British tourism industry.

The backpacker sector of the contemporary tourism industry is characterised by a relative paucity of research and market knowledge, especially in the British context. Current research originates almost exclusively from the Southern Hemisphere, especially Australia. The findings of this paper are based on research conducted in Britain in July / August 1999.

The paper identifies a significant relationship between backpacker travel and modern youth travel. The large youth travel market in Europe suggests that Britain could benefit more substantially, with extended provision aimed at this sub-sector of the British tourism market.

The paper identifies levels of interest and expenditure by international backpackers in Britain and their extended duration of stay. A combination of these factors indicates that international backpackers can be more significant economic contributors to the British tourism industry than is traditionally perceived.

The research also assesses backpacker attitudes, perceptions and experiences of the nature and structure of supply for backpacking visits to Britain. The paper highlights the need for an integrated transport and accommodation network that better caters for the needs of international backpackers, who constitute a substantial and valuable sub-sector of the British tourism industry, with significant growth potential. The research highlights that action could be taken by tourism organisations particularly to stimulate better provision for the backpacker market, in order to realise this potential.

Conclusions and recommendations from this paper concentrate on the future strategies required for marketing, accommodation provision, transport networks, the role of national/regional tourist authorities and areas for future research on the backpacker market in Britain.

Introduction

Backpacking is an example of a group of visitors, who due to their propensity to consume local products put money directly back into the local economy. However, one of the central themes of this research is that this potential is not being utilised in the British tourism industry, because the backpacker market niche is relatively unrecognised for its potential size and is undervalued.

While backpacking tourism is increasingly identified world-wide as a growth market, this valuable sub-sector of the British tourism industry remains largely ignored by tourism operators in Britain. In comparison, it is apparent that the 'quality' tourism sector is highly promoted and marketed. Backpacking continues to be overlooked by tourist boards in favour of more traditional tourists, especially those who are assumed to be higher spending visitors. The apparent neglect of the backpacker sector by tourism authorities is particularly surprising as this form of tourism fits the principles of 'sustainable' tourism, often highlighted in government and tourist board rhetoric.

The UK policy emphasis towards 'quality tourism' fails to account for the number of transactions that backpackers make in the countries visited. Backpackers are perceived to spend less than other categories of visitors and are therefore consigned to the foot of the promotional ladder. Initial spending is admittedly low per transaction, yet over the entire trip backpackers emerge as high spenders due to their extended duration of stay. Further, the volume of these visitors in terms of numbers involved makes this a valuable sub-sector of the UK tourism market.

This research is designed to have an influence on destination suppliers of backpacker travel products and upon tourism analysts and planners more generally. The British tourist economy could be failing to recognise and therefore capitalise on, the very features that make this market attractive to international budget tourists. While seeking to establish the economic significance of the backpacking market to the British tourism industry, a secondary aim is to identify what it is like to be a backpacker in Britain today. This may be valuable in better provision for this market and in contributing to an understanding of the characteristics, motivations and behaviour of backpackers.

Greater co-operation may be required at national level to address the needs of backpackers. Indicative data on the economic value of this sector suggests that action may be required to persuade national tourism organisations to accord a higher priority to backpacker travel. The current product appears to be fragmented. The research identifies the need for a more integrated network of accommodation and transport provision for the backpacker sector, rather than a series of isolated points of activity.

The reviewed research evidence that does exist might, lead one to the, not unreasonable, conclusion that the proportion of Britain's overseas visitors who are backpackers could be similar to that of other countries that have quantified this market. As an example, backpacking constitutes 8% of the overall tourism market in the case of Australia (Loker-Murphy and Pearce, 1995). This fact, coupled with data identified later in this paper, starts to indicate that there are likely to be over 1½ million overseas backpacker visitors to Britain annually.

Market definition

It is hard to formulate a comprehensive definition of what constitutes a 'backpacker', although many important characteristics have emerged. Keeley (1995) described backpacking as a distinct form of tourism because it is:

- Fuelled by motivations characteristic of younger people;

- Characterised by long stay, high activity holidays with an emphasis on informality and a minimum use of packaged products;

- Undertaken by an international group of adults from a range of social backgrounds.

Loker-Murphy and Pearce (1995) established certain characteristics, including backpackers:

- Preference for budget accommodation;

- Emphasis on meeting other people;

- Independently organised / flexible travel schedules;

- Longer than brief holidays;

- Emphasis on informal and participating holiday activities.

Riley (1989) offered an alternative, defining 'budget travellers' as people wanting to extend their trip beyond that of a brief annual holiday and faced with the necessity of living on a budget. They fall into the 'budget traveller' category rather than the 'tourist mode', often seen as being at a junction in their lives. Budget travellers invariably reject the tourist label on the grounds of lack of money and the extended length of time available to them. Riley identified that the main difference between the backpacker and the typical mass tourist was that tourists gain status from visiting prestige resorts or five star hotels, while the backpacker ego is enhanced from getting 'best value' and their status can be enhanced with tales of struggle and hardship.

Keeley (1995) identifies the motivation for travel as a mix of factors and rarely one driving force. Motivations were seen as:

- The notions that travel broadens the mind;

- A way that young people can postpone certain socio-economic decisions such as careers, marriage or settling down;

- Travel provides the opportunity to mix socially with other like-minded individuals;

- The experience of contrasting cultures helps to gain a greater understanding of others and ones own cultural values.

Attractiveness of backpacking to the international market

The backpacker market is an important sub-sector of the tourism market contributing economic benefits for the following reasons:

- Backpackers have a low propensity to import with their small backpacks and, therefore, a high propensity to spend on domestically produced goods and services;

- The only item purchased in their country of origin is the inbound travel ticket and personal insurance;

- Purchasing decisions are made daily due to the carrying limitations and so their entire spending is available to businesses in the places where they happen to be;

- Encouraging backpacking will increase and spread geographically the economic benefits from overseas tourism.

Backpacker tourism has unique features that could make it attractive to tourist authorities seeking to increase the commercial benefits from overseas markets. These include spreading economic benefits into areas as yet not experiencing it, avoiding the congestion of car borne tourism by using public transport, and avoiding the need for capital intensive resort development and infrastructure changes.

There are numerous attributes making Britain attractive to backpacker travellers. These include:

- A historic role in the world – attractive to young people hoping to know and experience Britain's past;

- A coastal and varied topography, for an extensive and diverse range of outdoor pursuits;

- Britain has the advantage that many young people from the main source countries have an adequate command of the English language to enable them to travel independently.

Negative interpretations of the contemporary backpacker are prevalent. In some parts of the world backpackers are perceived as people who leave little but resentment in their wake. Backpacking is seen as an almost compulsory addition to the college leaver's cirriculum vitae. In South East Asia, backpackers are accused of lacking respect for religion and cultures, demanding a westernised travel experience, having little interest in the places they visit and are only seeking a home from home (Hampton, 1998). However, it could clearly be argued that this is little different to a typical British sun/sea holiday in Spain or Greece and too broad to apply to backpackers on a global scale.

Research methodology

The main techniques for data collection were a questionnaire completed at four independent hostels, telephone interviews with representatives of four Regional Tourist Boards, interviews with independent hostel managers and owners, interviews with international backpackers, and participant observation field research.

Four independent backpacker hostels were chosen as sites to conduct the main section of this research study. The locations were Glastonbury, Cardiff, Oxford, and Stratford-upon-Avon. These locations were intended to provide access to a wide variety of international backpackers, avoided the bias that may result from the use of a single location and proved to be more desirable than conducting research at entry/exit points such as Gatwick airport or Victoria coach station in London.

The Lonely Planet guidebook (1999) proved invaluable during the research period as a source of information on accommodation and transport provision for budget travellers. The guidebooks are considered essential tools for the international backpacker in the UK.

Results

Backpacker profile

45.6% of respondents to the questionnaire were male and 54.4% were female, representing a balanced sample. The results confirmed that backpacking is dominated by people in the 16–29 years age range. 83% of those surveyed were under 30 years of age. Within this, the dominant ranges were 21-24 and 25-29, together accounting for 59.2% of the respondents.

Figure 1

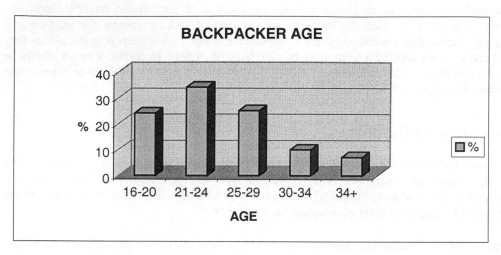

58% of backpackers were in the 16-24 years of age group, confirming previous findings that young people dominate backpacker travel. The growing youth market in Europe, identified by Seekings (1998) and the young age of many backpacker visitors, highlights the potential of this market for Britain at present.

Figure 2 demonstrates the prime countries of origin of backpackers to Britain, and again, the findings reflect the breakdown of numbers highlighted in the Annual Report of the YHA (1998). Australia accounted for 27.9% of respondents, followed by USA / Canada with 19.7%, New Zealand 9.5%, Germany 7.5% and Italy 6.1%.

Figure 2

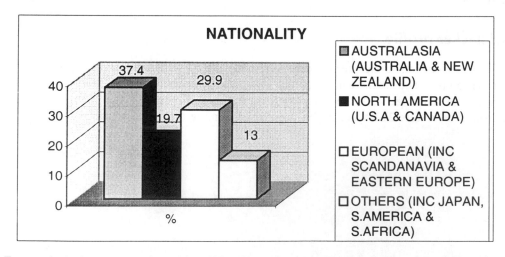

For analytical purposes the nationalities have been grouped into four broader categories (Australasia, North America, Europe [including Eastern Europe and the Scandinavian countries] and Others [including Japan, South Africa and South America].).

These aggregate groups were used because a full breakdown masks the impact of the European visitors, who were distributed over fifteen countries, including visitors from Eastern Europe and Scandinavia. It is important not to place too much emphasis on Australia (with a population of 18 million), while Europe has substantial market potential, with a population approaching 400 million.

Tourist authority perspective on backpacker travel

One of the questions this research aimed to address was the apparent neglect of the backpacker market by tourist authorities in Britain. Despite acknowledgement, positive action remains very limited.

Backpackers avoid the congestion that mainstream tourists bring to the city centres. Many cities are concerned with the influx of tourists aggravating the local community, with their high demand for the city centre attractions. 'Quality' tourists come to cities to visit the internal 'sights', while backpackers as independent travellers have more time available and can explore a 'wider net' of activities, not solely the central attractions that mass tourists are attracted to.

Backpackers have the potential to disperse economic activity to places that mainstream tourists do not visit, and this matches the aims of many Tourist Board's, who are trying to strike a balance between the beauty of the attractions and respect (and economic advantage) for the local communities.

Accreditation schemes

While regional Tourist Board's acknowledge the backpacker market, they appear to be unable to market or promote establishments that have not been granted an official accreditation from the Tourist Board. Each location would need to be visited and rated by a Tourist Board official. However, there is no rating system in place for hostel / YHA accommodation at present, and the only category for which these establishments could receive accreditation is as guesthouses or self-catering accommodation, which are not suitable criteria. Hostels find themselves in the middle ground with no suitable classification system, which is a problem that needs to be addressed in the short term.

Tourist Boards are faced with limited budgets and pressures from other areas of the tourism market, which have prevented a more thorough review of backpacker provision. It is likely that due to the relative paucity of figures on backpacker travel in Britain, many Tourist Boards are not fully aware of the potential of the market and have yet to react positively.

Travel intentions and duration of stay

This research indicates that 66.6% of backpackers arriving in the UK came directly from their country of origin. Britain would appear to be the first (or primary) destination for many international backpackers, who have yet to be exposed to the attractions of other countries. With two major international airports in London, it appears that a high percentage of travellers are flying directly into Heathrow or Gatwick at the start of their travels. If this market can be identified and convinced of the merits of staying in the UK, the economic benefits will increase and reduce departure to other destinations.

Other countries that backpackers were arriving from were predominantly European, especially France, Holland and Belgium. A high level of Australasian visitors had arrived in the UK from South East Asia. It appears that their tickets, purchased in their country of origin, allowed a stopover in Bangkok or Singapore and many took advantage of this opportunity for further travel before arriving in Britain.

Time away from country of origin

Figure 3 indicates that backpackers spend a relatively long period of time away from their country of origin. At the time of questioning, 39.4% of respondents had already been travelling for between 1-4 weeks and 21.7% had already been travelling for between 1-3 months.

Figure 3

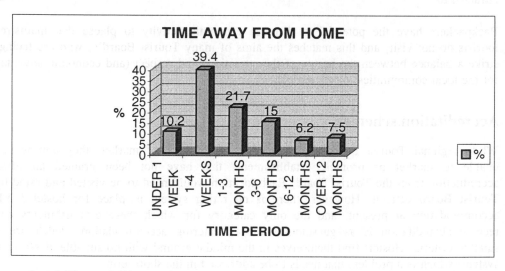

Figure 4 and Figure 5 illustrate the time that backpackers have been in the UK and how much longer they intend to stay. To collect comprehensive 'duration of stay' figures it would be desirable to conduct a complimentary post-travel survey. At this stage of questioning, any responses were purely outline plans or travel intentions. An analysis on how long visitors 'intend to stay', helps to indicate their contribution to the UK economy through tourism.

Figure 4

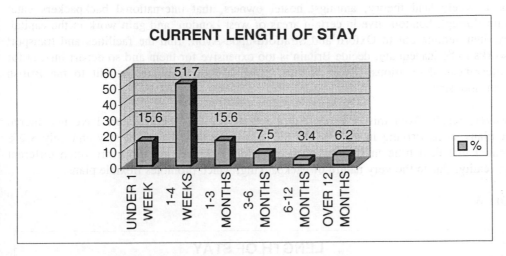

Both graphs indicate an extended length of stay for backpackers in the British Isles. 51.7% of respondents indicated that they had already been in Britain for between 1-4 weeks and 16% had been in the UK for between 1-3 months. These figures on the extended length of stay support the previous findings of Keeley (1995) and Loker-Murphy and Pearce (1995).

Figure 5

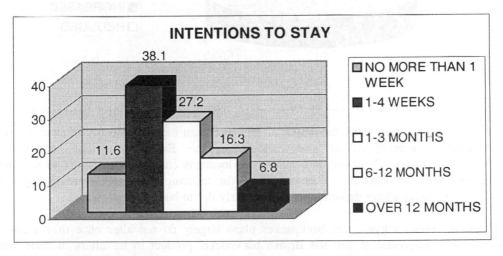

38% of respondents intended to stay for between 1-4 weeks, while 27.2%, over a quarter of the survey, intend to stay in Britain for 1-3 months and 23% intend to stay for a further 6 months or longer, in addition to whatever time they have already spent in the UK. The extended length of stay of backpacker visitors, coupled with their levels of expenditure, would indicate that they are significant contributors to the British tourism industry.

Changing travel plans

It is a widely held theory, amongst hostel owners, that international backpackers enter Britain through London, live in certain areas of west London, and gain work in the capital. They then venture out to Oxford and Stratford-upon-Avon, find the facilities and transport networks to be inadequate, decide Britain is too expensive for them and so depart instead for Mediterranean destinations. There is thus, potential lost economic benefit to the British tourism industry.

However, results from this research indicate that 78.2% of backpackers have not altered their plans since arriving in the UK, 13.6% increasing their length of stay and only 8.2% indicated that their time in Britain had been reduced. Travel intentions are often different from reality, due to the very nature of backpacking, which promotes flexible plans.

Figure 6

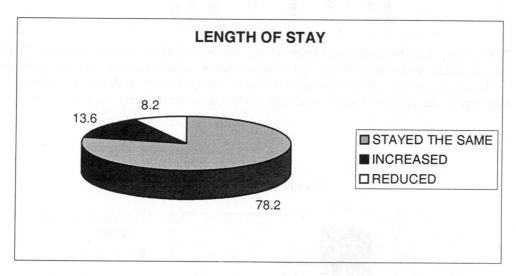

Reasons given for increasing the length of stay in Britain included more venues to see than anticipated, improvements in understanding of the English language, employment opportunities, 'word of mouth' information on locations encouraging visitors to visit new places and flexible itineraries. Reasons given for reducing the length were mainly cost-related, with backpackers departing to Europe early due to budgetary pressures.

The above results suggest that backpacker plans largely do not alter once they arrive in Britain. It is important to sell the British backpacker product to travellers in their home countries and try to influence their length of stay before they purchase their ticket. If travellers are aware that an extensive, integrated backpacker product exists in Britain, then this may convince travellers to plan to stay longer in Britain from the outset.

'Word-of-mouth' promotion remains a vital ingredient of backpacking. An increasing flow of 'word-of-mouth' information from experienced travellers to newcomer's results in a well-trodden network centred on established gathering places. The latest 'in' spots are communicated in this way, on the grapevine, via fellow travellers.

This is one of the characteristics that make the backpacking market so hard to define and assess. Many people arrive in a hostel or at friends or relatives houses, discuss itineraries and then, based on the recommendations and suggestions of their fellow travellers, routes will develop or change accordingly.

Hostel case study

Cardiff Backpacker Hostel, Cardiff, Wales

The independent hostel guide (1998) provides official statistics for budget accommodation in individual cities or locations. In Cardiff budget accommodation provision is 68 beds at the Cardiff YHA and 50 beds at Cardiff backpacker hostel. The guide estimates that Cardiff should be providing at least 190 beds, to have a comparative pro rata provision with cities like Edinburgh, York or London. There are only 108 beds per night in the city, an estimated deficit of approximately 72 beds for the backpacker market. These figures from the independent hostel guide (1998) suggest that Cardiff could support a larger supply in terms of accommodation provision. This is reflected by the 100% occupancy rates that both the Cardiff YHA and Cardiff backpacker hostel have at weekends from April to October.

Cardiff is a city with a growing reputation as a centre for young people. The hostel see it's main competition as the YHA and continues to promote their business with the distribution of 'flyers' and direct mailing campaigns, while embarking on networking through 'word of mouth' amongst other hostels.

The owner of 'Cardiff Backpacker' hostel, profiles his typical backpacker client as 'generally young (17-34 years old), resourceful, generally from ABC1 socio economic groups, with an empathy towards each other. They like socialising, drinking, staying out late and are generally 'green' friendly'.

The hostel requires a 40% occupancy rate to break even, however they continue to attract secondary markets and seek to target new potential market segments. Other markets include school and youth groups, university students on open days, visitors to Cardiff for rock concerts, special events, festivals or people on the way to or from Ireland. The Cardiff hostel was fully booked by mid May 1999 for the Rugby World Cup games played in Cardiff during October 1999.

Cardiff backpacker hostel gains revenue from the sale of guide books, batteries, camera film, T shirts, pens, maps, postcards, soap, shampoo and towels. The business generates economic benefits from franchise revenues, such as sales of soft drinks, snacks, cigarette machines, condom machines, in-house tours, fax and e-mail access, laundrette facilities, a jukebox and pool table. With the franchise revenue it is estimated that each backpacker spends £4.50 per person on top of the accommodation rate of £12.50 for a dormitory bed. These extensive services and the various daily deliveries of goods to the hostel are generating economic benefit to the local economy from backpacker travel.

If the Wales Tourist Board were fully aware of the high demand for backpacking, then they may consider supporting future accommodation development in Wales that would see the introduction of more international backpacker visitors.

Backpacker concessions

This research identified the need for the availability of concessions to backpackers. Often travellers are priced out of the market for mainstream tourist attractions because no reductions or concessions exist for backpackers.

In Cardiff it costs £5 to visit Cardiff Castle, with no concessions available. Tourist boards could investigate the possibility of approaching attractions with a view to offering discounts. In Cardiff hostel several backpackers expressed a desire to visit the castle, however they were not willing to pay £5. It may be more beneficial to allow two backpackers on a concession rate, paying £3 each, than to have both visitors not visit the castle at all.

It is possible that by not offering student or backpacker concessions, Cardiff Castle and many other attractions in Cardiff have eliminated a large potential market, particularly in not operating a tiered pricing structure. Lack of discounts could reflect the Wales Tourist Board's low priority towards backpackers, where the emphasis is on the short stay, high spending 'quality' tourists. It could also be that attractions in Cardiff are unaware of the scale of the backpacker market, and thus not offering discounts.

Location case study - Glastonbury

Backpacker visitors are heavily reliant on public transport while in Britain. To reach Glastonbury from London is an expensive and awkward journey by public transport. A train journey from London to Bath or Bristol costs £30 return. There is no direct link to Glastonbury. Independent travellers have to catch a bus from Bath to Wells and then catch another local bus to Glastonbury. There is one direct bus from Bath to Glastonbury, however this only operates on Sunday. This problem highlights the need for a more integrated transport system, providing ease of access to a prime backpacking location, such as Glastonbury. Potential visitors could be deterred from visiting the Southwest tip of England due to a fragmented transport system. This contrasts with the integrated transport network operating in Australia.

Glastonbury was a research location that provided access to a sector of the backpacking market that had made a conscious effort to move away from major cities and disperse their economic benefits to peripheral locations. Many of the backpackers questioned were en route to Cornwall to visit places like Penzance, Lands End, Newquay and Tintagel.

The hostel caters for the local population at weekends and the influx of 'new age' visitors around festival times. Glastonbury has the potential to become a 'Mecca' for backpackers, similar to the development of Byron Bay in Australia (Firth and Hing, 1999). The West Country tourist board and private transport operators could consider improving the transport links to enable the backpackers to reach Glastonbury.

Further research is needed to establish whether London based backpackers do actually travel to the other home countries or depart immediately to European destinations. One concern is that backpackers earning money in Britain, are not spending this money in destinations like Glastonbury or Cardiff, but it is going straight to mainland Europe when they choose to leave Britain, without having travelled extensively. These backpackers could be persuaded to stay in Britain longer, and spend their money in Britain. An integrated accommodation and transport system, supported by Tourist Boards, would help to convince international visitors of the benefits of staying in Britain.

Surveys and interviews conducted for this research indicate that a high percentage of Australian or New Zealand backpackers intend to spend a majority of their time in the UK working in London. This would suggest that future marketing plans would have limited impact, because these visitors never intend to travel extensively. Target markets for promotion could be the nationalities that move around during their stay. Too much emphasis may be given to the Australasian market, rather than to the much larger European market and their travel patterns.

Backpacker information sources

Results indicate that 70% of respondents obtain information from Tourist Information Centres. The range and quality of literature and information available at the Tourist Information Centres is restricted, possibly reflecting the low priority given to this sub-sector of the tourism market. The potential size of the backpacker market could be used to persuade the Tourist Information Centres to provide information suitable to the needs of backpackers. 33.3% of respondents to the survey are regular users of Internet sites, 86.4% of respondents use guide books, such as 'Lonely Planet' or 'Rough Guide' to gain information on the British Isles. 21.3% gained information on Britain from other sources that included friends, word of mouth, relatives and friends, newspapers, hostel 'flyers', assistance from hostel employees, previous trips to Britain and travel agents.

Internet promotion is an increasingly important medium for promoting the backpacker market. The Internet allows overseas visitors access to information on Britain, prior to arrival, and while in the UK. Private marketing consortiums such as 'Hostels in Europe', 'Backpackers Britain' and 'VIP' or 'Nomads' in Australia focus promotion on the Internet. Promotion on the Internet can convince travellers that an integrated product exists in the UK, that it is easy to travel with good accommodation provision. Much of this promotion and selling can be done before travellers buy their outbound ticket and leave their country of origin.

Travel experiences

Figure 7

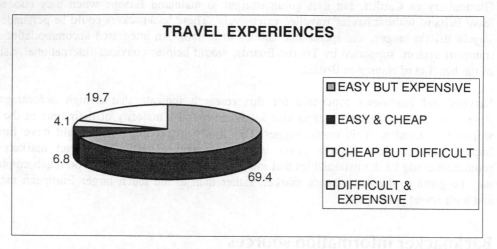

TRAVEL EXPERIENCES

19.7
4.1
6.8
69.4

☑ EASY BUT EXPENSIVE

■ EASY & CHEAP

☐ CHEAP BUT DIFFICULT

☐ DIFFICULT & EXPENSIVE

89.1% of respondents did find Britain to be expensive, however 76.2% indicated that they found travelling around Britain to be relatively easy. 69.4% of respondents rated Britain as easy but expensive and 19.7% found the UK to be both difficult and expensive.

A significant part of this research highlights the potential barriers and obstacles identified by backpackers, tourist boards, private transport providers and hostel owners in Britain. However, a major indication from this research was that backpackers did find it east to travel in the UK and cost was more of a consideration. Resourceful backpackers will reach their intended destination, although their journey could be made easier than at present.

Range of accommodation

Budgetary constraints limited the range of accommodation used by backpackers to the lower priced end of the accommodation market. Only 5.4% of backpackers used quality hotels, 32.6% stayed in Bed and Breakfast/budget hotels, 54.4% used YHA accommodation and 32.6% of respondents had stayed with friends or relatives.

Figure 8

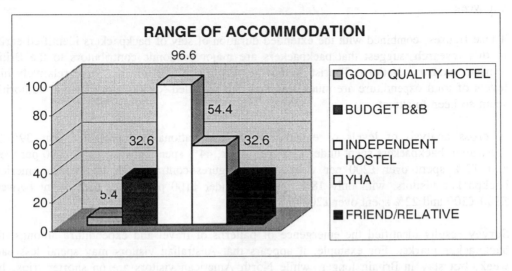

These results begin to illustrate that backpackers use a wide range of accommodation if the price is suitable. This is encouraging for any potential budget accommodation providers that may intend to diversify and try to attract backpacker visitors.

Expenditure

Expenditure levels of international backpacker's highlights the economic contribution that the backpacking market makes to the tourism industry in Britain. The most prominent ranges of weekly expenditure were £101-£150 accounting for 34.7% and £151-£200, which accounted for 25.8% of those surveyed.

Figure 9

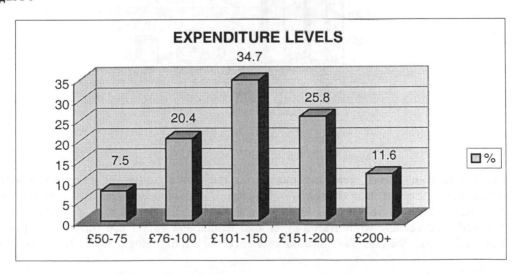

72.1% of respondents, almost ¾ of those surveyed, spent over £100 per week, while the top two categories £151-£200 and £200+, indicated that 37.4% of respondents spend over £150 per week.

These figures, combined with the extended duration of stay of backpackers identified earlier in this research, suggest that backpackers are major economic contributors to the British tourism industry. National Tourist Authorities could consider whether these relatively high levels of total expenditure are much less than the so-called 'quality' tourists that authorities seem so keen to attract.

A cross analysis of levels of expenditure against nationality highlighted that 39% of Australian backpackers spent under £100 per week, 44% spent between £150-£200 per week and 17% spent over £200 per week. These figures contrast with the North American backpacker visitors, with only 18% spending under £100 per week, 60% spent between £100-£200 and 22% spent over £200 per week.

Survey results identified the emergence of patterns of travel and expenditure amongst the backpacker market. For example, it appears that Australian visitors may spend less each week, but stay in Britain longer, while North American visitors are on shorter trips, but spend more money during their stay in Britain.

Transport

Figure 10

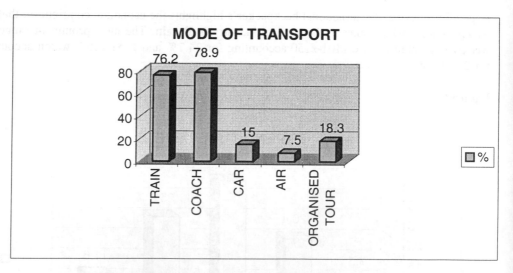

Coach and train travel were the most frequently used modes of transport amongst backpackers. At some stage of their travels, over ¾ of respondents had used both the train and coach. 78.9% of respondents had used coach travel and 76.2% had used trains. Only 15% had used car hire while travelling around Britain and 18.3% had travelled on private organised tours, such as the 'Stray Experience' or 'Hairy Hog'. Only 7.5% used air transport and these were the inexpensive flight offers to Ireland and Scotland with companies such as Ryanair or Easyjet.

These figures are useful for transport providers such as National Express, Stagecoach or railway franchise operators. They demonstrate that the backpacking market is using their services. The needs of backpackers could be considered when developing future transport strategies, given the potential significance of backpacker travel. Once again, many transport operators may be unaware of the size of the backpacker market, given the limited market research and promotion of this valuable sub-sector of the British tourism industry.

Transport provision is one area of provision criticised by independent travellers to Britain. Many international backpackers have an impression of a fragmented transport system in Britain. Several travellers were critical of National Express for not providing detailed travel maps of the UK, or details on possible routings and stop-off destinations. Many travellers could only obtain a price, arrival and departure time from one destination to another. In Australia, Greyhound coaches supply comprehensive details on routes and the times that coaches are due to pass through tourist destinations.

European integration

Results of this research indicated that almost 30% of backpackers questioned came from European countries. On a European level, backpacker development can be viewed as a positive influence towards greater European integration, by encouraging a youth market that have market potential for many years to come. These youth groups are the high spenders of the future. These groups have the opportunity to experience the cultural and heritage experiences of the UK and to appreciate what Britain can offer to Europe. Cultural experiences could help to increase the feelings of belonging to Europe, contributing to the development of European cultures, encouraging cultural activity and fostering co-operation.

Market size

In 1997, 25.2 million overseas visitors came to Britain, spending more than £12 billion pounds. The BTA (British Tourist Authority) estimate that by the year 2003, overseas visitors, estimated at 32 million, will spend around £18 billion a year in the UK, 47% more than in 1997 (www.star.co.uk).

It is logical that Britain could have a backpacker market presence equal to the 8% experienced in Australia. This prediction, compared with the figures above, provides an indication of the potential economic significance of backpacker travel to the British tourism industry. At 1997 levels, if it was assumed that backpackers constituted as little as 5% of all overseas tourists, this would equate to 1 ¼ million visitors. If the figure was compared to the 8% experienced by Australia then the number of international backpackers in Britain could be as high as 2 million each year.

In terms of expenditure levels, over £12 billion was spent in 1997. A backpacker contribution of 5% of total expenditure, once again a very realistic figure, would equate to a contribution of £620 million to the British economy each year. 8% of overseas expenditure would equate to spending of at least £960 million per year.

Future strategies

Marketing of the British backpacker product

Current marketing plans for the backpacker sector appear to be non existent in Britain. This research has identified the prime backpacker countries of origin, which could have implications for both tourist boards and private tourism marketing organisations. This could help facilitate provision to suit the needs and wants of these prominent backpacker-generating countries.

Tourist Boards could investigate and promote the marketing of the British backpacker product overseas. At present, it is not known in detail exactly what a young overseas backpacker to Britain hopes to see or the experiences that they wish to gain from their visit. It is necessary to establish the best way of communicating information on the British market to the prime countries of origin such as Australia, New Zealand, USA/Canada or Germany, to inform independent travellers of the product that is awaiting them in Britain. One challenge is to try to establish sales and distribution outlets in the host country and ensure that potential backpackers are presented with literature about Britain prior to the start of their travels. At present, this is rarely a focus of BTA outlets overseas.

Integrated accommodation and transport networks

There remains a need for an integrated accommodation and transport network for budget travellers in Britain. At present there is limited cohesive, integrated action or organisations working together to provide for this market. Potential exists for a network of integrated businesses providing transport, accommodation and activities, which informally co-operate to develop a defined, travel route, for their mutual financial gain. These include:

- Public and private transport operators, such as National Express, railway companies or regional bus companies;

- Potential for businesses, (shops, bars, cheap restaurants) in communities / districts often not regarded as hot spots for tourists;

- Budget accommodation providers;

- Outdoor pursuits / activity providers.

At present the principal weaknesses restricting independent travellers around the UK are:

- Lack of alternative supplies of budget accommodation other than the YHA;

- Lack of dedicated transport policy for independent travellers.

An integrated transport network is required to move backpackers away from gateway points like London and allow their economic potential to be dispersed. Co-operation between tourist boards, accommodation and transport providers would further facilitate and encourage backpackers to visit areas outside of London. Future developments may assist to increase local transport links to help connect travellers. This research demonstrates that only 18% of backpackers travelled on organised tours like the 'Stray Experience', 'Border Raiders', 'Haggis Tours' of 'Hairy Hog Tours'. Many backpackers want independent travel options and these are needed to help facilitate their movement around Britain.

Overview of budget accommodation provision

Quality grading

Any major accommodation expansion must see the introduction of quality grading schemes into the budget accommodation market to avoid the rise of poor quality accommodation and ensure that quality standards are maintained across all accommodation types.

London has numerous examples of low standard budget accommodation. It is unfortunate that these sub standard locations often provide backpackers with their first experience of the UK, which is often negative, and which may deter backpackers from travelling elsewhere to the hostels with higher standards. It is important to differentiate between good and poorer levels of provision, and low standard provision should be eliminated. A nationally agreed rating system was sought by all hostel owners interviewed in this research.

The Youth Hostel Association (YHA)

The present structure of the YHA in Britain is perceived as a major obstacle for many overseas visitors. The organisation is perceived as an unfriendly organisation and this 'dowdy' image often deters backpackers from staying, due to the perceived high level of rules and regulations. This very structure alienates potential customers. The following quote represents the general impression this research found regarding the YHA in Britain, from the backpacker/youth market perspective.

> *"The YHA in the early years appealed to ramblers, cyclists and people with a love for the countryside. Unfortunately it has got stuck with an image. The YHA has a major image problem amongst independent travellers. Adult independent travellers do not want to share a night with a bunch of ten-year-olds all singing ten green bottles or charging around doing treasure hunts. The current image is one of hairy knees, hot chocolate at ten o' clock, cleaning duties, girls and boys dorms, scrabble in the common room, disinfectant, born again evangelists and about as much chance of getting laid as of winning the lottery".* (Independent Travel Marketing Manager)

This research suggests the need for an image makeover for the YHA in Britain, to alter its current image amongst many overseas backpackers. In Britain, current accommodation provision is far too reliant on the YHA. The very problems that the organisation faces could act as an incentive for other budget accommodation providers to enter the budget traveller market.

Accommodation potential

There are various other providers of accommodation that could cater to the backpacker market. As long haul and European holidays have become cheaper, the traditional suppliers of accommodation have found themselves in a contracting market. The national and regional tourist authorities have advised them to upgrade facilities to attract 'second holiday' or 'bargain break' holidays from the domestic market. This cost of capital upgrading is high and it is also high risk commercially in an increasingly competitive market. These smaller establishments are also aware that they need to comply with catering, hygiene and safety standards.

The backpacker market could be attractive to some of these businesses that may consider it as an alternative market, which they are able to supply. It should be noted that independent travellers are quite happy with self-catering provision and the food preparation and hygiene regulations do not apply to establishments offering this form of accommodation.

Any continuing deficit in accommodation provision could provide opportunities for British universities, or similar establishments, offering accommodation during the vacation periods. Prime location university halls of residence could provide summer hostels. Other accommodation providers that could cater effectively for backpackers include Bed and Breakfast accommodation, Caravan parks, Camping grounds, Field study centres with surplus accommodation or Inns and Public houses.

Some of the above categories could even incorporate partial diversification into the backpacker market. For example, pubs with accommodation could allocate a certain number of rooms as backpacker rooms within their total capacity.

Activity centres are also budget accommodation providers, who have experienced difficult trading conditions in recent years, resulting from major changes and uncertainties in the schools group market and the impact of recession upon management training or development courses. It is precisely this type of business, which stands to benefit from the development of the backpacker market. Backpackers have a disposition to 'do' things, rather than merely 'see' things. The active holiday phenomenon opens up more activity provision.

Any new hostels or accommodation providers must be in good centres with good transport links, have owners and managers who empathise with the 'traveller' ideology and be able to create an atmosphere attractive to travellers. Ironically, many potential suppliers of budget accommodation do not realise the size of this market. However, they have the capacity to supply it and reap the economic benefits that backpacker travel can bring.

Transport provision

The potential for future transport routes exists. An integrated UK transport network could also become part of a wider European integrated transport route catering for backpacker travel. A round-Britain trip could be followed by a trip to Ireland or a ferry journey from the Northeast of England to Bergen in Norway, which would further allow access to the Scandinavian countries. Alternatively, travellers could reach Southwest England and take the ferry to Santander in northern Spain, allowing access to the southern Mediterranean countries and even Northern Africa.

Tourist Boards could identify the means of transport that allows travel both around a region / area and from one centre to another, further along the route. It should not be forgotten that backpackers are not generally car-borne. This is a major advantage over mainstream tourism, with its numerous trips and increasing congestion.

One further growing transport sector that the suppliers of low budget accommodation should investigate, and again one with small business potential, is that of the increasing interest in cycle tourism. The developing 'national cycle network' in the UK, under the direction of SUSTRANS, is being integrated into a number of European cycle routes, and this can be linked to be mutually reinforcing with the traditional backpacker market.

Community developments

Whole towns, villages and areas could flourish along well defined travel routes, which are themselves good places to spend time, not because they are 'full of sights', but because they offer, for example, a particular or certain set of activities which travellers are likely to be interested in. In addition, they provide access to the diversity that many of the travellers are seeking.

Regions could identify and highlight activities available in their areas, which may encourage the development of routes and centres. Adjacent regions could co-operate together to attract independent travellers along well-defined backpacker routes, such as on the East Coast of Australia. Development of communities like Byron Bay in Australia, have become self-supporting based on backpacker trade. This has particular potential for some peripheral areas grappling with the decline of traditional rural industries.

In Australia, towns flourish by 'word of mouth' promotion, as significant numbers 'migrate' to towns like Byron Bay. This is based largely on conversations and exchanges of travel experiences. Here, for example, Newquay in Cornwall attracts a large youth culture, based around both the night life and surfing cultures. Adjacent villages could prosper, based around attracting and providing for youth travellers to Cornwall. The whole process is self-perpetuating, which is the very nature of backpacker tourism. Byron Bay is an example of what can be achieved with the necessary support from tourist boards.

There remains potential for such development in the British context. In Britain there are towns, villages and entire regions that suffer high under employment or unemployment, where even small amounts of employment would be welcome. Backpacker tourism could increase local participation in real development, as part of a more sustainable long-term strategy, particularly in peripheral regions.

Areas for future research

Further research could focus on better understanding of backpacker needs and wants. It is important that authorities investigate, and take into consideration, community attitudes towards this group of international visitors and that the tourism industry caters for them. Visiting backpackers will not gain a positive experience of the UK if they are not welcomed by the locations they visit, and are instead perceived as a nuisance.

It would be desirable to conduct research studies based in London, to analyse the flow and travel directions of international backpackers. London tends to be the initial point of entry and place of departure for visitors to Britain. This research could identify where backpackers go to from London, and what are the opportunities and constraints to spread more effectively the market around the UK.

Research could conduct detailed interviews with the main transport providers to the backpacker market, such as railway franchises, National Express or Stagecoach, to identify how they value the significance of backpacker travel to their industry, and how they see the market developing.

A larger survey would demonstrate the development of different subsets of groups. For example, more extensive research could start to display the activities that American females like to participate in; what Japanese visitors spend money on; or the duration of stay of Australian backpackers. Such segmentation studies would greatly enhance both effective provision and promotion.

Travel plans can change dramatically amongst backpackers. It would be desirable to conduct detailed research studies that distribute questionnaires to the home address of identified respondents once they have finished travelling and returned home, asking them to reflect on their travel experiences, problems and observations.

National and regional Tourist Board support could be lacking due to the relative paucity of confirmed figures. Future support may be forthcoming if Tourist Boards are convinced of the size of this potentially valuable sub-sector of the British tourism market. No present research suggests that the relevant authorities are even aware of the market size, and this makes it hard to support further development of backpacker travel. More comprehensive research, along the same lines, would provide the BTA and national / regional tourist authorities with more evidence that this market sector of the British tourism industry is one that they cannot afford to continue to ignore and undervalue.

Summary conclusions

Britain has a profile highly likely to appeal to the international backpacker traveller. Their relatively low daily expenditure is more than compensated for by their extended length of stay and the fact that they distribute their spending more widely throughout the country they are visiting.

Although often perceived as a low value market, and therefore low priority, the results of this research show that the British backpacker market has many commercially attractive characteristics. It is long staying, shown by the extended duration of stay, backpackers buy locally produced products, especially in towns like Glastonbury, development does not need high capital investment, and the young age of those visitors surveyed represents the long 'shelf life' of backpackers.

Tourist authority priority has, however, recently focused on the 'shift to quality' marketing strategy in the British tourism industry, with 'bargain break' weekends, en suite bathrooms or country house hotels. The strategy of promoting Britain, first and foremost, to visitors from higher income groups should be modified. This is in view of the economic benefit of a market, which due to it's above average duration of stay and high propensity to spend domestically / locally, will facilitate financial benefits to regions and areas which do not benefit presently from the current emphasis on 'quality' visitors. It appears that today's backpacker visitors are tomorrow's 'quality' tourists.

National and regional tourist authorities may consider rethinking the lack of attention, which has been given to the backpacker market. This will demand a much greater understanding of the hidden benefits of backpacker travel. This market, like other tourism markets, is a potential tool for economic development and maintaining declining communities.

It is important that both government and industry endeavour to monitor all of the impacts (both positive and negative) associated with the backpacker segment of the British tourism industry. At present, heritage-oriented, high quality, mass tourism is king in Britain, and the backpacker sector is not even a footnote on local or tourist authorities main tourism development agendas. The results of this research suggest that this is unfortunate, and that this segment can contribute economically to local communities and provide a further selling-medium for tourism to the UK.

References

Callaghan, P., Long, P., and Robinson, M. (1994), *Travel and Tourism*, Business Education Publishers Ltd.

Cooper, C., Fletcher, J. et al. (1998), *Tourism Principles and Practice*, Second Edition, Longman.

Firth, T., and Hing N., (1999), "Backpacker Hostels and their Guests: Attitudes and Behaviour Relating to Sustainable Tourism". *Tourism Management*, Volume 20 (2): 251-254.

Hampton, M. (1998), "Backpacker Tourism and Economic Development:" *Annals of Tourism Research*, Volume 25 (3) 639-660.

Hostelling International, (1998), *Annual Report of the International Youth Hostel Federation, 1997-1998*.

Keeley, P. (1995), "The International Backpacker Market". *BTA Insights*.

Kotler, P. (1997), *Marketing Management*, 9ᵗʰ Edition, Prentice-Hall International.

Loker-Murphy, L., and Pearce, P. (1995), "Young Budget Travellers: Backpackers in Australia". *Annals of Tourism Research*, Volume 22 (4): 819-843.

Mintel International Group Ltd., (1999), *Mintel Market Intelligence*, "Budget Hotels", April 1999.

Riley, P. L. (1988), "Road Culture of International Long-term Budget Travellers". *Annals of Tourism Research*. Volume 15 (3): 313-328.

Seekings, J. (1995), "Europe's Youth Travel Market", *BTA Insights*.

Seekings, J. (1998), "The Youth Travel Market". *Travel and Tourism Analyst*, No 5, 1998.

Smith, C., and Jenner, P. (1997), "Educational Tourism". *Travel and Tourism Analyst*, No 3, 1997.

Thomas, B., Smallman, T., and Yale, P. (1999), *Britain – A Travellers Survival Guide*, Lonely Planet Publications Ltd.

YHA (England and Wales) Ltd (1998), *Annual Report of the Youth Hostel Association of England and Wales*, 1ˢᵗ March 1997 – 28ᵗʰ February 1998.

Other information sources

Web sites

www.yha.org.uk – The Youth Hostel Association of England, Wales and Scotland.

www.iyhf.org - Hostelling International.

www.backpack.co.uk – 'Backpacker Britain'.

www.staruk.org.uk – Statistics on Tourism and Research.

www.europa.eu.int/en/comm/dg23/tourisme – European Commission, DGXXIII (Enterprise Policy, Distributive Trades, Tourism and Co-operatives).

The meaning and provision of holidays for disadvantaged families

Vanessa J E Smith

Sheffield College, Sheffield

It is the purpose of this paper to contribute to the understanding of the diversity of the tourist experience by examining one particular group: Haukeland's (1990) 'Category C non-travellers.' In his Norwegian study, Haukeland (1990) defined non-travellers as those 'who had not been on summer vacation the previous season' (p 180) and his Category C non-travellers as those characterised as being in 'an unsatisfactory situation' (p 179). Although this group was involuntarily excluded from participation in regular holiday-taking for a variety of complex and often overlapping social and economic reasons, a lack of economic means and the need to care for others were significant constraints.

In Haukeland's (1990) study, the Category C non-travellers did wish to go on holiday and felt deprived by not being able to do so, to the extent that the lack of opportunity was viewed by Haukeland as possibly compounding social problems. For Haukeland (1990) 'Holiday travel has become an important element in one's social welfare' and, as such, 'should be treated like any other human right where social loss should be compensated by the welfare state' (p 178).

The term 'non-traveller' is used more loosely in this paper, referring to those who rarely or infrequently take a holiday. Holiday experiences are diverse and the meanings are, likewise, diverse. There is a tendency to assume the homogeneity of the tourist experience without allowing for differences in gender, age, employment status, domestic situation, social living circumstances etc. (Kinnaird and Hall, 1994; Stephenson and Hughes, 1995; Hughes 1997). It is unlikely that the meaning of the holiday would be the same for those who take regular holidays and are relatively affluent as it would be for those who rarely holiday and are relatively poor.

The aim, specifically, was to determine the meaning of the holiday experience for those who are considerably socially and economically disadvantaged and to consider the welfare implications of involuntary exclusion from regular holiday-taking.

Related studies

Relative deprivation and citizenship

The idea of a holiday as a necessity is not new, nor is the realisation that low income is a major factor in preventing participation. In 1927, the Editor of Lansbury's Labour Weekly wrote: 'Holidays are for those who can enjoy them. It is true that during Whitsun, many thousands left London for the sea and the countryside – some going as far afield as the Continent. All the same, most spent the holiday in and about the streets in which they live. More and more should we concentrate on the demand for less hours of work and higher and still higher rate of pay' (p 3).

It is however, only recently that the idea of a holiday as a necessity in today's society has been incorporated into the academic literature of poverty, the lack of a holiday (at least four days away from home, not with friends or relatives) being viewed as an indicator of deprivation. Supporters of the relativist tradition of deprivation (e.g. Townsend, 1979; Clarke and Critcher, 1985; Mack and Lansley, 1985; Oppenheim, 1990) view poverty as a dynamic concept relating to the resources and incomes enjoyed by the majority of the population at a specific time and in one particular place and thus susceptible to change. This notion of exclusion from a common way of life is particularly well-illustrated in Mack and Lansley's (1985) study with reference to holiday-taking. The study found that 74% of social classes A and B and 57% of social class E classified a holiday away from home as a necessity in today's society. The authors considered this to do with 'the quality of life, with enjoyment and with joining in social activities' (p 54). This view was supported by Clarke and Critcher (1985); who referred to the fact that, in 1979, 40% of the British population did not take a regular annual holiday away from home, a figure that was unlikely to have increased during the economic recession of the early 1980s. For Clarke and Critcher (1985): 'Containing as it must, the elderly, the sick and the poor, this group remains as deprived of holidays as it does most other things. If this is a leisure democracy, a substantial number remain disenfranchised' (p 174). Seaton (1990) estimated that between 20% and 30% of the population were still unable to participate in regular holiday-taking: 'In a society where tourism is increasingly visible on the social agenda as the apparent activity of all.....it is possible that the felt deprivation is sharp among the D, E underclass who are relatively excluded from the tourist boom' (p 110). A more recent study of poverty throughout the European Union member states has indicated that 36% of British households are unable to afford even one week's holiday away from home (Bates, 1999).

The relativist notion of poverty is closely associated with that of 'citizenship' or being a full member of one's community. In post war years, the classic exposition of the meaning of citizenship has been provided by Marshall (1950 and 1964). Marshall (1950) defined 'citizenship' as 'a status bestowed on those who are full members of a community. All who possess the status are equal with respect to the rights and duties with which the status is endowed' (p 28). In this sense, then, citizenship can be viewed as participation in, or membership of, a community. According to Bulmer and Rees (1996), questions of citizenship are as pertinent today as they were at the time of Marshall's writings, with 'citizenship' linking the social sciences to wider public debate.

A focus on social citizenship demonstrates the continuing relevance of sociology, social psychology, leisure studies and social policy to major issues relevant to contemporary society. Roche (1992) recognised that traditional forms of poverty persist whilst, at the same time, acknowledging the development of new forms, particularly associated with changes in family structure and the multiple deprivations related to gender, age and ethnicity. Limited access to leisure and/or regular holidays can now be seen as exclusion from a common way of life and from 'needs' which everyone has the right to be met in order to become a full citizen of a society or community. Bradshaw and Holmes (1989) considered that those families living in poverty 'may suffer what amounts to cultural imprisonment in their own home in our society in which getting out with money to spend on recreation and leisure is normal at every other income level' (p 50). Such 'cultural imprisonment' was clearly illustrated in Green, Hebron and Woodward's (1990) Sheffield study of women's leisure in which older women commented on the social isolation imposed by poverty. For them, this meant being deprived of access to the two most important local social forums: the pub and club.

Since the nineteenth century sport and recreation have gradually emerged as legitimate aspects of social policy, along with such services as health, housing and education. A belief in participation in sport for its own sake and in the universal availability of resources has been the catalyst behind government investment in sport and recreation, especially in the 1960s and 1970s. Haukeland's (1990) study led him to argue that an inability to participate in regular holiday travel should be compensated by the State. For many groups in poverty in the UK a holiday is only possible if assisted by special measures. However, access to holidays for the economically and socially disadvantaged is not viewed as a legitimate cause for government intervention, provision of such being left almost entirely to the voluntary sector.

Social tourism

Hughes (1991) has referred to the fact that low incomes are outside the control of the tourism industry and yet those of limited financial means can only afford to take a holiday away from home if assisted by a third party. According to the English Tourist Board (1976), 'It is a reflection of our social policy that those who are most in need of the benefits that a holiday can bring are least able to take one' (p 5). This trend can be summed up as one aspect of the Inverse Care Law, a concept put forward by Dr Tudor-Hart (1971) with reference to the distribution of healthcare. The provision of healthcare was said to be inversely related to the need for it, the force which created and maintained it being the operation of the market. The number of holidays taken varies directly with increasing socio-economic status (Seaton, 1992; Cahill, 1994). Any physical or psychological benefits of holiday-taking are thus more likely to be reaped by the higher socio-economic groups.

Since the 1950s, the concept of 'social tourism' has been used to refer to ways in which a society, through government initiatives or through voluntary organisations, can take responsibility for enabling its less fortunate members to participate in holiday-taking. In Britain in the 1970s, local authorities accounted for the bulk of social tourism, subsidising over 100,000 holidays, more than 60% of those being Inner London Boroughs with high levels of deprivation (Richards, 1992, p 2). However, cutbacks in public sector spending resulted in a drastic reduction of such services. The onus then fell on voluntary organisations. These tended to cater for low income groups such as the elderly, single-parents and, in particular, the disabled. Hughes (1991) commented on the fact that handicap attracted much financial support whilst certain other groups remained virtually neglected: 'Although assisting the disabled to have holidays requires no apology, the problems faced by other non-participants remain and need to be addressed' (p 195).

It is difficult to generalise about the voluntary sector in Britain, due to its heterogeneity, voluntary action itself covering a wide range of activities. Social tourism itself is provided by a mixture of official voluntary organisations, such as the Holiday Care Service and the Family Holiday Association, along with small, localised self-help initiatives.

A number of studies (Johnson 1981; Parry, 1990; Hughes, 1991) have highlighted the inequality in providing for the needs of some groups whilst neglecting those of others, particularly where financial support is dependent on private givers. The Child Poverty Action Group (CPAG) was cited by the Wolfenden Committee (1978) as exemplifying the uneven geographical distribution of voluntary organisations, the location of the Group's branches correlating more with the presence of Universities with departments of social administration than with low income. Hoggett and Bishop's (1985) study produced detailed findings indicating the existence of fewer voluntary organisations and resources in inner-city Leicester than in suburban Bristol.

Although no-one would deny the importance of voluntary organisations in meeting the needs of society, 'there is no guarantee that voluntary effort will necessarily materialise where need is greatest, that standards of service will be maintained, or that the sector as a whole will act in a co-ordinated manner' (Wolfenden Committee, 1978, p 28).

In reality, it may be impossible for the voluntary sector to meet the needs of particular groups alone without assistance from the public or commercial sector, yet social tourism remains one area of perceived social need almost entirely provided for by voluntary organisations.

Category C non-travellers

The study informants

The research reported in this paper focused on Category C non-travellers in the UK. who had recent experience of a holiday. The families interviewed had a number of criteria in common. The adults were all unemployed and in receipt of social benefits, they were living in deprived and/or difficult social and economic circumstances and were all resident in Yorkshire on large, urban estates which, according to the 1991 Census, were characterised by multiple indicators of deprivation. In addition, within the previous two years, they had participated in a week's holiday in Britain, not financed by themselves.

The Family Holiday Association (FHA) was launched in the U.K. in 1975 with the aim of providing financial assistance to families on low incomes and in difficult circumstances where, usually, the youngest child is at least two years old and where the family has not been away on holiday for at least four years. Referral is through a social worker or similar person attached to the family and, if the application is successful, the family may not reapply for a holiday for another four years. Approximately 1,000 families are helped each year and 2,000 applications are rejected, usually because of insufficient funds as the FHA relies entirely on voluntary donations.

Financial assistance for holidays is also available through the Joseph Rowntree Family Fund (FF) which was established by the Government in 1973 partly in response to the public outcry about thalidomide – damaged children (Lawton, 1993). The FF distributes approximately £15m per year, largely in cash grants to families with at least one severely disabled child, not just to finance holidays but to purchase items such as clothing, bedding and telephones. Families can apply directly to FF for assistance and approximately 70% of first-time applications are accepted. Families may be funded annually.

Most of the families interviewed in this study were contacted via the FHA or the FF. The samples were purposive in that a small number of people with certain common characteristics was selected. The samples were also opportunist in that, in both cases, a third person had to make the initial contact for reasons of confidentiality. In the case of the FHA, four families were interviewed; three lived in Rotherham and one in Sheffield.

A further four families were interviewed through the Family Fund; three living in Sheffield and one in Huddersfield. In addition, two single parent mothers from a self-help group in Bradford were interviewed. Contact with these was made through a social worker attached to the Family Service Unit in Bradford. The families belonged to a group which raised it's own funds to provide an annual caravan holiday at a British seaside resort for its members. Additional interviews were also held with Director of the FHA and with four social workers.

Official indicators of the levels of economic and social disadvantage existing in the areas where the informants lived were obtained from the 1991 Census data. The data for each estate covered in the study can be found in the Appendices (the actual names of estates have been changed).

Interviews and analysis

Initial familiarisation with the group (Category C non-travellers) providing the focus of this study was gained through an analysis of a random sample of letters written to the FHA by the clients themselves, or on their behalf, on return from a holiday. A number of meanings appeared attached to the holiday, with many overlapping and difficult to separate. The relative importance of each meaning was not established except by frequency of mention, nor did the researcher seek to determine the importance of a holiday relative to other aspects of contemporary society. Ideas generated by the content analysis of letters were subsequently systematically explored further through the use of in-depth, tape-recorded interviews. The intention was specifically to determine the meaning of the holiday experience for those who are economically and socially disadvantaged.

The interviews were carried out in the informants' own homes, with the exception of the self-help group who were interviewed, at their request, in the local community centre. Ages ranged between mid-twenties and late-thirties and the number of children per household from one to four, with ages ranging from two to eighteen years. None of the informants or their partners were in full-time employment. In this study 60% of families interviewed were single mothers. Any study of poverty and deprivation will include a significant proportion of single parents, the majority of whom will be women. The estates included in this study all had higher than average proportions of single-parent households, the majority more than twice the average for the Borough.

The non-standardised interview was selected as the main methodological tool, not only because it was considered the most suited to gathering large amounts of information of a delicate nature relatively quickly but because it permitted flexibility and adaptation. The subjects' responses were likely to be highly specific and spontaneous and this method would allow access to unexpected topics not initially considered by the researcher. An additional strength of the non-standard interview was viewed as its ability to allow 'verstehen' or empathy with the respondent. Commentators such as Holstein and Gubrium (1995) and Mason (1996) have argued that the validity of the interview depends largely on the establishment of such an effective relationship.

In order to develop rapport, the first 15-20 minutes of each interview were spent building up trust with the informant through engaging in 'small-talk' without the tape-recorder switched on. Finch (1984) discovered that rapport was easily built up by a female researcher interviewing other women, particularly when the interviews are conducted in the respondents' own homes: 'The interviewee feels comfortable with this precisely because the interviewer is acting as a family guest' (p74). In this study the majority of interviews were conducted in the informants' own homes. Like Finch (1984), the researcher felt genuinely welcomed into their homes. The women readily made coffee and, on two occasions, trusted the researcher to look after their child(ren) while they left the room. The only interview conducted with a male on his own did not flow as easily as the others and it was more difficult to build up initial rapport.

Inevitably, a certain amount of subjectivity is present in qualitative research where narration involves the fusing of opinion, emotion and recall of past events in an attempt to produce a coherent whole. Goffman (1959) doubted whether objectivity and complete honesty in narration could ever be achieved, although Mehan and Wood (1975) considered inconsistencies in narration as not being deliberate attempts to mislead but as arising out of the interview itself. This is because the prime purpose of the interview is 'to capture lived experience outside the interview' (Mehan and Wood, 1975, p51). In order to elicit accurate, spontaneous responses devoid of bias, careful attention was paid to the phrasing of questions. For example, instead of questioning informants directly with regard to their economic and social circumstances, they were asked why they considered their application for an assisted holiday to have been successful. They were also asked to describe the problems and difficulties they had experienced as a result of holiday-taking. This served as a 'permissive' question which allowed those who had experienced difficulties to respond truthfully. Consequently, a number admitted that the holiday had, in fact, left them in greater debt than previously, not all the families had possessed suitcases, the children did not have suitable 'holiday clothing' such as swimwear and shorts and a number of families had experienced problems using public transport.

The interview data were coded according to the process described by Fielding (1993) as 'coding up', whereby filing cards are used for each specific response and the cards sorted into related categories. This allows the categories to emerge from the data itself, thus avoiding interviewer-bias inherent in pre-determined categories based on the interviewer's own preconceptions.

Meaning of the holiday

Escape

Given the most importance (at least in frequency of reporting) was the escape or break aspect of a holiday. The break from routine was particularly welcome as the routine was often stressful. For the FF clients, the holiday had provided an escape from the tedium of hospital visits. The father of a five year old boy who was recovering from a recent kidney transplant commented: *"You've still got your problems with you but it doesn't seem as bad."* In all cases, holidays meant the lifting of restrictions that characterised life on the estate. Only one informant owned a car; with no access to private transport and through lack of confidence, few families left the estate. In addition, local parks were either no-go areas or, as in the case of a Rotherham estate, closed due to infestation by rats.

For one single parent, the holiday had offered a contrasting, safe environment where *"The kids could run around and do what they wanted at night-time – and that was the best part. I could have a drink and sit down. I can never let them go out on their own here after dark."* Another single-mother commented: *"Just to get away from the estate, from such deprivation, is really good. The kids see all the problems here and they don't want them. They see the fighting and the needles coming out of the drains."* The same mother reflected on a day-trip she herself had been on as a child: *"Lots of very bad things happened to me as a kid but the thing I look back on most is that day trip. It's the only one I ever had – we had a walk on the beach. We had no money; we couldn't even have an ice-cream, but it was away from my house. It gave me hope to carry on."*

Social workers interviewed were also of the opinion that holidays were necessary breaks from the tedium of everyday life. One commented that: *"For a lot of these families with young children, they need to pass on some sort of optimism for the future."* Another referred to the fact that few families ever leave the estate: *"A holiday is relaxation, a change from daily routine on the estate. They can see leisure in a purposeful way and it also legitimises not doing anything for a while ....."*

The informants in the study tended to emphasise the importance of 'escape' which holidays brought for their children rather than for themselves. Away from the estate, children could participate in activities taken for granted by most other families such as swimming and riding donkeys on the beach. 'Push' factors were particularly relevant, the destination itself being relatively unimportant. As one non-traveller said: *"It doesn't have to be abroad; just Skegness or Bridlington to give a person a break."*

The strengthening of family ties

This was a benefit mentioned by most parents. For those who had been on an FF- assisted holiday, it gave parents quality time to spend with the healthy child(ren) who had often been separated from their parents when time had to be spent with the sick child in hospital. In one family's case, it enabled the healthy sibling to form a closer relationship with her sister: *"It was the first holiday we'd had as a family – Clara and Leila are always fighting but, on holiday, Leila played with Clara and they got on really well. It brought the two sisters closer together – I think Leila understands more about Clara now."*

The FHA recipients also felt the holiday had brought them closer together. One couple had been on the verge of separating but the holiday encouraged them to stay together: *"We had a walk on the beach and flew a kite. It was raining but we went out and got wet. We all enjoyed being with each other. We're much more positive now."*

Children were able to see their parent(s) calmer and more relaxed in a different environment. One single-mother commented on the bonding which occurred on holiday whilst a social worker referred to a client whose daughter's name had been removed from the 'at risk' register after the family's return from holiday.

Health

A further meaning attached to the holiday was an improvement in physical and mental well-being. From the responses given , it was obvious that, in particular, the holiday enabled the families to 'cope'. One FF recipient commented: *"I admit it. I can't cope at times, especially in the summer holidays. If I didn't have a week away to look forward to, I don't know what I'd do."*

A number of respondents returned from the holiday more motivated. One couple commented that they now had the enthusiasm and motivation to complete the decorating they had begun but lost interest in.

The benefits of a holiday away from home in helping overcome physiological problems are less easy to measure although a number of informants believed their children had returned home healthier.

"She seems to have a bit more colour in her cheeks, to look healthier, not so stressed out." commented one father after the family's return from a week in Skegness.

Such considerations are clearly interrelated with other meanings mentioned such as the break from routine, establishing feelings of normality and building up relationships with significant others, all of which may contribute to physical and mental health.

Normality

Although only one informant referred directly to the feeling of 'normality' which the holiday had provided, this benefit was implied in comments made by others and was mentioned by several social workers. The two single-parents from the self-help group commented that an advantage of going away in August was that memories of it were fresh in the children's minds when they returned to school and they could share their holiday experiences with other children. The FF holiday recipients referred frequently to the long periods of time spent at hospital separated from the healthy child(ren) and the stress caused by the sick child's illness. Implicit in their comments was the view that such life was not 'normal'. This was explicitly iterated by one social worker attached to the FF: "It's very important for the parents to see their children living a 'normal' life away from hospitals and nurses."

The relative absence of reference to 'being normal' may, in part, have been a reflection of the relative importance attached to other perceived benefits. The informants in this study may have had little expectation of ever being able to go away. Although some had friends or relatives who had been on holiday and most would have seen adverts for holidays on television, holiday-taking was unlikely to have been a social convention on the estate. Not only would holiday-taking have been an insignificant element of the sub-culture of the estate, but also, for some respondents, there may have been a feeling that they did not have a right to receive the same rewards as the employed. A social worker commented on the prevailing view 'out there' that the unemployed do not need a break as they are not working and an informant felt guilt for having been offered an FHA holiday when there must be others "more deserving" of a holiday.

Other issues

Although all respondents agreed that a holiday had been beneficial overall, holidays were not always free of problems.

Two families had borrowed money to go on holiday and were having difficulty paying it back. For a number of FHA informants, unexpected costs whilst away, such as feeding electricity meters, had left them in greater debt. Those informants in receipt of FF-assisted holidays were given cash grants which were meant to cover all foreseeable expenses and none of these had incurred financial difficulties.

Applicants for FHA-funded holidays were often advised to apply out of season as this increased the chance of their application being successful. However, several of these families were already having problems with school attendance and this exacerbated the problem. An additional problem incurred as a result of going away out of season was mentioned by one mother: *"We had miserable weather. It sounds silly but I thought it would be nice because we were on holiday – so I took all the wrong clothes for the children."*

To some social workers attached to FHA recipients, the logistics of making an application for an assisted holiday was something of a mystery and thus few families obtained a holiday. For one social worker: *"There was so much paperwork, it was rather cumbersome this year ..... normally families raise it, not social workers ..... the assumption is that these holidays are in short supply. We always feel we shouldn't ask for too many."*

The Director of the FHA confirmed that this was a problem: *"... the degree of communication varies enormously. There are particularly high concentrations of applications from certain areas. Rotherham is a very active group – they know the system."*

The nature of funding also affects access to assisted holidays. The government-aided FF rarely rejects applications on the basis of inadequate funds whereas the FHA turns down approximately 2,000 applications each year, largely due to limited financial resources. The

FF allows successful applicants to re-apply after one year whereas the FHA's criterion is one application every four years. A related, unwelcome effect of FHA-assisted holidays was the raising of expectations: *"My little ones really enjoyed (the holiday) and wanted to go back to the seaside next year. You give it to them then take it away from them. There won't be another chance for at least four years"* commented one single-mother.

Conclusion

The most significant factor preventing access to holidays for this group of Category C non-travellers was low income, often exacerbated by debt. Enforced exclusion from a lifestyle common to the rest of society was expressed in terms of disability, the breakdown of familial relationships, limited horizons and lack of self-esteem. An inability to participate in regular holiday-taking, without third party intervention, was the indicator of such exclusion or marginalisation from wider society.

This study provides evidence relating to the meaning of the holiday for Haukeland's (1990) Category C non-travellers. Haukeland examined the category without examining the meaning of the holiday in any detail. This study extends his analysis and contributes to a greater understanding of the non-traveller.

A number of meanings were attached to the holiday but the separation of these is, to some extent, arbitrary, since many were interrelated. The meanings were interwoven but tended to focus particularly on 'change' or 'escape' from what was seen as a mundane, often boring domestic environment which presented little in terms of excitement and spectacle. These Category C non-travellers were far removed from Urry's (1990) 'gazers'. It would appear that Urry's 'tourist gaze' concepts are not universally pertinent. The view that particular sites, such as the British seaside resort, no longer hold an attraction clearly does not coincide with the experiences of the families in this study.

From the evidence presented, it appears that holidays have meaning for those without work as well as for those in work. Employment is not a necessary prerequisite for the holiday to be endowed with considerable meaning. For the unemployed, the holiday does have purpose; it also legitimises doing nothing. However, the unemployed are not an homogeneous entity and the meaning of holiday-taking for this group may be influenced by social divisions of race, gender and single-parent status as well as by caring responsibilities.

The findings of this study support those of, for example, the Wolfenden Committee (1978), Gratton and Taylor (1987) and Hoggett and Bishop (1988) that the voluntary sector is heavily dependent on local enthusiasm and experience. This results in a provision which is both socially and geographically uneven, with services not always provided at point of need.

This raises a number of social, economic and political questions regarding the role of the market and of social protection in the emergence of new forms of social exclusion in the twenty-first century. The State has a long history of involvement in recreational provision in the UK. Whilst not denying the inequalities in access to sport and leisure which persist for certain disadvantaged groups, the principle of State involvement in this sphere has been well established since the early twentieth century.. Although this study has identified a number of benefits of holiday-taking for low-income families, any further assistance or strategies from the State for widening participation would appear unlikely. In the short-term, at least, social tourism is likely to remain the prime responsibility of the voluntary sector.

References

Bates, S. (1999), Hard-up Britons who Cannot Afford Holidays *The Guardian* June 25, 1999, 6.

Bradshaw, J. R. and Holmes, H. (1989), *Living on the Edge* Tyneside: Child Poverty Action Group.

Brenton, M. (1985), *The Voluntary Sector in British Social Services* Harlow: Longman.

Bulmer, M. and Rees, A. M. (Editors) (1996), *Citizenship Today: The Contemporary Relevance of T H Marshall* London: UCL Press.

Cahill, M. (1994), *The New Social Policy* Oxford: Blackwell.

Clarke, J. and Critcher, C. (1985), *The Devil Makes Work: Leisure in Capitalist Britain* Basingstoke: The Macmillan Press Ltd.

English Tourist Board (1976), *Holidays: the Social Need* London: Macmillan Press Ltd.

Fielding, J. (1993), Coding and Managing Data, in Gilbert, N. (Editor) *Researching Social Life* Newbury Park, California: Sage Publications Inc., 218-237.

Finch, J. (1984) Its Great to Have Someone to Talk to: the Ethics and Politics of Interviewing Women, in Bell, C. and Roberts, H. *Social Researching: Politics, Problems and Practice* London: Routledge and Kegan Paul, 70-87.

Green, E; Hebron, S. and Woodward, D. (1990), *Women's Leisure, What Leisure?* Basingstoke: The Macmillan Press Ltd.

Goffman, E. (1959), *The Presentation of Self in Everyday Life* London: Pelican.

Haukeland, J. V. (1990), 'Non-Travellers – The Flip-side of Motivation', *Annals of Tourism Research*, 17, 172-184.

Hoggett, P. and Bishop, J. (1985), *The Social Organisation of Leisure: A Study of Groups in their Voluntary Sector Context* London: The Sports Council and Economic Research Council.

Holstein, J. A. and Gubrium, J. F. (1995), *The Active Interview* London: Sage Publications.

Hughes, H. (1997), Holidays and Homosexual Identity, *Tourism Management*, 18(i), 3-7.

Hughes, H. (1991), Holidays and the Economically Disadvantaged. *Tourism Management*, 12 (3): 193-196.

Kinnaird, V. and Hall, D. (Editors), (1994), *Tourism: a Gender Analysis* Chichester: Wiley.

Lawton, D. (1993), *The Family Fund Database* York: University of York Social Policy Research Unit.

Mack, J. and Lansley, S. (1985), *Poor Britain* London: George Allen and Unwin.

Marshall, T. H. (1950), *Citizenship and Social Class* Cambridge: Cambridge University Press.

Marshall, T. H. (1964), *Class, Citizenship and Social Development* New York: Doubleday and Co. Inc.

Mason, J. (1996), *Qualitative Researching* London: Sage Publications Ltd.

Mehan, H. and Wood, H. (1975), *The Reality of Ethnomethodology* New York: Riley.

Oppenheim, C. (1990), *Poverty: The Facts* London: Child Poverty Action Group.

Richards, G. (1992), *European Social Tourism: Welfare or Investment?* Conference paper.

Roche, M. (1992), *Rethinking Citizenship: Welfare, Ideology and Change in Modern Society* Cambridge: Polity Press.

Seaton, A. V. (1992), Social Stratification in Tourism Choice and Experience Since The War – Part I *Tourism Management,* 13 (1): 106-111.

Stephenson, M. and Hughes H. (1995), Holidays and the UK Afro-Caribbean Community, *Tourism Management*, 16(b), 429-436.

Townsend, P. (1979), *Poverty in the U.K.* Harmondsworth: Penguin Books.

Tudor-Hart, J. (1971), The Inverse Care Law *The Lancet,* 405-412.

Urry, J. (1990) *The Tourist Gaze* London: Sage Publications.

Wolfenden Committee (1978), *The Future of Voluntary Organisations* London: Croom Helm Ltd.

Appendix A: indices of economic and social disadvantage

Table 1   The Fielding Estate, Sheffield

Category	% Fielding Estate	Average % for Sheffield
Housing rented from the Local Authority	71.8	33.5
Unemployment	24.6	12.6
Households affected by long-term illness	22.3	16.1
Households affected by permanent sickness	12.3	8.6
Single parent households	9.7	4.3
Households without a car	75.0	44.9
Households without central heating	41.9	19.1

Table 2   Ainley Green, Huddersfield

Category	% Ainley Green	Average % for Huddersfield
Housing rented from the Local Authority	50.9	19.6
Unemployment (males)	25.5	10.3
Unemployment (females)	14.7	6.0
Households affected by long-term illness	27.6	24.9
Single parent households	13.9	4.9
Households without a car	62.4	37.1
Households without central heating	63.2	37.6

Table 3   The Farnborough Estate, Sheffield

Category	% Farnborough	Average % for Sheffield
Housing rented from the Local Authority	35.0	33.5
Unemployment	16.2	12.6
Households affected by long-term illness	20.0	16.1
Households affected by permanent sickness	5.1	8.6
Single parent households	3.8	4.3
Households without a car	56.7	44.9
Households without central heating	16.9	19.1

Table 4   West Lucking, Rotherham

Category	% West Lucking	Average % for Rotherham
Housing rented from the Local Authority	74.0	30.1
Unemployment	25.4	11.9
Households affected by long-term illness	22.8	15.5
Single parent households	7.6	3.7
Households without a car	66.5	38.2
Households without central heating	5.4	10.0

Table 5   The Meadowhead Estate, Sheffield

Category	% Meadowhead	Average% for Sheffield
Housing rented from the Local Authority	48.9	33.5
Unemployment	16.1	12.6
Household affected by long-term illness	18.7	16.1
Households affected by permanent sickness	4.4	8.6
Single parent households	4.8	4.3
Households without a car	47.3	44.9
Households without central heating	16.5	19.1

Table 6   The Aldersley Estate, Bradford

Category	% Aldersley	Average % for Bradford
Housing rented from the Local Authority	47.0	16.6
Unemployment	26.4	10.9
Households affected by long-term illness	18.2	13.4
Single parent households	10.0	1.7
Households without a car	68.3	40.9
Households without central heating	47.2	37.6

N. B.   All names have been changed.

Values as a basis for understanding motivations towards accommodation and activity choices

Maree Thyne and Rob Lawson

University of Otago, New Zealand

Introduction

Understanding tourist motivations and their link to the decision making process is vital to those involved in the tourism industry; in particular planners, marketers and managers. By understanding visitor motivations we get a better idea of the tourist's needs and wants, and thus are better equipped to satisfy them:

> ...*to market travel services and destinations well, there must be a degree of understanding on the part of travel sellers and suppliers about the motivating factors that lead to travel decisions and consumption behaviour* (Gee et al, 1984).

This paper will report on qualitative research undertaken in New Zealand that looked at tourist decision making motivations. Specifically, this paper will focus on values underlying accommodation choices and activity participation.

Goodall (1989) suggested accommodation to be a subsidiary to the main purpose of a vacation and that it is only chosen for somewhere to stay. Johnston-Walker (1999) however, suggests that tourists may be becoming more discerning in their accommodation choice, viewing it as much more than just a place to stay. Research on the decision making motivations for accommodation choice is very scarce. The majority of research on accommodation choice has concentrated on the influence of variables such as the travel party (Jamrozy, 1994) and the purpose of the trip (McCleary, et al., 1993). Often research has ignored consumer variables and concentrated on specifics of the accommodation, for example its location (Weaver and McCleary, 1991). Additionally, research on the motivations for participation in particular activities has been scarce in tourism literature, and links between values for accommodation and activity choices have basically been ignored.

This paper will focus on the values that underpin consumer choices for accommodation and activities. It will begin with an outline of research that has been undertaken on motivations for travel, accommodation choice and activity participation. Additionally, values research will be discussed. This paper will then move on to discuss qualitative research that was undertaken to ascertain the travel motivations of individuals. The laddering technique was implemented to determine these motivations. The results that will be discussed from this research will be the values' based motivations behind choosing particular accommodation and participating in specific activities.

Literature

Travel motivation

A major focus of consumer studies in the psychology of tourist behaviour is the study of travel motivation (McIntosh, et al., 1995). The motivation to travel refers to the set of needs which predispose a person to participate in tourist activity (Pizam, et al., 1978). Thus it is useful and important to ascertain these motivations so that consumers' 'needs' can be fulfilled. In fact Iso-Ahola (1982) states that motivation is a central concept in attempting to understand tourist behaviour.

Research on travel and tourist motivation has become quite specific over the years. Some examples include Shoemaker (1989) who looked at the motivations of the senior tourist markets, Cha, et al., (1995) who researched the motivations of Japanese overseas travellers, and Eagles, (1992) who determined the influences on Canadian eco-tourists' motivations. Finally, Cha and Jeong (1998) examined the influence of push/pull items of motivation on Korean pleasure travellers to New Zealand and Australia.

Also the motivations behind specific holidays have received some attention, for example Hill, et al., (1990) looked at the motivations of resort travellers, Quiroga (1990) researched the motivations of package tourists and Ross (1997) determined backpacker's motivations. In addition, there has been numerous research undertaken on the motivations behind visits to museums and other cultural attractions, (for example Davis and Prentice, 1995; Jansen-Verbeke and van Redom, 1996; Prentice, et al., 1997). However the majority of the research undertaken on travel motivations has been quantitative and has focused only on motivations and has thus ignored the influence of personal values. Additionally, consumer values' based motivations for accommodation and activity choices have generally been ignored.

Accommodation

Little research has been undertaken on the link between tourist behaviour and accommodation choice. A number of other variables have been considered as influencing accommodation choice, examples include the travel party (Jamrozy and Uysal, 1994; Loker and Perdue, 1992), the length of the trip (Loker and Perdue, 1992), the purpose of the trip (McCleary, et al., 1993) and the length of stay (Lieux, et al., 1994). However there has been a major lack of customer focused research, that has looked specifically at consumer behaviour. Studies that have looked into the motivations of accommodation stayers, have mainly concentrated on aspects of the actual accommodation, such as its location (McCleary, et al., 1993; Weaver and McCleary, 1991), the room rates (Lewis, 1984), the furnishings and décor (Mehta and Vera, 1990) and the staff professionalism (Lewis, 1984).

There are two main exceptions to this clear gap in consumer behaviour research, Zins (1998) and McCleary and Choi (1999). Zins (1998) used LOV items and psychographic constructs to ascertain hotel choice amongst themed hotels. Zins (1998) surveyed 389 guests of middle and upper class hotels in Austria, of five particular theme groups: tennis, golf, slim and beautiful, family apartments and Kinderhotels. Zins was interested in determining the influence of four psychographic concepts on hotel choice: values, lifestyle, vacation style and benefits.

With respect to the influence of values, respondents were asked to check and rank the three most important personal values from the list of LOV items. A logistic regression between personal values and four of the hotel choice variables was undertaken. Table one displays the values Zins found to be an influence on each type of hotel choice.

Table 1   Personal values found to influence hotel choice (Zins, 1998)

Hotel type	Influential Values
Tennis theme hotel	Excitement and Security
Golf theme hotel	Sense of belonging and being well respected
Beauty theme hotel	Elf respect and Self fulfilment
Family theme hotel	Being well respected and Seeking excitement

Zins (1998:10) advocated the usefulness in studying accommodation choice through psychographics and suggests that personal values actually play a superior role in explaining hotel choice.

McCleary and Choi (1999) administered a Rokeach Value Survey to a sample of business travellers from Korea and business travellers from the United States. McCleary and Choi (1999) point out that if different cultures have different personal values systems, then it seems likely that different cultures may also use different choice criteria when making buying decisions that reflect their different value systems (McCleary and Choi, 1999:4). Thus, if this is true, values may be a valuable segmentation base for relating cultural context to product purchase decisions across cultures (McCleary and Choi, 1999:4). Therefore, McCleary and Choi undertook a study of both US and Korean business travellers, to determine if they can be segmented by their personal values and to see if the segments differed between the two cultures. Both groups were successfully segmented (by their values) and different value structures were found to be related to different choice criteria for hotels. Additionally, sufficient evidence was found to suggest significant differences between the value systems of the two cultures.

Activities

Additionally, little literature has looked at tourist behaviour and activity choice. There are two main exceptions to this, Madrigal and Kahle (1994) and Gnoth (1999). Madrigal and Kahle (1994) examined whether or not holiday activity importance ratings differed across segments comprised of tourists homogeneously grouped on the basis of personal values. They distributed a survey questionnaire to tourists visiting Scandinavia. The survey consisted of four sections: reasons for visiting Scandinavia, a list of Scandinavian activities and their influence on choosing Scandinavia as a destination, LOV values (respondents were asked to check the most important values to them) and demographics.

Respondents were firstly segmented on their values through cluster analysis, then the ratings of 18 activities (in terms of how important each was in the respondent's decision to visit Scandinavia) were factor analysed. Following this, a one-way multivariate analysis of variance (MANOVA) was conducted, using the value-system segments as the independent variable and the four activity factor scores as dependent variables. The MANOVA indicated that significant differences did exist among value-system segments on the activity factors. Table two summarises the relationship found between the segments and the activity factors:

Table 2   The relationship between cluster segments and activity factors (Madrigal and Kahle, 1994)

Factor	Values included in factor	Activities participated in
Factor 1	Sense of belonging Being well respected Security	Visit historic sites Visit scenic sites Visit museums Learn about local culture
Factor 2	Fun and enjoyment in life Excitement	Camping Hiking/backpacking Hunting/fishing
Factor 3	Sense of belonging Self-fulfilment	Jogging Aerobics Tennis
Factor 4	Self-respect Warm relationships with others	Visit ancestral homelands Visit friends and/or relatives

Gnoth (1999) surveyed 385 camper van tourists in New Zealand, part of his research looked at the motivations behind their visit. Sixteen motivational items were included in the survey (for example, cheap, freedom, feeling of belonging and seeing nature), these were factor analysed, resulting in four factors. The factors were labelled Outer-Directed and Expressive (feeling of belonging), Outer-Directed and Instrumental (Fun and Enjoyment), Inner-Directed and Instrumental (Best way to travel around the country) and Inner-Directed and Expressive (see nature and have a sense of freedom). Gnoth analysed the association between motivations (the factors found) and various activities that the respondents had checked that s/he intended to pursue while in New Zealand. Table three outlines this association:

Table 3   The association between motivational factors and activities (Gnoth, 1999)

Factor	Motivations included in factor	Activities participated in
Factor 1 Outer-Directed and Expressive	I need a place where I belong It suits my style I don't feel as though I'm just a tourist It gives me the feeling of adventure I can live up to my full potential and by myself Driving a van is fun and enjoyable	Befriend Maori Eat Hungi food Visiting galleries
Factor 2 Outer-Directed and Instrumental	It guarantees holiday fun and enjoyment I enjoy not having to book ahead for accommodation	Go paragliding Go water-skiing
Factor 3 Inner-Directed and Instrumental	I can achieve more than with any other form of holiday It is the best way to travel the country	Mingle with local people Go on short walks
Factor 4 Inner-Directed and Expressive	I can really do what I want I want to be free and independent You get close to nature easily	Seek solitude Go on walks Find isolated country areas

The aforementioned sections have detailed tourist behaviour research that has been undertaken on accommodation choice and activity participation. Some research has included the measurement and importance of the consumers' values. However, as seen, it has all been undertaken quantitatively, and has lacked a direct association between the attribute (accommodation or activity) and the personal value that is being fulfilled. Additionally there have been no attempts to research a link between accommodation values' based motivations and those behind activity participation. This review will now move on to an overview of research that has been undertaken on values.

Values

To say that a person 'has a value' is to say that he or she has an enduring belief that a specific mode of conduct or end-state of existence is personally and socially preferable to alternative modes of conduct or end-states of existence (Rokeach, 1968:159-60). A value is a single belief that transcendentally guides actions and judgements across specific objects and situations, and beyond immediate goals to more ultimate end-states of existence. Also a value is an imperative to action, not only a belief about the preferable but also a preference for the preferable. Finally, a value is a standard or yardstick to guide actions, attitudes, comparisons, evaluations, and justifications of self and others (Rokeach, 1968:160).

Values can be contrasted to motivations, as motivations are more so a result of person-situation interactions. They contain motives influenced and operationalized by persons' values and their perception of given situations (Gnoth, 1999). Values are transcendent and deep-seated and are better suited for marketing purposes. Knowing that consumers endorse certain values more highly than other values, may be extremely useful in determining promotional appeals, product positioning and design, channel of distribution and pricing (Lawson, et al., 1996).

Although marketers realise the importance of values research, there is some debate over how values should be measured. Approaches include the Rokeach Value Survey (Rokeach, 1968), the LOV scale (Kahle and Kennedy, 1988), VALS (Mitchell, 1983) and the means-end technique. This paper will concentrate on the latter of these four approaches.

Numerous research has been undertaken on values, but Holt (1997) is especially relevant to the present study. Holt discusses various core principles that he found in his research, which he believes distinguishes his approach from previous research. One of which is the notion that people consuming the same category or brand of product, may be doing so for different reasons. This principle is highlighted in the current research, that people can invariably be choosing the same accommodation for quite different reasons, and because of the different values they hold.

Walker and Olson (1991) advocate that Marketing must persuade the consumer to associate a product or service with satisfying some benefit, goal, or value that is important to the consumer, this is the theory behind means-end. By influencing the degree to which consumers perceive a product or service to be self-relevant, marketers can affect consumers' level of motivation to learn about, shop for, and ultimately buy the sponsored brand (Walker and Olson, 1991). This theory can also be applied to tourism marketing.

A means-end chain is a model of consumers' cognitive structures, depicting the way in which concrete product characteristics are linked to self-relevant consequences. More specifically, it shows how a product characteristic (concrete or abstract) is linked to consequences (functional or psychosocial) or consumption, which in turn may be linked to the attainment of life values (instrumental or terminal) (Grunert and Muller, 1996).

One method in researching and measuring a means-end theory is through laddering. Laddering refers to an in-depth discussion with a consumer that focuses on linkages between personal values and consumer choice. Such a detailed discussion will uncover many consequences that are more immediately related to consumer choice than are personal values. That is, there is no direct connection between values and consumer choice behaviour. This suggests that there have to be some intermediate steps taken into account in explaining how values relate to consumer choice (Gutman, 1991).

To establish these steps, tailored interviews are undertaken, using a series of probes, mainly 'why is that important to you?' - with the express goal of determining sets of linkages between the key perceptual elements across the range of attributes (A), consequences (C), and values (V).

Figure 1   An example of the Laddering Technique

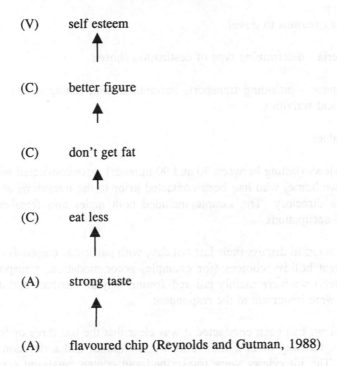

(V)   self esteem

↑

(C)   better figure

↑

(C)   don't get fat

↑

(C)   eat less

↑

(A)   strong taste

↑

(A)   flavoured chip (Reynolds and Gutman, 1988)

One criticism of the above example is the question of whether there really can be a relationship between a crisp and a personal value? Especially a value that is so removed from the product as self-esteem. It may be a more believable match if it were a low fat food such as that discussed by Grunert and Muller (1996). However, some products/services appear to be more suited to the laddering technique than say a crisp or something like a brand of sugar, such as accommodation choices and activities that a tourist participates in.

The laddering technique was chosen to be used in the interviews discussed in this paper, to gain an insight into how the product characteristic (for example staying at a camping ground) could be linked to life values (for example, freedom). The interviews were expected to immediately uncover consequences related to accommodation and activity choice and additionally link these to personal values.

Methodology

Twelve in-depth interviews were undertaken in Dunedin, New Zealand. Primarily the interviews were undertaken to gain information to develop questions for a national travel lifestyles questionnaire. However, with all the information attained in each interview, they stand alone, in their own right, as exploratory data. The interviews were conducted using the laddering technique. The different dimensions of a vacation that were covered in the interviews were defined from Woodside's model (Woodside and MacDonald, 1993) of vacation decision making which provides a comprehensive description in the different decision areas involved in tourist behaviour:

- purchasing behavior

- motivations / reasons to travel

- choice criteria - determining type of destination chosen

- travel behavior - including transport, accommodation, dining habits, as well as attractions and activities

- personal values

The in-depth interviews (lasting between 30 and 90 minutes) were conducted with individuals (usually in their own home) who had been contacted prior to the interview, at random from the local telephone directory. The sample included both males and females and a cross section of ages and occupations.

Respondents were asked to discuss their last holiday, with particular emphasis on the reasons behind their different holiday choices (for example, accommodation, transport and food). Specifically the interviews were mainly tailored around why an attribute and a consequence from that attribute were important to the respondent.

After twelve interviews had been conducted it was clear that the last three or four interviews had yielded little in the way of new motivations and attitudes and a decision was made to stop at that point. The interviews were transcribed and content analysed according to the categories established above.

In analysing the content of these interviews, the attributes and the consequences of the accommodation and activity choices were often clearly visible. These were then linked to a value that it was felt they most represented. Hierarchical maps were not designed in this study, because individual expressions were deemed more appropriate, rather than bringing all the interviews together in the attempt to determine one overall core value.

Results and discussion

Of the 12 interviews, the laddering technique (for both accommodation and activities) was successfully applied to 10. With these, the attributes of the accommodation and activity choices and the consequences of the visit were uncovered. As shown in tables four to thirteen, some interviews actually had more than one set of linkages between the key perceptual elements across the range of attributes, consequences and values. Thus respondents sometimes chose accommodation and/or activities to fulfil more than one of their values.

Most of the values in this research that consequences have been linked to, originated from LOV. However LOV appears to be missing values linked to freedom, friendship and a world of beauty, therefore relevant values to these dimensions were taken from RVS.

The following outlines and discusses the linkages between Attributes (A), Consequences (C) and Values (V) attained from the 10 interviews, for accommodation choice and the activities that the respondent participated in.

Table 4   Linkages from Attributes to Values attained for accommodation and activity choices from interview one

Interview one - Accommodation	Interview one - Activities
(V) Self fulfilment ↑ (C) Personal Satisfaction ↑ (C) It was important for my holiday to be a change from what I was doing, this includes the people I meet ↑ (C) Meet heaps of people ↑ (A) Stayed at a Youth Hostel	(V) Self fulfilment ↑ (C) Gives a good perspective of things and you realise how cool your country is ↑ (C) See something different, do different things ↑ (A) Very unique ↑ (A) Visited Rotorua
Interview one - Activities	**Interview one - Activities**
(V) Sense of belonging ↑ (C) Creates a sense of identity ↑ (A) Visited Cape Reinga	(V) Self esteem ↑ (C) Social acceptance ↑ (C) Keeping Fit ↑ (A) Fun and Excitement ↑ (A) Boogie boarding down a sand hill

This interview shows that the accommodation and one of the activities were chosen to fulfil the same values' based motivation - 'self fulfilment'. This respondent chose a youth hostel to stay in, for a change from his usual life. Also he wanted to meet people that were different from those he 'normally' meets. By staying somewhere different and meeting new people, he became personally satisfied and fulfilled. One activity that he did was visit Rotorua. Rotorua has a very strong Maori culture heritage, and is a lot different than the respondent's home town, so again he is immersed in a very different experience. The two remaining activities are quite different: one is very active and exciting (Boogie boarding), the other is more abstract and spiritual (visit to Cape Reinga - the top of the North Island). But both were undertaken to again fulfil very personal values. So it can be assumed that this respondent took this particular holiday very much for personal reasons, to fulfil personal needs and values.

Table 5   Linkages from Attributes to Values attained for accommodation and activity choices from interview two

Interview two - Accommodation	Interview two - Activities
(V) Security ↑	(V) Family security ↑
(C) We knew where it was and what it was like ↑	(C) Because we've got an intellectually handicapped son ↑
(C) We'd been there before ↑	(C) It's good to have somewhere safe where you can just throw a ball ↑
(A) Stayed in an apartment	(A) Walking along the beach

The accommodation and activities chosen by this respondent are the same with respect to which values' based motivation they fulfil. This respondent has very strong security values, and hence is motivated to seek safety for the family (a familiar apartment and somewhere safe to throw a ball). This may be enhanced by the fact that the family does include an intellectually handicapped son, which they are perhaps very protective of, hence emphasising the need for family security.

Table 6   Linkages from Attributes to Values attained for accommodation and activity choices from interview four

Interview four - Accommodation	Interview four - Accommodation
(V) Excitement ↑ (C) Part of going on holiday to somewhere different is to meet new people ↑ (C) Meet and chat to new people ↑ (A) A lot of other people there ↑ (A) Holiday park	(V) Family security ↑ (C) Makes it a better holiday for them and for the family as a whole ↑ (C) Fun and entertainment for the children ↑ (A) Heaps of children's activities ↑ (A) Holiday park

Interview four - Activities
(V) Family security ↑ (C) Family activities ↑ (C) The kids wanted to do these things ↑ (C) Fun for our children ↑ (A) Arana park/ QEII

The respondent in interview four also expressed strong family values, and again it was in line with making decisions to include the whole family (especially the children). This family stayed at a camping ground. The parents were motivated to do this for both their own reasons (to meet people) and also to fulfil an overall family value of warm relationships within the family. That is, if the children are kept happy and amused, then it is more likely to be a successful holiday for the entire family. The activities appeared to be chosen for this reason also. They participated in activities that the children mainly wanted to do, again to keep up these good, warm relationships.

This holiday appears to be a family holiday, in fact the respondent summed it up herself: "it was basically just what the kids wanted to do, it was their holiday just as much as ours".

Table 7   Linkages from Attributes to Values attained for accommodation and activity choices from interview five

Interview five - Accommodation	Interview five - Accommodation
(V) Warm relationships with others	(V) Freedom
↑	↑
(C) In camping grounds/cabins you are always stumbling over someone	(C) I really don't enjoy having to be somewhere at a set time
↑	↑
(C) Cheap and meet better people	(C) I hate that
↑	↑
(A) A cabin or tent	(A) You normally have to pre-book for hotels etc.
	↑
	(A) A cabin or tent

Interview five- Activities
(V) Freedom
↑
(C) If we liked a place we stopped, if few didn't we kept going
↑
(C) Which meant we could spend longer at one place, or less at another
↑
(A) Package deal of both sounds and glow worm caves over a two/three day period

The respondent in interview five also discussed a camping holiday he had recently been on. His values' based motivations for accommodation and activity choices were quite different to the previous interview. Although the accommodation was similar, this respondent was fulfilling 'freedom' values. He emphasised the need for a free, unplanned holiday. Additionally, he also valued 'warm relationships with others' but this was in a friends context, rather than family.

This difference with the previous interview could be attributed to the fact that children were not involved in the holiday discussed in interview five.

Table 8   Linkages from Attributes to Values attained for accommodation and activity choices from interview six

Interview six- Accommodation	Interview six- Accommodation
(V) Freedom ↑ (C) They are self contained ↑ (A) We stayed at camping grounds	(V) A world of beauty ↑ (C) I like being out there and seeing the stars at night ↑ (A) We stayed at camping grounds
Interview six- Accommodation	**Interview six- Activities**
(V) Freedom/self fulfilment ↑ (C) Which gives a feeling of getting away from everthing ↑ (A) There was not TV or telephone ↑ (A) We stayed at camping grounds	(V) Freedom/Self fulfilment ↑ (C) It's my idea of getting away from everything ↑ (C) I like being out there and being quite and peaceful ↑ (A) We went tramping

Interview six- Activities

(V) Warm relationships with others

↑

(C) There is a special sort of companionship with the people I go tramping with

↑

(A) We went tramping

Interview six was quite similar to interview five, there was a very strong connection between accommodation and activities chosen and the 'freedom' value. This interview also displayed the values of self-fulfilment and a world of beauty as important in the respondent's motivations. This probably reflects the fact that this respondent participated in more tramping activities, than the previous respondent.

Table 9   Linkages from Attributes to Values attained for accommodation and activity choices from interview seven

Interview seven - Accommodation	Interview seven - Activities
(V) Sense of security ↑ (C) We stay at the same motel and get rooms next to each other ↑ (C) Stay with friends at the same motel complex, we can pop into each other's room for a cup of tea, a matter or a game of cards ↑ (A) A motel is a home away from home ↑ (A) We stayed in a motel	(V) Sense of security ↑ (C) Know what to do because we play it in Dunedin ↑ (A) Played housie

Interview seven- Activities

(V) Sense of security
↑
(C) Then we just went back to the hotel and wathced sky TV
↑
(C) We had a walk around, but we didn't know how far to go in case we got lost
↑
(A) We just went next door to our hotel for a meal

The respondent in interview seven displayed very strong security values' based motivations for choosing a particular motel (always stay there) and activities, for example, the respondent did not venture far from her hotel in a strange city, she was scared to get lost. It appears that this respondent is happier holidaying with her friends, in the same motel, at the same place they always go to.

Table 10   Linkages from Attributes to Values attained for accommodation and activity choices from interview nine

Interview nine - Accommodation	Interview nine - Activities
(V) Friendship ↑ (C) You meet people around the pool, at the bar etc. ↑ (C) You can join in and meet people, you can't do that in a motel ↑ (A) We didn't want to cook ↑ (A) We stayed in one hotel for our whole stay in Fiji	(V) Friendship ↑ (C) Chatting with a lot of different people ↑ (A) Talk with people around the pool

Friendship and meeting people are the values' based motivations behind the accommodation and activity choices for the respondent in interview nine. This respondent was very driven to meeting people whilst on holiday.

Table 11   Linkages from Attributes to Values attained for accommodation and activity choices from interview ten

Interview ten - Accommodation	Interview ten - Activities
(V) Security ↑ (C) A safe place to stay ↑ (C) There was a security guard at the bottom of the elevator the entire time ↑ (A) There was a floor safe in your room for valuables ↑ (A) Stayed in a big hotel	(V) Security ↑ (C) With people watching the beach the whole time ↑ (A) It was just like something out of Baywatch ↑ (A) I liked surfing on the beach

Interview ten- Activities
(V) Sense of accomplishment ↑ (C) Just like something out of Baywatch ↑ (C) I quite like the surf, just really relaxing ↑ (A) I just liked the beach

This respondent was fulfilling safety/security values' based motivations in his accommodation and activity choices. He felt safe in his hotel (with security staff and locked safes available) and safe surfing on the beach (with lifeguards keeping watch). These values probably reflect the fact that this respondent was staying in a foreign country by himself, therefore he may have been more aware of security issues.

Table 12   Linkages from Attributes to Values attained for accommodation and activity choices from interview eleven

Interview eleven - Accommodation	Interview eleven - Activities
(V) Security/home comforts ↑ (C) We knew it was there ↑ (C) It was handy to my bother's house ↑ (A) It was somewhere we'd stayed before ↑ (A) We stayed at a motel around the corner from my brothers	(V) Warm relationships with others ↑ (C) We could do things with the kids ↑ (A) It's a big playground for kids ↑ (A) We went to Spencerville

This respondent had quite different values' based motivations behind her accommodation choice and activities she participated in. The accommodation was chosen mainly because she knew where it was and had been there before. Whereas the activity undertaken was mainly to do something with the children, thus make it a more pleasurable family holiday.

Table 13   Linkages from Attributes to Values attained for accommodation and activity choices from interview twelve

Interview twelve - Accommodation	Interview twelve - Activities
(V) Family security ↑	(V) Fun and enjoyment ↑
(C) Warmer in a motel in winter ↑	(C) It was a lot of fun ↑
(C) Better accommodation for our three year old daughter ↑	(C) Was good for our three year old daughter to see ↑
(A) We stayed in motels	(A) Visited a salmon farm

Interview twelve- Activities
(V) Warm relationship with others ↑
Rachel (daughter) is at the stage now that I can walk with her ↑
(A) Walking

The values that induced the motivations for this respondent's accommodation and activity choices were again family orientated, but were quite different. For accommodation, family security was very important, keeping their daughter warm and safe. Whereas the activities were chosen much more for fun and being together as a family.

In summary, these results show that eight out of ten respondents had the same values' based motivations for both their accommodation and activity choices. For example, in interview seven both the accommodation (motel) and activity (playing housie) choices are linked to the same value - security. These findings are very useful for the marketing and promotion of such facilities because they show the possibility of accommodation and activities working together, maybe creating a type of package deal for the client, that will include the activity and accommodation necessary to fulfil the client's values. Also, these results display quite different values behind accommodation and activity choices, an example of this is shown in table fourteen.

The results in table fourteen reveal two major findings; firstly that respondents chose quite different accommodation types to fulfil various values. For example, a Youth Hostel was chosen for self-fulfilment, compared to a motel that was often chosen for security. There are some possible patterns emerging in these accommodation choices, for example, freedom was associated by two of the respondents with camping/tents and three other respondents linked motels and apartments to security. Additionally, the results also show that people are not always consuming products for the same reason, for example a hotel was chosen by one respondent for friendship and by another for security. This finding is also discussed by Holt 1997, who advocates that people can choose the same product or service to fulfil totally different values.

Table 14   A summary of the values behind respondents' accommodation choices

Interview number	Accommodation choice	Value fulfilled
1	Youth Hostel	Self fulfilment
2	Apartment	Security
4	Holiday park	Excitement
	Holiday park	Family security
5	Tent/cabin	Warm relationships with others
	Tent/cabin	Freedom
6	Camping grounds	Freedom
	Camping grounds	World of beauty
7	Motel	Security
9	Hotel	Friendship
10	Hotel	Security
11	Motel	Security
12	Motel	Family security

Activities are more difficult to summarise, basically because respondents participated in many different activities (see Table fifteen). However, it appears that respondents who undertook familiar activities (that they had previously participated in) did so for 'security' reasons, either because they understood the activity or knew that it would be safe for themselves and/or their children. Conversely, more extreme and unfamiliar activities appeared to be chosen to fulfil such personal values as esteem, self-fulfilment and accomplishment. In addition, the value 'warm relationships with others' was generally connected to meeting people and having fun, and often family, holidays.

Table15   A summary of the values behind respondents' activity choices

Interview number	Activity choice	Value fulfilled
1	Visited Rotorua	Self fulfilment
	Visited Cape Reinga	Sense of belonging
	Boogie boarding	Self esteem
2	Walking along the beach	Family security
4	Arana Park / QEII	Family security
5	Package deal of sounds and glow worms	Freedom
6	Tramping	Freedom
	Tramping	Self fulfilment
	Tramping	Warm relationships with others
7	Played housie	Security
	Out for a meal close to accommodation	Security
9	Talk to people around the pool	Friendship
10	Surfing	Security
	Surfing	Sense of accomplishment
11	Visited Spencerville	Warm relationships with others
12	Visited a salmon farm	Fun and enjoyment
	Walking	Warm relationships with others

Conclusion

To conclude, this paper has outlined the findings of qualitative research undertaken in Dunedin, New Zealand. Interviews with 12 Dunedin residents (regarding their most recent holiday), using the laddering technique, were carried out and later transcribed. The content of 10 interview transcripts were analysed and several values were extracted that related to the respondent's motivations for choosing accommodation during their holiday and activities to participate in.

Overall the results outline the different values' based motivations behind accommodation and activity choice. It is apparent that quite often the same values' based motivations are emerging within the one respondent. That is, a single respondent may have the same motivations for choosing their accommodation type, as for participating in specific activities. An example being the respondent in interview five stating that he prefers to stay in a cabin or tent, because he does not enjoy having to be somewhere at a set time. Additionally this respondent was also motivated towards a package activity deal, which gave him freedom as to when he had to participate in each activity by.

This research has important marketing implications pertaining to the segmentation of vacationers, as it shows the possibility of accommodation facilities and activities working together to target specific markets. Respondents in this study were often fulfilling the same values' based motivations in their choice of accommodation and participation in particular activities. In fact, only the final two interviews showed some clear differences between their values' based motivations.

This research also shows that respondents sometimes had different values' based motivations for choosing the same type of accommodation or participating in similar activities. This factor emphasises the need for marketers to understand the multiple dimensions of the same consumption behaviour, for example, the various motivations for consuming a hotel room. Examples include the respondents in interviews nine and ten who both stayed in large hotels, however the values' based motivations in interview nine were friendship and warm relations with others, while the motivations in interview ten were seeking security and safety.

The methodology used in this study is a good, relevant method for determining the values' based motivations of tourists, especially with respect to their accommodation and activity choices. The means-end technique was more useful than a quantitative approach, because it is possible to determine the respondents' intrinsic values behind their motivations. For example, laddering enables a concrete attribute such as "we stayed in camping grounds" (Interview six - see Table eight) to be linked to an intrinsic value such as "freedom". It would be difficult to determine such information in a quantitative survey, because often respondents are limited to answering questions with specific responses, for example on a Likert scale.

There is a very definite need for further research on the values of tourists, specifically the relationship between values and the tourist decision making process. Emphasis should be on qualitative approaches to such research and the means-end technique is deemed appropriate for determining such values. This research has important marketing implications for accommodation and activity facilities, because it shows a potential relationship between the values' based motivations for accommodation choice and activity participation.

Acknowledgements

The authors would like to thank Tracy Young for her input and help with this research.

References

Cha, S., and Jeong, D. (1998), Travel Motivations of Korean Pleasure Travellers to Australia and New Zealand, *Pacific Tourism Review*, 2, pp.181-190.

Cha, S., McCleary, K. W., and Uysal, M. (1995), Travel Motivations of Japanese Overseas Travellers: A Factor-Cluster Segmentation Approach, *Journal of Travel Research*, 34 (1): 33-39.

Chen, J. S. (1998), Travel Motivation of Heritage Tourists, *Tourism Analysis*, 2, pp.213-215.

Davis, A., and Prentice, R. (1995), Conceptualizing the Latent Visitor to Heritage Attractions, *Tourism Management*, 16 (7): 491-500.

Eagles, P. (1992), The Travel Motivations of Canadian Ecotourists, *Journal of Travel Research*, 31 (2): 3-7.

Frauman, E., Norman, W. C., and Klenosky, D. B. (1998), Using Means-end Theory to Understand Visitors within a Nature-based Interpretive Setting: A Comparison of Two Methods. *Tourism Analysis*, 2, pp.161-174.

Gee, C., Swart W. W., and Var, T. (1984), *The Travel Industry*, AVI Inc, Westport, Connecticut.

Gnoth, J. (1999), Tourism Expectation Formation: The Case of Camper-van Tourists in New Zealand. In A. Pizam and Mansfeld, Y. (Editors), *Consumer Behaviour in Travel and Tourism,* New York, The Haworth Hospitality Press.

Goodall, B. (1989), Tourist Accommodation: A Destination Area Perspective, *Built Environment*, 15 (2): 78-91.

Grunert, S. C., and Muller, T. E. (1996), Measuring Values in International Settings: Are Respondents Thinking 'Real' Life or 'Ideal' Life? *Journal of International Consumer Marketing*, 8 (3,4): 169-185.

Gutman, J. (1991), Exploring the Nature of Linkages between Consequences and Values, *Journal of Business Research*, 22, pp.143-148.

Hill, B. J., McDonald, C., and Uysal, M. (1990), Resort Motivations for Different Family Life Cycle Stages, *Visions in Leisure and Business*, 8 (4): 18-27.

Iso-Ahola, S. E. (1982), Towards a Social Psychological Theory of Tourism Motivation: A Rejoiner, *Annals of Tourism Research*, 9 (2): 256-262.

Jamrozy, U., and Uysal, M. (1994), Travel Motivation Variations of Overseas German Visitors, *Journal of International Consumer Marketing*, 63 (3/4): 135-160.

Jansen-Verbeke, M., and van Redom, J. (1996), Scanning Museum Visitors - Urban Tourism Marketing, *Annals of Tourism Research*, 23 (2): 364-375.

Johnston-Walker, R. (1999), *Accommodation: Much More than just a Place to Stay? An investigation of the motivations and accommodation use patterns of international independent tourists staying in hotels and bed and breakfasts in Queenstown, New Zealand*, Master of Tourism, University of Otago, Dunedin, New Zealand.

Kahle, L. R., and Kennedy, P. (1988), Using the List of Values (LOV) to Understand Consumers, *The Journal of Services Marketing*, 2 (4): 49-56.

Lawson, R., Tidwell, P., Rainbird, P., Loudon, D., and Della Bitta, A. (1996), *Consumer Behaviour in Australia and New Zealand,* Sydney, McGraw-Hill, Inc.

Lewis, R. C. (1984), The Basis of Hotel Selection, *The Cornell Hotel and Restaurant Administration Quarterly*, 25 (1): 54-69.

Lieux, E. M., Weaver, P. A., and McCleary, K. W. (1994), Lodging Preferences of the Senior Tourism Market, *Annals of Tourism Research*, 21 (4): 712-728.

Loker, L. E., and Perdue, R. R. (1992), A Benefit-Based Segmentation of a Non-Resident Summer Travel Market, *Journal of Travel Research*, 31 (1): 30-35.

Madrigal, R., and Kahle, L. R. (1994), Predicting Vacation Activity Preferences on the Basis of Value-system Segmentation, *Journal of Travel Research*, 32 (3): 22-28.

McCleary, K. W., and Choi, B. M. (1999), Personal Values as a Base for Segmenting International Markets, *Tourism Analysis*, 4, pp.1-17.

McCleary, K. W., Weaver, P. A., and Hutchinson, J. C. (1993), Hotel Selection Factors as they Relate to Business Travel Situations, *Journal of Travel Research*, 32 (2): 42-48.

McIntosh, R., Goeldner, C., and Ritchie, J. R. B. (1995), *Tourism: Principles, Practice and Philosophies*, (7th Edition ed.), New York, Wiley.

Mehta, S. C., and Vera, A. (1990), Segmentation in Singapore, *The Cornell Hotel and Restaurant Administration Quarterly*, 31 (1): 80-87.

Mitchell, A. (1983), *The Nine American Lifestyles,* New York, Warner.

Pitts, R. E., and Woodside, A. G. (1986), Personal Values and Travel Decisions, *Journal of Travel Research*, 25, pp.20-25.

Pizam, A., Neumann, Y., and Reichel, A. (1978), Dimensions of Tourist Satisfaction with a Destination Area, *Annals of Tourism Research*, 5 (3): 314-322.

Prentice, R., Davies, A., and Beeho, A. (1997), Seeking Generic Motivations for Visiting and not Visiting Museums and like Cultural Attractions, *Museum Management and Curatorship*, 16 (1): 45-70.

Quiroga, I. (1990), Characteristics of Package Tours in Europe, *Annals of Tourism Research,* 17 (2): 185-207.

Reynolds, T. J., and Gutman, J. (1988), Laddering Theory, Method, Analysis and Interpretation, *Journal of Advertising Research*, 28, pp.11-31.

Rokeach, M. J. (1968), *Beliefs, Attitudes and Values,* San Francisco, Jossey Bass.

Ross, G. (1997), Destination Motivations among Backpacker Visitors to Northern Australia, *Pacific Tourism Review*, 1, pp.7-15.

Shoemaker, S. (1989), Segmentation of the Senior Pleasure Travel Market, *Journal of Travel Research*, 27 (3): 14-21.

van Veen, W. M. O., and Verhallen, T. W. M. (1986), Vacation Market Segmentation: A Domain-specific Value Approach, *Annals of Tourism Research*, 13, pp.37-58.

Walker, B. A., and Olson, J. C. (1991), Means-End Chains: Connecting Products with Self, *Journal of Business Research*, 22, pp.111-118.

Weaver, P. A., and McCleary, K. W. (1991), Basics Bring 'Em Back, *Journal of Hotel and Motel Management*, 206 (11): 29-38.

Woodside, A. G. and MacDonald, R. (1993), *General System Framework of Customer Choice Processes of Tourism Services,* Institute of Tourism and Service Economics International Conference, University of Innsbruck.

Zins, A. (1998), Leisure Traveller Choice Models of Theme Hotels using Psychographics, *Journal of Travel Research*, 36 (4): 3-15.

Rethinking tourists' e

Eugenia Wickens

Oxford Brookes University, UK

Abstract

Rethinking tourists' experiences

In his review of the sociological literature on tourists' experiences of a visited host community and its people, Cohen, (1979b: 198) found that 'the depth study of tourist experiences is not yet much developed although an endless number of surveys of tourist motivation has been conducted'. Twenty years on, little appears to have changed. Despite the quantity of writing on tourism, tourists themselves remain 'shadowy figures' in the existing literature and their voices are rarely heard. Tourists are typically treated as objects to be analysed rather than subjects with feelings, experiences of a host community, memories, and stories to tell. Our knowledge of this modern cultural experience is derived primarily from sources such as travel brochures, and from empirical studies where the touristic experience is conceptualised as a pre-programmed 'product' consumed by the 'tourist'. A key characteristic of research to date is that many scholars operate with undeveloped definitions of the term 'tourist', with some appearing to be oblivious to the need to define this term. Perhaps the definitional problem associated with the term 'tourist' is symptomatic of an inability to take seriously the orientations of the tourist. Furthermore, the notion of 'pseudo' or 'staged' events has been central to the sociological debate in tourist studies. There are those commentators who argue that such events subvert the tourist's search for 'authenticity', for experiences comparable to those of religious pilgrims. Other writers have suggested that 'the barbarians of our age of leisure' are unconcerned about artifice, desiring nothing more, or less, than 'a good time' while on holiday.

This ongoing debate concerning the nature of the touristic experience is the central theme of this paper. I shall examine critically the arguments of diverse thinkers, assess the strengths and weaknesses of their various positions, and explore their concepts of the 'tourist'. I then contrast these with my own ethnographic study of tourists' experiences in Chalkidiki, Northern Greece. A central conclusion to emerge from this review is that in order to obtain a deeper understanding of this phenomenon, research must go beyond the all-encompassing label of 'the tourist' by paying due attention to tourists' voices. It is also argued that, in order to obtain an adequate understanding of the touristic experience, a pluralist theoretical approach needs to be deployed.

...ction

...otion of 'pseudo', or 'staged', events has been central to sociological debate within ...ist studies. There are those commentators who argue that such events subvert the ...ourist's search for 'authenticity', for experiences comparable to those of religious pilgrims (MacCannell, 1976). Other writers have suggested that 'the barbarians of our age of leisure' (Turner and Ash, 1975) are unconcerned about artifice, desiring nothing more, or less, than 'a good time' while on holiday.

The central focus of this paper is the ongoing debate concerning the nature of the touristic experience and the factors identified by various writers as motivating people to leave their home environment for a holiday. I shall examine critically the arguments of diverse thinkers, assess the strengths and weaknesses of their various positions, and explore their concept of 'the tourist'.

A central conclusion to emerge from this survey is the growing realisation that in order to obtain a deeper understanding of tourism as a social phenomenon, research must go beyond the all-encompassing label of 'the tourist' by giving due attention to tourists' voices (Cohen, 1979a; Pearce, 1982; Crick, 1989). It is also clear that, in order to obtain an adequate understanding of the touristic experience, a pluralist theoretical approach needs to be deployed.

This paper commences with a review of the literature and then outlines a fresh perspective on tourists' experiences. This critique is informed by my ethnographic study of tourists' experiences in Chalkidiki, Northern Greece.

The literature: some generalisations

In his review of the sociological literature on tourists' experiences of a visited host community and its people, Cohen (1979b: 198) found that 'the in-depth study of tourist experiences is not yet much developed although an endless number of surveys of tourist motivations has been conducted'. Twenty years on, little appears to have changed and there is still 'little substance to the sociology of tourism' (Urry, 1991: 7). Thornton (1995) has recently made a similar observation on the absence of any solid empirical work on tourists' experiences. He argues that considerable research has been conducted by market researchers on tourist demand and tourist motivations, but the actual experiences and activities of tourists 'while on vacation have been a subject of less interest to researchers' (ibid.: 48).

Despite the quantity of writing on tourism, tourists themselves remain 'shadowy figures' in the existing literature, and their voices are rarely heard (Cohen, 1979a; Pearce, 1982; Crick, 1989; Thornton, 1995). Tourists are typically treated as objects to be analysed rather than subjects with feelings, experiences of a host community, memories, and stories to tell (Wickens, 1999)

Our knowledge of this modern cultural phenomenon is derived primarily from two sources. Secondary sources (such as travel brochures, travel books, tourist guide books, journals, TV and Radio programmes, newspapers, photographic representations, and novels), and empirical studies. In the latter, the touristic experience is conceptualised as a pre-programmed 'product' consumed by the 'tourist' (Buck, 1977; Dann, 1977; Papson, 1981; Moeran, 1983; Hilty, 1996). For instance, Hilty (ibid.) has used popular media, such as newspapers, as a data source on tourism, and Dann (ibid.) used travel brochures to explore the theme of the 'tourist as a child'.

More recently, postmodernist writers have drawn our attention to the consumers of the touristic experience, treating tourists as 'semioticians', in search of signs of cultural heritage and 'authenticity' (Urry, 1991; Harkin, 1995; Hughes, 1995). In his analysis of the touristic experience Urry (ibid.: 12), for instance, presents the tourist as a consumer of images and spectacles. However, the individual's experience of a visited place, as seen from his/her point of view, remains a relatively unexplored topic.

A key characteristic of research to date is that many scholars operate with undeveloped definitions of the term 'tourist', with some apparently oblivious to the need to define it. Many practitioners appear to be content to deploy the term tourist, albeit implicitly, as a label for a 'colourful-T-shirt-shorts-and-camera-round-his-neck' stereotype in their analysis of the touristic experience (Cohen, 1979b; Feifer, 1985). Feifer (ibid.: 219) caricatures this simplistic conceptualisation of the 'tourist'. In his straw hat, loud Hawaiian shirt, and Bermuda shorts' he is:

> *'armed for action. He has a camera slung round his neck and a wad of bills in his pocket. But, like a newborn chick to its mother hen, he stays close to the big bus. Nobody knows his name... staggering off the bus in yet another quaintly imposing grand place, he has no way to identify where he is except by dazedly scrutinising his itinerary - blinking, he utters the familiar caption. 'If it's Tuesday, this must be Belgium.... universally 'distasteful' but every marketer's favorite dish, he's simply and starkly the tourist.'*

What is also striking about the existing literature, is that 'the tourist' is primarily known 'by how many nights he spent at his hotel, what quantity of chips he consumed, the number of trips he made to museums as against trips to the beach' (Feifer, ibid.: 223). As Pearce rightly points out, the tourist is often conceived as a 'money-dispensing machine which requires regular serving' (Pearce, 1982: 7). Perhaps the definitional vagueness of the term 'tourist' is symptomatic of an inability to take seriously the orientation of the tourist.

There is also a tendency amongst some researchers to adopt one of two opposing orientations. One perceives the touristic experience of the visited host community as: 'superficial'; 'inauthentic'; 'genuine fake'; 'artifice'; merely a 'pseudo event'; a 'staged event'; 'staged specimens'; or a series 'of staged games' and 'spectacles'. (See, for example, Boorstin, 1964; Turner and Ash, 1975; MacCannell, 1976; Buck, 1977; Urry, 1991). The other sees the tourist's experience as: 'liminal'; 'hedonistic'; or a 'recreational' activity that provides the individual with release from everyday life. (See, for example, Graburn, 1977; Wagner, 1977; Moore, 1980; Lett, 1983; Shields, 1992). These two orientations may be seen as the ends of a spectrum of opinion with a variety of views lying between them (e.g., Smith, 1977; Cohen, 1979a; Pearce, 1982; Redfoot, 1984; Yiannakis and Gibson, 1992;).

Perspectives on Tourists

(a) The passive tourist

Early accounts of tourists' experiences were mainly descriptive and tended to mirror the negative attitude towards tourism, which is 'commonplace' among travel writers (MacCannell, 1976: 600). Hostility towards modern travel and package holidaymakers infuses Boorstin's writing. In 'The Lost Art of Travel' Boorstin argues that the transformation of foreign travel into a 'commodity' has diluted the 'authenticity' of the traveller's experience. Attractively packaged for touristic consumption, foreign travel now guarantees the consumer an experience of the 'strangeness' of the place from the secure vantage point of the 'environmental bubble' of the hotel complex. Before the ready availability of package holidays, the experience of a foreign country was a 'real' undertaking, involving an 'authentic' experience of a host community and its people. However, now:

> 'the multiplication, improvement, and cheapening of travel facilities have carried many more people to distant places. But the experience of going there, the experience of being there, and what is brought back from there are all very different.' (ibid.: 79).

He presumes that the modern tourist does not experience 'reality', but that what 'he really sees are specimens collected and embalmed especially for him', or 'attractions specially staged for him' (ibid.: 102).

A number of objections may be made to this analysis. First, as Ryan (1991: 45) stresses, 'the value of the tourist experience is not that of the academic writer imputing a set of normative judgements to the situation, but what is felt by the tourist him or herself'. Second, Boorstin overstates his case, by claiming that tourists disregard 'the real life' of the destination, passively enjoying the 'contrived attractions'. In so doing, he ignores differences between the wants, expectations and experiences of individual tourists (see, also, Cohen, 1988b).

Thirdly, the view that tourists go abroad 'not to see at all, but only to take a picture' (Boorstin, ibid.: 117) is too simplistic. My ethnographic evidence from Chalkidiki, Northern Greece, clearly indicates that not all modern tourists enjoy what Boorstin calls pseudo events (Wickens, 1999)

Boorstin is not the only commentator to take a negative attitude towards mass tourism and the modern tourist. The distinction he draws between the traveller and the modern tourist, and the hostility he expresses towards the package holidaymaker, is replicated in several other studies. For instance, the argument that there has been a loss of the 'art of travel', and the prejudice against modern tourists, who are seen as somehow different from travellers of the past, is also to be found in Levi-Strauss's (1993) work. By contrast, some commentators have questioned the distinction between tourist and traveller (e.g., Lytra, 1987; Bruner, 1991). Lytra (ibid.), for instance, presents historical evidence to show that early travellers to Greece were equally interested in antiquities and the Greek sunshine. According to the same source, these 'elite', Western European, travellers were not interested in the 'real' life of Greece, or in meeting the indigenous population. An observation which reduces, if not removes, the perceived distance between the traveller and the tourist as conceptualised by these thinkers.

(b) 'The barbarians of our age of leisure'

The conceptualisation of the mass organised tourist as a devotee of sun and 'synthetic fun', as someone who tries 'to get away from all the pollution and alienation' of modern societies and have a good time is developed in 'The Golden Hordes' (Turner and Ash, 1975: 15). This study, which is essentially a refinement of Boorstin's account of tourism, is also condescending towards the package holidaymaker. The assertions that the tourist industry plays an important role in shaping tourists' wants, and that tourists are 'mere suckers' of the tourist brochures, are found in this study. Echoing Boorstin, these commentators also suggest that tourism is a 'people processing' industry, which manipulates and influences people's desire to get away from everyday life, while 'at the same time providing the means by which these dreams can be fulfilled' (ibid.: 15). The assertion that the tourist does not experience the 'real life' of the visited host environment is also found in this study. Guided by their 'surrogate parents' - that is, tourist guides and hotel staff - the tourist is prevented from having any real contact with the host community. Again, several observations are necessary here. This interpretation of the touristic experience ignores the fact that:

> *'different language, different customs, different media, different climates, are initially disturbing. One does not know what to do if something goes wrong. One is in the midst of unfamiliar surroundings and practices.'* (Rojek, 1993: 176)

In 'Licensed for Thrills: Risk-taking and Tourism' (Wickens, 1997) I presented evidence which lends support to the view that the holiday reality for many tourists includes some discomfort; for example. minor health complaints associated with either food, drink or the sun (see also Ryan, 1991; Page, et al., 1994) A series of ethnographic interviews with foreign visitors to Chalkidiki, reveals that it is for this reason that tourists seek the security of the environmental bubble and the protection of their 'surrogate parents' (Wickens, ibid.). Choosing to go on a pre-packaged holiday, which is relatively free from physical hardship and health risks, 'need not be despised as evidence' of the lack of a desire to experience 'real' cultural events in the host community (Rojek, 1993: 176).

The shortcomings of this theoretical orientation become clear when the works in which it is found are put in context. Tourists are not the subjects of investigation. These writers are mainly concerned with the socio-cultural impact of tourism on the host community. Like other critics, these commentators adopt a negative stance towards mass tourism and package holidaymakers.

(c) The insulated tourist

The presumption that the tourist is unadventurous and insulated from the 'real life' of the host community is elaborated in Carroll's work. The touristic experience is said to be 'confined to a repeating series of jumbo jet flights, international airport interludes, air-conditioned taxi rides and International Hilton stops' (1993: 176). Contact between the holidaymaker and the host is said to take place in the context of service transactions and hence, apart from shopping and tipping, tourists are isolated and do not encounter any natives during their holidays.

This theme of the isolation of the tourist and the assertion that the tourist enjoys the superficiality and inauthenticity of artificially created touristic bubbles, or ghettos, are found in several other studies (e.g. Moynahan, 1985; Krippendorf, 1991). Krippendorf (ibid.: 34) writes:

> *'Not only are most tourist centres interchangeable but they all have the necessary capacity to process the tourist flood when it comes....They are completely sufficient and offer tourists, everything their hearts may desire - so they do not need to go outside them.....'*

(d) The alienated tourist

The argument that tourism is a sanctioned form of leisure that helps to keep the workforce compliant, is to be found predominantly in the work of Marxist-oriented analysts. From this perspective, foreign travel is viewed as a form of 'imperialism'. For instance, Nash (1989) suggests that this new form of 'imperialism' is based on the exploitation of the host destination and its people, and that it benefits only a few multinational corporations.

Such studies are primarily concerned with the impact of mass tourism on traditional societies. However, it is interesting to note that, escape from the 'alienation' caused by the oppressive 'capitalist societies' from which tourists originate, is singled out as the key factor motivating them to holiday abroad. Getting away from 'distasteful work roles' (Nash, ibid.: 35) is seen as the major impetus for people to participate in mass tourism. However, the reality is that travel motivation is much more complex (see Pearce, 1982; Dann, 1981; Wickens, 1995). Furthermore, as Cohen (ibid.) points out, there is scarcely a shred of evidence that all, or even most, tourists are alienated from their home environment.

Furthermore, the term 'tourist' is used by these analysts as a label for a:

> *'vacationer who insists on American fast-food hamburgers, coffee with his meals, hot running water in his bedroom and the use of the English language...'*(Nash, ibid.: 35)

It is interesting to note the pejorative language used by these critics to describe the tourist. For instance, modern tourists are portrayed as the 'new conquerors', and as 'colonialists' of the host community. Boorstin describes the tourist as a 'gullible' sightseer, and for Turner and Ash tourists are the 'sun-tanned destroyers of culture' (ibid.: 11). Terms such as 'ridiculous', 'naive', 'dupe', 'uncultured', 'like a sheep', 'ugly', 'polluting', 'irresponsible', 'licentious' and 'slothful' are commonplace in the literature (Krippendorf, 1991: 41). Other analysts have described mass tourists as 'cattle' and tourism as 'herding' (Godbey and Graefe, 1991: 219).

(e) The tourist in search of authenticity

In contrast to the view found in the above studies that the passive/alienated tourist is neither interested in the cultural attractions of a destination, nor in the 'real life' of the indigenous population, MacCannell (1976) maintains that attractions such as museums, historical and industrial monuments, parks and pageants, are important 'social symbols of modernity' (ibid.: 77).

Shadowing American tourists provided MacCannell with the evidence on which he bases his assertions about our quest for authenticity. He insists that 'by following tourists, we may be able to arrive at a better understanding of ourselves' (ibid.: 5). MacCannell, 'having discovered, like Trilling (1972) and Berger (1973) before him, authenticity as a basic value of modern culture..... goes on tacitly to ascribe such a quest to each and every individual modern tourist' (Cohen, 1988b: 34). The claim that the tourist is a middle class male traveller in a quest for authenticity, to borrow a phrase from Cohen, 'offends one's common sense' (Cohen, ibid.: 35). Moreover, even this theoretical approach ignores individual differences in the motivations and experiences of tourists.

(f) Post-tourists

The term 'post tourist' has been employed by some theorists to describe millions of holidaymakers (e.g., Culler, 1981; Feifer, 1985). In these writings, the separate categories of tourist and traveller are amalgamated into the new category of 'post-tourist' because the tourist/traveller dichotomy is seen as obsolete. There is no need for a tourist typology, we are told, since post-tourists live in an 'age of mass communications' and consequently are well informed about the cultures and lifestyles of potential hosts. From this theoretical perspective, the post-tourist knows very well that there is no authentic touristic experience to be found in the 'other'. The well-informed post-tourist knows that tourism is just 'a game', and that 'authentic' local entertainments are staged. Urry (1991:100) remarks that 'post-tourists know that they are tourists and that tourism is a game, or rather a whole series of games with multiple texts and no single, authentic tourist experience'. Likewise, Feifer (ibid.) writes that the tourist is not a 'time traveller when he goes somewhere historic; not an instant noble savage when he stays on a tropical beach; not an invisible observer when he visits a nature compound' (ibid.: 71).

According to these writers, the post-tourist can enjoy all kinds of tourism by choosing sometimes to be a package holiday maker, sometimes a freelance traveller, and sometimes not to be a tourist at all. Furthermore, Feifer (1985) argues that the post-tourist can now enjoy the experience of the 'other' (i.e., exotic sites) at home, at the 'flick of a switch', with TV programmes such as 'Wish You Were Here' or videos showing holiday destinations such as Greece. The post-tourist can imagine him/herself to be 'really there', enjoying the 'sunset' and the 'turquoise-coloured sea', without any physical discomforts (e.g., being bitten by mosquitoes). In this version of the post-tourist, travel is achieved via a touristic virtual reality (see, also, Sharpley, 1996).

It is important to note that this type of analysis stresses the 'de-differentiation', and the simulation, of the touristic experience. The term 'de-differentiation' attempts to capture the blurring of distinctions, for instance, between past and present and between work, leisure and travel (Rojek, 1995). Furthermore, it is argued that touristic worlds are reproductions, simulations. Proponents of this approach claim that we now live in a world of 'signs' without referents, where the artificial is more real than the 'real', i.e., it is 'hyperreal' (e.g., Baudrillard, 1997: 28). For Baudrillard, holiday locations such as sea-side resorts, theme parks and museums offer the tourist spectacles which are simulations. According to him, we now live in a 'world of sign and spectacle...one in which there is no real originality...Everything is a copy, or a text, where what is fake seems more real than the real' (1991: 85).

Echoing Boorstin and other like minded thinkers, Baudrillard argues that commercial interests promote and manipulate false pictures of holiday destinations, selling authentic paradises which do not exist (Baudrillard, 1988). For him, tourism is a way of providing a 'simulacrum of the world'. This postmodernist approach rejects the notion of 'authenticity' and, more significantly, the search for the 'authentic other' (as has been claimed by MacCannell, et al.), since everything is equally authentic, or, if you like, inauthentic. It places an emphasis on the 'superficial', the ephemeral, the trivial and the 'flagrantly artificial' in the touristic experience (Webster, 1996: 170).

The assertion that tourists are in search of 'signs of authenticity' and are consumers of 'signs and representations' is found in several other studies (e.g., Watson and Kopachevsky, 1996). Here, tourists are characterised as semioticians, reading the landscape for signs derived from various discourses of travel and tourism. Tourism is not only 'sign driven' but also 'media driven' (ibid.: 282). In this interpretation of the touristic experience it is the seeing of particular signs during the trip which are important to tourists. This argument rests on the assumption that 'people feel that they must not miss seeing particular scenes since otherwise the photo-opportunities will be missed....Indeed much tourism becomes in effect a search for the photogenic, travel is a strategy for the accumulation of photographs' (see Urry, 1991: 139).

(g) The tourist as contemporary religious pilgrim

A different approach to the touristic experience derives from Turner's work on pilgrimages (1973, and Turner and Turner, 1978). Van Gennep's (1960) theoretical heritage and Turner's work on pilgrimages, and, in particular, his notion of liminality, have informed several studies of foreign travel experiences (e.g., Graburn, 1977; Pfaffenberger, 1983; Gottlieb, 1982). Graburn was one of the first analysts to develop his thinking along lines similar to those of Turner. In conceptualising foreign travel as a contemporary form of pilgrimage, Graburn maintains that tourism is 'functionally and symbolically equivalent to other institutions' that people use to 'add meaning to their lives' (1977: 17). This functionalist model shifts the emphasis from the tourist's need for authenticity in the 'other' to the tourist's need for 'recreation'. Tourism is 'one of those necessary breaks from ordinary life that characterises all human societies... it is necessary for the maintenance of mental and bodily health' (Graburn, 1977: 15).

Influenced by Durkheim's work on religion, Graburn asserts that the passage of time alternates between 'profane and sacred' time. Life exhibits these two categories, or, put more simply, it contains both 'ordinary' and 'non-ordinary' time periods. He sees a contrast between the profane or ordinary, mundane everyday life of work and home and the 'sacred', 'non-ordinary', 'away from home', special time. Developing Durkheim's assertion that anything can be sacred, Graburn argues that tourism involves vacation time taken away from home, in a non-ordinary world, and therefore that it is, by analogy, sacred, in the sense 'of being exciting, renewing, and inherently self-fulfilling' (1977: 23).

From this point of view, tourism like religion in the past, makes human existence meaningful. It answers questions about the self and the world we live in. It is important to note here, that, unlike MacCannell, et al., Graburn's tourist is on a quest for a new self: 'we are a new person who has gone through recreation and if we do not feel renewed, the whole point of tourism has been missed' (ibid.: 23).

Summer vacations away from home are seen as being analogous to a sacred journey, since they mark a rite of passage from the profane experience of everyday life to the sacred experience of the holiday atmosphere in another place. Travel away from home functions as a rite of 'renewal' and 'recreation', marked by a beginning, a series of events along the way, and an end or a return to the ordinary home environment.

In arguing that the essence of tourism is recreation, Graburn makes too large a claim. It is not easily applicable to those tourists who seek adventure, as opposed to, or even as well as, recuperation and regeneration during their vacation. In 'Tourists' Voices: A Sociological Analysis of Tourists' Experiences in Chalkidiki, (Wicken's, 1999) I provide evidence which shows that a two week vacation in Kalimeria (a pseudonym for a holiday resort in Chalkidiki) appears to have multiple meanings, suggesting the need for an approach to understanding tourists' experiences which pays due regard to the differences, as well as the similarities, in tourists' needs and wants.

(h) The liminal tourist

In his study of the touristic experience in Gambia, Wagner (1977) applied Turner's concepts of communitas and anti-structure. In so doing, he attempts to explain the previously unexamined playful and permissive behaviour of tourists. According to him, the touristic experience is on the whole 'liminal'. In his study of charter tourism, Wagner writes that the Scandinavian tourists in Gambia indulge in 'spontaneous communitas' type behaviour. For him, this is 'the essence' of the tourist experience (ibid.: 44).

> *'The essence of being a mass tourist in many ways means the taking part in a spontaneous and existential communitas ......normless living during the holiday is probably of great importance as it may liberate the individual from the stresses... imposed by the formal structure of his own society and give him a chance to recuperate, to recharge the inner being, even to make it pleasurable to get back once again to work and to the order and regularity of everyday life.'*

From this point of view, tourism is seen as an escape from the bonds of everyday social structure. It is essentially a recreational activity in which the individual finds release and relief, and serves as a 'pressure-valve' for him or herself. Such touristic activities are functional in that they reinforce an individual's allegiance to the 'centre', i.e., the home environment. Hence, there is no need for a typology of tourists, since from this perspective the essence of the tourist experience is a spontaneous communitas in a liminal touristic space.

The value of this study lies in the fact that Wagner (ibid.) takes into consideration the encounter of tourists with locals, which is an important component of the touristic experience. Thus he notes that occasionally friendships may be formed as a result of these social contacts. Such friendships, for instance, between female tourists and young males are said to be of an instrumental nature. Wagner has observed that since Scandinavian charter tourists started to fly to Gambia, there has also been a small flow of young Gambians to Stockholm, the 'promised land'. Thus, as a result of their encounters with tourists, some young Gambians have been 'imported' by their 'lovesick paramours' or 'patrons'. He writes that it is doubtful that such friendships would ever have been made in 'ordinary life'.

Likewise, Lett's (1983) study of charter yacht tourism in the Caribbean provides ethnographic evidence that many tourists indulge in 'unlimited hedonism', that is casual sex and drink, thereby experiencing Turner's spontaneous communitas. For him, such conduct revitalises tourists for their return to their structured everyday life. In his interpretation, tourism is seen as functional for the individual and society. It compensates the individual for the demands of their working everyday life. Lett writes that 'the ludic and liminoid licence provides a temporary release from, but not a permanent alternative to, everyday life' (ibid.: 54). Thus, like Wagner, Lett also sees everyday life as arduous, and tourism as a source of liberation and compensation for the individual.

There are several other studies which offer a similar interpretation of the touristic experience (e.g., Moore, 1980; Gottlieb, 1982; Shields, 1992). The main thrust of these works is that in going away on holiday, people experience a 'non-ordinary' or a 'liminal' world that liberates the individuals and enables them to indulge in pleasurable pursuits. In contrast to those studies that are concerned with the authenticity of touristic spaces (e.g., Boorstin, ibid.; MacCannell, ibid.), from this functionalist perspective, holiday resorts are seen as the 'playgrounds' where tourists can enjoy the experience of liminality (Wickens, 1994b)

(i) Tourists in 'free areas'

Cohen and Taylor's (1992) study resonates with the notion of the 'liminal' world of tourism. Like many other commentators, they view tourism as an escape from everyday life into a 'free area', a notion which is isomorphic with the concept of a 'liminal space' (Lett, 1983; Shields, 1992). Drawing upon Goffman's work (1959), and employing the 'prison' metaphor, Cohen and Taylor perceive the modern world as a prison and tourism as a sanctioned escape route, a 'voyage of self-discovery'. Tourists, like the inmates of a prison, need to escape the unpleasant and monotonous reality of everyday life. People have a need to get away from everything, to 'let their hair down' (ibid.: 131).

Like Graburn (ibid.), they see tourism as a physical and mental escape from the reality of everyday life. Holidays are 'free areas' where 'lives are rejuvenated if not changed' (ibid.: 131). However, in contradistinction from Graburn's view, Cohen and Taylor argue that visiting a holiday resort changes only 'one part of the home such as the weather' (ibid.: 137). From this point of view, a holiday, for instance, in a Greek holiday resort is equivalent to England plus 'sunshine'. Tourists rarely experience the authenticity of the 'other', the real

Greece of traditional hospitality. What all tourists experience when they visit holiday destinations such as Greece is 'shops selling tea like mother makes'. And, although tourists return feeling relaxed, all that they have to show for it, is a 'suntan rather than a new self' (ibid.: 136).

While their study displays similar weaknesses to those of the studies discussed earlier, the value of Cohen and Taylor's model lies in the fact that it recognises that holidays also provide 'a taste of freedom', a fact which has not been considered by MacCannell, et al. What is suggested here is that the tourist may be either in search of the 'real self' or of 'a new cultural world'. This approach recognises that tourism provides an area of freedom, for free expression and self-development. In these free areas, 'tourists may also act out their fantasies' (ibid.: 115). Clearly this is still a global analysis of the touristic experience. More significantly, their analysis suggests that the flight from everyday life involves no more than an experience of home plus sunshine. The experience of the 'promised land' has become commodified and homogenised.

A fresh perspective

In 'Tourists' Voices: A Sociological Analysis of Tourists' Experiences in Chalkidiki, Northern Greece, (Wickens 1999), I reported on my ethnographic study of tourists' experiences in Chalkidiki, Northern Greece, conducted between 1993 and 1996. A fresh tourist typology is presented which is grounded on qualitative evidence derived from eighty-six respondents, and which challenges the assumption that 'the tourist' is a unitary type. The five types of tourists distinguished - the Lord Byron, the Cultural Heritage, the Heliolatrous, the Raver and the Shirley Valentine - are effectively sub-divisions within Cohen's category of 'institutionalised tourist' (Cohen, 1972). Each of these analytical categories 'brackets off' a set of respondents who exhibited similarities in their 'attachment' to a particular role. Goffman's (1967) concepts of 'role commitment, 'role attachment' and 'role embracement' were used as tools in the development of a theoretical understanding of these categories (see Wickens, 1999 and Wickens, 2000, forthcoming). One key finding from my study of tourists experiences in Chalkidiki is that people on an organised package holiday to Kalimeria (the research setting) commit themselves into Cohen's 'institutionalised' tourist role. An understanding of this commitment is developed in terms of three 'feeling states' (Giddens, 1992) which emerge strongly from the ethnographic data. These states, or motivational forces, are: 'familiarity', 'ontological security' (Giddens, 1991) and 'flight from everyday life'.

In addition, I have argued that, despite an individual's commitment to play the part assigned to them by the tourist industry, an individual may choose to step outside his/her role of individual mass tourist, and 'attach' himself/herself to one of the above types i.e., to be a Cultural Heritage, Raver, Shirley Valentine, Heliolatrous, or Lord Byron type. Employing Goffman's theoretical model, I have suggested that an individual's role attachment reflects his/her inclination to play an additional part during his/her vacation in Chalkidiki.

This fresh perspective recognises that while a slice of a participant's experience is structured by the tourist industry, the individual has the choice to 'stay in role' (e.g. the institutionalised role) or to 'go out or role' and enter into one of the five scenarios observed in this tourist setting and which are captured in my five-fold typology. This approach differs from current interpretations of tourists experiences in that, firstly it is derived from an analysis of what tourists said about their experiences, and secondly it provides an interpretation of their motivations within a pluralistic theoretical model. It recognises that tourism as an experience of the 'other' and as a behaviour is variable.

By using this approach, my study gives empirical reaffirmation to Cohen's (1988b: 43) observation that 'one way to accommodate the various approaches and moderate their extreme images of the tourist [found in the studies reviewed above] is to bring them to a common ground and build typologies which would bridge them'. Indeed, my classification has proved productive in making sense of tourists' experiences and motivations. In addition, it has been successfully applied to a study of tourist health (Wickens, 1997) and ethnicity (Lazaridis and Wickens, 1999).

Conclusion

As can be seen from the preceding review of the literature, a major focus of contention concerns the nature of the tourist (as opposed to the traveller of the past). Is s/he: a passive observer (e.g., Boorstin, et al.); or a serious traveller (e.g., MaCannell, et al); or a virtual tourist (e.g., Feifer); or a post-modern tourist (e.g., Urry, et al.); or a recreational spectator (e.g., Graburn, Cohen and Taylor)? Or is s/he merely a seeker of sexual pleasures, that is someone who wants to have a good time (Lett, et al). The theme of escape, whether it be from a boring, routinised, alienated, everyday life (Boorstin, Nash, MacCannell, and many others), or from a profane, ordinary, everyday life (Graburn, et al) unites all these approaches. They all suggest, either explicitly or implicitly, that modern society is inauthentic and alienating and that it drives people to leave their home environment. They differ however in their analysis of the 'pull' factors, which include: looking for meaning and authenticity in 'authentic places'; embarking on a journey, whether it be of self-discovery, or a journey of self-recovery; or seeking release into a free or ludic space warranting hedonistic excess.

Throughout this paper I have argued that the sample of studies reviewed display the same cavalier stance to defining 'the tourist' as a member of a self evident and homogeneous category. The voices of the tourists are hardly heard in the existing literature. However, without close attention to the tourist's voice, our work risks being descriptively and empirically flawed.

In addition, I have presented an outline of a fresh perspective on the touristic experience which is predicated on the view that while tourists commit themselves to playing the 'institutionalised' role, they may also choose to play an additional role. While it can be argued that a tourist typology cannot be applied to all tourists and at all times, my typology proved useful as an analytical tool in giving structure to my fieldwork in Chalkidiki. A central conclusion to emerge is that a tourist typology is an essential technique for a better understanding of this phenomenon. As Dann (1981: 195), points out, 'in the right hands a classificatory scheme represents a powerful instrument for understanding this phenomenon' of tourism.

References

Baudrillard, J. (1983), *Simulations*, trans. Foss, P., Patton, P. and Beitchman, P., New York: Semiotext Inc.

Baudrillard, J. (1988), *America*, trans. Turner, C., London: Verso.

Baudrillard, J. (1991), quoted in Featherstone, M. *Consumer Culture and Postmodernism*, London: Sage.

Baudrillard, J. (1997), *Simulacra and Simulation*, trans. Glaser, S., Ann Arbor: University of Michigan Press.

Berger, P. (1973), 'Sincerity and Authenticity in Modern Society', *The Public Interest*, Spring, 31: 81-90.

Boorstin, D. (1964), *The Image: A Guide to Pseudo-Events in America*, New York: Harper and Row.

Bruner, E. (1991), 'Transformation of Self in Tourism, *Annals of Tourism Research*, 18: 238-250.

Buck, R. C. (1977), 'The Ubiquitous Tourist Brochure: Explorations in its Intended and Unintended Use', *Annals of Tourism Research*, 4 (4): 195-207.

Carroll, J. (1993), quoted in Rojek, C. *Ways of Escape: Modern Transformations in Leisure and Travel*, London: MacMillan.

Cohen, E. (1972), 'Towards a Sociology of International Tourism', *Social Research*, 39 (1): 164-182.

Cohen, E. (1974) 'Who is a Tourist? A Conceptual Clarification', *Sociological Review*, 22 (4): 527-555.

Cohen, E. (1979a), 'A Phenomenology of Tourist Experiences', *Sociology*, 13: 179-201.

Cohen, E. (1979b), 'Rethinking the Sociology of Tourism', *Annals of Tourism Research*, 6 (1): 18-35.

Cohen, E. (1984), 'The Sociology of Tourism: Approaches, Issues and Findings', *Annual Review of Sociology*, 10: 373-392.

Cohen, E. (1988a), 'Authenticity and Commoditisation in Tourism', *Annals of Tourism Research*, 15 (3): 371-386.

Cohen, E. (1988b), 'Traditions in the Qualitative Sociology of Tourism', *Annals of Tourism Research*, Special Issue 15 (1): 29-46.

Cohen, S. and Taylor, L. (1992), *Escape Attempts: The Theory and Practice of Resistance to Everyday Life*, London: Routledge.

Crick, M. (1989), 'Representations of International Tourism in the Social Sciences: Sun, Sex, Sights, Savings, and Servility', *Annual Review of Anthropology*, 18 (1): 307-344.

Culler, J. (1981), 'Semiotics of Tourism', *American Journal of Semiotics*, 1: 127-140.

Dann, G. M. S. (1977), 'Anomie, Ego-Enhancement and Tourism', *Annals of Tourism Research*, 4 (4): 184-94.

Dann, G. M. S. (1981), 'Tourist Motivation: An Appraisal', *Annals of Tourism Research*, 9 (2): 187-219.

Dann, G. M. S., Nash, D. and Pearce, P. L. (1988), 'Methodological Issues in Tourism Research', *Annals of Tourism Research*, 15 (1): 1-28.

Dann, G. M. S. and Cohen, E. (1991), 'Sociology and Tourism', *Annals of Tourism Research,* 18 (1): 155-69.

Durkheim, (1967), *The Elementary Forms of the Religious Life*, New York: Collier Books. (First published in French, in 1912.)

Feifer, M. (1985), *Going Places*, London: MacMillan.

Forster, J. (1964), 'The Sociological Consequences of Tourism', *International Journal of Comparative Sociology,* 5: 217-27.

Fussell, P. (1982), *Abroad: British Literary Travelling Between the Wars*, Oxford: Oxford University Press.

Giddens, A. (1991), *Modernity and Self-identity*, Cambridge: Polity Press.

Giddens, A. (1992), *The Consequences of Modernity*, Cambridge: Polity Press.

Godbey, G. and Graefe, A. (1991), 'Repeat Tourism Play, and Monetary Spending', *Annals of Tourism Research*, 18 (2): 213-225.

Goffman, E. (1959), *The Presentation of Self in Everyday Life*, Harmondsworth: Penguin.

Goffman, E. (1961), *Encounters: Two Studies in the Sociology of Interaction*, Harmondsworth: Penguin.

Goffman, E. (1967), *Interaction Ritual*, Harmondsworth: Penguin.

Gottlieb, A. (1982), 'Americans' Vacations', *Annals of Tourism Research*, 9 (2): 165-87.

Graburn, N. (1977), 'Tourism: The Sacred Journey', in Smith, V. (ed.) *Hosts and Guests: The Anthropology of Tourism*, Oxford: Blackwell. (First Edition.)

Graburn, N. (1983a), 'To Pray, Pay and Play: The Cultural Structure of Japanese Domestic Tourism', *Les Cashiers du Tourisme*, Ser, B, 26: 1-89.

Graburn, N. (1983b), 'The Anthropology of Tourism', *Annals of Tourism Research*, Special Issue, 10 (1): 9-33.

Graburn, N. (1989a), 'Tourism: The Sacred Journey', in Smith, V. (ed.), *Hosts and Guests: The Anthropology of Tourism*, Oxford: Blackwell. (Second Edition.)

Harkin, M. (1995), Modernist Anthropology and Tourism of the Authentic', *Annals of Tourism Research*, 22 (4): 650-670.

Hiller, H. (1976), 'Escapism, Penetration and Response: Industrial Tourism in the Caribbean', *Caribbean Studies*, 16 (1): 92-116.

Hilty, A. (1996), 'Tourism and Literacy Connections: How to Manage the Image Created', in Robinson, M. (eds.) *Tourism and Culture: Towards the 21st Century, Conference Proceedings, Culture as the Tourist Product*, Newcastle: University of Northumbria.

Hughes, G. (1995), 'Authenticity in Tourism', *Annals of Tourism Research*, 22 (4): 781-803.

Iso-Ahola, S. (1982), 'Towards a Social Psychology of Tourism Motivation', *Annals of Tourism Research*, 9 (2): 256-62.

Krippendorf, J. (1991), *The Holiday Makers: Understanding the Impact of Leisure and Travel*, Oxford: Butterworth-Heinemann.

Lazaridis, G. and Wickens, E. (1999), 'Us and the Others: The Experiences of Different Ethnic Minorities in the Greek Cities of Athens and Thessaloniki', *Annals of Tourism Research*, 26 (3): 632-655.

Lett, J. (1983), 'Ludic and Liminoid Aspects of Charter Yacht Tourism in the Caribbean', *Annals of Tourism*, 10 (1): 35-56.

Levi-Strauss, C. (1993), quoted in Rojek, C. *Ways of Escape: Modern Transformations in Leisure and Travel*, London: MacMillan.

Lytra, P. (1987), *The Sociology of Tourism*, Athens: Interbooks. (In Greek.)

Lytra, P. (1989), *O Tourismos Pros to 2000*, Athens: Interbooks. (In Greek)

MacCannell, D. (1973), 'Staged Authenticity: Arrangements of Social Space in Tourist Settings', *American Journal of Sociology*, 79 (3): 589-603.

MacCannell, D. (1976), *The Tourist: A New Theory of the Leisure Class*, Basingstoke: MacMillan.

Moeran, B. (1983), 'The Language of Japanese Tourism', *Annals of Tourism Research*, 10 (1): 93-108.

Moynahan, B. (1985), *The Tourist Trap: The Hidden Horrors of the Holiday Business and How to Avoid Them,* London: Pan Books.

Moore, A. (1980), 'Walt Disney World: Bounded Ritual Space and the Playful Pilgrimage Center', *Anthropological Quarterly*, 53 (4): 207-218.

Nash, D. (1989), 'Tourism as a Form of Imperialism', in Smith, V. (ed.) *Hosts and Guests: The Anthropology of Tourism*, Oxford: Blackwell. (Second Edition.)

Page, S., Clift, S. and Clark, N. (1994), 'Tourist Health: The Precautions, Behaviour and Health Problems of British Tourists in Malta', in Seaton, A. et al. (eds.) *Tourism: The State of the Art*, Chichester: Wiley.

Papson, S. (1981), 'Spuriousness and Tourism: Politics of Two Canadian Provincial Governments', *Annals of Tourism Research*, 8 (2): 220-35.

Pearce, P. L. (1982), *The Social Psychology of Tourist Behaviour,* Oxford: Pergamon Press.

Pearce, P. L. (1993), 'Fundamentals of Tourist Motivation', in Pearce, D. and Butler, R. (eds.) *Tourism Research: Critiques and Challenges*, London: Routledge.

Pfaffenberger, B. (1983), 'Serious Pilgrims and Frivolous Tourists: The Chimera of Tourism in the Pilgrimages of Sri Lanka', *Annals of Tourism Research*, 10 (1): 57-74.

Redfoot, D. (1984), 'Touristic Authenticity, Touristic Angst, and Modern Reality', *Qualitative Sociology*, 7:291-309.

Rojek, C. (1985), *Capitalism and Leisure Theory*, London: Tavistock.

Rojek, C. (1993), *Ways of Escape: Modern Transformation in Leisure and Travel*, London: MacMillan.

Rojek, C. (1995), *Decentring Leisure: Rethinking Leisure Theory*, London: Sage.

Rojek, C. and Urry, J. (eds.) (1997), *Touring Cultures: Transformations of Travel and Theory*, London: Routledge.

Ryan, C. (1991), *Recreational Tourism: A Social Science Perspective*, London: Routledge.

Selwyn, T. (ed.) (1996), *The Tourist Image: Myths and Myth Making in Tourism*, Chichester: Wiley.

Sharpley, R. (1996), 'Tourism and Consumer Culture in Postmodern Society', in Robinson, M. et al. (eds.) *Tourism and Culture, Towards the 21st. Century Conference Proceedings: Tourism and Cultural Change*, Newcastle: University of Northumbria.

Shields, R. (1992), *Places on the Margin: Alternative Geographies of Modernity*, London: Routledge.

Smith, H. (1996), 'God's Own Country', *The Guardian*, February 11th, p.24.

Smith, V. (1977), 'Introduction', in Smith, V. (ed.) *Hosts and Guests: The Anthropology of Tourism*, Oxford: Blackwell.

Thornton, P. (1995), *Tourist Behaviour on Holiday: A Time-Space Approach*, Exeter University: Unpublished Ph.D.

Trilling, L.(1972), *Sincerity and Authenticity*, Cambridge: Harvard

Turner, L. and Ash, J. (1975), *The Golden Hordes: International Tourism and the Pleasure Periphery*, London: Constable.

Turner, V. (1973), 'The Centre Out There: Pilgrim's Goal', *History of Religions*, 12: 191-230.

Turner, V. (1974a), *The Ritual Process: Structure and Anti-Structure*, Harmondsworth: Penguin.

Turner, V. (1974b), 'Liminal to Liminoid, in Play, Flow, and Ritual: An Essay in Comparative Symbology', *Rice University Studies*, 60: 53-92.

Turner, V. and Turner, E. (1978), *Image and Pilgrimage in Christian Culture*, New York: Columbia University Press.

Urry, J. (1991), *The Tourist Gaze: Leisure and Travel in Contemporary Societies*, London: Sage.

Van Gennep, A. (1960), *The Rites of Passage*, London: Routledge.

Wagner, U. (1977), 'Out of Time and Place: Mass Tourism and Charter Trips', *Ethnos* 42: 38-52.

Watson, G. and Kopachevsky, J. (1996), 'Interpretations of Tourism as Commodity', in Apostolopoulos, Y. et al. (eds.) *The Sociology of Tourism: Theoretical and Empirical Investigations,* London: Routledge.

Webster, F. (1996), *Theories of the Information Society*, London: Routledge.

Wickens, E. (1994a), 'A Flight from Everyday Life: The Tourist Experience in Chalkidiki, Northern Greece', School of Social Sciences, Oxford Brookes University. (Paper presented at the BSA Annual Conference, University of Central Lancashire, Preston.)

Wickens, E. (1994b), 'Consumption of the Authentic: The Hedonistic Tourist in Greece', in Seaton, A. et al. (eds.) Tourism: The State of the Art, London: Wiley.

Wickens, E. (1995), 'The Exodus to the Sun', Social Science Teacher, (The Journal of the ATSS), Autumn.

Wickens, E. and Harrison, A. (1996), 'Staging Modernity: The Consumption of Hybrid Playful Experiences in Chalkidiki, Northern Greece', in Robinson, M. et al. (eds.) Tourism and Culture, Towards the 21st Century. Conference Proceedings: Culture as the Tourist Product, Newcastle: University of Northumbria.

Wickens, E. (1997), 'Licensed for Thrills: Risk-taking and Tourism', in Clift, S. and Grabowski, P. (eds.) Tourism and Health: Risks, Research and Responses, London: Pinter.

Wickens, E. (1999), Tourists' Voices: A Sociological Analysis of Tourists' Experiences in Chalkidiki, Northern Greece, Oxford Brookes University, Unpublished Ph.D.

Wickens, E. (2000), 'The Sacred and the Profane: A Tourist Typology', forthcoming.

Yiannakis, A. and Gibson, H. (1992), 'Roles Tourists Play', Annals of Tourism Research, 19 (2): 287-303.